T0211500

Lecture Notes in Computer Science　10297

Commenced Publication in 1973
Founding and Former Series Editors:
Gerhard Goos, Juris Hartmanis, and Jan van Leeuwen

More information about this series at http://www.springer.com/series/7409

Jia Zhou · Gavriel Salvendy (Eds.)

Human Aspects of IT for the Aged Population

Aging, Design and User Experience

Third International Conference, ITAP 2017
Held as Part of HCI International 2017
Vancouver, BC, Canada, July 9–14, 2017
Proceedings, Part I

 Springer

Editors
Jia Zhou
Chongqing University
Chongqing
China

Gavriel Salvendy
Purdue University
West Lafayette
USA

and

Tsinghua University
Beijing
P.R. China

and

University of Central Florida
Orlando
USA

ISSN 0302-9743   ISSN 1611-3349   (electronic)
Lecture Notes in Computer Science
ISBN 978-3-319-58529-1   ISBN 978-3-319-58530-7   (eBook)
DOI 10.1007/978-3-319-58530-7

Library of Congress Control Number: 2017939345

LNCS Sublibrary: SL3 – Information Systems and Applications, incl. Internet/Web, and HCI

Printed on acid-free paper

This Springer imprint is published by Springer Nature
The registered company is Springer International Publishing AG
The registered company address is: Gewerbestrasse 11, 6330 Cham, Switzerland

Foreword

The 19th International Conference on Human–Computer Interaction, HCI International 2017, was held in Vancouver, Canada, during July 9–14, 2017. The event incorporated the 15 conferences/thematic areas listed on the following page.

A total of 4,340 individuals from academia, research institutes, industry, and governmental agencies from 70 countries submitted contributions, and 1,228 papers have been included in the proceedings. These papers address the latest research and development efforts and highlight the human aspects of design and use of computing systems. The papers thoroughly cover the entire field of human–computer interaction, addressing major advances in knowledge and effective use of computers in a variety of application areas. The volumes constituting the full set of the conference proceedings are listed on the following pages.

I would like to thank the program board chairs and the members of the program boards of all thematic areas and affiliated conferences for their contribution to the highest scientific quality and the overall success of the HCI International 2017 conference.

This conference would not have been possible without the continuous and unwavering support and advice of the founder, Conference General Chair Emeritus and Conference Scientific Advisor Prof. Gavriel Salvendy. For his outstanding efforts, I would like to express my appreciation to the communications chair and editor of *HCI International News*, Dr. Abbas Moallem.

April 2017

Constantine Stephanidis

HCI International 2017 Thematic Areas and Affiliated Conferences

Thematic areas:

- Human–Computer Interaction (HCI 2017)
- Human Interface and the Management of Information (HIMI 2017)

Affiliated conferences:

- 17th International Conference on Engineering Psychology and Cognitive Ergonomics (EPCE 2017)
- 11th International Conference on Universal Access in Human–Computer Interaction (UAHCI 2017)
- 9th International Conference on Virtual, Augmented and Mixed Reality (VAMR 2017)
- 9th International Conference on Cross-Cultural Design (CCD 2017)
- 9th International Conference on Social Computing and Social Media (SCSM 2017)
- 11th International Conference on Augmented Cognition (AC 2017)
- 8th International Conference on Digital Human Modeling and Applications in Health, Safety, Ergonomics and Risk Management (DHM 2017)
- 6th International Conference on Design, User Experience and Usability (DUXU 2017)
- 5th International Conference on Distributed, Ambient and Pervasive Interactions (DAPI 2017)
- 5th International Conference on Human Aspects of Information Security, Privacy and Trust (HAS 2017)
- 4th International Conference on HCI in Business, Government and Organizations (HCIBGO 2017)
- 4th International Conference on Learning and Collaboration Technologies (LCT 2017)
- Third International Conference on Human Aspects of IT for the Aged Population (ITAP 2017)

Conference Proceedings Volumes Full List

1. LNCS 10271, Human–Computer Interaction: User Interface Design, Development and Multimodality (Part I), edited by Masaaki Kurosu
2. LNCS 10272 Human–Computer Interaction: Interaction Contexts (Part II), edited by Masaaki Kurosu
3. LNCS 10273, Human Interface and the Management of Information: Information, Knowledge and Interaction Design (Part I), edited by Sakae Yamamoto
4. LNCS 10274, Human Interface and the Management of Information: Supporting Learning, Decision-Making and Collaboration (Part II), edited by Sakae Yamamoto
5. LNAI 10275, Engineering Psychology and Cognitive Ergonomics: Performance, Emotion and Situation Awareness (Part I), edited by Don Harris
6. LNAI 10276, Engineering Psychology and Cognitive Ergonomics: Cognition and Design (Part II), edited by Don Harris
7. LNCS 10277, Universal Access in Human–Computer Interaction: Design and Development Approaches and Methods (Part I), edited by Margherita Antona and Constantine Stephanidis
8. LNCS 10278, Universal Access in Human–Computer Interaction: Designing Novel Interactions (Part II), edited by Margherita Antona and Constantine Stephanidis
9. LNCS 10279, Universal Access in Human–Computer Interaction: Human and Technological Environments (Part III), edited by Margherita Antona and Constantine Stephanidis
10. LNCS 10280, Virtual, Augmented and Mixed Reality, edited by Stephanie Lackey and Jessie Y.C. Chen
11. LNCS 10281, Cross-Cultural Design, edited by Pei-Luen Patrick Rau
12. LNCS 10282, Social Computing and Social Media: Human Behavior (Part I), edited by Gabriele Meiselwitz
13. LNCS 10283, Social Computing and Social Media: Applications and Analytics (Part II), edited by Gabriele Meiselwitz
14. LNAI 10284, Augmented Cognition: Neurocognition and Machine Learning (Part I), edited by Dylan D. Schmorrow and Cali M. Fidopiastis
15. LNAI 10285, Augmented Cognition: Enhancing Cognition and Behavior in Complex Human Environments (Part II), edited by Dylan D. Schmorrow and Cali M. Fidopiastis
16. LNCS 10286, Digital Human Modeling and Applications in Health, Safety, Ergonomics and Risk Management: Ergonomics and Design (Part I), edited by Vincent G. Duffy
17. LNCS 10287, Digital Human Modeling and Applications in Health, Safety, Ergonomics and Risk Management: Health and Safety (Part II), edited by Vincent G. Duffy
18. LNCS 10288, Design, User Experience, and Usability: Theory, Methodology and Management (Part I), edited by Aaron Marcus and Wentao Wang

Human Aspects of IT for the Aged Population

Program Board Chair(s): **Gavriel Salvendy, USA and P.R. China, and Jia Zhou, P.R. China**

- Panagiotis Bamidis, Greece
- Marc-Eric Bobillier Chaumon, France
- Julie A. Brown, USA
- Alan H.S. Chan, Hong Kong, SAR China
- Neil Charness, USA
- Shelia Cotten, USA
- Hua Dong, P.R. China
- Mireia Fernández-Ardèvol, Spain
- M. Anwar Hossain, Saudi Arabia
- Yong Gu Ji, Korea
- Jiunn-Woei (Allen) Lian, Taiwan
- Hai-Ning Liang, P.R. China
- Eugene Loos, The Netherlands
- Lourdes Moreno Lopez, Spain
- Lisa J. Molnar, USA
- Natalie Pang, Singapore
- Andraž Petrovčič, Slovenia
- Marie Sjölinder, Sweden
- Alvaro Taveira, USA
- António Teixeira, Portugal
- Wang-Chin Tsai, Taiwan
- Gregg C. Vanderheiden, USA
- Brenda Vrkljan, Canada
- Martina Ziefle, Germany

The full list with the Program Board Chairs and the members of the Program Boards of all thematic areas and affiliated conferences is available online at:

http://www.hci.international/board-members-2017.php

HCI International 2018

The 20th International Conference on Human–Computer Interaction, HCI International 2018, will be held jointly with the affiliated conferences in Las Vegas, NV, USA, at Caesars Palace, July 15–20, 2018. It will cover a broad spectrum of themes related to human–computer interaction, including theoretical issues, methods, tools, processes, and case studies in HCI design, as well as novel interaction techniques, interfaces, and applications. The proceedings will be published by Springer. More information is available on the conference website: http://2018.hci.international/.

General Chair
Prof. Constantine Stephanidis
University of Crete and ICS-FORTH
Heraklion, Crete, Greece
E-mail: general_chair@hcii2018.org

http://2018.hci.international/

Contents – Part I

Aging and User Experience

Digital Literacy and Training

Contents – Part II

Silver and Intergenerational Gaming

Health Care and Assistive Technologies and Services for the Elderly

Aging and Learning, Working and Leisure

Aging and Technology Acceptance

Age Differences in Acceptance of Self-driving Cars: A Survey of Perceptions and Attitudes

Chaiwoo Lee[(⊠)], Carley Ward, Martina Raue, Lisa D'Ambrosio, and Joseph F. Coughlin

Massachusetts Institute of Technology AgeLab, Cambridge, MA, USA
chaiwoo@mit.edu

Abstract. As self-driving cars begin to make their way on to the road, there is a growing need for research to understand acceptance of the technology among potential users. This study looked at responses from a national sample of 1,765 adults in the United States to uncover key determinants of the acceptance of self-driving cars and to understand how age and other characteristics relate to perceptions of and attitudes toward self-driving cars. Data from the online survey showed that perceived usefulness, affordability, social support, lifestyle fit and conceptual compatibility are key predictors of acceptance of self-driving cars across ages. A comparison across generational cohorts (i.e., Millennials, Generation X, Baby Boomers and the Silent Generation) found that age negatively affects perceptions of a self-driving car, interest in using it, and behavioral intentions to use one when it becomes available. Furthermore, experiential characteristics associated with age, including experiences with, knowledge of and trust toward technology in general, were found to have significant influence on how people felt about self-driving cars.

Keywords: Technology adoption · Automotive technology · Automated driving · Traffic safety · Technology experience

1 Introduction

A growing number of companies and organizations are working to bring self-driving cars – vehicles that can sense the surrounding environment and operate in it without requiring control, navigation or monitoring from a driver – to the road. Prototypes of self-driving cars and related technologies are continuously being tested for their functionality. Little is known, however, about how self-driving cars and their features are perceived and accepted by potential consumers and users.

There is a significant body of research around technology acceptance across various domains. Numerous studies have built on to earlier models such as the Technology Acceptance Model (TAM) [1] and the Diffusion of Innovations Theory [2]. In TAM, perceived usefulness and perceived ease-of-use are main factors that affect a user's attitudes toward using technology, which then influences the user's behavioral intentions and actual usage, as illustrated in Fig. 1. In the Diffusion of Innovations Theory, five characteristics – relative advantage, compatibility, complexity, trialability and observability – are the key factors that underlie adoption. Research stemming from

© Springer International Publishing AG 2017
J. Zhou and G. Salvendy (Eds.): ITAP 2017, Part I, LNCS 10297, pp. 3–13, 2017.
DOI: 10.1007/978-3-319-58530-7_1

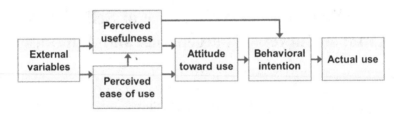

Fig. 1. Technology acceptance model [1]

these early models has described how perceived usefulness, ease-of-use, social influence, personal characteristics, cost and other factors also affect the adoption and use of technologies [3–8].

Recently, studies have begun to explore user perceptions and attitudes in relation to the acceptance of automotive technologies. In a study on automotive telematics, vehicle technologies that combine wireless communications technology and location-based services, Chen and Chen [9] tested different technology acceptance frameworks to understand the determinants of adoption and found perceived ease of use to be a key factor. Effects of individual characteristics on adoption have gained interest as well. For example, Son et al, [10] studied advanced driver assistance systems including forward collision warning and lane departure warning, and found differences by gender and age, with women and younger drivers showing lower acceptance. Efforts to understand user acceptance of automotive technologies are also beginning to focus on automated vehicles that do not require a human operator. For example, Madigan et al. [11] studied user acceptance of an automated public transport service for short-haul travel and found performance expectancy, effort expectancy and social influence to be key predictors. Abraham et al. [12] conducted a large-scale survey to understand acceptance of varying levels of automation in vehicles, and found that younger adults were more comfortable with the fully autonomous, or self-driving, mode compared to older adults.

Self-driving cars promise benefits for a diversity of road users, including drivers of various ages and abilities. With the aging of the population, the number of older drivers is expected to increase rapidly. The number of licensed drivers 70 years of age and older increased by 38% between 1997 and 2014 [13], and the trend is projected to continue. Age-related changes in physical and cognitive capabilities, however, can lead to declines in mobility and driving abilities [14, 15], leading many older adults to stop driving altogether. For this reason, they may be the primary beneficiaries of self-driving cars. Older adults, however, have knowledge of and experiences with technology that may differ from younger generations, which may cause them to perceive and accept self-driving cars differently [10, 12].

While research on technology adoption and transportation safety has begun to explore determinants of acceptance and age effects with regards to new automotive technologies, how different generations perceive and accept self-driving cars is not yet fully understood. In this study, a large-scale survey was conducted to investigate older adults' perceptions of and attitudes toward self-driving cars, and how their perspectives differ from other generations.

2 Data Collection

2.1 Questionnaire Design

A questionnaire was designed to gather people's attitudes toward and perceptions of self-driving cars, as well as interest in use and adoption. Questions explored various factors that contribute to technology acceptance and adoption identified in previous research [1, 8], as described in Table 1. In order to learn about other characteristics that may affect acceptance of a self-driving car, questions were also asked around experiences with technology in general, driving behavior and history, and demographics.

The questionnaire also included the following short description of a self-driving car: "For the purpose of this study, we define self-driving cars as those in which operation of the vehicle occurs without the driver controlling the steering, acceleration, and braking; the driver is not expected to constantly monitor the roadway. A self-driving car uses advanced sensors and software to navigate itself to your destination, understand the road environment, and react to various changes in the driving situation from traffic congestion to a pedestrian crossing the street. Some of the anticipated benefits from these vehicles include: more opportunity for people to use their time productively, increased safety on the road, and greater efficiency." Participants were shown the description before the questions displayed in Table 1 were asked, in order to establish a basic baseline knowledge.

Table 1. Technology adoption factors asked in the survey (adapted from [1, 8])

Category	Factor	Question statement	Response scale
Perceptions	Usefulness	How effective do you think that self-driving cars will be at preventing accidents?	1: Not effective at all–5: very effective
	Ease of use	Self-driving cars would be easy to use	1: Strongly disagree–5: strongly agree
	Affordability	Self-driving cars would be affordable for me	
	Accessibility	I will know where to find self-driving cars when they become available	
	Technical support	I will know where to go for technical support if something went wrong with a self-driving car	
	Emotional benefits	Self-driving cars would provide emotional benefits to users	
	Social support	My family and friends will approve of me using a self-driving car	
	Reliability	Self-driving cars will work reliably over time	

(continued)

Table 1. (*continued*)

Category	Factor	Question statement	Response scale
	Interoperability	Self-driving cars will work well with other smart technologies	
	Lifestyle fit	Using a self-driving car will fit into my lifestyle	
	Conceptual compatibility/fit	Self-driving cars will work in ways that make sense to me	
Attitudes toward use	Overall interest	How interested are you in using a self-driving car?	1: Not at all–5: very interested
Behavioral intention to use	Likelihood of adoption - general	How likely would you be to purchase a self-driving car?	1: Not at all–5: very likely
	Likelihood of adoption - conditional	How likely would you be to use a self-driving car if you were no longer capable of driving?	
External variables	Age (year of birth)	What is your year of birth?	n/a
	Technology experience	How would you rate your level of experience with technology in general?	1: Not experienced at all–5: very experienced
	Technology confidence	How confident are you generally in your ability to learn and use new technologies?	1: Not very confident–5: extremely confident
	Technology trust	How would you rate your overall level of trust toward technology?	1: No trust at all–5: very high trust
	Knowledge of new technologies	Select the technologies that you know about: smart glasses, smart watches, smart thermostats, smart TVs, drones, 3-D printers, tablets, smartphones, GPS navigation systems, fitness bands, cloud data storage, ridesharing services and mobile payment services.	0 (none checked)–13 (all checked)
	Driving experience	Do you have a current, valid driver's license?	Yes or no

2.2   Sample Profile

The survey was conducted in the United States, and responses were collected from a national sample of 1,765 adults. Data collection was completed online with a panel service provided by Qualtrics (http://qualtrics.com). The sample represented a wide age distribution and various demographic traits as summarized in Table 2.

Table 2. Participant profile (n = 1,765)

Characteristics	Descriptive statistics
Age (year of birth)	Silent Generation (born on or before 1945): 241 (13.7%)
	Older Baby Boomers (born 1946–1954): 303 (17.2%)
	Younger Baby Boomers (born 1955–1964): 341 (19.3%)
	Generation X (born 1965–1980): 332 (18.8%)
	Older Millennials (born 1981–1989): 307 (17.4%)
	Younger Millennials (born 1990–1998): 241 (13.7%)
Gender	Male: 933 (52.9%)
	Female: 815 (46.2%)
	Other or no answer: 17 (1.0%)
Education	Some high school or less: 36 (2.0%)
	High school diploma: 354 (20.1%)
	Some college: 442 (25.0%)
	Trade/technical/vocational school or associate's degree: 210 (11.9%)
	College degree: 449 (25.4%)
	Some post-graduate work: 75 (4.2%)
	Post-graduate degree: 199 (11.3%)
Marital status	Single, never married: 509 (28.8%)
	Married or living with a partner: 926 (52.5%)
	Divorced or separated: 230 (13.0%)
	Widowed: 99 (5.6%)
	Other: 1 (0.1%)
Ethnicity	White: 1411 (79.9%)
	Black or African-American: 147 (8.3%)
	Hispanic or Latino: 56 (3.2%)
	Asian or Asian-American: 77 (4.4%)
	Other or multiracial: 74 (4.2%)
Employment	Employed full-time: 526 (29.8%)
	Employed part-time: 172 (9.7%)
	Not employed: 197 (11.2%)
	Self-employed: 123 (7.0%)
	Retired: 501 (28.4%)
	Student: 80 (4.5%)
	Homemaker: 143 (8.1%)
Annual household income	Less than 25,000 USD: 451 (25.6%)
	25,000 USD or more but less than 50,000 USD: 529 (30.0%)
	50,000 USD or more but less than 75,000 USD: 365 (20.7%)
	75,000 USD or more but less than 100,000 USD: 237 (13.4%)
	100,000 USD or more but less than 150,000 USD: 133 (7.5%)
	150,000 USD or more: 50 (2.8%)

The majority of the participants had a valid driver's license at the time of data collection (89.2%). Most of them self-reported as frequent and safe drivers, with 57.2% driving at least five days per week; 69.8% reported they had never been stopped by a police officer for a moving violation, and 51.4% reported they had never been in a traffic accident.

3 Results

Statistical analysis was done to describe how perceptions of self-driving cars influence attitudes toward use and behavioral intentions to use them. Effects of age were analyzed to understand how potential users of different generations feel about self-driving cars and if they differ in terms of their willingness to use. Possible effects of past experiences with technology and driving behavior were also analyzed. The overall research model, which includes factors and measures described in Table 1, is illustrated in Fig. 2.

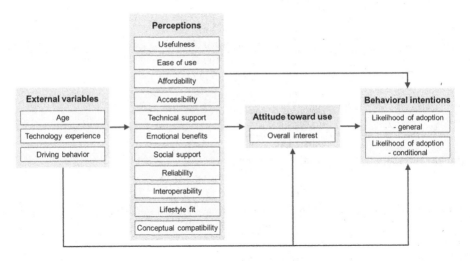

Fig. 2. Conceptual research model

3.1 Determinants of Self-driving Car Acceptance

The results of a regression analysis of acceptance measures on adoption factors are summarized in Table 3. The following factors were significant predictors of self-driving car acceptance: perceived usefulness, affordability, social support, lifestyle fit and conceptual compatibility. Across ages, those who perceived self-driving cars to be more practical, affordable, accepted by peers, and compatible with their lifestyles and conceptual mental models were more interested in getting and using them. Furthermore, attitudinal interest in self-driving cars strongly predicted behavioral intentions to use them.

Table 3. Regression results: effects of adoption factors (standardized β coefficients)

Independent measures		Dependent measures		
		Attitude	Behavioral intentions	
		Overall interest	General	Conditional
Perceptions	Usefulness	.294**	.274**	.219**
	Ease of use	.036	.101	.086**
	Affordability	.060**	.209**	−.053*
	Accessibility	−.017	.025	.004
	Technical support	.006	.024	−.050
	Emotional benefits	.028	.020	.090**
	Social support	.053*	.058*	.055*
	Reliability	.010	−.032	.046
	Interoperability	.001	−.032	.033
	Lifestyle fit	.389**	.336**	.265**
	Conceptual fit	.103**	.052	.132**
	R^2 (perceptions → attitude and behavioral intentions)	.721	.648	.549
Attitude	Overall interest	–	.891**	.775**
	R^2 (attitude → behavioral intentions)	–	.794	.600

* $p < 0.05$, ** $p < 0.01$.

3.2   Age Differences

Age was negatively associated with perceptions, attitudes and behavioral intentions toward the acceptance and use of self-driving cars. As summarized in Table 4, a comparison of average ratings across generations with analysis of variance (ANOVA) showed that older participants perceived self-driving cars as significantly less useful ($F = 33.033$, $p = .000$) and more difficult to use ($F = 26.965$, $p = .000$) compared to younger participants. Older adults were also more likely to think that self-driving cars would be more expensive ($F = 45.233$, $p = .000$) and more difficult to find where to purchase or access ($F = 8.025$, $p = .000$). Older adults indicated that they believed self-driving cars were less likely to be backed up with technical support ($F = 21.406$, $p = .000$), less likely to provide emotional benefits ($F = 20.853$, $p = .000$), less likely to be approved by their peers ($F = 27.341$, $p = .000$), less reliable ($F = 14.530$, $p = .000$), less likely to work with other technologies they have ($F = 21.637$, $p = .000$), and less likely to fit with their lifestyles ($F = 44.268$, $p = .000$) and mental models ($F = 21.483$, $p = .000$), compared to younger participants.

Strong inverse relationships with age were also found for overall level of interest in using a self-driving car ($F = 90.529$, $p = .000$) and likelihood of purchasing one in the future (general: $F = 82.792$, $p = .000$, if no longer able to drive: $F = 41.170$, $p = .000$), indicating that older adults are currently less interested in self-driving cars and less likely to use one when it becomes available. Millennials, those born between

Table 4. Age differences: mean comparisons (all measured on a 5-point scale, ANOVA results significant at $\alpha = 0.01$ for all factors)

		Silent generation ($\sim$1945)	Baby Boomers (1946–1964)	Generation X (1965–1980)	Millennials (1981–1998)
Perceptions	Usefulness	2.93	3.01	3.30	3.58
	Ease of use	3.15	3.28	3.58	3.78
	Affordability	2.12	2.18	2.55	2.95
	Accessibility	2.92	2.95	2.99	3.30
	Technical support	2.61	2.73	2.97	3.27
	Emotional benefits	2.89	2.99	3.19	3.50
	Social support	2.71	2.92	3.18	3.45
	Reliability	3.33	3.32	3.55	3.75
	Interoperability	3.30	3.39	3.58	3.87
	Lifestyle fit	2.47	2.77	3.17	3.49
	Conceptual fit	3.05	3.16	3.39	3.67
Attitude	Overall interest	2.15	2.48	3.10	3.57
Behavioral intention	General	1.92	2.11	2.77	3.14
	Conditional	2.85	2.97	3.48	3.77

1981 and 1998, were most favorable toward the use of self-driving cars. They indicated interest in using a self-driving car ($M = 3.57$ out of 5), and said they would consider getting one in the future generally ($M = 3.14$ out of 5) or if they were no longer able to drive ($M = 3.77$ out of 5). On the opposite end, the Silent Generation, those born in or before 1945, displayed low overall interest ($M = 2.15$ out of 5) and said that they are not likely to consider using a self-driving car in any case ($M = 1.92$ out of 5). Across ages, however, participants indicated that they would be more likely to use a self-driving car if they were no longer able to drive and less likely to use one if they were capable of driving.

3.3   Effects of Experience with Technology in General and Driving

In addition to age, experience with technology in general was strongly associated with self-driving car acceptance. Regression analyses showed that, across ages, participants who self-reported greater experience with technology in general and higher confidence in use of new technologies were significantly more interested in self-driving cars and more likely to purchase one in the future, as summarized in Table 5. Those who self-reported being more knowledgeable of new technologies were significantly more likely to purchase a self-driving car in the future if they were no longer able to drive. Trust toward technology in general had the strongest effect on self-driving car

Table 5. Effects of external variables on acceptance (standardized β coefficients)

Dependent measures		Independent measures – external variables					
		Year of birth	General technology experience and perceptions				R^2
			Experience	Confidence	Trust	Knowledge	
Perceptions	Usefulness	.004	.013	.031	.440**	.016	.217
	Ease of use	.013	−.011	.116**	.395**	.038	.219
	Affordability	.023	.178**	−.006	.308**	−.096**	.168
	Accessibility	−.023	.116**	.077*	.264**	.013	.152
	Technical support	−.015	.152**	.035	.313**	−.022	.181
	Emotional benefits	.012	.030	−.014	.397**	−.011	.162
	Social support	.025	.054	.020	.377**	.000	.175
	Reliability	−.005	−.006	−.002	.478**	.043	.233
	Interoperability	.029	−.013	.024	.430**	.096**	.215
	Lifestyle fit	.039	.043	.032	.409**	.007	.206
	Conceptual fit	.022	−.010	.082**	.414**	.035	.216
Attitude	Overall interest	.032	.117**	.071*	.396**	.020	.266
Behavioral intention	General	.017	.131**	.067*	.379**	−.008	.249
	Conditional	.029	.023	.071*	.354**	.054*	.180

* $p < 0.05$, ** $p < 0.01$.

acceptance. Among all technology experience measures, overall trust toward technology had the strongest effect on self-driving car acceptance as shown in Table 5.

As shown in Table 5, technology experience, confidence, trust and knowledge also had significant effects on self-driving car acceptance. These technology measures were not independent of age, however. The ages of participants, measured as year of birth, were correlated with self-rated level of experience with technology in general (Spearman's rank correlation $\rho = .390$, $p = .000$), confidence in ability to learn and use new technologies ($\rho = .325$, $p = .000$), overall level of trust in technology ($\rho = .196$, $p = .000$), and knowledge of new technologies ($\rho = .139$, $p = .000$). The findings suggest that while self-driving car acceptance varies across generations, as shown in Table 4, age may have an indirect effect on acceptance through experience with technology in general.

Additionally, current drivers and non-drivers showed minor differences in their attitudes toward using self-driving cars. Participants who did not have a valid driver's license were significantly ($p = .025$) more likely to be interested in using a self-driving car ($M = 3.12$ out of 5) than those who currently had a valid driver's license ($M = 2.86$ out of 5). No significant interaction effects were observed between age and possession of a driver's license.

4 Discussion and Conclusion

Self-driving cars have the potential to make transportation safer and more convenient for all users. Older adults, who are more likely than younger generations to experience difficulties with driving, are uniquely positioned to benefit from the enhanced mobility such technology could provide them.

In this study, a large-scale national survey was conducted to understand people's perceptions of and attitudes toward acceptance of self-driving cars, and to describe how age and other characteristics influence their thoughts. An online questionnaire was used to gather responses on evaluations of various technology adoption factors, overall interest in using a self-driving car, behavioral intentions to use, driving behavior, experience with technology in general, and demographics.

Across ages, perceived usefulness, affordability, social support, lifestyle fit and conceptual compatibility were significant determinants of self-driving car acceptance. The results from this study, however, suggest that older generations may not yet be ready to take their hands off the wheel and hop into a self-driving car. Age was inversely correlated with all predictors of self-driving car acceptance, as well as overall interest and behavioral intentions to use. While younger generations reported greater interest, older respondents thought of self-driving cars as less beneficial and were less interested in using them. An analysis with the effects of experience with technology in general further revealed that people who self-reported greater experience with technology in general, higher confidence in use of new technologies, higher overall trust toward technology, and greater knowledge of new technologies were more accepting of self-driving cars. These technology experience variables, which were all negatively associated with age, also showed significant effects on acceptance in addition to chronological age.

The findings indicate a need for further research on generational differences in relation to past experiences, perceived benefits of, and trust in adopting self-driving cars. While the results from this study found older adults to be less accepting of fully-automated self-driving cars, a few studies on advanced driver assistance systems suggest that older drivers were more likely to accept new in-vehicle technologies [10, 16]. Future studies can explore age differences around the acceptance of varying levels of vehicular automation. Additionally, research is needed to further explain potential links among age, technology experiences, trust and risk perceptions, and to describe how these relationships may affect acceptance of future systems.

Acknowledgment. The authors gratefully acknowledge research support from a grant from the United States Department of Transportation's Region One University Transportation Center at MIT.

References

1. Davis, F.D., Bagozzi, R.P., Warshaw, P.R.: User acceptance of computer technology: a comparison of two theoretical models. Manag. Sci. **35**(8), 982–1003 (1989). doi:10.1287/mnsc.35.8.982
2. Rogers, E.M.: Diffusion of Innovations, 4th edn. Free Press, New York (1995)

3. Lu, J., Yu, C., Liu, C., Yao, J.E.: Technology acceptance model for wireless internet. Internet Res. **13**(3), 206–222 (2003). doi:10.1108/10662240310478222
4. Sarker, S., Wells, J.D.: Understanding mobile handheld device use and adoption. Commun. ACM **46**(12), 35–40 (2003). doi:10.1145/953460.953484
5. Venkatesh, V., Morris, M.G., Davis, G.B., Davis, F.D.: User acceptance of information technology: toward a unified view. MIS Q. **27**(3), 425–478 (2003). doi:10.2307/30036540
6. Porter, C.E., Donthu, N.: Using the technology acceptance model to explain how attitudes determine internet usage. J. Bus. Res. **59**(9), 999–1007 (2006). doi:10.1016/j.jbusres.2006.06.003
7. Kulviwat, S., Bruner, G.C., Al-Shuridah, O.: The role of social influence on adoption of high tech innovations: the moderating effect of public/private consumption. J. Bus. Res. **62**(7), 706–712 (2009). doi:10.1016/j.jbusres.2007.04.014
8. Lee, C.: User-centered system design in an aging society: an integrated study on technology adoption. Dissertation, Massachusetts Institute of Technology (2014)
9. Chen, H., Chen, S.: The empirical study of autonomous telematics acceptance in Taiwan: comparing three technology acceptance models. Int. J. Mob. Commun. **7**(1), 50–65 (2009)
10. Son, J., Park, M., Park, B.B.: The effect of age, gender and roadway environment on the acceptance and effectiveness of advanced driver assistance systems. Transp. Res. F-Traf. **31**, 12–24 (2015). doi:10.1016/j.trf.2015.03.009
11. Madigan, R., Louw, T., Dziennus, M., Graindorge, T., Ortega, E., Grandorge, M., Merat, N.: Acceptance of automated road transportation systems (ARTS): an adaptation of the UTAUT model. Trans. Res. Procedia **14**, 2217–2226 (2016). doi:10.1016/j.trpro.2016.05.237
12. Abraham, H., Lee, C., Brady, S., Fitzgerald, C., Mehler, B., Reimer, B., Coughlin, J.F.: Autonomous vehicles, trust, and driving alternatives: a survey of consumer preferences. Paper presented at the Transportation Research Board 96th Annual Meeting, Washington, DC, 8–12 January 2017
13. Insurance Institute for Highway Safety – Highway Loss Data Institute: Older drivers (2016). http://www.iihs.org/iihs/topics/t/older-drivers/qanda. Accessed 30 Jan 2017
14. Baldwin, C.L.: Designing in-vehicle technologies for older drivers: application of sensory-cognitive interaction theory. Theor. Issues Erg. Sci. **3**(4), 307–329 (2002). doi:10.1080/1463922021000009029
15. Anstey, K.J., Wood, J.: Chronological age and age-related cognitive deficits are associated with an increase in multiple types of driving errors in later life. Neuropsychol. **25**(5), 613–621 (2011). doi:10.1037/a0023835
16. Yannis, G., Antonious, C., Vardaki, S., Kanellaidis, G.: Older drivers' perception and acceptance of in-vehicle devices for traffic safety and traffic efficiency. J. Transp. Eng. **136**(5), 472–479 (2010). doi:10.1061/(ASCE)TE.1943-5436.0000063

Mobile Technology Adoption Among Older People - An Exploratory Study in the UK

Jing Pan[1], Nick Bryan-Kinns[2], and Hua Dong[3(✉)]

[1] College of Architecture and Urban Planning,
Tongji University, Shanghai, China
2901candy@tongji.edu.cn
[2] School of Electronic Engineering and Computer Science,
Queen Mary University of London, London, UK
n.bryan-kinns@qmul.ac.uk
[3] College of Design and Innovation, Tongji University, Shanghai, China
donghua@tongji..edu.cn

Abstract. Although there are potential benefits of mobile technology, there are challenges and barriers for older people to adopting them. This exploratory study took place in East London in 2016, UK. It used questionnaire and interview, aiming at understanding how mobile technology is adopted among older people. Older people's adoption of mobile technology has been investigated and concluded from four aspects, i.e. getting, learning, using and adopting mobile technologies.

Keywords: Mobile technology · Technology adoption · Older people

1 Introduction

Aging and the speeding development of technology are two widely reported trends around the world.

Previous research shows that ICT can bring older people social and self-understanding benefits (e.g., increased access to current affairs and health information), interaction benefits (e.g., increased connectivity and social support), or task-orientated goals (e.g., ICT-assisted work, travel, shopping, and financial management) [1].

Although there are many benefits of ICTs, there are challenges and barriers for older people adopting them. The barriers have been reported as: poor visual and motor ability negatively impacting the use of ICT, resistance to change brought about by new technology, potential culture influences, etc. [2].

Mobile technology is a fast growing area of ICT with features of mobility, connectivity and the 'carry principle', referring to technologies that are small and ever present [3].

According to Adult's Media Use and Attitudes Report 2016 from Ofcom [4], there has been a considerable increase in the proportion of adults in the UK who only use devices (e.g. smartphones and tablets) other than a PC/laptop to go online, indicating that these devices are no longer just supplementing PCs/laptops, but are starting to replace them.

© Springer International Publishing AG 2017
J. Zhou and G. Salvendy (Eds.): ITAP 2017, Part I, LNCS 10297, pp. 14–24, 2017.
DOI: 10.1007/978-3-319-58530-7_2

Therefore, this study focused on the mobile medium, trying to understand older people's adoption and perceptions of mobile technology.

Technology acceptance has been thoroughly studied with many models and theories, such as the Theory of Reasoned Action (TRA) [5], the Technology Acceptance Model (TAM) [6], and the Theory of Planned Behavior (TPB) [7]. Most of the models consider a workplace setting and are used to predict how new technologies will be received by their potential users.

Since mobile technology is quite new in older people's life, instead of predicting, this study aims to understand how new technology is adopted.

Based on the Innovation Diffusion Theory [8], which explains how an idea, practice or object diffuse and be accepted by people, mobile technology adoption is a long process, getting through the Knowledge stage, Persuasion stage, Decision stage, Implementation stage and Confirmation stage. Therefore, this study investigated older people's adoption of mobile technology from many different aspects, including getting, learning, using and adopting mobile technologies.

Research questions of this study are as follows:

- How do older people get information about mobile technology?
- How do older people learn and use mobile technology?
- Why, or why not, do older people adopt mobile technology?

2   Methods

This study took place in the east part of London (Hackney and Tower Hamlets) in 2016. Questionnaires and interviews were used.

2.1   Participants

Usually, 'older people' are defined as people over 60 years old in accordance with the World Health Organization's convention for the definition of 'ageing' persons [9]. However, we included people between 50 and 60, for the consideration that this group of people are experiencing the evolvement of Internet and have been involved in different technologies to some degree, which may give us some predictive inspiration in future design and research work. We excluded people over 70 in this research, because few of them chose to have unlimited access to Internet or other technology devices.

30 participants took part in this study. They were balanced in gender and employment status, covering different education level and having different living arrangements (Table 1).

2.2   Process

The participants were recruited from a university and two social communities. All of them have signed a consent form, and agreed to take part in this study.

Table 1. Basic information of participants

Characteristics		N	%
Age	50–54	12	(40)
	55–59	6	(20)
	60–64	5	(16.7)
	65–70	7	(23.3)
Gender	Male	17	(56.7)
	Female	13	(43.3)
Living arrangement	Alone	10	(33.3)
	With partner only	6	(20)
	With child only	3	(10)
	With partner and child	7	(23.3)
	With other relative	1	(3.3)
	Other	3	(10)
Education level	Postgraduate or higher degree	11	(36.7)
	1st degree	4	(13.3)
	HND/HNC/Teaching	2	(6.7)
	A-Level	3	(10)
	BTEC/College diploma	7	(23.3)
	Lower degree	3	(10)
Employment status	Retired	7	(23.3)
	Employed part time	5	(16.7)
	Employed full time	9	(30)
	Unemployed	9	(30)

Firstly, each participant was given a printed questionnaire. Since some of the technical terms are unfamiliar with some older people, the questionnaires were done face to face. Each questionnaire took about 15 min to fill in. It was used to understand the general adoption of mobile technology among older people.

Then, each questionnaire was followed by an interview, based on the answers in the questionnaire. It aimed to find out the possible reasons why or why not older people adopt mobile technology.

3   Results

3.1   Information Channels of Mobile Technology

Information channels are important to people's early adoption of a new device or new App. Usually, people need information before making decision of whether to adopt the devices or apps.

From this study, information channels that older people get to know a new mobile device and new Apps are shown in Tables 2 and 3.

Table 2. Information channels of mobile devices

Information channels	N	%
Word of mouth by friends and family	22	73.3
High street stores	7	23.3
TV or Radio	5	16.7
Newspaper or magazines	8	26.7
Social media (such as Facebook and Twitter)	4	13.3
Relevant website	15	50.0
Advertisement in public place (in the underground or on the street)	5	16.7
Other: don't care about this kind of information	2	6.7
Valid N	30	

Table 3. Information channels of mobile apps

Information channels	N	%
Word of mouth by friends and family	12	50.0
App Store or Platform (such as Play Store, Galaxy Apps) in the smartphone or tablet	13	54.2
Newspaper or magazines	3	12.5
Social media (such as Facebook and Twitter)	3	12.5
Relevant website	11	45.8
Advertisement in public place (in the underground or on the street)	3	12.5
I only use the apps existed in my device and never get information about new apps	5	20.8
Valid N	24	

3.2   First Encounter with New Mobile Device or Apps

When facing a new mobile device such as a smartphone or a tablet, the study found that 43.5% participants think they have no difficulty in using a new device or the app 34.8% participants would like to have somebody explain and teach them how to use the new devices or apps.

Different people have different preference in the methods of learning a new function or a new app on mobile devices (especially the smart ones).

The preference of the participants in this study is shown in Table 4. Choices of participants with no mobile devices or only simple cellphones have been excluded in the result, as they have no or little demand for this kind of learning.

3.3   Mobile Technology Adoption Among Older People

Mobile Device Adoption. Among all the 30 participants, all of them have Internet, 14 participants (46.7%) have cellphones (simple mobile phones), 24 participants (80%)

Table 4. Preference of learning a new function or a new app

Methods	N	%
Try it myself	14	58.3
Watching an introduction video	4	16.7
Reading an introduction guide	3	12.5
One to One help from friends or family	7	29.2
One to One help from professionals	6	25.0
Learning within a group of people (like a training course)	3	12.5
Search online	1	4.2
Valid N	24	

have smartphones, 20 participants (66.7%) have personal tablets and 2 participants (6.7%) have smart wristbands.

The participants have rated the frequency of using each item with numbers 1 to 4:

1 = Never
2 = Occasionally
3 = Everyday within 4 h
4 = Everyday more than 4 h

The result is shown in Table 5.

Table 5. Frequency of ICT usage

ICT	Min	Max	Mean	SD
Internet	2	4	3.30	.702
Computer	1	4	2.90	1.029
Cellphone	1	4	1.67	1.028
Smartphone	1	4	2.83	.986
Tablet	1	4	2.20	1.031
Smart wristband	1	4	1.13	.571
Valid N	30			

As shown in the table, the usage of Smartphones has exceeded the usage of Cellphones and nearly the same with computer usage. Only two people in this research have smart wristbands. Both of them were using Fitbit. One got the wristband from her daughter and used it only occasionally, while the other was an IT specialist who used it everyday. Only one participant had never used any kind of mobile devices.

Mobile App Adoption. In total 24 (80%) participants have got a smartphone or tablet, which is capable for installing apps. Among them, 5 (20.8%) participants had never downloaded an app by themselves and rarely used the apps embedded in their smartphone or tablet. 2 (8.3%) participants had never downloaded the apps by themselves but often used the apps embedded in their smartphone or tablet. 17 (70.8%) participants have the experience of downloading some apps by themselves.

The apps they have downloaded include social apps such as whatsapp, twitter and facebook; traffic apps such as citymapper, bus time and national rail; video apps such as BBC Player and Youtube. Some people also download pdf readers to read ebooks or articles on their mobile device and some people could not really remember the names of the apps they had downloaded.

Adoption of Different Operations. People interact with their devices in different ways. Figure 1 shows how frequently the different operations are used.

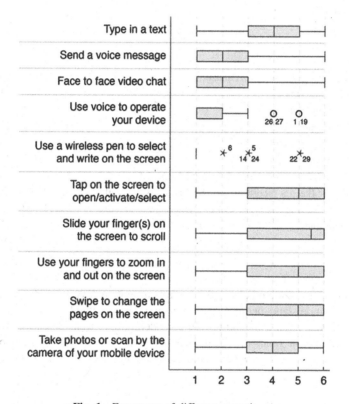

Fig. 1. Frequency of different operations

Frequencies are rated as:

1 = Never;
2 = Less than once a month;
3 = Every month;
4 = Every week;
5 = Everyday (less than 5 times on average);
6 = Everyday (more than 5 times on average).

Adoption of Different Functions. Today's mobile devices are integrating an increasing number of functions. Some people adopt mobile devices only as a mobile

Table 6. Adoption of different functions

Functions	N	%
Making a phone call	24	100.0
SMS, Text messaging	23	95.8
E-mailing	21	87.5
Using face to face video chat (such as Facetime, Skype)	14	58.3
Using social network (such as Facebook, Twitter)	11	45.8
Taking a photo	24	100.0
Filming/taking a video	11	45.8
Watching videos	12	50.0
Listening to music	13	54.2
Playing games	6	25.0
Online shopping (such as eBay Amazon)	6	25.0
Reading News or ebooks	11	45.8
Browsing/surfing website(s)	17	70.8
Mapping, Navigator (such as Google Map)	18	75.0
Online Banking or paying bill	4	16.7
Setting reminders (such as Calendar and alarm)	13	54.2
Sports tracker (count your steps and record your path)	2	8.3
Health monitor (keep a record of your health, such as google fit and healthkit)	4	16.7
Send voice messaging (using messenger, whatsapp or wechat)	7	29.2
Other: Traffic tracker	3	12.5
Valid N	24	

connect with others while other people may regard mobile devices as a small computer. Therefore, to understand people's adoption of mobile technology, their adoption of different functions should be taking into consideration as well. Since many functions are only available on smart mobile devices, only the answers of 24 participants who have smart mobile devices are taken into consideration. Results are shown in Table 6.

3.4 Reasons of Adoption and Non-adoption of Mobile Technology Among Older People

In this study, only one participant had never used a mobile device. He was a teacher who has not retired. He only uses a computer and telephone to get contact with people. The only time he will be out of reach to the people who he may want to contact is the "half hour walk from home to the office." He was satisfied with his lifestyle without mobile devices.

6 participants did not have any smart mobile devices, which could access a larger range of services other than making phone calls. The reasons for not getting this kind of device have been concluded in Table 7.

Table 7. The reasons for not getting a smart mobile device

The reasons for not getting a smart mobile device: (Similar expressions have been calculated as one reason)	N	%
"The cost of using a smartphone/tablet – I do not want to spend a lot of money when using a smartphone/tablet."	4	66.7
"I do not think a smartphone/tablet is useful."	4	66.7
"I want peace and quiet after my working hours"	3	50
"I have other devices such as a laptop or a netbook that can function as well, or better than a smartphone/tablet"	3	50
"A smartphone/tablet is too complicated and difficult to use, and it takes much efforts to learn it."	2	33.3
"I don't know how to use a smartphone/tablet and I don't know what to do when I have difficulties using it."	2	33.3
"Using a smartphone/tablet does not fit with my lifestyle."	2	33.3
"I do not feel comfortable using small screens and tiny keyboards."	1	16.7
"I'm worried about the negative consequences induced by the wrong operations and thus I avoid using new devices."	1	16.7
Valid N	6	

Only 2 of them planed to get a smartphone or tablet, and the reasons have been concluded in Table 8.

Table 8. The reasons for planning to get a smartphone or tablet

The reasons for planning to get a smartphone or tablet (Similar expressions have been calculated as one reason)	N	%
"Most of my friends have used smartphone/tablet, and have convinced me to get one."	2	100
"I want to have a new smartphone/tablet that has more functions such as taking a photograph, filming, and surfing the internet."	2	100
"I travel a lot and the smartphone/tablet will help me on my travels."	2	100
"I will get an upgrade from my provider"	1	50
"They offer apps for the learning apps for languages and composing music"	1	50
"I want to use a smartphone/tablet to keep a better connection with my friends or family"	1	50

Among the 24 participants who had a smart mobile device, 19 participants enjoyed using these devices while 5 of them did not really like using this kind of device. The reasons for not enjoy using smart mobile devices are shown in Table 9.

Table 9. The reasons for not enjoy using smart mobile devices

The reasons for not enjoy using smart mobile devices: (Similar expressions have been calculated as one reason)	N	%
"I don't want my life be taken over by mobile device."	4	80
"I don't want to spent too much time in a virtual world, I'd like to enjoy the real life."	4	80
"Things on mobile devices always change, I'm fed up with learning new figures."	2	40
"Sometimes, I would like to have someone explain and teach me the new functions or apps."	2	40
"Some apps are too complex to use, I can't remember how to use."	1	20

4   Discussion and Conclusion

From how older people get to know a mobile technology to how they use mobile technology, this study investigated mobile technology adoption among older people.

This study shows that more older people are using smartphones instead of simple cellphones. Normally, the fast growing smartphone market will contribute to this.

4.1   How Do Older People Get to Know a Mobile Technology?

Older people get information of mobile devices mainly from the "word of mouth by friends and family" (73.3%) and "relevant website" (50%). They get information of mobile devices mainly from "App Store or Platform (such as Play Store, Galaxy Apps) embedded in the smartphone or tablet" (54.2%). "Word of mouth by friends and family" (50%) and "relevant website" 45.8%) are also very important information sources of mobile apps.

4.2   How Do Older People Learn to Use Mobile Technology?

About 44% participants think they have no difficulty in using a new device or the apps on it. It suggests that older people are getting used to mobile device at a surprising speed, but it could in part because of the limited kind of apps and functions they use.

About 35% participants would like to have somebody explain and teach them how to use the new devices or apps. But 58% participants prefer to learn a new function or apps by "trying it myself". While mobile devices and mobile apps are easier to learn than computers and software, mobile devices have more private information. This is the most fast and safe way of learning a mobile device or mobile apps, especially for those who have confidence in using this kind of things.

This learning method is followed by "One to One help from friends or family" (29.2%) and "One to One help from professionals" (25%), showing that one to one help is the most preferable way for older people to get support on using a new mobile technology.

4.3   How Do Older People Use Mobile Technology?

This study suggests that many older people are already quite familiar with interacting with the touch screen, using "tap", "slide to scroll" and "swipe", even "zoom in and out". The most popular way for older people to input information is still typing text (Mean = 4.03). Taking photos or scanning by the camera of mobile device (Mean = 3.60) also has an extensive popularity among older users. However, using voice as an input (Mean = 1.73) hasn't been preferred by older people yet.

About 71% of the participants who have got a smartphone or tablet have experience in downloading an app. Although functions like "making phone calls" (100%), "SMS, Text messaging" (95.8%) and "E-mailing" (87.5%) show a great popularity among older people. Functions other than communication, such as "Taking a photo" (100%), "Mapping, Navigator" (75%) and "Browsing/surfing website" (70.8%) have also been used widely among older people. This may suggest that more and more older people begin to explore their smart devices, regarding mobile phone not only as a phone, and try to make full use of it.

4.4   Why, or Why not, Do Older People Adopt Mobile Technology?

The reasons for not getting a smart mobile device can be summarize in 2 points. The most important one is that older people cannot perceive enough usefulness of the device – not useful enough for them to pay an extra cost and not useful enough compared with other devices. The second point is lack of comfort, both physically and mentally, caused by mobile device. These two points are consistent with the "perceived usefulness" and "perceived ease of use" in Davis' Technology Acceptance Model [6].

People adopt devices first and adopt function and apps later. However, from the reasons for planning to get a smartphone or tablet, attractive functions and apps seems to be strong enough to promote the adoption of devices in reverse.

Although most participants are using smart mobile devices, many of them are unhappy with these devices. In order to avoid future abandonment of mobile technology, the reasons for not enjoying using smart mobile devices should be taken into consideration. The reasons come from two parts. On one hand, older people do not like the way that mobile technology interferes their life. On the other hand, they do not want to make much effort to keep up with the changing technology.

References

1. Selwyn, N.: The information aged: a qualitative study of older adults' use of information and communications technology. J. Aging Stud. **18**, 369–384 (2004)
2. Hill, R., Beynon-Davies, P., Williams, M.D.: Older people and internet engagement. Inf. Technol. People **21**(3), 244–266 (2008)
3. Foong, P.S.: The value of the life course perspective in the design of mobile technologies for older adults. In: Lim, S.S. (ed.) Mobile Communication and the Family. MCALIGI, pp. 165–181. Springer, Dordrecht (2016). doi:10.1007/978-94-017-7441-3_10

4. Adult's Media Use and Attitudes Report, Ofcom, 6–7 (2016). https://www.ofcom.org.uk/__data/assets/pdf_file/0026/80828/2016-adults-media-use-and-attitudes.pdf. Accessed 10 Feb 2017
5. Fishbein, M., Ajzen, I.: Belief, Attitude, Intention and Behavior: An Introduction to Theory and Research, pp. 561–562. Addison-Wesley, Reading (1975)
6. Davis, F.D.: Perceived usefulness, perceived ease of use, and user acceptance of information technology. MIS Q. **13**, 319–340 (1989)
7. Ajzen, I.: The theory of planned behavior. Organ. Behav. Hum. Decis. Process. **50**(2), 179–211 (1991)
8. Rogers, E.M.: Diffusion of Innovations, pp. 163–210. Simon and Schuster, New York (2010)
9. WHO: Definition of an older or elderly person. Who.int. Accessed 10 Feb 2017

Everyday Life Interactions of Women 60+ with ICTs: Creations of Meaning and Negotiations of Identity

Barbara Ratzenböck[✉]

Center for Inter-American Studies, University of Graz, Graz, Austria
barbara.ratzenboeck@uni-graz.at

Abstract. How do women 60+ use and ascribe meaning to "new" and "old" information and communication technologies such as cell phones, the Internet, computers, TV, and radio? To investigate this question, life-graph discussions, walking interviews in small domestic spaces, and semi-structured interviews with Austrian women aged 60–70 have been conducted. The analysis of the material collected has shown that both generation-specific experiences of media usage and individual biographical backgrounds influence the use of and ascription of meaning to ICTs. However, ICT usage does not only reflect collective generational experiences and individual biographical circumstances. ICTs are also actively used by women 60+ to creatively shape their identities as women and older adults. Thus, this paper discusses processes and strategies of identity negotiations of women 60+ in the context of ICTs, and explores how everyday life interactions with ICTs can be interpreted as a means of resistance against normative assumptions such as ageist stereotypes.

Keywords: Women 60+ · ICT experiences · Everyday life · Identity · Generations

1 Introduction

In Austria, as well as in Europe in general, age-related differences in terms of usage of information and communication technologies (ICTs) are well documented by empirical findings [1, 2]. Examining the data of Statistics Austria [1] regarding Internet usage by Austrians of different age groups more closely, one can moreover identify an intersectional digital divide, as not only age is statistically related to usage of the Internet, but also gender. Significant differences in Internet usage between older men and women can for instance be identified looking at the numbers of Austrians who in 2014 indicated to have never used the Internet. While almost every third Austrian man (roughly 31%) aged between 55 and 74 indicated to have never used the Internet, almost every other woman of the same group (roughly 47%) stated the same [1]. These intersectional digital divides are problematic, because digital platforms and services not only provide entertainment and opportunities for private communication, but are increasingly promoted as tools for the organization of life in general by political bodies such as the European Union [3, for example]. People who do not use digital communication technologies such as the Internet are at risk of being excluded on various societal levels [4].

© Springer International Publishing AG 2017
J. Zhou and G. Salvendy (Eds.): ITAP 2017, Part I, LNCS 10297, pp. 25–37, 2017.
DOI: 10.1007/978-3-319-58530-7_3

Thus, a current empirical study of the research project "Cultural Narratives of Age and Aging" at the Center for Inter-American Studies of the University of Graz, supported by funds of the Österreichische Nationalbank (Anniversary Fund, project no. 15849) explores processes of ascription of meaning to and strategies of use of various information and communication technologies (and particular 'new' ones, such as the Internet) by older women, a group that is being marginalized on the "digital spectrum" [5, p. 5] in the Austrian context. The project aims at understanding lifetimes of experiences with various information and communication technologies and how these past media biographies relate to older women's contemporary everyday life experiences with ICTs. As previous results of analyses conducted within the frameworks of this empirical study have shown [6], both generationally-framed media experiences in terms of a sense of "belonging" within time – in Heinz Bude's [7, p. 28] concept of generational experiences – and, in turn, individual biographic backgrounds, influence the use of and ascription of meaning to ICTs. Both collective reference points in terms of "media generations" [8, 9] and "generation-specific media practice cultures" – as Burkard Schäffer [8] termed practices that are particularly prominent among certain cohorts – and very personal and individual biographical contexts (e.g. work experiences), leisure interests (e.g. sports, music) and world views (spiritual beliefs, political opinions), influence older women's engagement with ICTs. Older women's interactions with ICTs in everyday life thus need to be understood as creative *interplays* of generational and individual experiences and interpretations thereof [6], as Christina E. Buse has also illustrated in her study on computer technologies and embodiment in later life [10].

However, ICT usage does not only reflect collective generational experiences and individual biographical circumstances, but information and communication technologies are also being *actively used* by older women to narrate their lives and thus negotiate their identities as members of social groups – families, communities, and society at large. Although a substantial percentage of studies in the context of seniors' interactions with ICTS primarily focuses on how ICTs can be used to "enhance" older peoples' lives, in terms of cognitive performance, connectivity, or life satisfaction [for example, 11–13], an increasing body of scholarly literature is emerging which highlights agency and creative potentials of older adults in their engagement with ICTs. There are numerous examples of such studies, among them works of Buse [10, 14], Kim Sawchuk and Barbara Crow [15, 16], Loredana Ivan and Shannon Hebblethwaite [17], Andrea Rosales and Mireia Fernández-Ardèvol [18]. This paper intends to contribute to this growing body of critical scholarly literature by examining how older women in Austria creatively engage with ICTs in everyday life and through these interactions negotiate their identities.

2   Method

Participants of this empirical study are women aged 60–70 years of different social backgrounds, residing in the Austrian province of Styria. The study thus focuses on women of the third age (young-old) [19, p. 9]. One assumption of this study is that generational factors, in terms of "historical location" [20, p. 137] as well as "historical participation" [20, p. 140] or "generation location" [21] influence usage of and ascription of meaning to ICTs across the life course. Thus, the age range of participants was limited to the age 60–70 years in order to create a somewhat comparable group in terms of a 'technology generation,' a concept denominating measurable cohort effects in relation to technology [22]. In Austria, the Internet became more widespread in the early 2000s [23]. Thus, women participating in the study are all likely to have been similarly confronted with decisions on (non-)adoption of new technologies, such as the Internet, both in their professional working environments and/or careers as family care workers, either on a discursive or practical level.

In terms of empirical methods, the study employs a three-part-methodology consisting of life-graph discussions [for an example, see 24] focusing on media biographies, semi-structured sit-down interviews, and "walking interviews in small domestic spaces" [25], all conducted at the same day at the home of the participant. All conversations are being recorded digitally. While the life-graph discussions are being used to biographically frame the conversations between interviewee and interviewer right from the start, the semi-structured sit-down interviews at the coffee or kitchen tables at participants' homes focus on a variety of specific media technologies, attitudes towards these technologies, specific everyday life strategies for interacting with these technologies, and general strategies of acquiring new knowledge on how to use ICTs across the life course.[1] The indoor walking interviews at the homes of the participants are conducted after the life-graph discussions and semi-structured sit-down interviews. Under the lead of the interviewee, interviewer and interviewee tour the interviewee's home, stop at different media devices, and have a casual conversation about them. As I have argued elsewhere [25], the main advantage of including walking interviews in small domestic spaces in the methodology design is that the method counters some of the power imbalances inherent to more traditional interview set-ups, allows for more informal glimpses of everyday life, and explicitly invites media objects into the research process. All of this enables a deeper understanding of the complex entanglements of older adults and ICTs [25].

So far, 10 life-graph discussions, 10 semi-structured sit-down interviews, and 10 walking interviews at the homes of participants have been conducted. In total, more than 24 hours of recordings of conversations have been transcribed, using a semi-detailed transcription scheme. The analysis of the transcriptions was based on the steps Udo Kuckartz suggested within the frameworks of "content-structuring qualitative content analysis" [27]. This form of analysis combines deductive categorization and inductive (open) coding inspired by Grounded Theory [28]. After carefully reviewing the entire interview material, main thematic categories were developed based on the main research question,[2] topics of the questionnaire for the semi-structured interviews, and notes taken during the initial review of the transcripts. The main six categories that were finally developed for the initial deductive analysis were "media biographies" (1), "information and communication technologies/devices" (2), "user strategies" (3), "attitudes towards ICTs" (4), "intergenerationality" (5), and "identity" (6). Using these six categories, the entire interview material was categorized.

---

[1] The questionnaire for the semi-structured sit-down interviews was developed on the basis of a questionnaire developed by Fernández-Ardèvol [26] for a case study on the adoption and use of cell phones by older adults.

[2] "How do Austrian women aged 60–70 years use and ascribe meaning to various ICTs?".

Subsequently, sub-categories for each main category were developed inductively, applying an open coding strategy [28]. The advantage of Kuckartz's approach is that it enables a creative and explorative interaction with the interview material while also ensuring a structured analytical procedure. Using content-structuring qualitative content analysis [27], more than 3,300 text segments could be categorized and coded.

In terms of a theoretical lens guiding the analysis, "anocriticism,"[3] [29] an interpretational approach developed by Roberta Maierhofer [29–32], was important for the review of the interview material. Anocriticism encourages the analysis of continuities *and* changes within an individuals' life course, as well as thinking of intersectional interrelations between age and gender. Much like in a feminist approach, anocriticism calls for a "search for a specific female culture of ageing" [31, p. 156], as well as for a distinction between chronological and cultural age [30, p. 129]. This interpretational lens was important for the present analysis, since it enabled a foregrounding of individual experiences in the context of ICT engagement, as well as adding the generational aspects to the context of the research [6]. However, anocriticism does not only help to emphasize individual *variations* in biographies that influence today's use of ICTs. Perhaps even more importantly, adopting an anocritical perspective enables the reader (in this case the reader of interview transcripts) to become a "resisting reader," as Maierhofer [31, p. 157] has argued building on Judith Fetterley's work. Resisting readers forgo traditional interpretations and investigate how a text challenges common understandings [31, p. 157]. In the context of analyzing older women's experiences and interactions with ICTs, this means to forgo mainstream interpretations of age as homogenous [5, p. 1] or generally related to missing technical competencies [33], and instead focus on the "subject of women growing old" [32, p. 334] and how these subjects actively and creatively use information and communication technologies (and talk about them) to negotiate their identities as human beings within time and society.

3 Results

By looking for *dominant images of self*, *common contexts* in which the use of ICTs was reflected on, and *points of resistance and explicit negotiation of identities* in the interview transcripts, three major thematic frameworks of participants' narrations of ICT experiences could be identified: "collective identities within time" (1), "social identities in the family context" (2), and "resisting identities" (3). In this context, identity is to be understood as referring to both a "thematization of self" [34, p. 151], and a *narration* or *construction* of self [34, pp. 151–152]. Within the frameworks of this study, identity thus comprises structural elements on the macro level, such as "generation location" [21] or gender as well as elements of meso and micro levels such as identities in a specific family setting or very personal life context.

---

[3] For a definition and etymology of anocriticism see, for example, source 29.

3.1 Collective Identities Within Time

The first thematic framework which proves to be important for participants' narrations of their ICT engagement comprises notions of *collectively shared identities with regards to experiences of time*. All interviewees expressed a sense of "temporal location in the historical process" [20, p. 139], as Alwin succinctly puts it. As stated elsewhere [6], this sense of cohort identity was often expressed by interviewees sharing childhood memories of "generation-specific" media experiences, such as having to be silent when parents listened to the radio or watching television as a group, in a family context. In addition, as the current analysis revealed, the experience of having had "little media" around when one was young was mentioned by multiple interviewees. Interviewee 3 (I 3), a 60-year old former secretary and homemaker living in a suburb of the Styrian capital Graz, stated that when she was young her family only had "[a] radio. That was it. There was nothing else."[4] But it was not only in terms of material realities that interviewees expressed an awareness of being historically located. Statements also reflected notions of generation in a Mannheimian sense, as "similarly 'stratified' consciousness" [21, p. 297] or "Zeitgeist" [20, p. 138]. As already illustrated in the discussion of previous intermediary results [6], multiple participants also expressed a feeling of generational belonging with regard to using media moderately and refusing to be part of a "throw-away-society" (I 3).

While notions of a cohort or generational identity with regard to media use were already prominent in previous analyses, more *dynamic* experiences of living within time only became apparent in the current analysis. Most interviewees believed that "the young" have media experiences different to their own. Interviewee 4, a woman from a small village in her mid-sixties, who used to work as an accounting clerk, thinks that "the young are just able to handle [media] differently." Interviewee 6, a woman in her early sixties who had migrated from Britain to Austria in her earlier years and used to work as a social worker before retirement, shares this perspective: "I think you [interviewer in her early 30s], you are of the Internet generation, you grew up with it. It is part of your life, it is just there, you can't imagine to be without it. We didn't. […] [T]he majority of young people knows stuff and if they know stuff or they don't know it, they know where to look for it. And if you are constantly part of that change – renew, renew – you are not having to make such big leaps, whereas [for] somebody of my age probably buying a tablet the first time is a big thing!" Also, interviewee 10, a woman in her early sixties living in a small village and who used to work as a bank clerk, shares this impression. Talking about how she does not like to look things up on the Internet to find out how to operate ICTs, she states: "It is somehow an effort […]. I think our generation did not grow with it [new ICTs], but rather entered [the situation] at some point. And, well, for me this close connection did not develop […]." Similar observations of notions of "being different from the young" were also reported in other studies, such as Crow and Sawchuk's investigation of mobile phone use among Canadian seniors [15, p. 501], Rebecca Hill, Paul Beynon-Davies, and Michael D. Williams'

---

[4] The majority of interviews was conducted in German. Only interview number 6 was conducted in English. Thus, with the exceptions of quotes from the transcript of interview number 6, all quotes from transcripts are translations from German to English by the author.

exploration of older people's Internet engagement [35, p. 257], Tiina Suopajärvi's findings [36, pp. 117–119] or Buse's study on embodiment and ICT use in later life [10].

In the current study, a lot of references to the smartphone were made in terms of an embodied age identity, for example by elaborating on how swiping as a movement has to be learned when purchasing a cell phone. Such findings are notable because they point to dynamic aspects of aging experiences, to experiences of time passing and things changing. They point to experiences of change of older ICT users and also to negotiations of age and cultural images associated with it. Negotiations of age particularly surfaced with regard to the questions of when one stops 'growing with' technologies and of when one is 'young' or 'old' with regard to media [37, pp. 6–8]. Although participants repeatedly stated that their media experiences and engagements are different from those of 'the young,' multiple participants also portrayed themselves as different from 'the old.' For example, talking about cell phones, interviewee 4 stated: "And the age-appropriate cell phone, I find that very good for the old folks. I say, well, I don't need it yet, but I have a sister who already is an old lady and she has such an age-appropriate phone and she can handle that quite well […]." Also interviewee 8, a woman in her early sixties who still works as a farmer in the Styrian countryside, negotiated her own aging identity noting that she would not like to take a traditional beginner's class for computer use "because if there are just seniors [in the class], then it probably won't be effective." Older adults, particularly older women, are often framed as the "Other" in terms of cultural narratives, as age critic Margaret Cruikhank [38, p. 5], among others, has noted. Also, participants of this study used this broader cultural reference point talking about their media experiences. These cultural images are negotiated in the interviews. Interviewee 6, for example, noted that she would not like to have a phone specifically designed for seniors: "I don't, in design, want to be different to everybody else. I am not gonna advertise 'Look, I need this big thing.'" Thus, interviewee 6 refused to be labeled as "different" from "everybody else" (the young) and indicated that she does not want to be seen with a device which is culturally coded as 'old.' As Suopajärvi [36, p. 117] notes, senior users engage in "boundary-making" between themselves and "old age." However, these boundaries are being negotiated ambivalently by emphasizing differences to "the young," but also to "the old" in terms of engagement with ICTs.

3.2   Social Identities in the Family Context

As the analysis of the interview material has shown, by far the most important reference point for participants to talk about their ICT experiences were social contexts, particularly family settings. After finishing the analysis, references to one's identity as a "socially-embedded" person (e.g. a mother, grandmother, member of a community or special interest group) in the context of ICT use amounted to more than 400 codings. Other possible reference points for the narration of ICT experiences, such as entertainment, were only rarely mentioned. This finding is supported by results of other studies on older adults' ICT use, such as Sawchuk and Crow's study on older Canadians' interactions with cell phones [15, p. 497]. Particularly often, interviewees talked about their own children and grandchildren when discussing their media experiences. Thus, regarding different frames for narrations of ICT experiences, participants' identity in terms of "kinship position" [20, p. 135] was key. Interviewee 2, a sixty-nine-year old woman from the suburbs of Graz who has been a homemaker and also used to work as a secretary in commerce and the social sector, referred to herself as a "cybermom" talking about her media use in comparison to her daughter and how she has always enjoyed shooting home videos with a super 8 early on.

In this context, it is important to note that participants' references to generation in terms of a specific phase within the life course were highly gendered. Interviewees frequently talked about their ICT experiences in the context of care work and household chores. Particularly often, they talked about their ICT use in the context of taking care of their grown-up children and grandchildren. For example, being asked where she uses her cell phone, interviewee 9, a sixty-two year old woman living in Graz who still works part-time as an accountant at an NGO, stated that "[...] the cell phone is like an umbilical cord. Without the cell phone I have to say, that might sound strange, but then [without the cell phone] I feel [that] something is missing. Then I am not connected with the world. You see, it is even in the bedroom. At night, I put it on silent mode but I am always afraid [that] the two sons [...], if they call and I am not available. I always have to be available for them." Many other participants talked about their ICT experiences in connection to performing care work as grandmothers. For example, interviewee 7, a woman in her early sixties living in the countryside, who used to run a grocery store together with her husband and continues to work part-time at a supermarket, stated with regard to gaining knowledge about new ICTs: "[...] I have always wanted to participate [in a computer class] at some point [...] but I never managed time-wise with the kids [referring to grandchildren] because at the beginning I had to watch [my grandson] and there was always something, so [...] I never managed time-wise." Also many other interviewees referred to their role as grandmother when it comes to engaging with ICTs. Interviewee 5, a sixty-two-year old woman from a small city in Upper Styria, who has been a homemaker and carer for most of her life, after having completed a seamstress apprenticeship in her youth, thinks that computers are for people who do not have grandchildren, like one of her friends. Her experience, however, is different: "[I]f there are also grandchildren, there is action and chaos anyways, thus a computer isn't of interest for us or very little because if all three [grandkids] are here during the weekend, there is action, so you are glad when they leave [again] and then I lie down and probably turn on the TV, but the computer, very little." As Ivan and Hebblethwaite [17, p. 12] have highlighted in their work on grandmothers' experiences of social networks, grandparent roles are still heavily gendered. Grandmothers are expected to take care of family bonding and maintain family relationships [17, p. 12]. This also became apparent in many ways in this study. Besides being available for their own kids on the phone and watching grandchildren, participants also shared other ways of performing their roles as family carers during the interviews. Interviewee 4, for example, reported that she keeps a kind of 'family log-book.' Because she has a big family and wants to remember details about each member, she started noting down facts about relatives in a word document: "[...] sounds weird, but [...] we have a big family and at some point I have noted down everybody with their siblings and their kids and there I note down certain things [...] because you cannot remember all of this [...]. [If] we did not get there [to her relatives' place] for a long time, I take a look [at the file], what was his name, what was the kid's name, how old is the kid, that helps a lot and prevents embarrassments." In addition to caring for relations with close and extended family, participants also repeatedly talked about their media experiences in relation to their identities as homemakers. As Buse [14, p. 1159] has found, gender roles are important in the context of negotiating boundaries of work, leisure, and retirement. Interviewee 8, for example, talking about her daily routines, stated that she combines household work and media engagement: "I have been cooking and it is a bad habit, but the TV is on, I actually never look at it [...] or during ironing, I watch something [...]. [I]t is a [...] habit, a bad one, to have the TV on while cooking. [...] I never used to turn the TV on while doing work [referring to household chores], except for ironing, I have always done that." Interviewee 8 perceives all the tasks she performs at home as "work," thus it is important to not only investigate older women's engagement with ICT in terms of leisure, but also with regard to their frequent and intense roles as "family manger[s]," as interviewee 2 referred to herself.

Another important aspect regarding participants' framings of their stories on their ICT use was intergenerational support with technologies, which already emerged as an important category early on in the study [6, 25], and has also been identified in other studies [39]. Also in this study, the most prominent strategy among interviewees to gain new knowledge about ICT use or acquisition of new devices was to ask their children (and the children's partners) for advice. Examples from the transcript are numerous in this context. Talking about using new ICTs, interviewee 7, for example, stated that her son's help was essential for her initial use of the computer: "[W]ithout [...] my older son being there and arranging everything, we would have probably not managed [...]. He helped us a lot then and actually from this point on I was also more interested [in computers] und then I took a computer class." As also noted by Fausto Colombo and Simone Carlo [40, p. 168], everyday family interactions are key when regarding the adoption of new ICTs and general approaches to using media. However, findings of the present study show that intergenerational support can be mutual between family members with different "kinship position" [20, p. 135]. While many participants supported their grown-up children in terms of care work for them and their children, they received support with ICTs. Older women use their experiences with ICTs to express images of gender roles and age, as Meika Loe [41] has argued. As the analysis has shown, also in the Austrian context, older women specifically use their experiences with ICTs to negotiate their gendered identities, such as the grandmother role.

3.3   Resisting Identities

Investigating generational perspectives – in terms of cohorts, Mannheimian generations, or positions in a family – helps to identify important aspects of older women's ICT engagement, such as intergenerational support. However, solely focusing on strongly collectively influenced identities regarding older women's ICT experiences, such as the grandmother role, can prevent us from seeing individuals in the context of their *unique* life narratives [42, p. 407]. Thus, examining "resisting identities" with regard to older women's ICT use is equally important. As Ivan and Hebblethwaite [17, p. 21] have argued, older adults' ICT choices need to be understood in the context of agency. As the interviews have shown, older women use – and sometimes also *do not* use – information and communication technologies to express their very individual identities, independent of references to generational experiences or family commitments. Examples from the interview material are numerous. Interviewee 1, a woman aged sixty-six, coming from the Styrian capital, who used to work part-time as a secretary in the public sector, besides being a homemaker, uses her stereo, cassette player, and record player to express her identity as chorister and music lover. For interviewee 4, new ICTs are a means of supporting environmental causes such as biodiversity, and thus strengthening her identity as an environmentalist. Interviewee 5, who generally identified herself as a non-user of new ICTs, only reads text messages to facilitate her work as a volunteer with an aid organization. And interviewee 10 interprets ICTs as a means supporting her training as a mystic and healer. In this context, approaches originally developed in the field of literary studies, such as Maierhofer's "anocriticism" approach [29–32], can enrich the analysis of empirical text material, such as interview transcripts, and help diversify the images of older ICT users. As Maierhofer [30, p. 141] has argued, interpreters of texts need to acknowledge the importance of self-definition of old "protagonists." In addition, the inclusion of the method of "walking interviews in small domestic spaces" into the design of empirical studies is promising with regard to the discovery of multiplicities of meaning and personal relevance related to older people's ICT engagement [25].

In the case of this study, besides identifying individual identities relevant to ICT engagement, such as being a musician or an esoteric, an analysis informed by anocriticism also allowed for the discovery of a strong sense of self-determination in many interviews. Most prominently, this sense of self-determination surfaced in the case of interviewee 5, who very consciously decided not to engage with technologies such as the Internet, and actively resists the general public discourse of the Internet as indispensable for life in the 21st century: "Well, and some do say, 'Don't you miss it [the Internet]? Or what?' I don't miss it because I don't know it, [and I] don't need it." Instead of using the Internet, she likes to walk her dog or walk down to the river, which seems more important to her: "I get more out of this." Also, with regard to concrete interactions with ICTs, a sense of self-determination was expressed by multiple interviewees. Particularly prominent was the notion of "being in charge" because one is able to simple turn off media devices by pushing the power button or deciding not to turn them on in the first place. As interviewee 2 said with regard to bad TV programs: "[O]ne must not complain all the time. I don't have to watch." For others, such as interviewee 6, self-determination also plays a role in the adoption of new technologies. Elaborating on her use of radio, interviewee 6 states: "[…] I hate listening to half a program on the radio and having to stand there till it's finished, so I tend to podcast in recent years and then I just take it around with my iPod and listen to it when I want." Thus, notions of self-determination are expressed in many different forms in the interview material.

4   Conclusion

What have I discovered and learned analyzing the interview material collected? When and how do communication and information technologies matter to women 60+? On the one hand, the analysis of the life-graph discussions, semi-structured sit-down interviews, and walking interviews at home confirmed previous findings obtained in the course of this multi-year study, namely the importance of intergenerational relationships and also the influence of generational factors on engagement with ICTs, as argued previously in the context of methodological reflections [25, p. 52] and presentation of interim results [6, pp. 61–64]. On the other hand, the current analysis suggests that the notion of "generation" is much more complex in the perspective of study participants than anticipated at first thought. While previous interim results of the study [6, pp. 61–62] suggested a relatively strong importance of childhood experiences for participants' current interactions with ICTs, present results show that notions of generation in the sense of "kinship positions" [20, p. 135] or "a period in the life course" [5, p. 2] are much more crucial for older women's narrations of ICT experiences. Besides cohort and generational notions, more dynamic experiences of living within time became apparent in the analysis as well. Talking about media experiences, many of the participants dismissed a binary notion of young and old by refusing to belong to "the old" (media users) and simultaneously distancing themselves from the radically different media experiences of "the young." Instead, interviewees put forward the idea of age as a relational category and portrayed themselves as being "old" and "young" at the same time. For participants, talking about ICTs thus is "doing age" [43, p. 89, for example].

Although identity references related to the macro level of society played an important role in the interviews, notions of generational identity in terms of family lineage prove to be even more important for the narrative framing of older women's experiences with ICTs. For participants of the study, talking about experiences with information and communication technologies also meant talking about caring for their grown-up children and grandchildren. In this context, gendered age identities were very prominent. Besides caring for their own kids and watching grandchildren, interviewees also fostered family relations in creative ways, for example by starting a 'family log-book' on the computer to keep track of extensive family networks (interviewee 4). In many ways, women participating in the study lived up to the role of a "grandmother" who is culturally expected to maintain family relationships [17, p. 12].

However, women also used other, more individual notions of self to frame their stories on ICT usage. These included, among others, identities connected to music, political orientations, volunteer work, and spiritual beliefs. Many women interviewed also voiced a sense of agency and of "being in charge" with regard to ICTs, for example in being able to just turn off a device. As this study has shown, theoretical tools such as "anocriticism" [29–32], as well as inclusive research methods, such as walking interviews at older peoples' homes, can help highlight more individual aspects of engagement with ICTs and "complicate" the image of older ICT users. This is crucial since older women's experiences with ICTs are multi-layered. They include multiple temporal perspectives, implicit and explicit references to larger cultural narratives on age and gender, as well as varying personal points of reference. Loe [41, p. 321] has argued that older women use technology for the "expression of womanhood, even in old age." Reviewing the interview material of the present study, I would like to take Loe's point even further by stating that older women do not only "express" their identities engaging with information and communication technologies, but *actively create, critically negotiate, and resist* their multiple identities as human beings within time.

5   Limitations and Implications for Future Research

This paper has discussed how Austrian women aged 60–70 years narrate their everyday life experiences with ICTs and identified central thematic frames of the stories they shared on their engagement with these technologies. In total, three dominant frames of narration could be identified analyzing the interview material collected: references to collective identities within time, references to social identities in the family context, and references to "resisting" identities pointing to unique personal life experiences. Although this study aims at contributing to the growing body of scholarly literature highlighting *agency* of older adults in their ICT engagement, it also acknowledges the importance social *structures* with regard to older adults' experiences with ICTs such as, for example, differences in socio-economic status. While interviewees of different social and economic backgrounds have been included in the sample, most interviewees belonged to the Austrian middle class. In addition to the focus on only one age-group (60–70 years) for reasons of comparability and feasibility, the relative homogeneity of the sample in terms of class and ethnicity represents another limitation of the study. Also the relatively small sample size due the exploratory design of the study is a limitation of this investigation. Recommendations for future studies are thus twofold. For future empirical studies the use of a larger sample – for example also in the context of a quantitative research design – is recommended in order to investigate frequency and distribution of different thematic framings of ICT experiences of older women in society as a whole. Yet, it is also important to reflect on the inclusivity or exclusivity of certain research methodologies. Thus, another recommendation for future studies on older women's ICT experiences is to include inclusive research methods such as "walking interviews in small domestic spaces" [25] in the design to ensure diversity in representation.

Acknowledgements. This work was supported by funds from the Österreichische Nationalbank (Österreichische Nationalbank, Anniversary Fund, project number: 15849). In addition, this work was also supported by a grant from the Social Sciences and Humanities Research Council of Canada to the Ageing, Communication, Technologies project 895-2013-1018 (actproject.ca).

References

1. Statistics Austria: Internetnutzerinnen und Internetnutzer (2014). http://www.statistik.at/web_de/statistiken/energie_umwelt_innovation_mobilitaet/informationsgesellschaft/ikt-einsatz_in_haushalten/073636.html (Internet users 2014)
2. Eurostat: Statistics in focus. http://ec.europa.eu/eurostat/documents/3433488/5585460/KS-SF-12-050-EN.PDF/39000dab-e2b7-49b2-bc4b-6aad0bf01279
3. European Commission: The European eGovernment Action Plan 2011–2015. http://eur-lex.europa.eu/LexUriServ/LexUriServ.do?uri=COM:2010:0743:FIN:EN:PDF
4. Richardson, M., Weaver, C.K., Zorn, T.: 'Getting on': older New Zealanders'. Percept. Comput. New Media Soc. **7**, 219–245 (2005). doi:10.1177/1444805050763
5. Loos, E., Haddon, L., Mante-Meijer, E.: Introduction. In: Loos, E., Haddon, L., Mante-Meijer, E. (eds.) Generational Use of New Media, pp. 1–9. Ashgate, Farnham (2012)
6. Ratzenböck, B.: Examining the experienced of older women with ICTs. Interrelations of generation-specific media practices and individual media biographies. Nordicom Rev. **37**, 57–70 (2016). doi:10.1515/nor-2016-0023
7. Bude, H.: Generation im Kontext. Von der Kriegs-zu den Wohlfahrtsstaatsgenerationen. [Generation Contextualized. From the War Generations to the Generations of the Welfare State] In: Jureit, J., Wildt, M. (eds.) Generationen. Zur Relevanz eines wissenschaftlichen Grundbegriffs [Generations. On the Relevance of a Basic Concept in Science], Hamburg, Hamburger edn., pp. 28–44 (2005)

8. Schäffer, B.: Mediengenerationen, Medienkohorten und generationsspezifische Medien praxiskulturen. Zum Generationenansatz in der Medienforschung. [Media Generations, Media Cohorts and Generation-specific Media Practice Cultures. On the Generational Approach in Media Studies] In: Schorb, B., Hartung, A., Reißmann, W. (eds.) Medien und höheres Lebensalter. Theorie – Forschung – Praxis [Media and Old(er) Age. Theory – Research – Practice], pp. 31–50. Verlag für Sozialwissenschaften, Wiesbaden (2009)

9. Bolin, G., Westlund, O.: Mobile generations: the role of mobile technology in the shaping of Swedish media generations. Int. J. Commun. **3**, 108–124 (2009)

10. Buse, C.E.: E-scaping the aging body? Computer technologies and embodiment in later life. Aging Soc. **30**, 987–1009 (2010). doi:10.1017/S0144686X10000164

11. Nascimento Ordonez, T., Sanches Yassuda, M., Cachioni, M.: Elderly online: effects of a digital inclusion program in cognitive performance. Arch. Gerontol. Geriatr. **53**, 216–219 (2010). doi: 10.1016/j.archger.2010.11.007

12. Cattan, M.: The use of telephone befriending in low level support for socially isolated older people – an evaluation. Health Soc. Care Commun. **19**(2), 198–206 (2011)

13. Lelkes, O.: Happier and less isolated: internet use in old age. J. Poverty Soc. Justice **21**(1), 33–46 (2013). doi:10.1332/175982713X664047

14. Buse, C.E.: When you retire, does everything become leisure? Information and communication technology use and the work/leisure boundary in retirement. New Media Soc. **11**(7), 1143–1161 (2009). doi:10.1177/1461444809342052

15. Sawchuk, K., Crow, B.: I'm G-mom on the phone. Remote grandmothering, cell phones and intergenerational dis/connections. Feminist Media Stud. **12**(4), 496–505 (2012)

16. Crow, B., Sawchuk, K.: New and old, young and old. Aging the mobile imaginary. In: Herman, A., Hadlaw, J., Swiss, T. (eds.) Theories of the Mobile Internet: Materialities and Imaginaries, pp. 187–199. Routledge, New York (2015)

17. Ivan, L., Hebblethwaite, S.: Grannies on the net: grandmothers' experiences of facebook in family communication. Rom. J. Commun. Public Relat. **18**(1), 11–25 (2016). doi:10.21018/rjcpr. 2016.1.199

18. Rosales, A., Fernández-Ardèvol, M.: Beyond WhatsApp: older people and smartphones. Rom. J. Commun. Public Relat. **18**(1), 27–47 (2016). doi:10.21018/rjcpr.2016.1.199

19. Vincent, J.A., Phillipson, C., Downs, M.: Part 1. The future of the life course. In: Vincent, J.A., Phillipson, C., Downs, M. (eds.) The Futures of Old Age, pp. 9–11. Sage, London (2006)

20. Alwin, D.F.: Who's talking about my generation? In: Silverstein, M., Giarrusso, R. (eds.) Kinship and Cohort in an Aging Society, pp. 134–158. John Hopkins University Press, Baltimore (2013)

21. Mannheim, K.: The Problem of generations. In: Kecskemeti, P. (ed.) Mannheim: Essays, pp. 276–322. Routledge, London (1952 [1927/28])

22. Sackmann, R., Winkler, O.: Technology generations revisited: the internet generation. Gerontechnology **11**(4), 493–503 (2013)

23. Growth for Knowledge Austria: GfK online monitor. http://www.e-government.steiermark.at/cms/dokumente/10103295_34808287/b8a4cf27/gfk_online_monitor_4_qu_stand_Juni_2012.pdf

24. Lancaster University: Transitions in practice: climate change and everyday life: the shower-bath path. http://www.lancaster.ac.uk/staff/shove/exhibits/showerv2.pdf

25. Ratzenböck, B.: "Let's take a look together": walking interviews in domestic spaces as a means to examine ICT experiences of women 60+. Rom. J. Commun. Public Relat. **18**(1), 49–64 (2016). doi:10.21018/rjcpr.2016.1.201

26. Fernández-Ardèvol, M.: Older people and mobile communication (2014). (Pers. E-Mail from Fernández-Ardèvol to Ratzenböck, B.)

27. Kuckartz, U.: Qualitative Inhaltsanalyse. Methoden, Praxis, Computerunterstützung [Qualitative Content Analysis. Methods, Practice, Computer Support]. Beltz Juventa, Weinheim (2012)
28. Strauss, A., Corbin, J.: Grounded Theory. Grundlagen Qualitativer Sozialforschung [Grounded Theory. Basics in Qualitative Social Research]. Beltz Juventa, Weinheim (1990)
29. Maierhofer, R.: Anocriticism. https://interamerikanistik.uni-graz.at/en/research/intersectionality-aging-studies/anocriticism/
30. Maierhofer, R.: Desperately seeking the self: gender, age, and identity in Tillie Olsen's "Tell Me a Riddle" and Michelle Herman's "Missing". Educ. Gerontol. 25(2), 129–141 (1999)
31. Maierhofer, R.: Third pregnancy: women, ageing and identity in American culture. An anocritical approach. In: Jansohn, C. (ed.) Old Age and Ageing in British and American Culture and Literature, pp. 155–171. LIT, Vienna (2004)
32. Maierhofer, R.: The old woman as the prototypical American – an anocritical approach to gender, age, and identity. In: Hölbling, W., Rieser, K. (eds.) What is American? New Identities in U.S. Culture, pp. 319–336. LIT, Vienna (2004)
33. Östlund, B.: Design paradigms and misunderstood technology: the case of older users. In: Jæger, B. (ed.) Young Technologies in Old Hands: An International View on Senior Citizen's Utilization, pp. 25–39. DJØF Forlag, Copenhagen (2005)
34. Lucius-Hoene, G.: Narrative Identitätsarbeit im Interview. [Narrative Identity Work in Interviews] In: Griese, B. (ed.) Subjekt – Identität – Person. Reflexionen zur Biographieforschung [Subject – Identity – Person. Reflections on Biography Research], pp. 149–170. VS Verlag für Sozialwissenschaften, Wiesbaden (2010)
35. Hill, R., Beynon-Davies, P., Williams, M.D.: Older people and internet engagement. Acknowledging social moderators of internet adoption, access and use. Inf. Technol. People 21(3), 244–266 (2008)
36. Suopajärvi, T.: Past experiences, current practices and future design. Ethnographic study of aging adults' everyday ICT practices – and how it could benefit public ubiquitous computing design. Technol. Forecast. Soc. Chang. 93, 112–123 (2015)
37. Loos, E.F.: Senior citizens: digital immigrants in their own country? Observatorio (OBS*) J. 6(1), 1–23 (2012)
38. Cruikshank, M.: Learning to Be Old: Gender, Culture, and Aging. Rowman and Littlefield, Lanham (2013)
39. Selwyn, N., Gorard, S., Furlong, J., Madden, L.: Older adults' use of information and communication technology in everyday life. Ageing Soc. 23(5), 561–582 (2003). doi:10.1017/S0144686X03001302
40. Colombo, F., Carlo, S.: Access and use of ICTs among the Italian young elderly: a field study. In: Zhou, J., Salvendy, G. (eds.) ITAP 2015. LNCS, vol. 9193, pp. 166–176. Springer, Cham (2015). doi:10.1007/978-3-319-20892-3_17
41. Loe, M.: Doing it my way: old women, technology and wellbeing. Sociol. Health Illn. 32(2), 319–334 (2010)
42. Wilińska, M.: An older person and new media in public discourses: impossible encounters? In: Zhou, J., Salvendy, G. (eds.) ITAP 2015. LNCS, vol. 9193, pp. 405–413. Springer, Cham (2015). doi:10.1007/978-3-319-20892-3_40
43. Nakao, C.: Käufliches Alter. Konstruktionen subjektiven Alterserlebens in der Marketingkommunikation. [Purchasable Age. Constructions of Subjective Experiences of Age in Marketing Communication]. Springer, Wiesbaden (2016)

Privacy, Data Security, and the Acceptance of AAL-Systems – A User-Specific Perspective

Julia van Heek[✉], Simon Himmel, and Martina Ziefle

Human-Computer Interaction Center, RWTH Aachen,
Campus-Boulevard 57, 52074 Aachen, Germany
{vanheek,himmel,ziefle}@comm.rwth-aachen.de

Abstract. Rising care needs, higher proportions of older, diseased, or disabled people, and an increasing deficiency of qualified care staff due to demographic changes are major challenges in western societies. Ambient Assisted Living (AAL) technologies represent one approach to face these challenges. Besides technological developments and implementations, focusing on user acceptance (including diverse stakeholder perspectives) is important for a successful rollout. As the most previous studies focus on age-related issues, this paper emphasizes especially on people with care needs due to a disability. In particular the acceptance of an AAL system is investigated considering the trade-off between perceived benefits (e.g., increasing autonomy) and perceived barriers (e.g., invasion in privacy, to "abandon" data security). Using a quantitative online questionnaire, decisive use conditions are identified, and the trade-offs and AAL-acceptance are evaluated comparing four user groups: "healthy people" without experiences with disabilities, disabled people, family members, and professional care givers. Results indicate that experience with disabilities influence the acceptance and relevant use conditions of AAL systems as well as the trade-offs between benefits and barriers. The results demonstrate the relevance to include diverse user groups (age, diseases, disabilities) and their specific needs and wishes into the design and evaluation process of AAL technologies.

Keywords: Ambient assisted living (AAL) technologies · Technology acceptance · User diversity · Privacy & data security · Disabilities & care needs

1 Introduction

Demographic change and a resulting increasing number of older people and people in need of care represent a major challenge for today's society and poses exceptional burdens for the care sector [1, 2].

The proportion of typical age-related diseases such as diabetes, dementia, or cardiovascular diseases increases continually and plays an important role for the care sector [3–5]. However, age-independent diseases and disabilities are also of importance and should be taken into account as they also effect huge needs of care and assistance [6]. In addition, it should be noted that there is a comparably new phenomenon of an first "old" generation of disabled people: on the one hand, due to medical and technical developments (e.g., innovative therapies and medicines), on the other hand, especially in Europe - due to the specific

© Springer International Publishing AG 2017
J. Zhou and G. Salvendy (Eds.): ITAP 2017, Part I, LNCS 10297, pp. 38–56, 2017.
DOI: 10.1007/978-3-319-58530-7_4

historical background of euthanasia murders during National Socialism [7]. Therefore, the three factors age, diseases, and disabilities are relevant and have to be considered concerning increasing care needs and related challenges.

In recent years, numerous single-case solutions but also complete ambient assisted living systems were developed in order to provide solutions for the care sector [8]. These systems are able to monitor medical parameters, to detect falls as well as to facilitate living at home using smart home technology elements [9–11]. Current research focuses specifically on holistic AAL systems, that combine various functions, are optimally economical, retrofittable, and customizable to individual needs of diverse users. Besides technological developments, it is important to investigate to which extent such AAL systems are desired and accepted by whom and under which conditions. Especially the trade-off between perceived advantages (mostly increased safety) and perceived barriers (e.g., data security, privacy) is discussed with regard to AAL technologies and their usage. As existing studies with regard to the acceptance of AAL technologies have mainly focus on age [12, 13] or gender [14] as affecting user factors and have not considered people with diseases and disabilities so far, this paper investigates the acceptance of AAL systems with focus on disabled people and people having experiences with disabilities (family members, caregivers). The study aims for a comparison of different user perspectives on use conditions, privacy, safety, data security, and the acceptance of AAL systems.

1.1 Ambient Assisted Living (AAL) Technologies

In the last years, different types of monitoring technologies (e.g., microphones, cameras, and movement sensors) are integrated into people's living environments in order to enhance safety by detecting falls and emergencies. Within this development, the number of commercial obtainable AAL systems as well as AAL research projects increased significantly. Currently, modular and multifunctional systems are available on the market and include smart home functions (e.g., sensors for lighting or heating control or automatic opening/closing of doors and windows), fall detection, and health care applications such as a reminder for blood sugar measuring. These systems are ready to be integrated in private home environments [15, 16], in hospitals [17], or nursing homes [18]. Besides commercially available solutions, some research projects put the main stress on a development of holistic AAL systems [19, 20]. In contrast to most commercial solutions, these research projects consider future users iteratively in the development process of AAL systems [21]. The future user should generally be considered in development processes, as the user's perspective is decisive for a successful integration of technologies in their everyday life [22].

Although AAL technologies and systems have the potential to increase safety and to facilitate the everyday life of older, diseased, or disabled people, they are presently not broadly integrated into private home environments. To understand this phenomenon, we have to focus on potential users of these systems (together with their individual characteristics), their perceptions, perceived use conditions, and their willingness to accept AAL technologies.

1.2 Acceptance of AAL Technologies

So far, AAL technologies have mostly been perceived and evaluated positive acknowledging the necessity and usefulness of technical support [20, 22]. In contrast, fears, caveats, and acceptance barriers - in particular a feeling of isolation [23], feeling of surveillance, and fears of an invasion of own privacy [24] - were present if people were asked to think about an integrated AAL system in their personal home environment. To understand this obvious trade-off between the perceived barriers (in particular enhanced safety) and perceived barriers (especially doubts on preservation of privacy and data security) it is necessary to consider technology acceptance and the diversity of potential AAL users.

Traditional technology acceptance models like TAM or UTAUT are only limited suitable, as AAL systems address especially older, diseased, and frail people with individual prerequisites, desires, and fears [25]. We presume that these user factors lead to a different prioritization of most important (perceived) benefits and barriers and to a different acceptance and willingness to use an AAL system. Hence, the following section presents an overview of research results focusing on the acceptance of AAL systems and different user groups.

Older people's perceived benefits and barriers of AAL technologies have widely been investigated using different methodological approaches such as focus groups [26, 27] or interviews [28, 29]. Older participants acknowledge the advantages of the possibility to stay longer in their own home, they understand the lack of care staff, and regard AAL technologies as a chance. In contrast, the participants express concerns about a dependency on technologies, a lack of personal contact ("replacing" staff by technology) as well as concerns about data security and privacy within the mentioned qualitative but also in quantitative studies, e.g., [30]. While numerous projects with regard to AAL technologies and smart homes focus solely on the technological parameters, some recent projects, e.g., [19], integrate future users into the system's development, design, and evaluation process [31].

So far, research for AAL technologies has mainly concentrated on older people with age-related chronic or physical illnesses. As assistive technologies could also be beneficial for people with disabilities (e.g., supporting mobility and communication, enhancing autonomy) and age-related illnesses come along with disabilities more frequently [7], disabled users should also be addressed.

Some occasional studies summarized and investigated to which extent different diseases and disabilities affect the use of medical technologies, e.g., [32, 33], and focus especially on the explanation why numerous existing technologies were not used or rejected. Existing research on disabled or diseased people's AAL acceptance are all on a comparatively unspecific, superficial, and on a theoretical level mostly not integrating or asking disabled people directly for their opinions, whishes, and needs. Hence, this is precisely where research is wanted: in particular disabled people have to be integrated in the development and design of AAL technologies and systems.

To do especially justice to people in needs of care, it is important to consider also the perspectives of professional care givers or family members in order to receive a preferably full picture about difficulties in the everyday live, desires, and ideas. Within AAL acceptance research, requirements as well as professional and family caregivers' perspectives on AAL systems have been considered separately and deliver first insights into different perspectives on the acceptance of AAL technologies [e.g., 34, 35]. However, they do not allow to directly compare the perspectives of different user groups (older people, diseased or disabled people, family members, professional care givers), as they each mainly focus on a specific user group and use no equivalent or comparable methodological approaches for different user groups.

The acceptance of AAL technologies has hardly been investigated with regard to disabled people and people with special care needs so far. As there is only sparse knowledge about the interaction of the described challenging factors (age, diseases, disabilities and resulting needs in assistance and care), these factors were addressed in the present study focusing on the perspectives of different user groups (disabled people, family members, professional caregivers).

2   Methodology

In this section, the applied research design is presented. First, the research approach with a preceding qualitative interview study is shortly introduced, which was taken as a basis for the subsequent quantitative study. Further, the quantitative study's empirical design and the sample are described. Our study addresses the following essential research questions:

1. How do participants evaluate the described AAL system and which use conditions are important?
2. Are perceived benefits (e.g., autonomy, independency) or barriers (especially privacy and data security) more important for its acceptance?
3. To which extent do age, experiences with disabilities, and current care needs influence the AAL system's evaluation and especially the trade-off between perceived benefits and barriers?

2.1   Research Design and Qualitative Pre-study

Previous studies on the acceptance of AAL technologies have mostly considered age as influencing user factor so far. Instead, developing AAL technologies especially for people with disabilities and investigating the acceptance of AAL technologies focusing on disabled users have prevalently not been considered. In addition, the inclusion of other perspectives (e.g., professional caregivers, relatives, and family members of disabled people) is also immensely important as they can support and complete the understanding of disabled and care-dependent user's wishes and requirements.

Within a qualitative interview study (with disabled people, caregivers, and family members of disabled people, n = 9, age 26–62, M = 36 years), perceived motives and perceived barriers of using an AAL system were initially identified. Further, use conditions were determined dependent on the different participant's perspectives and especially the trade-offs between perceived benefits (e.g., increased safety, relief) and perceived barriers (i.e. in particular privacy and data security) were intensely discussed. One major condition nearly all interview participants mentioned was the *customization* of the used technologies. Technical solutions should fit to individual and personal needs of users – which is not specific for disabled persons - but as all people are different, the wishes and grades for customization become even more essential for user acceptance. Therefore, also *user-centered design* within the development process is mentioned as a key condition. *Reliability* and *usability* are important factors for technology acceptance mentioned by most of the participants as well. Another condition for one interview partner was the *unobtrusiveness* of assistive devices, whereas it was mentioned that people (disabled by birth) have learned to deal with the fact the surrounding directly realizes their handicap. Therefore, this condition could have a diverse impact on acceptance. *Control* was also addressed by several participants and a simple on-off-switch for the whole AAL-technology was suggested as key condition to gain intimacy. Some interview partners not only mentioned user oriented individualization but also the *situational and smart technology adaption* – the AAL technology should realize "when to switch on lights" or "help getting up from the sofa". Besides these technical challenges, all participants mentioned the *funding by health insurance companies* as a major condition to actually use AAL-technologies and last but not least, the usage of these technologies should also be *fun*.

2.2 Questionnaire Design

The questionnaire consisted of several parts and its items were developed based on the findings of the preceding interview study. The first part addressed demographic aspects, such as age, gender, educational level, and income.

Following this, the participants were asked to indicate their attitudes towards technology using four items ($\alpha = .802$) [36], towards technological innovations ($\alpha = .808$) also using four items, towards privacy using 8 items ($\alpha = .718$; based on [37] and expanded by aspects from the interviews), and towards data security (using 14 items, $\alpha = .874$; also based on [37] and expanded by aspects from the interviews) including four different dimensions: general attitude towards data security, personal data usage, effects of data usage, and general handling of data. All items concerning data security and privacy are presented in Fig. 1 in Sect. 3.1.

The next part addressed experiences with disabilities: the participants were asked to indicate if themselves have a disability (a), if they are a family member of a disabled person (b), if they are a caregiver of a disabled person (c), or if they have no experiences with disabilities (d).

A scenario was designed in order to guarantee that all participants refer to the same basis according to the evaluation of an AAL technology. Depending on their expertise (need of care, experience with disabilities), the participants were introduced to the scenario specifically. For cases b, c, and d, the participants were asked to put themselves in a disabled person's position (respectively the person they are related with or they care (b,c)) while evaluating the AAL scenario. Participants without experiences with disabilities and need of care were asked to imagine that they would be in need of care. Within the scenario, the participants should imagine that an specific invisible AAL system was integrated in their personal home environment and included diverse functions: automatic opening and closing of doors and windows (by sensors), hands-free kit for phoning (by integrated microphones), monitoring of front door area (by cameras), fall detection (by sensors in floor and bed), automatic lighting control (by light sensors and position detection) and configuration of home temperature (by smartphone).

Subsequent to the scenario, the participants were asked to assess different use conditions (11 items, $\alpha = .808$; based on the qualitative interview study's findings, see 2.1), the trade-off between perceived benefits (e.g., to increase autonomy) and perceived barriers (e.g., feeling of surveillance, privacy, data security) (using 4 items; $\alpha = .866$), and the acceptance of as well as intention to use the described AAL system (using 8 items; $\alpha = .899$). All items are presented within the figures in Sect. 3.

Finally, the participants should evaluate eight different statements concerning the acceptance or rejection as well as the behavioral intention to use the described AAL system. Completing the questionnaire took on average 15 min and data was collected in an online survey in summer 2016 in Germany.

2.3 Sample

Overall, 279 participants volunteered to participate in our online questionnaire study. As we only used complete data sets for further statistical analyses, a sample of n = 182 data sets remained. 62.1% of the participants were female, 36.3% male (1.6% did not want to indicate their gender). The participants were on average 38.7 years old (SD = 13.95; min = 20; max = 81) and the educational level was high with 46.7% holding a university degree and 14.8% a university entrance diploma. In accordance with experience with disabilities, 51 participants indicated to be disabled (28.0%), 12.1% (n = 22) were professional caregivers, 35 participants were relatives of a disabled person (19.2%), and 40.7% (n = 74) had no experience with disabilities.

In addition, the self-reported technical self-efficacy was on average positive (M = 4.5; SD = 1.0; min = 1; max = 6) and the attitude towards technology innovations was slightly positive (M = 3.9; SD = 1.0; min = 1; max = 6).

Further, 79 (43.4%) participants indicated to need care or that the person they care or they are related with needed care (56.6% indicated to be not in need of care). These factors are related only in parts: age is not linked with experience with disabilities ($r = -.13$; $p = .08 > .05$) nor with current care needs ($r = -.10$; $p = .20 > .05$). In contrast, age is related with gender ($r = .20$; $p < .05$; 1 = female; 2 = male). As expected, experience with disabilities correlates with current care needs ($r = .61$; $p < .01$).

2.4 Data Analysis

Item analyses were calculated to ensure measurement quality before descriptive and inference analyses were carried out. Cronbach's alpha > 0.7 indicated a satisfying internal consistency of the scales. Data was analysed descriptively and with respect to the effects of user diversity, by (M)ANOVA procedures (level of significance was set at 5%). To analyze the impacts of experiences with disabilities and care needs on AAL acceptance and the evaluation of privacy and data security, we choose the factors age, experience with disabilities, and acute care needs for further analysis.

3   Results

Within this section, the study's results are presented and structured as follows: first, an overview of the evaluation of attitudes towards data security and privacy is presented. In a second step, the results concerning the acceptance of the described AAL system is detailed, followed by the results of acceptance-relevant use conditions. Finally, the evaluated trade-offs between data security, privacy, and the perceived benefits of an AAL system are described. In each case, the results are presented first for all participants and then potential influences of user factors (age, disabilities, care needs) are considered.

3.1   Attitudes Towards Privacy and Data Security

As it was shortly mentioned in the methodology section, the attitudes towards data security (Fig. 1) and privacy (Fig. 2) were assessed by using 14 or rather 8 items.

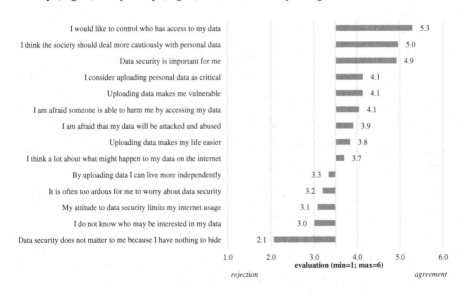

Fig. 1. Evaluation of data security items (all participants).

Data Security: The average needs for data security were on a moderate level with regard to all participants (M = 4.1; SD = 0.8; min = 1; max = 6). Zooming in the attitude items, *"...control who has access to data"* (M = 5.3; SD = 0.9) was the most important aspect, followed by *"...society should deal more cautiously..."* (M = 5.0; SD = 1.1) and *"data security is important for me"* (M = 4.9; SD = 1.0). In contrast, *"... does not matter to me because I have nothing to hide"* (M = 2.0; SD = 1.2) was the most rejected aspect, while four other items, e.g., *"I do not know who may be interested in my data"* (M = 3.0; SD = 1.5) and *"by uploading data I can live more independently"* (M = 3.3; SD = 1.4) were slightly rejected. The remaining items were evaluated rather positive, e.g., *"uploading* *data makes me vulnerable"* (M = 4.1; SD = 1.3) or *"I am afraid that my data will be attacked and abused"* (M = 3.9; SD = 1.4).

Interestingly, MANOVA analyses revealed that the attitude towards data security differed not with regard to age (F(28, 300) = .761; p = .805 > .05; n.s.), experiences with disabilities (F(42,453) = .933; p = .594 > .05; n.s.), nor with care needs (F(14,149) = .933; p = .642 > .05; n.s.).

Privacy: The average needs for privacy were also on a moderate level with regard to all participants (M = 4.4; SD = 0.7; min = 1; max = 6). The participants indicated that *"privacy is very important"* (M = 5.1; SD = 1.0), they want to *"be able to control own privacy..."* (M = 5.1; SD = 1.0), and they *"...respect the privacy of others"* (M = 5.1; SD = 0.9). The participants also agreed with the statements *"... should be handled more carefully"* (M = 4.7; SD = 1.1) and *"... I have enough privacy"* (M = 4.4; SD = 1.1). In contrast, the more concrete fear that *"private conservations and intimate details will be whispered"* (M = 3.6; SD = 1.4) was rated rather neutral, while the statements *"... no sense to worry about privacy as you can not protect it anyway"* (M = 2.4; SD = 1.2) and *"I wonder why such a hype is made about privacy"* (M = 2.3; SD = 1.3) were rejected.

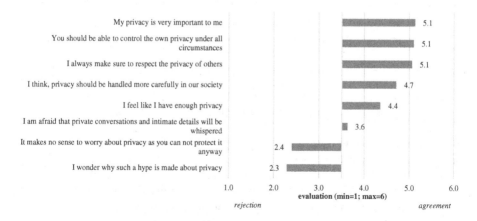

Fig. 2. Evaluation of privacy items (all participants).

Concerning the attitude towards privacy, MANOVA analyses also revealed that the attitude towards privacy differed not with regard to age (F(16, 308) = .636; p = .854 > .05; n.s.), experiences with disability groups (F(4,465) = .989; p = .479 > .05; n.s.), nor care needs (F(8,153) = .496; p = .858 > .05; n.s.). Instead, the combination of all three user factors (F(24,465) = 1.544; p < .05) and the combination of care needs and experience with disabilities (F(16,308) = 1.786; p < .05) influenced the attitude towards privacy significantly.

3.2 Acceptance of an AAL System

The attitude towards AAL technologies was on average positive (M = 4.6; SD = 1.0) and showed that the described AAL system was accepted by the participants. In detail (see Fig. 3), the items with regard to an intention to use the AAL system and care needs *("...due to care needs"* (M = 4.7; SD = 1.1); *"... reduce my care needs"* (M = 4.5; SD = 1.3)) were evaluated highest. The participants rated the three statements concerning a concrete intention to use the AAL system rather positive, while the item *"I would install..."* (M = 4.3; SD = 1.4) was assessed higher than the aspects *"I like to use these AAL technologies"* (M = 4.0; SD = 1.4) and *"I can imagine to use this AAL system now"* (M = 3.8; SD = 1.6). The three negative acceptance statements were all rejected (e.g., *"I think such AAL systems are superfluous"* (M = 1.9; SD = 1.1).

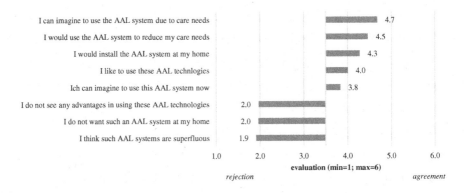

Fig. 3. Evaluation of AAL acceptance items (all participants).

Considering different user factors, MANOVA analyses revealed significant differences with regard to age (F(16,308) = 2.104; p < .01), experiences with disabilities (F(24,465) = 2.060; p < .01), and care needs (F(8,153) = 3.779; p < .01).

With regard to experiences with disabilities, the negative statements were rejected lowest by the professional caregivers (e.g., *"I do not want such an AAL system at my home"* (F(3,162) = 4.907; p < .01), which therefore seemed to have a higher negative attitude towards AAL systems than the other groups. This was also true for the intention to use an AAL system, to which statements all user groups agreed, while the professional caregivers showed the lowest agreement. The group of "not experienced" participants showed highest agreements concerning the *"in case of care needs"* items. This evaluation changed with regard to the statement *"I can imagine to use this AAL system now"*, which was evaluated clearly higher by the group of disabled people (M = 4.3; SD = 1.3) compared to the not-experienced participants (M = 3.5; SD = 1.7; post-hoc-tests: Tukey's HSD).

Concerning care needs, nearly all items with regard to the AAL system's acceptance differed significantly. The overall acceptance was a little higher for people with care needs (M = 4.7; SD = 1.0) than for people without care needs (M = 4.5; SD = 1.0; F(1,162) = 7.309, p < .01). The negative statements were significantly more rejected by people in need of care compared to people without care needs, e.g., *"I do not want such an AAL system at my home"* (F(1,162) = 10.187; p < .01). While the intention to use items with regard to care needs (e.g., *"...due to care needs"* (F(1,162) = 4.441; p < .05)) were only slightly more accepted by people with care needs than by people without care needs, the differences were more obvious considering the concrete intention to use items: participants in need of care showed clearly higher agreements for all items (e.g., *"I would install the AAL system at my home"* (M = 4.5; SD = 1.3; F(1,162) = 7.107; p < .01) than the participants without care needs (M = 4.1; SD = 1.5).

3.3 Conditions for Using an AAL System

As introduced before, the participants evaluated different conditions for using an AAL system at their own home. Figure 4 shows the descriptive results of all evaluated use conditions for all participants.

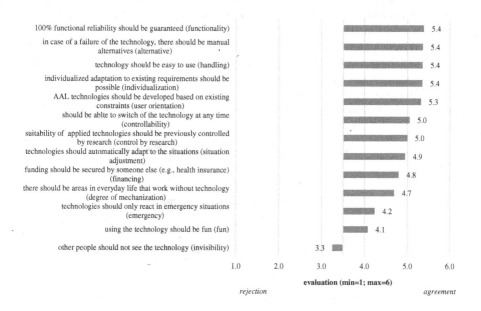

Fig. 4. Evaluation of use condition items (all participants).

"100% functionality" (M = 5.4; SD = 0.9), *"manual alternatives in case of failure of the technology"* (M = 5.4; SD = 1.0), an *"easy handling"* (M = 5.4; SD = 0.9), *"individualized adaption"* (M = 5.4; SD = 0.9), and *"user-oriented development based on existing constraints"* (M = 5.3; SD = 0.8) were rated highest and represented the most important use conditions. *"Controllability"* (M = 5.0; SD = 1.2), *"control by research"* (M = 5.0; SD = 1.1), *"situation adjustment"* (M = 4.9; SD = 1.0), *"financing"* (M = 4.8; SD = 1.1), and *"degree of mechanization"* (M = 4.7; SD = 1.4) received also agreement and are of importance for AAL system usage.

In contrast, the statements *"technologies should only react in emergency situations"* (M = 4.2; SD = 1.4) and *"using the technology should be fun"* (M = 4.1; SD = 1.3) were rather agreed and thus, they did not represent important use conditions. The fact that *"other people should not be able to see the technology"* (M = 3.3; SD = 1.4) was slightly rejected by the participants and thus, it constituted no relevant use condition.

MANOVA analyses revealed significant overall effects concerning the evaluation of use conditions for experience with disabilities (F(39,456) = 1.444; p < .05), but not for age (F(26,302) = .905; p = .602 > .05; n.s.) or care needs (F(13,150) = .963; p = .490 > .05; n.s.). Significant differences were found in particular with regard to the items *"control by research"* (F(3,181) = 2.576; p < .05), *"financing"* (F(3,181) = 2.863; p < .05), and *"degree of mechanization"* (F(3,181) = 4.288; p < .01). As it is shown in Fig. 5, *"control by research"* was most important for not-experienced persons (M = 5.2; SD = 0.9) and the group of professional caregivers (M = 5.2; SD = 1.0), while it was minor important for family members (M = 4.9; SD = 1.2) and especially disabled persons (M = 4.7; SD = 1.3). *"Financing"* (e.g., by health insurance) was comparatively most important for the group of disabled participants (M = 5.2; SD = 1.1) and professional caregivers (M = 5.1; SD = 1.0), followed by family members (M = 4.7; SD = 1.2), and least important for the group of not-experienced participants (M = 4.5; SD = 1.1). The *"degree of mechanization"* was clearly the most important use condition for the group of professional caregivers (M = 5.5; SD = 0.7), while it was minor important for not-experienced (M = 4.7; SD = 1.4) and disabled participants (M = 4.6; SD = 1.4), and least important for the group of family members (M = 4.3; SD = 1.5).

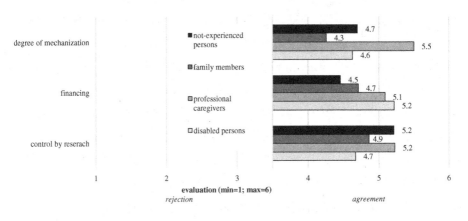

Fig. 5. Significant differences in the evaluation of use conditions (experience with disabilities groups).

3.4   Trade-Offs Between Benefits and Barriers

Figure 6 presents the results of a trade-off between different benefits (independency, autonomy, time savings) and barriers (data security, privacy) of AAL system usage. Overall, the participants rather agreed that it is fine to abandon a piece of privacy in favor for a *"more independent life"* (M = 4.1; SD = 1.2). Similarly, they showed also agreement concerning the statement that *"...autonomy will be more important than data security"* (M = 4.1; SD = 1.3). Likewise, the statement *"if AAL technologies need personal data for their automatic improvement, it will be okay to upload them"* (M = 3.9; SD = 1.3) was on average slightly endorsed by the participants. In contrast, *"time savings"* (M = 3.2; SD = 1.4) were slightly rejected and were not seen as a relevant benefit, for which the upload of sensitive data would be justified.

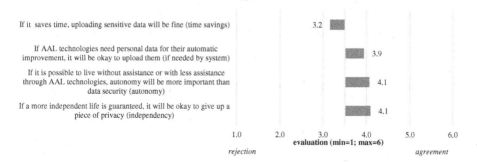

Fig. 6. Evaluation of items with regard to a trade-off between perceived benefits and data security as well as privacy (all participants).

MANOVA analyses revealed that this trade-off was affected by the user factor experience with disabilities but not by care needs (F(4,159) = 2.156; p = .076 > .05; n.s.) and age (F(8,320) = 1.631; p = .115 > .05; n.s.). In detail, *"independency"* (F(3,181) = 3.610; p < .05) and *"autonomy"* (F(3,181) = 5.019; p < .01) were evaluated clearly different by the four experience with disabilities groups (see Fig. 7):

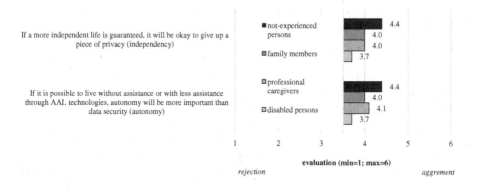

Fig. 7. Significant differences in the evaluation of the trade-off between benefits and barriers (experience with disabilities groups).

As it is shown in Fig. 7, in particular the not-experienced group and the disabled participants' group differed significantly in their evaluation (post-hoc-tests: Tukey's HSD): the not-experienced group agreed more clearly that *"independency"* (M = 4.4; SD = 0.9) and *"autonomy"* (M = 4.4; SD = 1.1) were more important than privacy and data security, while the disabled group evaluated both statements rather neutral *("independency"*: M = 3.7; SD = 1.4; *"autonomy"* M = 3.7; SD = 1.5).

Figure 8 presents the evaluation of three final statements concerning AAL usage, privacy, and data security for all participants. The statement *"since there is no unassailable network, you should avoid AAL technologies"* was rejected by the participants (M = 2.4; SD = 1.1) and hence, data security was no reason to avoid AAL technologies in general. Further, the participants rated the item *"the restriction of privacy by AAL technologies is wrong"* (M = 3.5; SD = 1.4) completely neutral. Finally, the participants endorsed that *"the use of AAL technologies requires 100% data security"* (M = 4.9; SD = 1.3).

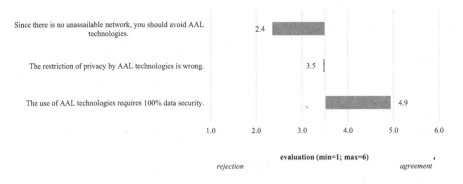

Fig. 8. Evaluation of items with regard to a AAL systems and their influence on data security and privacy (all participants).

MANOVA analyses revealed that the final evaluation of statements with regard to AAL usage, privacy, and data security was influenced by the user factor experience with disabilities ($F(9,486) = 2.474$; $p < .01$) as well. However, it was not affected by age ($F(6,322) = .715$; $p = .638 > .05$; n.s.) or care needs ($F(3,160) = 2.061$; $p = .108 > .05$; n.s.).

As it is shown in Fig. 9, the evaluation of the three respective items differed clearly referring to the experience with disabilities groups. The item *"...you should avoid AAL technologies"* ($F(3,181) = 2.972$; $p < .05$) was most rejected by the group of family members (M = 2.1; SD = 1.1), while the professional caregivers showed the lowest rejection (M = 2.7; SD = 1.2). The statement *"the restriction of privacy by AAL technologies is wrong"* ($F(3,181) = 3.693$; $p < .05$) was rejected by the not-experienced (M = 3.2; SD = 1.2) and the group of family members (M = 3.3; SD = 1.4), while the professional caregivers (M = 3.7; SD = 1.2) and the disabled persons slightly agreed (M = 3.9; SD = 1.6). Finally, the item *"the use of AAL technologies requires 100% data security"* ($F(3,181) = 2.972$; $p < .05$) was most endorsed by disabled persons (M = 5.2; SD = 1.1), professional caregivers (M = 5.1; SD = 0.9), and the not-experienced persons (M = 4.9; SD = 1.2), while the group of family members showed a comparatively lower agreement (M = 4.5; SD = 1.6).

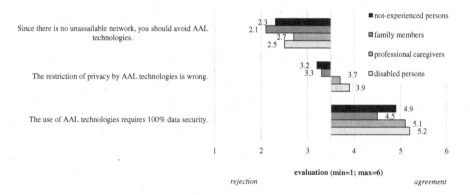

Fig. 9. Final evaluation of statements with regard to AAL usage, privacy, and data security (experience with disabilities groups).

4 Discussion

The present study revealed insights into acceptance patterns, relevant use conditions, and trade-offs with regard to AAL systems in home environments. We considered and compared different user perspectives (e.g., age, disabilities, and care needs) in order to understand specific needs of diverse potential users. The results provide valuable insights into user-specific as well as acceptance-relevant criteria in the context of AAL systems and should be taken into account for the development and design of AAL technologies.

4.1 User-Specific Acceptance of AAL Systems

First, it has to be mentioned that user diversity did not have a significant impact on the attitudes towards privacy and data security and thus, these factors are generic key conditions for AAL acceptance within all participants. However, user diversity had a significant influence on acceptance and on the direct trade-offs between perceived benefits and barriers (see Sect. 3.4), which is subsequently discussed for distinct results of selected user groups.

In line with previous research results, e.g., [20], our results demonstrate that a holistic AAL system with various functions is generally accepted and rated positive by all respondents. In particular, the intention to use the system is universally present (if care needs are mentioned within the items (see Sect. 3.2)) and differs only slightly with regard to the different user perspectives. In contrast, significant differences between the user perspectives are present, if a concrete intention to use was mentioned without the context of care needs: generally speaking, older people, disabled people, and people in need of care showed a clearly higher intention to use and acceptance of an AAL system than presumably healthy "not-experienced" people. Thus, the intention to use an AAL system is influenced by the user factors experience with disabilities and care needs.

Considering the different user perspectives, the *group of professional care givers* is striking with respect to their evaluations: in comparison with all other groups, they have a more negative attitude towards the described AAL system. Especially in contrast to users in need of care - who might be depending on assistive technologies and might have already experienced an intrusion of intimacy - the professional caregivers have a significantly more declining position towards AAL technologies. Although they might gain support in their everyday stressful job, the caregivers show least acceptance for technical solutions. This could be explained by diverse theories: on the one hand, the increasing use of technologies can come along with the fear of job loss due to a new technology or to be "replaced" by technology [e.g., 38]. Additionally, the use of technologies in the care sector raise ethical issues [39], for instance, to what extent is it acceptable that technological devices might replace time and everyday tasks usually caregivers would spent with residents? In the context of social jobs and working environments, individual influences of people and their perceptions are of major importance. Hence, much more research is necessary that not only focuses on scenario-based evaluations but moreover on real life scenarios, real working surroundings, and considers different stakeholder's perspectives.

This study's *disabled participants and participants with current care needs* perceived the in the scenario introduced AAL system as useful, helpful, comfortable, and future-orientated. However, these people in need for assistance have the most sensitive attitude towards privacy and data security concerns (similar to previous research results [40]). This group's results showed that the direct trade-off between perceived benefits (especially increased autonomy and safety) and perceived barriers (in particular data and privacy concerns) of ambient assisted living technologies are balanced and thus, both aspects influence the acceptance with a somehow similar weighting. To meet the individual requirements for privacy and data security, it is important to consider wishes and ideas, e.g., this study's participants suggested a selective on-off-switch of video monitoring functions (in line with previous studies [28]). Therefore, the early integration of people in need of care into the development process of AAL technologies is crucial for the acceptance and to reduce perceived barriers. The overall impression of this study was that the participating disabled people showed a high willingness to be part in the development and evaluation process and desired to be asked and involved more frequently.

4.2 Limitations and Further Research

The empirical approach of this study revealed valuable insights into the acceptance of AAL technologies, relevant use conditions, and trade-offs between perceived benefits and barriers focusing on different groups of future users. However, there are some limitations concerning the applied method and sample that should be taken into account for future research.

First of all, this study's evaluation based on a scenario and hence, a fictional system and not a real system was assessed. At a later stage, it will be possible to evaluate real systems within research projects. Then, it will be possible to compare the scenario and the real system evaluations. This way, it is enabled to investigate if the evaluations on a hypothetical level are comparable to the agreement or rejection of the real system [41]. Likewise, it will be very interesting to analyze whether the system really is efficient and beneficial for different user groups (e.g., relief in everyday life, increased autonomy).

Further, an entire AAL system with different functions and technologies was evaluated. In future studies it could be interesting to investigate if slightly different systems (e.g., adding or changing functions) will be assessed similarly.

In addition, a more detailed investigation of trade-offs (e.g., safety vs. privacy, increased independency/autonomy vs. invasion of privacy and data security) using other methodological approaches (e.g., conjoint analyses) would provide more information about concrete decisions between different motives that are relevant for AAL acceptance.

Also some aspects concerning the sample could be improved and continued in future research: first, this study's sample size was adequate, but the study should be replicated in even larger and especially more balanced samples. As this study contained a higher proportion of women than men, future studies should focus on a more gender-balanced sample. Further, age was not related to disabilities or current care needs within our study and thud, we reached similarly younger as well as older people with disabilities. To be able to focus also adequately on older disabled people [7], future studies should try to reach higher proportions of older and disabled people. Another important aspect is that our study focused on physically incapacitated people. However, the care needs of mentally disabled people pose a major challenge for the care sector and especially the care staff as well. Hence, it is very important to develop ideas and strategies how mentally disabled people could be integrated into future technology acceptance research.

A final remark refers to the fact that the present study focused on German participants and hence, it represented a perspective of a single country with a specific health care system. It would be very interesting to conduct this study in other countries in order to compare AAL acceptance as well as (disabled) users wishes, needs, and requirements depending on different cultures, countries, and backgrounds.

Acknowledgements. The authors thank all participants for their patience and openness to share opinions on novel technologies. Furthermore, the authors want to thank Lisa Portz for research assistance. This work was funded by the German Federal Ministry of Education and Research project Whistle (16SV7530).

References

1. Bloom, D.E., Canning, D.: Global demographic change: dimensions and economic significance. National Bureau of Economic Research, Report no. 10817 (2004). http://www.nber.org/papers/w10817
2. Walker, A., Maltby, T.: Active ageing: A strategic policy solution to demographic ageing in the European union. Int. J. Soc. Welf. **21**, 117–130 (2012)
3. Shaw, J.E., Sicree, R.A., Zimmet, P.Z.: Global estimates of the prevalence of diabetes for 2010 and 2030. Diabetes Res. Clin. Pract. **87**(1), 4–14 (2010)
4. Wild, S., Roglic, G., Green, A., Sicree, R., King, H.: Global prevalence of diabetes: estimates for the year 2000 and projections for 2030. Diabetes Care **27**(5), 1047–1053 (2004)

5. Roger, V.L., Go, A.S., Lloyd-Jones, D.M., Adams, R.J., Berry, J.D., Brown, T.M.: Heart disease and stroke statistics–2011 update: a report from the American heart association. Circulation **123**(4), e18–209 (2011)
6. Geenen, S.J., Powers, L.E., Sells, W.: Understanding the role of health care providers during the transition of adolescents with disabilities and special health care needs. J. Adolesc. Health **32**(3), 225–233 (2003)
7. Poore, C.: Disability in Twentieth-Century German Culture. University of Michigan Press, Ann Arbor (2007)
8. Schmitt, J.M.: Innovative medical technologies help ensure improved patient care and cost-effectiveness. J. Med. Mark. Device Diagn. Pharm. Mark. **2**(2), 174–178 (2002)
9. Cheng, J., Chen, X., Shen, M.: A framework for daily activity monitoring and fall detection based on surface electromyography and accelerometer signals. IEEE J. Biomed. Health Inf. **17**(1), 38–45 (2013)
10. Baig, M.M., Gholamhosseini, H.: Smart health monitoring systems: an overview of design and modeling. J. Med. Syst. **37**(2), 9898 (2013)
11. Rashidi, P., Mihailidis, A.: A survey on ambient-assisted living tools for older adults. IEEE J. Biomed. Health Inf. **17**(3), 579–590 (2013)
12. Fuchsberger, V.: Ambient assisted living: elderly people's needs and how to face them. In: Proceedings of the 1st ACM International Workshop on Semantic Ambient Media Experiences, pp. 21–24. ACM (2008)
13. Demiris, G., Hensel, B.K., Skubic, M., Rantz, M.: Senior residents' perceived need of and preferences for "smart home" sensor technologies. Int. J. Technol. Assess. Health Care **24**(1), 120–124 (2008)
14. Wilkowska, W., Gaul, S., Ziefle, M.: A small but significant difference – the role of gender on acceptance of medical assistive technologies. In: Leitner, G., Hitz, M., Holzinger, A. (eds.) USAB 2010. LNCS, vol. 6389, pp. 82–100. Springer, Heidelberg (2010). doi: 10.1007/978-3-642-16607-5_6
15. Casenio: Casenio - intelligente Hilfe- and Komfortsysteme [intelligent support and comfort systems] (2016). Webpage https://www.casenio.de/loesungen/
16. Essence: Smart Care - Care@Home Product Suite (2016). Webpage http://www.essence-grp.com/smart-care/care-at-home-pers
17. EarlySense: EarlySense all-in-one system. webpage (2016). http://www.earlysense.com/earlysense-one/
18. Tunstall: Tunstall - solutions for healthcare professionals (2016). Webpage http://www.tunstallhealthcare.com.au/healthcareprofessional
19. Sixsmith, A., Meuller, S., Lull, F., Klein, M., Bierhoff, I., Delaney, S.: SOPRANO – an ambient assisted living system for supporting older people at home. In: Mokhtari, M., Khalil, I., Bauchet, J., Zhang, D., Nugent, C. (eds.) Ambient Assistive Health and Wellness Management in the Heart of the City, pp. 233–236. Springer, Berlin Heidelberg (2009)
20. Gövercin, M., Meyer, S., Schellenbach, M., Steinhagen-Thiessen, E., Weiss, B., Haesner, M.: SmartSenior@home: acceptance of an integrated ambient assisted living system. Results of a clinical field trial in 35 households. Inf. Health Soc. Care **25**, 1–18 (2016)
21. Kleinberger, T., Becker, M., Ras, E., Holzinger, A., Müller, P.: Ambient intelligence in assisted living: enable elderly people to handle future interfaces. In: Stephanidis, C. (ed.) UAHCI 2007. LNCS, vol. 4555, pp. 103–112. Springer, Heidelberg (2007). doi: 10.1007/978-3-540-73281-5_11
22. Rogers, E.M.: Diffusion of Innovations, 4th edn. Free Press, New York (1995)

23. Beringer, R., Sixsmith, A., Campo, M., Brown, J., McCloskey, R.: The "acceptance" of ambient assisted living: developing an alternate methodology to this limited research lens. In: Abdulrazak, B., Giroux, S., Bouchard, B., Pigot, H., Mokhtari, M. (eds.) ICOST 2011. LNCS, vol. 6719, pp. 161–167. Springer, Heidelberg (2011). doi:10.1007/978-3-642-21535-3_21
24. Sun, H., De Florio, V., Gui, N., Blondia, C.: The missing ones: key ingredients towards effective ambient assisted living systems. J. Ambient Intell. Smart Environ. **2**(2), 109–120 (2010)
25. Wilkowska, W., Ziefle, M., Himmel, S.: Perceptions of personal privacy in smart home technologies: do user assessments vary depending on the research method? In: Tryfonas, T., Askoxylakis, I. (eds.) HAS 2015. LNCS, vol. 9190, pp. 592–603. Springer, Cham (2015). doi: 10.1007/978-3-319-20376-8_53
26. Kowalewski, S., Wilkowska, W., Ziefle, M.: Accounting for user diversity in the acceptance of medical assistive technologies. In: Szomszor, M., Kostkova, P. (eds.) eHealth 2010. LNICSSITE, vol. 69, pp. 175–183. Springer, Heidelberg (2011). doi:10.1007/978-3-642-23635-8_22
27. Demiris, G., Rantz, M., Aud, M., Marek, K., Tyrer, H., Skubic, M.: Older adults' attitudes towards and perceptions of "smart home" technologies: a pilot study. Med. Inf. Internet Med. **29**(2), 87–94 (2004)
28. Ziefle, M., Himmel, S., Wilkowska, W.: When your living space knows what you do: acceptance of medical home monitoring by different technologies. In: Holzinger, A., Simonic, K.-M. (eds.) Information Quality in e-Health, pp. 607–624. Springer, Heidelberg (2011)
29. Beringer, R., Sixsmith, A., Campo, M., Brown, J., McCloskey, R.: The "acceptance" of ambient assisted living: developing an alternate methodology to this limited research lens. In: Abdulrazak, B., Giroux, S., Bouchard, B., Pigot, H., Mokhtari, M. (eds.) ICOST 2011. LNCS, vol. 6719, pp. 161–167. Springer, Heidelberg (2011). doi:10.1007/978-3-642-21535-3_21
30. Himmel, S., Ziefle, M.: Smart home medical technologies: users' requirements for conditional acceptance. i-Com **15**(1), 39–50 (2016)
31. Brauner, P., Holzinger, A., Ziefle, M.: Ubiquitous computing at its best: serious exercise games for older adults in ambient assisted living environments–a technology acceptance perspective. EAI Endorsed Trans. Serious Games **15**, 1–12 (2015)
32. Harris, J.: The use, role and application of advanced technology in the lives of disabled people in the UK. Disabil. Soc. **25**(4), 427–439 (2010)
33. Gentry, T.: Smart homes for people with neurological disability: state of the art. NeuroRehabil. **25**(3), 209–217 (2009)
34. López, S.A., Corno, F., Russis, L.D.: Supporting caregivers in assisted living facilities for persons with disabilities: a user study. Univ. Access Inf. Soc. **14**(1), 133–144 (2015)
35. Mortenson, W.B., Demers, L., Fuhrer, M.J., Jutai, J.W., Lenker, J., DeRuyter, F.: Effects of an assistive technology intervention on older adults with disabilities and their informal caregivers: an exploratory randomized controlled trial. Am. J. Phys. Med. Rehabil. Assoc. Acad. Physiatr. **92**(4), 297–306 (2013)
36. Beier, G.: Locus of control when interacting with technology (Kontrollüberzeugungen im {U}mgang mit {T}echnik). Rep. Psychol. **24**, 684–693 (1999)
37. Wilkowska, W.: Acceptance of eHealth Technology in Home Environments: Advanced Studies on User Diversity in Ambient Assisted Living. Apprimus Verlag, Aachen (2015)
38. Broadbent, E., Tamagawa, R., Patience, A., Knock, B., Kerse, N., Day, K.: Attitudes towards health-care robots in a retirement village. Australas. J. Ageing **31**(2), 115–120 (2012)
39. Dorsten, A.-M., Sifford, K.S., Bharucha, A., Mecca, L.P., Wactlar, H.: Ethical perspectives on emerging assistive technologies: insights from focus groups with stakeholders in long-term care facilities. J. Empir. Res. Hum. Res. Ethics **4**(1), 25–36 (2009)

40. Himmel, S., Ziefle, M., Arning, K.: From living space to urban quarter: acceptance of ICT monitoring solutions in an ageing society. In: Kurosu, M. (ed.) Human-Computer Interaction Users and Contexts of Use, pp. 49–58. Springer, Heidelberg (2013)
41. Ajzen, I., Fishbein, M.: Understanding Attitudes and Predicting Social Behavior. Prentice-Hall, Englewood Cliffs (1980)

Domestic Robots for Homecare: A Technology Acceptance Perspective

Martina Ziefle[(✉)] and André Calero Valdez

Human-Computer Interaction Center, RWTH Aachen University,
Campus Boulevard 57, 52074 Aachen, Germany
{ziefle,calerovaldez}@comm.rwth-aachen.de

Abstract. In times of the demographic change and the increasing need of novel concepts to meet the requirements of older adults' care in the near future, health care robots could be a potent solution to meet shortcomings in the health care sector. Even though the potential of robotic home care assistance is promising, the question if older persons would accept a robotic assistance at home is still underexplored. Adopting a three-step procedure, older adults' perceptions towards home care robots are empirically explored. In a first step, focus groups were accomplished to understand older persons' perceptions on benefits and barriers. Second, a survey study was applied to determine acceptance criteria, the perceived usefulness and the extent and types of concerns toward a domestic robot in homecare. Finally, in a further survey study, specific care situations in the home care settings had to be evaluated in a third study, thereby comparing preferences for a human care persons vs. a robotic care assistant. Outcomes reveal both, age-sensitive as well as age-insensitive findings. While overall a positive attitude towards home care robots was found, serious concerns in terms of fear of loss of control and connection to family members are prevailing. Outcomes contribute to an understanding of social factors in the development and implementation of accepted home care solutions and might be helpful to develop age-sensitive information and communication concepts.

Keywords: Domestic robots · Technology acceptance · Demographic change · Older adults · User centered design · Smart home

1 Introduction

As a matter of fact: the profound demographic change and the growing aging population is a serious challenge for most industrialized nations in the world [1]. They all have to master the need to develop efficient, sustainable and humane solutions of medical care of the growing number of aged persons in times of overstrained health care systems and dwindling number of caregivers [2]. Demographic and financial constraints lead to a serious bottleneck, in which not enough caregivers for the growing number of patients remain. A critical shortage of public resources, doctors, nurses, and other healthcare personnel will

© Springer International Publishing AG 2017
J. Zhou and G. Salvendy (Eds.): ITAP 2017, Part I, LNCS 10297, pp. 57–74, 2017.
DOI: 10.1007/978-3-319-58530-7_5

arise within the next decades [3]. In situations, where persons cannot be treated in institutional settings alone anymore, individual and personalized care in the home environment plays a more and more important role [4, 5].

Along with this change an increased need exists for intelligent medical technologies covering diagnosis, treatment, and care, which enable seniors to live independently at home [6–9].

In the last decade, a huge number of innovative smart health care technologies have been developed that promise to deliver significant improvements in access to care, quality of care, and the efficiency of the health sector [3, 10, 11], thereby representing possible solutions to the soaring requirements of novel care concepts and bridging temporal and spatial gaps between patients and physicians.

The developments in the health care sector aimed at different implementation concepts, and the spectrum of emerging technical applications covers a broad variety of developments, reaching from internal technologies (implants for monitoring physiological signals) over devices integrated into clothes (wearable technologies) to healthcare robots or smart home technologies, which support older people in keeping up independent living [4, 12–14].

Even though the progress in these technical developments is significant and promising, still the social part of the developments is underexplored. Social and emotional aspects of humans' technology acceptance as well as the detailed study and the willingness of understanding individual usage motives and barriers have not been fully understood. Technology assistance—especially in the home-care and rehabilitation sector—can only fully deploy its huge potential for graying societies, if acceptance issues are considered and the willingness of older users to accept technical devices as care authorities in their homes. Usable systems and devices that meet users' expectations as well as respect their requirements to keep their individuality, dignity and their intimacy at home will be critical success factors [15–18] for a successful roll-out and a broad acceptance of such systems.

In this paper we concentrate on the social perception of domestic robots for the care of older persons at home. In the next section we describe the current state in the technical development of robot variants and also refer to recent acceptance studies which have been carried out to study human-robot interaction. On this base we develop the research question and the logic of empirical procedure undertaken in this study.

2   Robots for Healthcare

In the last years, many research projects and technical developments in research and industry have emerged to develop, implement and test health care robots in different settings, ranging from laboratory studies to field test or even in realistic settings such as senior homes [19, 20]. The majority of healthcare robots for older people are still in the development and validating test phases, even though some of them are already commercially available. Regarding the functionality, a huge range of functions and care situations has been addressed [21, 22].

In their overview article, Broadbent et al. [19] categorize health care robots into three large groups—all of them are designed to enhance the life quality of older people and to support their independent living at home. One type of robot is providing physical assistance, the second type of robot monitors health states and provides medical safety. The third category of healthcare robot offers social contact, entertainment or companionship [19]. In addition, there are also telepresence systems [23], which support social connectedness and communication of older adults with their family members and care personnel.

The Care-o-bot, which was developed at the Fraunhofer Institute in Germany [24], for example, is a robotic assistant that supports persons in their daily living at home, offering drinks, laying the table, waters plants and switches on the TV or the radio and is able to even call for the rescue service in case of emergency. Similarly, Pearl, a mobile autonomous robot developed at Carnegie Mellon university [25], was developed to support seniors' mobility at home and to support them to take medication or to remind them of appointments at the doctors' office. Another development is the hobbit, a care robot, which has been designed especially for fall detection and emergency detection. The robot is able to picking up objects from the floor in order to prevent falls and to call the ambulance, if necessary [23]. Also, the hobbit allows multimodal interaction for users with differing impairment levels.

Beyond these more or less functional robots, there are also social robot prototypes, as Aibo (http://www.sony-aibo.com), the robotic dog, or Paro the little seal from Japan (http://www.parorobots.com) that have been designed as social companions able to be much more than only a functional helper. Both robots have in common that they deliver social values which might be especially helpful for persons with only limited access to family members and persons with dementia [26, 27]. Like the Paro, the Hug [28] has a soft and warm surface and is equipped with sensors that react to physical pressure. By this, nonverbal communication behavior (sending and receiving hugs) between older adults and family members is enabled.

With the ever-increasing functionality, ability, and reach of health care robots, the question of technology acceptance and social aspects of human robot interaction is focused. On the one hand, the influence of robot attributes, form and personality on acceptance is under study [29] as well as the influence of user characteristics, e.g. cognitive abilities, gender, experience with technology, age, culture on the willingness to interact with the robot at home [30–33]. While most of the studies concerned with acceptance of robot assistance concentrate on older adults, there is a scarcity of research papers reporting on the different attitudes and preferences of all the different persons involved in the care process, as e.g. staff and residents of senior homes as well as family members and relatives of residents which could have different perspectives on the usefulness of health-care robots [34, 35]. A recent study in this context [35] showed that the concerns and the perceived benefits strongly depend on the respective perspective. Interestingly, the residents were more positive towards robotic assistance than the family members and the staff. While the staff was mostly concerned about the job loss, residents and family members feared the loss of personal care. The benefit reported by all stakeholders was the gain in time that allows increasing the care and communication quality with the residents. The target functions of the robots was seen in the detection of falls and getting quick help as well as support in lifting and monitoring locations.

Even though technology development in the homecare robotic sector is fast developing and the potential of robotic assistance in the field of domestic care of older persons at home is widely acknowledged, the research and technology development is mostly technology driven. The question if and if so, older persons would accept a robotic assistance at home—given that robotic assistance would be feasible and affordable—is still a research topic that needs deeper understanding [31, 35–37].

In addition, the general acceptance for or against a domestic robot is only one side of the coin. The willingness to allow a domestic robot to support us in sensitive and quite private care situations at home is another issue that needs to be examined in the older age group. This is an urgent research duty, as the integration of users in the technology development is indispensable for the success of the technology in the roll-out phase and therefore a mandatory requirement for sustainable solutions.

3 Research Questions and Purpose of the Study

Based on the acceptance-related research so far, the goal of this study was to explore all the acceptance-relevant criteria that people apply to the vision of using a domestic robot at home. In order to gain deeper insights, a three-step empirical procedure was applied.

In a first step, focus groups with users of all ages were run in which users discussed freely about potential benefits and drawbacks of having a robot at home. The argumentation patterns were recorded and used to develop the questionnaire instruments, which were used to quantify acceptance patterns in the next step. Focus groups allow a deeper understanding of mental models and hidden drivers for or against a novel technology as it might be the case in home car robots for which only very single persons might have experience with.

Second, a quantitative survey study was run, in which users of all ages evaluated the benefits and barriers of using a domestic robot. Also, they evaluated conditional usage criteria and prerequisites that should be given to reach positive acceptance or at least tolerance. Outcomes allow to quantify the relative benefits and barriers to estimate the overall willingness to adopt homecare robots.

While in the second study quite general benefits and barriers of domestic robots were explored, the third study addressed specific actions and daily assistive functions a robot could do to be an accepted helper at home. Here, the focus was laid on sensitive care situations which might be accomplished by a domestic care robot. In order to compare the relative acceptance, participants evaluated both, the acceptance of a home care robot doing these tasks and a human care person.

For the analysis, we took an aging perspective, thereby determining if users of different ages and technology education might have a different perspective on the acceptance of a domestic robot.

4 Study 1: The Focus Group Approach

4.1 Participants

Three focus groups were run, in which younger and older adults volunteered to take part. Overall, 27 persons in an age range between 22 and 65 years took part. 60% were females. Participants were recruited from the social network of the authors. All of them were open to novel technologies, from different backgrounds and educations, but did not have experience with using a robot by themselves. Participants were not gratified for their efforts.

4.2 Procedure and Instruction

In the beginning of each focus group, the topic was introduced to participants by giving them a scenario in which the role and the functions of the domestic robot was characterized in a functional and neutral way. The household robot was introduced as an assistive device that can support persons in their independent living at home, in the following areas: (1) Tasks of housekeeping (Fetching and passing household items, laying the table, using the microwave, cleaning, controlling heating, light, front door, shutters) (2) Personal assistant (safe mobility in the house, communication and exchange with the environment but also as a support to get help in emergency situations, reminder of appointments and intake of medication). Participants were instructed to freely comment on these functions and to envisage to have such a robot at home. The focus groups lasted around 1.5 h and were carried out on university campus. Data were collected by note-taking by assistants who were not involved in the discussion.

4.3 Results

Overall, the discussion was vivid, revealing both, positive as well as negative aspects. As the perception of assistive domestic robots was not age-sensitive, revealing similar benefits and barriers across ages, results are reported alongside three categories which have been formed out of the argumentations.

Accepted usage contexts: A first category dealt with visions of using contexts in which such a robot would be welcome. In the first place, the robot was perceived as a relief in everyday life for handicapped or disabled persons which need assistance (stairs, moving around) with the goal to be more flexible in old age. In addition, the robot was perceived as a possibility to get things efficiently done, whenever care costs are too expensive or people are lazy or oblivious, but also for time savings for busy people. But the robot was also seen helpful as a social companion, if no relatives are living nearby, for entertainment reasons or just for having fun. The use of a robot was also seen positive in a situation in which an older person lives with the relatives, and the robot is then helping to have both the independency of being cared for but still the presence of family members for personal contact.

Fears and barriers: When it comes to the barriers, the discussion centered around three main topics:

One referred to the vision that the robot is not controllable anymore and decides for humans even if they do not want this. Here, it was obvious that the fears were nurtured by irrational scenes and movies in which robots took over the control and "got crazy". In this context, it was also discussed that participants have concerns of data protection and privacy loss and that third parties could have access to their physiological data or emotional states ("Occurrence of wrong functions through potential manipulations which I do not understand as old person").

The second type of barriers referred to usability issues. In this context, participants (especially the middle-aged and older ones) were concerned about the ease of handling the robot, the unpredictability of technical errors and system failures ("short circuit", "system crash", "attrition of parts", "unreliability") but assumed that the robot would be also complicated to program and use ("too many functions at once", "missing maintenance service"). They also assumed that the robot would be too slow to react and that the robot would be too bulky and difficult to maneuver in the apartment.

The third type of barriers regarded the dependency on the robot and the feeling to be at the mercy of the robot. In this context, participants not only mentioned the unlikable personality (the interaction was assumed to be "impersonal", "cold", "sterile", "imbalanced"), but also suspected that the presence of the robot would prevent family members to stay in contact, thus the robot was made responsible for social isolation and for a "life without life quality". Singularly, also health concerns were raised in terms of probable electric shocks that could occur when persons have wet hands and when robots mingle with water.

4.4   Discussion

Overall, discussions regarding the acceptance of a domestic robot were fruitful and participants—independently of their age and gender—were very engaged, seeing both, benefits and drawbacks. Positive perceptions were prevailing about the usefulness of such a robot in case of being old and needing help, but also for daily assistance whenever people are lazy, busy or oblivious.

When focusing on the barriers, concerns raised seemed to be triggered by movies in which robots are taking over the control over the world and human beings having nothing to do against it. Here three types of (mis-)information might be responsible for the types of concerns raised: The vision of a robot made from steel, that must be cold, technical, impersonal and bulky and could provoke electricity issues (shock, smog).

The vision of robot care which makes people lonely either because relatives would then not care for the older persons any more (as the robot is doing this), or the general vision that technical assistance is the opposite to human assistance. Finally, the vision of being helpless in terms of complexity of functions, problems with using and handling the interfaces and technical errors. Apparently, the everyday experience with technical failure in devices might have triggered the usability issues raised by participants.

5   Study 2: Determining Benefits and Barriers Towards a Domestic Robot

5.1   Participants

Overall, 260 participants, in an age range of 20–88 years completed the online survey. The sample was split into three age groups. In age group 1 (younger), there were 92 participants, 51% women, from 20–30 years of age ($M = 24.7$, $SD = 3$). Age group 2 (middle-aged) consisted of 101 persons in an age range of 40–65 years of age ($M = 51.5$, $SD = 6.2$), with 45% men and 54% women. Finally, in age group 3 (older group), there were 69 persons, 57% women (41% men), in an age range from 66–88 years ($M = 75.8$, $SD = 6$). Participants were asked via email to take part in the study. Completing the questionnaire took about 30 min. Younger persons were mostly students from different fields of study, the middle-aged and older age group came from different professional fields (e.g., engineers, administrative officers, secretaries, teachers, nurses, architects and craftsmen). All of them reported to use ICT for private and business purposes regularly and were quite technology affine. Neither of them had experience with using a robot.

5.2 Questions in the Survey

The survey contained the following sections: The first part of the questionnaire dealt with demographical data like gender, age and educational level.

In a second part, the general usefulness of a domestic robot was asked for. Participants had to answer the following questions (see Table 1):

Table 1. Items to the questions: "Do you think ... Items had to be answered on a 4-point Likert scale (1 = no, 2 = probably not, 3 = probably, yes 4 = yes).

Do you think...
that the use of the devices could increase your life-quality?
to use a home robot to live longer independently at home?
that the home robot is generally useful?
that the use of the devices will make your life easier?

Table 2. Items to the questions: "I would accept the usage of a domestic robot, if.... Items had to be answered on a 4-point Likert scale (1 = no, 2 = probably not, 3 = probably, yes 4 = yes).

I would accept the usage of a domestic robot if...
I can retain my independence
I can spare my relatives from intensively caring for me
I can live with dignity in independency for a longer time
I can avoid familial disputes concerning my care
I do not have to be a burden to anyone
I do not become dependent on other people
I do not have to bear the ignobility of strange care persons
I can save care costs

In a third part, the reasons for using the robots were explored (see Table 2). Participants had to affirm/deny the following items on a 4 point Likert scale.

Finally, we assessed the concerns participants have when using a domestic robot. Again, participants answered the items by confirming or denying the respective items (see Tables 3 and 4) on a 4-point Likert scale.

Table 3. Items to the questions: "I am worried that... Items had to be answered on a 4-point Likert scale (1 = no, 2 = probably not, 3 = probably, yes 4 = yes).

I am worried that...
the device sends too many error messages and that no one takes me seriously anymore
the purchase or maintenance of the device costs too high
the device has a technical defect and fails
I am not my own master anymore
my family would have too much control over me
I might look older or sicker than I am actually, when I use the device
my doctor has too much control over me

5.3   Results

Data was statistically analyzed by ANOVAs. The level of significance was set at 5% level. Due to the higher inhomogeneity of the older sample significance levels of $\alpha = 0.1$ are reported as marginally significant.

Results are presented according to the structure of the questionnaire, i.e., first we report the ratings with respect to the usefulness of the domestic robot, then acceptance criteria and barriers. For each of the sections, descriptive data with the focus on the age groups are reported as well as the inference statistical testing of differences.

5.3.1   Usefulness of Domestic Robots

Participants had to firstly answer how they generally evaluate the usefulness of a domestic robot. In this context, they were given four questions which they had to answer on a 4-point scale (1 = do not agree at all, 4 = do fully agree). Statistical testing showed a significant age effect ($F(2, 253) = 2.6, p < .05$). In Fig. 1, descriptive outcomes with respect to the three age groups can be seen.

When asked if home robots increase life quality, the younger group showed the highest confirmation ($M = 2.9, SD = 0.8$), followed by the middle-aged group ($M = 2.6, SD = 0.9$) and finally the oldest group, who showed the lowest confirmation in this regard ($M = 2.4$,

Fig. 1. Rated usefulness of domestic robots (means) in the three age groups

$SD = 0.9$). A very similar pattern was found for the question if domestic robots would enable independent living at home.

While the younger group shows the strongest affirmation ($M = 3$, $SD = 0.8$) to this statement, the middle aged ($M = 2.8$, $SD = 0.9$) and the older participants ($M = 2.4$, $SD = 0.9$) are more reluctant.

Asked if home robots would be generally useful, again affirmation to that vision is strongly age-sensitive. The younger group ($M = 3.14$, $SD = 0.8$) is convinced that this is the case, while the middle-age ($M = 2.9$, $SD = 0.8$) and the older group ($M = 2.6$, $SD = 1$) are not so positive.

Finally, the vision that domestic robots would make things easier was evaluated with the very same answering pattern, with the youngest showing the highest confirmation ($M = 3.2$, $SD = 0.7$), followed by the middle-aged persons ($M = 2.9$, $SD = 0.9$) and the oldest group ($M = 2.6$, $SD = 0.9$).

5.3.2   Acceptance Criteria for Using Domestic Robots

In a second part, participants were asked to answer eight different reasons that could be in favor of accepting a domestic robot at home. Answers again had to be given on a 4-point scale (high numbers indicate high confirmation). Again, age had a significant effect on the acceptance ($F(2, 253) = 2.3$, $p < .05$).

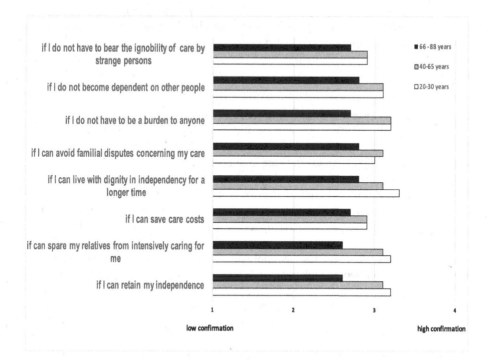

Fig. 2. Ratings of acceptance criteria (means) in the three age groups

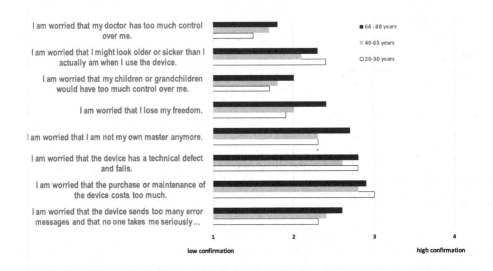

Fig. 3. Rated worries when using domestic robots (means) in the three age groups

Descriptive outcomes can be taken from Fig. 2. Overall, the younger participants are much more willing to accept domestic robots, but also the middle-aged adults which showed a similar willingness to adopt domestic robots in comparison to the younger group. Again, only the senior group showed a more reserved attitude towards the acceptance criteria.

5.3.3 Worries Towards Using Domestic Robots

In the third part of the survey, participants indicated the extent of concerns or worries they have in the context of using a domestic robot. Their answers were given on a 4-point Likert scale (high numbers indicate high confirmation).

In Fig. 3, descriptive outcomes are depicted. Again, there was a significant age effect, showing that the extent and type of worries is indeed age-specific ($F(2, 253) = 2.6$, $p < .05$). Still however, age patterns in the context of worries are less "linear" (in the sense: the younger participants are the higher the approval of the domestic robot as care authority).

Apparently, there are worries that apply also for the younger group. For example, the worry that persons would look older and sicker than they are (when using the robot), was most strongly confirmed by the younger group. The same applied for the worries that purchase and maintenance costs for the domestic robots would be high, which was also most strongly confirmed by the younger age group in comparison to the middle-aged and the aged persons.

But there were also worries which were most pronounced in the senior group. As such, the worry that older adults lose their freedom or the worry that they would not be able to master their own life was confirmed most strongly by seniors.

5.4 Discussion

The survey yielded both, age-insensitive and age-sensitive findings in the context of using a domestic robot at home. Independently of age, participants attested a considerable usefulness of having a domestic robot and saw a lot of reasons in favor of using them. As such, independency and the possibility to live longer in the own four walls were strong arguments, as well as not being a burden for relatives which might have the duty to care for them.

Beyond this age-insensitive positive view, the relative extent of confirmation to the respective reasons was indeed age-sensitive, as the younger and middle-aged persons were more positive than the seniors which showed more reluctance in this context. When it comes to worries, a more complex picture emerged. Especially the older group reported to have stronger concerns in the vision of losing their freedom or the ability to master their lives when relying on the support of domestic robots. Also, usability issues seem to be a strong concern of the senior group as well as the fact that assistive devices could be stigmatizing in the sense that persons look older and sicker than they factually are. Particularly, this was also a serious concern that has been raised by the younger group. Obviously, the fact that assistive devices—domestic robots—are in use is perceived as a negative stigma, rather than as a valuable assistance for specific situations.

6 Study 3: Exploring the Acceptance of Specific Functions in Robotic Assistance

In the third study, we focused on more specific functions in the context of personal care and compared the willingness of participants to accept a domestic robot in comparison to a human care person.

6.1 Sample

Overall, 304 participants, took part in the study. Due to an ad-hoc sampling method, the age distribution was quite asymmetrical with a considerably higher number of younger than middle-aged and older persons. Overall, participants were between 21 and 99 years of age, with 60% women and 40% men. Three age groups were formed: In age group 1 (younger), there were 198 participants, 51% women, from 20–30 years of age ($M = 24.3$, $SD = 2.1$). In age group 2 (middle-aged) they were consisted of 72 persons in an age range of 31–53 years of age ($M = 44.7$, $SD = 8.3$), Age group 3 (older group) consisted of 34 persons, in an age range from 57–99 years ($M = 62.3$, $SD = 9.3$).

Respondents were asked by email to take part in the study. Completing the survey took about 20 min. Again, the younger persons were mostly students from different fields of study, while he middle-aged and older age group had different educational backgrounds and professional fields. All of them reported to use ICT for private and business purposes regularly. None of them had experience with using a robot.

6.2   Questions and Design of the Study

Within the questionnaire design, there were two independent variables.

(1) One independent variable referred to the age group (comparing three different age groups)
(2) the other independent variable was the care authority, comparing a robotic care assistant vs. a human care person.

Participants had to evaluate the willingness to accept a robot as well as a human care person for the following care situations (Table 4).

Table 4. Care situations to be executed by either a human care or a robotic care assistant Items had to be answered on a 6 point Likert scale (1 = no, 6 = yes).

	Human care	Robotic care
Putting s.o. to bed		
Spoon feeding s.o.		
Giving medication		
Applying cream to the body		
Helping s.o. to wash hair		
Helping s.o. into the bath tube		
Giving s.o. a wash		
Helping s.o. to visit the toilet		
Helping s.o. to cream the face		
Helping s.o. to comb hairs		

Acceptance had to be answered on a 6-point Likert Scale (1 = not at all and 6 = in any case, yes). A dependent measurement design was applied thus participants evaluated both care authorities with respect to the willingness to accept them in the respective care situations.

6.3   Results

Data was statistically analyzed using MANOVAs with repeated measurements. The level of significance was set at 5%. Due to the higher inhomogeneity of the older sample significance levels of $\alpha = 0.1$ are reported as marginally significant. Descriptive data with the focus on the age groups are reported as well as the inference statistical testing of differences.

In a first step, we provide an overall analysis, summing up the answers across all care functions for the robot assistance and the human care person, respectively. Outcomes can be seen in Fig. 4.

The analysis revealed a significant main effect of the care authority ($F(1, 276) = 14.5$, $p < 0.001$) while there was no significant age effect. Thus, independently of age the human care person was preferred over the robotic assistant.

When looking at the single care functions (Table 5) differences showed up. We found both, situations in which humans are clearly preferred (e.g., giving s.o. medication, spoon-feeding s.o.) as well as care situations in which the robotic care assistant seems to be the "better" care authority (e.g., putting s.o. to bed; helping s.o. to visit the toilet).

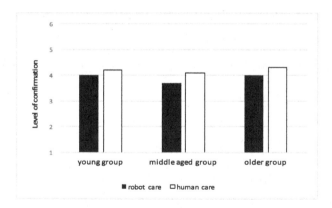

Fig. 4. The willingness (means) to be cared by a robot (black bars) and a human care persons. Answers have been summed up across the different care situations

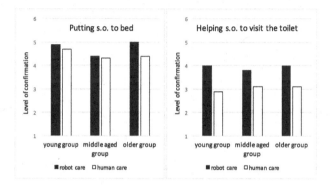

Fig. 5. Care situations (putting s.o. to bed, left side and helping s.o. to visit the toilet, right side) in which confirmation levels (means) are higher in the robotic assistance (black bars) in comparison to a human care person (white bars).

In Fig. 5, those care situations are depicted, in which participants indicated to prefer the human care. Statistical testing revealed a significant effect of care authority in the case of putting s.o. to bed ($F(1, 270) = 3, p < .1$) as well as in the case in which persons are supported to visit the toilet ($F(1, 270) = 30, p < .001$).

Figure 6 depicts, in contrast, the situation in which the human care person is clearly favored over the robot. For giving medication ($F(1, 270) = 24.9, p < .001$), statistical analysis revealed a significant effect of the care authority as well as when spoon-feeding s.o. ($F(1, 270) = 10.7, p < .001$).

In Table 5, descriptive outcomes for all care situations are given, thereby differentiating age groups and both care authorities.

Table 5. Means and standard deviations in the single care situations

Care functions	Care authority			Significance
	Age-groups	Human care	Robot care	
Putting s.o. to bed	Young (20–30)	4.7 (1.2)	4.9 (1.3)	*authority:* p < 0.1; *age:* p < .05
	Middle (31–50)	4.4 (1.1)	4.3 (1.3)	
	old (51, +)	4.4 (1.1)	5.0 (1.3)	
Spoon-feeding s.o.	Young (20–30)	4.3 (1.3)	3.9 (1.5)	*authority:* p < 0.01; *age:* n.s.
	Middle (31-50)	4.2 (1.1)	3.8 (1.3)	
	old (51, +)	4.3 (1.2)	3.6 (1.2)	
Giving medication	Young (20-30)	4.9 (1.1)	4.2 (1.6)	*authority:* p < 0.01; *age:* n.s.
	Middle (31-50)	4.6 (1.0)	3.9 (1.0)	
	old (51, +)	4.9 (0.6)	4.1 (1.3)	
Applying cream to the body	Young (20-30)	3.7 (1.4)	3.5 (1.5)	*authority;* p < 0.01; *age:* n.s.
	Middle (31-50)	3.8 (1.3)	3.2 (1.3)	
	old (51, +)	4.1 (1.3)	3.6 (1.5)	
Helping s.o. to wash hair	Young (20-30)	4.7 (1.1)	4.2 (1.5)	*authority:* p < 0.01; *age:* p < .05
	Middle (31-50)	4.4 (1.3)	3.8 (1.4)	
	old (51, +)	4.8 (0.8)	4.3 (1.3)	
Helping s.o. into the bath tube	Young (20-30)	3.9 (1.5)	4.5 (1.6)	*authority:* p < 0.01; *age:* n.s.
	Middle (31-50)	4.3 (1.3)	4.3 (1.3)	
	old (51, +)	4.7 (1.3)	4.7 (1.4)	
Giving a wash	Young (20-30)	3.5 (1.4)	3.5 (1.6)	*authority:* n.s. *age:* n.s.
	Middle (31-50)	3.6 (1.3)	3.8 (1.5) ·	
	old (51, +)	3.7 (1.4)	3.9 (1.6)	
Helping s.o. to visit the toilet	Young (20-30)	2.9 (1.4)	4.0 (1.7)	*authority:* p < 0.001; *age:* n.s.
	Middle (31-50)	3.1 (1.3)	3.7 (1.4)	
	old (51, +)	3.1 (1.4)	4.0 (1.7) ·	
Helping s.o. to cream the face	Young (20-30)	4.2 (1.3)	3.4 (1.5)	*authority:* p < 0.001; *age:* p < 0.0 1
	Middle (31-50)	4.1 (1.3)	3.2 (1.4)	
	old (51, +)	4.3 (1.2)	3.4 (1.4)	
Helping s.o. to comb hairs	Young (20-30)	4.8 (1.2)	3.8 (1.6)	*authority:* p < 0.001; *age:* p < 0.05
	Middle (31-50)	4.5 (1.1)	3.2 (1.1)	
	old (51, +)	4.6 (1.1)	3.9 (1.6)	

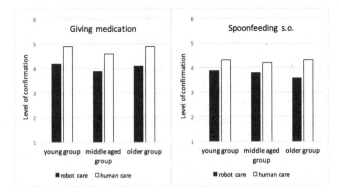

Fig. 6. Care situations (giving medication left side and spoon-feeding s.o., right side) in which confirmation levels (means) are higher in human care assistance (white bars) in comparison to robotic assistance (black bars).

6.4   Discussion

The study provided interesting insights into specific care situations and the tolerance of participants towards robotic care. Across all care situations under study there was a significant preference of human care over robotic assistance. A closer look in specific care situations however, revealed that the preference of human care over robotic assistance seems to be specific. There are care situations, as for example, the medication support or the spoon-feeding that should be in the responsibility of a human care person. In contrast, there are also care situations which are preferred to be accomplished by a robotic nurse, as e.g. putting s.o. to bed or helping s.o. to visit the toilet.

Interestingly though, no significant age effect was found showing that preferences in this context are quite age-insensitive. This is special as the acceptance of a robotic assistant was higher in younger age groups whenever general acceptance was in the focus of the study. However, whenever it comes to concrete and quite sensitive care situations, the preferences are quite stable across age groups. Surprisingly and seemingly contradicting previous findings, age is neither related to a clear preference of one over the other care authority, nor does age influence the overall extent of acceptance. Here, it should be critically kept in mind that the sample was asymmetrically young (with a larger number of younger adults) in comparison to the middle-aged and aged group. We speculate that this finding could be a result out of the asymmetrical age distribution and that age (in combination with a higher need of medical care) will influence the perception of a robotic care authority if this present sample is mirrored with significantly older participants.

7   Conclusions

In this research, we have looked at human-robot interaction in the context of caring for elderly people at home. We have seen that research in this context is mostly focused on designing the interaction of robots from a technical point of view. In contrast the willingness to accept a robot as a home care device is not easily understood. We conducted focus groups and two survey studies to understand the intricacies of robot acceptance in potential users and future users.

It is interesting to note that both qualitative and quantitative data show that the users' worries with the use of robots stems from the technological side of the equation. Risks such as technical defects and high maintenance costs are pervasive across age groups. Familiar risks—such losing control over ones' autonomy—become more palpable with age, while abstract risks—such as the fear of seeming to be more ill than one actually is—are also strongly shared by younger people. Surprisingly, loss of autonomy, when phrased as a benefit of robot use (i.e., maintaining independence), is perceived more beneficial by younger people. These seeming contradictions might be caused by differences in age-related risk perception and risk-taking personality aspects. Overall, the acceptance of a domestic robot seems to be rather high, given that no experience with such devices has been made by any of the participants.

When we look at the individual care acts that should be conducted and into the comparative analysis, we see that the subtext of the act has a strong influence on preferences. Acts that are traditional acts of human interaction (e.g., feeding someone, or giving someone medicine) are still preferred from a human care authority. Explanations for this might come from affects related to medical mistreatment (the care person knows what he is doing and can adapt). The possible risks associated with giving medication are high while going to the bathroom or being put to bed is seemingly risk free. One can argue that participants do like human care, when it is associated with the affective nature of the caring process (feeding, hair brushing, applying skin-cream), but still prefer the non-personal care of a robot in situations of bodily exposure (taking a bath, going to the bathroom). The shame-affect caused by exposing the nude body in a possibly degrading situation to a human care person could also be a relevant explanation for this result.

Overall it is necessary to further investigate how these judgments come to be. The reasoning behind these preferences has not been surveyed and would probably need further qualitative and quantitative data for a deeper understanding. It is also crucial to incorporate the participants' health status and their own experience in caring contexts. Experience with real-life care might modulate perception of human care as well as robot care. The aim of our study was to explore untainted perceptions of human-robot interaction regarding home caring. As soon such technology becomes financially viable and readily available, perceptions are bound to change. By integrating users' perceptions into the development process, early adopters of care robots—be it out of curiosity, wealth or necessity—might benefit from technology better suited to their needs. In the long term, we will have to ask ourselves: Humans or robots? Who cares?

Acknowledgement. We would like to thank the following students for conducting the survey studies: Anna Chatzopoulos, Marcel Derichs, Vi Anh Do, Theresa Eichhorn, Patrick Halbach, Christian Henn, Corinna Körner, Alexander Kwiatkowski, Dennis Lohse, Vivian Lotz, Dirk Nettelnbreker, Lorena Niebuhr, Oliver Oschmann, Hava Osmanbeyoglu, Yulia Ponomarenko, Nina Rußkamp, and Valerie Scharmer. In addition, authors thank Lisa Schwier, Anais Habermann, Sylvia Kowalewski and Carola Caesar for supporting this research. The authors would like to thank the German Research Foundation DFG for the kind support within the Cluster of Excellence "Integrative Production Technology for High-Wage Countries".

References

1. Salmond, S.W., Echevarria, M.: Healthcare transformation and changing roles for nursing. Orthop. Nurs. **36**(1), 12 (2017)
2. Holzinger, A., Röcker, C., Ziefle, M.: From smart health to smart hospitals. In: Holzinger, A., Röcker, C., Ziefle, M. (eds.) Smart Health. LNCS, vol. 8700, pp. 1–20. Springer, Cham (2015). doi:10.1007/978-3-319-16226-3_1
3. Leonhardt, S.: Personal healthcare devices. In: Mekherjee, S., et al. (eds.) Malware: Hardware Technology Drivers of Ambient Intelligence, pp. 349–370. Springer, Dordrecht (2006)
4. Demiris, G., Hensel, B.K., Skubic, M., Rantz, M.: Senior residents' perceived need of and preferences for "smart home" sensor technologies. Int. J. Technol. Assess. Health Care **24**, 120–124 (2008)

5. Gaul, S., Ziefle, M.: Smart home technologies: insights into generation-specific acceptance motives. In: Holzinger, A., Miesenberger, K. (eds.) HCI for eInclusion, pp. 321–332. Springer, Heidelberg (2009)
6. Kleinberger, T., Becker, M., Ras, E., Holzinger, A., Müller, P.: Ambient intelligence in assisted living: enable elderly people to handle future interfaces. In: Stephanidis, C. (ed.) UAHCI 2007. LNCS, vol. 4555, pp. 103–112. Springer, Heidelberg (2007). doi: 10.1007/978-3-540-73281-5_11
7. Ziefle, M., Röcker, C.: Acceptance of pervasive healthcare systems: a comparison of different implementation concepts. In: 4th ICST Conference on Pervasive Computing Technologies for Healthcare and Workshop User-Centred-Design of Pervasive Health Applications (UCD-PH 2010) (2010)
8. Mynatt, E.D., Rogers, W.A.: Developing technology to support the functional independence of older adults. Ageing Int. **27**(1), 24–41 (2002)
9. Meyer, S., Mollenkopf, H.: Home technology, smart homes, and the aging user. In: Schaie, K.W., Wahl, H.-W., Mollenkopf, H., Oswald, F. (eds.) Aging Independently: Living Arrangements and Mobility. Springer, Heidelberg (2003)
10. Mynatt, E.D., Melenhorst, A.-S., Fisk, A.D., Rogers, W.A.: Aware technologies for aging in place: understanding user needs and attitudes. Pervasive Comput. IEEE **20**(3), 36–41 (2004)
11. Warren, S., Craft, R.L.: Designing smart health care technology into the home of the future. In: Engineering in Medicine and Biology, vol. 2, p. 677 (1999). http://www.hctr.be.cua.edu/ HCTworkshop/HCT-pos_SW-FutureHome.htm
12. Weeks, L.E., Branton, O., Nilsson, T.: The influence of the family on the future housing preferences of seniors in Canada. Hous. Care Support **8**(2), 29–34 (2005)
13. Ziefle, M., Schaar, A.K.: Technology acceptance by patients: empowerment and stigma. In: Handbook of Smart Homes, Health Care and Well-Being, pp. 167–177 (2017)
14. Lalou, S.: Identity, social status, privacy and face-keeping in the digital society. J. Soc. Sci. Inf. **47**(3), 299–330 (2008)
15. Necheles, T.: Standards of medical care: how does an innovative medical procedure become accepted. Med. Health Care **10**, 15–18 (1982)
16. Zimmer, Z., Chappell, N.L.: Receptivity to new technology among older adults. Disabil. Rehabil. **21**, 222–230 (1999)
17. Wilkowska, W., Ziefle, M.: Privacy and data security in e-health: requirements from users' perspective. Health Inf. J. **18**(3), 191–201 (2012)
18. Bedaf, S., Huijnen, C., Heuvel, R.V.D., Witte, L.D.: Robots supporting care for elderly people. In: Robotic Assistive Technologies: Principles and Practice, pp. 309–332. CRC Press (2017)
19. Broadbent, E., Stafford, R., MacDonald, B.: Acceptance of healthcare robots for the older population: review and future directions. Int. J. Soc. Robot. **1**(4), 319 (2009)
20. Broekens, J., Heerink, M., Rosendal, H.: Assistive social robots in elderly care: a review. Gerontechnology **8**(2), 94–103 (2009)
21. Karabegović, I., Doleček, V.: The role of service robots and robotic systems in the treatment of patients in medical institutions. In: Hadžikadić, M., Avdaković, S. (eds.) Advanced Technologies, Systems, and Applications. LNNS, vol. 3, pp. 9–25. Springer, Cham (2017). doi:10.1007/978-3-319-47295-9_2
22. Fischinger, D., Einramhof, P., Papoutsakis, K., Wohlkinger, W., Mayer, P., Panek, P., Vincze, M.: Hobbit, a care robot supporting independent living at home: first prototype and lessons learned. Robot. Auton. Syst. **75**, 60–78 (2016)
23. Graf, B., Hans, M., Schraft, R.D.: Care-o-bot II—development of a next generation robotic home assistant. Auton. Robots **16**(2), 193–205 (2004)

24. Pollack, M.E., Engberg, S., Matthews, J.T., Thrun S, Brown, L., Colbry, D., Orosz, C., Peintner, B., Ramakrishnan, S., Dunbar-Jacob, J., Mc-Carthy, C., Montemerlo, M., Pineau, J., Roy, N.: Pearl: a mobile robotic assistant for the elderly. In: AAAI Workshop on Automation as Eldercare, Edmonton, Canada (2002)
25. Tamura, T., Yonemitsu, S., Itoh, A., Oikawa, D., Kawakami, A., Higashi, Y., Fujimooto, T., Nakajima, K.: Is an entertainment robot useful in the care of elderly people with severe dementia? J. Gerontol. Biol. Med. Sci. **59**, M83–M85 (2004)
26. Banks, M.R., Willoughby, L.M., Banks, W.A.: Animal-assisted therapy and loneliness in nursing homes: use of robotic versus living dogs. J. Am. Med. Dir. Assoc. **9**, 173–177 (2008)
27. Stiehl, W.D., Lieberman, J., Breazeal, C., Basel, L., Cooper, R., Knight, H., Lalla, L., Maymin, A., Purchase, S.: The huggable: a therapeutic robotic companion for relational, affective touch. In: Proceedings of the 3rd IEEE Consumer Communications and Networking Conference, Las Vegas, Nevada, pp. 1290–1291 (2006)
28. Mutlu, B., Osman, S., Forlizzi, J., Hodgins, J., Kiesler, S.: Task structure and user attributes as elements of human–robot interaction design. In: Proceedings of 15th IEEE International Symposium Robot Human Interactive Communication, RO-MAN 2006, p. 74 (2006)
29. Kuo, I.H., Rabindran, J.M., Broadbent, E., Lee, Y.I., Kerse, N., Stafford, R.MQ., MacDonald, B.A.: Age and gender factors in user acceptance of healthcare robots. In: The 18th IEEE International Symposium on Robot and Human Interactive Communication, RO-MAN 2009, pp. 214–219. IEEE (2009)
30. Young, J.E., Hawkins, R., Sharlin, E., Igarashi, T.: Toward acceptable domestic robots: applying insights from social psychology. Int. J. Soc. Robot. **1**(1), 95 (2009)
31. Beer, J.M., Smarr, C.A., Chen, T.L., Prakash, A., Mitzner, T.L., Kemp, C.C., Rogers, W.A.: The domesticated robot: design guidelines for assisting older adults to age in place. In: Proceedings of the Seventh Annual ACM/IEEE International Conference on Human-Robot Interaction, pp. 335–342. ACM (2012)
32. Parette, P., Scherer, M.: Assistive technology use and stigma. Educ. Train. Develop. Disabil. **39**(3), 217–226 (2004)
33. Dijkers, M.I., deBear, P.C., Erlandson, R.F., Kristy, K., Geer, D.M., Nichols, A.: Patient and staff acceptance of robotic technology in occupational therapy: a pilot study. J. Rehabil. Res. Dev. **28**, 33–44 (1991)
34. Broadbent, E., Tamagawa, R., Patience, A., Knock, B., Kerse, N., Day, K., MacDonald, B.A.: Attitudes towards health-care robots in a retirement village. Australas. J. Ageing **31**(2), 115–120 (2012)
35. Heerink, M.:. Exploring the influence of age, gender, education and computer experience on robot acceptance by older adults. In: Proceedings of the 6th International Conference on Human-Robot Interaction, pp. 147–148. ACM (2011)
36. Flandorfer, P.: Population ageing and socially assistive robots for elderly persons: the importance of sociodemographic factors for user acceptance. Int. J. Popul. Res. (2012)
37. Smarr, C.A., Prakash, A., Beer, J.M., Mitzner, T.L., Kemp, C.C., Rogers, W.A.: Older adults' preferences for and acceptance of robot assistance for everyday living tasks. In: Proceedings of the Human Factors and Ergonomics Society Annual Meeting, vol. 56, no. 1, pp. 153–157. SAGE Publications, Los Angeles (2012)

User-Centred Design for the Elderly

Co-creation Methods: Informing Technology Solutions for Older Adults

Lupin Battersby[1(✉)], Mei Lan Fang[1], Sarah L. Canham[1], Judith Sixsmith[2], Sylvain Moreno[1], and Andrew Sixsmith[1]

[1] Simon Fraser University, Vancouver, Canada
{lbatters,mlfang,scanham,sylvainm,ajs16}@sfu.ca
[2] University of Northampton, Northampton, UK
judith.sixsmith@northampton.ac.uk

Abstract. With the demographic shift towards an aging population, there is an increasing need for and interest in technologies that address challenges associated with aging. The AGE-WELL Network of Centres of Excellence is developing and building capacity in researchers and partners affiliated with the network and beyond to co-create solutions with older adults and other stakeholders. In this paper three projects using different approaches to co-creation are explored: community-based participatory research, integrated knowledge translation, and transdisciplinary working. The projects span different focus areas and disciplines: (1) a seniors' affordable housing redevelopment evaluation; (2) a realist review of middle-aged and older adults and the digital divide; and (3) development of rehabilitation software for older adults' cognitive health. Based on these projects, opportunities for enriching the research process through co-creation methods are highlighted. In addition, factors to consider when choosing and implementing co-creation methods, such as the type of research project, level of project development, ethical issues, and resources available will be discussed. We conclude the paper with a call for researchers using co-creation in technology development to evaluate the impact of such approaches.

Keywords: Community-based participatory research · Co-creation · Integrated knowledge translation · Transdisciplinary working · Aging · Technology · Innovation

1 Introduction

With the demographic shift towards an aging population, there is an increasing need for and interest in technologies that address challenges associated with aging. In Canada adults 65 and older account for over 16% of the population; this proportion is expected to rise to 20% by 2024 [1]. A similar trend is seen globally. To meet the needs and expectations of older adults, it is imperative that technologies currently being developed are relevant, usable, appealing, and are suited to the everyday lives of older adults. This could be supported by using co-creation research approaches.

AGE-WELL NCE, a pan-Canadian research network on aging and technology is focused on developing innovative methods and technologies to support adults to age

© Springer International Publishing AG 2017
J. Zhou and G. Salvendy (Eds.): ITAP 2017, Part I, LNCS 10297, pp. 77–89, 2017.
DOI: 10.1007/978-3-319-58530-7_6

well. This transdisciplinary network of experts derives from several disciplines and professions, including gerontology, neuropsychology, health sciences, engineering, software development and more. Together they are working on a number of research initiatives focused on engaging older adults in research; one of which is a scoping review to better understand transdisciplinary working practices, in particular, the barriers, facilitators and added value to enhance research outcomes and positive transformation in real world contexts [2]. Another is looking at how best to support meaningful engagement of older adults throughout the research process. These are amongst a number of the key projects that are working towards evaluating, improving, and innovating opportunities to develop technological solutions that are relevant and accessible for integration into older adults' everyday lives. Through this work, AGE-WELL NCE is developing and building capacity in researchers and partners affiliated with the network and beyond to co-create solutions with older adults [3].

Developing technologically innovative solutions *with* rather than *for* older adults requires a degree of visioning and understanding of co-creation that extends beyond revealing and collecting accounts of older people's experiences. The authors, affiliated with AGE-WELL NCE, contribute to building capacity for innovative ways of working with older adults based on their experiences with co-creation research approaches utilized prior to and within the context of AGE-WELL NCE.

Co-creation is often associated with product development in the business literature. A number of seminal works articulate co-creation in the business management literature for value creation, such as Ramaswamy and Ozcan [4] who define co-creation as: "joint creation and evolution of value *with stakeholding individuals*, intensified and enacted through *platforms of engagements*, virtualized and emergent from *ecosystems of capabilities*, and actualized and embodied in *domains of experiences*, expanding *wealth-welfare-wellbeing*" (italics in original, p. 14). Co-creation articulated in business, as defined here, focuses on value creation for the company and the consumer. However, the value that researchers are seeking to gain through co-creation in their work may be somewhat different (for example, academic publications versus increased profits). The critical element that crosses the boundary from business and marketing to academic research and innovation is that all stakeholders have goals being met through the process. Moving beyond user input, into collaboration, towards what Gibbons [5] refers to as 'context-sensitive' or 'Mode 2' science, where the boundaries between science and society are blurred and the resulting interaction is producing new questions, methods, knowledge sources, and solutions that serve a broader objective.

With this broad view of co-creation - context-sensitive, collaborative, socially engaged, and interactive - we reflect on our experiences with research related to older adults using the following co-creation approaches: community-based participatory research, integrated knowledge translation, and transdisciplinary working. Each of these approaches has overlapping or complimentary components, yet stem from different disciplinary bases or paradigms. Community-based participatory research, often associated with social sciences, involves stakeholders as research participants and producers, working toward the co-creation of applied solutions. Integrated knowledge translation derives from health sciences and emphasizes early stakeholder engagement and an iterative synthesis of available evidence prior to implementation. Finally, transdisciplinary working emphasizes the engagement of all relevant disciplines, sectors, and stakeholders in a collaborative process that transcends disciplinary boundaries to contribute to the development of innovative solutions to real world problems.

In this paper, these approaches are examined through three illustrative research projects, detailing the theoretical and practical aspects of the identified approaches. The projects span different focus areas and disciplines: (1) a seniors' affordable housing redevelopment evaluation (community-based participatory research); (2) a realist review of middle-aged and older adults' access to and use of information and communication technology (integrated knowledge translation); and (3) development of rehabilitation software for older adults' cognitive health (transdisciplinary working).

Based on these projects, we illustrate opportunities for enriching the research process through co-creation methods rather than provide instructions on how to conduct a co-creation project. We do explore factors to consider when choosing and implementing co-creation methods, such as the type of research project, level of project development, ethical issues, and resources available. We conclude the paper with a call for researchers using co-creation in technology development to evaluate the impact of such approaches.

2 The Projects and Co-creation Approaches

Three research projects that explore the nuances, complexities, and value of co-creation approaches, including key features and strategies that can be applied in research and development for technology solutions for older adults are described and discussed.

2.1 Community-Based Participatory Research

This project explored the experiences of older adults transitioning from a deteriorating 3-storey low-rise affordable seniors' housing community into two newly built 16-storey high-rise towers. Of particular focus was the integration of seniors' sense-of-place and strategies for rebuilding the 'feeling of community' among the original tenants of the low-rise building. This project applied a number of strategies for user engagement, including photovoice sessions, experiential group walks, and mapping exercises with service providers and older adults, which incorporated action-oriented components.

Traditionally, the planning process for housing redevelopment initiatives has taken a top-down approach with the regeneration professional acting as the expert and decision-maker [6]. However, this approach has been challenged as it largely excludes the knowledge of local residents, which is important to ensure that any change reflects the community needs, resources, and assets [7]. Resident insight has been identified as crucial for the success of redevelopment projects [8]. Despite having extensive neighbourhood context and place experience, residents of a community, particularly older people, are seldom engaged in regeneration initiatives [9]. Since the new trend is to make cities more age-friendly, involving older people in the creation and maintenance of such environments is key for producing urban environments that facilitate health and well-being [9]. Achieving this objective will require a shift from developing urban places *for* older people to building meaningful environments *with* and *by* seniors [9].

To prioritise the perspectives of older adults, a community-based participatory research study design was chosen to provide seniors with the 'space' and platform to have their voice heard and generate collaborative dialogue (with the researchers). This research approach brought together researchers and community stakeholders (e.g., older adults, developers, municipal government, housing society, and service providers) to formulate equitable partnerships for the co-creation of research with the shared goal of improving community health and social outcomes and knowledge production and exchange [10, 11]. To engender community-based participatory research principles in the research process, experiential group walks, participatory mapping exercises, and photovoice sessions with service providers and older adults were conducted. These methods were selected because they offered community stakeholders a nuanced mechanism to share lived experiences via voice and vision triggering their emotional ties to place, observations of their physical surroundings, and ideas generated through mutual knowledge exchange [12].

For instance, photovoice is a visual method [13] grounded in qualitative participatory research principles that is used as a way of exploring personal experiences of a particular phenomenon [7]. First established by Wang and Burris, this method has been used to facilitate community engagement while simultaneously producing powerful images that have the potential to influence policy agendas in the areas of public health, education, and social work [14]. During photovoice sessions, participants can take or direct the taking of photographic images to illustrate their everyday experiences, engage in visual narrative interviews, and work with each other and researchers to discuss related themes and potential actions [15]. For participants, this process provided an avenue to visually portray experiences, and share and discuss personal knowledge about issues that may be challenging to express through words alone [13]. Photovoice was selected for this study because it provided a space that empowered older people to share stories of place though creative and collaborative photo taking and analysis. Critical to the success of the photovoice process in this project was the relationships established by the researcher with the older adults. The trust and bond developed over the course of the project supported the open and creative sharing of their experiences.

Meanwhile, participatory mapping is a research process that provides the opportunity to create a tangible display of people, places, and experiences that make up a community [16]. Over the last decades, participatory mapping was used by various disciplines for an array of different research and development purposes, such as land use, crime prevention, education, and health [17]. Similarly, experiential group walks involved researchers walking with older adults and stakeholders to explore the neighborhood context, enabling participants to be the expert, highlighting (in real-time) meaningful places, public spaces, and activities in their local environment [18]. Experiential walks enabled the research team to access older peoples' attitudes and knowledge, and further understand the types of relationships they maintained within their community [19]. Experiential group walks and mapping exercises offered visual cues to help participants describe their relationship to place; such triggers were captured via audio recording and photography [12]. Visual methods [20] provided opportunities for understanding unique cultural and social nuances of participants' everyday lives. One of the challenges faced in this method was the mobility of the participants, not all of the older adults were interested in or able to do an extended walk. The researchers accommodated the needs of the groups by shorter routes and frequent breaks. In addition part of the process involved identifying the spaces and places important to the older adults on physical maps of their community.

Findings from this project are rich, qualitative, and contextualized themes that capture a number of issues that are important to older adults for aging well in the right place. For instance, the theme of 'positive sense-of-place' identified key areas that planners could support: access to physical activities; safe and familiar spaces for social activities; convenient proximity to community resources; and maintaining a sense of control over their lives [12]. Stakeholder participants identified ideal characteristics of affordable housing as: adaptable, well-appointed, affordable, and centrally located. And recommended an inclusive design and development process similar to the co-creation approaches described in this paper.

From these, and further findings of the project, multiple applied and academic outputs have been generated. The former included working with the housing provider and residents in the development of an implementation and sustainability plan for the new affordable housing towers to support social interaction and sense of community; supporting the commitment to action of the housing provider, municipality, and developers to work collaboratively with residents; and recommendations for the municipality and housing society to consider for housing policies and future developments. For the tenants of the towers involvement in the project has supported their community engagement in the new building and as sense of validation for their expertise and experience. They can see themselves in all of the activities, impacts, and the research process. For academic outputs, the team has presented at national and international conferences on the methods and project findings. In addition, the relationships established with the different stakeholder groups (including older adults) have generated further collaborations, initiatives, and user engagement in other research projects.

2.2 Integrated Knowledge Translation

This project set out to explore the digital divide for middle-aged and older adults concerning their access to and use of information and communication technologies (ICTs). The project began in collaboration with a community partner organization, which contributed to the development of the research questions and other research decisions. In addition, two World Cafés were conducted with stakeholder groups to guide, inform, and contribute to the data analysis, synthesis, and knowledge mobilization.

Given the potential of digital technologies to support aging well, we were interested in exploring the current state of what is often referred to as the 'digital divide'. The digital divide was understood in the project as the unequal and/or inequitable access to the benefits of ICTs due to limitations of motivation, physical access, or capacity to use [21]. The integrated knowledge translation project included a realist synthesis review, two World Café events, and dissemination materials.

Integrated knowledge translation refers to the integrated, collaborative working of academic researchers with knowledge users throughout the entire research process to produce evidence that is useful and relevant to practice and to moving science forward

[22–24]. Critical to understanding integrated knowledge translation is the concept of knowledge translation itself. There are over 100 terms used for this concept, such as knowledge exchange, knowledge mobilization, and evidence-based practice, depending on the context and discipline [25]. For the purposes of this project, we used the Canadian Institutes of Health Research definition:

> "A dynamic and iterative process that includes synthesis, dissemination, exchange and ethically-sound application of knowledge to improve the health of Canadians, provide more effective health services and products and strengthen the health care system. This process takes place within a complex system of interactions between researchers and knowledge users which may vary in intensity, complexity and level of engagement depending on the nature of the research and the findings as well as the needs of the particular knowledge user" [24].

In keeping with this definition of knowledge translation, we sought to synthesize available literature published over the last decade on the current state of the digital divide as it pertains to middle-aged and older adults. The integrated portion of the knowledge translation process speaks to the degree of engagement of stakeholders in the process. We chose an integrated knowledge translation approach to ensure that: relevant questions were asked; channels for dissemination developed; and relevant knowledge and expertise beyond what was available through academia were included in the knowledge synthesis. The three primary strategies used in the project included: collaborating with community partners; conducting two World Café dialogue events with diverse community members and stakeholders; and producing accessible dissemination materials.

The first strategy of community partner collaboration involved team meetings with our partner to develop and refine our research goal and objectives prior to submitting the grant application for funding. Subsequently, we worked closely with our partner to refine our knowledge synthesis questions. The research objectives were to identify: knowledge gaps relating to middle-aged and older adults access to and use of ICTs; and recommendations for policy, service, and research to address the digital divide. One challenge we faced was that our primary contact at the community partner organization left the position approximately two-thirds into the project period, and her successor did not prioritize the research partnerships to the same degree. This is a perennial challenge to collaborative research initiatives. Given the probability for this to occur memorandums of understanding [26] should be established prior to the project being undertaken and having multiple community partners can reduce the impact. For this project other community partners were involved to differing degrees such that the project was able to move forward successfully.

The second strategy used was the World Café. World Cafés are often used as a participatory method for effective dialogue, knowledge exchange, and relationship building. Through the application of this approach, Fouche and Light [27] found "the impetus on collective discoveries enables the harnessing of resourcefulness and a sense of hope, while the drive towards collaborative learning allows for equitable and collective participation" (p. 46). As such, these interactive Cafés were an excellent approach for the project such that interdisciplinary and inter-sectoral groups were empowered to engage in dialogue that focused on a topic of shared interest (i.e., the use of ICTs by middle-aged and older adults). The aims of the World Café events were twofold: to capture the tacit knowledge of others' experiences of ICT use by middle-aged and older adults; and to develop interest and engagement to support the knowledge mobilization of the findings.

The World Café method incorporates the following five key components: a comfortable setting, a welcome and introduction, small group rounds, questions, and large group discussion. World Cafés are meant to foster open and relaxed dialogue, which is in part achieved through emulating a casual café-like setting where participants will be seated around tables with a café ambiance and refreshments [28]. Our two events were organized differently, with the first focused on generating understandings and meanings of the digital divide through everyday lived experiences and the second focused more on identifying gaps, validation of the findings, and knowledge mobilization.

At the first World Café, 6 tables of 5–7 participants (older adults, service providers, and researchers with vested interest in the area) were set up with one facilitator and one note-taker. Paper and pens were provided to enable creative expressions or hand written notes to supplement the verbal dialogue. The second event was held after the synthesis was completed as a workshop prior to gerontology conference with two tables of 5–7 participants. Participants included researchers and service providers focused on older adults and technology. We found that the World Café method worked particularly well for the first event, allowing for rich exploratory conversations with the variety of stakeholders involved. It was essential to have older adults' voices at the tables to contextualize their experiences of using ICTs, which provided real world examples of what was emerging in the literature. Participants at the events appreciated to networking and learning opportunity that the World Café afforded, as well as an opportunity to hear different experiences and strategies for exploring and addressing these issues.

Central to this integrated knowledge translation project was producing accessible outputs to share with participants, stakeholders, and the broader community. The research synthesis and World Café dialogue informed the development of a final report which was designed and written to be engaging and useful for policy makers, service providers, and other researchers [see 29]. The report describes the key messages, in brief these are: (1) There continues to be a gap in ICT access and use between younger cohorts that have grown up with the technology (generation X and younger) and the next previous cohort (baby boomers and older); (2) Tailored, relevant, and ongoing training and support can help to increase access; (3) Ageist representations of older adults and ICT use serves to perpetuate the digital divide; and, (4) Usable and accessible design can enhance use of ICTs as some adults experience physical challenges such as declines in vision and hearing, and increased arthritis in their hands. Highlighting the key findings, or points of interest, to the front of the report with details of the research near the end.

This report was shared at an academic gerontology conference, a multidisciplinary knowledge mobilization event hosted by the funding organization, and is available online. Additionally, a manuscript for peer-reviewed publication is in progress in order to reach the wider academic community.

The integrated knowledge translation approach ensured the project explored a relevant question that had practical implications. The context and specific examples provided through the first World Café event enriched the project report, making it more useful and user friendly for policy and service provision, while the second validated the work, increased knowledge sharing, and identified gaps to address in future research.

An additional benefit of the engagement process was building new relationships for future collaborative research initiatives.

2.3 Transdisciplinary Working

This project focused on developing rehabilitation software for older adults with the goal of improving the cognitive health of seniors. The software was created in collaboration with seniors, neuropsychologists, scientists, and music teachers and directly targets cognitive functions while inspiring high engagement and motivation. The research team adapted the content of the software based on the guidance of the different stakeholders.

A transdisciplinary scoping review completed by the AGE-WELL transdisciplinary working research team identified three features of transdisciplinarity: (1) is of mutual benefit for science and society; (2) is an interactive process involving co-production and integration of research and experiential knowledge; and (3) includes implementation or mobilization to create real-world impact [2].

The rehabilitation software development project applied a transdisciplinary approach in order to develop their curriculum of music training for children into one that would support the cognitive health of older adults [30]. Thus, experts from several fields (music, teaching, psychology, clinic practice, neuroscience, programming, engineering) and older adults were brought together. The technology undertook a unique approach to brain fitness by using musical training to improve different cognitive skills, such as language, reading, attention, memory, self-esteem, and intelligence. The software integrated scientific findings related to the effects of musical training, benefits of various teaching methods, and cognitive aging. Emerging evidence indicates that music training is an effective method to counteract age-related declines in cognitive ability suggesting that engaging in musical activity late into life may preserve cognitive functioning in old age [31].

The research development panel for the project identified that having a transdisciplinary team was the reason for successfully creating musical training software to improve different brain skills. Throughout the project, each skill and diverse expertise of the transdisciplinary team was critical. However, transdisciplinary working was not straightforward and many difficulties were encountered due to the diversity of the team. The difficulties experienced are reflected in the transdisciplinary literature. An initial challenge to overcome was language difference, as team members often used the same words for different purposes as specified by their discipline. This created many misunderstandings and was overcome by developing a common vocabulary, an issue confronted in other transdisciplinary contexts [32–34]. Another challenging element was the lack of understanding of the scope and limitations of different disciplines [35–37]. Thus, a fluid communication channel was critical to ensuring clear understandings of what each team member could contribute. Finally, coordinating the schedules, restrictions, and productivity of a large, dispersed, transdisciplinary team was challenging as members were dependent on each other for different aspects of the work. In this case, as in other transdisciplinary projects [33, 35, 37, 38], effective facilitation, sufficient resources, and good management skills were necessary to keep the project moving forward. The challenges were outweighed by the productivity of the team [37, 39–42];

developing scientific and social understanding of a real world problems [39, 41, 42]; and the production of better solutions to the complex problem at hand [32, 35, 37, 38, 43, 44].

3 Discussion

As with any type of research, a number of factors contribute to determining the 'optimal' research approach. As a result, decisions to adopt a co-creation approach, such as the research paradigm and methods, are dependent upon the suitability of the project for co-creation and available resources. As illustrated by the small sample of diverse projects and co-creation approaches described here, there are a variety of strategies to support active engagement of older adults and other stakeholders.

Prior to beginning a co-creation project, researchers and innovators need to identify if, when, and how, older adults and other stakeholders should be involved in their research and development projects. For example, basic scientific research may not lend itself to active knowledge user engagement, but could benefit from advisory group input. In the context of aging and technology for supporting older adults to age well, most, if not all projects, will benefit from active and integrated user engagement. In addition, the project needs to be of interest to older adults. If the project or the involvement strategy does not meet the interest or needs of older adults their participation and engagement will be challenging.

For projects that are under development, an integrated knowledge translation approach is a viable option for ensuring relevant questions are being addressed and the full range of available evidence and knowledge is synthesized toward developing the solutions or answers to those questions. This approach can serve to address and support the engagement of older adults. If an older adult is engaged at the research question phase, they are bound to find the experience more fulfilling. For projects that have a community partner interested in solving a problem specific to their community, using community-based participatory research can create actionable outputs the community partner can implement and build on with further research and development. Community organizations serving older adults can often facilitate the active engagement of older adults in projects that they are serving their members. Finally, taking a transdisciplinary working approach is well suited to projects that seek to address complex problems and create social and scientific change.

To assist in determining 'if and when' co-creation approaches should be used, research teams could identify their stage of product development. There are a number of Product Readiness Scales that can assist with identifying the stage of development a project has attained (see [45]). This can inform the type of user engagement and feedback needed for moving the project forward. AGE-WELL NCE is developing a product readiness level framework to be utilized by AGE-WELL and other aging and technology projects that has integrated concepts of user engagement and transdisciplinary working.

In addition to the suitability of the project, determining the resources available and required is necessary before choosing a co-creation approach. User engagement can be resource heavy in regards to time, skills, and funding. The time required for actively engaging knowledge users and stakeholders may require extra meetings and coordination, development of materials that are accessible to multiple audiences, working through differences, and potential refinement or redirection of the project. It is critical to build in the time and care required to foster meaningful engagement so that older adults have a positive and enriching experience. The AGE-WELL transdisciplinary scoping review found the following factors useful for facilitating transdisciplinary working: institutional support [37, 38, 46]; a diverse, heterogeneous team [34, 35, 38]; using in-person and digital communication (including both a social and working component to engagement) [35, 40, 43]; and having strong team leadership with brokering skills [35, 38, 40, 47]. These facilitators are essential to all co-creation approaches.

From our experiences, critical to co-creation is having team members with the experience, interest, and relationship building skills to engage knowledge users and stakeholders in the process. While content and disciplinary knowledge are essential to research and innovation, co-creation approaches require skills for facilitating collaborative working. As Muller and Druid [48] state in regards to using participatory design methods in computer specification and design, "You can't just add users and stir" (p. 3). It is important to recognize that projects will require space for the researcher or developer as well as older adults and other stakeholders to work through their differences of experience and knowledge, creating opportunities for learning and development for all involved. Essential here is to remember the human component: co-creation requires the messiness of getting to know people - sharing meals, laughter, frustrations, and creating new shared experiences together.

To support the creation of this space, capacity building within the team or hiring someone with engagement experience (e.g., a knowledge broker) should be integrated into co-creation projects. A sufficiently skilled team can support active engagement and ensure that work is conducted in an ethical manner, which is important given the unique challenges that emerge when using co-creation approaches. Ethical considerations of co-creation projects include the knowledge user requesting the product under development that may not be available beyond the life the project [49], non-disclosure and confidentiality agreements, intellectual property, and the return on investment of time and resources of the knowledge user [see 50, 51]. Thus, co-creation needs to address what it will be like for the older adult to be involved, including what they will get in return for their investment in the project and what will happen for them at the end of the project.

4   Conclusion

Many researchers are using co-creation methods to varying degrees. The co-creation experiences described here (community-based participatory research, integrated knowledge translation, transdisciplinary working) were dynamic, enriching, and appear to have real world impact. While each project had their own challenges, pitfalls, and resource demands, we found the approaches to be essential to the integrity and applicability of the process and outputs produced. We expect the success of technology solutions for older adults to increase if all stakeholders are thoroughly engaged in the research and development process because the solutions will be more accessible and useable to the target population. However, comprehensively evaluating the impact of co-creation approaches on the research and implementation process and outcomes is challenging. Co-creation based research projects that demonstrate impact with a cost-benefit analysis are needed. Determining outcome indicators of co-creation projects that are measurable and contextually relevant will be challenging.

References

1. Statistics Canada: The Canadian population in 2011: Age and sex (2012). http://www12.statcan.gc.ca/census-recensement/2011/as-sa/98-311-x/98-311-x2011001-eng.pdf. Accessed 12 Jan 2017
2. Sixsmith, J., Grigorovich, A., Kontos, P., Fang, M.L.: Using transdisciplinarity to inform technologies for older adults: a scoping review. In: Paper presented at the 45th Annual Scientific meeting of the Canadian Association of Gerontology, Montreal, Canada, 20–21 October 2016 (2016)
3. AGE-WELL: Annual Report 2015–2016, Toronto, Ontario (2016)
4. Ramaswamy, V., Ozcan, K.: The co-creation paradigm. Stanford University Press, Stanford (2014)
5. Gibbons, M.: Mode 2 society and the emergence of context-sensitive science. Sci. Public Policy **27**(3), 159–163 (2000)
6. Davitt, J.K., Lehning, A.J., Scharlach, A., Greenfield, E.A.: Sociopolitical and cultural contexts of community-based models in aging: the village initiative. Public Policy and Aging Report pru055 (2015)
7. Nowell, B.L., Berkowitz, S.L., Deacon, Z., Foster-Fishman, P.: Revealing the cues within community places: stories of identity, history, and possibility. Am. J. Commun. Psychol. **37**(1–2), 29–46 (2006)
8. Halpern, R.: Rebuilding the Inner City: A History of Neighborhood Initiatives to Address Poverty in The United States. Columbia University Press, New York (1995)
9. Buffel, T., Phillipson, C., Scharf, T.: Ageing in urban environments: developing 'age-friendly' cities. Crit. Soc. Policy **32**(4), 597–617 (2012)
10. Jagosh, J., Bush, P.L., Salsberg, J., Macaulay, A.C., Greenhalgh, T., Wong, G., Pluye, P.: A realist evaluation of community-based participatory research: partnership synergy, trust building and related ripple effects. BMC Public Health **15**(1), 1 (2015)
11. Minkler, M., Wallerstein, N. (eds.): Community-Based Participatory Research for Health, 2nd edn. Jossey-Bass, San Francisco (2008)
12. Fang, M.L., Woolrych, R., Sixsmith, J., Canham, S., Battersby, L., Sixsmith, A.: Place-making with older persons: establishing sense-of-place through participatory community mapping workshops. Soc. Sci. Med. **168**, 223–229 (2016). doi:10.1016/j.socscimed.2016.07.007
13. Wang, C., Burris, M.A.: Photovoice: concept, methodology, and use for participatory needs assessment. Health Educ. Behav. **24**(3), 369–387 (1997)
14. Catalani, C., Minkler, M.: Photovoice: a review of the literature in health and public health. Health Educ. Behav. **37**(3), 424–451 (2010)
15. Hergenrather, K.C., Rhodes, S.D., Cowan, C.A., Bardhoshi, G., Pula, S.: Photovoice as community-based participatory research: a qualitative review. Am. J. Health Behav. **33**(6), 686–698 (2009)
16. Corbett, J.: Good Practices in Participatory Mapping. International Fund for Agricultural Development, Rome (2009)

17. Chambers, R.: Participatory mapping and geographic information systems: whose map? Who is empowered and who is disempowered? Who gains and who loses? Electron. J. Inf. Syst. Dev. Countries **25**, 1–11 (2006)

18. Garcia, C.M., Eisenberg, M.E., Frerich, E.A., Lechner, K.E., Lust, K.: Conducting go-along interviews to understand context and promote health. Qual. Health Res. **22**(10), 1395–1403 (2012). doi:10.1177/1049732312452936

19. Carpiano, R.M.: Come take a walk with me: the "go-along" interview as a novel method for studying the implications of place for health and well-being. Health Place **15**(1), 263–272 (2009). doi:10.1016/j.healthplace.2008.05.003

20. Rose, G.: Visual Methodologies, 3rd edn. SAGE, London (2012)

21. van Dijk, J.: Digital divide research, achievements and shortcomings. Poetics **34**(4–5), 221–235 (2006). doi:10.1016/j.poetic.2006.05.004

22. Bowen, S., Graham, I.: From knowledge translation to engaged scholarship: promoting research relevance and utilization. Arch. Phys. Med. Rehabil. **94**(1), S3–S8 (2013)

23. Phipps, D., Shapson, S.: Knowledge mobilisation builds local research collaborations for social innovation. Evid. Policy **5**(3), 221–227 (2009)

24. Canadian Institutes of Health Research: about knowledge translation (2009). http://www.cihr-irsc.gc.ca/e/29418.html. Accessed 4 Jan 2011

25. Shaxson, L., Bielak, A., et al.: Expanding our Understanding of K*(KT, KE, KTT, KMb, KB, KM, etc.): A Concept Paper Emerging from the K* Conference Held in Hamilton, Ontario, Canada, April 2012. UNU-INWEH, Hamilton (2012)

26. Adams, A., Miller-Korth, N., Brown, D.: Learning to work together: developing academic and community research partnerships. WMJ-MADISON **103**(2), 15–20 (2004)

27. Fouche, C., Light, G.: An invitation to dialogue: 'The World Café' in social work. Qual. Soc. Work **10**(1), 28–48 (2010)

28. Brown, J., Isaacs, N.M.: Hosting conversations that matter at the world cafe. Whole Syst. Assoc. **1**, 1–20 (2002)

29. Battersby, L., Canham, S.L., Fang, M.L., Sixsmith, J., Sixsmith, A.: Middle-aged & older adults' information and communication technology access: a realist review. SSHRC Knowledge Synthesis Report (2016). sfu.ca/grc

30. Moreno, S.: System and method for providing music based cognitive skills development. U.S. Patent No. 2012/0090446 (2012)

31. Hanna-Pladdy, B., MacKay, A.: The relation between instrumental musical activity and cognitive aging. Neuropsychology **25**(3), 378–386 (2011)

32. Simard, M., Gagné, A.M., Lambert, R.D., Tremblay, Y.: A transdisciplinary approach to the decision-making process in extreme prematurity. BMC Res. Notes **7**(1), 1 (2014)

33. Olson, B.D., Fauchald, S.K.: A transdisciplinary approach to developing a web-based nursing experiential log system for advanced practice nursing clinical experiences. Comput. Inf. Nurs. **29**(11), 630–636 (2011)

34. Daudelin, G., Lehoux, P., Abelson, J., Denis, J.L.: The integration of citizens into a science/policy network in genetics: governance arrangements and asymmetry in expertise. Health Expect. **14**(3), 261–271 (2011)

35. Orozco, F., Cole, D.C.: Development of transdisciplinarity among students placed with a sustainability for health research project. EcoHealth **5**(4), 491–503 (2008)

36. Lambert, R.D., Monnier-Barbarino, P.: Transdisciplinary training in reproductive health through online multidisciplinary problem-solving: a proof of concept. Eur. J. Obstet. Gynecol. Reprod. Biol. **123**(1), 82–86 (2005)

37. Loisel, P., Hong, Q.N., Imbeau, D., Lippel, K., Guzman, J., MacEachen, E., Corbiere, M., Santos, B., Anema, J.R.: The work disability prevention CIHR strategic training program: program performance after 5 years of implementation. J. Occup. Rehabil. **19**(1), 1–7 (2009)
38. Schensul, S.L., Nastasi, B.L., Verma, R.K.: Community-based research in India: a case example of international and transdisciplinary collaboration. Am. J. Commun. Psychol. **38**(1–2), 125–139 (2006)
39. Hall, K.L., Stokols, D., Stipelman, B.A., Vogel, A.L., Feng, A., Masimore, B., Morgan, G., Moser, R.P., Marcus, S.E., Berrigan, D.: Assessing the value of team science: a study comparing center-and investigator-initiated grants. Am. J. Prev. Med. **42**(2), 157–163 (2012)
40. Stokols, D., Harvey, R., Gress, J., Fuqua, J., Phillips, K.: In vivo studies of transdisciplinary scientific collaboration: lessons learned and implications for active living research. Am. J. Prev. Med. **28**(2), 202–213 (2005)
41. Ottoson, J.M., Green, L.W., Beery, W.L., Senter, S.K., Cahill, C.L., Pearson, D.C., Greenwald, H.P., Hamre, R., Leviton, L.: Policy-contribution assessment and field-building analysis of the Robert Wood Johnson Foundation's active living research program. Am. J. Prev. Med. **36**(2), S34–S43 (2009)
42. Gutman, M.A., Barker, D.C., Samples-Smart, F., Morley, C.: Evaluation of active living research: progress and lessons in building a new field. Am. J. Prev. Med. **36**(2), S22–S33 (2009)
43. Pelletier, D.: Food and nutrition policy: a biological anthropologist's experiences from an academic platform. Am. J. Hum. Biol. **27**(1), 16–26 (2015)
44. Mâsse, L.C., Moser, R.P., Stokols, D., Taylor, B.K., Marcus, S.E., Morgan, G.D., Hall, K.L., Croyle, R.T., Trochim, W.M.: Measuring collaboration and transdisciplinary integration in team science. Am. J. Prev. Med. **35**(2), S151–S160 (2008)
45. Canadian Institutes of Health Research: Stages of the Innovation Pipeline (2014). http://www.cihr-irsc.gc.ca/e/48839.html. Accessed 8 Feb 2017
46. Snow, M.E., Salmon, A., Young, R.: Teaching transdisciplinarity in a discipline-centred world. Collected Essays Learn. Teach. **3**, 59–65 (2010)
47. Kneipp, S.M., Gilleskie, D., Sheely, A., Schwartz, T., Gilmore, R.M., Atkinson, D.: Nurse scientists overcoming challenges to lead transdisciplinary research teams. Nurs. Outlook **62**(5), 352–361 (2014)
48. Muller, M.J.: Participatory design: the third space in HCI. Hum.-Comput. Interact. Dev. Process **4235**, 165–185 (2003)
49. Munteanu, C.: Ethical dilemmas during field studies of emerging and disruptive technologies – is our current state of knowledge adequate? SSHRC Knowledge Synthesis Report (2016)
50. Katz, J.S., Martin, B.R.: What is research collaboration? Res. Policy **26**(1), 1–8 (1997)
51. Minkler, M.: Ethical challenges for the "outside" researcher in community-based participatory research. Health Educ. Behav. **31**(6), 684–97 (2004)

Addressing Issues of Need, Adaptability, User Acceptability and Ethics in the Participatory Design of New Technology Enabling Wellness, Independence and Dignity for Seniors Living in Residential Homes

Joan Cahill[1(✉)], Sean McLoughlin[2], Michael O'Connor[2],
Melissa Stolberg[2], and Sean Wetherall[2]

[1] School of Psychology, Centre for Innovative Human Systems (CIHS),
Trinity College Dublin, College Green, Dublin 2, Ireland
cahilljo@tcd.ie
[2] Oneview Healthcare, Blackrock Business Park Co., Dublin, Ireland

Abstract. This paper reports on human factors research concerning the advancement of new technology facilitating seniors leading fulfilling, meaningful and independent lives, with dignity in the community. Specifically, this paper provides a roadmap for the specification of new technology for use in residential homes - which seeks to establish the appropriate balance between enabling the independence and well-being of residents (including supporting their privacy) and protecting residents from potential hazards. This research adopts a stakeholder evaluation/participatory approach to requirements elicitation and user interface design. The technology is defined from the perspective of addressing specific end user and stakeholder needs, and achieving relevant states/benefits associated with well-being, successful ageing, and relationship centred care. This research is being undertaken as an industry/academia collaboration involving Trinity College Dublin (TCD) Ireland and Oneview Healthcare.

Keywords: Assisted living · Ageing and technology acceptance · Health care technologies and services for the elderly · Relationship centered care · Social connection · Stakeholder evaluation · Well-being · User acceptability · Ethics · Privacy

1 Introduction

1.1 Ageing and Models of Successful Ageing

Ageing is a normal part of life. Although certain diseases occur in old age, old age itself is not a disease. As we age, we face many changes and losses. This includes changes in physical health and cognitive ability, changes in way of life (and living environment), and loss of friends and family. Ageing and old age is also associated with maturity, wisdom and acceptance of life challenges. In addition, with increased time availability,

J. Zhou and G. Salvendy (Eds.): ITAP 2017, Part I, LNCS 10297, pp. 90–109, 2017.
DOI: 10.1007/978-3-319-58530-7_7

there is the potential for personal growth, strengthening social relationships and engaging in purposeful activity.

Biomedical models focus on the absence of chronic disease, independent physical functioning, performance, mobility, and cognitive functioning [1]. Rowe and Kahn distinguish between usual ageing/normal decline and successful ageing [2]. According to Rowe and Kahn, successful aging is multidimensional, encompassing the avoidance of disease and disability, the maintenance of high physical and cognitive function, and sustained engagement in social and productive activities [2]. Psychosocial models focus on life satisfaction, social participation, functioning, and psychological resources [3, 4]. Psychological resources include a positive outlook and self-worth, self-efficacy or sense of control over life, autonomy and independence, and effective coping and adaptive strategies in the face of changing circumstances [5]. Such psychological resources are important to maintaining positive mental health as we age. Seniors are at risk for developing anxiety and depression, given increased frailty, medical illnesses and medication and the potential for loss, reduced social connection and trauma (arising from injuries/accidents such as falls).

1.2 Underpinning Concepts

Discussions of ageing make reference to several theoretical concepts including well-being, autonomy, independence, quality of life, social connection and community. According to biopsychosocial models of health and well-being, medical and psychological factors, family and social factors are some of the different determinants impacting on a person's health and well-being [6, 7]. This is supported by trends in the prescription of (1) physical activity, (2) social activity, (3) the practice of hobbies and artistic/cultural activity and (4) specific relaxation techniques (i.e. yoga and meditation), by physicians and other health practioners.

In relation to senior living, the concept of autonomy refers to exercising individual choice, freedom of will, and assuming responsible for one's own behavior and/or self [8]. As human relationships are based on mutual dependence and partnership [9], autonomy cannot be viewed as separate from the relationships within which individuals are embedded [10]. Accordingly, the concept of relational autonomy has been posited [11].

Independence is often discussed in the context of a senior's ability to complete specific activities of daily living (ADL). Basic ADLs consist of self-care tasks that include, but not limited to functional mobility, bathing and showering, dressing, self-feeding, personal hygiene and grooming and toilet hygiene. Instrumental activities of daily living (IADLs) are not necessary for fundamental functioning, but they let an individual live independently in a community. This includes housework, preparing meals, taking medications as prescribed, managing money, shopping for groceries or clothing, use of telephone or other form of communication and transportation within the community. Quality of life is a more nebulous concept, referring to the standard of health, comfort, and happiness experienced by an individual or group. Several studies substantiate the link between self-determination/autonomy and quality of life for seniors [12, 13].

A community is a most commonly referred to as a social unit or population living and/or interacting with one another in a specific environment. An individual's social relations/ties within a community are often characterized as either personal or professional. Theories of social capitol [14–16], emphasize the enabling role of relevant actors within ones community, in terms of supporting both healthy behavior and behavior change.

1.3   Care Models

In care contexts, patients want a personal relationship, quality communication and empathy from medical/care professionals. To this end, patient-centered care replaces our current physician centered system with one that revolves around the patient [17]. Some argue that the concept of patient-centered care must be supplemented with the concept of person-focused care [18]. Patient-centered care focuses on visits involving care of generally chronic diseases [18]. In contrast, person-focused care 'extends beyond communication because much of it relies on knowledge of the patient (and of the patient population) that accrues over time and is not specific to disease-oriented episodes' [18]. More recently, there has been a move towards relationship centered care [19–21]. Advocates of relationship centered care emphasize the importance of personhood and relationships. As human beings are active relational beings, nurturing positive relationships is essential to well-being, and has a bearing on health care experiences and outcomes [22].

1.4   Care Models and Contexts/Settings

According to research by the American Association of Retired Persons, nearly 90 percent of seniors want to stay in their own homes as they age [23]. 'Ageing in place' is associated with many positives, including the comfort of being in ones' own environment (with associated implications of user control and privacy), and enabling continuity/access in terms of social arrangements. However, the home is not always the ideal environment for fostering independence and quality of life. Studies also highlight the potential for social isolation [24] and disempowerment [25]. This is often the case, if the home is the location for medical treatment and service intervention [26]. Many seniors attend day service which usually involves commuting to a nearby health-care service facility (i.e. ambulatory care model). Such facilities offer a broad range of services outside the acute hospital system, including Primary Care, Social Care, Mental Health and Health & Wellbeing Services. Continuing care retirement communities and/or assistive living refers to a system that provides a place to live and medical care for people (such as elderly or disabled people) who need help with daily activities.

1.5   Residential Care and Nursing Role

Residential care/nursing homes provide twenty four hour care to seniors. The decision to transition into a residential care facility is frequently related to changes in health and/or personal circumstances (i.e. loss of spouse/partnèr or caregiver). Residential/care homes have been associated with certain negatives. For example, hospital-like rooms, regimented routines (i.e. lack of control in relation to when eat, wash, sleep and wake), lack of freedom, reduced social connection [27], boredom and issues adapting to privacy [28]. Others highlight a lack of purposeful activity (i.e. passive group entertainment), and a tendency to treat residents like preschool children, where life designed to be safe and supervised, but devoid of meaning [29]. A recent qualitative review of quality of life (QoL) in care homes identified four key themes affecting good QoL (1) acceptance and adaption to their living situation, (2) connectedness with others, (3) a homelike environment, and (4) caring practices [30]. As highlighted by Gawande [29], residential care facilities have historically addressed societal goals (for example, freeing up hospital beds, taking burdens off families, coping with poverty amongst elderly), as opposed to addressing the goals of those domicile in them.

While many nurses and care assistants report the value and dignity associated with their work, senior care is not without its own challenges. Physical and emotional fatigue, stress, burnout and compassion fatigue is a common experience for geriatric nurses and care assistants. In this regard, nursing goals of avoiding bedsores, maintaining weight and protecting a patient's safety, can be at odds with an individual's desire for personal freedom, strengthening social bonds and engaging in meaningful activity. To this end, charters of rights for seniors living in care homes have been advanced both generally [31] and in the memory care context [32].

More recently, there has been a 'culture change' in residential care. There is now more attention to relationships, resident preferences and promoting intergenerational contact/communications. The 'inside out' approach advocates the integration of the community with senior residents so as to support the socialization needs of all, while providing opportunities for more partnerships. As evidenced in the Eden project, the use of pets, plant- life and buddying systems (i.e. community volunteers) encourages meaningful activity and social relationships [33]. This in turn bolsters wellbeing and has an impact on health outcomes. Equally, evaluations of Green House programs (i.e. care facilities staffed by 24-hour caregivers with 8–10 bedrooms and common living rooms and dining rooms) indicate enhanced quality of life for residents [34].

1.6   New Assisted Living Technologies

New technologies are being advanced to support the needs of seniors living both independently and in assisted living contexts. In parallel, technologies are being advanced for other stakeholders – in particular, carer's, family/informal carers' and healthcare providers (i.e. GP, hospital, specialists and community nurses). Such technologies provide diverse functions including: self-management of health, care coordination, health information/care plan access, entertainment, communications, education, telecare, ADL monitoring, medication adherence, emergency alerting, exercise and diet management, fall prediction, wander management, security management, mood and well-being, life logging, wayfinding and digital signage, brain training, resident administration and room administration. Generally, this involves the use of a range of connected devices (i.e. TV, tablets, smart phones, wearables, environmental sensors).

In relation to the nursing role, new tools are being introduced to enhance the assessment of patient acuity (and associated management of nursing assignment/staffing), to support nurse rounding and allied care tasks, and to manage and report on work related stress [35].

In general, the new technologies outlined above follow from (1) certain broad spectrum technology trends (i.e. the Internet of things, sensors in everything, big data, interoperability of new technology), and (2) specific health care trends (i.e. connected health, electronic healthcare pathways, technology-enabled caregivers and ambient assisted living). In most cases, these technologies are underpinned by concepts of ageing in place, autonomy, personalized care, social capitol, community, social connection and quality of life. However, the specific technologies are not articulated in relation to specific health and well-being models (i.e. biopsychosocial), and models of successful ageing (i.e. biomedical, psychosocial or some combination of these).

1.7   New Assisted Living Technologies: User Acceptability

It is argued that the purpose and functionalities of gerontechnologies are often led by the requirements of their social and caregiving environments [36]. Often, their functionalities do not match their intrinsic motivations and expected benefits. This has an impact on user acceptance [36]. Acceptance is critical if technologies are to be embedded in a person's life [37]. Chen and Chan found that technology acceptance and usage behavior in elderly people are predicted by certain (1) user characteristics (i.e. age, education, gerontechnology related self-efficacy and anxiety, and health deficiencies), and (2) environmental factors (i.e. accessibility, assistance and guidance) [37], rather than attitudinal factors, as proposed in the technology acceptance model [38]. Research, by Lee, Lee and Hwang [39] illuminates the connection between self-determination and user acceptance. When technology supports self-determination, it positively impacts acceptance. That is, seniors are 'intrinsically motivated' by technology that promotes autonomy.

1.8   New Assisted Living Technologies: Ethics

Human beings value their privacy and the protection of their personal life [40]. The privacy debate has advanced with the development of information technology. Indeed, technological changes are influencing privacy norms [41]. Many of the available technologies pose fundamental questions in relation to ethics and user acceptability. In advancing new AL technology, the following questions might be asked:

1. For whom is this technology for?
2. How should this technology be designed to deliver the appropriate benefits to seniors and other relevant stakeholders?
3. Whose rights need to be considered and who has priority?
4. How to the rights and need of seniors and other stakeholders interrelate?

2   Methods and Research Status

2.1   Research Design

This is an action research study combining several qualitative research methods including ethnography (interviews and observations) and participatory design [42]. Overall, the human factors design approach is premised on the assumption that solutions for seniors and other actors are necessarily interrelated. As such, a stakeholder evaluation based approach is adopted [43]. Human factors research involves active and ongoing participation of end users (i.e. seniors) and other key stakeholders. As detailed in Table 1, system development follows several iterative activities pertaining to (1) needs analysis, benefits analysis, processing mapping and requirements elicitation, (2) user interface design prototyping and (3) evaluation.

Table 1. Research phases and activities

#	Research phases/activities	Stakeholder involvement
1	Literature analysis (theory, research projects, competitors/industry)	Internal stakeholders
2	Preliminary definition of philosophy/approach, concept, high level requirements and associated personae specification	Internal stakeholders
3	Requirements elicitation (interviews and observations with end users and stakeholders) and process mapping	External Stakeholders
4	Elaboration of concept and philosophy and specification of detailed requirements and personae	Internal stakeholders
5	User interface design prototyping	Internal stakeholders
6	Co-design and evaluation	Internal & External Stakeholders
7	Final specification and design	Internal & External Stakeholders

Certain research phases are sequential (phases 1 and 2), while others are running in parallel (to an extent) and iterative (phases 3, 4, 5 and 6).

In relation to needs and benefits analysis, interviews and observations are being undertaken with end users and other stakeholders. The methodological approach is underpinned by phenomenological approaches to eliciting information about 'lived experience' [44], and specifically, interpretative Phenomenological Analysis [45]. The emphasis is on understanding the context and meaning of experience, and in particular, the interactions between seniors and relevant stakeholders in their personal and professional community (i.e. family members, carer's, friends, GP etc.).

In relation to participatory design activities, the methodology draws upon person centered design approaches – specifically, 'personae based design' [46], and 'Scenario Based Design' [47]. Personae's have been advanced for seniors in different contexts. This ensures that the proposed technology will take into account (1) the experiences and needs of end users in different settings and situations (i.e. lifespan perspective – home,

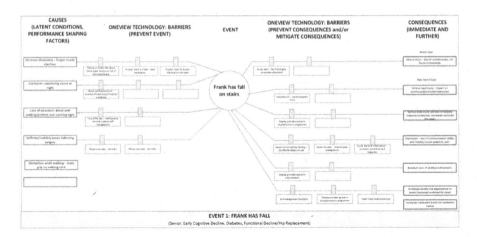

Fig. 1. Bow tie (Frank has fall).

assisted living community), and (2) the specific needs of end users and other stakeholders in the residential care context.

Further, as depicted in Fig. 1, bowties are used to elicit and validate technology requirements in relation to addressing latent conditions and states/benefits to be achieved. Specifically, the bowties enable joint/collective problem solving with respect to user need/requirements and user interface design solutions. Co-design activities focus on how the proposed technology installs barriers to (1) prevent the event from occurring and, (2) to recover the situation, if the hazard is encountered (thereby reducing/mitigating the consequences of the hazardous event).

There are two strands of evaluation, (a) ongoing participatory design/evaluation with stakeholders, and (b) discrete evaluation using an aged care Living Lab. The qualitative data analysis software NVivo is being used to support the thematic analysis of data relating to lived experience and need. Following, the analysis of all data, co-design activities will be undertaken with the participant panel (internal and external stakeholders).

2.2 Community of Practice and Participant Profiles

In support of stakeholder design/evaluation activities, a 'Community of Practice' (COP) [48] has been formed comprising both internal and external stakeholders. As detailed in Table 1 above, both internal and external stakeholders participate in different research activities. Internal stakeholders (N = 10) include members of the assisted living project/research team (i.e. human factors researchers, user experience designers, developers, product owners, clinicians, nurses and experts in health informatics). External stakeholder comprises two participant groups (1) end users and (2) other stakeholders (N = 30 to 40 participants). (1) End users are split into four sub-groups – comprising seniors living independently and living in residential homes, potentially living with one or more morbidities, with different levels of functional and cognitive ability and an age range of 60 to 90 years. (2) Other stakeholders include three sub-groups, (a) family members, (b) formal aged care staff – (i.e. aged care nurses, care assistants and community nurses) and (c) other stakeholders (i.e. GPs, geriatricians, experts in ageing, volunteers in active ageing groups and volunteers/staff of relevant groups/societies). In terms of the research design, the participants are being considered as independent of each other. End users and other stakeholders are participating in research phases 3, 6 and 7.

2.3   Research Status

Research phases 1 and 2 are complete and phases 3, 4 and 5 are currently underway (these are running in parallel and iterative). Interviews and observations have provided feedback about lived experience, stakeholder need, expected benefits and underlying process facilitators and blockers. Personae's have been defined for different end users and stakeholders, in specific contexts including residential care, home-care, assisted living and palliative care. High level requirements have also been defined (see Appendix 3). Preliminary prototypes for (1) seniors and (2) nurses have been defined. These will be further elaborated in co-design activities (see Appendices 5 and 6). It is anticipated that co design activities with end users and other stakeholders (phase 6 research) will enable problem solving around need and issues pertaining to acceptability/ethics.

3   Results

3.1   Lived Experience of Seniors

The lived experience of seniors (and associated perceived quality of life and autonomy) varies according to a senior's overall life course, individual characteristics, activity levels (i.e. level of self-care and requirement for assistance) and levels of social interaction. In relation to levels of physical and social activity, this usually depends on the older person's general health (i.e. if managing one or more morbidities), physical/functional ability and cognitive ability (i.e. level of cognitive decline). The availability of family and friends in relation to transportation support has an impact on attendance at 'outside' social events.

Adaptation is a feature of the ageing experience (i.e. concentrating on strengths rather than weaknesses). Seniors use many strategies to cope with loss of function/independence and change. This includes the use of external aids (i.e. walking frames), getting help from others, engagement in purposeful activities (i.e. bridge, gardening, volunteering, bowling and dancing) and social participation (i.e. attendance at community and family events). Overall, there is an interest in active and healthy ageing.

In different contexts (home and residential care), loneliness and boredom is a common experience. Spending time and interacting/communicating with family members and friends is highly valued. Such social engagement supports a sense of 'belonging', 'having a role' and 'feeling needed'.

The transition to residential care is often precipitated by health changes (i.e. worsening illness) and different care constraints (i.e. key family member's not living close-by, difficulties of providing suitable 24 h care in the home and so forth). This decision is usually made with family members. There is often significant apprehension in relation to transitioning to residential care. This includes fear in relation to loss of control over daily activities, loss of privacy and loss of identity.

3.2   Community Concept

Well-being is strongly influenced by the quality of a senior's relationships with members of their personal and professional community. Specifically, different members of a person's community can be associated with different spheres of well-being – albeit these are all related. A senior's personal community includes family members, friends, neighbors and members of active retirement groups. The professional community includes care assistants, nurses, Dr's, specialists, hairdressers and the postman.

3.3   Stakeholder Need, Benefits and States

Seniors. Seniors represent a diverse group with different physical and cognitive abilities and needs. Successful ageing is multidimensional and includes psycho social elements. In this regard, research outlines several states (1) to be promoted, (2) to be managed and/or mitigated and (3), to be avoided. For more, please see Appendix 2. Seniors want more than just safety and care support (i.e. ADL's, management of disease). In general, seniors want to avoid 'being a burden' for friends and family. Seniors want care with dignity and choice. They want the option to live as independently as possible - while availing of community/ambulatory services when required. Overall, there is a strong need for self-fulfillment, being mentally aware and strengthening relationships with friends and family. In both home and residential settings, seniors miss friendship, having a purpose to their day and being needed. There is an interest in fostering independent and purposeful activities (i.e. not just formal events in the residential home), and to promote organically occurring activities between residents. The risk of personal injury (and specifically injuries from falls) is a big concern for seniors both in home and residential contexts. In general, seniors are keen to improve their own health literacy and to adopt self-management approaches. This provides a degree of self-fulfillment and autonomy.

Carer's and Family. For carer's and family members, systems should support relevant care and activity/safety monitoring tasks, along with enabling empathy and social connection. Technology might support resident transition to the new care situation. For example, it might be used to familiarize the resident with the new environment, care routines, how technology is used, and how privacy is addressed (thereby managing fear and supporting their ability to deal with change). Further, preferences, interests and their personal story might be elicited at the beginning, and recorded in an electronic resident record. Providing care staff with information about 'who they are' and 'what matters to them' might enhance care activity and ensure that structured leisure activities are both meaningful and purposeful. From a nursing perspective, future systems might address issues around assessing patient acuity and enabling efficient and real-time access to resident information. Electronic rounding systems might capture well-being information (i.e. level of physical activity, pain, sleep, diet and social activity). It is anticipated that this will support quality care delivery, particularly in high workload periods. Further, it will address fatigue and stress management (thereby mitigating/reducing burn-out). In addition, such systems might enable nurse interaction with family members and other clinicians and specialists (both on and off site).

GP and Specialists. Integration of health documentation is a key need for both primary and secondary care providers.

3.4 Ethics, Privacy and User Acceptance

Future systems should not be used to replace person centred care and/or to reduce the time that nursing and care staff spend with residents. Such systems should respect a senior's privacy and choice. Residents should have control over the personal sphere - including any information captured about the biopsychosocial dimensions of their health and well-being. Residents should have the option to opt in and out of sensors. Appendix 4 includes a list of issues/considerations in relation to ethics and user acceptability.

3.5 Initial Concept, Preliminary Requirements and User Interface Design

Overall, the concept is to develop a range of self-decided services (opt in/out), based on what matters to older people, and to allow for personalization. The proposed functionality is (1) conceptualized in relation to stakeholder relationships. According, there a suite of inter-related technologies are being advanced for seniors and other stakeholders (i.e. nurses, family members, GP etc.). The proposed technology (2) addresses all three pillars of well-being and the interrelationship therein. Specific functions promote wellness and map to the underpinning biopsychosocial model of health and well-being. Further, (3) the functionality takes into account models of successful ageing - supporting social participation, addressing stress, mood and engagement, providing entertainment functions and promoting self-management and purposeful ageing. For more, see Appendix 3. Moreover, (4) the availability and level of personalization reflects an 'ability' philosophy.

The design solution is adaptive in terms of age-related changes and characteristics (see Appendices 5 and 6). The design concept avoids known problems with current WIMP (windows, icons, menus, point-and-click devices). Interactions are natural using touch (and potentially speech and gesture). At present, outputs are primarily text/image based. Research is currently addressing multimodal aspects – voice synthesis and haptics. It is intended that design interactions will be natural and engaging. It is not likely that mid to late stage memory care patients, will have significant interaction with Tablet/TV systems. Here the focus will be on delivering smart and emphatic solutions for carer's and family. Critically, solutions for these actors will yield benefits for memory care patients.

4 Discussion

4.1 Role of Technology

In a residential context, technology has a role beyond that of (1) managing and reporting on a resident's physical health and security (and associated clinical and care tasks), and (2) supporting operational and organisational goals (for example, staffing, risk management and compliance). Technology has a role in terms of supporting the well-being of both patients and staff alike, enabling life/job satisfaction and social participation, and fostering an environment that provides a sense of purpose for all (i.e. residents, staff and families).

Importantly, future technology has the potential to address (and possibly ameliorate) many of the issues identified in relation to quality of life, user control and privacy in care homes. As mentioned previously, technology can be used to familiarize the resident with the new environment, care routines, technology usage and procedures in relation to privacy – thereby supporting a senior's ability to deal with change. Technology can improve care practices and quality of care by enabling holistic approach to care delivery and reporting (i.e. biopsychosocial). Intelligent and unobtrusive sensors can be embedded in the environment. Lighting and door locking can reflect user need and patterns (linked to data analytics). In principle, the provision of choice in relation to meal selection, supporting self-decided activities, enabling organically developed social relationships goes a significant way towards fostering independence. However, we cannot simply pay lip service to the idea of autonomy. This needs to extend into data protection practices and staff/care procedures too.

4.2 Technology Enabling Relationship Centered Care

Relationship centered care provides the framework for thinking about need, and the context for thinking about concepts such as independence, quality of life and community. As stated earlier, independence (and quality of life for seniors) is linked to interdependence (i.e. support from other actors in a senior's personal and professional community). The different care models outlined previously focus on personhood and nurturing social/care relationships. By implication, future technology needs to consider both (1) the person and (2) enabling positive relationships and communications between seniors and relevant actors in their personal and professional community. Specifically, the achievement of benefits in relation to resident experience, autonomy and well-being, is dependent on situating technology development in the context of enabling these relations. There are issues/barriers on both sides and these must be addressed in a 'joined up' way. This is not necessarily straightforward. Critically, it requires a commitment to a 'relationship centred' approach, underpinned by ethical principles centred on respect for seniors and their circle of care. Overall, the approach is to develop technology from the perspective of understanding the relationship/interdependencies between different stakeholders. These interdependencies are modelled in terms of workflow and user interface design, so that the states/lived experience outlined in Appendix 2 are realized. Further, this stakeholder approach has implications in terms of the overall technology offering. Future assisted living technology cannot be advanced for seniors alone. Corresponding applications are required for other relevant stakeholders with whom seniors communicate/have interactions with. It is this communication/interaction that has an impact on well-being and health. This is the key to promoting the positive states as outlined in Appendix 2.

4.3   Focus on Personhood

Technology has the potential to (1) support personhood, and (2) enable both person-centered and relationship centered care by (a) eliciting the right information at the right time about relevant actors (i.e. resident's, carer's and their families), and (b) sharing this information at the right time with relevant actors. Critically, this frees up time for value based care practices and meaningful social interactions. The advancement of person centred resident records which address the three pillars of well-being (i.e. biological, psychological and social) and includes detailed information about life history and what matters to the resident is critical. This should be supplemented by real-time information about the resident, so a dynamic and evidence based profile is captured. This 'live' record can form the basis for all social and clinical interactions with the resident (and their families) and associated decisions. For example, if the resident completes a wellness report, this information should be made available to the nurse so that he/she is armed with the right information, to enable meaningful care/social interactions. Further, self-report data can be coupled with observational data and data arising from any clinical assessments. Over time, a rich picture of the resident and their wellness can be advanced – facilitating person centered and relationship centered care. Equally, the provision of real-time access to health, well-being and medication information captured by different actors (i.e. GP's, specialists, pharmacists, occupational therapists, dieticians, psychologists, psychiatrists, well-being coaches etc.) enables person centred care.

Evidently, if seniors are to use this technology, then the benefits need to map to what matters to them (i.e. appeal to intrinsic motivation). It is anticipated that the direct experience of benefits in relation to quality of life, social connection and improved care practices will be a motivating influence for seniors. As is evidenced in the Eden project and others, such benefits have knock on impact in relation to resident medication requirements, mortality rates, along with staff workload and retention.

4.4   Ethics and User Acceptability

Technology should not be used to minimize or replace person centered care. Further, it should reflect a careful balance between optimizing the ability/strengths of the person, while taking into account the needs (and workload) of carer's. This technology will be implemented in different care contexts with different business models (i.e. for profit/not for profit, government funding). The motivation for introducing such technologies may vary and there is the potential that organizational needs (i.e. staff costs, keeping residents safe) may conflict with end user needs (i.e. independence, privacy and social interaction). It is important that residents have the option to opt in/out of the use of sensors. The role and use of data analytics in terms of (1) tracking and responding to an individual resident's clinical needs and (2) addressing issues relating to managing risk/safety, needs to be carefully considered. Where possible, resident consents should be established in relation to who has permission to access resident data and how this data is used. In certain cases, different interests may need to be balanced (i.e. memory care).

4.5   Technology is One Part of the Solution

The objective is to advance technology which supports well-being, successful ageing, and relationship centred care (and associated positive behaviors for relevant end users and stakeholders). It is important to be mindful of the complexities and challenges of ageing, and the opportunities to advance technology which manages and mitigates potential challenging states and behaviors. Technology is only one part of the solution, and does not replace person centered interaction/care. Further, the implementation of new assisted living technology needs to take into account other socio-technical dimensions (i.e. people, process, environment, culture and training). Relationship/patient centered care necessitates happy well trained staff, working with the right level of resources (i.e. staffing, equipment) and supported by person friendly processes that foster communication, trust and open disclosure.

5   Conclusions

There are need/benefits on different sides (i.e. residents, families, Dr's, nurses and care assistants). Evidently, supporting resident autonomy, independence and quality of life is important. However, such autonomy cannot be conceptualized outside an understanding of the relationships seniors have in their personal and professional community. Independence (and quality of life for seniors) is linked to interdependence (i.e. support from other actors in a senior's personal and professional community). Accordingly, the approach is to develop technology from the perspective of understanding, modelling and transforming the social, information and process relationships between seniors and associated stakeholders in the community.

The overall technology solution is predicated on (1) successful models of ageing, and (2) biopsychosocial models of well-being. Further, it directly addresses (3) the lived experience/states to be achieved for relevant end users and stakeholders. Further, (4) it is based on an ability philosophy. Overall, the outlook is positive – there is a strong potential for using assisted living technology to deliver on these states, both directly and indirectly.

Future assisted living technology should promote active ageing, engagement with life, independent living, self-management of health, well-being and mental health awareness. Such technology should be predicated on positive accounts of ageing and avoid ageism and negative stereotypes. The future is positive. New technology affords the possibility for improved social relationships, better quality of care and user control/independence, in residential care contexts. Nonetheless, such technologies require careful consideration in relation to ease of use, adapting to age/condition and issues around ethics and user acceptability. Seniors should be able to opt in and opt out of all services. Critically, the proposed technology must uphold people's dignity and supports their right to make their own choices (promoting independence and quality of life).

Appendices

Appendix 1: AL Stakeholders and Community Concept

See (Table 2).

Table 2. List of stakeholders

Stakeholder	Category	Persona
Senior (primary end user)	Active and healthy senior	Richard
	Senior with early stage functional decline	Anne
	Frail elderly/senior	Lucy
	Senior with early cognitive decline and underlying morbidity/medical condition	Frank
	Memory care patient (early stage dementia)	Tom
	Memory care patient (middle stage dementia)	Zena
	Memory care patient (late stage dementia)	Edward
Personal community	Spouse 1 (male)	Barry
	Spouse 2 (female)	Emily
	Family/daughter	Jane
	Buddy from local school community programme	Peter
	Friend	Alan
	Neighbour	Paul
	Other residents (care home/residential home)	Jenny
	Gardener/maintenance	Bob
	Club member	Susan
Professional community	Formal carer (care assistant/nurse)	Angela
	GP	Kate
	Pharmacist	Robert
	Community nurse	Sandra
	Care service/community (administration)	Louise
	Emergency room doctor	Mike

Appendix 2: Lived Experience, States and Benefits

See (Table 3)

Table 3. Lived experience, states and benefits

Promote/Support	Manage/Mitigate & reduce	Avoid
Quality of life	Loss of identity	Deception
Wellness	Loss of privacy	Infantilization
Independence	Loss of physical liberty	Isolation
Social participation	Physical discomfort	Elder abuse
Privacy and protection of	Communication difficulties	Objectification of the
personal sphere	Fear	dementia patient
Communication	Boredom	Unsafe behaviour
Safety	Sense of powerlessness	Reduction in human contact
Ability	Difficulty with new	Neglect
Identity	information	Other...
Empowering person	Difficulty with change	
Dignity/respect	Restlessness	
Purposeful activity	Feeling lost	
Active and healthy living	Overstimulated	
Sense of continuity	Stress	
Sense of belonging	Apathy/loss of interest	
Sense of purpose	Wandering	
Sense of usefulness	Frustration	
Acceptance	Confusion	
Resilience/coping	Agitation	
Self-management of health	Negative thinking	
Engagement	Depression	
Calmness	Aggression/anger	
Sense of confidence	Sleep disturbances and sun	
Awareness (including sensory	downing	
awareness)	Suspicion and delusions	
Nurturing person	Self-neglect	
Citizen participation		

Appendix 3: Proposed High Level Technology Functions/Requirements

See (Table 4)

Table 4. Technology functions

#	High level function/requirement
1	Activity monitoring
2	Wellness reporting (include mood, pain, sleep/fatigue, social activity, eating etc.)
3	Social engagement and events
4	Communications
5	Entertainment
6	Emergency Alerting
7	Education and coaching
8	Care plans, care records, care co-ordination
9	Telecare
10	Medication management
11	Reporting (care needs, problems, safety events)
12	Exercise and wellness
13	Nutrition and Meal ordering
14	Wander management
15	Wayfinding and digital signage
16	Storytelling/life logging
17	Transport co-ordination

Appendix 4: Issues Pertaining to User Acceptability and Ethics

See (Table 5)

Table 5. Issues pertaining to user acceptability and ethics

#	Issue	Examples
1	Privacy and use of technology	Use of close circuit television (CCTV) to record resident activity/behavior in own rooms, social rooms, in corridors, in gardens Use of wearable sensors to track resident movement and falls Use of bed sensors to track activity at night Use of RFID tags – tracking identity and location Use of wearables – biomarkers (track health condition and risk)

(*continued*)

Table 5. (*continued*)

#	Issue	Examples
2	Protecting dignity and autonomy	Should a senior be able to opt out of the use of ambient sensors? Of the personal information recorded about a senior, what information should be treated as sensitive? If a family is paying for a loved persons care, should the family interest in accessing their loved ones clinical/care data, supersede the senior's right to privacy?
3	Encroachment on moral autonomy	If lack of privacy can expose seniors to outside forces that influence their choices, is it fair to share personal data with these others?
4	Brain health and challenging the user/senior	Should the technology challenge the user (stretching person to contribute to brain health), or should it just give the person access to the information they want (keeps them happy but not necessarily optimizing/extending brain health)?
5	Managing risk/safety	Loss of physical liberty versus freedom of movement a. Use of automatic door locking b. Use of sensors tracking location and movement Should technology raise an alarm for staff members and others, if specific care tasks not undertaken?
6	Data protection	Data analytics and clinical decisions Resident access to own data Permissions for others to access (sharing of data with family members)
7	Lifestyle choices and responsibilities	Use of technology to manage distribution of food (prevent resident eating food that might make them sick) Use of technology to track eating habits and behavior of resident (frequency, swallow risk)
8	Resident surveys	Should a resident be required to complete surveys capturing data about what food eating, pain levels and management of pain, stress and mood?
9	Unethical/illegal behavior	Use of technology to detect and manage unethical or illegal behavior of residents or carer's or family

Appendix 5: Senior User Interface

See (Fig. 2)

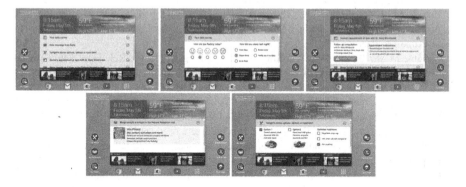

Fig. 2. Resident screens – example prototype

Appendix 6: Nurse User Interface

See (Fig. 3)

Fig. 3. Nurse rounding screens – example prototypes

References

1. Seeman, T.E., Charpentier, P.A., Berkman, L.F., Tinetti, M.E., Guralnik, J.M., Albert, M., et al.: Predicting changes in physical performance in a high-functioning elderly cohort. MacArthur studies of successful aging. J Gerontol. **49**(3), M97–108 (1994)
2. Rowe, J.W., Kahn, R.L.: Successful Aging. Pantheon Books, New York (1998)
3. Silverstein, M., Parker, M.G.: Leisure activities and quality of life among the oldest old in Sweden. Res. Aging **24**(5), 28–47 (2002)
4. Leonard, W.M.: Successful aging: an elaboration of social and psychological factors. Int. J. Aging Hum. Dev. **14**(3), 23–32 (1981)
5. Bowling, A., Iliffe, S.: Which model of successful ageing should be used? Baseline findings from a British longitudinal survey of ageing. Age Ageing **35**, 7–14 (2006)

6. Engel, G.: The need for a new medical model: a challenge for biomedical science. Science **196**, 6–9 (1977)
7. Havelka, M., Lucanin, J.D., Lucanin, D.: Biopsychosocial model – the integrated approach to health and disease. Coll. Antropol. **33**(1), 303–310 (2009)
8. Rodgers, V., Neville, S.: Personal autonomy for older people living in residential care: an overview. Nurs. Prax. NZ **23**(1), 29 (2007)
9. Barnes, M., Blom, A., Cox, K.: The social exclusion of older people: evidence from the first wave of the English Longitudinal Study of Ageing (ELSA) final report. Office for the Deputy of Prime Minister (2006)
10. Perkins, M.M., Ball, M.M., Whittington, F.J., Hollingsworth, C.: Relational autonomy in assisted living: a focus on diverse care settings for older adults. J. Aging Stud. **26**(2), 214–225 (2012)
11. Hillcoat-Nallétamby, S.: The meaning of "independence" for older people in different residential settings. J. Gerontol. Ser. B Psychol. Sci. Soc. Sci. **69**(3), 419–430 (2014)
12. Ferrand, G., Martinent, N., Durmaz, N.: Psychological need satisfaction and well-being in adults aged 80 years and older living in residential homes: using a self-determination theory perspective. J. Aging Stud. **30**(1), 104–111 (2014)
13. O'Connor, B.P., Vallerand, R.J.: Motivation, self-determination, and person environment fit as predictors of psychological adjustment among nursing home residents. Psychol. Aging **9**(2), 189–194 (1994)
14. Bourdieu, P.: The forms of capital. In: Richardson, J.G. (ed.) Handbook of Theory and Research for the Sociology of Education. Greenwood, New York (1986). Putnam RD
15. Putnam, R.D.: Bowling Alone: the Collapse and Revival of American Community. Simon & Schuster, New York (2000)
16. Morgan, A., Swann, C. (eds.): Social Capital for Health: Issues of Definition, Measurement and Links to Health. Health Development Agency, London (2004)
17. Institute of Medicine: Crossing the Quality Chasm. Crossing the Quality Chasm: A New Health System for the 21st Century. National Academy Press, Washington, D.C (2001)
18. Starfield, B.: Is patient-centered care the same as person-focused care? Permanente J. **15**(2), 63–69 (2011)
19. Kitwood, T.: Dementia Reconsidered: The Person Comes First. Open University Press, Buckingham (1997)
20. Nolan, M.: Relationship-centred care: towards a new model of rehabilitation. Int. J. Ther. Rehabil. **9**, 472–477 (2002)
21. Soklaridis, S., Ravitz, P., Adler, G., Nevo, A., Lieff, S.: Relationship-centered care in health: a 20-year scoping review. Patient Exp. J. **3**(1), 130–145 (2016)
22. Beach, M.C., Inui, T.: Relationship-cantered care research network. Relationship-centered care: a constructive reframing. J. Gen. Int. Med. **21**(Suppl 1), 3–8 (2006)
23. American Association of Retired Persons: Aging in Place: A State Survey of Livability Policies and Practices A Research Report by the National Conference of State Legislatures and the AARP Public Policy Institute. AARP Public Policy Institute, Washington (2011)
24. Milligan, C.: There's No Place Like Home: Place and Care in an Ageing Society, 1st edn. Ashgate, Farnham (2009)
25. Rabiee, P.: Exploring the relationships between choice and independence: experiences of disabled and older people. Brit. J. Soc. Work **43**, 1–17 (2012)
26. Baldwin, N., Harris, J., Kelly, D.: Institutionalisation: why blame the institution? Ageing Soc. **13**, 69–81 (1993)
27. Kane, R.A.: Definition, measurement, and correlates of quality of life in nursing homes: toward a reasonable practice, research, and policy agenda. Gerontologist **43**(II), 28–36 (2003)

28. Forbes-Thompson, S., Gessert, C.E.: Nursing homes and suffering: part of the problem or part of the solution? J. Appl. Gerontol. **25**(3), 234–252 (2006)
29. Gawande, A.: Being Mortal: Illness, Medicine and What Matters in the End. Profile Books, London (2015)
30. Bradshaw, S.A., Playford, E.D., Riaz, A.: Living well in care homes: a systematic review of qualitative studies. Age Ageing **41**(4), 429–440 (2012)
31. European Commission: European Charter of Rights and Responsibilities of older people in need of long term care and assistance (2010)
32. Alzheimer's Society: Human rights and older people in Ireland (Policy Paper), December 2013
33. Ransom, S.: Eden alternative: the Texas project (2000). https://digital.library.txstate.edu/handle/10877/4087. Accessed 20 Jan 2016
34. Kane, R.A., Lum, T.Y., Cutler, L.J., Degenholtz, H.B., Yu, T.C.: Resident outcomes in small-house nursing homes: a longitudinal evaluation of the initial green house program. J. Am. Geriatr. Soc. **55**, 832–839 (2007)
35. Frost and Sullivan: Acuity-based staffing as the key to hospital competitiveness: why the smartest hospitals are tying their nurse labor investment to patient care. Frost & Suillivan White Paper (2015). http://www.quadramed.com. Accessed 20 Jan 2016
36. Dupuy, L., Consel, C., Sauzéon, H.: Self determination based design to achieve acceptance of assisted living technologies for older adults. Comput. Hum. Behav. **65**, 508–521 (2016)
37. Chen, K., Chan, A.H.S.: A review of technology acceptance by older adults. Gerontechnology **10**(1), 1–12 (2011)
38. Davis, F.D.: Perceived usefulness, perceived ease of use, and user acceptance of information technology. MIS Q. **13**(3), 319–339 (1989)
39. Lee, Y., Lee, J., Hwang, Y.: Relating motivation to information and communication technology acceptance: self-determination theory perspective. Comput. Hum. Behav. **51**, 418–428 (2015)
40. van den Hoven, J., Blaauw, M., Pieters, W., Warnier, M.: Privacy and information technology. In: Zalta, E.N. (ed.) The Stanford Encyclopedia of Philosophy, Spring edn. (2016). http://plato.stanford.edu/archives/spr2016/entries/it-privacy. Accessed 20 Jan 2017
41. Boenink, M., Swierstra, T., Stemerding, D.: Anticipating the interaction between technology and morality: a scenario study of experimenting with humans in bionanotechnology. Stud. Ethics Law Technol. **4**(2), 1–38 (2010)
42. Bødker, S., Burr, J.: The design collaboratorium. A place for usability design. ACM Trans. Comput. Hum. Inter. **9**(2), 152–169 (2002)
43. Cousins, J.B., Whitmore, E., Shulha, L.: Arguments for a common set of principles for collaborative inquiry in evaluation. Am. J. Eval. **34**(1), 7–22 (2013)
44. Lindseth, A., Norberg, A.: A phenomenological hermeneutical method for researching lived experience. Scand. J. Caring Sci. **18**(2), 145–153 (2004)
45. Smith, J.A., Osborn, M.: Interpretative phenomenological analysis. In: Smith, J.A. (ed.) Qualitative Psychology: A Practical Guide to Methods, 2nd edn. Sage, London (2008)
46. Pruitt, J., Grudin, J.: Personas: practice and theory. In: Proceedings of the 2003 Conference on Designing for User Experiences (2003)
47. Carroll, J.M.: Scenario-based design: envisioning work and technology in system development. Wiley, New York (1995)
48. Wenger, E.: Communities of Practice: Learning, Meaning, and Identity. Cambridge University Press, Cambridge (1998)

Towards Accessible Automatically Generated Interfaces Part 2: Study with Model-Based Self-voicing Interfaces

J. Bern Jordan[✉] and Gregg C. Vanderheiden

University of Maryland, College Park, Md., USA
{jbjordan,greggvan}@umd.edu

Abstract. The automatic generation of personalized user interfaces is a potential strategy to enable people with disabilities to enjoy wider access to devices and systems. The Functionality Input Needs and User Sensible Input (FIN-USI) model was created to make it easier to both model the devices and functionality to be controlled and for the automatic generation of personalized, accessible user interfaces. In order to study the feasibility of the model, two basic interface generators were created that used the FIN-USI model and users' interactor preferences to generate self-voicing, mobile-device interfaces intended for people who are blind. The efficacy of the FIN-USI model and generators was then tested using 12 blind and 12 inexperienced, blindfolded participants. In the user study, participants' performance, preference, and satisfaction were measured and compared on four interfaces: two interfaces that were manufacturer created and two that were automatically generated from each user's preferences. All usability measures in the study were better significantly for the automatically-generated interfaces compared to the manufacturer-created ones, including a manufacturer-created interface specifically designed for people who are blind.

Keywords: Automatic UI generation · Personalization · User interface model · Screen reader · Self-voicing interfaces

1 Introduction

People with disabilities often have difficulty using mainstream user interfaces (UIs) because of a poor fit with their individual needs and constraints. The automatic generation of user interfaces is a potential solution to this problem [1]. With auto-generated interfaces, alternative user interfaces can be generated in a one-size-fits-one manner to fit individual needs and preferences that cannot be easily met through other strategies. The auto-generation of user interfaces is based on an underlying model of the interface or functionality to be controlled.

Many interface models have been created that could be used for generating interfaces, but there has been little practical progress towards real-world applications suitable for people with disabilities. Many of the models that have been developed are too complex for their potential benefit [2, 3]. Other models, such as those used in [1, 4] are simpler, but have been focused on limited types of interaction and input. In order to be useful and usable to industry and to make it beyond research to application, a model

© Springer International Publishing AG 2017
J. Zhou and G. Salvendy (Eds.): ITAP 2017, Part I, LNCS 10297, pp. 110–128, 2017.
DOI: 10.1007/978-3-319-58530-7_8

needs to be both robust and easy-to-apply to many different products and functionality. It also should be validated for improved accessibility and shown to be useful to people with disabilities and others who need alternative user interfaces.

The FIN-USI model (detailed in Part 1, this volume) was developed to address the shortcomings of currently available models. It is intended to be simpler to apply to products and functionality than many of the current models. This would potentially make it easier for industry to adopt and build into their own products. The FIN-USI model also covers a wider range of input and interaction styles than other current models, which may allow it to be used for more devices and functionality.

Much of the user research to date has been around gathering user requirements and preferences that might be used in generating or adapting user interfaces (for example [5, 6]). However, relatively few user studies have been conducted to verify that personalized, auto-generated interfaces improve access for people with disabilities over the interfaces and accessibility strategies that are employed by industry today. User testing in the Personal Universal Controller (PUC) project showed a reduction of errors and an increase in user speed with automatically generated interfaces on touchscreen personal digital assistants (PDAs) for copiers, especially for interfaces that were generated to match an interface on which a person was previously trained [7]. The PUC graphical user interface generation system did not account for users' preferences, characteristics, or abilities. In the SUPPLE project, graphical user interfaces could be generated to fit varying screen sizes and users' pointing performance. User testing with people with physical disabilities showed that participants generally performed better with the SUPPLE system than with other graphical user interfaces [1]. However, to reduce performance variance, participants in the SUPPLE study were explicitly led through the interface and told where to point and click. Such an experimental design is helpful for teasing out differences in pointing performance, but cannot be generalized more broadly to the actual usage and usability of auto-generated systems.

This study explores the use of auto-generated interfaces for people with functional limitations. In this study, the FIN-USI model was used as the basis for the auto-generation of two self-voicing interfaces. Both self-voicing interfaces accepted gesture input on a mobile device touchscreen.

2   Experimental Design

The main purpose of the experiment was to compare auto-generated interfaces to manufacturer interfaces. Specifically, blind users' performance, preference, and satisfaction were compared for manufacturer-created interfaces, including one interface designed for blind users by the manufacturer, and automatically-generated interfaces built using participants' interactor preferences. The auto-generated interfaces in this experiment were created on the base of the FIN-USI model (described in Part 1 in this volume), which aims to be a simple model that can cover a broad range of applications and functionality. With the FIN-USI model, each input element of an interface can be modeled as type of input (data type) and characteristics (input cardinality, time dependence, and validity characteristics) that are applied to that input. In the model, inputs may be further grouped in logical or functional groupings. From the model of each target device, the interface generators created self-voicing, mobile device-based interfaces suitable for people who were blind or who had very low vision.

The research questions this study was designed to answer are:

Primary research question: Is there evidence of improved usability (performance, preference, and satisfaction) over manufacturer-created interfaces of either or both FIN-USI auto-generated interfaces that use each person's preferred interactors?

Secondary research questions: Are any usability differences moderated by the user group (which have different levels of self-voicing interface experience) or the target device? Even if usability is moderated by interacting factors, do the main effects of interface still stand?

While the study was not designed to specifically answer a further research question, we were also interested to see if there was any evidence that a novel loop-navigation interface (one of the auto-generated interfaces) showed improved usability over a more typical (but also auto-generated) interface layout.

To answer the research questions, the experiment was conducted as a 4-Interface × 2-Device × 5-Task(Device) within-subjects design with 2 groups of participants (between subjects).

2.1   Participants

Both participants with sight and participants who were blind were invited to be a part of the study of the screen reader and self-voicing interfaces. Blind participants who regularly use screen readers on computers or mobile devices are the primary target of such interface generators and thus were included in the study. While it is recognized that it is best to study representative users in controlled experiments [8], we were also interested in exploring a greater diversity of experience levels. Screen reader users tend to be technically savvy because current screen readers are complex—effectively using a screen reader requires one to memorize many keyboard shortcuts or gestures and switch between modes of operation. Could automatically-generated, preference-built interfaces be useful to people who had no prior experience with screen readers or other strategies that technically-savvy blind people might use? To have a greater diversity of technology experience, sighted participants were invited to participate in the study while wearing blindfolds. The recruitment target was for 12 people who were blind and 12 people who were sighted. Participants were paid for travel expenses and at a rate of $15 per hour for their participation.

Blind participants were recruited by making an announcement at a state blind convention, sending study advertisements to various local and statewide email lists that were of interest to people who are blind, and by having an e-mail message sent by a local vocational rehabilitation counselor to clients. Sighted participants were recruited through posters that were placed in stores and libraries in the local community. All participants completed a short set of screening questions over the phone. Participants were screened out of the study if they reported significant physical difficulty that would hinder their ability to use a smartphone or if sighted participants felt that they could not wear a blindfold for at least 20 min at a time.

In total 12 people who were blind and 15 people who were sighted were initially recruited into the study. Three sighted individuals were dropped from the main study. The first two sighted individuals were dropped as run-in participants as the researchers identified issues with the experimental methods. One sighted participant was also screened out of this study because of observed difficulty in making the required interface gestures and completing the tasks during Phase 1, which took him 75 min (42%) longer than the next longest Phase 1 session with increased errors. This participant was invited back later to be part of a case study which had additional interfaces available for testing, including manufacturer-created and auto-generated interfaces that did not require gestures on a touchscreen. From the case study with this participant, no evidence was found that would contradict the findings of this study.

A total of 12 blind participants (6 female) with an average age of 37 (SD = 12.0) and 12 blindfolded participants (8 female) with an average age of 37 (SD = 15.5) completed both phases of the study. The blindfolded group had more racial diversity (11 white, non-Hispanic and 1 Hispanic blind participants compared to 8 white, 3 black, and 1 Asian blindfolded participants) and educational diversity than the blind group (all 12 blind participants had education beyond high school, whereas 3 of the 12 blindfolded participants had a high school education or less). A few sighted participants reported disabilities that might have had an effect on their performance during the sessions: two participants had ADHD, one of whom also had a diagnosed nonverbal learning disorder. It was also observed during the study that one of the blind participants had hand tremor, with the observed result that the iPod Touch would sometimes misinterpret the participant's gestures.

2.2 Instrumentation

During the experiment, participants frequently interacted with an iPod Touch (Model ME643LL/A, Apple Inc., Cupertino, Calif.) running iOS 8.2. The iPod Touch was connected to a computer and a mixer for recording and to a speaker to allow for louder and clearer audio. The iPod Touch was placed in a modified OtterBox (Fort Collins, Colo.) Defender Series case that had the screen protector removed for better responsiveness and a 1.9-mm-thick plastic piece added to block the top 4.3 mm of the screen with the iOS clock, icons, and notifications bar. For some parts of the experiment, participants used VoiceOver (a screen reader built into iOS) and for other parts of the experiment, the interface was programmed using JavaScript to provide speech output using the same voice as VoiceOver.

Participants also interacted with the physical controls of a smart thermostat (Model CT80, Radio Thermostat Company of America, San Francisco, Calif.) and a multifunction copier (Model X654de, Lexmark International, Inc., Lexington, Ky.), both of which are pictured in Fig. 1. These two devices were chosen as representative of common, every day-use devices in home and office environments that also had applications or web-interfaces that could potentially be used with a screen reader on a smartphone or other mobile device. The multifunction copier was chosen for study because its web-based interface was specifically designed for use with screen readers. Both devices in the study had their interfaces modeled using the FIN-USI model. The two interface generators were basic: they used the FIN-USI model of the interfaces and then built an interface for the iPod Touch using the interactors that each participant preferred for each modeled input or output. There were no nuances or extra information included in the interface models or generators that could tune interfaces to particular tasks.

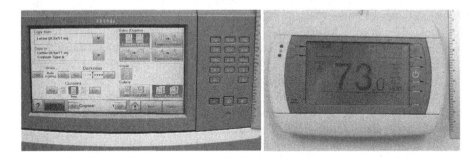

Fig. 1. Photographs of the physical interfaces of the copier (left) and thermostat. Both devices had a touchscreen and physical buttons. Rulers in the photos are marked in centimeters.

Participants used both the thermostat and iPod Touch on a table to make it easier to video record their interactions.

2.3 Methods

In this experiment, four general interface types were tested (where the prefix *Mfr*-denotes manufacturer-created interfaces and *Gen-* denotes auto-generated interfaces): Mfr-Physical, Mfr-Item, Gen-List, and Gen-Loop.

- Mfr-Physical: The manufacturer-created physical interfaces on the tested devices (see Fig. 1 above). Both UIs had physical buttons and touchscreens for control. Neither UI had speech output.
- Mfr-Item: Manufacturer-created UIs that were run on the iPod Touch using Voice-Over.
  - The thermostat had a native iOS application, which was not specifically designed for accessibility. Its UI failed two WCAG 2.0 [9] provisions (2.4.2 & 2.4.6), but could be used with VoiceOver if one figured out its idiosyncrasies.
  - The copier was chosen because it had a web-based interface specifically designed to be accessible and usable to people using screen readers on computers. Its UI used links and form fields and met all level-AA WCAG 2.0 provisions.
- Gen-List: Auto-generated, personalized interfaces that were generally laid out in a conventional list layout, with one interactor or element per row. The gestures used on this interface were a subset of the ones in iOS VoiceOver.
- Gen-Loop: Auto-generated, personalized interfaces with a novel interface layout and gestures [10]. In the Gen-Loop interface, all of the interactors and elements were

arranged around the edges of the screen in a clockwise direction. It was designed to be used by dragging around the edges of the screen (although it could also be used with many of the same gestures as the Gen-List interface) to find and activate elements.

When participants were introduced to the interfaces, they were called the Physical, Item, List, and Loop interfaces, respectively. Figure 2 shows example interfaces that were tested.

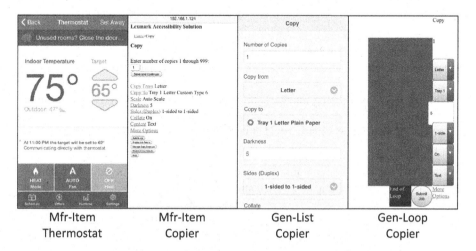

| Mfr-Item | Mfr-Item | Gen-List | Gen-Loop |
| Thermostat | Copier | Copier | Copier |

Fig. 2. Screenshots from the iPod Touch of representative interfaces that were tested. The first two were manufacturer-created interfaces. The last two screen shots were auto-generated and took somewhat different forms during the experiment for each user depending on individual preferences.

The experiment was in two phases. In the first phase, each participant's preferences for interactors was elicited. The second phase was the comparative study of the manufacturer-created interfaces and auto-generated interfaces using the participant's Phase 1 preferences. Sighted participants wore a blindfold while training and performing tasks. The interfaces were covered when participants took breaks from the blindfold.

Participants were told at the outset of the study that the researchers were comparing different interfaces for people who were blind. They were told neither the hypotheses of the experiment nor that they were choosing interactors and having customized interfaces generated for them. Furthermore, the experimenters who interacted with the participants during the study sessions were also not told the hypotheses of the experiment. They were familiar only with the procedures for interacting with participants and carrying out the data collection.

Before the experiment was conducted, the significance (α) level of 0.05 was chosen for all statistical tests.

Phase 1: Preference Elicitation. After participants arrived for the first session, a consent form and demographic questionnaire were administered. The volume and rate of the iPod's text-to-speech output was then adjusted. The speech rate was incrementally slowed until the participant could correctly repeat five consecutive, random phrases that the system spoke from a list of phrases that the system was likely to say during the latter phase of the experiment. Finally, before training, participants double-tapped the screen many times to set their baseline double-tap rate (constrained to be between 250–1000 ms).

Participants then went on with training on the three touchscreen interfaces (Mfr-Item, Gen-List, and Gen-Loop) on the iPod Touch. All three of the introductory training interfaces had a set of on-screen buttons, one for each letter of the alphabet.

- With the Mfr-Item training interface, which utilized iOS's VoiceOver feature, the alphabet buttons were arranged in a grid with 3 buttons per column. VoiceOver would step through them in alphabetical order when the horizontal swiping gestures were used.
- With the Gen-List training interface, the alphabet buttons formed a single column, like a list.
- The Gen-Loop training interface had alphabet buttons arranged around the periphery of the screen.

The order of the three training interfaces was randomly ordered and balanced between participants. Participants were instructed how to navigate (i.e., move the focus around) the self-voicing interfaces by stepping (making short right or left swiping gestures) or by dragging their finger around the interface. Participants were told how to change pages (three-finger swipes up or down on the Mfr-Item and Gen-List interfaces and a continuing looping gesture on the Gen-Loop interface) and how to activate items (double-tapping anywhere on the screen when an element is highlighted). Finally, to ensure that participants had a basic understanding of the three interface styles, they were instructed to find and activate randomly named on-screen buttons until they had activated five buttons correctly in a row. After training on all the iPod self-voicing interfaces, participants ranked them by preference and commented on them.

The last and longest part of the Phase 1 session was eliciting the participants' preferences for particular interactors for specific types of input. Preference elicitation interfaces were constructed using the same two interactors of interest (for example, two dropdown menus or two sets of radio buttons). For each preference elicitation task, participants had to navigate past the first interactor on the screen to get to the second interactor, which they would need to manipulate. Participants would start by trying a random pair of interfaces with the same task and choose their favorite (ties were allowed). Their favorite interface from the prior pair was then paired with a random challenger interface, and they were then to try and rank those two interfaces. This pairwise comparison process was repeated until the favorite interface of all of the available ones was identified. Then the entire process was repeated for the next task and interface style. Participants started with the Gen-List interface and performed three sets of tasks in order: select-one-from-two, followed by select-one-from-seven task, and then numeric entry task. They then repeated the three sets of tasks and interactor comparisons with the Gen-Loop interface.

If there were two or more interactors tied for favorite for a given task, then the system automatically chose the interactor to be used for the auto-generated interfaces. The system's choice was based on the participant's tied interactors and a listing of interactors in a preference order determined before the study by the researchers.

Phase 2: Comparative Interface Testing. The main purpose of Phase 2 of the experiment was to gather performance, preference, and satisfaction data comparing the four interfaces on the two devices. Phase 2 was split into two sessions for the participants who were slower: one session for the initial factorial experiment and the second session for its replication.

Each Phase 2 session started with setting the three personal parameters as in Phase 1: volume, speech rate, and double-tap baseline. Afterwards, participants tried a short gesture practice session to become familiar again with the basic gestures used in the experiment: swiping right and left to navigate, double-tapping to activate, swiping up and down to change values, and three-finger swiping up and down to change pages. In the gesture practice sessions, participants were told a randomly-ordered task they were to accomplish (e.g., "Next", "Activate", or "Earlier Page"), and they would respond by making a gesture. Participants had to get four of each gesture correct the first time they were cued before they could continue to the training.

Participants were also trained on the interfaces that they were to use: the copier's Mfr-Physical interface, the thermostat's Mfr-Physical interface, and the Mfr-Item, Gen-List, and Gen-Loop interfaces on the iPod Touch. For the three iPod Touch interfaces, participants were trained using the preference elicitation interfaces and tasks (from Phase 1) with their favorite interactors (the Mfr-Item training interface used interactors that were like those that participants would use on the copier's Mfr-Item interface). The five interfaces were trained in random order. After completing the training, participants answered a questionnaire verbally before continuing with the factorial experiment.

The bulk of the data was gathered during the factorial experiment where participants tried every combination of Interface and Device with a set of five device-specific tasks (see Table 1). Participants would start with a random device (either the copier or the thermostat) and try each of the four interfaces (Mfr-Physical, Mfr-Item, Gen-Loop, and Gen-List) before moving on to the other device. The order of the interfaces was counterbalanced for each participant using a Latin Square. Participants were told to perform each task "as quickly and as accurately as possible." Participants were given no more than 2 min to complete a task, after which point the participant was told to move on and the task was recorded as a failure. After each task, participants verbally answered the Single Ease Question (SEQ) [11]. After each of the iPod-based interfaces, participants were verbally administered the System Usability Scale (SUS) questionnaire [12] modified to have 7-point Likert-scale items instead of the original 5-point. This modification was made to reduce the confusion observed during pilot testing with users switching between 5- and 7-point scales and because there is evidence that a 7-point SUS scale may provide more accurate measures than the original scale [13]. Participants were asked to rank and comment on all four interfaces after trying all of them for a given device.

Table 1. The device-specific tasks participants attempted on the different interfaces. Simple tasks were chosen so that participants would have higher rates of success. The asterisks denote tasks that would require the use of the (non-voicing) touchscreen on the Mfr-Physical device in order to complete the tasks.

#	Copier tasks	Thermostat tasks
1	Make a single copy	Raise the target temperature 2°
2	Make a darker copy*	Set the target temperature to 70°*
3	Make 5 copies	Turn the fan on*
4	Make a 2-sided copy from a 2-sided original*	Change the mode to cool*
5	Set the Content setting to "Photograph"*	Set the target temperature to 75° and turn hold on*

Depending on the time, participants would replicate the factorial experiment in the same session or come back for a second Phase 2 session. To reduce frustration, participants did not replicate the tasks on the Mfr-Physical interfaces that were a priori considered to be inaccessible because they required the use of non-voicing touchscreens for success. Participants were allowed breaks between devices and whenever they requested one.

3   Results

The mean Phase 1 session length (including breaks) for blind participants was 124 min. (SD = 39) and that for blindfolded participants was 137 min. (SD = 33). The difference between Phase 1 session times between groups was not significant; $t(22) = 0.880$, $p = 0.388$. A total of nine blind participants completed Phase 2 in one session with a mean length of 163 min. (SD = 23); nine blindfolded participants also completed Phase 2 in a single session (M = 184 min., SD = 22). The difference in single Phase 2 session times was not significant ($t(16) = 1.933$, $p = 0.071$). Of the three blind participants who had two Phase 2 sessions, the two sessions averaged 205 min. (SD = 18) and 128 min. (SD = 23) long, respectively. The three blindfolded participants who had two Phase 2 sessions had mean session times of 160 min. (SD = 10) and 132 min. (SD = 35), respectively.

3.1   Preferences for Interactors

To get each participant's favorite interactors for the automatic generation of Gen-List interfaces, participants tried all five available interactors for a Select-1-of-2 task, then all five available interactors for a Select-1-of-7 task, and then all four interactors for a number input task. Ties were allowed in the preferences. Several of the tested Gen-List interface interactors had the same behaviors and interaction as pre-existing interactors that were used in the copier's accessible Mfr-Item interface or the native iOS VoiceOver screen reader. Analyzed with exact binomial tests (see Table 2), participants favored the new interactors created for this study over the pre-existing interactors.

Table 2. Exact binomial tests of new interactors being favored over pre-existing interactors.

Task	P	k	n	Significance
Select 1 of 2	3/5	22	23	<0.001
Select 1 of 7	3/5	23	24	<0.001
Number input	2/4	15	19	0.010

Where P is the probability of success (i.e., favoring new interactors) due solely to chance, k is the number of participants who favored new interactors (i.e., the number of binomial successes), and n is the number of participants who did not have tied favorites between new and pre-existing interactors.

Participants also choose their favorite interactors in a similar manner for Gen-Loop interfaces. However, since the Gen-Loop interface is a novel interface style, there were no pre-existing interactors against which to compare.

3.2 Preferences for Interface Types

Participants were asked to rank the interfaces by preference at seven points during the two phases of the study. For analysis, each separate ranking can be treated as a binomial experiment where a "success" is defined as both automatically-generated interfaces (Gen-List and Gen-Loop) being ranked higher than both of the manufacturer-created interfaces (Mfr-Physical and Mfr-Item). The auto-generated interfaces were not favored with the first ranking ($p = 0.406$, exact binomial test with probability of 1/3, $k = 9$, and $n = 24$) after the Phase 1 training on the iPod Touch interfaces. For each of the subsequent rankings, however, both auto-generated interfaces were strongly favored by participants over both manufacturer-created ones ($p < 0.001$ for all exact binomial tests).

When blind participants were asked to rank the three mobile-device interfaces at the end of the experiment, 8 participants preferred the Gen-Loop interface, 3 preferred Gen-List, 0 preferred Mfr-Item, and 1 participant had a first-place tie between Gen-Loop and Gen-List. When blindfolded participants were asked to rank the interfaces at the end of the experiment, 10 participants preferred the Gen-Loop interface, 2 preferred Gen-List, and 0 preferred Mfr-Item. The difference between the number of blind participants who favored the novel Gen-Loop interface to the Gen-List interface was not significant (two-sided Wilcoxson signed rank test, $z = 1.31$, $p = 0.190$). However, blindfolded participants preferred the Gen-Loop interface over the Gen-List interface (two-sided Wilcoxson signed rank test, $z = 2.02$, $p = 0.043$).

3.3 Comparative Study Results

Four measures were collected as participants performed the various tasks. Success/failure and successful task time were recorded for each task on all four interfaces. The Single Ease Question (SEQ) responses were collected for each task on the three mobile-device interfaces (Mfr-Item, Gen-Loop, & Gen-list). The System Usability Scale (SUS) questionnaire was verbally administered after participants had completed all the tasks on each of the iPod Touch-based interfaces (Mfr-Item, Gen-List, & Gen-Loop). The Spearman's rank correlations between these measures were significant ($p < 0.001$ for all correlations) and are shown in Table 3.

Table 3. Spearman's rank correlation coefficients for the four Phase 2 study measures.

	Rank-transformed performance	Success/fail	SEQ	SUS
Rank-transformed performance [b]	1			
Success/fail [b]	−0.902	1		
SEquation [a]	−0.760	0.720	1	
SUS [a]	−0.616	0.613	0.810	1

[a] *Measures were collected for the three iPod Touch interfaces.*
[b] *Measures were collected for all four interfaces.*

Each measure was analyzed separately for significance of the Interface factor and any Interface-factor interactions using methods appropriate for each type of data.

Success/Fail Data. The success/fail binary data was analyzed using Generalized Estimating Equations (GEE) with a binomial logit link function. This technique allows for correct inferences of repeated measures binomial data [14]. A full factorial model with Group (2) × Device (2) × Interface (4) × Replication (2) was run and then the most non-significant terms were iteratively removed from subsequent GEE models until a parsimonious model was found with the lowest Corrected Quasi-likelihood Information Criterion (final model QICC = 1656.137). The terms of the model and significance tests of their effects is shown in Table 4.

Table 4. Factors in the final GEE model of the success/fail data and their significance.

Source	Wald Chi-Square	df	Significance
(Intercept)	1.516	1	0.218
Group	9.991	1	0.002
Device	10.589	1	0.001
Interface	214.503	3	<0.001
Replication	18.593	1	<0.001
Group × Device	2.460	1	0.117
Group × Interface	18.918	3	<0.001
Device × Interface	24.228	3	<0.001

All the main effects were significant at a 0.05 α-level. The Group, Device, and Interface factors were also involved in two-way interactions. Pairwise post hoc tests were conducted on the significant interactions using the sequential Sidak procedure.

The Group × Interface interaction (see Fig. 3) was significant. Between the blind and blindfolded groups on the Mfr-Item interfaces, blind participants had a success rate

0.44 points (0.20–0.67 95% Wald difference CI) higher than that of the blindfolded participants (p < 0.001). There were no other significant differences between the groups on particular interfaces. For both groups, the Mfr-Physical and Mfr-Item interfaces had significantly lower success rates than the Gen-List and Gen-Loop interfaces (both with p < 0.001). For the blindfolded participants, the Gen-List interfaces had a success rate that was 0.60 points (0.43–0.77 difference CI) higher than on the Mfr-Item interfaces. For blind participants, the Gen-List interfaces had a success rate that was 0.36 points (0.21–0.50 difference CI) higher than on the Mfr-Item interfaces. Differences between success rates on the Gen-List and Gen-Loop interfaces within each group were not significant.

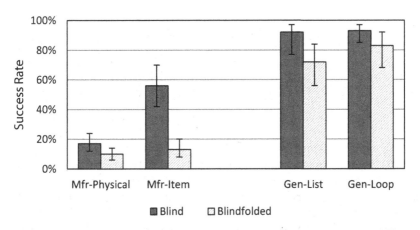

Fig. 3. The estimated marginal mean success rates for the Group × Interface interaction. Error bars show 95% Wald confidence intervals for the marginal estimates.

The Device × Interface interaction was significant. With both devices, participants were more successful on the Gen-List and Gen-Loop interfaces than the Mfr-Physical and Mfr-Item interfaces. On the copier, the Gen-List interface had a success rate 0.42 (0.22–0.63 95% Wald difference CI) points greater than on the Mfr-Item interface (p < 0.001). Similarly, participants using the thermostat were successful 0.61 (0.40–0.81 difference CI) points greater when using the Gen-List interface than when using the Mfr-Item interface (p < 0.001). Differences between the Gen-List and Gen-Loop interfaces on particular devices were not significant.

Performance Data. The success/fail data is folded into the performance data, because task times were only recorded for successful tasks (see Fig. 4). Because the users failed significantly more often on the manufacturer-created interfaces, the performance differences were only compared between the two auto-generated interfaces. To test the differences in performance, the task time and failure data were converted to a comparable scale, which was done by rank transforming the data (where all failures were given tie rankings). Repeated measures ANOVA was then used to analyze the ranked performance data partitioned by device.

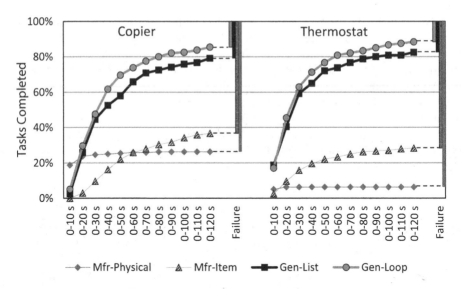

Fig. 4. Cumulative distributions of task performance on the copier and thermostat.

For the copier, the Interface main effect (F = 3.346, df = 1) was not significant (p = 0.082). The only significant interaction involving the Interface factor was the Interface × Task interaction (F = 3.382, df = 4, p = 0.013). Further investigation with sequential simple effect Sidak post hoc tests indicated that participants performed better on the Gen-Loop interface for two of the five tasks (with p = 0.005 and p = 0.015).

For the thermostat, the Interface main effect (F = 1.149, df = 1) was not significant (p = 0.295). No interactions involving the Interface factor were significant.

Single Ease Question (SEQ) Data. The single ease question (SEQ) on a 7-point scale anchored with 1 = "very difficult" and 7 = "very easy" was asked after each task. A full factorial Type III Sum of Squares GEE model on the Group (2), Device (2), Interface (3), and Replication (2) factors was run on the interval-type SEQ data with a multinomial cumulative logit link function. Only the three iPod interfaces (Mfr-Item, Gen-List, and Gen-Loop) were included in the analysis because the Mfr-Physical interface was low

Table 5. **Factors** in the final GEE model of the SEQ data and their significance. Only the Mfr-Item, Gen-List, and Gen-Loop interfaces were included in this analysis because they had complete factorial data.

Source	Wald Chi-Square	df	Significance
Group	6.874	1	0.009
Device	0.364	1	0.546
Interface	98.308	2	<0.001
Replication	19.532	1	<0.001
Group × Interface	7.395	2	0.025
Device × Interface	9.626	2	0.025

scoring and did not have complete factorial data for the replication. The GEE model was run iteratively removing 4-, 3-, and 2-way interactions that were obviously non-significant one at a time. The significance data of the resulting final model is shown in Table 5. The two auto-generated interfaces scored significantly higher (Mdn = 7 for Gen-Loop and Mdn = 6 for Gen-List) than the Mfr-Item interface (Mdn = 2, IQR = 4).

As a post hoc comparison of the Gen-List and Gen-Loop interfaces, the data was partitioned to remove the Mfr-Item interface and the full factorial GEE multinomial cumulative logit model was run again with iterative removal of non-significant effects. The factors and significance data of the resulting final model is shown in Table 6. On the SEQ, participants rated the tasks on the Gen-Loop interface as easier (Mdn = 7, IQR = 1) than the Gen-List interface (Mdn = 6, IQR = 2).

Table 6. Factors in the final GEE model of the SEQ data for the two auto-generated interfaces and their significance

Source	Wald Chi-Square	df	Significance
Group	1.463	1	0.227
Device	0.759	1	0.384
Interface	6.290	1	0.012
Replication	21.435	1	<0.001
Group × Replication	3.722	1	0.054

System Usability Scale (SUS) Data. The 10-question Likert SUS questionnaire was answered by participants after completing all five tasks of each replication with the three iPod interfaces (Mfr-Item, Gen-List, and Gen-Loop). A Cronbach's alpha reliability score was calculated for each of the 12 times the SUS was administered. Agreeing with the literature (e.g., [15, 16]), the individual SUS scale items were highly consistent for each administration in this experiment; the average Cronbach's alpha for the items in the SUS in this experiment was 0.931 with values ranging from 0.865–0.973. Because of this high reliability, the individual items were transformed and summed, as is typical with SUS measurements, for the subsequent analysis.

The SUS data was analyzed as a Group (2) × Device (2) × Interface (3) repeated measures ANOVA, as is typical [17]. The main effect of Interface was significant $(F(2) = 77.800, p < 0.001)$, as was the Interface × Replication interaction $(F(1.525) = 5.148, p = 0.018$ with Greenhouse-Geisser correction for significant asphericity of the data), which is shown in Fig. 5.

Sequential simple effect post hoc tests with the sequential Sidak correction were performed on the Interface × Replication interaction. These tests indicated that participants scored the Gen-List interface 8.56 points higher on the replication (p = 0.015), the Gen-Loop interface 7.00 points higher on the replication (p = 0.001), and no significant SUS score change on the Mfr-Item interface with the replication (p = 0.273). Both the Gen-List and Gen-Loop interfaces significantly outscored the Mfr-Item interface at both time points (p < 0.001). The SUS scores for the Gen-List and Gen-Loop interfaces for the first block were not significantly different (p = 0.059), but the Gen-Loop did score 9.58 points higher (0.39–18.78 95% difference CI) than the Gen-List interface with the replication (p = 0.039).

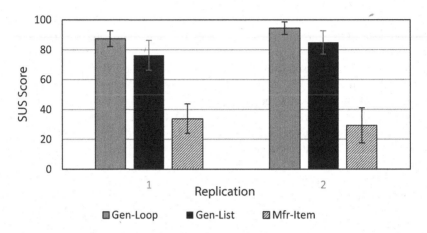

Fig. 5. The Interface × Replication interaction showing the marginal means of the SUS scores. The error bars show 95% normal-distribution confidence intervals for the marginal interaction means.

4 Discussion

When choosing their favorite interactors in Phase 1, participants had strong preferences for the Gen-List interactors that were designed for this experiment over "pre-existing" interactors. Particularly notable was the dislike of the Picker interactor (which is what is presented to people using the iOS VoiceOver screen reader whenever a person encounters a dropdown list (e.g., a <select> element in HTML). One blind partici-pant, who had used pickers before on her own device, said bluntly that, "Pickers could go to hell." Nobody in the experiment chose the Keyboard interactor, which was closely modeled after the iOS keyboard mode that was presented for numeric entry (e.g., entry into a <input type = "number"> element in HTML). Both the Picker and Keyboard interactors were examples of layered interfaces—where people use a screen reader interface layer that is reading (and interacting with) a graphical user interface that was specifically designed for mainstream users with vision. Having automatically generated interfaces can eliminate this layering of interfaces, because the interactors can be designed with users' primary modalities in mind. For this experiment, the "new" interactors were designed specifically with speech output and touchscreen gesture manipulation in mind; any visual representations were secondary and mostly included to make it easier for the sighted researchers to observe.

While participants liked the "new" interactors, several of the blind participants wished that additional gestures were supported by the two auto-generated interfaces.

For example, two blind participants use the VoiceOver drag-and-tap-with-a-second-finger gesture on their own iPhone devices to make selections rather than the double-tap that was required by the research system. Others had difficulty with the gestures required by both VoiceOver and the research systems and would rather have substituted their own gestures. The blind participant with tremor suggested having a dedicated area on the touchscreen or button on the device for activation rather than double-tapping anywhere on the screen. Such user preferences could be supported by personalized, automatically-generated interfaces.

In Phase 1, the interactors that participants chose and the reasons that they reported for making the choices did not always seem optimal to the researchers. For example, one blindfolded participant chose a double-tap interactor for the Select-1-of-7 task (which requires a person to double-tap to change values and thus double-tap multiple times to cycle through all the values). This participant reported some frustration in Phase 2 when he used Gen-List interfaces, because he would sometimes overshoot the desired selection and have to double-tap through the entire list all over again. Other participants occasionally wished that the Gen-List or Gen-Loop interfaces were a little different when they were trying the study tasks of Phase 2 rather than the preference elicitation tasks. For example, a blind participant who chose radio button interactors in both the Gen-List and Gen-Loop interface reported later in Phase 2 that it was awkward to have to switch pages so much when completing the copier or thermostat tasks (which is the tradeoff with choosing radio buttons over menu-based or other interactors). This suggests that a different approach to preference elicitation may be helpful. It is also possible that users who knew ahead of time that they are choosing interactors for personalized interfaces might choose differently than participants who are just told to pick favorite interactors without context as in the study. Users may also pick better interactors if they were to do a first pass to screen out the interactors that they strongly dislike, and then try more comparisons with more realistic interfaces and the finalist interactors. Creating a better preference elicitation process would be a good avenue for future work.

Even with some participants' interactor choices seeming to be suboptimal, the two automatically-generated interfaces tested better than the manufacturer-created interfaces for all measures on both the copier and thermostat devices. The magnitude of the difference was greater than expected. Before conducting the experiment, it was expected that at least the copier's accessible web-based interface (i.e., the copier's Mfr-Item interface designed specifically for blind screen reader users) would have been a much closer match to the two automatically-generated interfaces, because it had been hand-crafted specifically for people who are blind and using screen readers. One blind participant said that copier's Mfr-Item interface was "100-percent do-able," and that she probably would have scored it more highly on the usability questionnaire (SUS) if she had not just tried a superior interface beforehand (in her case, the Gen-List interface). For participants in this experiment, the automatically-generated interfaces were consistently better than the manufacturer-created ones.

The results of the sub-study of the performance and preference differences between the two automatically-generated Gen-List and Gen-Loop interfaces are not as clear, however. The subjective measures (ranking, SEQ, and SUS) showed limited evidence that the Gen-Loop interface may be better than the Gen-List interface, but the success/

failure and performance data did not. The fact that the Gen-Loop interface was perceived as generally preferred to or better than the Gen-List interface might also be a bias related to the good-subject effect [18]. The Gen-Loop interface was obviously the most different interface to people who were blind, so "good" participants might have felt that the study's aim was to show that the Gen-Loop interface was better and "good" participants might respond in such a way to support that perceived hypothesis. It would be fair to say that participants had different and sometimes changing preferences between the Gen-List and Gen-Loop interfaces. One blind participant strongly disliked the Gen-Loop interface concept in general because he felt it was confusing and unintuitive. Other participants liked how the Gen-Loop interface felt logical and efficient. Some participants did not have much of an opinion either way because they used both the Gen-List and Gen-Loop interfaces with swiping navigation gestures. If participants chose particular interactors, then they could potentially have exactly the same user experience when swiping to navigate with both Gen-List and Gen-Loop interfaces. Many participants did not like the Gen-Loop interface at first with only limited exposure and use, but later after becoming accustomed to the interface style, many participants' preferences changed. One participant had his own hypothesis and said that the Gen-Loop interface violated the two ways that blind people have interacted with user interfaces so far: (1) navigation using arrow keys, tabbing, or swiping and (2) scanning through the interface as with a visual magnifier or dragging on a touchscreen. He said that the Gen-Loop interface was good, but that he did not like it at first because it required him to break the force of habit: "Forget all that. [The Loop interface] might be a better, more efficient way to do this."

This lack of a clear difference between Gen-List and Gen-Loop interfaces may lend more support to model-based generation of user interfaces. Model-based, automatic interface generation can support people's preferences, even for very different layouts and interaction styles. People who prefer and perhaps better comprehend a more typical, linear interface could have automatically-generated interfaces that look and behave like a Gen-List interface. Other people might prefer to use a Gen-Loop interface because it is intuitive and more efficient for them.

While group differences were not the focus of the study, the data supported the expectation that people who were blind perform better with blind-specific interfaces than people who were blindfolded and had no prior experience with those interfaces or techniques and strategies that are used by people who are blind. It was remarkable that the blindfolded participants did as well as they did. VoiceOver and screen readers in general have a steep learning curve that can be particularly difficult for elders and others who are not technically savvy (K. M. Fountaine, personal communication, August 31, 2015). The two-way Group × Interface interaction of the success/fail data (plotted in Fig. 3 above) could be interpreted along with the flexibility and experience of participants. Blind participants were more flexible and experienced and thus did better on the Mfr-Item interface than the blindfolded participants. However, the automatically-generated interfaces studied here were very consistent and had relatively few interactors and gestures, which seemed to make it easier for even novice blindfolded users to experience success.

5   Conclusion

The self-voicing interfaces that were automatically generated using each participant's preferred interactors were statistically better on all performance and usability measures than the manufacturer-created interfaces. While preferences varied in the beginning when participants were first learning about the different interface styles, participants also preferred the auto-generated interfaces once they had finished training and started performing the actual tasks. These results are notable because the model and interface generators were both relatively simple.

This study supports the ability of the FIN-USI modeling approach to automatically generate user interfaces that participants prefer and on which they perform better compared to the manufacturer-created interfaces, including one interface designed by the manufacturer specifically for people who are blind. It also supports the sufficiency of even simple interface generators created using the model to outperform manufacturer interfaces. In the future, model-based auto-generation of interfaces could support a wide range of user needs and preferences, where people could choose the type of interface they want and from what components interfaces are built.

Acknowledgements. The contents of this paper are based on work carried out with funding from the National Institute on Disability, Independent Living, and Rehabilitation Research, U.S. Department of Health and Human Services, grant number H133E080022 (RERC on Universal Interface and Information Technology Access). However, the contents do not necessarily represent the policy nor imply endorsement by the funding agencies.

References

1. Gajos, K.Z., Weld, D.S., Wobbrock, J.O.: Automatically generating personalized user interfaces with Supple. Artif. Intell. **174**, 910–950 (2010). doi:10.1016/j.artint.2010.05.005
2. Meixner, G., Paternò, F., Vanderdonckt, J.: Past, present, and future of model-based user interface development. i-Com **10**, 2–11 (2011). doi:10.1524/icom.2011.0026
3. Myers, B., Hudson, S.E., Pausch, R.: Past, present, and future of user interface software tools. ACM Trans. Comput. Hum. Interact. **7**, 3–28 (2000). doi:10.1145/344949.344959
4. Nichols, J., Myers, B.A., Higgins, M., Hughes, J., Harris, T.K., Rosenfeld, R., Pignol, M.: Generating remote control interfaces for complex appliances. In: Proceedings of the 15th Annual ACM Symposium on User Interface Software and Technology, pp. 161–170. ACM, New York (2002). doi:10.1145/571985.572008
5. Coelho, J., Duarte, C., Biswas, P., Langdon, P.: Developing accessible TV applications. In: The Proceedings of the 13th International ACM SIGACCESS Conference on Computers and Accessibility, pp. 131–138. ACM, New York (2011). doi:10.1145/2049536.2049561
6. Peissner, M., Häbe, D., Janssen, D., Sellner, T.: MyUI: generating accessible user interfaces from multimodal design patterns. In: Proceedings of the 4th ACM SIGCHI Symposium on Engineering Interactive Computing Systems, pp. 81–90. ACM, New York (2012). doi:10.1145/2305484.2305500
7. Nichols, J., Chau, D.H., Myers, B.A.: Demonstrating the viability of automatically generated user interfaces. In: Proceedings of the SIGCHI Conference on Human Factors in Computing Systems, pp. 1283–1292. ACM, New York (2007). doi:10.1145/1240624.1240819

8. Sears, A., Hanson, V.: Representing users in accessibility research. In: Proceedings of the SIGCHI Conference on Human Factors in Computing Systems, pp. 2235–2238. ACM, New York (2011). doi:10.1145/1978942.1979268
9. Caldwell, B., Cooper, M., Reid, L.G., Vanderheiden, G., Chisholm, W., Slatin, J., White, J. (eds.): Web Content Accessibility Guidelines (WCAG) 2.0 (2008). http://www.w3.org/TR/WCAG20/
10. Jordan, J.B.: A circular direct-selection interface for non-visual use. IPcom Prior Art Database. Disclosure Number: IPCOM000241004D (2015)
11. Sauro, J., Dumas, J.S.: Comparison of three one-question, post-task usability questionnaires. In: Proceedings of the 27th International Conference on Human Factors in Computing Systems, pp. 1599–1608. ACM, New York (2009). doi:10.1145/1518701.1518946
12. Brooke, J.: SUS: A "quick and dirty" usability scale. In: Usability Evaluation in Industry. Taylor and Francis, London (1996)
13. Finstad, K.: Response interpolation and scale sensitivity: evidence against 5-point scales. J. Usability Stud. **5**, 104–110 (2010)
14. Lee, J.-H., Herzog, T.A., Meade, C.D., Webb, M.S., Brandon, T.H.: The use of GEE for analyzing longitudinal binomial data: a primer using data from a tobacco intervention. Addict. Behav. **32**, 187–193 (2007). doi:10.1016/j.addbeh.2006.03.030
15. Bangor, A., Kortum, P.T., Miller, J.T.: An empirical evaluation of the system usability scale. Int. J. Hum. Comput. Interact. **24**, 574 (2008). doi:10.1080/10447310802205776
16. Sauro, J., Lewis, J.R.: Correlations among prototypical usability metrics: evidence for the construct of usability. In: Proceedings of the 27th International Conference on Human Factors in Computing Systems, pp. 1609–1618. ACM, Boston (2009). doi:10.1145/1518701.1518947
17. Sauro, J., Lewis, J.R.: Quantifying the User Experience: Practical Statistics for User Research. Morgan Kaufmann, Waltham (2012)
18. Nichols, A.L., Maner, J.K.: The good-subject effect: investigating participant demand characteristics. J. Gen. Psychol. **135**, 151–166 (2008). doi:10.3200/GENP.135.2.151-166

Towards Accessible Automatically Generated Interfaces Part 1: An Input Model that Bridges the Needs of Users and Product Functionality

J. Bern Jordan[(✉)] and Gregg C. Vanderheiden

University of Maryland, College Park, Md., USA
{jbjordan,greggvan}@umd.edu

Abstract. Automatic model-based generation of user interfaces is a potential strategy to enable individuals with disabilities to control products and services with an interface that fits their specific needs. Most of the existing work and models have been focused on mainstream users and have evolved into complex, multilayered approaches. In this paper, we describe a new, simpler input model, the FIN-USI model, which is a bridge between the basic input a system/device needs for functionality (the Functionality Input Needs; FINs) and the basic input that users provide as input in an abstract, modality independent manner (User-Sensible Inputs; USIs). An abstract model of a user interface can be made up of FIN and USI elements. Each FIN and USI element consists of a type of input and characteristics that are applied to that input type. Input elements may be grouped for functionality or usability reasons. All the components of the model are described and examples of application are given in this paper.

Keywords: Abstract user interface model · Accessibility · Functionality needs · Input requirements · Personalization · Universal design · User input · User needs

1   Introduction

People with disabilities often find it difficult or impossible to complete tasks with user interfaces (UIs) that do not meet their needs or are not operable with their abilities. There are many potential strategies for creating accessible interfaces for people with disabilities [1]. Built-in interfaces may be designed using a universal/inclusive design process to try to accommodate as many users as is commercially feasible [2]. Software and web UIs may be designed in accordance with accessibility standards, such as the Web Content Accessibility Guidelines (WCAG) 2.0 [3] and application program interfaces (APIs), such as IAccessibile2, AT-SPI, UIAExpress, NSAccessibility, UIAccessibility, MSAA, UIA, and others [4–6] so that assistive technologies can be used. A manufacturer may also go so far as to create several alternative UIs for different expected user populations. All of these strategies require deep knowledge of accessible design and the resources necessary for development and testing with all of the different types, degrees, and combinations of the disabilities targeted. Furthermore, these accessibility strategies also focus on common disability groups—they are not personalized. This makes accessibility difficult to extend

© Springer International Publishing AG 2017
J. Zhou and G. Salvendy (Eds.): ITAP 2017, Part I, LNCS 10297, pp. 129–146, 2017.
DOI: 10.1007/978-3-319-58530-7_9

to people who have needs and preferences that are uncommon or conflict with those of other users.

Automatic, model-based generation of user interfaces is potentially a powerful strategy for creating interfaces that fit each person's needs and preferences [7]. Using underlying models of a UI, an interface generator on a person's Personal Alternative User Interface (PAUI) device (such as a mobile phone running special interface software) could create an interface tailored to the user [1]. The PAUI's interface might have features for the person, such as a dynamic braille display, text-to-speech, or alternative input modalities. The one-size-fits-one approach of automatic interface generation could then provide a usable interface even if no manually-designed interfaces for the device are accessible to the individual. This paper does not specifically focus on the generation of UIs, but instead on models that could support UI generation.

Models for the generation of UIs have been developed as standards and as the output of research projects. Many of the research-oriented models suffer from being too complex and difficult to implement for their resulting benefit [8, 9] and have not been used by industry in any meaningful way. Models that have been successfully tested with users (e.g., [7, 10]) have tended to be simpler. Unfortunately, models that have been developed to this point have generally been focused on relatively limited types of interaction and input, such as input that can be handled by form-like interfaces, rather than considering a broader range of what various systems might require for input. There is a need for a simple model for user interface generation that covers a broader range of user input that systems need for operation, yet is practical enough for industry use. In this paper, we describe such a model and its development.

2 Background

Model-based UI generation relies on a separation between the user interface and the functionality that is to be controlled. This separation of concerns was introduced with the Seeheim model [11] and is now a common software architecture pattern that underlies Model-View-Controller [12], Model-View-Presenter [13], Model-View-ViewModel [14], and other patterns. In COUSIN [15], an early user interface management system, this separation was emphasized to automatically generate a UI from an abstract definition of the functionality. Several potential advantages were found with this approach: reduced effort for UI design, UIs with more user support, easier involvement of human factors experts, more consistent UIs, and the ability to provide multiple UIs [15]. This separation between the user interface and functionality also potentially allows for alternative UIs to communicate with the underlying system functionality. Despite seemingly potential benefits, the automatic generation of UIs has made little headway in mainstream UI development.

2.1 Models for User Interface Generation

A number of models have been developed to facilitate the generation of user interfaces. Many of the models that have been developed can be categorized using the CAMELEON reference framework [16, 17], which foresees models at four levels:

- *Concept & Task Models* define the tasks a user is expected to perform and the domain objects with which a person will interact.
- *Abstract UI Models* define interface elements independently of specific interaction modalities.
- *Concrete UI Models* specify the interactors (widgets) that will be used, which are targeted to a particular platform, environment, and modality.
- *Final UI* is the runnable user interface that can be executed as binary code or an interpreted language.

A user interface generator may take models at any of these levels and may incorporate other models and information about the user, the context of use, and the environment to generate the final UI. Fully automatic generation of UIs is challenging [9]. Because of this, many of the model-based interface generation research programs have limited their work to semi-automatic generation of user interfaces [8]. This hand-tuning of interfaces is unacceptable as a scalable solution for providing customized or close-fitting access to people with disabilities. Most model-based user interface projects have focused only on mainstream users, leaving the creation of interface generators for people with disabilities as future work, with two notable exceptions. In the SUPPLE project, a constraint-based approach was used to layout graphical user interfaces (GUIs) for people with physical disabilities [7]. In the MyUI project, a pattern-based approach was used to create UIs for older people interacting with specific applications on a television [18].

Early model-based systems were developed to generate interfaces because, at the time, creation of UIs was a particularly difficult process. Modern UI toolkits and visual editors were not yet available. With the Mickey system [19], basic menus and dialog boxes were generated from specialized function signatures and comments in the application logic code. The Jade system [20] utilized a basic textual specification of seven types of inputs.

' As frameworks were further developed, they generally became more complex. The MASTERMIND system [21] was one of the first to include a task model, which was modeled in terms of goals and preconditions. Since then, many model-based UI generation projects have included a task model or other higher-level model of the interface. The TRIDENT system [22] relies on task models in the form of an Activity Chaining Graph. ConcurTaskTrees [23] is a hierarchical task model that is included as a component of the TERESA [24] and MARIA [25] projects. The UsiXML project uses FlowiXML [26] as a task model, which is itself an extension of ConcurTaskTrees. The task models can be helpful in improving an interface by providing information that can be used in grouping and navigation [27]. Producing task models also requires more effort, which may not be worth the investment for manufacturers.

There are some notable exceptions to the general trend towards increasing model complexity. The SUPPLE system [7] represents abstract UIs with a combination of primitive input types and container types. The Personal Universal Controller (PUC) system [28] defines interfaces in a similar way, with a limited set of input elements and a tree interface structure that can be adjusted based on dependency information. Both systems were tested with users and showed performance and other benefits over manufacturer and other one-size-fits-all UIs [7, 10].

A widely-used type of model at the Concrete and Final UI levels are GUI toolkits. Many GUI toolkits are available. Toolkit widgets may support input from multiple modalities (e.g., keyboard, mouse, and touch input), which can make them easier to use by people with disabilities. Toolkits for GUIs may also have built-in support for accessibility APIs. Assistive technology, such as screen readers, can use these APIs in their functioning to present an alternative UI to users. Without accessibility APIs, using assistive technology can be more difficult or impossible. There are strategies, such as off-screen models [29] that can be used, but these are more difficult and may only be available for the most commonly used applications. However, basing an adapted or alternative interface on an accessible graphical user interface may result in layers of interface. For example, a person with a screen reader listens to and interacts with an audio representation (layer 1) of a graphical interface (layer 2) to control a system's functionality (layer 3). This layering and indirection can lead to unnecessary complexity and confusion.

Some interface models at different levels of abstraction have been standardized. The HyperText Markup Language (HTML) is ubiquitous on the web and evolved from a language initially for the publication and exchange of documents to one that supports complex applications. Markup in HTML5 [30] can be extended with scripts to enhance the type of applications and interactions that can be created, but this can lead to inaccessible interfaces if care is not taken. XForms [31] offers a potentially more flexible way of specifying forms with richer processing logic than HTML, but is used much less in practice. To better support assistive technology in dynamic HTML, WAI-ARIA [32] was developed and can be used to provide compatible assistive technology with enhanced metadata about elements' roles and states. The Universal Remote Console (URC; ISO/IEC 24752:2014) is a system that can discover and allow remote control of compatible target devices through an interface socket [33]. This socket is defined in an XML language with a resource layer that defines different groupings and dependencies and uses XML Schema [34] data types. Interfaces for a URC controller may be manually designed or automatically generated for simple target systems [35]. Although not a system for user interface generation, the Common Access Profile (ISO/IEC 24756:2009) uses a two-sided approach for assessing the matching quality of a system's capabilities with a user's needs. However, this approach is focused on modality-matching and does not accommodate individual user interface elements.

All the models and projects discussed so far work for form-like interfaces, where users interact with buttons and enter data into sequential fields in a time-independent manner. Form fill-in is only one of a range of interaction styles [36]. Not all interactions with systems fit this paradigm.

2.2   User Input Beyond Forms

Several taxonomies of user input have been created (forms are a subset of each). In an early attempt to categorize input, six elemental tasks were proposed for graphical computer systems: Select, Position, Orient, Path, Quantify, and Text [37]. These elemental tasks could potentially be accomplished through different interface techniques. This list of elemental tasks is not a list of perceptual tasks that people do on a computer, but was proposed instead as a different way to think about and categorize input for those systems. Other taxonomies of input characterize input devices rather than the tasks one might perform. Buxton focused on continuous input devices and characterized their properties sensed and number of dimensions supported [38]. This work was extended to other devices and dimensions of input in [39].

For creating interfaces for people with disabilities a modality-independent approach, like that of [37] is more appropriate. However, it is still important to consider these other, broader taxonomies of input as well. Novel and modality-dependent input may be used to provide input that is outside the form input paradigm.

3   The FIN-USI Model

There were four goals for the model as it was developed.

1. *Allow for the creation of UIs that meet the needs of users.* All users have needs and preferences when interacting with UIs. People with disabilities may have different needs from others. A PAUI and UI generator must use the model and create an interface that meets these individual needs.
2. *Model a broad range of input that systems need for proper functioning.* Users need to be able to control functionality of a variety of systems and should not be limited to systems that only have form-like input requirements.
3. *Require as few base components as possible.* Complex models are more difficult to implement for both manufacturers and PAUI developers. With a limited vocabulary of required inputs that must be supported, PAUI developers do not need to create as many interactors and UI generation rules for users who have unique input needs.
4. *Allow for extensions to improve usability.* Expressiveness is limited with a small vocabulary. Optional extensions can enable richer interface generators that support a wider range of interactors that are tuned for particular types of inputs.

The user interface needs of all users fall into three broad categories [1]. All users, including people with disabilities, must be able to *perceive* all information, must *understand* that information, and must be able to *operate* all controls necessary for all functionality. Interfaces generated via a suitable UI generator on a PAUI would cover the user needs of perception and operation (i.e., a generator should only use interactors that use a modality that the individual can perceive and interactions that the individual can operate). The user's ability to understand the input they are to provide and how to do so is a function of both the interface model and generated interface.

3.1   Model Development Process

To create a simpler yet more comprehensive model than those that currently exist, the authors started by examining a variety of sources and literature. By better understanding the limitations and successes of other models, the best features of these models could be incorporated into the new model. The model was developed in an iterative process. First a potential model was proposed, and then real-world interfaces were modeled. When the model could not accommodate a real-world interface, the model was revisited and revised. The FIN-USI model is the result.

3.2 Description of the FIN-USI Model

A user interface is a bridge between the user and the functionality they wish to control. The FIN-USI model is an abstract model of input that is provided through a user interface. Like a bridge, the FIN-USI model has two ends. The Functionality Input Need (FIN) end models the input needs of the functionality of the device, software, or system. For example, what does the tuner part of a television or the refrigeration functionality of a refrigerator need as user input in its most basic, modality-independent form? The FINs are very different from what a user interface needs a user to provide. A user needs to be able to find and push the Channel Up and Down buttons on a specific remote control to tune the television, but the TV only needs to know the channel number (the FIN). With refrigerators, the user needs to find and twist a knob on the inside of one, or push buttons on another to set the temperature, but both refrigerators only need to know the settings and do not care how it is entered. If users cannot fulfill the FIN using an available user interface (because the available UI does not fit their needs), and no alternate interface is available to them, then they will be unable to use that functionality.

The User-Sensible Input (USI) end is a model of abstract, modality-independent interactors that a user needs to be able to perceive, understand, and operate in order to fulfill the system's FINs. The FIN and USI components of the model are related by transformation functions which translate user-understandable input into the system-understandable input that the device requires. In this way, USIs fulfill FINs. The double-ended aspect of the FIN-USI model is unique among interface models and accounts for situations where the needs that a system has differs from what a user needs and understands. The relationship between USI and FIN elements (where each element is an input component) is shown in Fig. 1.

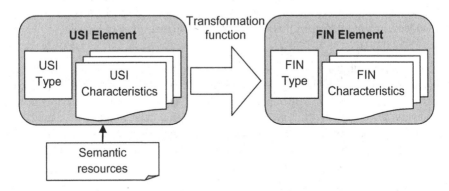

Fig. 1. The relationship between a USI and FIN Element and their subcomponents. The value that a user inputs to a user-sensible input (USI) element is transformed to fulfill a functionality input need (FIN). Semantic resources are applied to USI elements to make the purpose of the input understandable to users. An individual FIN or USI element is comprised of a type and any applicable characteristics.

Both the FIN and USI models have three major components:

- *Types*: The FIN Types are the raw data or other input that a system needs, whereas the USI Types are user- understandable forms of data and other input.

- *Characteristics*: The FIN/USI Characteristics define the manner in which the FIN/USI types must be provided.
- *Groups*: The FIN Groups identify data that must be grouped together for submission on the functionality end, while the USI Groups organize and provide context to the user input.

In short, the FIN/USI types are what a system needs and a user must provide, the FIN/USI characteristics are how the inputs are provided, and the FIN/USI groups are how the inputs are organized and submitted.

FIN Types. The FIN Types are a hierarchical organization of the types of input that functionality needs (see Fig. 2).

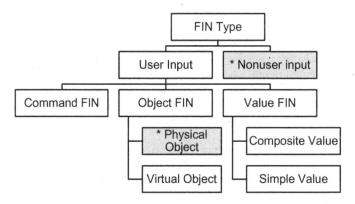

Fig. 2. Hierarchical class diagram of the upper levels of the Functionality Input Need (FIN) Types. Classes that are not the focus of the paper (Nonuser and Physical Object Input classes) are marked with asterisks and shaded. They are included in the FIN model for completeness.

The input to a system may come from the user or from non-user sources (e.g., data from sensors, such as GPS, from network sources, or other channels). The User Input FIN type can be further broken down into Command, Object, and Value FIN types. With Command FINs a system requires a request or command to be issued by the user for the system to enact some functionality. With Object FINs a system requires physical (objects, environments, or events in the real physical world—for example, a copier needs paper) or virtual objects (data or files) for functionality. Physical objects (such as using a biometric scanner, loading paper into a copier, having a voice recorded for speaker recognition, providing printed text for optical character recognition and translation, or use of a specific physical control) have inherent barriers to some people with disabilities that cannot easily be ameliorated with software-based changes to an interface. Value FINs are variables or data that a system accepts as input and are among the most common types of input. These values are understandable to the system and may or may not be understandable to users in their raw form. Simple Value FINs correspond to atomic data types that a system accepts, including Boolean, text, and scalar values. Composite Value FINs are comprised of other Value FINs. For example, an ISO-8601-format date-time FIN is a Scalar FIN with a representation like "2007-01-06T15:20:55-06:00". Another system might use a different date-time scale, such as a UNIX-epoch-date-time FIN (also a Scalar FIN) with a representation like "1168118455". As another example, systems that need the user to input a color might internally use different representations of color with different color models: for example, RGB, RGBA, HSV, HSL, CMYK, and others (which are all Composite Value FINs with multiple Scalar FINs along different dimensions) or color spaces such as Pantone, which can be described with ID numbers (which is a type of Text FIN). Value FIN types are practically unlimited because they must meet the specific needs of a system's functionality which may vary broadly between systems.

An interface generator based solely on FINs does not meet Goal 1 (because FINs may not be understandable in raw form to users) or Goal 3 (because there are a practically infinite variety of FIN types). Instead, it is proposed that an interface generator use the USI Types, which are limited in number, and which can be converted with transformation functions to fulfill the FIN Types.

USI Types. The USI Types are a hierarchical organization of types of basic input that are understandable to users (see Fig. 3). It is restricted to user input that can be provided through software-based interactors. The USI Type model does not fulfill the Nonuser Input and Physical Object FIN Types because those needs cannot be met with the software-based interactors of PAUIs. The USI types can be used to fulfill FINs directly or with transformation functions (which are discussed later).

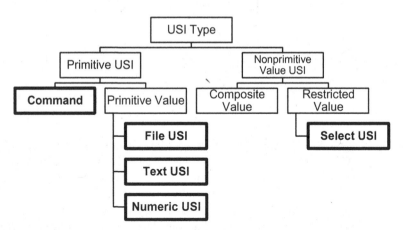

Fig. 3. Hierarchical class diagram of the User-Sensible Input (USI) Types. Classes marked in bold (Command, File, Text, Numeric, and Select USIs) are base USI types.

There are two categories of input in the USI model: Primitive and Nonprimitive USIs. Primitive USIs are atomic inputs that cannot be subdivided further into multiple user-sensible inputs. Nonprimitive USIs are composed of other Value USIs, and some are included as base USIs, which must be supported by all UI generators because they are very common in user interfaces.

A Primitive USI can be either a Command USI or a Primitive Value USI. The Command USI directly fulfills the Command FIN as a request or command issued by the user. In UIs, there are many ways by which users may issue a command: for example, they may click a button or menu item on the screen, press a shortcut key combination on a keyboard, make a gesture or swipe on a touchscreen, or enter a command at a prompt.

The Primitive Value USI class is further subdivided into three types of input: File, Text, and Numeric USIs. A File USI is a reference to a data file or an entity in a specific file that a system needs as input. The File USI directly fulfills the Virtual Object FIN. A Text USI is a string of character data that a system needs to function, and directly fulfills the Text FIN. A Numeric USI is any rational number that can be represented in decimal form. With appropriate transformations, Numeric USIs can be used to fulfill many types of Scalar FINs.

The USI Types are further extensible by creating Nonprimitive USIs in two ways: by specifying validation rules which restrict the values of one of the base types (Restricted Value USIs) or by defining Composite USIs which are composed of multiple Value USIs. A Composite USI is a group of related Value USIs that can be used to model more complex FIN types that can be decomposed into individual atomic values. For example, a system may need a date in ISO 8601 extended format, such as "2009-04-04." While the date could be directly entered by the user in that form as a Text USI, in many cases, it would be better to use a Composite USI with the date split into three atomic Primitive Value USIs: year, month, and day.

Restricted Value USIs can be defined by restricting the values of Primitive Value USIs. There are many ways of restricting values, but one of the most important and common restrictions is enumerating all possible values so that users must select from that list—a Select USI. A Select USI can fulfill a Simple Value FIN directly (e.g., selecting a mode from a list) or through a name-value pair transformation function if that is more understandable to users (e.g., a user picks names from a list which are then transformed to the database ID numbers associated with each name). In mainstream UIs, there are many ways to make a selection, including choosing an option from a drop-down menu, clicking radio buttons or checkboxes on a form, keying a code for an item from a vending machine, or using a touch-tone phone to choose an option in an automated voice menu system.

Interface generators must at a minimum support all the base USI types. Interface generators may also optionally support some extended USI types with specialized interactors, especially for common types of entry with widely-used interface generators. For example, a Date Composite USI (which contains the primitive USIs: year, month, and day), could have its own interactor for some platforms and PAUIs. A specialized date-interactor might look like a calendar picker for some users and a set of dropdown menus for others. Not all generators will have specialized interactors for a given extended USI, however. In these cases, users will use the interactors associated with the base USIs.

FIN & USI Characteristics. The FIN and USI models share the same characteristics, which relate to the manner in which input must be provided to the system in order to be accepted.

Input Cardinality and Order. Input cardinality is the count of the number of individual object or value inputs that a system requires or allows. Minimum cardinality is the minimum number of values/objects that are required for valid input. FIN/USI elements with a minimum cardinality of 0 are optional. The maximum cardinality characteristic defines the maximum number of values or objects that can be input. For example, "Vote for up to 5 candidates," has a minimum cardinality of 0 and maximum cardinality of 5.

For multiple inputs, the order of the values may or may not be important to the system's functionality—the order dependent FIN/USI characteristic. For example, the order of input is important if users are supposed to rank their choices or provide a two-dimensional path, which is a series of XY values.

Input Time Dependence. Time dependence is an important characteristic of input that can be applied to all FINs and USIs. Input is time dependent if the meaning or success of the user's input depends on when the input is submitted. If the same input submitted at a different time or for a different length of time, yields a different effect, it is time dependent. There are three types of time dependence: (1) *none*, where there is no time dependence; (2) *momentary*, where only the moment of time at which the command is activated or value is submitted is important; and (3) *continuous*, where values require continuous control or adjustment.

Input Validity. To function properly, a system needs values that are valid. There are many possible ways to validate data ranging from very simple rules to extraordinarily complex algorithms that rely on formulas that relate multiple values and internal state variables. From the system's perspective, an invalid value simply needs to be replaced by a valid one, but things are more complicated from the user's perspective. Users need to know the location of invalid values, what they did wrong, and what types of values are expected. Note that validation properties may be different between a FIN and related USIs where there is a transformation between different FIN and USI value domains.

Validation can always be handled by notifying the user what inputs have invalid values with a helpful error message. However, it is better to prevent user input errors than to have the users fix errors after making them [22]. Many interactors prevent users from entering invalid data: for example, a slider widget does not allow a user to enter a value that is outside of a defined range. Despite the practically infinite number of methods of validation, there are some that are very common. Numeric values may be bounded by maximum and minimum values and further validated by conforming to a fixed step size between subsequent valid values. Text values may be validated by being compared to minimum or maximum string lengths and to regular expression patterns. Enumeration, which forms the Select USI base type, is a particularly common and important method of validation that allows for convenient interactors that list the available choices.

FIN & USI Groups. All but the simplest user interfaces have groups or container elements (such as screens, windows, dialog boxes, toolbars, tabs, and fieldsets) that are used to structure and organize the elements. Some functionality requires several inputs to be provided simultaneously—these are FIN groups. USI groups may also group simultaneous input, but they can also provide structure to make a UI potentially less cluttered and easier to understand and use. Groups can be nested to further organize the input.

There are three types of groupings in the model. A *semantic group* is a USI-only group that contains USI elements that are grouped in a logical manner to provide context and aid understanding. A *simultaneous group* is a set of time-dependent FIN or USI elements that must all be available to the user at the same time. A *submission group* is a set of non-time-dependent, value FIN or USI elements that must be submitted simultaneously to the system at the same time for validation, processing, or other reasons. Both simultaneous groups and semantic groups agglomerate elements that should be in the same interaction context (e.g., controls that must be on the screen at the same time or that make sense as a coherent whole). In contrast, submission groups do not require all elements to be in the same interaction context; the elements may instead be in a sequence, such a wizard interface, if that is what a user needs or prefers.

USI Semantic Resources. The USI elements are input that a user understands. However, a user also needs to know the purpose and context of their input. The functionality does not need these semantics, but users need them to understand an interface. This information can be provided to users through semantic resources: instructions, helpful error messages when invalid data is submitted, group titles, and input labels. These semantic resources are task specific and may also be specific to a particular language, culture, and output modality. Semantic resources for a USI element can potentially be provided in multiple versions, which might have different lengths and modalities (e.g., abbreviated text suitable for a small screen or dynamic braille; long, descriptive text; and icons as labels). An interface generator could choose the most appropriate resource from the multiple versions.

Labels and titles are an important way to help users understand the current context and what input they are to provide. Labels are required in accessibility standards (e.g., [5, 18]). Each USI element should have a label so the person knows the purpose of the element's input. A Composite USI must have a label for the composite and each Primitive Value USI (e.g., "Birthday" for a date Composite USI and then "Year," "Month," and "Day" for the primitive inputs).

Transformations: FIN-USI Relationships. A USI and a FIN may have a one-to-one relationship or there may be multiple FINs or USIs that are related to each other. A USI is sensible to users by definition; however, systems only understand the FIN-form of input, which may or may not be the same as the USI form. A transformation layer is necessary to convert one or more USIs to one or more FINs. It is envisioned that the transformation layer would be provided by the manufacturers, but third parties could potentially define alternative transformation functions from USIs to FINs. The transformation layer is not a new concept; in software, it is common to check, transform, and normalize user input into something that is useful to the system.

There are several possible relationships between FIN and USI elements. With a direct relation, the USI is the same as the FIN (identity transformation). Other USIs and FINs may have a one-to-one relationship but require a transformation from one value domain to the other. Many-to-one relationships are also possible. In the most frequent case, multiple USIs may be transformed and combined into a single FIN (e.g., the components of a date into a single date entity in the proper format). It is also possible that a single Text USI be parsed to fulfill several FINs, although parsing may be problematic if the user's input is not in the expected form. It is also possible to define multiple, alternative USIs to fulfill a FIN. An interface generator would pick the one that is the best fit for the user. For example, a system might internally represent time in a 24-hour format: one USI might be the original 24-hour format while an alternative USI might allow for 12-hour time entry with an AM or PM designation.

3.3 Application of the FIN-USI Model

The two-sided nature of the FIN-USI model makes explicit the separation between the input needs of systems' functionality and what the user must do to provide those inputs. The USI-side of the model may be used as a base vocabulary of modality-independent inputs for an abstract UI. The USI elements can straightforwardly be applied to typical form input widgets found in GUIs. The USI model can also be used to describe other types of input that do not fit into a form fill-in interaction style. See Table 1 for examples of the USI model applied to different types of input.

Table 1. The USI model applied to various user inputs.

Input or task GUI widgets	USI type	Card. Min.	Card. Max.	Order Dep.	Time Dep.
Form input: Text GUI: single & multi-line text fields, command line prompt	Text	0 or 1	1	–	None
Form input: Numeric GUI: text box, spinner, or slider	Number	0 or 1	1	–	None
Form input: single selection GUI: drop-down list, listbox, or radio buttons	Select	0 or 1	1	–	None
Form input: multiple selection GUI: multi-select listbox or checkboxes	Select	n_1 $(n_1 \geq 0)$	n_2 $(n_2 \geq 2,$ $n_2 \geq n_1,)$	False	None
Form input: Date (YYYY-MM-DD) GUI: text field, text fields & drop-downs set, or calendar picker	Composite: Number, Select, Number	0 or 1	1	–	None
Drawing program: Path of xy-coordinates	Composite: Number, Number	1	∞	True	None
Teleconferencing: Hand-raising functionality	Command	–	–	–	Momentary
Live auction: Bidding	Number	1	1	–	Momentary
Voting: Select up to 3 candidates	Select	0	3	False	None
Voting: Select & rank up to 3 candidates (rank voting system)	Select	0	3	True	None
Basic driving: simultaneous control over (1) wheel angle, (2) brake pressure, & (3) throttle.	Simultaneous group: Number, Number, Number	1, 1, 1	1, 1, 1	–	Continuous (×3)

For each example, the table lists the USI Type along with the USI characteristics: cardinality minimum, cardinality maximum, order dependence, and time dependence.

3.4 Inherent Task-Related Barriers to Access

It has been recognized that certain types of tasks cannot currently be made accessible to people across disabilities [40]. With current technology, we do not know yet how to create interfaces or interactors that allow access to some kinds of input, for example time-dependent input.

Time dependence can be one of the main barriers to accessibility. With some forms of input (such as scanning), there is no known way for users to provide the input in the expected time frame with the expected level of accuracy, especially when input is time dependent in a continuous manner. These barriers may be caused by a wide variety of factors that cannot easily be mitigated by changing an interface's interactors. Some people move more slowly than average because of physical disabilities. Those who must use an interface in which they navigate and step through options are typically slower than those who can directly select options or commands with a mouse or touchscreen. Some people might be using interaction styles that have their own time dependence (such as automatic scanning interfaces) and they cannot generate input at any arbitrary rate. Getting information through speech output or reading braille is inherently slower in many situations than looking at a screen and reading text.

The need for simultaneous input (i.e., FIN/USI simultaneous groupings of inputs) can also be a barrier to accessibility. These interactions are time-dependent and also require a person to manipulate two or more controls at the same time. Some people can only easily manipulate one control at a time because of paralysis or other physical disabilities. Other people can only focus on one task and control at a time and would have difficulty trying to coordinate interactions with multiple controls.

4   Comparison to Existing Models

Existing models for the generation of user interfaces cover basic form and data entry interfaces well. However, they have poor coverage of other forms of input. The FIN-USI model was created to address this systematic shortcoming. Table 2 is a comparison of several UI models. The USI model has fewer base input types than other models, which was a conscious decision (Goal 3). Having more input types is both a benefit and a liability: more differentiation potentially allows for finer control and tuning of interfaces to fit particular types of input, but it also increases the number of interactors that must be created in order to support the differentiated input. For people with uncommon disabilities and for those who need novel methods of interaction, it is likely that relatively few interactors will be available or be created. The number of types is not the main difference of note between the USI and other models however.

The set of FIN-USI characteristics are a novel contribution of the model. Most other models allow for multiple selections, but, except for UsiXML and limited HTML input elements, the models do not allow for multiple inputs (i.e., cardinality maximums greater than 1) of arbitrary data. The order of multiple input values (the order dependence characteristic) may be important in some cases. Only the UsiXML abstract user interface model [39] captured this consideration, but only for a specific array datatype. The time-dependence of an input is also an important consideration which may preclude some interactors and indicate others. The other models do not natively support timed input except implicitly with a command, trigger, or button input that could be used to invoke a command or submit values at a point in time. Timed input can potentially be added to

Table 2. A comparison of selected interface models.

Model	Comments	Input elements in model	Cardinality support	Order Dep. support	Time Dep. support
HTML 5 [30]	A few of the input elements in HTML are redundant and serve the same purpose.	26 input elements	/	0	/
WAI-ARIA 1.0 [32]	WAI ARIA specifies non-abstract input roles that can annotate controls. States and properties can be applied to modify their features.	12 input roles	/	0	/
XForms 1.1 [31]	XForms has a limited number of core input elements, but may rely on additional extended datatypes, which are not specified in XForms.	9 core input form control elements	/	0	/
XML Schema datatypes [34]	While not a standard for UI models, the XML Schema Datatypes are used in other specifications, such as that of URC (ISO/IEC: 24752:2014)	44 built-in datatypes	/	0	0
UsiXML AUI model [41]	UsiXML has many layers. Applicable abstract UI layer components are considered here.	13 abstract input interaction units	X	/	/
PUC [42]	The PUC specification language was designed to support UI generation for appliances.	8 inputs	0	0	/
SUPPLE [43]	The focus of the SUPPLE project was not on modeling UIs but on generating GUIs from a declarative model.	7 primitive inputs	/	0	/
USI	A USI input element is fully specified by a base input (or composites) and its characteristics.	6 base inputs	X	X	X

Key: X = complete support, / = partial support, 0 = no support for the characteristic.

some interfaces with scripting (e.g., JavaScript in HTML). However, this does not add these time dependencies to the UI model. Without these time dependencies in the UI model, a UI generator would be unable to choose interactors most appropriate to the needs of both the user and the system's functionality.

The two sides of the FIN-USI model also make explicit that users and systems may have different needs. Other models (except for the Common Access Profile) tend to take for granted that the input required by the functionality is already in a user-sensible form. In reality, systems may require input that is not user-understandable in raw form. This model underscores that transformation steps may be required for some input to be understandable to both users and systems.

5   Summary of User Testing

A user study with participants who were blind or blindfolded was conducted to compare interfaces that were automatically generated from the FIN-USI model against both physical interfaces and mobile-device-based interfaces that were manually-created by manufacturers. The experimental design and results are detailed in an accompanying paper (Part 2, in this volume), but are summarized here.

Two FIN-USI interface generators were created, both of which created self-voicing interfaces for a mobile PAUI device for people who could not see. Participants tried different interactors for various USI types and chose their favorite interactors. The interface generator then used each participant's favorite interactors to generate personalized interfaces for two products: a copier and a thermostat. As part of a factorial experiment, participants tried a series of tasks on four interfaces: the physical interface of the products, a manufacturer-created interface for a mobile device used in conjunction with a screen reader, and the two self-voicing auto-generated interfaces.

With a study of 24 participants (12 blind and 12 blindfolded), all the measured usability metrics indicated that participants were better with the FIN-USI auto-generated interfaces than either of the manufacturer-created ones—including one (the web-based interface for the copier) that was specifically designed to be used in conjunction with screen readers. Participants were successful more often, and felt that tasks were easier on the auto-generated interfaces. Participants also rated the auto-generated interfaces as significantly more usable and preferred over either of the manufacturer-created ones (including the one specifically designed by the manufacturer for use without sight).

6   Conclusion

There has been significant work done in the field of model-based UI generation. However, the complexity and general inadequacy of current UI models have hindered their real-world usage, which would have benefits for people with disabilities. Complex models make both the creation of product-specific abstract UIs and the creation of specialized interface generators more complex. Furthermore, models are inadequate when they cannot cover the range of inputs that devices require. The FIN-USI model is a simpler model of input that builds on existing work by proposing a set of characteristics that can be applied to different input types to support more paradigms of input. A simpler-to-implement, yet broader application model, such as the FIN-USI model, may be more attractive to industry. Furthermore, the USI model might itself be used as a base abstract user interface model for input to a system, or the concepts may be used in the development of new or revised abstract UI modeling languages.

Acknowledgements. The contents of this paper are based on work carried out with funding from the National Institute on Disability, Independent Living, and Rehabilitation Research, U.S. Department of Health and Human Services, grant number H133E080022 (RERC on Universal Interface and Information Technology Access). However, the contents do not necessarily represent the policy nor imply endorsement by the funding agencies.

References

1. Vanderheiden, G.C.: Accessible and usable design of information and communication technologies. In: Stephanidis, C. (ed.) The Universal Access Handbook, pp. 3-1–3-26. CRC Press, Boca Raton (2009). doi:10.1201/9781420064995-c3
2. Vanderheiden, G.: Fundamental principles and priority setting for universal usability. In: Proceedings on the 2000 Conference on Universal Usability, pp. 32–37. ACM, New York (2000). doi:10.1145/355460.355469
3. Caldwell, B., Cooper, M., Reid, L.G., Vanderheiden, G., Chisholm, W., Slatin, J., White, J. (eds.): Web Content Accessibility Guidelines (WCAG) 2.0 (2008). http://www.w3.org/TR/WCAG20/
4. Gibson, B.: Enabling an accessible web 2.0. In: Proceedings of the 2007 International Cross-Disciplinary Conference on Web Accessibility (W4A), pp. 1–6. ACM, New York (2007). doi: 10.1145/1243441.1243442
5. Gonzalez, A., Reid, L.G.: Platform-independent accessibility API: accessible document object model. In: Proceedings of the 2005 International Cross-Disciplinary Workshop on Web Accessibility (W4A), pp. 63–71. ACM, New York (2005). doi:10.1145/1061811.1061824
6. Watson, L., McCathie Nevile, C.: Accessibility APIs: a key to web accessibility. http://www.smashingmagazine.com/2015/03/web-accessibility-with-accessibility-api/
7. Gajos, K.Z., Weld, D.S., Wobbrock, J.O.: Automatically generating personalized user interfaces with Supple. Artif. Intell. **174**, 910–950 (2010). doi:10.1016/j.artint.2010.05.005
8. Meixner, G., Paternò, F., Vanderdonckt, J.: Past, present, and future of model-based user interface development. i-Com **10**, 2–11 (2011). doi:10.1524/icom.2011.0026
9. Myers, B., Hudson, S.E., Pausch, R.: Past, present, and future of user interface software tools. ACM Trans. Comput. Hum. Interact. **7**, 3–28 (2000). doi:10.1145/344949.344959
10. Nichols, J., Chau, D.H., Myers, B.A.: Demonstrating the viability of automatically generated user interfaces. In: Proceedings of the SIGCHI Conference on Human Factors in Computing Systems, pp. 1283–1292. ACM, New York (2007). doi:10.1145/1240624.1240819
11. Pfaff, G.E. (ed.): User Interface Management systems, Proceedings of IFIP/EG Workshop on UIMS. Springer, Heidelberg (1985)
12. Krasner, G.E., Pope, S.T.: A cookbook for using the model-view controller user interface paradigm in smalltalk-80. J. Object Oriented Program. **1**, 26–49 (1988)
13. Potel, M.: MVP: model-view-presenter, the Taligent programming model for C++ and Java (1996). http://citeseerx.ist.psu.edu/viewdoc/download?doi=10.1.1.189.782&rep=rep1&type=pdf
14. Smith, J.: Patterns-WPF apps with the Model-View-ViewModel design pattern. MSDN Mag. **24**, 26–49 (2009)
15. Hayes, P.J., Szekely, P.A., Lerner, R.A.: Design alternatives for user interface management systems based on experience with COUSIN. SIGCHI Bull. **16**, 169–175 (1985). doi: 10.1145/1165385.317488
16. Calvary, G., Coutaz, J., Thevenin, D., Bouillon, L., Florins, M., Limbourg, Q., Souchon, N., Vanderdonckt, J., Marucci, L., Paternò, F., Santoro, C.: The CAMELEON Reference Framework (2002). http://giove.isti.cnr.it/projects/cameleon/pdf/CAMELEON%20D1.1RefFramework.pdf
17. Calvary, G., Coutaz, J., Thevenin, D., Limbourg, Q., Bouillon, L., Vanderdonckt, J.: A unifying reference framework for multi-target user interfaces. Interact. Comput. **15**, 289–308 (2003). doi:10.1016/S0953-5438(03)00010-9

18. Peissner, M., Häbe, D., Janssen, D., Sellner, T.: MyUI: generating accessible user interfaces from multimodal design patterns. In: Proceedings of the 4th ACM SIGCHI Symposium on Engineering Interactive Computing Systems, pp. 81–90. ACM, New York (2012). doi: 10.1145/2305484.2305500

19. Olsen Jr., D.R.: A programming language basis for user interface. In: Proceedings of the SIGCHI Conference on Human Factors in Computing Systems, pp. 171–176. ACM, New York (1989). doi:10.1145/67449.67485

20. Vander Zanden, B., Myers, B.A.: Automatic, look-and-feel independent dialog creation for graphical user interfaces. In: Proceedings of the SIGCHI Conference on Human Factors in Computing Systems, pp. 27–34. ACM, New York (1990). doi:10.1145/97243.97248

21. Szekely, P.A., Sukaviriya, P.N., Castells, P., Muthukumarasamy, J., Salcher, E.: Declarative interface models for user interface construction tools: the MASTERMIND approach. In: Proceedings of the IFIP TC2/WG2.7 Working Conference on Engineering for Human-Computer Interaction, pp. 120–150. Chapman & Hall Ltd., London (1996)

22. Bodart, F., Hennebert, A.-M., Leheureux, J.-M., Provot, I., Sacré, B., Vanderdonckt, J.: Towards a Systematic building of software architecture: the TRIDENT methodological guide. In: Palanque, P., Bastide, R. (eds.) Design, Specification and Verification of Interactive Systems '95, pp. 262–278. Springer, Vienna (1995)

23. Paternò, F.: Model-Based Design and Evaluation of Interactive Applications. Springer, London (2000)

24. Mori, G., Paternò, F., Santoro, C.: Design and development of multidevice user interfaces through multiple logical descriptions. IEEE Trans. Softw. Eng. 30, 507–520 (2004). doi: 10.1109/TSE.2004.40

25. Paternò, F., Santoro, C., Spano, L.D.: MARIA: a universal, declarative, multiple abstraction-level language for service-oriented applications in ubiquitous environments. ACM Trans. Comput. Hum. Interact. 16, 19:1–19:30 (2009). doi:10.1145/1614390.1614394

26. Guerrero Garcìa, J., Vanderdonckt, J., Gonzàlez Calleros, J.M.: FlowiXML: a step towards designing workflow management systems. Int. J. Web Eng. Technol. 4, 163–182 (2008). doi: 10.1504/IJWET.2008.018096

27. Montero, F., López-Jaquero, V.: IdealXML an interaction design tool. In: Calvary, G., Pribeanu, C., Santucci, G., Vanderdonckt, J. (eds.) Computer-Aided Design of User Interfaces V, pp. 245–252. Springer, Dordrecht (2007)

28. Nichols, J., Myers, B.A., Higgins, M., Hughes, J., Harris, T.K., Rosenfeld, R., Pignol, M.: Generating remote control interfaces for complex appliances. In: Proceedings of the 15th Annual ACM Symposium on User Interface Software and Technology, pp. 161–170. ACM, New York (2002). doi:10.1145/571985.572008

29. Schwerdtfeger, R.S.: Making the GUI talk. BYTE, 118–128 (1991)

30. Hickson, I., Berjon, R., Faulkner, S., Leithead, T., Navara, E.D., O'Connor, E., Pfeiffer, S. (eds.): HTML5 (2014). http://www.w3.org/TR/2014/REC-html5-20141028/

31. Boyer, J.M. (ed.): XForms 1.1 (2009). http://www.w3.org/TR/2009/REC-xforms-20091020/

32. Craig, J., Cooper, M., Pappas, L., Schwerdtfeger, R., Seeman, L. (eds.): Accessible rich internet applications (WAI-ARIA) 1.0 (2014). http://www.w3.org/TR/2014/REC-wai-aria-20140320/

33. Zimmermann, G., Vanderheiden, G.: Use of user interface sockets to create naturally evolving intelligent environments. In: Proceedings of the 11th International Conference on Human-Computer Interaction (HCII 2005). Lawrence Erlbaum Associates, Las Vegas (2005)

34. Biron, P.V., Halhotra, A. (eds.): XML Schema Part 2: Datatypes Second Edition (2004). http://www.w3.org/TR/2004/REC-xmlschema-2-20041028/

35. Zimmermann, G., Jordan, J.B., Thakur, P., Gohil, Y.: GenURC: generation platform for personal and context-driven user interfaces. In: Proceedings of the 10th International Cross-Disciplinary Conference on Web Accessibility, pp. 6:1–6:4. ACM, New York (2013). doi: 10.1145/2461121.2461139

36. Shneiderman, B., Plaisant, C.: Designing the user interface: strategies for effective human-computer interaction. Addison-Wesley, Boston (2010)

37. Foley, J.D., Wallace, V.L., Chan, P.: The human factors of computer graphics interaction techniques. IEEE Comput. Graph. Appl. **4**, 13–48 (1984)

38. Buxton, W.: Lexical and pragmatic considerations of input structures. SIGGRAPH Comput. Graph. **17**, 31–37 (1983)

39. Card, S.K., Mackinlay, J.D., Robertson, G.G.: The design space of input devices. In: Proceedings of the SIGCHI Conference on Human Factors in Computing Systems, pp. 117–124. ACM, New York (1990). doi:10.1145/97243.97263

40. Jordan, J.B., Vanderheiden, G.C.: Modality-independent interaction framework for cross-disability accessibility. In: Rau, P.L.P. (ed.) CCD 2013. LNCS, vol. 8023, pp. 218–227. Springer, Heidelberg (2013). doi:10.1007/978-3-642-39143-9_24

41. UCL ed: D1.3: UsiXML Definition (UsiXML Deliverable) v 1.4.3 (2013). https://itea3.org/project/workpackage/document/download/1583/08026-UsiXML-WP-1-D13v3UsiXMLDefinition.pdf

42. Nichols, J., Myers, B.A., Litwack, K., Higgins, M., Hughes, J., Harris, T.K.: Describing appliance user interfaces abstractly with XML. In: Proceedings of the Workshop on Developing User Interfaces with XML: Advances on User Interface Description Languages, Gallipoli, Italy, pp. 9–16 (2004)

43. Gajos, K.: SuppleType: Supple API (2005). https://www.cs.washington.edu/ai/supple/docs/edu/washington/cs/supple/rep/SuppleType.html

Representing Meaning in User Experience by Visualizing Empirical Data

Eui Chul Jung[1] and Eun Jeong Kim[2(✉)]

[1] Seoul National University, YeSulkwan #49-303, Gwanak-ro 1, Gwanak-gu,
Seoul 151-742, Korea
jech@snu.ac.kr
[2] Yonsei University, Samsungkwan #703, 262 Seongsanno, Seodaemungu, Seoul 120-749, Korea
eunjeong@yonsei.ac.kr

Abstract. The study aimed to represent insightful meaning in user experiences by transforming empirical data into visible structural formats in a variety of aspects. To achieve the goal, components of user experience and the process of information visualization from the literature were reviewed. The general process consists of four steps: (1) defining the dimension to construct the data structure, (2) setting the topology to develop the visual structure, (3) giving the relation among the plotted data on the topological map, and (4) integrating the maps to find insightful data patterns by extending and modifying the visual structure. A case study was conducted to demonstrate how the process can be applied. The finding shows how the components and structure have been organized and transformed to provide perceivable information for user experience design.

Keywords: Visualization · Data transformation · User experience · User centered design · Design methodology

1 Introduction

In the current situation of design paradigm shifting from the technology-focused platform to the human-centered platform (Krippendorff 2006), designers are making every effort to understand the problematic situation of users' complex and undefined experiences for better problem-solving. Citing Mitchell's (1993) argument, Redström (2006) explained that design should be focused, not on the problem of a product itself, but on the user experience based on the rich knowledge and deep understanding of the user. Hassenzahl and Tractinsky (2006) devoted their efforts to researching the user experience and emphasized the importance of understanding user experience and applying the insights to the design process.

Wright and McCarthy (2010) asserted that designers should have a holistic approach that human emotion, knowledge, and activity is handled as a comprehensive and inseparable model, instead of a separate analysis of each entity, if they are to view and understand the diverse aspects of user experience in a problematic situation. To have a holistic approach to the user experience, Owen (2007) introduced a few capabilities that designers should adopt, including a perspective focusing on humans and surrounding

© Springer International Publishing AG 2017
J. Zhou and G. Salvendy (Eds.): ITAP 2017, Part I, LNCS 10297, pp. 147–159, 2017.
DOI: 10.1007/978-3-319-58530-7_10

environment, a tendency toward versatility, a subjective use of language, a friendly bond for good teamwork, a combination of potential components instead of making a decision among the imperfect and inflexible answers, and flexibility and communicability through visualization (Razzouk and Shute 2012).

To view the problem in a structured frame, the ability to visualize plays an important role. Visualization can work as an effective medium to transform the abstract concept into a specific and visible element in an orderly layout by organizing and reconstructing massive information identified from the problematic situation.

Information visualization, which has been applied widely in the computer science research field, is a useful methodology to analyze a large amount of information structurally and to interpret the meaning that arises from the information structure succinctly. This method has great potential for designers to adapt a new problem analysis method in the design process. Information architecture is also a general method to organize, systematize, and visually represent massive amounts of data in various research areas. Garrett (2011) explained that this, as a technical method, could help designers view users' experiences in a visible and structural way.

The main goal of the study was to understand meaning in user experience by transforming empirical data into visible structural formats in a variety of aspects.

To achieve the goal of the study, the research is divided into three phases. In the first phase, we looked at comprehensive characteristics of user experience to understand the main components and sub-components of this construct. The second phase explained the process of information visualization. Finally, in the third phase, we applied the process to the in-class design project how to understand meaning in user experience along with visualizing empirical data.

- Phase 1: Understanding of the components and sub-components of user experience
- Phase 2: Review of the process and the principles of information visualization
- Phase 3: Representing meaning with visualization

2   User Experience

2.1   The Components of User Experience

Many researchers have defined the concept of user experience emphasizing the relationship with context. Alben (1996) viewed user experience as a consequence of the interaction between a user and an object that deals with feelings about a product, a user's level of understanding, emotion aroused while using a product, functionality of a product, and accordance with the context of the product-use environment. Goto (2004) and ISO 9241-210 (2010) explained that user experience is the overall user response to a product, system, service, or interaction.

Among the definitions of user experience, the most frequently adapted definition by other researchers is that of Hassenzahl and Tractinsky (2006). They explained that user experience is a series of comprehensive consequences that result from the combination of a user's internal mentality, an attribute of a system, an environment, or context where interactions take place. Based on previous studies, Law et al. (2009) suggested a comprehensive model of user experience that consists of three essential dimensions: person, artifact and context.

From the review of definitions illustrated above, user experience is a consequence of a user's interaction with a product, service, or system. Most researchers agreed that the critical components of user experience include a user and his/her emotion, an artifact's functionality, technology and aesthetics, a diverse context involving time, space, personality of a user, etc. Therefore, as illustrated in Fig. 1, user experience mainly involves a user, artifact, and context, and these components are not independent from each other but rather are interrelated.

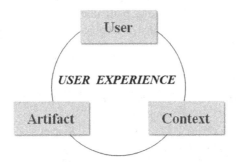

Fig. 1. The three components of user experience: user, artifact, context

According to <User Experience White Paper> (2011), the design elements and assessment criteria in the past have comparatively emphasized the functionality and usability of an artifact, whereas user experience design, at present, focuses on the influence an artifact has on a user and the interpretation of meaning aroused from the interaction between the user and artifact. Supporting this statement, Carlos et al. (2011) explained that successful user experience does not result from the analysis of a big data, but relies on a direct and focused user-centered approach to better identify a problem situation and to better collect problematic information. In summary, the important issue is to collect, analyze, and interpret diverse problematic information in the UX-centered design field.

2.2 The Sub-components of User Experience

The holistic approach in user experience covers from functionality of an artifact to the emotional aspects of a user. <User Experience White Paper> (2011) discussed three components of context, state of a user (motivation, feeling, emotion, expectation, etc.), and system property (from functionality, aesthetics, and response to brand identity) would critically affect user experience, and context could be divided into five sub-categories: social, physical, task, technical, and information context.

Lim and Rogers (2008) divided the design information components into three categories: action, interaction, and object-description. A user's action to an artifact is relevant to an object, location, and time as well as a user and his/her activity. Interaction involves both subject-user and object-user, activity, and time. Object-description refers to information that is relevant to the attributes and functioning of an artifact. They argued that the visualized framework developed based on the above three components could work as a useful lens to organize, save, share, and analyze user experience data.

Goodman et al. (2012) introduced four principles to structure information, people, situations (value, preference, usefulness), activities (level of understanding, satisfaction, a user's skill level), and processes/systems (extra needs, possibility to combine more than two different artifacts).

Carlos et al. (2011) synthesized ideas about the components of user experience and defined the essential components to user experience as following: the user, the artifact (e.g., a product or system), interaction between a user and an artifact, and the context in which a user interacts with an artifact (e.g., particular location and time). They especially emphasized the importance of the context, and categorized it as physical, social, cultural, situational, and temporal.

Table 1. The components of user experience from diverse researchers

UX components	USER	Between user and artifact	Artifact	Context
UX white paper (2011)	User (a person's motivation, mood, current mental and physical resources, and expectations)		System properties (functionality, aesthetics, designed interactive behavior, responsiveness); the properties added or changed in the system, the brand, or the manufacturer's image	Context-social, physical, task, technical, information context-time (before, during, after, long-term)
Carlos et al. (2011)	User	Interaction between user and product	Artifact (product or system)	Context-physical, social, cultural, situational, temporal context
Lim and Rogers (2008)	Action (User, act, object, location, time)	Interaction (Subject-user, act, object-user, tool, time)	Object-description (functionality and attribute)	
Goodman et al. (2012)	People, activity (level of understanding, satisfaction, skill level)		Process or system	Situation-value, preference, usefulness

Based on the various discussions on user experience explained above, the key components of UX can be organized as seen in Table 1. The researchers had slightly different preferences on the terminology, but shared the big picture of the concept that user experience involves a user, an artifact, a context, and an interaction between the user and artifact. The synthesized sub-components for each component of user experience from multiple UX-related authors are classified in Table 2.

Table 2. The UX components & sub-components adapted from UX-related researchers

UX components	USER	Between user & artifact	Artifact	Context
Sub-components	*User's emotion* *User's activity* *User's skill Level*	*Interaction between user and artifact*	*Functionality* *Aesthetics* *Attribute*	*Social context* *Physical context* *Temporal context*-Before/ during/after/ long-term usage *Situational context*

Table 2 shows that the components of user experience are classified into four viewpoints: User, artifact, context, and interaction between the user and the artifact. The user includes both internal and external aspects, such as emotional response and specific activity as well as the user's skill level to access the artifact. Artifact consists of the functionality, aesthetics, and attributes of a product or a system. Context covers diverse aspects, such as social, physical, temporal, situational, etc.

3   Process of Information Visualization

As we discussed in the previous chapter, user experience is constructed from the interaction between a user and an artifact within a diverse context, which results in some meaning. To fully and deeply understand user experience, it is important to interpret the relationship between the entities and the change that occurs during the experience in a comprehensive and holistic way. Cognitive psychologists Restrepo and Christiaans (2004), viewed user experience as a problem-solving process, thus, design can also be considered as a process to find a solution within a problem space. The problem space is not a physical location; rather, it is more like a metaphorical area where diverse problem-solving activities take place. Restrepo and Christiaans explained that this space includes all the information that could be identified in the process of experience, such as information directly related to the problem, information about the transformation from the problem to a solution, and information related to the potential solution. When we apply this viewpoint to the problematic space in design, user, artifact, context, and interaction can be considered as various types of information that construct the experience.

Therefore, making the UX design information structure more intuitive and insightful requires that designers actively adapt the concept of information visualization, which has been widely used as the information analysis method in various fields since Bertin (1967/1983) and Tufte (1983) introduced the method (Card et al. 1999). Dahl et al. (2001) pointed out that visualization has already been playing an important role in the design process; therefore, it could be a useful method to explore the design problem and its potential solution. They also explained that it is possible to create, interpret, and control information by representing the data in the space through visualization.

Visualizing user experience design information effectively requires understanding the visualization mapping process, which consists of three phases (Card et al. 1999). Card et al. (1999) explained that raw data collected from user research can be transformed into a visual structure that we can recognize through the process of visual mapping by applying spatial attributes, signage, graphical components, etc. The visual mapping process can be summarized as follows: (1) Raw data are organized as a data table through data transformation. The data transform from abstract to structural property, including metadata, by classifying data using variables. (2) The data table is again transformed into a visual structure through visual mapping. The transformed visual structure includes both visibility and topological properties by combining them with spatial substrate, mark, and graphical components. (3) The visual structure is specified and developed into a more recognizable structure by applying graphical parameters through the process of viewing the transformation (Card et al. 1999).

Wurman et al. (Wurman et al. 2000) explained that a process of information visualization consists of three steps: (1) classify data by similarity, (2) arranging data by intention or data meanings, (3) organizing and establishing relations amongst data

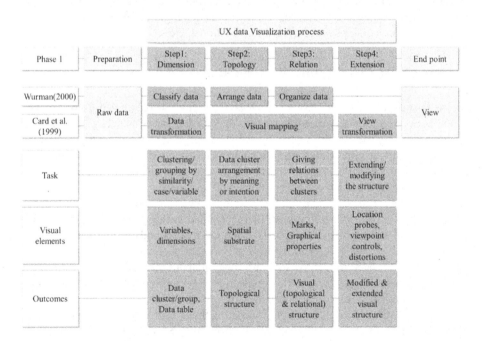

Fig. 2. The process of UX data visualization based on the information visualization process Adapted from the models of Wurman et al. (2000) and Card et al. (1999).

groups or between data entities. By looking at Card et al.'s (1999) model with an overlay of Wurman's processes), visualizing UX data can be inferred as four steps (see Fig. 2) based on the process of information visualization.

The first step in Fig. 2 is a process of transforming UX raw data into a data table. UX raw data can be classified into UX components such as user, artifact, context, and interaction, and their sub-components; these classified UX components are transformed into a data table. In this step, it is important to understand an attribute of data, and then transform that attribute into a proper variable by project or research goals because the variables work as dimensions to transform the data table into a topological structure.

The second step is to transform the data table into a topological structure by applying a spatial substrate. To better interpret UX data, the key principle of this step is to make full use of the visual mapping process that transforms a data table consisting of invisible and non-topological data entities or data clusters into a visual structure that has a visible attribute based on topology. Spatial substrate is an essential element to construct a visual structure, and it plays a key role in transforming non-topological data attributes into a location-based attributes.

The third step is to transform a topology-applied data structure into a more visible structure. In this step, the relations amongst data can be revealed more clearly by organizing the data using marks and graphical properties. Marks create relations and flow amongst location-based attributes to deal with the four types of point, line, area, and volume. Graphical properties help the data of which location and relation are pre-defined to be presented in more structured way using position, gray scale, orientation, color, texture, shape, etc.

The fourth step is to modify the visual structure to add a dynamic visibility using graphical variables such as location probes, viewpoint controls, and distortions. This step enables people to better perceive visual structures by bringing a dynamic interaction between human and data (Card et al. 1999).

4 Case Study: Anti-crime Project at University Area

The case study was used an anti-crime design project for university students living apart from their families, and renting rooms around the university. The goal of this UX design project was to provide students with safety when commuting to and from school. Team members conducted user research on student lifestyles regarding commuting patterns, and followed the design process based on the visualization framework to analyze the UX data. The result led to two meaningful insights drawn from the analysis: (1) a safe zone as a place of refuge in case of an emergency, (2) an easy and quick way-finding system in a winding and narrow alley. The following case study is used to explain the process of applying the visualization framework to the anti-crime design project to assess its practical use and offer a rationale for each step.

Firstly, in the <Dimension> step, the data collected from the UX research on anti-crime for university students was classified into the three UX components: user, artifact, and context. To define sub-components, the dimensions were defined as shown in Table 3 considering the attribute of data and project goal. For the user component, data were classified into the three user types: a student living apart from his/her own family who was the main target of the project, a police officer who was in direct charge of local anti-crime, and an employee working at a store/café/shop during the day and night who had a potential influence on students by frequently interacting with them in business. For the artifact component, all environmental elements that had the possibility to either induce or prevent a crime were included, as were public facilities provided for local anti-crime efforts. As latent elements for safety, business stores and landmarks in the area were also included to the artifact. For the context component, the data were classified into day/night by temporal aspects and main street/alley by the aspect of physical context with consideration for the fact that the crime rate could be highly affected by timeline and locational character.

Table 3. The UX components & sub-components by dimensions regarding safe return home

UX components	Dimension	Sub-component	
User	Main target	Student	-usual path
	Direct influence	Police officer	-daily lifestyle & commuting pattern -emotional state & experience on crime
	Indirect influence	Employee at business store	
Artifact	Safe	Public facility (street light, CCTV)	
	Non-safe	Blind spot, broken/unattended facility	
	Latent/neutral	Business store, landmark	
Context	Temporal	Day/night	
	physical	Main street/alley	

To reach the goal of a safe return home, one must understand the contextual meaning of safety regarding the collected data. In the second step, to interpret the classified data shown in Table 3 from the aspect of safety, two topological spaces were formulated: the geographic map and the Venn diagram. Firstly, as illustrated in Fig. 3, the geographic map was chosen because of the common geographical position of users' paths and the

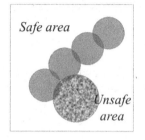

Fig. 3. The two different types of topological map formulated for anti-crime design project: geographic map (left) & Venn diagram (right)

sub-components of the artifact (facility, landmark, stores, etc.), and because the meanings of data could be easily identified by the dimensions of safe/non-safe/potential viewpoints based on the geographical distribution of data on the map.

On the map, the users' paths and locations of artifacts could be visually identified, and temporal/physical contexts at a particular area could be represented using the x and y axes to indicate geographical positions. Secondly, the Venn diagram was used to distinguish relative areas according to the frequency of crime and the degree of anxiety considering that crime rate and users' emotional states could be affected by temporal and locational characters. In this case study, judging from the brightness of light by day and night, the openness and crowdedness of areas, and students' anxiety about crime, the Venn diagram consisted of two different categories: safe versus unsafe areas.

In the third step, the team members actually plotted the UX data on the topological maps formulated in the previous step, and gave visible relations between the data entities. To identify the pattern of data distribution clearly regarding safe/unsafe aspects, the visual structure (see Fig. 4) was developed by overlaying the network map onto the plotted data on the topological map.

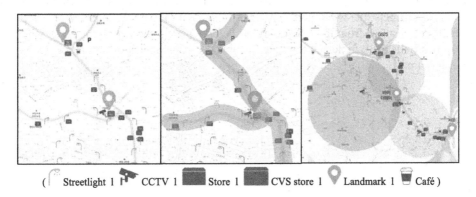

(Streetlight 1   CCTV 1   Store 1   CVS store 1   Landmark 1   Café)

Fig. 4. The visual structures developed with the application of topology and relation: the geographic map (left), the network map (middle), and the Venn diagram (right)

The left and center images in Fig. 4 were partial results of the developed visual structure. The left image shows the location of street lights belonging to the safe element on the geographic map, while the center image represents the overlay of the network map onto geographic map using a thick translucent line following the regular distribution of streetlights. The left image in Fig. 4 also visually represents the locations of stores, landmarks, and CCTV using different icons for each artifact; locations of streetlights are also included. Comparing the left and center images, the topological map (left image) itself does not reveal a meaningful pattern because the plotted data entities were meaninglessly scattered on the map. However, the visual relation given among the data entities, which shared the same attributes, could suddenly reveal a meaningful visible pattern. For example, the network map overlaid onto the topological map in Fig. 4 (middle image) could be interpreted that the regular distribution and high frequency of streetlights work as positive elements for students' safe returns home and correspond mainly to the main streets.

Meanwhile, the right image in Fig. 4 was the result of the Venn diagram distinguishing between the safe and unsafe areas according to crime rate and users' emotional states, which could be affected by the timeline (day and night) and locational characters (openness, crowdedness, etc.). For better distinction between the areas, safe areas with low crime rates and less anxiety is colored in green, while the unsafe areas with relatively high crime rates and more anxiety for crime are colored in red. In summary, by plotting the UX data and visualizing the relation between the data on topological maps, the meanings of data clusters formulated by the dimensions and attributes applied to classify the UX data and the independent meanings of each data entity could be interpreted more clearly.

In the fourth step of <Integration>, to draw meaningful insights from the data patterns for the safe return home, the geographic map with relations and the Venn diagram were integrated into a map using the medium of shared attributes between the visual structures. The geographic map was developed based on the locational attribute of artifacts, and the Venn diagram was formulated using the dimension of safe/unsafe area. Accordingly, the two topological maps turned out to share the attribute of space. The Fig. 5 resulted from the integration of the two maps centering on the geographic map that holistically reflected the space attribute of geographical position and distinguished area.

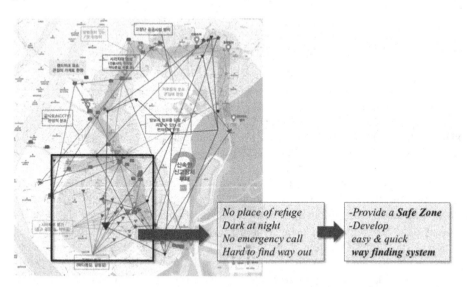

Fig. 5. The integrated analysis map developed through the visualization framework

For example, as shown in Fig. 5, insights were drawn from the integration of the network map for streetlights and convenience stores and the Venn diagram as follows. The streetlights located on the allies were irregularly and rarely distributed unlike those on the main street, which aroused students' anxiety because of blind spots and darkness.

The interesting fact resulting from the integration of the maps was that the convenience stores and the employees could be potential safe places and guards for crime because of their around-the-clock business hours. Referring to this fact, the safe areas (a convenience store, a police station, including the anti-crime checkpoint) for commuting were specifically identified. Accordingly, it was discussed that the design possibility of how a police officer, an employee at a convenience store, and a pedestrian could cooperate in case of an urgent crime in the area. As a result of the discussion, the two key insights drawn were as follows. (1) The safe zone could function as a shelter in case of emergency. In addition, the UX design concepts were discussed on how to transform the blind spots as potentially threatening elements for safety in the safe areas, and how to provide immediate and better access to these potential safe guards and/or places. (2) The easy and quick way-finding system in the potentially unsafe zone, such as narrow and winding allies, was suggested from the visualized analysis. Figure 5 illustrates the final integrated analysis map for the anti-crime project developed through the visualization framework of the four steps in which the plotted UX data regarding anti-crime on the geographic map and the Venn diagram was integrated into a map in relation to the data.

From a review of the first case study, it was found that the meaningful information could be drawn from the data using the visualization framework. It was also revealed that the information could be transformed into the principles for design concept development using integrative interpretation.

The rationale used for the visualization framework in this case study is illustrated in Fig. 6. Firstly, to reach the project goal of safe return home and define the safe zone for university students, the UX data collected from the research were classified into categories by adding dimensions considering the goal. Secondly, both a geographic map capable of representing location of data and a Venn diagram to conceptualize the safe attributes were defined as topology for the primary visualization of UX data. Thirdly, the classified data were plotted onto the map, followed by setting the network relations among the data to reveal the visible data patterns. Finally, the topological maps with relations were integrated into a map centered on the attributes of safety, which led to

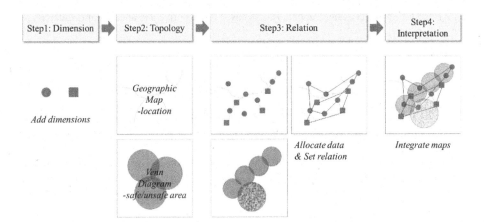

Fig. 6. The rationale used for each step of the visualization framework in case study 1

the integrative interpretation of UX data patterns regarding a safe return home as the project goal.

5 Conclusion

To better interpret the insightful meanings of UX data, this study attempted to establish four-steps-visualization-process. The first step, <Dimension>, constructs the data structure by classifying the UX components into the user, artifact, context, and interaction, with consideration for a project goal. The second step, <Topology>, sets the basic structure of the topological space according to the meaningful attributes of UX components to intuitively interpret the data. The third step, <Relation>, develops the visual structure by giving process or network relations to the topological space with the UX data plotted onto that space. The fourth step, <Integration>, involves the comprehensive interpretation of insightful meanings according to the project goal based on the complex relationships among the data patterns identified from each visual structures as well as the integration of multiple visual structures developed with topology and relation applied in the previous step.

From the above case study, this paper concludes that the four-steps-visualization-process shows the possibility of being applied to a design project in the form of a flexible visual structure with various combinations of topology and relation according to a design goal. It can also be concluded that the process is useful to structurally interpret meaningful insights by visualizing the UX data patterns within the process of each step. Further research should be done to develop a general framework and design toolkit for the visualization process by conducting a variety of case studies and iterating the refinement of the process. It is also expected that various types of methods for interpreting UX data meaning be suggested with examples using a combination of topology and relation according to the UX project goals and subjects.

Acknowledgement. This work was supported by the Ministry of Trade, Industry & Energy (MOTIE, Korea) under Industrial Technology Innovation Program. No. 10060517, 'Development of user-centered product design support system based on cognitive and affective information'.

References

Alben, L.: Quality of experience: defining the criteria for effective interaction design. Interactions **3**(3), 11–15 (1996)

Card, S.K., Mackinlay, J.D., Shneiderman, B.: Readings in information visualization: using vision to think. In: Card, S.K., Mackinlay, J.D., Shneiderman, B. (eds.) Information Display. Morgan Kaufmann, San Francisco (1999)

Carlos, J., Nicolás, O., Aurisicchio, M.: A scenario of user experience. In: International Conference on Engineering Design, ICED11, pp. 1–12 (2011)

Dahl, D.W., Chattopadhyay, A., Gorn, G.J.: The importance of visualisation in concept design. Des. Stud. **22**(1), 5–26 (2001)

Garrett, J.J.: The Elements of User Experience: User-Centered Design for the Web and Beyond, 2nd edn. New Riders, Berkeley (2011)

Goodman, E., Kuniavsky, M., Moed, A.: Observing the User Experience, 2nd edn. Morgan Kaufmann, Waltham (2012)

Goto, K.: Brand value and the user experience. Digital Web Magazine (2004). http://www.digital-web.com

Hassenzahl, M., Tractinsky, N.: User experience-a research agenda. Behav. Inf. Technol. **25**(2), 91–97 (2006)

ISO 9241-210: 2010 Ergonomics of human-system interaction-Part 210: human-centred design for interactive systems. In: International Organization for Standardization ISO, pp. 759–768 (2010)

Krippendorff, K.: The Semantic Turn: A New Foundation for Design. CRC, Boca Raton (2006)

Law, E.L.-C., Roto, V., Hassenzahl, M., Vermeeren, A.P.O.S., Kort, J.: Understanding, scoping and defining user experience: a survey approach. In: Proceedings of the 27th International Conference on Human factors in Computing Systems - CHI 2009, pp. 719–728. ACM Press (2009)

Lim, Y., Rogers, Y.: A framework and an environment for collaborative analysis of user experience. Int. J. Hum. Comput. Interact. **24**(6), 529–555 (2008)

Mitchell, W.J.: A computational view of design creativity. In: Gero, J.S., Maher, M.L. (eds.) Modeling Creativity and Knowledge-Base Creative Design, pp. 25–42. Lawrence Erlbaum Associates, Hillsdale (1993)

Owen, C.: Design thinking: Notes on its nature and use. Des. Res. Q. **2**(1), 16–27 (2007)

Razzouk, R., Shute, V.: What is design thinking and why is it important? Rev. Educ. Res. **82**(3), 330–348 (2012)

Redström, J.: Towards user design? On the shift from object to user as the subject of design. Des. Stud. **27**(2), 123–139 (2006)

Restrepo, J., Christiaans, H.: Problem structuring and information access in design. J. Des. Res. **4**(2) (2004). doi:10.1504/JDR.2004.009842

Roto, V., Law, E., Vermeeren, A., Hoonhout, J.: User experience white paper. Bringing clarity to the concept of user experience (2011)

Seminar, D., Experience, D.U.: User experience white paper. In: Roto, V., Law, E., Vermeeren, A., Hoonhout, J. (eds.) Dagstuhl Seminar on Demarcating User Experience, pp. 1–12. Acta Materialia (2011)

Wright, P., Mccarthy, J.: Experience-centered design: designers, users, and communities in dialogue. Synth. Lect. Hum. Centered Inf. **3**(1), 1–123 (2010)

Wurman, R.S., Leifer, L., Sume, D.: Information Anxiety 2 (Hayden/Que), 2nd edn. Que, Indianapolis (2000)

A Study on Interactive Explanation Boards Design and Evaluation for Active Aging Ecotourism

Li-Shu Lu[(✉)]

Department and Graduate School of Digital Media Design,
National Yunlin University of Science and Technology, Douliou/Yunlin, Taiwan
luls@gemail.yuntech.edu.tw

Abstract. According to the advanced aging society and the change of travel style, the advanced age groups are active in joining ecotourism to increase knowledge and experiences that raise their qualities of living. Therefore a solution to enhance ecotourism experiences of the advanced age group would be a major considera-tion in the future. A tendency of elevating knowledge and experiences of the active aging group with assistance of technology is anticipated. As a consequence the study focus on literature analysis of active aging group, ecotourism, interac-tive design and related design principles. Through a demand investigation, design and building of principle-based interactive interpretive signs prototype, a revised proposal of the prototype design is come up based on user reports regarding eval-uation and review of the interactive prototypes. The study results are as following: (1) A fulfillment of recording, knowledge, safety and convenience of ecotourism is brought to the active aging group through the assistance of technology. (2) From the investigation of technology demand, the study developed consistency, flexi-bility, efficiency, artistic and simplified design, visibility, feedback, attraction, instruction, sustainability, satisfaction, assistance and directions, user control and unrestrained 11 prototype design characteristics. The design and building of interactive interpretive sign prototypes are based on the above characteristics. (3) In accordance with the user report, an induction of "Hardware Performance Issue" of interactive prototypes are able to increase knowledge of the active aging group, so as to improve the height, layout, narration, icons and information guidance, etc. For the interactive narration time design in "Information Media", long time consumption of active aging group in a fixed location should be avoided. It may cause inconvenience to other users. The guiding information should be more detailed and screen size should be increased. The "Interactive Operation" is smooth. Manipulating both graphics and words simultaneously, as well as the efficiency of operation system should improve the guidelines. The listening expe-rience in "Sharing their Experience" is one of the most important elements to enhance the interactive narration quality. As for the vision experience, an advancement of the narration screen and the story content is required. The study results expect to enhance the ecotourism experience of the active aging group, also to provide references for related studies operations.

Keywords: Active aging · Ecotourism · Interactive design · Explanation boards · Usability

© Springer International Publishing AG 2017
J. Zhou and G. Salvendy (Eds.): ITAP 2017, Part I, LNCS 10297, pp. 160–172, 2017.
DOI: 10.1007/978-3-319-58530-7_11

1 Introduction

As predicted by Taiwan government, Taiwan will enter the stage of super population ageing in 2025, with people aged 65 years and over accounting for more than 20% of the population or one of every five people aged 65 years or over (Department of Statistics, Ministry of the Interior 2012). With rapid population ageing and changing demographic structure, the well-being of the aged population group will be increasingly important to the social development of Taiwan. Ecotourism, or tourism that incorporates ecological preservation, is increasingly valued (Lang et al. 2011). The premise of ecotourism is environmental conservation and experiential enhancement, and the ultimate goal is sustainable development. Specifically, ecotourism is a model of tourism that is aimed at educating the tourists environmentally, increasing their environmental awareness, inducing environmentally responsible actions, and finally bringing economic benefits to the local community to enable continuous improvement of preservation efforts and well-being of the local people, with explanation resources play an essential role in realizing the purpose of ecotourism not just helping the tourists understand and appreciate the unique natural and human environment (Wu and Hung 2004; Lin and Weng 2002). Leisure tourism is one of the factors that have impact on life satisfaction and life quality of senior citizens. They take leisure travels mainly for learning and experiential purpose; besides learning and experiencing new things, they may also participate in tourism experience activities for improving emotional bond with their families and friends (Chang et al. 2009; Lee and Liu 2011). Some elderly people are also active in ecotourism, in order to improve knowledge and life quality. The tourism demand of those aged 55–64 and 65–74 is trending high, and these two population groups are becoming more active in social relation activities (Matsubara 2010). Wang and Hsu (2012) indicated that, while the potential demand of the elderly for travelling should be satisfied, the deterioration in their physiological function and cognitive capacity has to be considered. Only with a balance kept between these two aspects can the elderly achieve active ageing through tourism experience. "Le ling zu" (literally people who are happy with their age), originally a respectful address to the elderly in Singapore and Malaysi, is now used to motivate them to learn happily and enjoy actively the ageing process (Wang 2012). Besides, as more of the elderly are using new technology, appropriate application of new technology can improve the experiential and learning appeal of ecotourism and compensate for the physical confinement of the elderly, in order to provide healthy life to the elderly, to increase their social participation level, and to improve their life quality through product development and design (Hsu and Liu 2013). In recent years, the research in application of augmented reality (AR) technology for outdoor navigation is valued across the world (Kuo and Cheng 2008). With Taiwan's initiatives to propel the tourism industry and the changed tourism demand of the elderly, the experiential and learning appeal is becoming an important index of ecotourism service quality. With the elderly's travelling demand for improved leisure quality and learning experience in recent years, a tour guide, when not able to cope with the needs of all of the tourists he is supposed to service, uses outdoor explanation boards for his tour guide service. That is, outdoor explanation boards are used by both tour guides for transmitting knowledge and the elderly tourists for absorbing knowledge. Besides, the elderly take travelling mainly for learning and experience purpose but, owing to deterioration of physiological function, may be faced with obstacles in experiencing the tour guide service. Therefore, this study is aimed at defining the interactive prototype of the elderly's experience with ecotourism explanation boards and optimizing explanation board design with the latest technology. Specifically, the objectives of this study include: analysis of the technology need of the elderly for ecotourism experience; prototype design of technology enabled explanation board as a gadget assisting the elderly in ecotourism experience; and evaluation of interactive explanation board for enhancing the elderly's ecotourism experience.

2   Literature Review

2.1   Active Ageing and Ecotourism

In recent years, the number of elderly tourists has been increasing continuously. In terms of the purposes of their travelling, there have also been obvious changes. In terms of travelling mode, the traditional leisure tourism has developed to experiential tourism that is characterized by aspiration for learning and in-depth understanding (Hsu et al. 2007; Neuhofer 2012). Ecotourism has been increasingly valued across the globe and now is obviously the future development mode pursued by the world tourism industry. The ecotourism of Taiwan started late but has been expanding the fastest among all sectors of the tourism industry (Tourism Bureau 2013; Tsao 2001). The premise of Ecotourism experience activities is environmental conservation and enhanced tourist experience, and the ultimate goal is sustainable development. Centered at simplicity, preservation, appreciation, and spiritual experience, ecotourism is aimed at promoting the latest environmental knowledge to the whole society, educating the tourists environmentally, inducing environmentally responsible actions, and finally bringing economic benefits to the local community to enable continuous improvement of preservation efforts and well-being of the local people, with explanation resources playing an essential role in realizing the purpose of ecotourism, not just helping the tourists understand and appreciate the unique natural and human sites (Wu and Hung 2004; Lin and Weng 2002).

2.2   Experience of Outdoor Interactive Explanation Resources

With technological advancement, Ciavarella C (2004) proposed to apply mobile devices and location detection technology in indoor tour guide service and create an indoor information environment where users can access and share information anytime. Chou et al. used PDS and infra-red devices to detect the location of users in museum tour guide service, and created a mobile learning environment where users can access linguistic and audio information about exhibits (Chou et al. 2004). Institute for Information Industry (2014) found in a study that about 13% of the interviewed used smart phones and about 6.5% used tablet PC, and predicted that, with increasing popularity of smart phones, 52.5% of the population in 2015 will use at least one of the two mobile devices, the driving force for new development of content and service. When a tourist wants to know more about the tourism resources, he can use a mobile device to navigate for tour guide service, which is interactive and always available. As smart phone is becoming increasingly popular, mobile devices will certainly play a more important role in ecotourism on-site service. AR technology is now widely used in outdoor tour guide service, and involves two types of location detection technology: detective device and imaging. Therefore, if the latest technology is incorporated in outdoor explanation board, specifically using the location detection by smart phone imaging, DIY tour guide service will be easy to use for elderly tourists and enable richer and more diversified interactive tour experience.

2.3 Design Principle of Interactive Explanation Device

Norman (1988) argued that, in order to avoid cognitive confusion during the operating process, the operational procedure of a product should be simple and direct and should follow the conceptual pattern of the user. According to Preece, Rogers and Sharp, design principle is the abstract ideas that enable a designer to produce utility, and the many aspects of design principle originates from various theories, basic knowledge, experience, and common sense (Chen 1999). Human Computer Interaction (HCI), one of the most important design principles, is a concept governing the entire process of information system design, and in its essence is about whether the user of an information system can experience good efficiency and reliability (You et al. 2009). As proposed by scholars in the field, the design principles of a product interaction interface include: rich and comprehensive in message, predictable, easy to learn and use, reliable, natural in interaction, and intelligent in application (Norman 2007; Liu 2011). Therefore, the design principles applicable to the design of interaction prototype roughly include controllability and freedom, aesthetic and simple design, coherence, appeal, safety, intuitive and straightforward visual presentation, flexibility, and efficiency, help and illustration, feedback, educational effect, satisfaction, motivation, and continuity. In summary, the elderly has changed their tourism consumption habit from the traditional leisure tourism to the cultural tourism that is characterized by aspiration for learning and in-depth understanding. Technology can help the elderly's physiological and conceptual experience of ecotourism.

In recent years, mobile device enabled QR code technology and AR technology have been used in tour guide service. Especially, AR can effectively appeal to the attention of the elderly, enables real-time interaction, and help build social bond between those with similar life experience. Therefore, AR technology combined with explanation board is used in this study as the enabling technology for outdoor tour guide service.

3 Methods

The study is divided into three stages. At the first stage, the technological needs and principles for ecotourism were confirmed. Tourists to the **Sun-Link-Sea** region (Fig. 1) were observed for their behaviors and interviewed for their needs. The experiential needs for ecotourism was analyzed based on human computer interaction principle and workshops participated by tourists. The principles for explanation board design were preliminarily defined at the first stage. At the second stage, the prototype was built. Based on the analysis conducted at the first stage, interaction prototype was designed and built. At the third stage, the interaction system was valued. Elderly users of the system were observed for how they operated the system for interaction purpose following the typical tasks method and coach method. Also a questionnaire investigation was conducted to collect the trial users' questions about operating the system. Finally, modifications were proposed to improve the system.

Fig. 1. The research filds- Sun-Link-Sea

3.1   Defining Technological Needs and Principles for Ecotourism

Investigation of the Elderly's Mobile Devices and Verification of Needs. First, some elderly tourists (not aware of being observed) were observed for what they did when and where and interviewed for how they were equipped for ecotourism and their opinions. Next, some elderly people participated in an ecotourism travel as research subjects and were interviewed after the travel for their physiological and emotional needs during ecotourism.

Reference Design Principles for Interactive Explanation Board. At this stage, design principles for ecotourism interactive explanation board intended for the elderly were further defined based on research literature on technology enabled explanation board and results of need investigation. These principles served as the starting point for the prototype design and build. See Table 1.

Table 1. Description of design principles

Design principles	Description
User's freedom in control	Simple operating steps and easy to operate
Aesthetic and simple design	Stylistic and content design tuned to the elderly's needs
Coherence	Coherent throughout the system, following certain standard or logic
Appeal	Appealing to the elderly's attention, inducing further reading and learning
Safety	Minimum safety hazards during the operating process
Straightforward presentation	Clear presentation of required devices and information
Flexibility and efficiency	Fast and effective detection of the device
Help and illustration	Providing guidance, easy for the elderly to learn
Feedback	Providing the elderly with audio, visual, sensual, and linguistic information
Educational effect	What the elderly can learn from the presentation
Satisfaction	The elderly is satisfied with the operating experience
Motivation	Able to motivate the elderly to further learning
Continuity	How long an elderly user continuously uses the presentation

3.2   Prototype Build

Prototype Design and Build. APrototype is a person's conceptual system of the form and classification of a certain object, and the conceptual system is characterized by certain level of cognitive impression (Wang and Lee 2005). There are 5 steps in the Prototype build stage (Fig. 2): STEP-01 planning for the interaction prototype: summarized research literature and user needs, defined style and multimedia content, and confirmed interactive operations; STEP-02 hardware build: built hardware according what had been planned at STEP-01; STEP-03 hardware design: incorporated digital media and software into the hardware; STEP-04 preliminary testing: preliminarily adjusted the prototype to the actual onsite environment and confirmed correct functions of the prototype; STEP-05 Prototype sign-off.

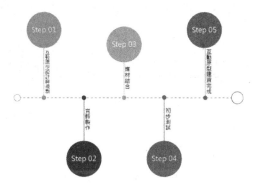

Fig. 2. Development steps of prototype build stage

Operating Steps of Interaction Prototype. There are four steps to operate the proto-type (Fig. 3): STEP-01: Download Aurasma, APP of the tour guide service system via wireless connection; STEP-02: take photograph of the explanation board with smart phone and initiate tour guide service; STEP-03: view the presentation and take photo-graph; STEP-04: share tourism experience on the internet platform. Interview questions for the typical tasks were generated concerning the 4 steps above.

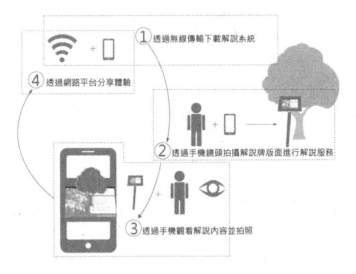

Fig. 3. Four steps to operate the prototype

3.3 Prototype Valuation

Planning for Prototype Valuation. The major activities at this stage included collec-tion of valuation materials, development of valuation criteria, defining typical tasks, development of valuation method, analysis and collection of materials for implementing the valuation, and analysis of usability questions and proposal. as shown in Fig. 4.

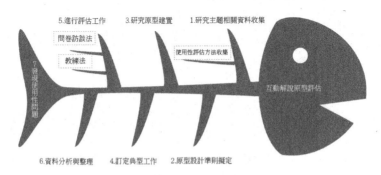

Fig. 4. Process of prototype valuation

Typical Tasks. The typical tasks for operating the prototype were defined as in Table 2. Prototype valuation covered the hardware, interactive operations, and multimedia experience. The usability issues with the interaction prototype were identified through trial use by elderly research subjects.

Table 2. Typical tasks

Step 01	Introduction to the system prototype
Step 02	View the operating steps of the explanation board
Step 03	View the content of the explanation board
Step 04	Start operation with smart phone
Step 05	Click and select interactive tour guide system
Step 06	Click to select presentation of the plant on smart phone screen
Step 07	View the presentation of the plant on smart phone screen
Step 08	Listen to the audio information of the plant
Step 09	Click on the camera function of smart phone
Step 10	Click on the "Share" button
Step 11	Share experience

4 Result and Discussion

4.1 Confirmed Technological Requirements and Principles for Ecotourism

Investigation of the Elderly's Mobile Devices. During the study, 46 groups of elderly tourists were investigated for how they were equipped with mobile devices. The results are: 52% were equipped with smart phone; 7% with non-smart phone; 3% with tablet PC; 29% with digital camera; 6% with both smart phone and digital camera; and 3% with both smart phone and tablet PC. The investigation results showed that most of the elderly had traveled to ecotourism sites and smart phone was more popular than digital camera and tablet PC. That is, smart phone is increasingly popular among the elderly.

Technological Needs of the Elderly. Through retrospective interview the following five aspects were identified in terms of the elderly's technological needs during ecotourism: (1) Need for recording: most of the elderly consumers of ecotourism liked to take individual or group photographs as a means of recording the travelling experience for emotional collection in the future; (2) Need for safety: the elderly are more prone to emergency situation during ecotourism experience activities than your people and thus are worried about safety and prefer traveling destinations where better sense of safety is provided; (3) Need for knowledge: introduction to unique or rare species or scenery beauty can induce the elderly to further learning; (4) Need for convenience: simple operation, comfort, convenience, and easy information can increase the elderly's willingness to learn to use new things; (5) Need for sharing: Some of the elderly took photographs of scenery sites for the purpose of emotional collection in the future, and uploaded the photographs onto internet platform and share the scenery beauty with families and friends.

Defining Design Principles of Interactive Explanation Tools. Design principles were defined on the basis of literature review and needs analysis, including (1) Need for recording: appeal, feedback, (2) Need for safety: safety, satisfaction, (3) Need for knowledge: educational effect, continuity, motivation, aesthetic and simple design, held and illustration, and (4) Need for convenience: visual presentation, user's freedom of control, coherence, flexibility and efficiency. (5) Need for sharing satisfaction, feedback, and educational were used for the prototype design. See Table 3.

Table 3. Defining Design Principles of Interactive Explanation

Design principles	Description
Appeal	Inducing the elderly to further reading and learning through the use of appealing objects
Feedback	Providing the elderly with visual, sensual, and linguistic information
Safety	Minimizing safety hazards during operation
Satisfaction	Satisfying the elderly emotional needs
Educational effect	Learning something new from the presentation
Continuity	Appealing to the elderly and motivating them to further learning
Motivation	Tuning the stylistic and content design to the taste of the elderly
Aesthetic and simple design	Appealing to the elderly, motivating them to further learning
Held and illustration	Providing help and illustration to facilitate the elderly's learning process
Feedback	Providing the elderly with audio, visual, sensual, and linguistic information
Visual presentation	Straightforward presentation of information required by the elderly
User's freedom of control	Simply operation steps, improving the usability to the elderly
Coherence	Coherent through the system, following certain standard and logic
Flexibility and efficiency	Fast and effective detection of the device
Satisfaction	Satisfying the emotional needs of the elderly
Feedback	Providing the elderly with audio, visual, sensual, and linguistic information
Educational	Learning something new from the tourism experience

4.2   Results of Prototype Design

Description of the Production of Interactive Explanation Board. Interactive explanation board intended for the elderly was produced following the design principles of aesthetic and simple design, straightforward presentation, and coherence. The size of the board is 20 cm (L) by 15 cm (W). The heading of the board, or the name of the plant is in 72# type size. The main text, or explanative words of the species are in 24# type size. There are 85 characters in the main text, which is served as a compact introduction to the plant and divided into several groups of characters by topic. 60% of the presentation area is used for illustration, and 40% for linguistic information. The board is established 80 above the ground and the inclination angle is 30°. Besides, QR code, AR, and smart phone (Android operating system) are incorporated in the interactive explanation resource. As to AR design, the hardware is smart phone SONY-XPERIA S and software/APP is Aurasma.

Multimedia Content and Interactive Operation. The production of interactive multimedia was mainly based on the video of retrospective interview. The designer and programmer planned together for what content about the plant in question should be extracted from the video based on the pre-defined design principles. During the study, more than one minute of multimedia was developed to introduce peony, a representative plant of the tourism site, and an interactive tour guide system was developed. After Effect and Premiere are the two main software tools used to develop the multimedia content, which was presented 30 s of time-lapse photos. See Fig. 5.

Fig. 5. Multimedia content and interactive operation

There were 3 stages with the process of the interactive tour guide system: (1) Preparation stage: click to select the interactive tour guide system and view the multimedia content; (2) Experience stage: when smart phone camera is aligned to the explanation board, the system automatically plays the multimedia content. When clicking on the camera button on smartphone, the system automatically saves the screen and indicates the cloud space available for sharing experience. If the smart phone camera is moved away from the alignment to the explanation board when the multi-media is being played, the system stops the multimedia and presents camera image instead. The operating methods above are available on the explanation board. (3) Closing stage: After clicking on the "sharing" button, the system enters the closing screen.

4.3 Prototype Evaluation and Testing

During the study, 26 elderly tourists were interviewed. Among them 10 were male and 16 female; 16 were aged 51–60, 9 aged 61–70, and 1 aged 71–80. Evaluation and analysis were conducted concerning the hardware form, information multimedia, and interactive operation experience. Finally, modifications to the prototype were proposed.

1. Hardware form (Fig. 6): (1) Height of explanation board: It was proposed to change the height to 100 cm based on the best viewing angle for the elderly; (2) size of explanation board: It was proposed to increase the sizes to 30 cm by 18 cm; (3) Topics coverage: it was proposed to divide the linguistic information into groups and increase the sizes of illustrative pictures; (4) User guide: It was proposed to add illustrative and linguistic user guide to the upper right area of explanation board, in order to facilitate fast and easy use.

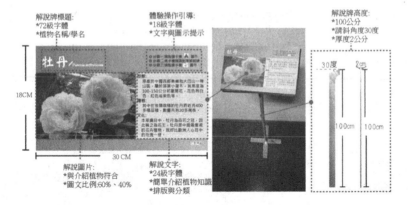

Fig. 6. Description hardware form

2. Information multimedia: (1) Duration of presentation: It was found the best duration is 1 min; (2) Content of presentation: It was proposed to add heading and duration of flowering so elderly tourists can read the information while listening to the audio message. (3) Screen page sizes: most of the elderly tourists proposed to increase the sizes of the video presentation screen page.
3. Interactive operation: It was proposed to increase the efficiency of the system in retrieving and sharing video presentation for future interaction prototypes.
4. Experience sharing: (1) Audio experience: The volume of sound should be adjustable; (2) Photograph sharing: It was proposed to put a reminder on the explanation board that photographs taken can be shared.
5. Operating concept of overall explanation board (Fig. 7): (1) Download f interactive explanation system: the elderly should be able to download the interactive tour guide system onto their smartphone; (2) Clicking to run the interactive tour

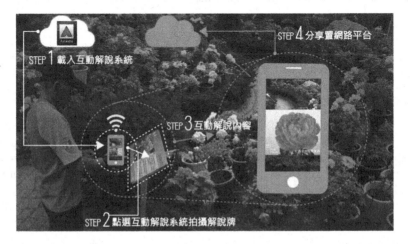

Fig. 7. Schematic diagram of ecotourism interactive tour guide system for the elderly

guide system and taking photograph of the explanation board: clicking to run the pre-downloaded interactive tour guide system and taking photograph of the explanation board to start the tour guide service. (3) Multimedia content: It was proposed to combine the multimedia content with actual scenery of tourism site on smart phone screen, in order to enable a three-dimensional presentation and enrich the elderly ecotourism experience; (4) experience sharing: able to share ecotourism experience on the platform.

5 Conclusion

To summarize the valuation results concluded from the empirical study, a good interaction prototype should have unique appeal to the elderly in terms of hardware form, the presentation of explanation board should be straightforward and self-explanative, the aesthetic design of the information should be simple, the linguistic information should be accurate and concise, the information multimedia of the prototype should provide comprehensive visual information, the visual and audio information should complement each other, the interaction prototype as a whole should have good user control and freedom, flexibility, efficiency, and coherence, as incoherent operating mode may easily lead to increased difficulty for the elderly to use, illustrative and linguistic user guide can be added to facilitate fast operation and avoid any confusion. In terms of experience sharing, both visual and audio experience of the elderly should be satisfied to a high degree, and the content should have educational effect. Besides, concerning topic design of explanation board, it was proposed to improve the linguistic navigation function for future technology enabled interaction prototype and to incorporate ergonomic factors into the screen page design, in order to improve the level of pleasure during the elderly's ecotourism experience activities. Therefore, the user experience of technology enabled interactive tour guide system must be intuitive and easy, in order to help the elderly achieve the best experience. Finally, the prototype developed for ecotourism interactive navigation system can be used a reference for designing and developing explanation boards at parks or botanical gardens.

Acknowledgment. This research is partially supported by the "104 Interactive scenario design on ecotourism for active ageing" of National Yunlin University of Science and Technology (College of Design), sponsored by the Ministry of Science and Technology, Taiwan, R.O.C under Grant no. MOST 104-2410-H-224-024.

References

Chang, K.W., Shih, J.Y., Lai, S.F.: Research trend analyses on older leisure and tourism market in Taiwan. Tamsui Oxford J. Tourism (27), 13–49 (2009)

Chen, C.H.: Interface usability in user-centered interaction design. In: Ming Chuan Universit, Essays of Design Group of Trans-century Symposium, Ming Chuan University, vol. 88, pp. 92–109 (1999)

Chou, L.-D., Lee, C.-C., Lee, M.-Y., Chang, C.-Y.: A tour guide system for mobile learning in museums. In: Proceedings of the 2nd IEEE International Workshop on Paper presented at the Wireless and Mobile Technologies in Education (2004)

Ciavarella, C.: The design of a handheld, location-aware guide for indoor environments. Pers. Ubiquitous Comput. **8**(2), 82–91 (2004)

Department of Statistics, Ministry of the Interior (2012), Key Interior Statistics, 31 December 2012. http://www.moi.gov.tw/stat/index.aspx

Hsu, C., Cai, L., Wong, K.: A model of senior tourism motivations eanecdotes from Beijing and Shanghai. Tourism Manag. **28**, 1262e73 (2007)

Hsu, Y., Liu, T.S.: Discussion of product design of the orange technology. Ind. Des. (128), 49–54.6 (2013)

Huang, F.S., Huang, M.Y.: White paper -towards an aging society - the elderly education (2008)

Institute for Information Industry: FIND: About 3 Million Citizens Domestically Use Smartphone (2014), About 3 Million Citizens Domestically Use Smartphone (2014), 18 March 2014. http://www.ithome.com.tw/node/68869

Wang, K.-H.-C., Xu, H.-L.: A study of discovery the needs of travel service for senior. J. Gerontechnol. Serv. Manag. **1**(1), 107–118 (2012)

Kuo, C.G., Cheng, T.S.: The research of augmented reality registration technology applying on architecture and urban outdoor guiding systems-using "cultural heritage guiding system" and "invisible shop signboard" as examples. Architectural J. (66), 145–166 (2008)

Lang, Y.C., Lei, W.G., Chang, S.Y.: A study on the relationship between environ mental qualification, attitude, and preservation of ecotourist. Sport Health Leisure J. National Chiayi Univ. **10**(3), 23–36 (2011)

Lee, C.S., Liu, D.Y.: Literature review on seniors' tourism motivation and con straint. J. Sport. Recreation Res. **6**(2), 30–58 (2011)

Lin, H.J., Weng, L.H.: A tentative study on forest ecotourism development. Taiwan Forestry **28**(1), 63 (2002)

Liu, X.X.: A study on the intelligent product design for seniors. Ind. Technol. Forum (9), 92–93 (2011)

Matsubara wulang, General Historic and Cultural City and World Heritage: General Tourism Design. Gakugei Publishing House (2010)

Matsubara, 観光のユニバーサルデザイン:歴史都市と世界遺産のバリアフリー. 学芸出版社 (2010)

Neuhofer, B., Buhalis, D., Ladkin, A.: Conceptualising technology enhanced destination experiences. J. Destination Mark. Manag. **1**, 36–46 (2012)

Norman, D.A.: The Psychology of Everyday Things. Basic books. (1988)

Norman, D.A.: The Design of Future Thing. Basic Books, New York (2007)

Tsao, S.H.: Analysis on Taiwan's ecotourism market. In: Essays of the 1st Sustainable Ecotourism Symposium, pp. 65–77. Taiwan Ecotourism Association, Taipei City (2001)

Bureau, Tourism: Ministry of Transportation and Communications, Ecotourism White Paper. Tourism Bureau, Ministry of Transportation and Communications, Taipei City (2002)

Tourism Bureau, Ministry of Transportation and Communications, Survey on Citizen's Travelling in 2013 (2013). http://admin.taiwan.net.tw/statistics/market.aspx?no=133

Wang, M.T.: Possible design directions of healing toys for caring the aging group. J. Des. **17**(2), 1–24 (2012)

Wang, K.C., Hsu, M.T.: A study of discovery the needs of travel service for senior. J. Gerontechnol. Serv.Manage. 1(1), 107–118 (2012)

Wang, C.L., Lee, C.F.: A study of Taiwan styling furniture-archetypal design with canopy bed as example. J. Des. Res. (5), 112–119 (2005)

Wu, H., Hung, C.-W.: The Research on Residents" Perception and Development Attitude toward Ecotourism in Penghu Area, pp. 277–289. China Science and Technology Press, Beijing (2004)

You et al.: User-oriented interactive design research. Ind. Des. **121**, 189–194 (2009)

A Pyramid Model of Inclusive Design to Get Outdoors for China's Ageing People

Guoying Lu[✉] and Ting Zhang

School of Design and Art, Shanghai Dianji University, Shanghai, China
normee@126.com

Abstract. To help people aged 60 years or older who are experiencing the functional loss be self-reliant and go out activities happily and safely is an urgent issue. This paper conducts a preliminary study on what developed countries or regions have done to cope with the ageing people in terms of inclusive design and then analyses the challenges in China. A Pyramid model to help create an inclusive outdoor environment for China's aged people is suggested through literature review.

Keywords: Ageing people · Getting outdoors · Inclusive design · Pyramid model

1 Introduction

"World Population Ageing 1950–2050" by United Nations, reveals China has the largest number (12 million) aged 80 years or older presently. In 2050, the number will reach 99 million, whilst the number aged 60 years or older will reach about 480 million, exceeding one-third of the total Chinese population. Figure 1 demonstrates average annual population growth rate at age 60 or older, 65 or older, and 80 or older from 1950 to 2050 [1]. In the meantime, about 49.7% of urban Chinese senior citizens with families live apart from their offspring who are well known as elderly "empty-nesters" [2]. These "empty-nesters" have to look after themselves.

Functional loss of aged individuals in the ageing society is more or less experienced at different levels. Inclusive design toolkit developed by the University of Cambridge, Engineering Design Center introduces a framework for related data to measure a person's capability, or assess the ability level that a product demands to use it. It contains seven categories of capabilities: vision, hearing, thinking, communication, reach & stretch, dexterity and mobility [3]. The most relevant capability with getting outdoors is the mobility. It involves combination of locomotion, reach & stretch, and dexterity. All too often, people with low dexterity also have locomotion or reach & stretch disadvantage. As illustrated in Fig. 2, 14.7% of the Great Britain (GB) adult population has less than full ability in one or both of seven categories in the Disability Follow-up Survey conducted by GB, while at that time the total number of population is 45.6 million.

© Springer International Publishing AG 2017
J. Zhou and G. Salvendy (Eds.): ITAP 2017, Part I, LNCS 10297, pp. 173–183, 2017.
DOI: 10.1007/978-3-319-58530-7_12

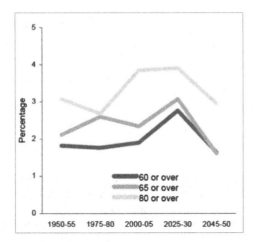

Fig. 1. Average annual population growth rate at age 60 or older, 65 or older, and 80 or older: world, 1950–2050 [1]

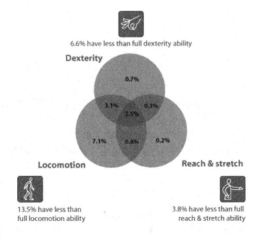

Fig. 2. Prevalence of the population with less than full ability in locomotion, reach & stretch, and dexterity, where the overlapping circles indicate the population that has capability losses in one or more categories [3]

As little as five minutes of exercise a day in the outdoors can improve mental health, according to a British study published in the journal Environmental Science and Technology. P. John Clarkson and R. Coleman [4] addressed "Older people go out into their local neighborhoods very frequently, regardless of season, and walking is very much the predominant form of transport. The three major reasons given for going out are: socializing, getting physical exercise and fresh air and contact with nature."

Yet, despite their desire for walking out, the most impaired capability is locomotive within the population aged 75 years or older in GB, older people have to stay at home for long time rather than getting out due to overburdened public resources and the lack of health care providers. To be self-reliant, they should be able to commute from home to the outdoors or other destinations even with functional loss. This situation urges governors, researchers, designers and manufacturers take inclusive design seriously into account. In such developed countries as UK, USA, Japan, inclusive design regarding the outdoor environment from research to knowledge base and product production has been in progress.

Compared with the developed countries or regions, the barriers for China's old people to get outdoors are much higher for reasons such as China's rapid urbanization, high population density and basic facilities deficiency. As designers as well as future aged people, the authors aim to make a preliminary study on how to help aged people take an active part in built environment and lead a quality life. This paper focuses on the following issues:

- What capabilities impact on ageing people's quality outdoor life?
- What developed countries or regions did to make an inclusive environment for aged people?
- What challenges China is encountering with concerning ageing population?
- How can China learn from developed countries or regions?

2   Literature Review

2.1   Origins of Influences and Ideas on Inclusive Design

Inclusive design, a concept coined in 1994 in UK, is employed often as a design approach in design field. It focuses on design for the whole population. There are three origins of influences and ideas on it [4], as Fig. 3 illustrates.

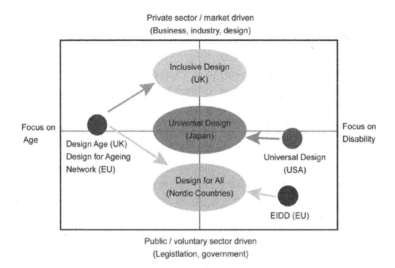

Fig. 3. Three origins of influences and ideas on inclusive design [4]

- Firstly, universal design in the USA, originated as a disability-inclusive architectural design approach, and a major influence on the emergence of universal design in Japan.
- Second, DesignAge, Design for ageing network (EU) and the European Institute for Design and Disability EIDD (EU) emerging with other groups, giving rise to Inclusive Design in the UK and Design for all in Europe. Inclusive design in UK is mostly private sector or market driven, while design for all are mostly public or voluntary driven due to Nordic country's strong welfare.
- Japan's universal design reflected the reality of the most advanced society in terms of population ageing. The famous Ubiquitous (U)-Japan made information and communications technology (ICT) available tools for disabilities.

2.2   Three Approaches in Terms of Legislations and Initiatives

Accordingly, disability civil rights legislations and initiatives have been launched or implemented. I. Audirac [5] argued there were three broad approaches on inclusive design in above developed countries or regions. Table 1 shows disability civil rights legislations and initiatives in Europe, USA and Japan.

Table 1. Disability civil rights legislations and initiatives [5]

Countries or regions	Disability civil rights legislations and initiatives
Europe	European Commission (EC) White Paper on European Transport Policy to 2010
	EU's e-Inclusion 2005 and e-Accessibility
	UK Disability Discrimination Act (DDA), 1995
USA	Americans with Disabilities Act, 1990
	Architectural Barriers Act, 1968
	Rehabilitation Act, 1973
	Safe, Accountable, Flexible, and Efficient Transportation Equity Act, 2006 (aims to reduce barriers to transportation and provide services beyond ADA requirements)
Japan	e-Japan Strategy, 2001, and U-Japan Strategy, 2004
	"Heart Building Law" or Law for Promoting Easily Accessible and Useable Building for the Aged and the Disabled, 1994, 2002
	"Barrier-Free Transportation Law" or Law for Promoting Easily Accessible Public Transportation Infrastructure for the Aged and the Disabled, 2000

Europe. Governmental and non-governmental organizations (NGO)-led approach of planning at all levels for accessible products, services, and environments with an eye on the older market.

USA. Inclusive network of think tanks, advocacy NGOs, consultancy groups, and university in which architects, industrial designers, and engineers lead the way, intend to influence their respective industries about the social and market benefits of designing for the widest possible usability beyond the Americans with Disabilities Act (ADA) accessibility standards.

Japan. Japanese multinational and corporate-led approach directed on access to the information society, chiefly post-industrial and production oriented, and focused on industrial procurement guidance and design standards with a global market scope.

2.3   Design Guidance

USA: 2010 Americans with Disabilities Act Standards for Accessible Design Guidance on the 2010 ADA Standards for Accessible Design. "The US was the first nation to fully embrace and codify design as a civil right for people with disabilities." [6] The Department of US Justice published revised regulations for Titles II and III of ADA 1990 in the Federal Register on September 15, 2010. The 2010 Standards set minimum requirements: both scoping and technical, for newly designed and constructed or altered state and local government facilities, public accommodations, and commercial facilities to be readily accessible to and usable by individuals with disabilities, typically mandated [7].

UK: Guidance of Inclusive Mobility by the Department of Transportation 2005. Guide published by the department of transportation in UK is to provide good access for disabled people; designs that satisfy their requirements also meet the needs of many other people. Those who are travelling with small children or are carrying luggage or heavy shopping will all benefit from an accessible environment, as will people with temporary mobility problems and many older people. Thus, the overall objective of this guide is to provide inclusive design and through that achieve social inclusion [8].

2.4   Research Programs

UK: I'DGO Research Program (2003–2012). I'DGO research program funded by Extending QUAlity Life (EQUAL) in UK [9], aims to support old people's quality life and demand in built environment through inclusive design. Its first phase was started in 2003 and finished in 2006. Follow-up project named I'DGO TOO was launched in 2007, and the findings were reported in 2012 [10].

Based on evidence from their research, I'DGO publishes a 13 part toolkit. Each part addresses a different environmental feature of streets and neighborhoods. Each guide proposes recommendations for the inclusive design of the environmental feature. And recommendations are for all scales from urban form to street furniture. In addition, WISE proposed a concept "Streets for life" as well as design strategies and guidelines. Their findings have been published in China named "Inclusive urban design: streets for life". In this book, six guidelines are given: familiarity, legibility, uniqueness, accessibility, comfort, safety [11].

UK: i~design Research Program. I'design research program is funded by EQUAL in UK. It is carried out in three phases: i~design1, i~design2, i~design3. The i~design team plays a key role in developing BS:7000-6 (2005) which provides the guidelines for adoption of inclusive approach to design of products in UK. I~design program brings a number of outputs including inclusive design toolkit and design with people toolkit.

2.5 Design Toolkits

Inclusive Design Toolkit (IDT). IDT answers three questions in UK context. It contains: What is inclusive design? Why do inclusive design? How to design inclusively? On this site, the toolkit provides information about user capabilities such as vision, hearing, thinking and mobility. Take the example of mobility, the toolkit presents mobility which is divided into fourteen mobility levels and related design guidance, etc. [3].

Design with People Toolkit (DWPT). Developed by the team of i-design 3, DWPT has been created by the Helen Hamlyn Center for Design at the Royal College of Art to share ways to design with people. The toolkit provides ten real individuals with different degrees of functional loss across the spectrum of capability as well as five categories of case studies and other resources such as design methods, developing protocols for ethical practice [12].

3   Methodology

The authors explored the web source to acquire the latest demographic and reviewed the literatures to find out capability variation and what developed countries carried out to help build an inclusive outdoor environment. Additionally, the lead author utilized observations of how ageing people to get outdoors during her stay in the USA as a visiting scholar. In order to get deep design strategies, this paper made case studies to see how improve outdoor environment through products and services design as well. Based on the analysis of challenges of inclusive design in China, the authors proposed a model of Pyramid to help aged people getting outdoors more happily and safely.

4   Case Studies

Besides law enforcement and design guidelines engages in inclusive built environment in UK, there are also a number of product or service related designs, which help mobility-disadvantaged people to get outdoors. Figures 4 and 5 are two case studies designed for people with limited mobility published by i~design program. In these cases, designers respond to the Disability Discrimination Act (DDA), adopt inclusive approach through design process, and help people with locomotive loss get outdoors easier as well as meet the needs of many other people.

Fig. 4. The four-wheel mode (left), the two-wheel mode with the case open (right) [12]

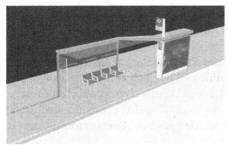
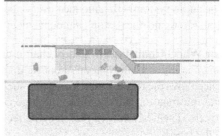

Fig. 5. Physical layout of the "smart" bus shelter with easy access to waiting area (left), the waiting area for bus (right) [12]

4.1   Caddy: A Combined Mobility Aid and Roller Suitcase (2006) [12]

The Caddy™ is designed as a mobile case which works as granny trolley, the mobility aid and roller suitcase with aesthetic innovation. It provides storage, support and seating. It can be pulled with one hand, or pushed with two, enabling use by people of all abilities. Users can easily switch between the two and four-wheel modes through the pivoting rear-leg frame and lockable castors. There is a rigid polymer outer shell, with all features and fixing points molded in. A removable fabric case sits within the shell to form the storage compartment, and is accessible through the top from both front and back, as illustrated in Fig. 4. Large diameter wheels with integral axles and rubber tyres help them negotiate uneven terrain and small kerb and reduce jarring. Compression brakes engage when the user is seated, avoiding the need for lever brakes, which are difficult for people with reduced grip. A large curved handle allows different gripping and leaning options, with adjustment levers integrated into the form.

4.2   Is that My Bus?: A "Smart" Bus Shelter (2004) [12]

The bus shelter is reconsidered to make boarding a bus easier for older people with limited mobility or vision. It involves bus shelter environment, smart cards, disabled travelers, information systems, and service design. Design solutions are generated after the team identifies the key problems. The layout of the bus shelter has been reconfigured and existing telecommunication technologies have been integrated into the physical design of the shelter. It avoids the complex access by simple interaction at the point of need, as shown in Fig. 5. How does the "smart" bus work for visually impaired people and wheel chair users?

For Visually Impaired People. Visually impaired people take the Smartcard "Freedom Pass" which contains limited information about their condition. They have Proxim add-on to their cards. Before they leave for the bus stop, Proxim device will be activated to make sure they won't walk pass the bus stop. The Proxim reader fitted to the bus stop detects them and the bus stop identifies with an audio message to tell what routes and direction. When they touch down the reader in the shelter, it will collect fares. But when they touch down the reader in the bus, it will activate the speaker in the bus. The audio system will announce every approaching bus stop in time to request desired stop. (Note: no "next-stop" announcement in common buses in UK.)

For Wheel Chair Users. Wheel chair users take the Smartcard "Freedom Pass" which contains limited information about their condition. When they arrive at the stop, they touch down the reader embedded in the shelter. It will identify them as wheel chair users. The information will highlight the logo on the flag/RTI and is communicated to the drivers. Then drivers will pull in at the recommended position. Users can easily access in the bus.

5   A Model of Pyramid to Help Get Outdoors

5.1   Challenges in China

As a developing country with the largest ageing population in the world, China has to face bigger challenges. Basically, China's inclusive design is government and experts led approach. Being a vulnerable social group, aged people intend to be overlooked by the country's top-down planning system. Though several legislations related barrier-free design have been published in past decades, inclusive design hasn't seized the Chinese popular imagination nor shaped the personal or professional identity of most designers. Currently, there are around four challenges China is encountering with:

Inefficient & Deficient Existing Inclusive Facilities. One of the most often example of inefficient inclusive facilities is that lots of sidewalk for the blind couldn't work well due to maintenance problem. And deficient facilities to get outdoors mainly are reflected on the accessible transit. Though China has the largest aged population, they can't be seen often on the streets.

Focus of Inclusive Design Shift. In the international dimension, inclusive design cares for not only disabled people, but also people of all ages. China's decision makers should catch up with this focus shift. They should give the opportunity to aged people to have their voice. Government and experts should reconsider the demands of ageing people from city scale, neighborhoods or community to even small lanes.

Research Organizations Engagement. Based on literature review, so far there are only two inclusive research organizations across China: Inclusive Design Research Center (IDRC) at Tongji University and Tianjin Barrier-Free Research Institute at Tianjin University. Underlying cause is the lack of public sectors, private sectors even market drivers.

Design Education Involvement. Inclusive design hasn't been a common set of design curriculums in colleges or universities. All very often, it is an elective course or a coursework. This fact indicates educators haven't reached the consensus that inclusive design should be considered as one of important design approaches. As future designers, the students must put old people at the heart of design process.

5.2   A Model of Pyramid

Based on above research findings, the authors summarised a preliminary model of Pyramid to tackle ageing challenges in China as illustrated in Fig. 6. The Pyramid model builds upon a tiered government and experts led approach to establish a powerful network of inclusive design. Tiered approach as a pyramid contains:

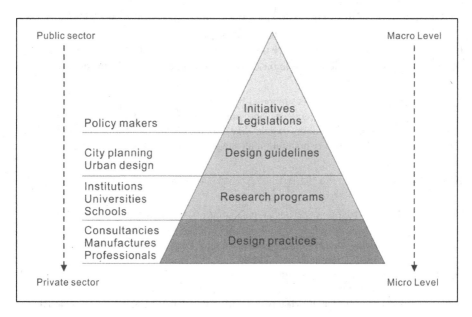

Fig. 6.   Model of pyramid (Color figure online)

Red Tier: Design practices at micro level could be booming and driven by private sectors including the design consultancies, manufactures and design professionals.

Blue Tier: Research programs mainly conducted by institutions, universities and schools.

Green Tier: Design guidelines formulated by city planning and urban design-related governmental organizations.

Top Tier: Legislations and initiatives launched by policy makers to support other tiers.

Through four parties' engagement in the Pyramid, happier and safer outdoor environment might be built.

6   Conclusion and Future Work

Aged people are getting to be included in outdoor environment in developed countries or regions where inclusive design has been delivered since last century. These countries or regions already acquired great achievements and rich experiences. A wealthy of inclusive products and services are emerging though new design challenges are coming out. Whether legislations making, design guidelines formulated with minimum mandated requirements, research programs engagement or detailed product designs involves a large number of stakeholders and is time consuming. Considering the complexity of each tier of Pyramid model, getting outdoors more happily and safely in China has a long way to go.

The limitation of this paper is the lack of quantitative research and pilot study for a specific outdoor activity problem. The Pyramid model should be refined in next stage. Further studies will focus on inclusive product design such as outdoor shopping facilities and street furniture for older people based on a typical ageing neighborhood.

Acknowledgments. This paper is supported by 2016 Domestic Visiting Scholar Program for Young Backbone Teachers in colleges and universities by Ministry of Education, China (A1-0217-16-004-08). The authors would like to acknowledge all the literature source contributors. They also feel very grateful for all suggestions from IDRC at Tongji University.

References

1. IV. Demographic Profile of the Older Population. World Population Ageing 1950–2050. http://www.un.org/esa/population/publications/worldageing19502050/pdf/90chapteriv.pdf
2. China sees growing elderly 'empty-nesters'. China Daily. http://www.chinadaily.com.cn/bizchina/2012-09/22/content_15947771.htm
3. Inclusive design toolkit website. http://www.inclusivedesigntoolkit.com/betterdesign2/UCframework/framework.html
4. John Clarkson, P., Coleman, R.: History of inclusive design in the UK. Appl. Ergon. **46**(Part B), 235–247 (2015)
5. Audirac, I.: Accessing transit as universal design. J. Plan. Lit. **23**(1), 4–16 (2008)
6. Fletcher, V., Bonome-Sims, G., et al.: The challenge of inclusive design in the US context. Appl. Ergon. **46**(Part B), 267–273 (2015)
7. ADA Standards for Accessible Design, Guidance on the 2010 ADA Standards for Accessible Design. https://www.ada.gov/2010ADAstandards_index.htm
8. Guidance of Inclusive Mobility. https://www.gov.uk/government/publications/inclusive-mobility

9. Hua, D.: Inclusive design: new practice in interdisciplinary engineering in UK. J. Eng. Stud. **3**(1), 19–25 (2011)
10. I'DGO Research Program. http://www.idgo.ac.uk/about_idgo/index.htm
11. Burton, E., Mitchell, L.: Inclusive Urban Design: Streets for Life. China Architecture & Building Press, Beijing (2009)
12. Design with People Toolkit. http://designingwithpeople.rca.ac.uk/people/moblity-case-studies

Using Care Professionals as Proxies in the Design Process of Welfare Technology – Perspectives from Municipality Care

Marie Sjölinder[1(✉)], Isabella Scandurra[2], Anneli Avatare Nou[1], and Ella Kolkowska[2]

[1] RISE, SICS, Box 1263, 164 29 Kista, Sweden
marie@sics.se
[2] School of Business, Örebro University, 701 82 Örebro, Sweden
Isabella.Scandurra@oru.se

Abstract. Bringing real users into the design process is often seen as a successful way of creating useful IT systems. However, when it comes to designing for elderly, this is not always possible since many elderly suffer from age-related decline, both with respect to physical and cognitive abilities. This paper elaborates on the approach of working with proxies, in this case elderly care personnel. Different groups of people (N = 117) working with elderly and well familiar with needs and contexts around elderly were engaged in this study. Using a question-naire and a more in-depth workshop we explored with municipality care profes-sionals their experiences as well as the need to create a framework to improve such a proxy approach, and whether a method using care professionals as mediators could be possible to establish in elderly care. The results described in this paper are complementary to ours and others previous knowledge and show promising commitment and willingness to work in accordance with the proposed method.

Keywords: Welfare technology · Elderly · Community-based participatory research · Participatory design · User-centred design · Community networks · Professional-patient relations · Proxy

1 Introduction

From research literature we know that usability and user-centred aspects should be brought in early in the information technology (IT) design process [1, 2]. Bringing real or potential users into the design process is often seen as a successful way of creating useful IT systems and devices. However, there is a need to develop technology towards the demands of older adults in the future, but for people in this target group it may be difficult to participate in a design process. Many of the elderly suffer from age-related decline, both with respect to physical and cognitive abilities, which hinders an active involvement in the design of new technology.

This fact places the design of new technology and new services in a situation where participatory design [3] are not enough and where we need to get feedback about user needs in other ways. Inspired by Boyd-Graber et al. [4] and their work regarding using people close to the intended user in the design process, we explored this concept in the

© Springer International Publishing AG 2017
J. Zhou and G. Salvendy (Eds.): ITAP 2017, Part I, LNCS 10297, pp. 184–198, 2017.
DOI: 10.1007/978-3-319-58530-7_13

context of elderly users of technology. In a number of studies people familiar with elderly persons' presuppositions were involved and different ways of using care personnel as mediators of the needs of the elderly was investigated [5]. In this approach the aim was to involve the senior end-users as much as possible, but when this inclusion was not entirely feasible, elderly care personnel was also involved. The authors adhere to human computer interaction (HCI) as research field and apply user-centred and participatory design methods as main methodologies. Nevertheless, the possibility of using people close to the end-users became useful in this setting and was therefore elaborated further. It should be noted however, that this approach was adopted only when the information could not be gathered from the elderly themselves and is thus a deviation of the recommended standard methods in HCI. As a colleague of ours put it: "You always want to work with the elderly end-users, but sometimes you just can't".

Based on our experiences from involving care personnel in different ways in the design of new technology targeted towards elderly, a number of lessons learned can be drawn. These insights are related to aspects such as the perception of the personnel regarding technology experience of elderly users as well as the involvement and engagement of elderly in trials and evaluation sessions. Other important aspects are when in the design process the care professionals contribute and how their cooperation with the elderly users takes place.

A dilemma arises when you want to keep a participatory and cooperative design approach but cannot fully involve the end-users in the process: how to keep the needs of the elderly still in focus and not accidently placed aside? And how to assess that this is actually done? In order to cope with the loss of real end-users involved in the design, we made an effort to develop a method for using care personnel juxtaposed the elderly in the process. The method targeted "elderly care personnel as proxies for elderly" and was applied in a larger welfare technology development project and subsequently evaluated in the context where it took place [5]. Insights from previous studies formed the basis for aspects to take into consideration when care professionals are used as proxies for elderly end-users.

The purpose with the study described in this paper was to further explore those aspects together with municipality care personnel in order to start building a methodological framework containing important issues that will contribute to a set of recommendations for working with proxies in the welfare technology design process. The goal, of which this is a step, is to improve the use of proxies by creating a framework of methods with concrete easy-to-use recommendations.

2   Background

Human-computer interaction (HCI) research has come a long way in understanding the importance of involving users in the process of developing new technology. This work is conducted within the framework of action research projects that adhere to Participatory Design (PD) [6, 7], as one of the HCI theories that regards system development with user participation and that considers designing a social process.

2.1 Proxy Usage

Previous studies have been conducted using care personnel or relatives as mediators for elderly, here called proxies. For example, with respect to judging functional state and medical history of the elderly person [8]. When evaluating, in several aspects the judgements of the proxy was quite in line with the answers of the elderly person. However, the perceptions of a proxy could also point in the opposite direction. In a care-giving situation the perceptions of the proxy was shown to be related to perceived care burden; the heavier care burden the proxy felt, the larger was the risk that the proxy overestimated disability or loss of functionality [8]. Another aspect also related to judgement of health conditions of elderly by proxy persons was the relationship between the elderly person and the proxy. The closer relationship is the better concordance between the answers of the elderly person and the proxy [9].

As described above, some studies that use proxies as mediators of the needs of the elderly were conducted in the area of judging health conditions. A larger area of research is using proxies in understanding the needs or the situation around people with disabilities. These results also show that the closer the relationship, the better concordance between the answers. For example, responses of spouses are more accurate than other proxies, and professionals and caregivers provide more accurate information than lay proxies [10].

With respect to using proxies in the design of technology and services, Boyd-Graber et al. [4] conducted work regarding using people close to the intended user in the design process. In their study care professionals that worked close to users with aphasia were involved in the design process. This study showed that overall it worked well since supporting staff was very familiar with the needs and demands of the user groups. However, some difficulties were found regarding the testing of prototypes since it was impossible to imagine another person's usage context all the way and in all details [4].

In our first study [5] inspired by Boyd-Graber et al. [4] we investigated the use of care personnel as mediators for elderly using an information and communication technology system for sharing information and for keeping in touch with friends and family.

In this work care personnel and elderly living at a nursing home participated in workshops around the technology and some of the elderly tested the technology in their own apartments. The personnel managed the work and they were also involved in work regarding creating personas representing different categories of elderly living at the nursing home. One lesson learnt from this work was the importance of having a dialogue with the personnel about needs and relevant target groups. Initially the care personnel involved elderly users that had access to a computer and were, as they thought, experienced with technology. That was a mistake since this group already had access to services for interacting with others. However, after this misunderstanding with respect to need of technology among the elderly the care personnel changed their view and suggested new ways of using the technology. First they provided the technology to elderly that had no other technology (besides a telephone) for communication with others. When this was done the usage of the system increased to some extent, however in this situation we realised that many of the elderly had too small social networks to benefit from this kind of technology. This insight led to a suggestion by the personnel to place the devices in dining areas as something to gather around, e.g. to show each other pictures of friends and family. This turned out to be a success and finally the system became used, although in another way than what was initially the intention. We believe that increased usage was achieved thanks to the increasing understanding of the personnel that regarded the need of technology and its potential benefit among the elderly during the entire project [5].

Results from this project indicating that the care personnel initially overestimated the importance of having computer experience and also that they underestimated the elderly's general technology literacy is in line with other studies. Other studies have shown that proxies over-report disabilities for people aged 65 or older, but under-report disabilities for persons under 65 [11]. Unfortunately, these results reveal a general view of elderly as weak and less capable, both with respect to use of technology and in other situations.

In another study, also conducted by us, the use of proxies as mediators of elderly users was further elaborated. Within this project a Kinect™ sensor tool for stroke rehabilitation at home was developed [12] and the study aimed at exploring whether or not usage could be broadened to other user groups than stroke patients. The system was installed at three activity centres for elderly and there the aging users tested a Kinect sensor for conducting exercises, although the technology was designed for home usage. Each centre had responsible care personnel doing observations during tests. After the session both aging users and staff filled in a questionnaire about usage of the system and the exercises. Aging users answered from their perspective and the staff based their answers on the support given to the users when using the system. Even though it was a prototype containing flaws, the aging users managed to test it and contributed with suggestions for improvements. When evaluating the questionnaires, there were no direct contradictions between the answers given by aging users and care professionals. However, the care professionals provided a deeper insight since they had a more holistic perspective on the situation. They provided valuable information about how and why features and interaction should be changed. The shared experience between care professionals and aging users contributed to a similar view of the situation and of the usage of the technology [13].

Finally, in line with the results of Boyd-Graber [4] our first study also showed that proxies report what they see or what they can observe. Initially the care personnel that worked in the project only saw the elderly as care taking elderly without experience of technology. After working with the elderly in the project they gradually realised that many of the elderly previously in life had been working with technology and that they were not that alienated from technology as the personnel had thought.

2.2 Aspects Affecting the Use of Proxies

Assumptions and increased understanding of the elderly: Assumptions of the personnel about the technology experiences of elderly users could be very misleading. The important aspect is to which extent a potential user would benefit from the technology - not if he/she is experienced in other technologies.

It was evident that although the personnel were acquainted with the persons living at the nursing home, they were not familiar enough with their previous lives or connections to the life outside the nursing home. The fact that care personnel often sees a patient through his/her condition or diagnoses rather than the individual has been recognized since long and many now strive to keep a salutogenic approach [14]. We note that this was relevant also here, not only in terms of frail elderly, but also as the elderly were seen as technology illiterates rather than curious of which benefit the device could give them.

Engagement from the personnel: When the personnel became engaged in their role as proxies a positive outcome was that they started to think about how and where this technology or device could meet the needs and be beneficial to its potential users. This could increase the possibility to find new and meaningful areas of usage and also find aspects and functionalities that make the technology better suited for the target group at hand. With respect to this and from a methodological point of view, the challenge is to find ways to engage the personnel/proxies to the extent that they start to think about usage in new ways. In terms of proxy usage, the relationship between the elderly and the personnel is also important, the closer relationship the better the elderly's needs will be conveyed [10].

Sharing the experience: In two of our studies we found positive effects of personnel and elderly sharing the experience of trying new technology. In this situation it becomes something that you do together and it makes it easier for the personnel to actually observe the needs of the elderly. In this situation it reveals itself both which services that are perceived as meaningful and how the interaction can be improved [5]. A further advantage is that they share the experience but will have the possibility to give feedback on the usage from different perspectives. The elderly user can describe what is easy and what is difficult, and the observing personnel can provide insights about why something does not work and also provide alternative solutions [13]. When testing the technology together, there is also less difference between the feedback given by the personnel and the elderly user.

Participating personnel: Another important aspects is to choose and involve care personnel that are interested and also provide them with the possibility to engage in this work. There has to be time to engage in the role as proxy along with the ordinary work tasks. This part has to be considered in a way that does not affect the other personnel in terms of a heavier workload. In the long run they will get involved and if their first encounter is a heavier workload, it may be a bad start.

Development - challenges and opportunities: One added value that the proxy approach can give are insights that only reveal themselves in the meeting of different groups of people. For example, in the dialogue between the elderly testing the technology and the personnel helping/observing. When also bringing in the developers into this context they will get the possibility to observe and gaining knowledge that are not possible to gain from a second source. In this context and also together with researchers and designers, the possibility to draw attention to new insights from the personnel (and or the developers) increases.

3   Method and Materials

Qualitative and quantitative methods were chosen to investigate the empirical field in order to illuminate socio-technical and socio-cultural aspects affecting the use of proxies, using the participants' experiences. The aim was to develop knowledge that can contribute to a broader understanding of human actions and experiences in a socio-technical and -cultural context with regard to working with proxies in the welfare technology design process.

Data collection was performed during a conference entitled Meeting Point Welfare Technology and E-health, 24 of January 2017 in Stockholm, Sweden. During a 45 min plenary session given by the authors, the audience was asked to take part in a *survey*, using an online questionnaire tool [https://www.mentimeter.com] containing 12 questions. The material was stored online (see section of Materials).

A *workshop* was short thereafter organized as part of the conference programme, where the same topics were discussed in a focus group to gain more depth to each aspect. During the focus group discussion the results from the survey were shown as a catalyst for the discussion. The five aspects illustrated above were explored in the workshop group during 90 min, using pre-defined open questions. The focus group discussion was documented verbatim by one of the authors, whereas the other acted as chair.

Data analysis of the two data collecting sessions followed the procedure of systematic text condensation [15] which is a descriptive and explorative method for thematic cross-case analysis of different types of data. The procedure is rather pragmatic, and consists of the following steps: (i) reading the material to obtain an overall impression, bracketing previous preconceptions; (ii) identifying units of meaning, representing different aspects of the participants' experiences and coding for these; (iii) condensing and abstracting the meaning within each of the coded groups; and (iv) summarizing the contents of each code group to generalized descriptions and concepts reflecting the most important challenges reported by the participants [15, 16] to merge data from the survey with the qualitative data, developing categories from empirical data, rather than using a preconceived theoretical framework.

3.1   Materials: Participants and Tools

The audience during the plenary session consisted of over 120 delegates of the conference, interested in/experts of the needs and contexts around elderly. They were asked to participate in the survey during the talk, and 113 persons choose to provide their opinions and experiences regarding the proxy approach in elderly care (Table 1). Nine persons participated in the focus group discussion during the workshop (plus two of the authors); some of them had attended our plenary session before.

Table 1.   Roles at work of the respondents and the participants in the workshop

Role in organisation	Number of respondents in the survey (N = 113)	Number of participants in the workshop (N = 11)
Registered nurses	1	
Nurses	12	
Administration (incl. mgm, econ etc)	42	2
IT	19	1
Physiotherapist	1	
Occupational therapist	3	
Researcher	3	2
Other[a]	42	6

[a]As the question asking about the roles of the audience also was used as the first question to try out the system, there may be erroneous answers, or the alternatives given here did not match the roles the respondents actually have.

The workshop participants (N = 9) also carried out the questionnaire, providing their experience of working with development of IT in elderly care on a scale ranging from 1 (not at all) to 5 (to a great extent). Four graded their experience [2]; two answered medium experience [3], whereas three stated [4]. Five of the nine graded their experience of developing technology together with elderly to [1: none at all], whereas three participants graded their experience [2] and one graded medium on the scale [3].

The online survey tool used was Mentimeter.com. It provides to the audience the questions on their own smart mobile phones, if they entered a unique code before the start of the presentation of the questions. The statements and questions (presented below) were created on beforehand and launched stepwise during the presentation. When answering the questionnaire, the voting results of the audience was immediately shown on the projector screen. The results of the survey were saved online and are presented in the results section.

Mentimeter Questionnaire. All questions were of a multiple answer format, where it was possible to select only one option. Many of them were similar to a Likert scale. The first question was a test, to try out the system. Questions 2–4 regard the experience of the respondent. In question 4 the answers are based on the "citizen participation ladder" developed by Arnstein [17] and recently modified by Östlund [18] to suit older people

Table 2. The 12 questions posed to the audience via the interactive online tool

1. What is your role in your organization? [Reg. nurse; Nurse; Admin (Manager/economy/ similar); IT; Physiotherapist; Occupational therapist; Physician; Researcher; Other]
2. What experience do you have of working with development of IT in elderly care? 1–5: [None at all - Very much experience]
3. What experience do you have of developing technology together with the elderly? 1–5: [None at all - Very much experience]
4. What are the roles older users mostly carry in the projects you are involved in? [No control - controlled by the decisions of others; Get information about things that happen; Contribute with their views; Participate as experts; Drive the development and change]
5. Are you currently working in a similar manner what we have described (e.g. the staff can influence the design of welfare technology for the elderly) 1–5: [Not at all - to a great extent]
6. Does your organization wish to increase the knowledge about design and technology development among the staff? (e.g. ambassadors/motivators are encouraged) 1–5: [Not at all - to a great extent]
7. Is it feasible to apply this approach in your organisation? 1–5: [Not at all - to a great extent]
8. Are you interested in working according to this approach? 1–5: [Not at all - to a great extent]
9. To which extent is it important that the staff understands the technology experience of the elderly users? 1–5: [Not at all - to a great extent]
10. To which extent is it important that the staff is skilled in using welfare technology themselves? 1–5: [Not at all - to a great extent]
11. To which extent is it important that the entire group of personnel somehow is involved in implementation of welfare technology? 1–5: [Not at all - to a great extent]
12. To which extent is it important that the elderly and the staff try out the welfare technology together? 1–5: [Not at all - to a great extent]

in the innovation and design process. The assumption here is that older users may "climb" the steps if the environment becomes more aware and knowledgeable of how to deal with elderly in the design process.

Questions 5–8 regard how work is conducted today, 9–12 regard whether the respondent finds it important to adhere to the aspects discussed (Table 2).

Themes Discussed During the Workshop. The objective of the workshop was to gather participants from the municipalities to get feedback on the aspects that were derived from previous studies [5, 13] and to learn about their ideas of the feasibility of adopting such approach in elderly care. The discussion was equally interesting for the participants as for the authors, as the questions regarded how to deal with the challenges following the willingness to innovate elderly care using welfare technology.

Table 3. Themes with survey questions (Qn) to the left and sub-questions to discuss to the right.

Assumptions and increased understanding of the elderly	
Q2: Experience of development of IT in elderly care Q3: Experience of developing technology together with elderly Q4: Roles older users mostly carry Q9: Important that staff understands the technology experience of elderly users?	– Do you have suggestions on how to work for a more nuanced picture of the elderly and their technology skills. – How to avoid stereotypes in the design of new technologies? – On what premises are participants selected in these contexts? – How were the elderly chosen in the contexts you know of?
Engagement of the personnel	
Q10: Important that staff is skilled in using welfare technology themselves	– What is required for the staff to get involved at a level so that they can see where new technologies could be of use?
Sharing the experience	
Q12: Important that elderly and personnel try out welfare technology together	– How can you achieve a favourable test environment for both staff and the elderly?
Participating personnel	
Q11: Important that entire group of personnel somehow is involved in implementation of welfare technology	– How to select staff who will be involved? How to manage involvement/ lack of involvement of "others"? – What are the conditions for this in your organizations?
Development – challenges and opportunities	
Q5: Personnel affects the development of welfare technology Q6: Organization's wish to increase knowledge about design and development among staff Q7: Feasibility of this approach in your organisation Q8: Important that staff understands the technology experience of elderly users?	– Why can you (not) to use this kind of method in your organization? – What is required in your organization to start using this approach? – What would you do if you want to pursue this type of development in your organization?

The focus group discussion was based on five themes, coinciding with the aspects derived from previous studies. They were handled both during the plenary session and in the survey. Some sub-questions were added during the workshop to support the group discussion (Table 3).

4   Results and Analyses

Below, the results are presented around identified themes related to the use of care personnel in understanding user needs when designing technology together with elderly.

4.1   Assumptions and Increased Understanding of the Elderly

Experience: The experience, of development of IT within elderly care, among the audience was quite high considering the large number of administrative personnel in the audience. However, not many had previous experience of developing technology together with elderly users (Table 4).

Table 4. Experience of developing technology together with elderly

Survey questions	1	2	3	4	5	m	N
2. Experience of development of IT in elderly care	19	22	38	22	12	2,88	113
3. Experience of developing technology together with elderly	65	28	8	5	1	1,59	107

Participation: According to Arnstein [17] the amount of participation in society, or as in this case in design, could be described in a participation ladder. The lowest step on the ladder is "No control - controlled by the decisions of others"; continuing with higher steps in terms of "Get information about things that happen", "Contribute with their views" and "Participate as experts". At the final step the person has taken control and "Drive the development and change".

Opposite to the actual situation, shown by the questionnaire, where most of the respondents reported that the elderly participated on the lower steps of the ladder (Fig. 1) the discussions in the workshop placed a focus on the importance of showing the elderly meaning and benefits with the technology. They pointed out that this is a demanding group of users that needs strong incentives if they should be engaged and interested in using the technology.

Treating everyone in an equal way: In the questionnaire the participants rated it to be important that the personnel understood the elderly users' actual technology experience (Table 5), and not based their judgements on assumptions about elderly having no or little experience of technology. Further the participants in the workshop placed a focus on the importance of treating all the elderly in an equal way and invite all that were interested to participate; instead of selecting the ones they thought were best suited.

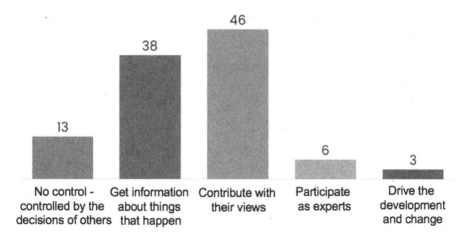

Fig. 1. Survey question 4: What are the roles older users mostly carry in the projects you are involved in?

Table 5. Understanding the needs of the elderly

Survey question	1	2	3	4	5	m	N
9. Extent to which it is important that the personnel understand the technology experience of elderly users	0	2	7	22	78	4,61	109

Attitudes: Another important issue that was mentioned in the discussions was attitude towards elderly technology users. There is both a risk of treating the person in a superior way as if he/she is a child, and also in a too enthusiastic way describing them as "cool" or "cute". On the other hand it is a difficult balance between these approaches and the care taking role the personnel has. However, this might be more pronounced in cultures where old age is associated with weakness rather than wisdom and knowledge; and also with an old fashioned view of elderly and their interests and knowledge.

Vocabulary: In the discussion the participants mentioned the importance of selecting the right words when introducing technology to older people. Technology and services should be named and described with the usage and benefits in focus. Words like "robot reader" for example should be avoided.

4.2 Engagement of the Personnel

Benefits and perceived meaning: In the discussions the participants mentioned the importance of showing the personnel the meaning and the usefulness of the technology. It has to be perceived as meaningful to both the elderly and to the personnel, and it cannot make the work more difficult for the personnel. One solution to make the threshold lower is to introduce the technology stepwise, this will demand less resources initially. The respondents to the questionnaire also reported high importance in having personnel skilled with the technology and that time has to be spent on introducing and learning the technology to the personnel (Table 6).

Table 6. Importance of personnel skilled in using technology

Survey question	1	2	3	4	5	m	N
10. Extent to which it is important that the personnel are skilled in using welfare technology themselves	0	2	10	29	65	4,48	106

Attention and appreciation: Another important aspect to achieve engaged personnel is to increase their feeling of being valued and appreciated for their work. Time should be set aside so that the personnel can work with elderly and technology without a feeling of high pressure.

4.3   Sharing the Experience

Focusing on the need of elderly persons: In previously conducted work we mainly discussed sharing experiences in terms of testing the technology together. In this workshop participants discussed this matter in relationship to address needs by different technical solutions. The needs should be discovered and discussed in person-centred individual meetings. The needs of elderly persons should be in focus in discussions about finding the right solution and adjust it to the specific needs of the user. It is important to show the benefits of the technology to users, but in a realistic way without giving the users too high expectations.

Testing the technology together: In the survey respondents reported that they thought it was important that elderly and personnel tested the technology together (Table 7). In many situations this could be a quite equal context since many of the younger elderly are skilled and experienced in using technology and ICT services; and there is increasing technology literacy among the personnel. This will provide new possibilities to gather around new technology and provide input to design and development. The increased experience and awareness of existing technology will also reduce difficulties in imagining new services and areas of usage. However, in this context there might be a risk that elderly gets to enthusiastic and are not critical enough towards new technical solutions.

Table 7. Importance of trying the technology together

Survey question	1	2	3	4	5	m	N
12. Extent to which it is important that the elderly and the personnel tries out welfare technology together	1	0	9	32	63	4,49	105

4.4 Participating Personnel

Increasing the opportunities for the personnel: In the survey the respondents reported it important that the entire group of personnel is involved in implementation of welfare technology (Table 8). To achieve this, time and resources need to be put aside. This could be a challenge with current practice; high workload and little time to introduce new ways of working. The awareness of this risk needs to be included and handled accordingly throughout the process.

Table 8. Involvement of the entire group of personnel

Survey question	1	2	3	4	5	m	N
11. Extent to which it is important that the entire group of personnel somehow is involved in implementation of welfare technology	0	0	18	28	60	4,40	106

Further, it was considered important to involve the entire group of personnel to avoid a feeling of a small group being selected to work with the technology. In general, avoiding the feeling of being left outside is important with respect to all involved and the success of the implementation of the technology. Both elderly and personnel needs to be involved and engaged in an open way where everyone are welcome to participate.

The attitude of the managers: As mentioned, the managers could have an important role in engaging and inspiring the co-workers but they could also hinder the involvement by transmitting a negative attitude and making tasks more complicated than they should be.

4.5 Development – Challenges and Opportunities

In the survey 102/111 respondents showed a clear interest (value 4 and 5 to involve personnel in design of new technology. However, they rated the actual feasibility a bit lower, 63/109 answered value 4 and 5 (Table 9).

Table 9. Organisational aspects.

Survey question	1	2	3	4	5	m	N
5. To which extent the personnel currently affect the development of welfare technology in the organisation	39	32	19	13	4	2,17	107
6. Wish of organisation to increase knowledge about design and development among the staff	4	14	32	24	36	3,67	110
7. Feasibility of this approach in your organisation	3	9	34	38	25	2,75	109
8. Interest of working according to this approach	1	1	7	31	71	4,53	111

With respect to design of new services a great challenge was to get the involved elderly (and the personnel) to envision future solutions and services that not yet exist. There could be needs that we are unaware of until the service is created to support and fulfil these unknown needs. One way of better understanding existing needs could be by using own stories and narratives to create concrete situations where different needs could be addressed by new technology. Another approach could be to gather information from follow-up systems since they contain much data about activities that had been conducted to meet the needs of the elderly.

5 Discussion

With respect to user involvement, the result from this work showed a difference between the real life situation and the ideal situation. The participants responding the survey thought it was important that elderly were involved in the development and that they perceived the technology as meaningful. However, when thinking of many real life situations the participants estimated the elderly to be on a level of the participation ladder [17] where they just receive information or contribute with their views. The results also supported previous insights about the importance of the personnel's broad understanding of the technology experience of the elderly participants; and that the personnel should not exclude participants based on the assumption of the staff [5]. Instead all the elderly should be treated equally and invited to participate. The result from this work added knowledge to the first theme regarding understanding of the elderly in terms of placing attention to the fact where personnel should use a vocabulary that did not exclude possible elderly participants.

With respect to engagement of the personnel it was pointed out that it was important that the technology was perceived as meaningful. The personnel should have the possibility to learn about the technology, time should be set aside for this specific purpose and finally needs appreciation for the effort they put in this work.

The initial themes included one aspect regarding sharing experiences of trying and using technology. The workshop discussion focused on earlier phases in the design process, and pointed out the importance of individual meetings and an approach that was centred on needs of the individuals. This was in line with previous research showing that "the closer relationship between proxy and elderly, the better the needs of the elderly will be conveyed" [10]. It was also pointed out that in many situations, both elderly and personnel are actually already skilled in using technology, as opposed to what many believe. This is important to take advantage of in testing and refining existing technology.

With respect to personnel that participates in designing technology together with elderly it is important that time is set aside, that the manager is positive, supporting and appreciate their work. The participators reported 'to a great extent' their own interest to work with methods involving personnel. At the same time they were thoughtful about the extent to which it was feasible within own organizations.

Finally, the original theme focused around the added value from meetings where all different stakeholders participated. The results from this work broadened to include previously gained knowledge such as information from follow-up systems.

6   Conclusions

Through this work, one step further is taken in the development of a method for using care professionals in the development of welfare technology. Although the best source of information is the actual user, we cannot give up the thought of using others in situations where the users cannot speak for themselves. We recommend using care professionals as proxy where it is suited as through the engagement that the professionals spread, users could start reaching higher steps on the participation ladder [17]. Among participants there was an interest and willingness to work according to this method. It could contribute to technology being perceived as more meaningful, both to elderly and personnel.

References

1. Grudin, J.: Interactive systems: bridging the gaps between developers and users. Computer **24**(4), 59–69 (1991). doi:10.1109/2.76263
2. Constantine, L., Lockwood, L.: Software for Use: A Practical Guide to the Essential Models and Methods of Usage-Centered Design. Addison-Wesley, Reading (1999)
3. Schuler, D., Namioka, A.: Participatory Design Principles and Practices. Lawrence Erlbaum Associates, Inc., London (1993)
4. Boyd-Graber, J., Nikolova, S.S., Moffatt, K.A., Kin, K.C., Lee, J.Y., Mackey, L.W., Tremaine, M.M., Klawe, M.M.: Participatory design with proxies: developing a desktop-PDA system to support people with aphasia. In: Computer-Human Interaction (2006)
5. Sjölinder, M., Scandurra, I.: Effects of using care professionals in the development of social technology for elderly. In: Zhou, J., Salvendy, G. (eds.) DUXU 2015. LNCS, vol. 9194, pp. 181–192. Springer, Cham (2015). doi:10.1007/978-3-319-20913-5_17
6. Greenbaum, J., Kyng, M.: Design at Work: Cooperative Design of Computer Systems, pp. 3–24. Lawrence Erlbaum Associates, Inc., Hillsdale (1991)
7. Schuler, D., Namioka, A.: Participatory Design Principles and Practices. Lawrence Erlbaum Associates, Inc., London (1993)
8. Long, K., Sudha, S., Mutran, E.J.: Elder-proxy agreement concerning the functional status and medical history of the older person: the impact of caregiver burden and depressive symptomatology. J. Am. Geriatr. Soc. **46**(9), 1103–1111 (1998)
9. The Medical Research Council Cognitive Function and Ageing Study: Survey into health problems of elderly people: a comparison of self-report with proxy information. Int. J. Epidemiol. **29**(4), 684–697 (2000). doi:10.1093/ije/29.4.684
10. Elliott, M.N., Beckett, M.K., Chong, K., Hambarsoomians, K., Hays, R.D.: How do proxy responses and proxy-assisted responses differ from what medicare beneficiaries might have reported about their health care? Health Serv. Res. **43**(3), 833–848 (2008). doi:10.1111/j.1475-6773.2007.00820.x. PMCID: PMC2442242
11. Todorov, A., Kirchner, C.: Bias in proxies' reports of disability: data from the National Health Interview Survey on disability. Am. J. Public Health **90**(8), 1248–1253 (2000)
12. Sjölinder, M., Ehn, M., Boman, I-L., Folke, M., Hansson, P., Sommerfeld, D.K., Nylander, S., Borg, J.: A multi-disciplinary approach in the development of a stroke rehabilitation tool. In: Proceedings of HCI International 2014, Crete, Greece, 22–27 June 2014
13. Sjölinder, M., Scandurra, I., Avatare Nöu, A., Kolkowska, E.: To meet the needs of aging users and the prerequisites of innovators in the design process. In: Zhou, J., Salvendy, G. (eds.) ITAP 2016. LNCS, vol. 9754, pp. 92–104. Springer, Cham (2016). doi:10.1007/978-3-319-39943-0_10

14. Antonovsky, A.: Health, Stress and Coping. Jossey-Bass, San Francisco (1979)
15. Malterud, K.: Systematic text condensation: a strategy for qualitative analysis. Scand. J. Public Health. **40**(8), 795–805 (2012)
16. Crabtree, B.F., Miller, W.L.: Doing Qualitative Research, pp. 20–24. Sage, Thousand Oaks (1999)
17. Arnstein, S.: A ladder of citizen participation. Am. Inst. Plan. J. **35**(4), s216–s224 (1969)
18. Östlund, B.: The benefits of involving older people in the design process. In: Zhou, J., Salvendy, G. (eds.) ITAP 2015. LNCS, vol. 9193, pp. 3–14. Springer, Cham (2015). doi: 10.1007/978-3-319-20892-3_1

Technology Experience Café—Enabling Technology–Driven Social Innovation for an Ageing Society

Johannes Tröger[1]([✉]), João Mariano[2], Sibila Marques[2], Joana Mendonça[2],
Andrey Girenko[1], Jan Alexandersson[1], Bernard Stree[3], Michele Lamanna[4],
Maurizio Lorenzatto[4], Louise Pierrel Mikkelsen[5],
and Uffe Bundgård-Jørgensen[5]

[1] DFKI – German Research Center for Artificial Intelligence, Saarbrücken, Germany
{Johannes.Troeger,Andrey.Girenko,Jan.Alexandersson}@dfki.de
[2] ISCTE – Instituto Universitário de Lisboa, CIS-IUL, Lisboa, Portugal
{Joao_Mariano,Sibila_Marques,Joana_Mendonca}@iscte.pt
[3] CEA – Commissariat à l'énergie atomique et aux énergies alternatives,
Grenoble, France
BERNARD.STREE@cea.fr
[4] CITTA DI TORINO, Torino, Italy
{Michele.Lamanna,Maurizio.Lorenzatto}@comune.torino.it
[5] InvestorNet-Gate2Growth, Copenhagen, Denmark
{lpm,ubj}@gate2growth.com
http://www.dfki.de, http://www.cis.iscte-iul.pt

Abstract. Effective technology innovation process management in the context of active healthy ageing has the potential to improve older adults' quality of life, allowing them to maintain their independence and age in their own homes for longer. But as older adults significantly differ from the general population in technology use and its impact on their quality of life, tools are needed that (1) involve this target group into the innovation process, as well as (2) capture the diverse needs of technology for various stakeholders involved in this process. This paper presents the framework called Technology Experience Café (TEC), developed within the European project SIforAGE, answering exactly this need. Detailed information on the methodology and its implementation in five sites, in four different countries across Europe, focusing on participating stakeholders, general design of the TEC, and used evaluation tools, is provided. Preliminary results show, that (1) the target group's perception of the TEC as a framework was thoroughly positive and TECs had a positive impact on older adults' technology related attitudes and (2) that stakeholders' benefits affiliated with their involvement in the TECs are manifold. Implications and limitations are discussed.

Keywords: Social innovation · Innovation process management · Technology acceptance · Older adults · Productive interactions

J. Zhou and G. Salvendy (Eds.): ITAP 2017, Part I, LNCS 10297, pp. 199–210, 2017.
DOI: 10.1007/978-3-319-58530-7_14

1   Introduction

The world's population is ageing faster than ever. The number of persons at the age of 60+ has increased substantially in recent years in most countries and regions, and that growth is projected to accelerate in the coming decades; globally, this figure is expected to more than double by 2050 and more than triple by 2100[1]. According to the European Commission's report on *Population ageing in Europe*, the shift in age composition and decline in population growth is even more accentuated in Europe compared to other continents[2]. This demographic change presents new societal challenges which set a new policy context for the upcoming decades, especially in the domain of health and well-being. Addressing this challenge, the introduction of innovative technology in the context of active healthy ageing has the potential to improve quality of life of older adults, allowing them to maintain their independence and age in their own homes for longer [12]. However, older adults significantly differ from the general population in terms of technology use and, consequently, its impact on their quality of life. This imposes a serious challenge on the management of the technology innovation process, within the scope of the aforementioned societal challenge. Succeeding in this process, it has been argued that new emerging trends in innovation management have to be taken into consideration: users should be involved in the process of innovation during all stages and technology providers should not innovate in isolation, but as part of a societal system of different very heterogeneous stakeholders [10]. Consequently, there is a growing need for tools for the technology innovation process that are (1) geared towards the specificities of involving older adults in this innovation process and (2) effectively involve all stakeholders by a systemic approach.

This paper presents the *Technology Experience Café (TEC)*, an evidence-based tool aiming to involve older adults in research, technology development and innovation activities, within the scope of innovation process management in a systemic fashion. TEC was an important component of the international project *SIforAGE – Social Innovation on Active and Healthy Ageing for Sustainable Economic Growth*[3], which promotes active and healthy ageing through research and innovative products for longer and better lives. Subsequently specific challenges of involving older adults in technology innovation activities are discussed and a methodological overview of TEC as a framework, as well as its implementation in five events across four countries is provided. The results are presented and discussed according to the above-mentioned requirements.

---

[1] https://esa.un.org/unpd/wpp/publications/files/key_findings_wpp_2015.pdf; accessed: 2016-12-12.

[2] https://ec.europe.eu/research/social-sciences/pdf/policy_reviews/kina26426enc. pdf; accessed: 2016.12.12.

[3] The SIforAGE consortium comprised many different partners with complementary backgrounds and expertise at the European and International levels, working together for a society for all ages—http://www.siforage.eu.

2 Technology Innovation Process for Older Adults

Involving older users in the technology innovation process represents a challenge in itself, as they face age-related declines in perceptual, cognitive and motor skills which affect their interaction with technology [11]. This significantly restrains technical innovations' perceived usefulness and the perceived ease of use, preventing the acceptance of novel technical solutions by this group. In addition, attitudinal factors, such as self-efficacy and anxiety have been found to underlie age differences in technology use [6]. Reviewing this body of research, it can be argued, that in order to understand older adults' adoption of innovative technology, holistic models need to combine individual characteristics and social contexts of use [9]. Taking this into account, the TEC framework promotes multiple factors positively affecting older adults' engagement with technology: (*i*) supportive environments, (*ii*) social support and (*iii*) consideration of individual characteristics.

Supportive Environments. Studies suggest that the environment in which older users engage with technology has important implications for their user experience. Environments which allow for training and experimenting, such as guided courses or simulations, should be organised in sensitive settings, with adequate support for learning, since older adults need considerably more support than younger adults [2, 15].

Social Support. To provide adequate social support, older adults' efforts, learning to use innovative technology, should be valued [3]. Positive reinforcement and encouragement has shown to enhance learning [4]. Positive role models also help to overcome potential negative attitudes held by older adults towards technology [3]. Older technology literates who have positive attitudes towards technology can be used as role models for older learners. Video-based instructions provided by role models have been found to enhance knowledge acquisition among older adults learning the use of technological [8]. Similarly, there is evidence that even social comparisons with younger adults can improve older adults' performance, as long as it is within a positively stereotyped domain, like solving crosswords [14].

Individual Characteristics. Adaptations that minimise the individual effects of age-related decline on interactions with technology are important tools to improve user experience [4]; increased font size and contrast are valuable adaptations for the visually impaired elderly. Similarly, larger and simpler keyboards, touch screens and other alternative input devices may also be used to accommodate older adults' motor limitations.

The development of the TEC framework within the SIforAGE project was based on this comprehensive evidence, considering the full complexity of properly involving older users in the process of innovation management for societal change.

3 Technology Experience Café as a Framework

The following section provides detailed information on the methodology of TEC and how it was implemented in five sites in four different countries across Europe, focusing on (*i*) participating stakeholders, (*ii*) the general design of the TEC, (*iii*) the used evaluation tools, across all five TECs within the SIforAGE project, respectively.

3.1 Participating Stakeholders

TECs allows for a dialogue between older adults and various stakeholders on a wide range of issues related to science and technology. In addition to older adults themselves, this includes R&D stakeholders, representatives of a broader public participants—such as family members and societal institutions—public health and care services, NGOs or associations of older people, and also enterprises—such as manufacturers, providers, insurers, distribution or marketing companies. The concrete set of stakeholders varied across all five venues, see Table 1. This is due to the fact that each TEC's effectiveness, in terms of objectives, hinges on the presence of the appropriate set of stakeholders. Particular TEC objectives can be related to presented technologies' particular stage within the innovation cycle, as well as scientific and/or economic goals of participating stakeholders. The following section contains an overview of the involved stakeholders' profiles.

Table 1. Overview of the site-specific variations of the TEC-design elements; DU = Direct Users, IU = Indirect Users (median of age), N = Nursing Students, TE = Technology experience stations, IS = Individual Schedule, GE = Group Experience, BE = Blended Experience.

Site	DU	IU	Day	TE	Schemes	Café
Denmark, Frederiksberg	9 (73)	22N	1	4	IS+Helpers	Socialising with helpers and entertainment with non-technical media
Denmark, Glostrup	18 (69)		1	2	IS	Socialising and entertainment with non-technical media
France, Troyes	32 (71)	9	2	5	IS	Socialising and entertainment with non-technical media
Germany, Saarbrücken	25 (71)	16	1	2	GE	Socialising and round-table discussion
Italy, Torino	30 (69)		2	1	BE	Socialising

Direct Users. They were approached according to a definition of the target audience: Senior citizens, age 55/60/65 or older, with no or minor health-related limitations, allowing active and independent participation in the TEC activities. The Danish TEC had a broader target audience including persons with mild health-related limitations requiring support of their caregivers.

Indirect Users. Entities benefiting from data provided or actions stimulated by the technology during its usage by the direct user; whose activity consists in helping the direct users in their daily life, partially or totally, within a professional or voluntary activity, such as helpers, relatives, caregivers or practitioners. This also includes persons who coordinate and/or fund activities of care and home services, such as local, regional or national authorities, caregiving companies, NGOs, insurers, banks, or charities.

Technology Representatives. These are: scientists presenting new technologies in the context of scenarios and collecting opinions aiming at directing scientific endeavours, technology developers presenting prototypic solutions and collecting feedback within the UCD development cycle, providers, manufacturers, and marketing agents presenting early-on-the-market products and collecting feedback for designing marketing strategies, and middle-man entities organising TECs on behalf of the above mentioned groups of technology representatives, compare also the paragraph on Technology Experience Stations.

3.2 TEC Design

Similar to the involved set of stakeholders, each TEC's design depends on the objectives and the available resources and facilities. Across all five TECs, typical elements included: ($ii.a$) plenaries, ($ii.b$) technology experience stations, ($ii.c$) experience schemes, ($ii.d$) social spaces—cafés and ($ii.e$) supporting services. Beyond that, the TEC events differed in the way these key elements were organised; overall some events were organised on two succeeding days and some were held in one day, compare Table 1 and (Fig. 1).

Plenaries. These were held as general meetings, briefing participants on the event, expected outcomes and organisation. Plenaries may include introductory presentations and also other stakeholders' presentations. They are typically held at the beginning—briefing—and at the end—debriefing—of the event.

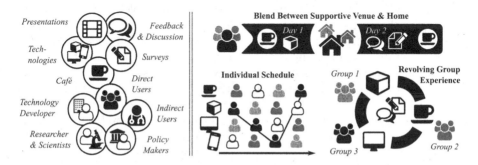

Fig. 1. The left panel presents the variety of activities and stakeholders encompassed by the central component—the café; the right panel presents the three different experience schemes implemented over the fives sites.

Technology Experience Stations. One of the main goals of TECs is to provide users with the opportunity to interact with a particular technology, preferably to try it in a realistic scenario and, with the support of qualified personnel to receive explanations and consultations. Within SIforAGE, all TECs contained more than one technology, providing several stations; time allocated to each station depends on the nature of the technology and the scenario. In general, the pace of acquainting with any new technology has to be taken into consideration. According to the afore-mentioned adaptation for older adults' individual characteristics, software and hardware adaptations were used during the TECs to accommodate potential age-related declines in perceptual, cognitive, and motor abilities, see Sect. 2.

The following technologies could be experienced at the five sites: Denmark, Frederiksberg—DukaBOX, InCare, Brain+ & Who am I?; Denmark, Glostrup—El-pris tavlen & E-box; France, Troyes—ARPEGE, Mobile application evaluation, EELEO, Robot, Social TV; Germany, Saarbrücken—Smartphone In-Door Navigation, Intelligent Speaking Kitchen; Italy, Torino—Torino Facile.

Experience Schemes. Ranging from group-experimentation to assisted single person experimentation, different schemes were implemented. Again, the decision upon the experience scheme depends on the technology experience stations and their tasks, the outcome, feedback the technology representatives opt for, as well as the direct users' abilities and profiles. In the Danish and French TECs, the direct users followed an individual schedule to experience all demonstrated technologies in an *Individual Experience* set-up together with the respective technology representative. In the Danish TEC in Frederiksberg, the direct users' profile required additional assistance whereby helpers facilitated the technology experience towards an *Individual Assisted Experience*; one helper accompanied one direct user during all technology experience stations. In the German TEC, direct users where split into three groups which allowed for a revolving *Group Experience Scheme*. In this scheme, they stayed within one group and rotated from one technology experience station to the next thereby jointly reflecting on the technologies. The group also spent the break—the café—together. As in the Torino TEC, direct users experienced only one technology, the experience scheme was changed towards a *Blended Experience*. Hereby the TEC workshop atmosphere was blended with the direct users' personal life. In the two-day TEC, direct users were given the opportunity to sign up for a platform, self test it in the scaffolded venue environment, receive demonstrations of the systems' capabilities and ask questions. Most importantly, at the end of the first day, there were given a technology-specific task as homework. This private experience with the technology was then discussed in the subsequent session and enriched with dedicated exercises. This blended experience scheme has also proven to be very powerful in *mobisaar*, a German active healthy ageing project; therefore, this scheme helps to accompany and keep a fixed user base in lasting operational tests of technology demonstrators with *Technology Readiness Level* (TRL)[4] of six or higher [1,15].

---

[4] https://en.wikipedia.org/wiki/Technology_readiness_level; accessed 2017.02.08.

Cafés. This constitutes the social aspect in SIforAGE and represents one of the most important features of TECs, being a social place where people meet technology and technology meets people in a casual way. Above all, the café allows people to meet people; by mentioning people, representatives of all discussed stakeholder groups are comprised. To facilitate this social aspect, nice environments, small food, soft drinks, and non-technical entertainment was and should be foreseen. Cafés also serve a far more practical goal which was especially relevant for the direct users in SIforAGE: Even healthy older adults get tired and distracted faster than younger users which can lead to loss of motivation, as well as biased or even unusable evaluation results. Within this line of thoughts, the café also represents a technology-distant space were users can reflect on their technology experiences amongst themselves or moderated by skilled facilitators; this transforms the café into an additional valuable source for feedback and a tool in the UCD process. Building upon its beneficial effect on older adults' performance, the French TEC provided crosswords in the café section to activate positive stereotypes [14].

Supporting Services. Overarching the technology stations, the experience schemes and the café, all TECs provided comprehensive support to all participants on any issue throughout the event. This was organised in the form of a help desk and local supporters at the TEC venue, ensuring that no older participant was left unattended at both the technology stations and inbetween the session, including also the evaluation.

3.3 Evaluation Tools

All TECs comprised two main phases of evaluation: (*iii.a*) the evaluation of the technology during or immediately after experience at the stations and (*iii.b*) the framing evaluation; the French TEC even featured a framing pre-post-test evaluation design. The evaluation of the technology during experience is highly dependent on the technology itself and the goal of its representatives, considering also the respective TRL. Therefore, multiple technology representatives used tailored surveys for their technologies. Conversely, the framing assessment was independent from the technologies and standardised across all five TECs. These dedicated surveys covered the following dimensions: (*iii.b.1*) perceived usefulness and perceived ease of use, (*iii.b.2*) stereotypes of the elderly in combination with technology, (*iii.b.3*) demographic information, (*iii.b.4*) previous experience with technology, (*iii.b.5*) feedback on the TEC and demographic profiles. Given their conceptual complexity, the first two dimensions stated are shortly introduced.

Technology Acceptance Model (TAM). Introduced in 1986 [7] its basic assumption is: An individual's behaviour intention to use a system is determined by *perceived usefulness*, defined as the extent to which a person believes that using the system will enhance their performance, and *perceived ease of use*, defined as the extent to which a person believes that using the system will be free of effort. TAM-2 marks an extension in terms of social influence and cognitive processes [16] and also comes in a modified version evaluating the acceptance and characteristics of technology for older users, which was used within the SIforAGE TECs [17].

Stereotypic Perceptions. This is commonly identified as one of the main barriers to technology use by older adults. Critically, the associated societal phenomenon of *Ageism*[5] has shown to be internalised by older adults themselves [4]. This effect turns into a barrier when it comes to technology, as the elderly might be convinced that they are too old to learn using computers even before attempting to do so [3]. In order to measure the impact of ageing stereotypes, items measuring *stereotype threat, stigma consciousness, stereotype content*, in general and specifically related with the use of technology by older people, were included in the questionnaire.

Each TEC contained an upfront available *Informed Consent (IC)* ensuring ethical issues handling in-line with the EU legislations on private data handling. Each IC contained the event's objectives, activities and procedures users will be involved in, the intended use of the results, the arrangements concerning audio/video recording and other issues according to national regulations or practices.

4   Results

In line with the overall scope of this paper, this section will provide results, from all five conducted TECs, on (1) older adults perception on the TEC as a framework, as well as the TECs' impact on technology related attitudes and (2) on other stakeholders' benefits affiliated with their involvement in the TECs.

4.1   Feedback and Impact on Technology Attitudes

Due to organisational issues, the two TECs held in Denmark did not include standardised questionnaires in the post-evaluation, compare Sect. 3.3. Therefore, older adults' perception, is only reported for France, Italy and Germany; in France, not all direct users filled out the post-experimentation surveys: 22 of 32 participants. Descriptive statistics indicate that the TECs were positively perceived across the three evaluated sites, Italy, France and Germany, compare Table 2.

Qualitative analysis of the post-survey's open feedback section underlines this result. Respectively, participants across all four countries consistently expressed their positive reception. They enjoyed participating in TEC characterising it as an *entertaining and pleasant experience*: "I really liked the event. The presentation was perfect and I really enjoyed my time. Keep it up!" (60 years-old participant, Germany) TECs were also very often described as *interesting, informative, and useful* for them: "I appreciated this meeting which interested me a lot." (90 years-old participant, France) "It is useful to know how the citizens can benefit from the services and what the difficulties are." (65 years-old participant, Italy) Others highlighted the importance of *involving older users themselves* in

---

[5] The systematic stereotyping and pervasive negative view of older persons in society.

Table 2. Older adults' perceptions of the TEC conducted in France (n = 22), Germany (n = 25), and Italy (n = 30); median (range) values ranging from 1 = "strongly disagree" to 7 = "strongly agree".

Statement	Median (range)		
	Italy	France	Germany
The overall TEC experience was pleasant	7 (2)	7 (1)	6 (3)
The TEC was conducted in an easy way	7 (2)	7 (2)	6 (5)
The quality of the provided instructions was good	7 (3)	7 (1)	6 (3)
The chosen technology evaluation methods were adequate	7 (3)	6.5 (2)	6 (4)
I learned new ways of interacting with technology	7 (3)	6 (4)	5.5 (6)
I learned new things about the tested technologies	7 (3)	7 (3)	6 (5)
Participation improved my technology knowledge	6.5 (3)	7 (3)	6 (5)
Participation was very useful for me	7 (2)	7 (2)	6 (4)

the innovation process: "It is nice you are asking people directly." (63 years-old participant, Denmark) Some were inclined to *participate in similar initiatives in the future*: "Interesting! I would like to participate in further studies as well. Thank you for this opportunity!" (67 years-old participant, Germany) However, some participants also *expressed difficulties* while participating: "It is difficult to answer precisely some of the questions." (80 years-old participant, Denmark)

The pre-post-test evaluation setup in France allowed for a comparison of direct users' perceived usefulness, perceived ease of use and perceived stereotypes in combination with technology, before and after the technology experimentation. One-tailed t-tests were conducted, showing significant increases on the TAM-2 sub-scales intention to use technologies ($T(21) = -1.92$, $p = .038$), perceived usefulness ($T(21) = -1.96$, $p = .064$) and self-efficacy ($T(21) = -2.05$, $p = .052$), as well as a significant decrease in stigma consciousness ($T(21) = -1.90$, $p = .072$).

4.2 Benefits for the Technology Innovation Process

Indirect Users. The broad involvement of indirect users in the TECs becomes very evident in the case of Turin: indirect users from multiple organisations ($\Sigma = 11$) attended, including NGOs ($N = 1$), trade unions ($N = 1$), organisations representing older people ($N = 3$), local authorities and policy makers ($N = 3$), foundations for regional development ($N = 1$) and associated European projects ($N = 1$). Within the scope of the innovation process management, involving local authorities and policy makers, as well as foundations for regional development is especially interesting. In the case of Turin, they stated that their participation was for conceptualising new tools for decision-makers responsible for the definition and implementation of municipal policies for the older people. They also explicitly aimed at developing new models of collaboration, knowledge transfer and projects clustering, in order to align the region as a hub of technology and innovation.

As a result of the German TEC, the research institution DFKI gained new insights from the round-table discussions, setting of an innovation project funded by the German Federal Ministry of Education and Research (BMBF) – DiDiER[6]. Similarly the Portuguese research institution ISCTE-IUL used the lessons learned from the TECs to successfully include the topic *Positive Role Models and Facilitators for Older Adults' Use of Technology* into their nationally funded research roadmap.

Technology Providers. Across the five TECs, the presented technologies ($\Sigma = 14$) can be categorised as follows: scientific tools (N = 1), prototypes under development (N = 4) and early-on-the-market products (N = 9). When subscribing to the event, technology providers had to state their expected outcome. Revealing that the main reasons for participating were indeed to receive feedback from direct users and collect requirements for new products (N = 5), to test or benchmark close-to-market products with target users (N = 3), to use the TEC as dissemination and marketing platform (N = 4), and to network with important stakeholders and policy makers (N = 2).

5   Discussion and Conclusion

This paper set out to present the Technology Experience Café, a tool aiming at involving older adults in the innovation process in a systemic way. Concretely, the TEC framework is presented as a tool for the technology innovation process that is (1) geared towards the specificities of involving older adults in this innovation process and (2) effectively involve all stakeholders through a systemic approach. The preliminary results show that, across four countries in five TECs, (1) older adults, direct users, positively perceived the TECs and in one site evidentially changed their attitude towards technology after participation and (2) a broad variety of stakeholders were effectively involved, ranging from technology providers to policy makers.

Positive Perception and Change in Attitude. The post-TEC survey results of three out of four sites illustrate well that the TEC framework was perceived throughout positively. The descriptive statistics are also reflected in the comments and feedback. Most promisingly, the TEC in France demonstrates how the proposed format can significantly affect older adult attitudes towards innovative technology. The 22 direct users significantly changed their attitudes towards innovative technology after participating in the TEC, reporting a higher intention to use technology in every day life, perceiving innovative technology as more useful, feeling more self-efficient when using technology and thereby also lowering the consciousness of technology related stigma according to their age. Especially the latter shows how tools like TECs can positively influence a phenomenon like ageism, by changing internalised beliefs in older adults and thereby shaping also their societal perception [4].

---

[6] See http://www.didier-projekt.de/wp/.

Innovation Process Management and Social Impact Assessment. According to the SIAMPI project [5], which aims at narrowing the gap between technology research and social impact, so called *Productive Interactions* are a powerful indicator for innovation's social impact; "exchanges between researchers and stakeholders in which knowledge is produced and valued that is both scientifically robust and socially relevant." [13, p. 212] Within this scope, TECs can clearly be classified as productive interactions which are a blend of direct interactions—aiming at behavioural change through direct contact between users and other stakeholders—and indirect interactions—aiming at technology uptake and dissemination through exhibitions, demonstrators and other media. Technology providers from the private sector attending the TECs stated explicitly that they aimed at retrieving requirements and feedback through face-to-face interaction with target users, as well as using the venue for marketing and dissemination. From a broader perspective, the participation of local authorities and policy makers serves even more directly as evidence for the capabilities of the TEC framework in the sense of strategic innovation process management.

Conclusion. The presented framework called Technology Experience Café, very promisingly, answers the growing need for tools for the technology innovation process that are (1) geared towards the specificities of involving older adults in this innovation process and (2) effectively involve all stakeholders through a systemic approach. Results have shown, that TECs can be a powerful tool to address the serious societal challenge, imposed on the process of technology innovation management. By involving older adults in this process during all stages and rendering technology innovation as part of a system of different, very heterogeneous stakeholders, TECs can play an important role in the arena of technology driven innovation for active healthy ageing in a demographically changing society.

Future Work. Though very promising, the here reported work has some limitations. The fact that methodology and especially evaluation tools were not consistent over all five TECs represents a major flaw in terms of the results' generalisability; mainly regarding positive perception and change in attitude of direct users. The fact that experience schemes differed across all TECs can be also seen as a methodological weakness, but on the other hand provides a variety of very practically oriented scenarios and best practices. Nevertheless, in order to better accomplish the goal of evaluating the impact of technology on market, as well as society, more effort has to be spent on incorporating tools for social impact assessment within the TECs themselves but also, more importantly, in their follow-up.

Acknowledgements. The underlying research is partly funded by the SIforAGE and the mobisaar project. SIforAGE is a Seventh Framework Programme collaborative project funded by the European Commission, grant agreement number: 321482. mobisaar is an InnovaKomm framework project funded by the German BMBF under the support code 16SV7431.

References

1. Alexandersson, J., Banz, D., Bieber, D., Britz, J., Rekrut, M., Schwarz, K., Spanachi, F., Thoma, M., Tröger, J.: Oil in the machine: technical support for a human-centred service system for public transport. In: Wichert, R., Klausing, H. (eds.) Ambient Assisted Living, pp. 157–167. Springer, Heidelberg (2015)
2. Blažun, H., Saranto, K., Rissanen, S.: Impact of computer training courses on reduction of loneliness of older people in finland and slovenia. Comput. Hum. Behav. **28**(4), 1202–1212 (2012)
3. Broady, T., Chan, A., Caputi, P.: Comparison of older and younger adults' attitudes towards and abilities with computers: implications for training and learning. Br. J. Educ. Technol. **41**(3), 473–485 (2010)
4. Chaffin, A.J., Harlow, S.D.: Cognitive learning applied to older adult learners and technology. Educ. Gerontol. **31**(4), 301–329 (2005)
5. Commission, E.: Social impact assessment methods for research and funding instruments through the study of productive interactions between science and society (2012). http://www.siampi.eu/. Accessed 14 Dec 2016
6. Czaja, S.J., Charness, N., Fisk, A.D., Hertzog, C., Nair, S.N., Rogers, W.A., Sharit, J.: Factors predicting the use of technology: findings from the center for research and education on aging and technology enhancement (create). Psychol. Aging **21**(2), 333–352 (2006)
7. Davis Jr., F.D.: A technology acceptance model for empirically testing new end-user information systems: theory and results. Ph.D. thesis, Massachusetts Institute of Technology (1986)
8. Gramß, D., Struve, D.: Instructional videos for supporting older adults who use interactive systems. Educ. Gerontol. **35**(2), 164–176 (2009)
9. Lee, C., Coughlin, J.F.: Perspective: older adults' adoption of technology: an integrated approach to identifying determinants and barriers. J. Prod. Innov. Manag. **32**(5), 747–759 (2015)
10. Ortt, J.R., Smits, R.: Innovation management: different approaches to cope with the same trends. Int. J. Technol. Manag. **34**(3–4), 296–318 (2006)
11. Rogers, W.A., Stronge, A.J., Fisk, A.D.: Technology and aging. Rev. Hum. Factors Ergon. **1**(1), 130–171 (2005)
12. Soar, J.: The potential of information and communication technologies to support ageing and independent living. Ann. Telecommun. annales des télécommunications **65**(9), 479–483 (2010)
13. Spaapen, J., Van Drooge, L.: Introducing 'productive interactions' in social impact assessment. Res. Eval. **20**(3), 211–218 (2011)
14. Swift, H.J., Abrams, D., Marques, S.: Threat or boost? Social comparison affects older people's performance differently depending on task domain. J. Gerontol. Ser. B Psychol. Sci. Soc. Sci. **68**(1), 23–30 (2013)
15. Tröger, J., Alexandersson, J., Britz, J., Rekrut, M., Bieber, D., Schwarz, K.: Board games and regulars' tables — extending user centred design in the Mobia project. In: Zhou, J., Salvendy, G. (eds.) ITAP 2016. LNCS, vol. 9754, pp. 129–140. Springer, Cham (2016). doi:10.1007/978-3-319-39943-0_13
16. Venkatesh, V., Davis, F.D.: A theoretical extension of the technology acceptance model: four longitudinal field studies. Manag. Sci. **46**(2), 186–204 (2000)
17. Wong, A.M., Chang, W.H., Ke, P.C., Huang, C.K., Tsai, T.H., Chang, H.T., Shieh, W.Y., Chan, H.L., Chen, C.K., Pei, Y.C.: Technology acceptance for an intelligent comprehensive interactive care (ICIC) system for care of the elderly: a survey-questionnaire study. PLoS ONE **7**(8), 1–7 (2012)

Research on Age-Adaptive Design of Information Interaction Based on Physiological Characteristics of the Aged

Ming Zhou[(⊠)] and Yajun Li

Nanjing University of Science and Technology,
200, Xiaolingwei Street, Nanjing 210094, Jiangsu, China
zhouming0829@126.com, lyj5088@163.com

Abstract. The research on age-adaptive design of information interaction based on physiological characteristics of the aged is carried out to make functional reconstructions to the interactive information output from the perspective of interaction mechanism according to interactive demands on the basis of the life styles, behavioral characteristics and behavior patterns of the elderly population. The structure form is manifested as cognitiom-understanding-decision-imple-menting-feedback, which constructs the information interaction prototype for observing and understanding, the information interaction prototype for exploring and iterative design, the information interaction prototype for communication and evaluation. These prototypes are applied to look into the information exchange mechanism and pattern of the products for aged people and the mapping and correlation between behavior pattern of the old and the way of interaction of products. This is combined with the principles and methods of information inter-action design to obtain the rules and integrate the behavioral paradigm of the innovation of product information interaction, thus constructing an innovative method system of "age-adaptive design of information interactive". With the information interactive performance of the products for the elderly improved from aspects including inclusiveness and usability, the information exchange between elderly users and products is more accurate, natural, smooth and easy, so that products designed for the elderly become more safe, comfortable, healthy and efficient, more "useful, easy to use, want to use", in which way the validity and reliability of the information exchange of the products for the aged is deepened and the breadth and depth of information interaction design of the products for the elderly are expanded.

Keywords: Elderly · Age-adaptive design · Information interaction

1 Introduction

Ministry of Civil Affairs authoritative statistics show that as of the end of 2015, China's elderly population aged 60 and over 22200 million, accounting for 16.1% of the total population, of which 65 years and over population of 143.86 million, accounting for 10.5% of the total population, China has entered a serious Of the aging society. With the

© Springer International Publishing AG 2017
J. Zhou and G. Salvendy (Eds.): ITAP 2017, Part I, LNCS 10297, pp. 211–220, 2017.
DOI: 10.1007/978-3-319-58530-7_15

growth of age, the physiological capacity of the elderly, habits and adaptability to the external environment are rapidly declining, especially in the context of the ever-changing information technology interactive information technology products has been far beyond the way the elderly Based on the physiological characteristics of the elderly population, this paper studies the appropriate aging design strategy of information interaction, and improves the information interaction performance of elderly products from the aspects of inclusiveness and usability so as to make the information exchange between the old users and the products Information exchange is more accurate, natural, smooth, easy, so that older products more secure, comfortable, healthy, efficient, more "useful, easy to use, want to use."

2 Elderly Physiological Characteristics Extraction and Information Interaction Demand Mining

Cognitive ability includes intelligence, attention or alertness, language, memory and learning function, visual spatial ability, psychomotor ability and executive function. Cognitive ability of the elderly mainly presents two significant features: (1) degenerative changes, that is, the general trend of decline or aging rather than growth or development. (2) differences in changes. On the one hand, the performance of different psychological functions of the early and late aging, and different rates, such as the perception of recession earlier and faster, and slow aging and other thinking; the other hand, between individuals: some elderly and even elderly people As senior government officials or managers of large and medium-sized enterprises or decision-makers, showing unusual insight and a very high intelligence, but some elderly memory significantly recession, mental significantly passivation, thinking serious delay. When they are in their 60s, cognitive abilities begin to decline, but decline slowly. By the time they are in their 80s, the speed of performance declines rapidly. Speech and verbal memory decline dramatically. Digital ability and intuitive speed The most obvious decline. The current study shows that the cognitive decline in the elderly is mainly due to information processing and slow response rate caused.

2.1 Changes in Intelligence

If the intelligence is divided into language ability (crystal intelligence) and fast learning ability (liquid intelligence) of these two parts, the liquid intelligence increases with age and a large degree of decline, the decline in liquid intelligence is mainly due to slow processing speed. Therefore, the need to quickly complete a number of designated tasks in a short time, the elderly showed greater difficulties. The crystalline intelligence is acquired mainly acquired, and it is knowledge, culture, experience accumulation and ability to understand. As the elderly experienced a wide range of experience, crystal intelligence easy to maintain. Senile mental decline, mainly for the memory impairment, stubborn thinking, attention is difficult to focus on.

2.2 Memory Changes

According to the cognitive load theory, the working memory capacity of the individual is extremely limited, especially in the elderly with cognitive deficits. The memory of the elderly tends to decline with age, but the decline is not significant. The general trend is: after the age of 40 there is a more pronounced decline stage, and then maintained at a relatively stable level, until after 70 years of age there is a more pronounced decline stage. Assuming an average score of 100% (highest) for memory between 18 and 35 years of age, the average score for memory at age 35–60 is 95% and 80–85% for 60–85 years of age. It can be seen that most of the elderly, the general trend of memory changes with the aging decline, mainly as follows: mechanical memory decreased significantly, significantly slower memory speed, memory span smaller, memory capacity decreased significantly.

2.3 Visual Function Changes

The increase of age has almost all negative effects on the visual system. Most of the visual function changes of the elderly show narrowing of vision, absolute threshold of brightness, decrease of visual acuity, decrease of contrast sensitivity, increase of glare sensitivity and color Discrimination decreased. In particular, the elderly have decreased visual acuity at night. In order to see objects, 60-year-old people need 20-year-old 5 or 6 times the light, and need to use magnifying glass to see the writing, an increase of about 20% of the lighting. In addition, the focus of the eye slows down, especially for low-frequency wave color recognition ability, often on the green, blue and purple and other low-frequency wave color is unclear, doubling the eye reaction time, glare to make eyes blind time doubled. Most of the elderly suffer from astigmatism, presbyopia, myopia and hyperopia of the disease. With increasing age, visual spatial capabilities and execution speed have declined.

2.4 Changes in Behavioral Functions

In the process of interaction, the important factors that affect the motor function of the elderly mainly include: independent activities, physical and range of activities, physical flexibility and coordination, daily living ability. With age, the elderly there is the phenomenon of muscle atrophy. Ordinary people reduce the muscle tissue from about 50 years of age, 60 years after the greatly accelerated. Therefore, once the elderly limb function degradation is more serious or suffering from certain diseases caused by limb can not be flexible operation of the mouse, for example, some elderly people will tremble, as well as amyotrophic lateral sclerosis (amyotrophic lateral sclerosis (ALS) patients Fingers lose the ability to exercise, the elderly it is very difficult to interact with the machine.

3   Aging Information Exchange Decision-Making Mechanism

Interaction design is a complex decision-making logical process, which involves the use of context, behavior pattern, cognitive psychology, meaning construction and so on. "After abstraction, process of behavior, acting on refining the general information structure, and make it has a positive feedback".

Information architecture focused on product information, the core task is to organize information, so that information is ordered. Concerned about the structure of product content, but also concerned about the behavior used to access the content, and how to present the content to the user; behavioral logic describes the user may occur interactive behavior, and the use of product-specific behavior of the process of the process, Behavioral design, but also concerned about how the behavior and form and content to contact. Adaptive aging information exchange decision-making is described from the origin of interactive design decision-making rules that match the information architecture and behavioral logic, so that the formation of symbiotic relationship between man and machine.

In the interaction design derives the product frame from the user demand process, the information architecture and the behavior logic match is the vital point of convergence. Behavioral logic does not exist in the imagination, it is the interface for the media to the information structure under the interface as the foothold and carrier. It is precisely because of the existence of information architecture, making the behavior of interactive design logic can be extended over time to happen. Design process to improve the information structure and behavior of the degree of matching logic, you can enhance the user control and the corresponding user experience.

The matching mechanism between information architecture and behavior logic can be summarized into three levels: the implicit layer: Alan Cooper points out the existence of mental model and realization model from the perspective of user cognition, and the cognitive friction existing between them results in the user operating product obstacle; Interactive layer: the interaction designer does not directly design the psychological model and implementation model, directly deal with the information architecture and behavioral logic, the important work is to match the construction of a user-oriented performance model; explicit layer: the user operating the product, Of the behavior directly on the interface of information, performance model in the user and the product plays a connecting role between the link. Interaction between User Behavior and Product Information A situation occurs where the context can help people act on information in a manner that is necessary for accomplishing the goal. Interaction design is the logical relationship between behavior and information of the explicit layer, and the matching process is based on the mental models of the implicit layer and the realization model matching, and finally through the expression model with real structure or concept structure.

4   Aging Design of Information Interaction Task Based on Cognitive Characteristics of the Aged

4.1   Information Exchange Interaction Channel Selection for Cognitive Characteristics of the Elderly

The decline of physiological function of the elderly population, the formation of a certain degree of cognitive and interaction barriers, need a simple, natural visual, auditory and tactile channel interaction to achieve "useful, easy to use" goal.

Visual, auditory and tactile effects channels are designed in parallel. Users can choose one or several interactive ways to interact with the interface according to their special physical condition or preferences. For example, if the eyes turn right or "right" When the voice or the right mouse button is pressed, the task dialog box bounces to the right. One visual and auditory (voice) channel in the interactive process, users can more directly and more naturally to express their ideas, to the user with a friendly, humane feeling. This user-friendly experience can greatly reduce the user of the traditional human-computer interaction in the machine gives a cold feeling, especially for the elderly, they are more in need of such a sense of relevance. This is the visual, auditory (voice) channel relative to the mechanical channel unparalleled advantage. However, visual and auditory (speech) channels also have some problems: for example, visual channels have "Midas contact" problems, and auditory (speech) channels are susceptible to background noise. Therefore, to interact with other means, such as tactile interaction, one or several interactive ways to operate the interface in parallel, allowing users to more comfortable and convenient way to convey their orders, while improving interface efficiency. In recent years the rise of multi-channel interaction is to solve similar problems with these.

4.2   Definition of Information Interaction Task for Elderly Cognitive Features

For example, for a person with a disability, "I want to eat" is to meet the people's cognitive semantic requirements of the information organization, and "I want to listen to the network," said, "I want to listen to the Internet," the task of the user's interaction is not chaotic but to meet certain cognitive semantics, While satisfying the grammatical rules does not meet the normal semantic requirements of cognition. Different information regions constitute cognitive semantics according to human's cognitive rules. Therefore, the essence of information interaction is that the user constructs the dialog box combination of cognitive semantics through the physiological channel as the input to finish the series interactive task and the intelligent response process of the computer (or machine).

Such as the line of sight to track human-computer interaction system is divided into $n + 2$ interactive interface dialog box, respectively, for the dialog box $1 \sim n$ and the dialog box "start" and "end." The symbol di ($i = 1, 2, ..., n$) represents a staring dialog i, $\{di, ..., dj\}$ representing a stare dialog combination which is related in sequence and constitutes a specific cognitive semantics. S, E, respectively, stare at the dialog box "start" and "end", the development of interactive tasks: $Ti = \{S, di, ..., dj, E\}$, that stare at the dialog box "start" to confirm the user began to interact, Then the dialogs "di", "dj", which contain specific cognitive semantics on the interface, are stared, and the end of the interactive task is confirmed by looking at the "end" of the dialog. The time taken to view the Start dialog box to the End dialog box is recorded as the task execution time t. K represents the number of times a single dialog box continuously responds to a single dialog in the interactive dialog Ti, ..., dj, and the number of successive responses di is num (di), then:

$$K = \max\{\text{num}(di), \ldots, \text{num}(dj)\} \tag{1}$$

For example, Ti = {"Start", "I", "To", "Drink", "End"}, the user to complete this interactive task need to stare at the dialog box "Start", "Water" and "end", that is, by ①→②→③→④→⑤ orderly stare at the dialog box, the task contains the cognitive semantic information "I" drink water.

4.3   Information Exchange Appropriate Aging Design of the Principle of the Gestalt

- The principle of Gestalt: proximity

The proximity principle is that the relative distance between objects affects whether we perceive them as well as how they are organized together. A number of objects closer to each other appear to belong to one group relative to other objects, and those that are far away do not belong to that group. The principle of proximity is closely related to the layout of the operator panels and dialogs in software, websites, and electrical equipment. Designers often use a column bar to separate the action buttons and parameter settings on the interface. However, according to the principle of proximity, we can not need the column lines, but only by the same category of objects to be closely arranged to open this group of operational objects and other objects from the distance, so that this group of operating objects in the user To belong to a group, they can meet the same task requirements. Many graphical user interfaces use this approach to reduce visual clutter and the amount of code on the user interface. On the other hand, if the operational objects are placed improperly, for example, the distance between the relevant operational objects is too long, it becomes difficult to perceive them as relevant and the software becomes more difficult to learn and memorize.

- The principle of Gestalt: similarity

Gestalt similarity principle points out another visual perception rule that affects our cognitive classification: people tend to regard visual objects with the same or similar shapes, colors, and structural features as a group. If several objects in an interface are the same in shape, color, structural features, etc., then the user will see them as a class to meet the needs of the same task components; If the designer to allow users to quickly Effectively differentiate between the different operational objects, they will be for each category of operational objects to set a unique shape, color, structural characteristics.

- The principle of Gestalt: continuity

The principle of continuity is that our vision tends to perceive continuous forms rather than discrete fragments. The volume slider control is an example of a user interface that uses the continuity principle. The slider bar represents the threshold of the sound, and there is an icon on the slider bar where the user does not regard the icon as a separator for the slider, but instead treats it as a volume that adjusts the volume, because of the continuity principle Drag-and-drop controls. Even showing the sliders at the ends of the icons in different colors does not completely break our awareness of the slider as a continuous whole, although choosing a strongly contrasting color will definitely affect people's perception of continuity slightly.

- The principle of Gestalt: closed

Related to continuity is the principle of Gestalt Closure: Our vision system automatically tries to close an open pattern, perceiving it as a complete object rather than a fragmented fragment. Our visual system has the tendency to organize the objects in the field of view to obtain a stable, independent graph, a trend known as Gestalt in Gestalt psychology. The closure principle is often embodied in the graphical user interface. For example, when users open multiple software interfaces on the screen at the same time, the operation interface of these software is superimposed on each other. The software interface arranged in the back only exposes a part, but the user will still recognize this part as a certain border Complete interface, but the rest of it is obscured.

- Gestalt principle: symmetry

Gestalt symmetry principle is that when our field of vision of the object has multiple cognitive possibilities, our visual system will be in accordance with the most simplified form to recognize the object, symmetry is a simplified tendency in a common organization form. Human brain in the cognitive process to take up some cognitive resources, but the brain's cognitive resources are limited, subject to short-term memory capacity constraints, so the human visual system is often the most simplified form of organization to interpret To the object, because this is the most savings cognitive resources, but also to speed up the speed of cognition. In the interactive interface layout design, using symmetrical, balanced or appropriate proportion of composition methods, users can simplify the process of cognitive page layout, to speed up the user identification information.

- Gestalt principle: the main/background

The subject/background principle states that our brains divide the visual area into subjects and backgrounds. The main body consists of all the elements in the scene that occupy our main attention, and the rest is the background. The subject is located above the background and usually has a well defined profile with a smaller area than the background; the background is relatively vague and often has no definite edge. The reason our brains distinguish objects in our vision is to simplify our cognitive processes so that we can identify visual information as quickly as possible and place the visual focus on important objects for primitive humans in the grasslands or forests Rapid identification of food and natural enemies have a crucial role. In the user interface design, the subject/

background principle has two purposes. First, to provide operational feedback to the user, the feedback information can be pop-up dialog box in the form of highlights in the current user interface above, as the subject is our attention and interpretation; Second, the dialog box form of feedback does not occupy the user interface Of the total space, the user can still know through the background information they are in the current environment in which the whole process of that stage.

- Gestalt Principle: common destiny

The six Gestalt principles are for static (non-motion) graphics and objects, and the last Gestalt principle - common destiny, involves moving objects. The principle of common destiny is related to the principle of proximity and the principle of similarity, which affects whether or not the objects we perceive are grouped. The common fate principle states that objects that are moving together are perceived as belonging to one group or are related to each other. For example, if there are multiple files in a folder, if you want to move several files of any distribution, you can set the file to move with the mouse, the file will follow the movement of the mouse displacement, the movement Feedback gives the user a sense of whether their actions are valid and whether multiple or fewer occurrences occur.

Of course, in the real-world visual scene, the various Gestalt principles do not operate in isolation, but work together.

4.4   Research on Aging Design Based on Information Interaction Task

According to the information interaction task and the interaction decision mechanism, the task Ti is judged if the task satisfies the cognitive semantics in the specified time. F (Ti) to determine the principle is:

$$F(Ti) = 1 \text{ The task is completed as required}$$

$$F(Ti) = 0 \text{ The task is not completed as required} \tag{2}$$

(Ti) and the error rate Pf (Ti) for the interactive task Ti are: () () () () () () () ()

$$Ps(Ti) =? F(Ti)Ni \tag{3}$$

$$Pf(Ti) = 1 - Ps(Ti) \tag{4}$$

Set t0 as the maximum time allowed to complete a task Ti, k0 is the maximum number of consecutive responses allowed for a single dialog in the process Ti, and PT is the probability threshold of the system state judgment. According to formula (2) and (3), the total execution power of each task is calculated according to cognitive judgment semantics, time criterion, single dialogue box continuous response times and other judging criteria. When the success rate Ps (Ti) < PT, it indicates that the system can not meet the normal human-computer interaction requirement, and the system is not working properly. (2) If the total power is not less than the set threshold PT, the system does not need re-calibration.

Information adaptive aging is as follows:

Step 1: Select the parameters. The interaction task Ti is selected. According to the usage experience of the line-of-sight tracking human-computer interaction system, the maximum time t0 allowed for the execution of the task is set. The single dialog box allows the continuous response times k0 and the system operating state judgment probability threshold PT.

Step 2: The implementation of interactive tasks and records. According to the selected interactive task cognitive semantics request to start the task, record the task execution time t, a single dialog box continuous response times k.

Step 3: To judge the implementation of the task. According to the joint judgment criterion, we can judge the performance of this task, f (Ti) = 1 if t $\neq$ t0 and k < k0, otherwise f (Ti) = 0 when the task completion process satisfies cognitive semantic requirements.

Step 4: Identify the working status of the system. (Ti) is calculated according to the formula (3) and compared with the set probability threshold value PT to determine the current system operating state.

5 Discussion

The design of interactive information aging has a bright future in the field of helping the old and disabled, especially for people with loss of language expression and limb movements such as ALS patients, but the mental normal people, information exchange design can be used to help them through the available channels To achieve the expression of will. The main research work in this paper is:

(1) According to the cognitive rules of the elderly group design interactive tasks, to effectively prevent misunderstanding of information generated by misuse of older users, which is only the basic cognitive capacity of the elderly incapacitated mobility, people with disabilities is particularly important to reduce its Cognitive load and memory burden.

(2) According to the set of interactive tasks, when the implementation of personnel in the calibration position when the system has a high reliability, the accuracy of the implementation of interactive tasks up to 90%; with the implementation of personnel to leave the system calibration position, system reliability and leave The farther the calibration, the worse the reliability.

(3) According to the cognitive ability of the elderly population, the information interaction channel should try to make the interaction mode simple, natural and easy. In the selection of the effect channel, although the accuracy of the line-of-sight tracking interaction technique is not very high, the vision is the most direct and natural channel for information acquisition and consciousness expression. 80% of the human information is obtained by the visual, and most of the elderly executive dysfunction, the eye is the normal rotation, so the system to select the visual channel as one of the effect channel.

(4) The results show that based on the method proposed in this paper, the design of interactive tasks combined with the history of the implementation of interactive tasks can effectively identify the status of the current system to avoid the Midas contact

problems, local miscarriage of justice on the system working conditions, Reduce the system calibration caused by misjudgment. In addition to the above findings, this study also needs to be improved, mainly in: the method does not apply to all user groups, cognitive decline will significantly affect the accuracy of system state identification.

6   Conclusion

Based on the analysis of the cognitive changes of the elderly and the multi-channel characteristics of human-computer interaction, the paper presents a simple, natural interactive multi-channel information interaction based on the visual, auditory (haptic) and tactile effects channels Very suitable for a certain cognitive impairment of the elderly use. In addition, in addition to a certain cognitive impairment of the elderly, for the use of ordinary interactive means of the disabled people with disabilities, the system also has a certain applicability.

According to the requirements of cognitive interaction semantics, the interactive task is set up, the execution of interactive task is judged and the results of task execution are statistically analyzed. The current system working state is estimated according to the probability and statistics of historical interactive task execution. The experimental results show that the method can judge the working status of the current system more accurately, and avoids the miscarriage of the working state of the system caused by Midas contact problem.

Acknowledgement. My paper is supported by the Project supported by the Young foundation of the Humanity and Social Science of Ministry of Education of China (Project No. 15YJCZH243), the Fundamental Research Funds for the Central Universities (Project No. 30920130132029), the National Social Science Foundation of China (Project No. 16BSH127).

References

1. Drewes, H.: Eye gaze tracking for human computer interaction. Ludwig-Maximilians University (2010)
2. Nakano, Y., Conati, C., Bader, T.: Workshop on eye gaze in intelligent human machine interaction. In: Proceedings of the 16th International Conference on Intelligent User Interfaces, IUI 2011, pp. 479–480 (2011)
3. Liang, J., Lam, J.: Robust state estimation for stochastic genetic regulatory networks. Int. J. Syst. Sci. **40**(1), 47–63 (2010)
4. Inbar, Y., Botti, S., Hanko, K.: Decision speed and choice regret: when haste feels like waste. J. Exp. Soc. Psychol. **47**(3), 533–540 (2011)
5. Liu, S.-l., Guo, J.: Study on multifunctional bed design for the elderly. Furnit. Inter. Decor. **1**, 28–31 (2016)

Product Design for the Elderly

Study on PSD Model with FAHP Method in the Product Design for Older Adults

Yongyan Guo$^{(\boxtimes)}$ and Minggang Yang$^{(\boxtimes)}$

East China University of Science and Technology,
Shanghai, People's Republic of China
gyymemory@163.com, yangminggang@163.com

Abstract. There is a large aging population in China, not only because the old population base is huge, but also the growth rate is relatively fast there. Health care policy has become a way to improve the aging life. Fitness will effectively improve the physical condition of the older adults, but there is a big problem for them in terms of fitness awareness. Therefore, there is a big gap in the design of the fitness products for older adults. This research is about how to persuade the older adults to be willing to exercise by the product design. The motivation and ability of older adults' fitness are weighted with FAHP method. According to the PSD model, the product is decomposed into different semantic information elements and the weight of the elements will be the guidance in the product design.

Keywords: PSD model · FAHP method · Older adults · Intelligent product design

1 Introduction

There is a huge demand for intelligent fitness products in the Aging society. China is the world's aging population, not only the old population base is huge, but also the growth rate is relatively fast. At the end of 2015, China's population of 60 years old and above is 221 million 820 thousand people, accounting for 16.15%, of which the population of 65 years old and above is 143 million 740 thousand people, accounting for 10.47% [1].

Fitness will effectively improve the physical condition of the older adults, but there are some big problems in the physical fitness awareness and fitness condition for them. (1) The exercise environment is not suitable for the older adults doing outdoor sports because of the air pollution, long fog and haze, etc. Lacking of exercise place is another problem for the elder's fitness. (2) For older people with relatively weak physical functioning, the impact of the weather and other external conditions on the body should be considered. For example, climatic characteristics of winter are low temperature and the dry air. The older adults exercise in such weather conditions can easily lead to colds and respiratory diseases. (3) Lack of awareness of movement. Exercise is not only for lose weight, but more important for the health of the body. For the older adults with normal BMI and body fat composition, exercise can change the structure of muscle and fat, improve the corresponding health indicators, and improve the function of all aspects of the body.

© Springer International Publishing AG 2017
J. Zhou and G. Salvendy (Eds.): ITAP 2017, Part I, LNCS 10297, pp. 223–232, 2017.
DOI: 10.1007/978-3-319-58530-7_16

Exercise can enhance physical fitness, improve the body state, but on the contrary, it is a wear process for the knee joint. Old people can't exercise too much. The special guidance is needed. Professional guidance and monitoring can help to prevent sports injuries [2].

Therefore, there is a big gap in the fitness product design for the older adults. The challenge of this research is how to design fitness product with persuade design (PSD) model to persuade the older adults to be willing to exercise. According to the PSD model, the product is decomposed into different semantic information elements. The weight of the factors which is got by the fuzzy analytic hierarchy process (FAHP) method is the guidance in the design progress.

2   Persuasive Design Model

2.1   Fogg's Model

The model of persuasive tech is a tool to describe the user's behavior change, which is studied in the Persuasive Technology Lab of Stanford University. According to BJ Fogg's article, there are three important events in the model: motivation, ability and triggers. A trigger is something that tells people to perform a behavior now. In fact, for behaviors where people are already above the activation threshold – meaning they have sufficient motivation and ability – a trigger is all that's required (Fig. 1). Triggers are divided into three types: sparks, facilitators, and signals. A spark is a trigger that motivates behavior. A facilitator makes behavior easier. And a signal is to indicate or remind the user [3].

Fig. 1. Fogg's model

This model constructs the individual ability based on the persuade design framework. It is a model with the most extensive impact to design. The advantage of the model is that it puts forward the correlation of motivation and capability of the persuasion design, pointing out the decomposition levels of each factor. The disadvantage of the model is that it is a qualitative analyze model of ability and motivation, so that it is difficult to provide direct guidance to design and strategies.

2.2   Persuasive Systems by Oinas-Kukkonen and Harjumaa

In the Persuasive Systems by Oinas-Kukkonen and Harjumaa, there are four design classification for persuasion design, the Primary Task support, the dialogue support, the System Credibility Support and the social support. Each category is divided into a number of design strategies. According to this system model, the intelligent products

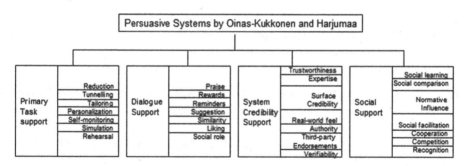

Fig. 2. Persuasive Systems by Oinas-Kukkonen and Harjumaa

can be divided into the 28 criterias (Fig. 2) [4]. Each criteria can be weighted based on the system hierarchy.

It is characterized by persuading users by computers, and it focuses on design of user interface graphics (GUI) and digital products. The model is mainly used to guide the interface design of network, but it is rarely used to guide the design of intelligent products.

2.3 DWI Model

At the persuasive conference, Dan Lockton et al. defined the concept of "design from the perspective of intent" (DWI) as "the change of design intent or the change of some user behavior" (Lockton, Harrison and Stanton 2008; Lockton, Harrison, Holley and Stanton 2009; Lockton 2013) [5] DWI method is generally applied to the model of user behavior, and its influence is determined by two modes: "Inspiration" and "Prescription". In the inspiration mode, the designer combines six different lenses (lens) from a wide range of target behaviors, representing the principles that can be used to influence behavior through design. In the prescription pattern, the designer has summed up a series of expression patterns of behaviors. Lens are methods for organizing design model which share understanding of how to influence the way of user's thinking and related behaviors.

The six lenses are: (1) Architectural Lens (2) Error-proofing Lens (3) Persuasive Lens (4) Visual Lens (5) Cognitive Lens (6) Security Lens. These lenses are a very specific way to help stimulate a variety of design patterns when the designer is to use these lenses to obtain a viable solution (Lockton 2013). The six lens are applied in different fields that range from interface design to product design and environmental design. It is used to help designers have more concept designs. The disadvantage is that although the model provides many guiding lenses, but it lacks of detailed and feasible evaluation method in the specific product design, and lacks of weight of each lens in the design.

2.4 Review Summary of PSD Models

In the intelligent product development, the composition of the product is more complex. Combined with the above models, the comprehensive PSD model will help to provide guidance for the selection of product design strategy.

3   AHP (Analytic Hierarchy Process) and FAHP (Fuzzy Analytic Hierarchy Process)

3.1   AHP and FAHP

The Analytic Hierarchy Process (AHP) is proposed by the Professor T.L. Saaty (1980). He used the AHP when he studied the "emergency plan" for the U.S. Defense Department in 1971. In 1977 he issued a "Modeling of Unstructured Decision Problems—Analytic Hierarchy Process" on the International Conference on mathematical modeling; then AHP has been applied in many fields of decision-making problem, while the same time AHP theory has also been developed [6]. Fuzzy analytic hierarchy process (FAHP) can be used to deal with fuzzy decision-making problems. A fuzzy concept was added to the analytic hierarchy process by Grann (1980) first [7].

3.2   Steps of Fuzzy Analytic Hierarchy Process

The basic idea of Fuzzy AHP is based on the nature of multiple objective evaluation and overall goal. The problem itself is decomposed to the hierarchy structure. Therefore, in the use of FAHP decision-making, the progress can be broadly divided into the following four steps.

(1) To analyze the problem and determine the causal relationship between the various factors in the system, to establish a multilevel hierarchical structure model for the various elements of the decision-making problems.
(2) The elements of the same level are pairwise compared with the criterion of above element. According to the evaluation criteria, the relative importance of the degree is determined, and the fuzzy judgment matrix is established finally.
(3) The relative importance of each factor is determined by certain calculation.
(4) Through the calculation of the comprehensive importance degree, all alternatives are ranked in order to provide the scientific basis for decision making.

3.3   The Mathematical Model of FAHP

The establishment of fuzzy complementary judgment matrix. In the fuzzy analytic hierarchy process (FAHP), the fuzzy judgment matrix is obtained by the quantitative pairwise comparison $A = (a_{ij})_{n \times n}$, when the factors are with the factors as follows:

(1) $a_{ii} = 0.5$, $i = 1, 2, \cdots, n$;
(2) $a_{ij} + a_{ji} = 1$, $i, j = 1, 2, \cdots, n$;

The judgment matrix is called fuzzy complementary judgment matrix. In order to give a quantitative description of the relative importance of criterion for any two compared schemes, quantity scale is usually given by the method of 0.1–0.9 scale, as shown in Table 1.

Table 1. Quantity scale and the explain

Scaling	Definition	Explain
0.5 Equally important	Comparison of two elements	Equally important
0.6 Slightly important	Comparison of two elements	One element is more important than the other
0.7 Obviously important	Comparison of two elements	One element is more important than the other
0.8 Much more important	Comparison of two elements	One element is more important than the other
0.9 Extremely important	Comparison of two elements	One element is more important than the other
0.1, 0.2, 0.3, 0.4	Anti comparison	If judgment of r_{ii} is obtained by comparing of element a_i and element a_j, the judgment obtained by comparing element a_i and a_j is to be $r_{ji} = 1 - r_{ij}$

$a_{ii} = 0.5$ means the factors are as important as themselves; if $a_{ij} \in [0.1, 0.5)$, means factor x_j is more important than x_i; if $a_{ij} \in [0.5, 0.9]$, means factor x_i is more important than x_j.

Based on the above numerical scaling factors, a_1, a_2, ..., an pairwise comparison fuzzy complementary judgment matrix is obtained.

$$A = \begin{bmatrix} a_{11} & a_{12} & \cdots & a_{1n} \\ a_{21} & a_{22} & \cdots & a_{2n} \\ \cdots & \cdots & \cdots & \cdots \\ a_{n1} & a_{n2} & \cdots & a_m \end{bmatrix} \tag{1}$$

Weight formula of fuzzy complementary judgment matrix. A general formula is deduced for solving the fuzzy complementary judgment matrix. The formula for solving the weight of fuzzy complementary judgment matrix is as follows:

$$W_i = \frac{\sum_{j=1}^{n} a_{ij} + \frac{n}{2} - 1}{n(n-1)} \tag{2}$$

Consistency checking method of fuzzy complementary judgment matrix. If the weight value obtained by formula (2) is reasonable, the consistency test should be carried out. When the offset consistency is too large, it is proved that the calculation result of the weight vector is not reliable. The principle of consistency of fuzzy judgment matrix is derived to test the consistency principle.

Define 1: Set matrix $A = (a_{ij})_{n \times n}$ and $B = (b_{ij})_{n \times n}$ are both fuzzy judgment matrix, call

$$I(A, B) = \frac{1}{n^2} \sum_{j=1}^{n} \sum_{i=1}^{n} a_{ij} + b_{ij} - 1 \qquad (3)$$

is compatibility criteria for A and B.

Define 2: Set $W = (W_1, W_2, \cdots, W_n)^T$ is the weight vector of fuzzy judgment matrix A, $\sum_{i=1}^{n} W_i = 1, W_i \geq 0 (i = 1, 2, \cdots, n)$, It is said n order matrix:

$$W\star = (W_{ij})_{n \times n} \qquad (4)$$

In order to judge the characteristic matrix of matrix A, the decision maker's attitude is A. When the consistency criteria is $I(A, W) \leq A$, the judgment matrix is considered satisfied. The smaller the A indicates that the higher the consistency of the fuzzy judgment matrix is for the decision maker. A = 0.1 is better.

For the actual problem, the same factor set X pairwise comparison judgment matrix $A_K = (a_{ij}^{(k)})_{n \times n} (k = 1, 2, \cdots, m)$ is usually given by a number of experts (set $k = 1, 2, \cdots, m$).

They are all fuzzy complementary judgment matrices, and the set of weights can be obtained $W^{(k)} = (w_1^{(k)}, w_2^{(k)}, \cdots, w_n^{(k)}) (k = 1, 2, \cdots, m)$.

In order to test the consistency of fuzzy complementary judgment matrix, the following two aspects should be done:

(1) Checking the consistency of m judgment matrix A_k: $I(Ak, W^{(k)}) \leq A$, $k = 1, 2, \cdots, m$
(2) Test satisfactory compatibility between judgment matrices: $I(A_k, A_l) \leq A, k \neq l; k, l = 1, 2, \cdots, m$ can test that if the fuzzy complementary judgment matrix $A_k (k = 1, 2, \cdots, m)$ is acceptable, their comprehensive judgment matrix is also acceptable. Weight vector expression:

$$W = (W_1, W_2, \cdots, W_n) \qquad (5)$$

Formula (5):

$$W_i = \frac{1}{n} \sum_{k=1}^{n} W_i^{(k)} (i = 1, 2, \cdots, n)^2$$

As long as (1) and (2) are fulfilled simultaneously, it is reasonable and reliable to treat the mean value of m weight sets as the weight distribution vector of factor set X.

4 Case Studies

4.1 Analysis of the Older Adult's Fitness Behavior Model Based on FAHP and Fogg's Model

Methods: First, questionnaire survey of *Older Adults Fitness Motivations and Needs was done* in this study, and data on their demands of fitness products was collected, then the criteria of Fogg's persuasion design model (motivation, ability and trigger) is studied with FAHP method. The user behavior and the importance weight of fitness were investigated, and the main factors were found to motivate the old adult's fitness behavior. Then the workshop was held to make focus group discussion on the weights of factors one by one, which is proposed to improve the product.

In the end, the existing products are discussed by the brainstorming. Combined with the Oinas-Kukkonen & Harjumaa system framework and DWI, the new PSD model is made for the older adults' product design. Then the criteria of product and the weight of hierarchy criteria are got by fuzzy analytic hierarchy process. This persuasive design model can be used to design relative products for the older adults' fitness products.

4.2 The Results of Data Analysis

Combined with the user research and Delphi method, the fitness motivation - ability hierarchy model of older adults (Fig. 3) is got, and the FAHP was carried out by seven experts.

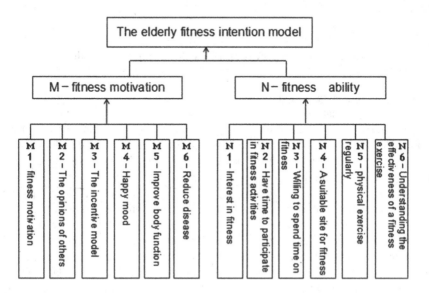

Fig. 3. The fitness motivation - ability hierarchy model of older adults

Table 2. The ordering weights of the elements in the decision level

Hierarchical structure	Weight	Uniformity	
M Fitness motivation	0.6667	0.0940	< 0.1
N Fitness ability	0.3333	0.0914	

Alternative	Weight	Alternative	Weight
M1 Self will	0.2117	N1 Interest in fitness	0.1311
M4 Happy mood	0.1367	N6 Understand a fitness effect	0.0634
M2 Evaluation of others	0.1136	N4 Have the right place for exercise	0.0483
M3 The incentive model	0.0873	N5 support for long periods of Physical exercise	0.0519
M6 Reduce chronic disease	0.0842	N3 Have time to participate in fitness	0.0206
M5 Improve body function	0.0331	N3 Willing to spend money on fitness	0.0180

The results of weight are calculated. The consistency of each judgment matrix is <0.1, indicating that the validation is valid.

According to above results, the rank weights that elements in the scheme layer to the decision goal is in the Table 2. The top three factors of influence to aging users' will of fitness are as follows: M1 Self will, M4 Happy mood and M2 Evaluation of others. The top three factors of influence to aging users ability of fitness are as follows: N1 Interest in fitness, N6 Understand a fitness effect and N5 support for long periods of Physical exercise.

4.3   The Strategies and Classification of Health Persuasion Model of the Older Adults

According to the Fogg's model, the health willingness of the older adults can be divided into four categories: high willingness-low capacity, to improve product usability strategies to reduce obstacles mainly by reducing the difficulty in the use of product. High willingness-high capacity, users has the high ability and high motivation themselves, so there is no need to improve their behavior by more triggering factors. Rich experiences of the product should be designed to meet the needs, with more enjoyable using process. Low willingness - low ability, not only lacking of physical exercise motivation, but also lacking of the exercise ability, this kind of users are difficult to be triggered by design. To improve their behavior, easy to use strategy is suitable, with the intelligent software to provide more incentives. Low willingness - high ability, this kind of users is characterized by having the basic ability to exercise, which can complete the fitness behavior independently, but because of lack of motivation, maintaining healthy behavior is difficult for them. The intelligent system should be used to improve their experience. With the help of the Oinas persuasion system, the interest and social interaction of the product will be added to improve the user's awareness and willingness to fitness.

Users with low motivation-low ability will be difficult to trigger. Users with high willingness-high capacity need little trigger to support them. Users with high willingness-low ability and low willingness-high capacity are the main objects to trigger design.

A total of 26 old persons (above 60 years old, 6 males, and 20 females) were randomly divided into two groups in the workshop. First of all, the ordering of weights above are shown to them, and brainstorming discussion are held among them, then their opinions and suggestions of the trigger design are recorded to improve the motivation and ability of elder's fitness.

Finally, the existing older adults fitness products are shown to users (including fitness bicycle and other products), the persuasion design model of aging fitness products are proposed.

4.4   PSD Strategy Model of Older Adults' Fitness Product

According to the FAHP, 7 experts are invited to make the matrix evaluation, and weight coefficients of criteria of the PSD model are calculated. The consistency of each judgment matrix are <0.1, indicating that the validation is valid (Fig. 4).

Hierarchical structure	Weight	Ranking	Uniformity	
A Appearance matrix	0.6870	1	0.0516	
B Control interface matrix	0.1265	3	0.0794	< 0.1
C Interaction strategy matrix	0.1865	2	0.0442	

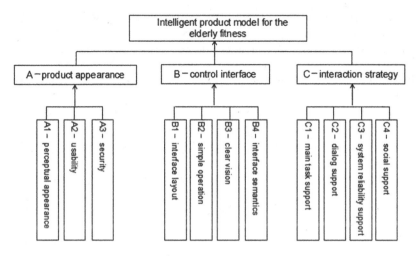

Fig. 4. PSD model of older adults' fitness product

5 Conclusion

In the intelligent product design for older adults, the PSD strategy according to the order of weight is: the appearance, the entity interface and the control interface, that respectively weight is 0.6870, 0.1865 and 0.1265. For the user of high willingness-low capacity, the usability design strategy is mainly adopted, and the appearance design is improved; on the user of low willingness-high capacity, the trigger motivation strategy is mainly adopted, and interactive interface design is focused on to enhance the user's interest in fitness.

Based on user research, the corresponding level of persuasion model of intelligent product is got, and the weight of every criterion is calculated. This evaluation method will provide design methods and strategies for designing of intelligent health products in the context of aging society. In the future research, we will analyze the influence factors of persuasion and satisfaction of using the product for the older adults.

Acknowledgments. This research was supported by Undergraduate Key Course Construction Project through the Research Foundation of ECUST (No. YZ0126104).

References

1. Yan, Z.: Investigation and analysis of physical fitness and exercise behavior of urban old adults. Business **44**
2. van Turnhout, K., Jeurens, J.: The healthy old adults: case studies in persuasive design. Interact. Des. Archit. J. IxD&A **23**, 160–172 (2014)
3. Fogg, B.: A behavior model for persuasive design. In: Proceedings of the 4th International Conference on Persuasive Technology (Persuasive 2009), Claremont, CA, pp. 1–7 (2009)
4. Oinas-Kukkonen, H., Harjumaa, M.: Persuasive systems design: key issues, process model, and system features. Commun. Assoc. Inf. Syst. The Berkeley Electronic Press (bepress). http://aisel.aisnet.org/cais
5. Lockton, D., Harrison, D., Stanton, N.A.: The design with intent method: a design tool for influencing user behaviour. Appl. Ergon. **41**(3), 382–392 (2010)
6. Saaty, T.L.: Decision making with the analytic hierarchy process. Int. J. Serv. Sci. **1**(1), 83–98 (2008)
7. Chang, D.Y.: Applications of the extent analysis method on fuzzy AHP. Eur. J. Oper. Res. **95**, 649–655 (1996)

User Experience Design Research of New Types of Home Appliances Based on the Analysis of the Learning Curve of the Elderly

Bin Jiang[✉], Lili Tian[✉], and Di Zhou[✉]

School of Design Arts and Media, Nanjing University of Science
and Technology, 200 Xiaolingwei Street, Nanjing 210094, Jiangsu, China
jb508@163.com, 1091268286@qq.com, zhoudi@njust.edu.cn

Abstract. Based on the learning curve of the elderly, this paper analyzed the user experience design of new types of home appliances. Firstly, it gave an introduction to user experience design and its social meaning. On the basis of the special characteristics of the elderly, the user experience design of the new types of small home appliances will bring great convenience to the elderly. Secondly, this paper analyzed the user experience design of home appliances used by the elderly. At present, due to the problem of excessive functions, complex operation and "younger tendency" of small home appliances in the market, it conducted an analysis of the physical and psychological factors of decreased learning ability of the elderly by making use of these problems. Then this paper illustrated the necessity of the elderly to use user experience design. At last, it put forward the principles of easy operation, easy function, humanization and fault tolerance according to the problems encountered by the elderly when they use new types of home appliances.

Keywords: User experience design · The elderly · Learning ability · New types of small home appliances

1 User Experience Design

1.1 User Experience Design

Based on appropriate appraisals of user's real expectation and purpose, user experience design is a user-oriented research. It revises the design product so as to guarantee a perfect interaction during the communication between people and machines. User experience is the response of the individual after being stimulated by the outside world. Viewing from different angles, it has different division. In his book *Emotional Design*, Norman analyzed levels of human cognition from the perspective of cognitive psychology (Fig. 1). According to him, it could be separated into instinct, behavior and reflection level [1]. The design of the instinct level refers to the external image of the product. At this level, product experience is only the preparation period which focused on the development of external factors like color, form and material in order to

© Springer International Publishing AG 2017
J. Zhou and G. Salvendy (Eds.): ITAP 2017, Part I, LNCS 10297, pp. 233–243, 2017.
DOI: 10.1007/978-3-319-58530-7_17

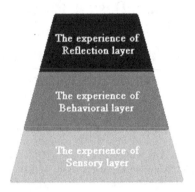

Fig. 1. The levels of user experience

stimulate users favorable initial instincts toward the product. Only at the behavior level will the design relates to the interaction between users and products. After using the product, users will have a more clear understanding of the function, performance and utility of products. During the interaction process, the design of an excellent product from the aspect of behavior level is based on the behavioral characteristics of users. By dong so, it can generate perfect experience from users towards products. The design of the reflection level tries to materialize ideological values and it enters into the feedback period of user experience. Designers try to express values through products' designs so as to meet users' demands and fulfill their aspirations. During all periods of using the product, the ideal user experience degree curve is supposed to be a straight line (Fig. 2). However, present user experience design put much emphasis on the preparation and interaction period which can bring benefits to developers. This initiative has exerted negative influence on the small home appliances used by the elderly, that's to say, the lack of efforts on products' feedback period will render it impossible to solve problems caused by the universal "younger tendency" home appliances presently used by the elderly. This can greatly affect old people's use of small home appliances. As a result, this paper focused on the analysis of special psychology of old people's unwillingness to use small home appliances due to decreased learning ability and gave a conclusion of the principles that old people should follow when using new types of small home appliances (Fig. 3).

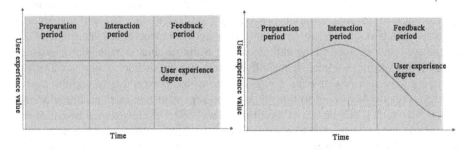

Fig. 2. The levels of user experience   **Fig. 3.** The levels of user experience

1.2   Social Meaning of User Experience Design

User experience design was developed according to the analysis of users' needs. By analyzing the characteristics of the elderly and designing small home appliances which meets their specific needs, it has the social meaning of bringing convenience to the elderly and making them feel willing to use these products.

2   User Experience Design Analysis of New Types of Small Home Appliances for the Elderly

2.1   Current Problems with Small Home Appliances Design

As a kind of daily necessities which is closely related to human life, the development of current home appliances is tightly combined with high technology. The new types of small home appliances mentioned in the paper mainly refer to those united with high technology. With the improvement of people's living standard, there is more and more demands for small home appliances. However, despite its fast development, there exist some major problems in terms of the design:

(1) Excessive functions. Presently, many manufacturers of small home appliance tend to improve their competitiveness by add more functions to products. Although it can attract lots of consumers, it can also bring the problem of because of complex operation result in inconvenient for use. For example, general microwave oven sold in the market has 80 to 160 kinds of functions. There are 100 to 400 kinds of functions on its menu [2]. The rice cooker was firstly invested to cook rice. But at present, new types of rice cookers (Fig. 4) can make cakes, cook porridge and dumplings. In fact, the elderly don't need so many functions. The repetition of function will only render it more inconvenient for the elderly to use them, not to mention operating them.

(2) Complex operation. The increment in functions results in more and more operation keys and the more complex operation interface. Faced with a wide range of functions and operation keys, the elderly feel at a loss on how to operate them, sometimes they even feel disappointed and annoyed towards these designs.

Fig. 4. New types of rice cooker

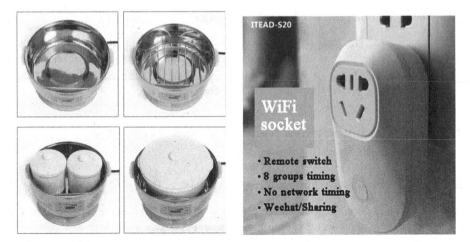

Fig. 5. Multifunctional cookware   **Fig. 6.** Outlet connected with WIFI

Giles Colborne, an English designer, stated in the book *Above Simplicity* that users want to feel that they are controlling the technology they are using now [3]. So in terms of many high-tech products, the elderly only hope that this product can finish a certain task in a more convenient way.

(3) "Younger tendency" [4]. Now the design of small home appliances in the market does not cater to the characters and needs of the elderly. For instance, the continual upgrading of the functions of new types of small home appliances (Fig. 5), the connection of products with WIFI for operation (Fig. 6) and so on all lead to failure in use of the elderly, which even brings "techno-phobia" among them. This tendency results in old people's unwillingness to use these small home appliances.

2.2 Current Problems with Small Home Appliances Design

People's learning ability generally won't decline with the increase of age, but the following factors can affect the learning ability of the elderly and lead to decreased learning ability among them. This paper analyzed it from the physical and psychological aspects:

(1) Physical factors

Physical factors can be viewed from two aspects. On the one hand, the increase in age and decline in memory (Fig. 7) will affect the learning ability of the elderly. Faced with complex functions and computer menu setting of small home appliances, an increasing number of the elderly feel the difficulty in operating and memorizing all the steps. On the other hand, the elderly will face declined physical functions with the increase in age. Physical functions influencing their use of small home appliances include vision, hearing, touch, hand and foot dexterity and brain activity, etc. All these physical factors have weakened old people's perception of and control over small home appliances and

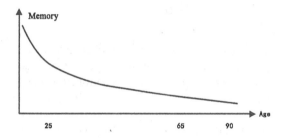

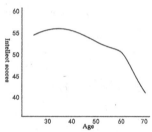

Fig. 7. The change of memory curve with the increase in age

Fig. 8. The change of intelligence curve with the increase in age

thus reduced their efficiency in operating them and increased the probability of incorrect manipulation. The research has found that ole people's average ability of using home appliances is 3.63 [5]. The reason behind that is the decline of old people's intelligence under the influence of physical factors with the increase in age (Fig. 8), but the design of new types of small home appliances gives no specific consideration of the elderly.

(2) Psychological factors

The change of psychological features is bound to exert influence on psychology [6], which also has to be viewed from two aspects. For one thing, the elderly lack motivation for learning and they tend to make analyses by experience. With the increase in age, they become more conservative which reduces their curiosity for new things. For another, the elderly have fewer opportunities for learning and face declined ability for learning new knowledge after retirement. These psychological factors hinder their use of new types of small home appliances so that they even harbor dull and fearful feeling towards these products.

2.3 The Necessity of Highlighting User Experience Design of New Types of Small Home Appliances for the Elderly

Now, user experience design has penetrated into every aspects of our life which has exerted positive influence on our quality of life, lifestyle and society. It's influence on old people's use of small home appliances are stated as follows:

(1) Meeting old people's needs of sensory experience

Sensory level experience means the experience of people's sensory organs stimulated by outside existence. When using small home appliances, the relevant sensory experience include vision, hearing and touch. The form, material, color and finishing process of products will bring stimulation to users' vision and touch. Some of them even have speech control which can bring stimulation to users' hearing. So after the process of designing user experience and understanding old people's special sensory needs, we can design new types of small home appliances that satisfy their sensory experience.

(2) Meeting old people's needs of behavioral experience

Behavioral experience is the one that occurs during the interaction between users and products. When using small home appliances, users make the most frequent interaction with products by their two hands. Foe example, they have to press the button when using rice cooker. Moreover, some of the current smart TVs can be controlled by hand and body gestures. On the basis of understanding problems like inflexible physical activity faced by the elderly when they become older, after user experience design process, we can avoid some complex interactions so as to provide products which are easier to use.

(3) Meeting old people's needs for emotional experience

Emotional experience is a kind of response generated after the interaction between users and products. On the one hand, after user experience design, new types of small home appliances can enable the elderly to have control over products by their good functions, ways of operation and interactions. On the other hand, their design of outer appearance can show great concern for the elderly.

3 Principles of User Experience Design of New Types of Small Home Appliances Based on Decreased Learning Ability of the Elderly

3.1 The Principle of Easy to Use

Easy to use is the most fundamental principle when designing new types of small home appliances. The principle of easy to use for products used by the elderly mainly include easy to learn, easy to memorize and easy to identify. New types of small home appliances based on the principle of easy to use can help users to learn instructions quickly and bring more convenience to them.

(1) Easy to learn

The elderly tend to think in a certain manner and they are very slow in learning new knowledge. They will only recognize things that are familiar to them. New types of small home appliances now sold in the market have too many varieties and functions which are very complex to operate for the elderly. They feel very confused about using these products. As a result, it is very necessary for the products to be easy to operate for the elderly, especially those small home appliances like kitchenware which are indispensable in our daily life. When designing these products, we have to ensure that the elderly can learn and use them directly by referring to their experiences without any specialized instruction. We can realize the principle of easy to learn by reducing products' functions so that the elderly can learn to operate by their experience.

(2) Easy to memorize

With the increase in age, the elderly will face declined memory and even have Alzheimer's disease which can greatly hinder their ability in using small home appliances.

So it is also very necessary to design products which are easy to memorize for the elderly. When design products, we should reduce their memorial burden so that they don't need to relearn instructions after initial learning. We all know that our ability of using products relies on two kinds of knowledge [7]: internal knowledge within our mind (long-term memory) and external knowledge (in the form of suggestions presented by products' design to give right instructions). As a result, we can reduce old people's memorial burden of using small home appliances in two ways. One way is to design products by taking advantage of users' long-term memory (designing products in the way that is easy to operate from ole people's memory); the other is to make proper use of users' short-term memory by applying suggestions like vision, hearing and touch to inform design.

(3) Easy to identify

With the increase in age, the elderly will have difficulty in identifying items like buttons, keys and text because of the decline in their vision, hearing, hand and feet dexterity and mental flexibility. For instance, although new types of home appliances like TV, washing machine and STB have already united with high technology, they still use the traditional remote controls. At this time, it comes to the question of identifying these messages faced by the elderly. Kitchenware is still operated through pressing different kinds of buttons which also relates to the identification problems faced by the elderly. The use of small home appliances is to improve the quality of our life rather than indispensable items. So most users of this kind of products are youngsters, there are few old people using them now. Moreover, these products are often operated by pressing buttons. The only problem remains for the elderly id the identification of different functions of these buttons. So it also turns out that the design of small home appliances should be easy for the elderly to identify them. By conducting surveys on the behaviors of the elderly when they use small home appliances, designers can design products which are able for the elderly to operate by their experience.

3.2   The Principle of Easy to Operate

With the increase in age, the elderly also witness changes in their heights. For instance, they will have problems like hunchback and decline in heights. So the principle of easy to operate can be reflected from the following two aspects. That's to say, the ease of operation in terms of interface and ways.

At present, new types of small home appliances all have interface. The design of interface is also a critical factor influencing users' choice of a particular product. The existing products in the market generally ignore the problems faced by the elderly. For one thing, the interface design of current products doesn't take into consideration the problem that the elderly have to face the decline in heights and sensory functions when identifying prompt tone and indicator light. To cite as an example, some rice cookers (Fig. 9) will automatically turn to heat preservation when the rice is ready. There are prompt tones during the process. However, if the sound is too small, it will be of no use for the elderly who are experiencing declined hearing. So designers have to take declined hearing of the elderly when choosing prompt tones, great attention should be

Fig. 9. Rice cooker

paid to choosing appropriate warning tones. Besides, the choice and layout of products' interface shows no concern for the elderly. For instance, the text on some rice cookers is so small that the elderly are unable to see that because of the decreased vision. That will in turn lead to old people's failure in using products. As a result, designers have to make appropriate choice and arrangements of elements like buttons, keys and text according to the visual features of the elderly when designing products.

The widespread use of new types of small home appliances brings about one problem. That's to say, faced with excessive functions and complex operation, the elderly feel very confused when using them. Say, smart TVs, which are popular now, have added functions like downloading software, watching movies online and playing games. Although more functions can provide more experience for users, the problem is that the remote control will have more buttons (Fig. 10) and the setup of STB (Fig. 11) which renders them more difficult for the elderly to use them. There are even some old people don't watch TV because of the difficulty of setting STB. So firstly, designers have to put aside unnecessary functions and try to improve the core functions by taking old people's needs and liking into consideration. Secondly, the process and ways of

Fig. 10. Remote control

Fig. 11. STB for TV

operation should be as easier as possible. If these products are indeed to be complex, they should be able for the elderly to operate them by simple learning based on experience.

3.3 The Principle of Humanization

Humanized small home appliances are centered on the elderly. During the design process, designers take full consideration of the elderly and making them feel the care and concern when using products. The principle of humanization can be illustrated through three aspects: humanized sensory experience, humanized behavioral experience and humanized emotional experience.

(1) Humanized sensory experience

Humanized appearance of products can express a feeling of concern to users by their visual messages. Humanized sensory experience of new types of small home appliances used by the elderly comes from vision, hearing and touch. In terms of their vision, they generally encounter the problem of declined eyesight. So products with humanized sensory experience have the following advantages. For one thing, designers take into consideration of the visual features of the elderly when choosing visual elements by avoiding the use of bright colors so as to avoid incorrect manipulation of products. For another, designers try to make sure that the text and pictures are bid enough for the elderly to identify. From the perspective of hearing, now nearly all products have prompt and warning tones. Old people's decline of hearing will pose threats to their use of products so products with humanized sensory experience also have the following merits. Firstly, when choosing buttons, designers try to use those which can be identified through touch so as to reduce the probability of incorrect manipulation. Secondly, due to the fact that old people's touch flexibility decreases with the increase of age, products demands little touch flexibility of users. At last, small home appliances used by the elderly have so many buttons that the elderly may have the difficulty in operating them because of their inflexible movements. So designers will try to expand the distance between different buttons without influencing everyone's performance.

(2) Humanized interaction experience

During the process, the elderly will have interactions with products. Only good interaction can encourage the elderly to continue their use of these new types of small home appliances. Because of decreased learning ability of old people, interaction experience of products should give concern to two aspects. Firstly, when choosing ways of interaction, designers should prefer those which are subconscious to the elderly like ways that has already been used in products. Sub consciousness is the fundamental motivation for awareness [8]. For the elderly, subconscious interaction is a kind of motivation. Only when they feel motivated will they be willing to use these products. Secondly, the process of interaction can lead to the operation of the next step. To a certain extent, it can be used to motivate the elderly to use new types of small home appliances and reduce their burden of learning.

(3) Humanized emotional experience

The purpose of products' humanized emotional experience is to create an emotional connection between users and products. According to Norman, emotion belongs to the reflection level of product design. Products with humanized emotional experience should provide users with good experience, convenient interface in order to make users feel happy, pleasant and secure during the whole process.

3.4   The Principle of Fault Tolerance

Fault tolerance is the ability to withstand false performances of products. Fault tolerance design of products can promote the smooth communication between users and products [9]. Fault tolerance mechanism of product design (Fig. 12) can improve the reliability of products. Fault tolerance should definitely be implemented to the design of small home appliances used by the elderly. It can be introduced from two aspects. On the one hand, designers should avoid incorrect manipulation. Certain literature pointed out that meaningful control of elements can reduce users' incorrect use. Fault tolerance of mew types of small home appliances reaches its aim of design control by physical constraints. For example, kitchen home appliances in the picture (Fig. 13) are controlled by rotate buttons. The design of buttons renders it unable to be operated by other means. On the other hand, all the incorrect manipulation that happened can be saved. For instance, the backspace key of the remote control (Fig. 14) just displays this principle.

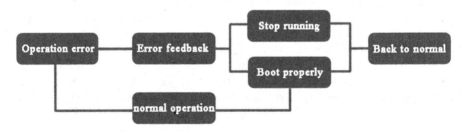

Fig. 12. Fault tolerance mechanisms for product design

Fig. 13. Smart rice cooker   **Fig. 14.** Remote control

4   Conclusion

The design of new types of small home appliances is for the benefit of human life. However, for the elderly who have "techno-phobia", it fails to bring convenience to them. As a result, when designing these products for the elderly, designers should take into consideration of psychological problems like declined memory and physical activities, lack of motivation and decreased learning opportunities so that the elderly will be more willing to use these products. Only when designers find the reason for old people's reluctance to use new types of small home appliances will they design products favored by the elderly.

References

1. Huang, S.: Application of user experience in APP design. Master's degree thesis, School of Design and Arts, Xi'an University of Science and Technology, Xi'an (2012)
2. Li, M.: Discussion on the interface design of smart small appliances from the user's needs. Acad. Res. **4**, 117–118
3. Colborne, G.: Simplicity First: Interactive Design Four Strategies (Turing Interactive Design from the book), pp. 39–40. People's Posts and Telecommunications Press, Beijing (2016)
4. Degrees [EB/OL]: Baidu Encyclopedia, 2 January 2017. http://www.hbrc.com/rczx/shownews-4014667-19.html
5. Quan, L.U.: Analysis on the demand of household appliances with the weak feature of the old. Packag. Eng. **36**, 81–84 (2014)
6. Xu, H., Xu, Y.: Interacting design of home sphygmomanometer for the elderly. Design (5), 121–122 (2015)
7. Norman, D.: Psychology of Design, pp. 133–172. CITIC Publishing House, Beijing (2010)
8. Huang, H.: On the existence and function of the subconscious. J. Ningbo Inst. Educ. (6), 52–56 (2004)
9. Yan, X., Nie, P.: Fault tolerance thinking in product design. J. Donghua Univ. (Nat. Sci.) (38), 636–639 (2012)

Analysis and Study on the Furniture Used by the Aging Population Based on the Quality of Sleep

Bin Jiang$^{(\boxtimes)}$, Hui Niu$^{(\boxtimes)}$, and Di Zhou$^{(\boxtimes)}$

School of Design Arts and Media, Nanjing University of Science and Technology,
200, Xiaolingwei Street, Nanjing 210094, Jiangsu, China
jb508@163.com, 939425664@qq.com, zhoudi@njust.edu.cn

Abstract. As China has already stepped into an aging society, it is of great importance to care more for the aging population. Compared with the speed of the aging of population, products designs for the elderly can't meet the needs of market. Due to the change of social roles and the increase of leisure time, now the elderly can have close interaction with furniture. However, there are little furniture specially designed for the elderly and they can't meet old people's basic needs. Sleep is a basic psychological process which is closely related to human health. A good sleep can relieve fatigue and refresh our mind. With the increase in age, one of the many physiological changes of the elderly is the change of sleep structure. They tend to wake up easily and have less sleep which leads to the decline of efficient sleep time as well as sleep disorders under the influence of other unfavorable factors. By researching old people's sleep disorder and its influential factors and combing the relationship of prone position with health, this paper focused on furniture used by the aging population to discuss the furniture's influence on the quality of sleep and proposed the design direction for this kind of furniture.

Keywords: The elderly · Sleep state · Prone position · Furniture design

1 Elderly-Orientation

1.1 The Aging of the Chinese Population

Since China stepped into an aging society in 1999, the aging of population has become increasingly serious day by day. According to the sixth nationwide population census, until 1st November 2010, 178 millions of the population is the elderly who accounted for 13.26% of the whole population. During the Twelfth Five-Year Plan period, China encountered the first drive for the aging population which kept an annual increase of 8.6 million [1]. The following two decades will be a period with the fast increase of the aging population. It is estimated that there will keep in annual increase of 10 million and reach the number of 400 million by 2030 (Fig. 1). At that time, China will have more old people than Japan and become a country with the highest degree of the aging of population in the world. By 2050, China will enter into an advanced aging society and reach the state of super aging. As a country facing with the most serious aging issue, there are exists huge unprecedented challenges in every aspect of the aging population.

© Springer International Publishing AG 2017
J. Zhou and G. Salvendy (Eds.): ITAP 2017, Part I, LNCS 10297, pp. 244–254, 2017.
DOI: 10.1007/978-3-319-58530-7_18

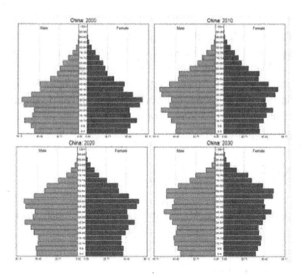

Fig. 1. The change of China's aging population

1.2 Aging

With the increase of age, people will witness changes in their physiological functions. It is also called aging. Aging means that people have weaker physiological functions compared with younger age, but it is different from being sick [2]. People's muscle strength becomes weaker when they reach the age of 30. If one's physical strength is 100 in his or her twenties, it will to fall to only one half of that figure with the increase of age. The result is that daily activities like standing up, going up and down stairs and open and close the door or window will also be significantly influenced.

Physical function		Middle aged(45-64)	Pre aging(65-74)	Late aged(Above 75)
Body motor function	Changes in body size and weight	Height slightly lower, weight slightly gain	Height and weight decreased significantly, Personal differences increase	Individual differences are smaller than before, Height and weight decreased significantly
	muscle strength	A slight decline in muscle strength and respiratory function	weak muscle strength and weak respiratory, Skeletal weakness	Decreased muscle strength and respiratory function, Obvious osteoporosis
	Balance ability and locomotivity	No difficulty moving, Balance ability decreased slightly	Balance ability decreased obviously, Move slightly difficult	Significantly impaired balance ability, Move quite limited

Fig. 2. Aging of physiological functions (parts)

Aging is also related with all the human organs. Apart from the before-mentioned muscle strength, eyesight and hearing, other ability like balance, adaptability to darkness, reaction capability, attention and application of knowledge will also begin to fall (Fig. 2). Aging can lead to the change of excretion and sleep. The change of daily routine itself is not serious, but the corresponding mental distress and conflicts with family members will cause many problems. Just like the aging of body, the aging of mentality is also unavoidable. Research found that the degree of mental aging is closely related with people's health, mood, heredity, nutrition, study, habits, physical activities and environment (such as water quality, temperature, economic condition, labor intensity, the density of social group, interpersonal relationship and pollution).

1.3 Elderly-Oriented Design

Elderly-oriented design conforms to the principle of" based on the elderly". From the perspective of the elderly, designers try to understand old people's different needs so as to design a living environment fitting for old people's physical and psychological needs.

2 Sleep States of the Elderly

Sleep is one of our basic physiological processes which can concern a lot with our body and mental health. A good sleep can help you to relieve fatigue, refresh your mend and recharge your body. With the increase of age, the elderly will witness changes in their physiological functions. One of them is the change of sleep structure. The elderly tend to wake up easily and have less sleep which leads to the decline of efficient sleep time as well as sleep disorders under the influence of other unfavorable factors [3].

2.1 Characteristics of Sleep

With the increase of age, old people have to face declined physiological function and sleep quality (Fig. 3). It can be reflected in the following aspects:

(1) Less sleep. The average sleep time for babies is 16 to 20 h. Adults have to sleep for 7 to 8 h, while the elderly have to sleep for 6.5 h everyday. Lack of sleep can have significant influence on human body. Research found that sleep inadequacy can lead to declined physiological function, neuroendocrine system disorders, negative feelings like stress and disappointment which can worsen the condition and even cause new health problems.

(2) The change of sleep structure. The result of a Meta analysis from abroad showed that:With the increase of age, the percentage of FWS (fast wave sleep) will decline, while that of SWS (slow wave sleep) will increase. It's also said that SWS keeps an annual growth of 2% before the age of 60. When reaching the age of 65, the elderly only have 10% of FWS. But when they are 75, they nearly have no FWS [4].

(3) Foreign scholars believe that due to the change of physiological function which gives rise to forward leading of their sleep patterns, the elderly will sleep early and get up early. Domestic reports stated that with the increase of age, the elderly will sleep earlier and have a longer sleep.

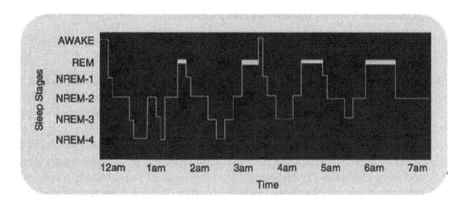

Fig. 3. Sleep efficiency in the elderly

2.2 Single Factors Influencing Sleep Quality

General condition: old people's sleep quality has close relation with their education level and marital status. Old people with education background lower than college degrees will suffer less from sleep disorders with the improvement in education. Those with degrees higher than bachelors tend to suffer more. Those windowed and divorced people have a higher percentage of suffering from sleep disorders than married ones.

Psychological condition: old people's sleep quality has correlation with their mental symptoms and negative sexual life. Moreover, those who have mental symptoms and negative sexual life tend to be easier to suffer from sleep disorder.

Physical condition: old people's sleep quality is related with their heath status, ability for daily living, uncomfortable time with 6 month and degree of physical pain. Old people with the above-mentioned problems tend to suffer more from sleep disorder.

Daily habits: daily habits like drinking, smoking, sports, community activities, interests are all related with old people's sleep quality. The elderly who often drinking and smoking have more sleep problems. Those who have fewer sports and community activities and fewer interests tend to suffer more.

Chronic disease: old people's sleep quality also has relation with disease like high blood pressure, diabetes, heart disease and brain stroke. People with the above-mentioned chronic disease can be more prone to sleep problems.

Interpersonal environment: old people's sleep quality have correlation with social support conditions, family functions and time of communication with children. Old people enjoy poor interpersonal environment have a higher percentage for having sleep disorders.

Economic status: old people's sleep quality concerns with their monthly wage, balance situation, endowment insurance and medical insurance. Old people with a monthly wage less than 5000 Yuan are more prone to sleep problems while those with a monthly wage more than that figure tend to suffer more.

2.3   Psychological Factors Influencing Sleep Quality

(1)   The influence of uncomfortable time within 6 months and physical pain on old people's sleep quality.

By analyzing many factors, the research found that uncomfortable time within 6 months and physical pain can greatly affect old people's sleep quality. If they suffer more from sickness and have a longer uncomfortable time, they will be more likely to have sleep problems. Physical pain can make it much difficult for the elderly to get to sleep. From the perspective of neuroantomy, noxious stimulation will reflect on cortical sensory area and induce painful and emotional feeling which in turn results in poor sleep quality and sleep disorders [5]. Research found that pain and discomfort, cough and asthma and forced posture can all lead to sleep disorder. Reports from abroad said that patients suffer from chronic disease have an incidence rate of insomnia up to 50%–88%. Besides, the study of using fibromyalgia and chronic fatigue syndrome as models to research the neurobiological effect of pain found that there are interactions between neural-endocrine-immune system and sleep-wake system. Pain can lead to sleep disorder, while sleep disorder in turn can reduce the threshold value of pain. Sleep deprivation may affect the synthesis of endogenous opiate and thus reduce the threshold value of pain which can make old people become more sensitive to pain and cause a vicious circle. As a result, the elderly should have timely treatment so as to reduce their pain and the occurrence of sleep problems.

(2)   The influence of common chronic disease on old people's sleep quality.

High blood pressure: the research found that high blood pressure is a factor influencing old people's sleep. Old people with high blood pressure have higher incidence rate for having sleep problems. It is mainly related with their physical and psychological factors. People with high blood pressure are more prone to have nerve dysfunction and facing impairment of the circulation system between heart and its surrounding areas. They will have excessive release of vaso-active substance (like norepinephrine, angiotensin and endothelin) which can lead to the increase of aortic stiffness and the decrease of affinity to β-adrenoceptor. During the aging process, these changes will affect the stability of blood pressure, cause fluctuation of blood pressure as well as other problems. Old people are prone to have discomfort like headache, dizziness and shortness of breath which will be very difficult for them to fall asleep. Moreover, they worry a lot about their state of illness and treatment efficiency which can strengthen their psychological burden and thus have a great influence on their sleep quality. At the same time, people with high blood pressure have to take medicine regularly. For example, antihypertensive drugs like captopril can cause increased urination frequency and thus affect sleep to varying degrees. Research showed that as long as people's blood level increase one level, the number of people suffering from sleep disorder will increase by 1.62 times. Regardless of the illness course, people will have improved sleep quality if they can keep their blood level in well control.

Heart disease: according to the research result, heart disease is an illness which can affect old people's sleep state. The elderly who have heart disease have a higher level of having sleep disorders. One research from abroad found that 79% of people with chronic heart disease have poor sleep. It is rather commonplace to see patients with apnea. These people are very easy to encounter problems such as apnea, daytime sleepiness and nighttime sleeplessness because of fast heartbeats and overexcited sympathetic nervous system. All these cal lead to old people's poor sleep quality. Apart from that, atrial fibrillation and palpitation can also affect sleep. It is very necessary to inform the elderly to have timely treatment so as to relieve their symptoms and improve their sleep.

3 The Comfort of the Human Bed Interface

3.1 Prone Position and Sleep Quality

Human body which has contact with the mattress will have symptoms like ischemia. Metabolites caused by ischemia will stimulate sensitive nerve endings and force people to change their postures when feeling the pain. The change of postures can avoid the pressure overloading of soft tissues and muscle stiffness. Most people like to have their own sleep postures. There is also situation that they change postures for 20 times overnight. It can't be referred to as ideal sleep state. Sleep postures also have relation with people's age. Children like to sleep in different ways. But the elderly like to lie on the side (especially the right side). They are less likely to lie prostrate. They have less sleep time and don't change their postures frequently.

By conducting research, Professor Kris, a specialist in sleep, has confirmed six types of common sleep postures [6]. They are: curling up like a fetus, sleeping on one side like a log, the pining position (sleeping on one side with arms extending out at right angles to the body), the soldier position (flatting on one's back with arms at his or her sides), lying prostrate and the starfish position (lying on the back with outstretched arms and legs) (Fig. 4).

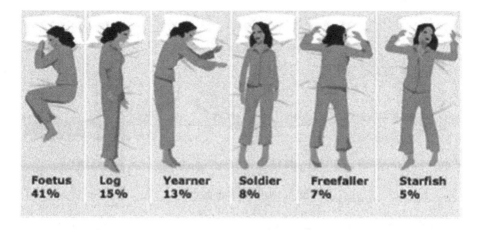

Fig. 4. Six types of sleep postures

When working in daytime, people's weight is corresponded with the direction of spinal canal (Fig. 5). Sudden physical exercise and incorrect postures for a long time will increase the stress on spinal canal which can fasten the speed of dehydration and cause illness. The research found that 80% of people had once suffered from back pains. Prone position is the best way for having a rest because it exerts less tress on spinal canal intervertebral disc can regain water and restore flexibility. If the mattress can not provide enough support, the spinal canal will lie in an unnatural way. If so, the spinal canal can't get recovered and even cause problems on themselves. As a result, mattress support, especially the part which supports the spinal canal is of great importance.

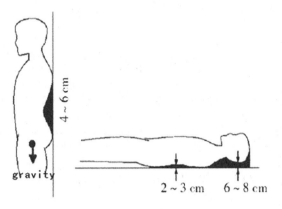

Fig. 5. The difference of the spinal curvature between sanding and lying on one's back

Mattress support is different from people's sleep habit. People have different sleep postures (Fig. 6). Besides, age can also the mattress support condition. The elderly like to lie on one side and have fewer changes of sleep postures.

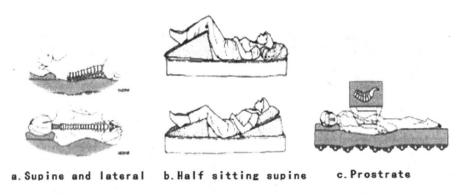

a. Supine and lateral   b. Half sitting supine   c. Prostrate

Fig. 6. Natural sleep postures

Of course, people do not adapt to mattress support in a passive way. They can keep their spinal canal in an ideal state by optimizing their sleep postures consciously or subconsciously [7]. Different sleep postures have their specific advantages. Due to the difference of people's pressure distribution and spinal structure and their own health condition, they have different best postures. As a result, unreasonable human bed interface relationship will not only influence spinal support, but also increase their adjustment of structures and behaviors which can cause more energy consumption and affect sleep quality. For the elderly who have declined physiological functions and suffer from pain and chronic illness, it is very important to rationalize the human bed interface relation.

3.2 Furniture and Sleep Quality

Apart from meeting the need of size, designers also have to take into consideration of the softness and the focus of human body support. With the increase of age, the elderly have to suffer from a more serious osteoarthritis which usually occurs in areas like ankles and knees. It can be in the form of problems such as arthralgia, swelling, limited activity, stiffness, cervical spondylosis and lumbar disc herniation. Furniture used by the elderly should be enable them to have a good rest, relieve fatigue, recover strength and reduce the incidence rate of the above-mentioned diseases [8].

(1) Mattress

The function of mattress is to provide consumers with healthy and comfortable sleep. Good mattresses have two features. One is that people can keep their spinal canal straight in different sleep postures. The other one is that the mattress has equal pressure so that people can relax themselves freely when lying on it. A good mattress needs to have three basic functions at the same time. It should have cushioning effect which can reduce muscle's pressure on furniture. The second function is heat preservation. It should be able to provide a certain temperature so as to ensure excellent blood circulation. The last one is effectiveness. People can prevent complications like burn and bedsore. Hardness and supportability are two important features closely related with sleep comfort.

Hardness: a mattress should not be too hard or soft. If it is too hard, the pressure distribution of the human bed interface will be very concentrated so that the back lacks enough support. As a result, it will be difficult for people to keep a natural state. When people lying on one side, there will be much pressure centering on their shoulders and bottoms (Fig. 7). There will be more pressure on intervertebral disc if people lie on their side. Moreover, due to the centralized pressure and the increasing frequency of turnover, people will have more difficulty to sleep [9]. When the mattress is very soft, the force of rolling friction needed to turn over and adjust postures will increase because of the increased contact area. So people will consume more energy. It will be more difficult to send away moisture and relax muscles and nerves. At the same time, when the mattress is rather soft, people will have the difficulty in keep their natural states.

Supportability: mattress chassis has seen a development course of from soft to hard ones and then a return to soft ones. At first, people didn't realize the importance of mattress chassis design but focused on achieving soft support. Initial types of chassis also had good flexibility and air permeability, but they are very easy to get sunken (Fig. 8a). Hard bed can partly reduce the possibility of lying on one side, but it can not completely avoid that (Fig. 8b). At the same time, hard bed is very bad in air permeability. Now, many of the skeleton structures have already been in widespread use. People can adjust the distance and

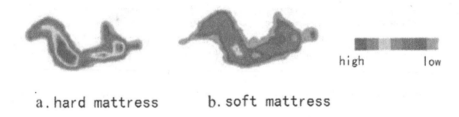

a. hard mattress   b. soft mattress

Fig. 7. Pressure distribution of human bed interface

height when using them. This structure is very ideal in aspects like flexibility, air permeability and Supportability (Fig. 8c). However, it's worth noting that this structure has to match with the type of mattress.

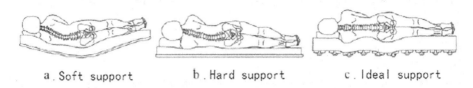

a. Soft support   b. Hard support   c. Ideal support

Fig. 8. Support effects of mattress chassis

The elderly like to lie on one side due to their declined physical strength. So they have to keep their spinal canal relaxed in a natural way. As a result, mattress that is too hard and too soft will cause abnormal bends which is very comfortable and can even cause skeletal injury.

(2) Condition of temperature and humidity

When sleeping, people will continuously expel the moisture. Part of it can be dispersed into the air through breathing, but the rest is dispersed by the skin among which 25% are absorbed by mattress and 75% by bed sheets, bedding and pillows. The air permeability of the mattress and bedding has direct influence on moisture's ability to disperse itself. When the air permeability is rather poor, people will feel humid. The mattress chassis will also be prone to mildew. Besides, the thermal conductivity of the mattress material should not be too high or too low. When the thermal conductivity is too high, people will have lower temperature and stiff muscle. When it is too low, the interface will have higher temperature which may make people feel humid. Both of these two features can do no benefit to a good sleep.

4   Design Trend of Furniture for the Aging Population

4.1   The Improvement of Basic Functions

Mattress's performances depend not only on materials but also their combination methods. Factors influencing its comfort are not materials, but overall performance, flexibility and distribution presented by materials, structures and their combinations. Besides, a mattress should not be sued for a very long time. The research found that its flexibility will reduce by 10% to 15% after a period of ten years. With more research conducted on this aspect, there is still much room for its development.

4.2 The Improvement of Prone Position

Free and comfortable gesture adaptation has significant influence on reducing spine deformation, improving sleep quality and promoting physical health. The softness and hysteresis play a significant part on gesture adaptation. Moreover, human activity and gesture adaptation need sufficient space. Human consumption of energy mainly comes from two aspects. One is the fact that the mattress's hysteresis is too large or it's too soft. The other one is the frequent gesture adaptation. They all can hinder good sleep. So when designing mattress, designers should take old people's physical activities and gesture adaptation into consideration. They should design mattress with reasonable flexibility, hardness, hysteresis and size so as to help the elderly find the posture fitting them most.

4.3 Disease Prevention

Generally, with the increase of age, most people will suffer from a serious of health problems. As sleep state has close relationship with many diseases, the elderly can reduce their pain and promote blood circulation by changing sleep postures and controlling the temperature and humidity of their bodies.

4.4 Mattress-Type Sleep Monitoring System

With the advancement of technology, there also should be changes in furniture. Using mattress as a carrier and testing heart beat, breath and other pressure changes, this system can evaluate old people's sleep quality, recognize sub-health state, detect cardiovascular function and identify arrhythmia.

5 Conclusion

The fast speed of the aging of the population makes people concern more about old people's health conditions. The improvement of sleep quality can directly affect their health status. This paper mainly analyzed the sleep quality of the elderly from the perspective of physiology and furniture. However, there are many factors that can influences their sleep quality such as mental condition, daily habits, interpersonal relationship and economic status. When designing furniture for the elderly, we must have a clear understanding of their needs and design products that are fit for their use so as to improve their quality of life.

References

1. Wu, Y.: China Aging Development Report. Social Science Literature Press (2013)
2. Human Engineering in Highly Mature Societies, pp. 247–250. Japan Science and Technology Corporation (1997)
3. Kang, J., Zeng, H., Shi, P.: Study on the correlation between sleep quality and cognitive function of the elderly in community. Chin. Gen. Pract. **14**(2A), 439–445 (2011)
4. Liu, L., Shi, R., Liu, X., et al.: Sleep quality and its related factors in the elderly. Chin. J. Gerontol. **22**(11), 437–440 (2002)
5. Wu, R., Zhang, C., Deng, J.: A comparative study on coping style and sleep behavior in patients with chronic insomnia. Chin. J. Ment. Health **17**(10), 716–718 (2003)
6. De Koninck, J., Lorrain, D., Gagnon, P.: Sleep positions and position shifts in five age groups: an ontogenetic picture. Sleep **15**(2), 143–149 (1992)
7. Dolan, P., Adams, M.A., Mutton, W.C.: Commonly adopted postures and their effect on the lumbar spine. Spine **13**(2), 197–201 (1998)
8. Chen, Y., Shen, L., Guo, Y.: The effect of human design of mattress on sleep health. Packag. Eng. **33**(12) (2012)
9. Xu, M., Xia, Q.: Index of body pressure distribution. China Mech. Eng. **8**(1) (1997)

A Sensory Emotion Data System for Designing Information Appliances

Yan Jin[✉], Long Xu, and Sangwon Lee

Yonsei University, Seoul, Korea
xyz110844@hotmail.com

Abstract. Under the growing competition in the manufacturing industry, more and more companies are focusing on users' emotional experiences to make their products attractive to the potential buyers. Driven by the recent shift of the consumer trend to smart life style, companies are striving to release their products with not only their high functionality but also their design that fully consider end users' cognitive and emotional parts. However, they are faced with a significant challenge of securing time, effort, and expertise to gather and utilize such information. The purpose of our study is to construct a database system that provides basic information to field experts so as they can utilize to improve the design of information appliances. For the construction of the system, we first conducted literature review to set data types of sensory emotion data, and explored concept and definition of each type. After collecting emotional data modules, we conducted an in-depth interview with field experts to confirm the relevance. Finally we suggest the design of the system that can be utilized in the actual design step within the product design progress. The main contribution of our study is that we propose a systematic process for constructing a scalable tool that can automatically provide sensory emotional data to industrial experts.

Keywords: Sensory emotion data · Information appliance · Automated system

1 Introduction

With the emergence of a smart life style, consumer demands for information appliances are growing. The characteristic of this trend is diversification of products considering personal taste. In order to be competitive with the nature of this market, companies need to consider product design in terms of not only functionality but user's sense of cognition and emotion.

In product design, the importance of user-centered design has been emphasized for a long time in practice as well as in academia. Particularly, visual, auditory, and tactile senses have a critical impact on the added value of products because they play a crucial role in how people form emotion by communicating with the external environment. Therefore, understanding the sensory information transmitted via these three senses and the emotional data induced from it is an essential element in user-centered product design.

However, collecting and applying relevant information requires a lot of time and cost for many companies. Small and mid-sized businesses that have a short product development cycle and a high reliance on a single product tend to be more subjective to this problem.

© Springer International Publishing AG 2017
J. Zhou and G. Salvendy (Eds.): ITAP 2017, Part I, LNCS 10297, pp. 255–263, 2017.
DOI: 10.1007/978-3-319-58530-7_19

This study aims to make the sensory emotion data more available in the form of online database so that designers in the small and mid-sized businesses can apply them to actual practices more easily.

We first summarize the product design process from the literature on new product development and user experience design. Second, we define the sensory emotion data based on the theories on visual, auditory, and tactile perception and transform them into modules of a database system. Finally, we design the user interface of the sensory emotion data system based on the interview with the product designers of information appliances.

2   Background

In the information science field, having recognized the importance of user's emotional factors, a group of researchers began to explore their effects (Beaudry et al. 2010). They created sensor-based theoretical framework for the acceptance of information technology: technology acceptance models, UTAUT (Venkatesh et al. 2003), innovation diffusion theory, and planned behavior theory. In recent years, however, since the use environment of information technology has become complex and multidimensional, the above mentioned theories have limitations in grasping the preceding variables of user's behavior. Therefore, this study starts with a comprehensive understanding of the design process that will involve emotional data by limiting the scope of the product called information appliances. Next, we review the literature on the concept and role of sensory information and on the visual, auditory, and tactile sensory emotion data.

2.1   Design Process of Information Appliances

Product design process represents the linkage system between activities for designing a product. The user-centered design process consists of five stages: an understanding stage that defines the problem, a research stage that examines the interaction between people and objects, a design stage that explores pain points or new values, a prototype stage in which an idea or a demo version is tested, and an evaluation stage to evaluate the likelihood of use and performance results. (Roozenburg and Eekels 1995) There is also a double-diamond design process that is used in the UX design methodology aimed at spreading and defining the scope of thinking through the process of diffusion and convergence, and then to derive innovative ideas from this. This process consists of four steps: Discover, Define, Develop, and Deliver (Council 2005).

2.2   Visual, Auditory and Tactile Senses in Information Appliances

Visual perception information: the overall visual perception process proceeds as shown (Fig. 1). Visualization occurs through selection, structuring, simplification, and clustering as the iterative process of searching and fixing through eye movement occurs, followed by cognitive judgment. Thinking and judgments arise to solve problems according to human sensory models.

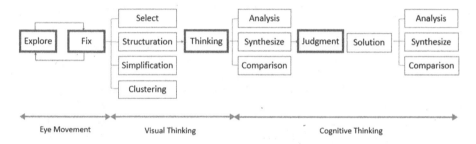

Fig. 1. Visual perception Process (Arnheim 1969)

Visual information in information appliances allows users to use products more efficiently. The goal of the visual information design is to design user-friendly, natural and pleasant interactions and also includes solving various problems that exist in human-computer interface (Jacobson 2000). The visual representation of information is composed of elements such as shape, color, texture, layout, typography, metaphor, etc. (Byung Keun and Sung Jung 2008). The visual information module of the system includes space between letters, stroke width ratio (Alexander 1986), and color of text (Alexander 1986).

Auditory cognitive information: the auditory information is processed through various stages where physical stimulation by the sound source and the vehicle is transformed to nerve energy. The auditory information in the information appliances design is the user interface related to the hearing. The hearing interface in information appliances helps to establish the identity of a product. Auditory information is the sound heard by the user, and can be largely defined by three factors: size, height, and tone. The auditory module of the system consists of volume, tone, and pitch.

Tactile cognitive information: unlike the visual and auditory sense described above, the tactile sense is spread throughout the entire body. Sense is a process of primary information processing, in which external stimulus information is converted into signals of the internal nervous system and input. In the information appliances design, the tactile sense can form either a particular emotion from the surface material of the product, or a tactile interface for interacting with the product. In this study, we constructed a tactile cognitive module that compares the difference threshold (Matsumoto et al. 2011) and absolute threshold data (Parsons and Griffin 1988; Yonekawa et al. 1999) with reference to document (11, 14, 20).

2.3 Emotional Data in Information Appliances Design

Emotional data is the result of primary perception and subjective interpretation. In the general process of Kansei Engineering, (1) the basic adjectives are selected from dictionaries, magazines, surveys, and observation methods, (2) secondary representative adjectives are selected according to experts and observers' evaluation, frequency and suitability and (3) emotional factors are identified through psychological evaluation and physiological evaluation (Seung-Hwa and Myung-Suk 2001).

Visual emotion data: This is emotion information generated from a user's visual perception on a product's design elements (Mini et al. 1996). When the user chooses the product based on the design, the color and the shape are the main criteria for the product selection; especially the color which has a great influence on the emotion is selected as the visual emotion module. IRI emotion scale (IRI color research institute 2011) and Kobayashi color emotion scale (Kobayashi 1991) which are representative color emotion scale were gathered.

Auditory emotion data: This is the emotion generated from a product's auditory design elements. There are limitations on the number of emotions to deal with and there is a sensitivity that should be emphasized according to the characteristics of the product. The auditory sensibility module was formed using Russell's emotional adjectives (Russell 2003).

Tactile emotion data: This data provides information between a user's emotion and a product's design variables during the usage of the product (Chen et al. 2009). When the user interacts with the product, the material perceived by the tactile sensor influences the emotional aspect (preference/non-preference) of the user (Dépeault et al. 2009; Karlsson and Velasco 2007; Kawasegi et al. 2013; Park et al. 2013).

3   Designer Interview

3.1   Goal

In this study, an in-depth interview was conducted with designers of information appliances in order to establish a user's visual, auditory, tactile emotion data. Through the interview, we tried to confirm the need of user's visual, auditory, tactile emotion data and how such information is utilized. Table 1 summarizes the interviews with 6 field designers.

Table 1. Interview summaries

		Details
Target products	Information appliances	Humidifier, Door-lock, Black box, Robot, Display module, Monitor, Educational display etc.
Companies	Small to mid-size	(1) Miro (2) Ever-net (3) SOC (4) Yujinrobot (5) Tovis (6) Neocartek
Schedule	2016. 3	Six times during March to June 2016
Questions	4 categories (21 in total)	– Work processes and UX capacity – Key design features for product manufacturing – The required data for designing key factures – The method of collecting data

4   Result

Two evaluators coded the recording of the interview independently and agreed to a single version after a few iterations. The analysis is as follows.

Design process of information appliances: The information appliances product design process has basic steps such as Planning, Design, Prototype, and Evaluation, but it differs from the research in the user-centered design process described in above literature review. The user-centered research method focuses on user's direct observations and observes behavior, pattern, experience, and potential desire. On the other hand, planning stage research in the design process of information appliances does not consider user's direct observation but the competitor's models and given functions. You can validate the finding through the interview with Ever-net Co.

> From planning to release, there is almost no step that tries to satisfy the consumer's needs
> [...] Plan the process according to the merchandising schedule and
> [...] also choose the design accordingly.
> (Tovis Designer Interview)

> If a certain product needs to be planned, we have a meeting with the development team regarding the price range, hardware, software of a competitive product A, and go through a design phase that reflects the price and specifications of the most popular product in the market.
> (Evernet Designer Interview)

From a process perspective, there was a company who executes a sequential process: clarifies the purpose of a product, decides the function that fits the purpose, sets the concept, and determines the material within the budget. On the other hand, there also was a nonlinear process where a design and function are decided by a scenario and adjusted based on the manufacturability. It is assumed that the nonlinear product process is preferred when the technology is not yet mature or the new product has little user experience data.

> I think the scenario is the most important thing. We first work on the scenario that determines the target, content, and place of the service and on the design. During the process, we discuss with the engineers on the possibility of implementing certain functions.
> (SOC Interview)

Utilizing sensory emotion data: As designers perform specific sub-design tasks, there was a need for a sensory emotion data that helps to determine design variables. Due to the limitations on cost and stability, they preferred materials and colors commonly used in the industry, for existing voice database. However, they were also willing to look into the sensory emotion data as long as it matches the target product function and the design characteristics. In addition, interviewers confirmed that data reflecting the rapid changes in consumer trends are necessary.

> The industry is conservative. We hardly seldom our practice.
> (Neo Café Interview)

> The babies have such a sensitive hearing that we couldn't find a sound that only adults can wake up to. We are willing to provide auditory functions if the data support such information.
> (Miro Interview)

> The products are almost the same. The material is fixed.
> [...] Previously customers liked red so much they sold a lot of red. Now it's black. We have to reflect these things.
> (Evernet Interview)

5   Sensory Emotion Data Support System

5.1   System Interface

The sensory emotional data support system can be largely divided into two parts: the input of design variable for the design of particular product and the output of the sensory emotion data related to it. The main structure of the interface is based on these two components (Fig. 2). The input part of the system is the design information by the designers at each stage of the design process, and the output is the result composed of data modules of visual, auditory, and tactile senses constructed from literature review.

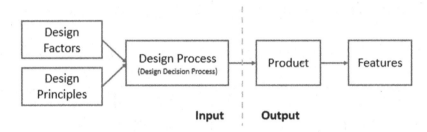

Fig. 2.   Interface design input and output basic structure

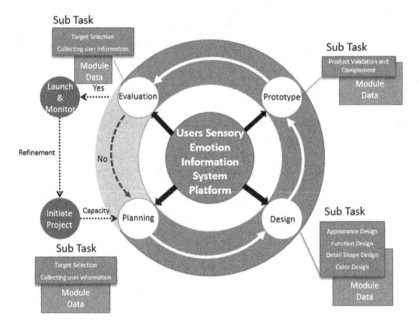

Fig. 3.   System framework

Figure 3 shows the integrated process framework of the user cognitive/emotional information system. Based on the product design process, detailed design activities were defined in each stage (Planning, Design, Prototype, and Evaluation). The system provides sensory data modules relevant to the sub-tasks in each product design stage.

5.2 Sensory Emotion Database

The function of the database is to enable users to receive relevant sensory emotion data at each stage of design activity. Through interviews with practitioners, we have found that at each step of the design process, designers need to determine a certain set of design variables and sensory emotion data can help the decision-making. We created totally six modules where emotion data are extracted.

Figure 4 shows an example of the sensory data module of the visual information (letter, symbol, and figure) for the display design of information appliances. If there is a design variable called readable font size, the database system shows the sub-variables such as the distance, luminance, font type, and the number of strokes.

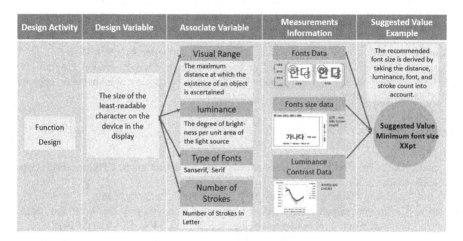

Fig. 4. Visual module example

6 Conclusion

Although the industry recognizes the necessity to utilize sensory emotion data in product development, it is still a challenging task to collect and present such information in a structured way. Therefore we extracted the required information through interviews and literature reviews and tried to establish an interactive system with corresponding modules. In the process of implementing the system, the following conclusions could be drawn.

First, a platform-based sensory emotion data system of open source concept is more suitable than a static data library. According to the interview with the designers, even the companies' manufacturing the same type of projects in the same industry sector have different design processes with different sensory information requirements at each stage depending on the product development cycle and the portfolio. Therefore an open-platform with flexible interface is more desired than a fixed database based on single process in order to serve different scenarios by different designers. Also, emotion tends to change and evolve by social events and trends. The user context shifts rapidly as numerous information systems affect our life style. An open-platform allows adapting the sensory emotion data more quickly.

Second, while the contribution of our study lies in collecting and providing the sensory emotion data to the industry, our feeling is that there still is a large empty area in terms of the emotion data. Human emotion is affected by social and physical environment and hard to be quantified or systemized. There is a certain set of generalized emotion data but they do not serve particular target consumers or products. Therefore there exists a need for further development of emotion data particularly those differentiates different contexts.

We hope that the system help designers improve their products by providing the relevant sensory emotion data. In future research, the user evaluation should be conducted to verify the usability which will enhance the reliability of the system.

Acknowledgments. This material is based upon work supported by the Ministry of Trade, Industry & Energy (MOTIE, Korea) under Industrial Technology Innovation Program. No. 10060517, 'Development of an user-centered product design support system based on cognitive and affective information'.

References

Alexander, D.C.: The Practice and Management of Industrial Ergonomics. Prentice Hall, Upper Saddle River (1986)

Arnheim, R.: Visual Thinking. University of California Press, Berkeley (1969)

Beaudry, A., Pinsonneault, A.: The other side of acceptance: studying the direct and indirect effects of emotions on information technology use. MIS Q. **34**(4), 689–710 (2010)

Chen, X., Shao, F., Barnes, C., Childs, T., Henson, B.: Exploring relationships between touch perception and surface physical properties. Int. J. Des. **3**(2), 67–76 (2009)

Design Council: The 'Double Diamond' Design Process Model (2005)

Dépeault, A., Meftah, E.-M., Chapman, C.E.: Tactile perception of roughness: raised-dot spacing, density and disposition. Exp. Aging Res. **197**(3), 235–244 (2009)

Jacobson, R.: Information Design. MIT press, Cambridge (2000)

Karlsson, M., Velasco, A.: Designing for the tactile sense: investigating the relation between surface properties, perceptions and preferences. CoDesign **3**(S1), 123–133 (2007)

Kawasegi, N., Fujii, M., Shimizu, T., Sekiguchi, N., Sumioka, J., Doi, Y.: Evaluation of the human tactile sense to microtexturing on plastic molding surfaces. Precis. Eng. **37**(2), 433–442 (2013)

Kobayashi, S.: Color image scale. Kodansha America Incorporated, New York (1991)

Matsumoto, Y., Maeda, S., Iwane, Y., Iwata, Y.: Factors affecting perception thresholds of vertical whole-body vibration in recumbent subjects: gender and age of subjects, and vibration duration. J. Sound Vib. **330**(8), 1810–1828 (2011)

Mini, A., Palomba, D., Angrilli, A., Bravi, S.: Emotional information processing and visual evoked brain potentials. Percept. Mot. Skills **83**(1), 143–152 (1996)

Park, J., Park, K., Yu, J., Choe, J., Jung, E.S.: Effects on the tactile affections of touch behaviors and materials of vehicle interior. In: Paper Presented at the Proceeding of the 2013 Fall Conference of the Ergonomics Society of Korea (2013)

Parsons, K., Griffin, M.: Whole-body vibration perception thresholds. J. Sound Vib. **121**(2), 237–258 (1988)

Roozenburg, N.F., Eekels, J.: Product Design: Fundamentals and Methods, vol. 2. Wiley, Chichester (1995)

Russell, J.A.: Core affect and the psychological construction of emotion. Psychol. Rev. **110**(1), 145 (2003)

Seung-Hwa, P., Myung-Suk, K.: A study on the design of visual-auditory haptic interface - with emphasis on embodying haptics using visual and auditory perception. Arch. Des. Res. **14**(2), 15–25 (2001)

Venkatesh, V., Morris, M.G., Davis, G.B., Davis, F.D.: User acceptance of information technology: toward a unified view. MIS Q. **27**(3), 425–478 (2003)

Yonekawa, Y., Maeda, S., Kanada, K., Takahayashi, Y.: Whole-body vibration perception thresholds of recumbent subjects. Ind. Health **37**(4), 398–403 (1999)

Color Research Institute IRI.: Color Combination (Revised Edition) (Hardcover) (2011). YoungJin.com

Byung Keun, O., Sung Jung, K.: Infographics Design Textbook. Ahn Graphics, Seoul (2008)

Users' Affective Response to Furniture Design Based on Public Openness

Yein Jo[1], Jeebin Yim[1], Hyeonsu Park[2], and Younah Kang[1(✉)]

[1] Information and Interaction Design, Yonsei University, Incheon, South Korea
trie60@gmail.com, jeebiny@gmail.com, yakang@yonsei.ac.kr
[2] Graduate School of Communication and Arts, Yonsei University, Seoul, South Korea
park10714@gmail.com

Abstract. Furniture directly affects users' emotion, since it forms the overall atmosphere of the space where it is placed. While previous research projects and furniture design practitioners rarely consider the spatial context of furniture, we sought to understand users' emotional aspect and spatial context of furniture. In this study, we focused on users' affective responses to visual aesthetic attributes of furniture design. We conducted observations and expert interview sessions in order to find what factors would influence the spatial context. From the initial study, we assumed that the level of "public openness" might influence users' affective responses and preferences to furniture design. To explore our research question, we conducted in-depth interviews with ten participants who recently engaged in the purchasing process of furniture items. Through the analysis, we found that there is a correlation between the level of public openness of the space and users' affective responses to furniture design. We explain how such openness affect users' affective responses to the furniture design.

Keywords: Furniture design · Public openness · Affective response · Visual aesthetic attribute · Qualitative study

1 Introduction

While numerous researchers and current industry of furniture have emphasized functionality when planning and designing a single or a set of furniture, functionality alone cannot cover the entire context of furniture usage. It is important to consider the special context of furniture, because furniture greatly influences the overall atmosphere of the space where it is placed, which can be directly linked to users' emotional aspect. With such significance, we narrowed down our focus on users' affective responses to furniture design in our study. We conducted observations and interview sessions to see what other factors would affect people's design preference to furniture other than functionality, and were able to find another significant factor, the public openness. We found that based on the level of openness, rooms or spaces of a house can be classified into rooms with high or low level of public openness, so as it would affect users' design preferences. We conducted an in-depth interview with users, to fully investigate what visual aesthetic attributes of furniture design affect users' affective responses and preferences and how they differ based on the level of public openness.

J. Zhou and G. Salvendy (Eds.): ITAP 2017, Part I, LNCS 10297, pp. 264–274, 2017.
DOI: 10.1007/978-3-319-58530-7_20

The contributions of our study include:

- We found the public openness as a novel factor that affects the spatial context.
- We confirmed that the public openness influences users' affective responses to furniture design
- We examined the details about how the level of public openness affects users' affective responses and preferences to furniture design.

2 Discovering Spatial Context

It is important to consider the special context of furniture since it plays a key role in deciding the overall atmosphere of the space, which can be directly linked to users' emotional aspect. Thus, we conducted a field study to find what factors influence space context besides aesthetic design elements of furniture. We conducted observations and expert-interview sessions. For the observation session, we visited a furniture store of Hanssem, one of the most dominant furniture brands in Korea. While exploring the store, we found several factors that mold space context, such as the purpose of the room, users' social standing, and the size of the space. For example, there was a room named as a study room with a set of furniture including a desk, a chair, and a lamp. Another room was decorated with a queen-sized bed with white curtain, indicating that a room is for a new married couple. Moreover, we were able to collect several keywords about users' affective responses to furniture design through promotion phrases written on the wall and conversations between users and salesmen.

We also conducted one-on-one interviews with four experts, including a vice-president of a bedroom company, a CEO of a furniture consulting company, a marketing director from a design department of a furniture company, and a wood craftsman. Each interview session took about an hour, and the interviewees received $20 as their incentive.

Through observation and interview sessions, we constructed our research question that the level of public openness would affect users' affective responses as well as their design preferences to furniture.

"When people buy items, they usually consider how it will form the atmosphere of their home places." (Expert 01)

"Actually, the top selling item is sofa, because people place sofa in their living room, the place where they show to others." (Expert 02)

3 Public Openness

Privacy is an important factor to consider when it comes to understanding a space. Altman [1] defines privacy as a dynamic process, in which it is under continuous negotiation and management with the boundary that separates privacy and publicity according to circumstance. Privacy is a process where people manage their accessibility along the range of "openness" and "closedness" based on context. Privacy can also be interpreted in terms of individuality, communality, and public and private dimensions [2]. It is described in physical, psychological, social, and informational dimensions [3].

In this study, we concentrated on spaces' physical dimension of privacy regarding public openness. We defined public openness as a level of accessibility of a space to the public. The public includes friends, neighbors, strangers, and other individuals who are not residing in that space. Level of public openness of a space ranges from high to low. Space with high level of public openness tends to have less physical privacy, and space with low level of public openness tends to have high level of physical privacy.

There are various dimensions that determine a meaning and value of a space, especially in the context of a home. According to Roderick J. Lawrence [4], the design, meaning, and use of home interiors are related to a range of cultural, sociodemographic, and psychological dimensions. Lawrence states that house is designed to distinguish public and private domains. Also, different spaces in home have different cultural dimensions, and those dimensions relate to the design, meaning, and use of home interiors.

Displaying status symbols using objects with high social value could be a reason for decorating and furnishing rooms [5–7]. Functions are not the only aspect people consider when decorating home interior, people also consider the values attributed to specific rooms and objects [8]. An object's value is determined by its private and public meaning, as mentioned in Marsha L. Richins' study [9]. According to Richins, every object has its meaning assigned by its owner and meaning given to it by others and society. Therefore, public and private meanings are also ascribed to furniture. Furniture represents utilitarian values, financial aspects, and owner's interpersonal ties and identity.

In the past, these contextual dimensions of a space and furniture, including public openness, were not fully addressed when designing furniture. However, users' growing interest in interior decoration in Korea led furniture designers and companies to take functional aspect, aesthetic elements, and contextual information into consideration.

"We no longer think that bed is used only for sleeping, but we also think about how users will spend their time watching TV, reading books, and going on their laptops on the bed [...] We recently designed a bed that could adjust the header and mattress to better accommodate users' various activities on the bed." (Expert 04)

4   Interaction Model of a Furniture Item and a User

In the field of product design, previous research projects proposed several consumption frameworks. They have described similar frameworks that include a product (or a producer), a user (or a consumer), and the environment that bridges the product and a user. Within such frameworks, researchers have defined detailed factors with two perspective: a product and a user.

From the perspective of a product, a product has several attributes that affect users' purchase decision. According to a diagram proposed by Tahira N. Reid [10], a single product possesses decision variables including price, geometry, and stylistic elements, and such variables affects physical and perceptual attributes of the product.

From the perspective of a user, a user responses to the attributes of a product. According to a model of consumer responses to product form proposed by Peter H. Bloch [11], a product influences a user's psychological responses that includes cognitive and affective responses, and thus affect behavioral responses that decides whether a user decide to approach to the product. In this model, cognitive responses include one's belief about the product or the brand. Affective responses refer to aesthetic and other positive/negative responses.

Another framework proposed by Nathan Crilly, James Moultrie and P. John Clarkson [12], also described a similar framework with different detailed constructs within the model. It presented that the user's responses cover all three elements: cognition, affect, and behavior. It added one depth further addressing three different factors of the cognitive response: aesthetic impression, semantic interpretation, and symbolic association.

Based on several frameworks, we developed our own model (Fig. 1), before conducting a user study. While a furniture item has various attributes including, price, shapes, colors, and performance, we exclusively focused on visual aesthetic attributes of an item. Also, we brought the perspective of a user, defining a user's reaction as affective response, to see how one responds to such visual aesthetic attributes. We defined affective responses as any emotion-related reaction to the product or the brand. We set the term as *affective*, since the term *affect* commonly used to describe all the emotional related words including, emotions, mood, and feelings [13]. Following quotations are the examples of users' affective responses:

"I think the bed should be comfortable. [...] I think the texture of the real wood gives me comfortable feeling because it feels like natural. [...] When the legs of a bed are high, it is really uncomfortable to climb up, so I think the lower one gives me much comfortable feeling." (P05)

"I bought an elegant sofa, [...] the grayish color and the expensive leather give me such feeling." (P02)

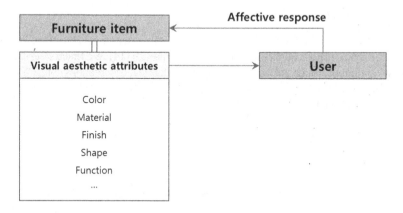

Fig. 1. Interaction model of users' affective response to visual aesthetic attributes of furniture

5 Study

To examine our research question, "how the level of public openness is related to users' affective responses and preferences to furniture design," we conducted a study with users

5.1 Procedure

Setting items: We selected two furniture items for the interview session – a bed and a sofa because we believed that a bed is a relatively private item and a sofa is a relatively public item.

Pre-interview session: We carried out one pre-interview session as a pilot to validate and modify our interview questions.

In-depth interview session: After a pre-interview session, we conducted an in-depth interview session with ten participants. We asked questions about the level of public openness of rooms and spaces in their home places, and their considerations when purchasing furniture items based on such openness. About an hour of in-depth interview was conducted either face-to-face or through telephone.

5.2 Participants

We had a total of 10 participants, with three males and seven females, ranging in age from 28 to 56 years. We recruited participants with following criteria:

- People who have any experience of participating in the purchase process of a bed and a sofa within one year.
- People who clearly separate spaces of their living place regarding where to open and where close to others.

5.3 Data Collection and Analysis

All interviews were audio recorded and transcribed later. After all sessions were done, the data were analyzed using a qualitative data analysis approach [14]. We first transcribed each interview's audio recording and then coded the transcripts and observations notes. We began by identifying major themes and keywords from the text. Throughout the coding process, we iteratively refined the information. We then elaborated on supporting evidence from the data through a deductive approach.

6 Findings

6.1 Users Have Different Perceptions on Level of Public Openness Regarding a Space

Through the analysis, we found that each person perceives a level of public openness of a space differently. How much and to whom a space is opened to determines the level of perceived public openness of a space. When the participants explained each space of their currently residing home, we noticed that they consider "living room is a space opened to others" and "bedroom is a space that cannot be opened to others." This indicates that the participants decide the space's level of public openness based on the degree of open and closedness of a space to the public.

The level of public openness is different for various spaces within a house. Participant 03 explained different levels of public openness for each segment of her home. She perceived a living room as a space opened to others, a space with high level of public openness, while she considered a bedroom as a space that cannot be opened to others with low level of public openness:

"When I have a housewarming party or sometimes invite friends over, I give a tour of my living room to everyone. However, I never show my bedroom to anyone because it is a secret space for just my husband and I." (P03)

Another finding was that each person perceives the level of public openness differently even for the same type of space.

While participant 03 regarded a bedroom as a space with low level of public openness, participant 09 viewed his bedroom as a space with high level of public openness, as shown in following quotation:

"When people come over, I show them both my living room and bedroom. I don't refrain from showing my bedroom to people. We don't have privacy specific for bedroom, living room and bedroom is same to us." (P09)

The degree of public openness could change over time or due to altered environmental factors. For example, participant 07 initially thought a bedroom had low level of public openness. However, as more guests frequently visited his home and viewed his bedroom, he started to perceive his bedroom as a space with high level of public openness.

"As my wife's friends frequently visit our home, more and more people viewed and toured our bedroom. Since we opened up various spaces of our home to people, my thoughts on our bedroom being a private room for just my wife and I changed." (P07)

The level of perceived public openness of a space influences users' affective responses toward furniture design.

6.2   When the Level of Public Openness Is High, Visual Aesthetic Attributes Are Considered Important

User consider aesthetic impression of furniture important when they are placed in a space with high level of public openness. Users expect furniture located in the space with high openness to be viewed by others. Because it is opened for others to see, users think that furniture placed in that space reflects who they are and it determines how they are viewed by others. For that reason, users place importance on the image of themselves presented to public through their furniture. When choosing furniture design, users consider the elements of visual aesthetic attributes of the furniture (color, shape, material, finish, function, etc.) to display affective response consistent to images of themselves they want others to perceive. For example, participant 02 contemplated how others may view her through the design of a sofa during the purchasing process of a sofa for her living room. As following interview quotation shows, she wanted others to think of her as a person who has a luxurious taste. Accordingly, she purchased an expensive-looking luxurious grey-toned sofa made out of cowhide (Fig. 2).

"We wanted to emphasize this is who we are! [...] Anyone who look at it will think, it looks expensive! That is why we purchased this expensive cowhide couch. It looks luxurious because of the material, [...] we chose grey tone because we wanted it to look fancy." (P02)

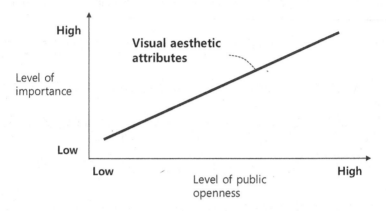

Fig. 2. Relationship between the level of public openness and users' perceived importance

Users, such as participant 02, consider visual aesthetic attributes of furniture that give identical objective affective response if they are concerned about how they will be perceived by others. They want others to feel the identical affective responses with themselves through the furniture design. Participant 02 chose to purchase grey-toned cowhide sofa because it gives luxurious affective responses to anyone who views it. Similar observation has been made during the interview with participant 11.

"I redesigned my home interior into grand, classical style that shows our couple is still stylish. [...] We bought luxurious-looking real leather couch made in Italy." (P11)

Users consider furniture located in a space with high level of public openness as an equipment to display their design taste. Users tries to deliver identical affective response with their design taste to the audience through the furniture design. To do that, they have to take account of furniture's visual aesthetic attributes based on their taste. participant 07 viewed his living room as a showroom where numerous guests visit. He purchased a sofa for the living room to show his design taste based on visual aesthetic attributes. Following interview quotation demonstrates that participant 07 implemented corky style furniture to show his design sense. He also purchased a sofa with a vintage style color and shape.

"Our living room is like a showroom. We don't even have a TV. [...] Since I work in design industry, I think furniture design that exhibits my style is important. [...] I placed a corky style couch, [...] to show vintage style, I chose color and leather, [...] interestingly arms and back has same height. [...] totally my personal taste." (P07)

6.3 Furniture in a Space with High Level of Public Openness Are Used as Expression Equipment

In Sect. 6.2, we discovered that furniture is used as expression equipment in a space with high level of public openness. There are two different ways furniture are used as expression equipment. Firstly, users express through furniture by attaching social significance (object with social recognition) to its design. Participant 11 chose luxury as her furniture's visual aesthetic attribute after considering the social significance. As a result, individuals who view her furniture will experience affective responses to social significance of the luxurious furniture.

> "My husband is now retired after working as corporate executive, we still cannot lose our style. [...] The concept of my living room furniture is luxury." (P11)

Secondly, users express through furniture by depicting his/her personal design taste to its design. Participant 10 purchased a customized table and sofa for her living room in order to express her personal design taste, affective responses to antique style, to the audience.

> "I really like antique furniture. [...] Table and sofa in the living room are antique style, [...] I customized all wood materials and finishing touches to personalize. [...] Neighbors often visit, and whenever they do, they compliment the furniture and ask where I got them from." (P10)

6.4 When the Level of Public Openness Is Low, People Place Less Importance on Visual Aesthetic Attributes

Users consider visual aesthetic attributes of furniture to be less important when it is placed in a space with low level of public openness. Users recognize that furniture located in a space with low level of public openness is less viewed by the public and thus, visual aesthetic attributes of furniture are less important to them. Regarding the furniture located in the low level of public openness, users tend to consider furniture's usability (or functionality) more than its visual aesthetic attributes when they purchase furniture items. For example, participant 04 defined her bedroom as a place where she could fully rest without worrying about others. She bought her bed for her bedroom, to give comfortable affective responses. The bed is pastel-toned color that tends to evoke comfortable feelings, and it has stable-looking design with less height.

> "Bedroom needs to be a space where I can comfortably rest, not bothered by anyone. [...] It was important for the bed in the bedroom to have a comfortable-looking design. [...] pastel colors rather than strong vivid colors. [...] bed without leg parts." (P04)

Participant 11 also perceived bedroom as a space with low level of public openness. She thought affective responses in perspective of usability (or functionality) were vital. She chose visual aesthetic attributes that can give her cozy feeling. During the process of purchasing a bed, she selected a soft textured latex mattress, a light-colored oak frame, and a comfortable head made of fabric.

> "I did not really care about styling my bedroom, since no one will see it. [...] Bedrooms have to be cozy! [...] I chose latex mattress so that it will be comfortable, [...] oak material for cozy atmosphere, [...] fabric header to lean on it. [...]" (P11)

6.5   When the Level of Public Openness Is Low, Users Consider Visual Aesthetic Attributes that Reflects Their Personal Design Taste Important

In the Sect. 6.2, we identified that, when the space's level of public openness is high, users tend to consider visual aesthetic attributes of furniture are important. These characteristics also can be occurred when the level of public openness of a space is low, however, different kind of visual aesthetic attributes are pursued. In the space with high level of public openness, furniture is frequently viewed by the public and visual aesthetic attributes that could be recognized by others have the tendency to be pursued. For example, furniture items that are arranged in a space with low level of public openness, viewed less by the public, tend to pursue visual aesthetic attributes that reflects personal taste. Participant 01 considered a bedroom as a space with low degree of public openness. Because it is not opened for others to see, she applied personal design taste when choosing her furniture items. In other words, she pursued visual aesthetic attributes that display her personal design taste, that normally she would not expose to the public. Participant 01 wanted to have a princess-like bed, but before getting married, she lived in a one-room apartment where people often visited. She could not decorate her space as she wanted to because she did not want to be judged by those who visit and see her space. Recently, she purchased an ivory bed with large curvy shaped legs and a header for her new home, which was a romantic and antique style. Following quotation states that she placed her new bed in the bedroom with low level of public openness.

> *"I slightly have a desire for princess-style interior. [...] When I lived alone, friends used to frequently visit me to keep me company. [...] I don't think anyone knows that I like princess-style. [...] I think they might have judged me if I had princess style furniture. [...] Recently, while I was preparing for wedding, I purchased a princess style ivory colored bed with long legs, and header with large curves [...] I placed it in the biggest bed room of my new home." (P01)*

7   Discussions and Limitations

The study discovered that each person differently perceives the level of public openness and it can change depending on time and context. Such level influences one's affective responses and design preferences in visual aesthetic attributes of the furniture. When a user perceives a space with high level of public openness, one would think visual aesthetic attributes of the furniture item in the space is important. Likewise, when the level of public openness is low, a user might think visual aesthetic attributes is less important. However, it is hasty to conclude that there is an absolute value in the relation between the level of importance in visual aesthetic attributes of the furniture design based and the level of public openness. This is because the level of public openness and the level of importance in visual aesthetic attributes vary based on one's personal and cultural backgrounds. For example, participant 10 answered that she perceives her bedroom with low level of openness, because she believes that it is a courtesy not getting into the bedroom in Korea:

"It is rude to get into the bedroom in Korea, so I think the bedroom is a place where others cannot see!" (P10)

Likewise, one's cultural background might affect his/her affective responses to visual aesthetic attributes including shapes, textures, materials and other factors. Since we conducted our study in Korea, participants' standard to the level of public openness and the level of visual aesthetic attributes might be influenced by the Korean culture. However, we believe that our study is significant in a way that we confirmed the relationship between the level of public openness and the one's affective responses to level of visual aesthetic attributes in furniture. That is, even for the same furniture items, visual aesthetic attributes would be vary based on the space's level of public openness perceived by users. Thus, we suggest considering the public openness of the space where the item would be placed when planning or designing furniture items.

Also, it is not possible to quantify the results of ten participants, as the level of public openness differs based on one's personality and cultural background. Furthermore, the number of participants was not enough to reflect various demographic variables including, age range, gender, and social status. Thus, for the future study, we are planning to increase the data size so that we can hopefully generalize the relationship between the level of public openness and one's affective responses to visual aesthetic attributes. Also, how such relationship would differ by demographic variables including age, gender, and social status needs to be considered.

8 Conclusion

In this study, we explored how the level of public openness of the space influences users' affective responses and thus affect their preferences to visual aesthetic attributes of furniture items. In spaces where the level of public openness is high, one would consider visual aesthetic attributes of the furniture as an important factor, since the space can be revealed to others. Also, one would like to present oneself and deliver the same or similar affective responses to audiences through visual aesthetic attributes of the furniture in the space where the level of public openness is high.

In the space with low level of public openness, a user tends to consider visual aesthetic attributes of the furniture less significant. With the low level of public openness, we found the tendency that participants purchase the furniture by considering its usability, functionality, and personal tastes rather than visual aesthetic attributes. Likewise, through this study, we confirmed that there is a correlation between the level of public openness and users' affective responses. We suggest that it is important to consider the space's level of public openness when it comes to planning and designing furniture.

Acknowledgements. This material is based upon work supported by the Ministry of Trade, Industry & Energy (MOTIE, Korea) under Industrial Technology Innovation Program. No. 10060517, 'Development of a user-centered product design support system based on cognitive and affective information'.

References

1. Altman, I.: The Environment and Social Behavior: Privacy, Personal Space, Territory, and Crowding. Brooks/Cole, Monterey (1975)
2. Altman, I., Gauvain, M.: Cross-cultural and dialectic analysis of homes. In: Liben, L.S., Patterson, A.H., Newcombe, N. (eds.) Spatial Representation and Behavior Across the Life Span: Theory and Application. Academic Press, New York (1981)
3. Leino-Kilpi, H., Välimäki, M., Dassen, T., Gasull, M., Lemonidou, C., Scott, A., Arndt, M.: Privacy: a review of the literature. Int. J. Nurs. Stud. **38**(6), 663–671 (2001)
4. Lawrence, R.J.: What makes a house a home? Environ. Behav. **19**(2), 154–168 (1987)
5. Bernard, Y., Jambu, M.: Espace habité et modèles culturels. Ethnologie française **8**, 7–20 (1978)
6. Kron, J.: Home-Psych: The Social Psychology of Home and Decoration. Clarkson N. Potter, New York (1983)
7. Russell, J.A., Ward, L.M., Pratt, G.: Affective quality attributed to environments: a factor analytic study. Environ. Behav. **13**(3), 259–288 (1981)
8. Mary, D., Isherwood, B.: The World of Goods: Towards an Anthropology of Consumption. Basic Books, New York (1979)
9. Richins, M.L.: Valuing things: the public and private meanings of possessions. J. Consum. Res. **21**(3), 504–521 (1994)
10. Reid, T.N., Frischknecht, B.D., Papalambros, P.Y.: Perceptual attributes in product design: fuel economy and silhouette-based perceived environmental friendliness tradeoffs in automotive vehicle design. J. Mech. Des. **134**(4), 041006 (2012)
11. Bloch, P.H.: Seeking the ideal form: product design and consumer response. J. Mark. **59**, 16–29 (1995)
12. Crilly, N., Moultrie, J., Clarkson, P.J.: Seeing things: consumer response to the visual domain in product design. Des. Stud. **25**(6), 547–577 (2004)
13. Norman, D.: Emotion & design: attractive things work better. Interactions **9**(4), 36–42 (2002)
14. Strauss, A., Corbin, J.: Basics of Qualitative Research, vol. 15. Sage, Newbury Park (1990)

Emotions in Material Surfaces for Product Design

Donghwan Kim, Yun Jae Lee, Jiwon Kim, Hyerin Park, Min Hee Shin, Ji Hyun Lim,
Choeun Kim, Taezoon Park, and Wonil Hwang[✉]

Department of Industrial and Information Systems Engineering, Soongsil University,
369 Sangdo-ro, Dongjak-gu, Seoul 06978, Korea
wonil@ssu.ac.kr

Abstract. Nowadays tactile emotions on product surfaces gain more attention. This study aims to investigate what emotions consumers expect from product surfaces through tactile perception. A questionnaire was designed with 12 emotional expressions and 7 product categories, and data was collected through online survey. 121 participants took part in the survey, and the data was analyzed using ANOVA and Tukey multiple comparison test to examine significant difference among product categories for expected tactile emotion on product surfaces. It is concluded that each of product categories can be significantly differentiated by expected tactile emotions, and also age groups show significant interaction effects with product categories.

Keywords: Emotional expressions · Tactile emotion · Emotional design · Product surfaces

1 Introduction

Product design is the process of designing a product by implementing the target performance or function based on the specifications that were set in the product planning stage. Product design can be divided into concept design, functional design, detailed design, and production design according to the stages of design processes. Therefore, the function, structure, and shape of a product are determined through four steps. In the design process, the design of surface is typically done at the later stage of product development, usually called as the design of color, finish and material design. Especially for the products that require direct contact and interaction with human, the surface design is important. If the product designer does not consider the surface of specific products properly, the user may feel uncomfortable when using the product and consequently will not buy the product. For example, when designing a yoga mat, if the area of contact with the body is too rough or hard, it will not satisfy both the designer's intention and the consumer's expectation. In this sense, the surface design have mainly focused on functional aspects of the product, such as ease of handling, convenience, and usability of handles, buttons, and sticks. However, as the design guideline gradually becomes clear, emotional design that emphasizes not only ease of manipulation, convenience, usability but also human tactile sensibility gains more attention. Although it depends on the product characteristics, emotional appeal is closely related with the purchase decision.

© Springer International Publishing AG 2017
J. Zhou and G. Salvendy (Eds.): ITAP 2017, Part I, LNCS 10297, pp. 275–283, 2017.
DOI: 10.1007/978-3-319-58530-7_21

Therefore, when designing the surface of product, it is necessary to reflect human tactile sense appropriately to meet the needs of the customer. However, it is not systematically investigated what expectation consumers have depending on the product categories. Thus, in this study, we focused on the surface characteristics of consumer products to check the expected emotions from the surface feeling.

2   Related Works

Among the various classification schemes for products to explain the purchase behavior Foote, Cone, & Belding grid (FCB grid) is one of the most cited. The FCB Grid is a comprehensive model created by Vaughn [9], for analyzing consumers' purchase decisions. It analyzes the purchase decision process into two dimensions of high involvement and low involvement, thinking and feeling, it is used to establish appropriate advertising strategies depending on their location in the grid. For the 'feel' type product with low involvement are more likely to be influenced by affective appeals whereas 'think' type products with high involvement depends more on rational decision making processes. Along this line, the locations of tested products in FCB grid were identified o check proper coverage of interested consumer product set.

The surface of the product refers to the outermost or topmost part of the product. Therefore, the product surface differs depending on the material constituting the surface, and the surface stimulus varies depending on the characteristics of the material. Studies on tactile sensibility emerging from a material or a surface can be classified into a study on emotions according to physical characteristics related to surface roughness and a study on emotions according to vibro-tactile stimuli. For the first part, Chen et al. [1] investigated the physical characteristics of the surface in order to confirm the relationship between the tactile perception and the physical properties of the surface. A questionnaire consisting of 37 samples and 6 pairs of adjectives (warm-cold, slippery-sticky, smooth-rough, hard-soft, bumpy-flat, wet-dry) constructed the relationship between the characteristics and emotions. Kawasegi et al. [4] fabricated 14 different samples with different physical properties (pitch, height) to develop plastic molded parts with tactile properties to be used in various industrial fields. Morishima et al. [7] tried to express the tactile sensibility according to the physical properties of fibers by using 18 adjectives with five samples including nylon in order to obtain the physical properties of fibers to express tactile sensibility. Kim et al. [5] classifies the mechanical properties of automobile seat skin material into four types (Resilience, Bending Moment, Thickness, Friction) to make a prediction model for development of the skin material considering the mechanical characteristics and sensitivity of automobile seat skin material. The neural network model was constructed by expressing the mechanical properties of leather (natural, PU, PVC) using four kinds of sensibility (Softness, Elasticity, Volume, Stickiness) by using fuzzy logic. Dépeault et al. [2] classified the physical properties of surface roughness into 3 types (Longitudinal spacing, Transverse spacing, Dot density) and measured the physical properties and evaluated the surface roughness by making a cylindrical sample with protrusions on the surface. Park et al. [8] classified the degree of roughness of six different materials used in automobile interior materials into two physical property values (Ra, Rz) in order to investigate the change of emotion when contacting with various car skin materials. In order to investigate the emotional changes caused by various fingertip vibrations, Hwang and Hwang [3] studied 29 emotional stimuli with frequency and sensory levels, Kim et al. [6] evaluated the responses of 10 types of adjectives to 15 stimuli with different frequencies and amplitudes.

Still, tactile sense is not fully known and understood yet, and many studies are under way to find the relationship between emotions and physical characteristics. Especially, studies on tactile sensibility that changes according to physical characteristics are limited to specific samples and materials. Therefore, in order to investigate various aspects of tactile sensibility, this study intends to identify the emotions that are related with the surface of a specified product groups.

3   Methods

To investigate the expected tactile emotions for material surfaces of products, online questionnaire was designed with 7 product categories and 12 emotional expressions, and data was collected from 121 participants.

3.1   Design of Questionnaire

Participants were asked to respond to the extent of agreeability for emotional expressions, which consumers expected to perceive from the material surfaces of products when they thought of a particular product. 12 (or 6 pairs of) emotional expressions for tactile perceptions of material surfaces were prepared from prior studies in the literature: cold/warm, sticky/slippery, hard/soft, dry/wet, flat/uneven, and rough/smooth. The extent of agreeability for each of 12 emotional expressions were measured with 7-point interval scales (1: strongly disagree, ..., 4: neutral, ..., 7: strongly agree).

7 product categories, such as bed, kitchen tool, VR (virtual reality) headset, body fat analyzer, yoga mat, digital door lock and electric drill, were presented to participants, who were supposed to think a preferred product that belonged to the presented product category, and described by words and pictures in the questionnaire. 7 product categories were selected because they were familiar to consumers and located in four spaces based on the FCB Grid. 'High involvement/think' includes 'bed', 'VR headset', 'body fat analyzer'; 'high involvement/feel' includes 'kitchen tool'; 'low involvement/think' includes 'electric drill' and 'digital door lock'; and 'low involvement/feel' includes 'yoga mat'.

3.2   Participants and Procedure

A total of 121 participants took part in the survey. They were 52 males (43.0%) and 69 females (57.0%). 87 participants (72.0%) belonged to the age group of 20 to 29 years old, and 27 participants (22.3%) were between 40 and 49 years old. The others were 4 participants (50–59 years old), 2 participants (30–39 years old) and 1 participant (equal to and more than 60 years old). Thus, with regard to age, majority of participants belonged to two age groups, '20–29 years old (72.0%)' and '40–59 years old (25.6%)'.

Survey was conducted based on the online questionnaire, which was opened during a week and advertised by emails and SNS to Korean consumers. Thus, even though the questionnaire did not contain questions for ethnicity or nationality, it seemed that all of participants were Korean consumers. Participants were expected to respond to 12 questions for each of 7 product categories, while they thought of a preferred particular product from the presented product category, and the responses were automatically collected by online.

4 Results

The data collected from online survey was analyzed using ANOVA (analysis of variance) to find out whether there was significant difference among product categories for the expected tactile emotions. In addition, it was analyzed whether there were significant interaction effects between product categories and age groups for the expected tactile emotions.

4.1 Expected Emotions for Products

ANOVA was conducted for each of 12 expected tactile emotions to examine significant difference among 7 product categories, and Tukey multiple comparison tests were conducted to find out where there was significant difference.

'Cold'/'Warm'. For 'cold' emotion, there is significant difference among product categories ($F_{6,819} = 15.35$, $p = 0.000$). According to Tukey multiple comparison test, 'digital door lock (mean = 4.65)' and 'electric drill (mean = 4.42)' show significantly higher value than 'bed (mean = 3.03)' and 'yoga mat (mean = 3.03)' (see left graph in Fig. 1). Likewise, for 'warm' emotion, there is significant difference among product categories ($F_{6,819} = 21.05$, $p = 0.000$), but 'bed (mean = 3.94)' show significantly higher value than 'digital door lock (mean = 2.12)' according to Tukey multiple comparison test (see right graph in Fig. 1). Therefore, it could be inferred that consumers expect 'cold' emotion from the surface of 'digital door lock' and 'electric drill', and that consumers associate 'warm' emotion with the surface of 'bed' rather than the others but the association strength is not high.

'Sticky'/'Slippery'. For 'sticky' emotion, there is significant difference among product categories ($F_{6,819} = 13.18$, $p = 0.000$). According to Tukey multiple comparison test, 'yoga mat (mean = 2.35)' show significantly higher value than the others (see left graph in Fig. 2). Meanwhile, for 'slippery' emotion, there is significant difference among product categories ($F_{6,819} = 5.34$, $p = 0.000$), and 'digital door lock (mean = 3.34)' show significantly higher value than 'bed (mean = 2.36)' and 'electric drill (mean = 2.43)' according to Tukey multiple comparison test (see right graph in Fig. 2). Therefore, it could be inferred that consumers do not usually expect 'sticky' and 'slippery' emotions from the surfaces of all 7 product categories, but relatively associate 'sticky' and

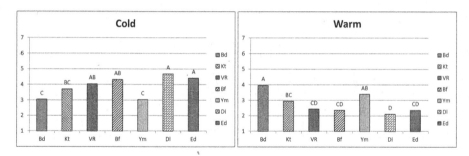

Fig. 1. Products and 'Cold'/'Warm' (*Bd*: Bed, *Kt:* Kitchen tool, *VR:* VR headset, *Bf:* Body fat analyzer, *Ym:* Yoga mat, *Dl:* Digital door lock, and *Ed:* Electric drill; alphabets indicate Tukey multiple comparison groups)

'slippery' emotions with the surfaces of 'yoga mat' and 'digital door lock', respectively, compared to the others.

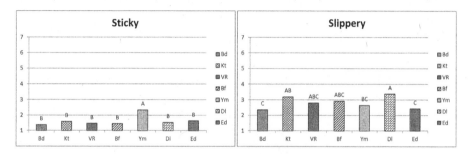

Fig. 2. Products and 'Sticky'/'Slippery' (*Bd:* Bed, *Kt:* Kitchen tool, *VR:* VR headset, *Bf:* Body fat analyzer, *Ym:* Yoga mat, *Dl:* Digital door lock, and *Ed:* Electric drill; alphabets indicate Tukey multiple comparison groups)

'Hard'/'Soft'. For 'hard' emotion, there is significant difference among product categories ($F_{6,819} = 70.35, p = 0.000$). According to Tukey multiple comparison test, 'kitchen tool (mean = 4.74)', 'VR headset (mean = 4.49)', 'body fat analyzer (mean = 4.85)', 'digital door lock (mean = 4.96)' and 'electric drill (mean = 5.12)' show significantly higher value than 'bed (mean = 2.48)' and 'yoga mat (mean = 1.97)' (see left graph in Fig. 3). On the contrary, 'soft' emotion ($F_{6,819} = 106.2, p = 0.000$) shows the exact opposite pattern to 'hard' emotion with product categories (see right graph in Fig. 3). Therefore, it could be inferred that consumers expect 'hard' emotion from the surface of 'kitchen tool' 'VR headset', 'body fat analyzer', 'digital door lock' and 'electric drill', and 'soft' emotion from the surfaces of 'bed' and 'yoga mat'.

'Dry'/'Wet'. For 'dry' emotion, there is no significant difference among product categories ($F_{6,819} = 1.44, p = 0.197$) (see left graph in Fig. 4). Meanwhile, for 'wet' emotion, there is significant difference among product categories ($F_{6,819} = 12.6, p = 0.197$), and 'kitchen tool (mean = 2.63)' show significantly higher value than the others according

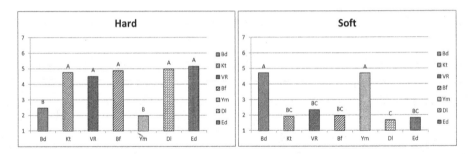

Fig. 3. Products and 'Hard'/'Soft' (*Bd:* Bed, *Kt:* Kitchen tool, *VR:* VR headset, *Bf:* Body fat analyzer, *Ym:* Yoga mat, *Dl:* Digital door lock, and *Ed:* Electric drill; alphabets indicate Tukey multiple comparison groups)

to Tukey multiple comparison test (see right graph in Fig. 4). Therefore, it could be inferred that consumers are neutral to all of product categories for 'dry' emotion, and that consumers do not usually expect 'wet' emotion from the surfaces of all 7 product categories, but relatively associate 'wet' emotion with the surfaces of 'kitchen tool' compared to the others.

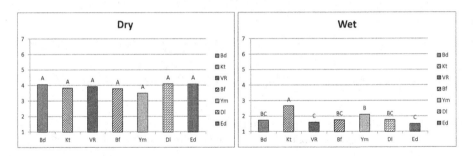

Fig. 4. Products and 'Dry'/'Wet' (*Bd:* Bed, *Kt:* Kitchen tool, *VR:* VR headset, *Bf:* Body fat analyzer, *Ym:* Yoga mat, *Dl:* Digital door lock, and *Ed:* Electric drill; alphabets indicate Tukey multiple comparison groups)

'Flat'/'Uneven'. For 'flat' emotion, there is significant difference among product categories ($F_{6,819} = 17.53, p = 0.000$). According to Tukey multiple comparison test, 'digital door lock (mean = 4.57)' show significantly higher value than 'VR headset (mean = 3.77)' and 'electric drill (mean = 2.41)' (see left graph in Fig. 5). Meanwhile, for 'uneven' emotion, there is significant difference among product categories ($F_{6,819} = 18.62, p = 0.000$), and 'electric drill (mean = 3.65)' show significantly higher value than the others according to Tukey multiple comparison test (see right graph in Fig. 5). Therefore, it could be inferred that consumers expect 'flat' emotion from the surface of 'digital door lock', and that consumers do not usually expect 'uneven' emotion from the surfaces of all 7 product categories, but relatively associate 'uneven' emotion with the surface of 'electric drill', compared to the others.

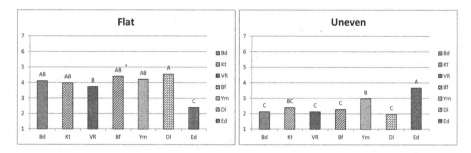

Fig. 5. Products and 'Flat'/'Uneven' (*Bd:* Bed, *Kt:* Kitchen tool, *VR:* VR headset, *Bf:* Body fat analyzer, *Ym:* Yoga mat, *Dl:* Digital door lock, and *Ed:* Electric drill; alphabets indicate Tukey multiple comparison groups)

'Rough'/'Smooth'. For 'rough' emotion, there is significant difference among product categories ($F_{6,819} = 25.35$, $p = 0.000$). According to Tukey multiple comparison test, 'electric drill (mean = 3.53)' show significantly higher value than the others (see left graph in Fig. 6). Meanwhile, for 'smooth' emotion, there is significant difference among product categories ($F_{6,819} = 12.47$, $p = 0.000$), and 'kitchen tool (mean = 4.90)' and 'digital door lock (mean = 4.83)' show significantly higher value than 'yoga mat (mean = 3.98)' and 'electric drill (mean = 3.19)' according to Tukey multiple comparison test (see right graph in Fig. 6). Therefore, it could be inferred that consumers expect 'smooth' emotion from the surface of 'kitchen tool' and 'digital door lock', and that consumers do not usually expect 'rough' emotion from the surfaces of all 7 product categories, but relatively associate 'rough' emotion with the surface of 'electric drill', compared to the others.

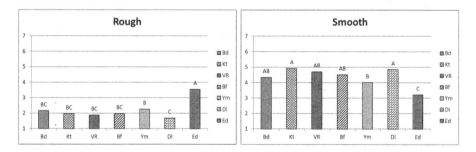

Fig. 6. Products and 'Rough'/'Smooth' (*Bd:* Bed, *Kt:* Kitchen tool, *VR:* VR headset, *Bf:* Body fat analyzer, *Ym:* Yoga mat, *Dl:* Digital door lock, and *Ed:* Electric drill; alphabets indicate Tukey multiple comparison groups)

4.2   Interaction Effects Between Products and Age Groups

Majority of participants were divided by age into two groups: 'younger group: 20–29 years old ($n = 87$)' and 'elder group: 40–59 years old ($n = 31$)'. Interaction effects between product categories and age groups were investigated for each of 12 emotions, and it was found that 'soft ($F_{6,805} = 2.66$, $p = 0.015$)' and 'uneven ($F_{6,805} = 3.99$, $p = 0.001$)' emotions showed significant interaction effects. For 'soft' emotion, younger group (mean = 5.08) shows significantly higher value than elder group (mean = 3.66) in 'bed' product, according to Tukey multiple comparison test (see Fig. 7). Meanwhile, for 'uneven' emotion, younger group (mean = 3.97) shows significantly higher value than elder group (mean = 2.62) in 'electric drill' product, and likewise, younger group (mean = 3.39) shows significantly higher value than elder group (mean = 1.83) in 'yoga mat' product, according to Tukey multiple comparison test (see Fig. 8). Therefore, it could be inferred that younger consumers expect softer beds than elder consumers, and that all consumers do not usually expect 'uneven' emotion from the surfaces of electric drills and yoga mats, but younger consumers would like to easily associate 'uneven' emotion with the surfaces of 'electric drill' and 'yoga mat' rather than elder consumers.

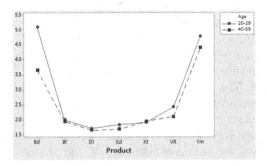

Fig. 7. Products and 'Soft' by age groups (*Bd:* Bed, *Kt:* Kitchen tool, *VR:* VR headset, *Bf:* Body fat analyzer, *Ym:* Yoga mat, *Dl:* Digital door lock, and *Ed:* Electric drill)

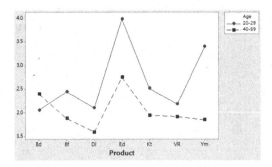

Fig. 8. Products and 'Uneven' by age groups (*Bd:* Bed, *Kt:* Kitchen tool, *VR:* VR headset, *Bf:* Body fat analyzer, *Ym:* Yoga mat, *Dl:* Digital door lock, and *Ed:* Electric drill)

5   Discussion and Conclusions

This study investigated what emotions consumers expected from the surfaces of products through their tactile perceptions. 7 product categories were selected to represent all spaces of FCB grid, and 12 emotional expressions were used to measure tactile emotions perceived from surfaces of products. Based on the data collected from online survey, we can conclude what emotions consumers expect from the tactile perception on product surfaces as follows.

First, consumers expect 'soft' emotion from 'bed' and 'yoga mat' surfaces. Especially, younger consumers expect soft emotion from bed more than elder consumers. Second, consumers expect 'hard' and 'smooth' emotions from 'kitchen tool' surfaces. Third, consumers expect 'hard' emotion from 'VR headset' and 'body fat analyzer' surfaces. Fourth, consumers expect 'cold', 'hard', 'flat' and 'smooth' emotions from 'digital door lock' surfaces. Finally, consumers expect 'cold' and 'hard' emotions from 'electric drill' surfaces. These conclusions show what emotions product designers should focus on relatively when designing the product surfaces, even though product surfaces have many emotions perceived by consumers.

Since this study is an exploratory study for expecting consumer's tactile emotions for product surfaces, there are some limitations to achieve research goals. This study only measure consumer's expectation based on online questionnaire. Survey participants responded the questions depending on their memory related to using a particular product. More elaborate experiments with a number of variables related to product surfaces would be needed for further study rather than the survey.

Acknowledgments. This work is supported by the Ministry of Trade, Industry and Energy, (MOTIE, South Korea) under Industrial Technology Innovation Program No. 10060517, 'Development of user-centered product design support system based on cognitive and affective information'.

References

1. Chen, X., Shao, F., Barnes, C., Childs, T., Henson, B.: Exploring relationships between touch perception and surface physical properties. Int. J. Des. **3**, 67–77 (2009)
2. Dépeault, A., Meftah, E.M., Chapman, C.E.: Tactile perception of roughness: raised-dot spacing, density disposition. Exp. Brain Res. **197**, 235–244 (2009)
3. Hwang, J., Hwang, W.: Perception and emotion for fingertip vibrations. Arch. Des. Res. **23**, 127–137 (2010)
4. Kawasegi, N., Fujii, M., Shimizu, T., Sekiguchi, N., Sumioka, J., Doi, Y.: Evaluation of the human tactile sense to microtexturing on plastic molding surfaces. Precis. Eng. **37**, 433–442 (2013)
5. Kim, J.Y., Lee, C.J., Kim, A.N., Lee, C.H.: Comforts evaluation of car seat clothing. Sci. Emot. Sensib. **12**, 77–86 (2009)
6. Kim, S.-C., Kyung, K.-U., Sohn, J.-H., Kwon, D.-S.: An evaluation of human sensibility on perceived texture for real haptic representation. J. KISS Soft. Appl. **34**, 900–909 (2007)
7. Morishima, M., Morikawa, A., Shimizu, Y., Takatera, M., Gocho, H., Jojima, E.: Evaluation of tactile sensation for fabrics of various fiber fitness. Kansei Eng. Int. **2**, 27–32 (2001)
8. Park, J., Park, K., Yu, J., Choe, J., Jung, E.S.: Effects on the tactile affections of touch behaviors and materials of vehicle interior. In: Fall Conference of the Ergonomics Society of Korea, Korea, pp. 42–46 (2013)
9. Vaughn, R.: How advertising works: a planning model revisited. J. Advert. Res. **26**, 27–30 (1986)

Study on the Product Packaging Color Identification of Elder Men and Elder Women

Jiajie Lyu$^{(\boxtimes)}$ and Delai Men

School of Design, Guangzhou Higher Education Mega Center,
South China University of Technology, Panyu District,
Guangzhou 510006, People's Republic of China
371049310@qq.com

Abstract. The main purpose of this paper is to study the difference of Chinese elder men and elder women on the product packaging color identification visually. The elderly aged between 65 and 75 are selected as the research targets, to test the impact of three major attributes of color on the elderly of different genders and obtain data, by referring to the Munsell color system color lightness variation diagram, to make tests according to the contrast effects of the color ring. Test the lightness, purity and saturation of color respectively, and record and analyze the test reactions of the elderly. Half of the data recorded are elder men, and the other half are elder women. There are subtle differences in the physical function between the male and the female, and SPSS software is used to sum up.

The three attributes of color are the keys of this study. The analytical results can not only be used as data support for the study of product design and packing design, but also provide reference data for the living space of the elderly. With an aging trend world wide, the aged population and its proportion are increasing year by year. China particularly entered aging society totally around the year of 2000, with the population aged above 65 reaching 138 million in 2014, accounting for 10.1% of the total population, which is expected to reach 12.8% in 2020 [1]. Under this circumstance, it is necessary to enhance the design study of the elderly. This paper mainly tests and studies the visual identification of the product packaging color of the elderly. This article also studies the impact of the colors on product packaging used by the elderly on their psychology, physiology and other aspects, and probes into the study of how to increase and optimize this impact of colors. It will be a key point as to how to offer a unique product packaging for the elderly through color design, and the elderly of different gender have different acceptance and preference of the package, which will change from the virtual functional level to the psychological level gradually. The elderly are their own protagonists, that is to say, designs focusing on the use benefit of the elderly will be preferred.

At the same time, different colors can express different emotions, and each color has an independent feature bringing unique feeling to people. At the same time, color preference will change along with the increase of people's social experience, the improvement of cultural level, the social environment and other factors. The elderly will definitely have unique aesthetics after experiencing so many years of worldly affairs, combined with aesthetics on special product packaging design, using color to attract the elderly to make purchase is a method for sales promotion in packaging design. The color sensitivity of the elderly

© Springer International Publishing AG 2017
J. Zhou and G. Salvendy (Eds.): ITAP 2017, Part I, LNCS 10297, pp. 284–303, 2017.
DOI: 10.1007/978-3-319-58530-7_22

began to decrease, the color information in the image can help the eyes to distinguish between the main figure or object and background clearly.

Therefore, the study takes the elderly as the research object, taking into account the three attributes of color, the age, gender, culture and other factors of the subject, in order to obtain more convincing research results. Through the study of the visual characteristics of the elderly, it obtains the data analysis and the emotional characteristics of color, to explore the design methods suitable for the emotional characteristics on color of the elderly. The basic content of this paper is to get the color emotion of the elderly with the use of the basic knowledge of color and the analysis methods of visual design. And then, it makes detailed data analysis of the time of the elderly's eyes resting on the cool colors and warm colors, and certain color range. In the selection of research objects, investigation will be made on the elderly with different cultural backgrounds and living environments according to the actual situation, while making efforts to ensure the reality and accuracy of the survey results, to provide useful data for the subsequent design process.

Keywords: Color identification · Elder women · Elder men · Visual characteristics

1 Introduction

Nowadays, the world population is faced with the trend of aging and China is completely entering into the aging society around 2000. The latest survey data shows that the population of 65 years old or above reached 109.56 million in 2008, accounting for 8.3% of the total population, with an increase of 0.2% over the previous year [1]. In China, more and more elderly people live alone, and more and more their children work far away from home. China's national conditions determine that the elderly's life is arduous and complicated. Therefore, it is necessary to study how to improve and design the living environment of the elderly.

When entering the old age, people will be faced with the decline in various abilities, such as physical function including vision, hearing, language ability and limb movement function and cognitive ability including perception, memory, attention and learning ability degradation. More than 80% of the necessary information received from people's social life comes from the visual system, [2] mainly through visual sensitivity of human body, visual field, color vision and the minimum recognition critical value on vision and a series of visual function which can apperceive the surrounding environment [3]. When it comes to the photopia vision, the human body can apperceive different colors of visible light to form the color vision [4]. The human eyes not only improve the acceptance speed, but also enrich daily life through rapid screening and identification of color information the outside world. However, the vision of the elderly usually declines, and the field of vision shrinks; the color recognition weakens, especially for blue and green color; visual sensitivity weakens, especially for the sensitivity of dynamic objects.

The trend of product packaging is required to consider the actual needs of the elderly and the product packaging design based on the needs. In order to improve the life quality of the elderly and facilitate the daily life of the elderly, color recognition and analysis have been taken into consideration for packaging design, which minimizes the cost and maximize the effect, as well as realizes the subtle discrepancy on the physiological function between men and women.

2   Characteristics and Differences of Body Function and Visual Between Male and Female

The human eye tissue structure changes with age, and gradually there will be some phenomenon of visual degradation, which causes certain inconvenience to the daily life of the elderly. Based on the known theory about the color vision of the elderly and environmental aspects, the color selection of the elderly daily product packaging is analyzed, emphasizing two analysis aspects including the color recognition between male and female and the color preference of different genders, which provides reference for the color design suitable for the packaging of elderly's product. There are great differences in the vision between men and women: women have stronger color recognition than men, and men have the visual advantages in the sensitivity of the details on the distant objects and the ability to track fast moving objects. The researchers claim that this distinction starts form the ancient times because men and woman have different roles in the long-term social labor division.

2.1   Physical Function and Visual Characteristics of the Elderly

Compared with the young, the eye tissue structure of the elderly has a series of changes occurred, which results in a visual degradation. On the one hand the aging cornea and lens lead to color perception change and light transmission performance weakens, which cause the visual effects of the elderly turn yellow and the corresponding human perception changes. It is difficult to recognize the color blue and green, but the rest color of red, orange, yellow and others are relatively easy to identify. Human recognition ability for the discrepancy of color, brightness and saturation correspondingly decline, thereto there is little changes for the recognition for brightness difference. In addition, with age, changes of human cornea lead to the light scattering, and the pupil becomes smaller, which causes sensitivity for light declines and the adjustment function of eyes declines due to the changes of vitreous structure and retina. Changes of eye tissue structure are expressed by a series of phenomenon of physiological changes on the eyes such as physiological presbyopia, changes on bright and dark vision, decline of contrast sensitivity, sensitivity of glare and decline of vision and depth of field, even cataract, glaucoma and senile ocular lesion [5].

2.1.1   Common Functional Degradation of the Elderly

(A)   Cataract: the elderly with cataract cannot see things clearly and the sight seems be blocked because transparent lens produce sclerosis, turbidity and other lesions. Severe cataract has the following symptoms: blurred vision, photophobia, darker image color, when reading light is low, the degree of glasses changes.

(B)   Presbyopia: As time goes, the lens of the eye will gradually harden and lose the original flexibility, which cause the adjustment function of eyes weakens and make it difficult to work and read in the close distance with the symptoms [2] of fatigue, pain and swelling, and even headache, nausea etc. [6].

2.1.2   The Data Is Old

At present, data collection about the elderly in China is still in the stage of infancy. There are very few studies on the visual discrepancy of color discrimination between the male and female elderly. There is some information on visual illusion and visual degradation and visual characteristics of the elderly etc. However, there are few specific distinctions visual differences between the male and female elderly. So the reference data in terms of color identification for the elderly is relatively poor.

2.2   Research on Color Identification Between the Male and Female Elderly

Because there are still differences of color vision between the male and female elderly, this study is to make the elderly of different genders identify and choose the best option by Munsell color system, PCCS color card and the color of the common packaging in life, as well as, summarize visual difference between the male and female elderly according to statistical data of SPSS analysis.

3   Experiment

3.1   Experimental Objectives

This article aimed at the target group of the elderly between 65 and 75 years old, whose physical function drops significantly compared with the younger old people between 60 and 65 years old. However, the elderly more than 75 years old are on the stage of relative self-reliance and capable of completing necessary trivia in life and going to the supermarket to buy products. Therefore, 50 elderly male between 65 and 75 years old and 50 elderly female between 65 and 75 years old are chosen as the objects of study. In this study, those objects of research are from Guangdong and Inner Mongolia respectively, which shows the difference between the north and south and universal meaning.

3.2   The Measurement Parts

Thought the Munsell lightness color card, PCCS color ring and product packaging, the elderly are interviewed to choose more clear color and the code of color ring preferred in accordance with the contrast effects of the samples. The experimental data is received through investigation and interview to the objects of study.

3.3   The Measurement Methods and Tools

In order to ensure the accuracy of data, we invited a professional to participate in the whole experimental process. The main method is to show fifty elderly men and fifty elderly women all these three experimental samples including PCCS hue circles, six color packaging samples with main colors of red, yellow, blue and green, and three color rings with high, medium and low brightness and then choose their most recognizable and favorite color, packaging sample and color ring respectively. The date recorded is used to make the graph and analyzed (Figs. 1, 2 and 3).

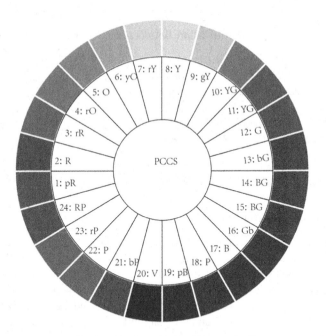

Fig. 1. Sample 1 (Color figure online)

Fig. 2. Sample 2 (Color figure online)

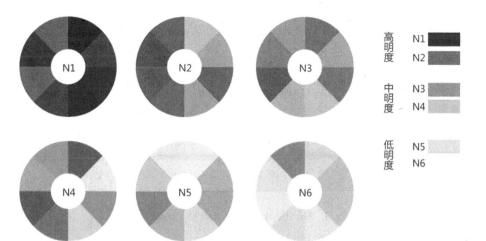

Fig. 3. Sample 3 (Color figure online)

4 Data Analysis

4.1 The Data Prepossessing

In order to ensure the accuracy and reliability of data, 100 elderly people between 65 and 75 are chosen as the object of study. Measurement data are processed and some repeated data are deleted after checking. 100 valid data are received with effective rate of 100%.

4.2 The Analysis Methods

SPSS data analysis software is used to analyze the data, and then the differences of visual color identification between male and female elderly from north and south are summarized and compared.

4.3 The Analysis of Data

After statistics and analysis of the data, we can learn about the histogram of experimental materials (Figs. 4, 5, 6, 7, 8, 9, 10, 11, 12, 13, 14 and 15).

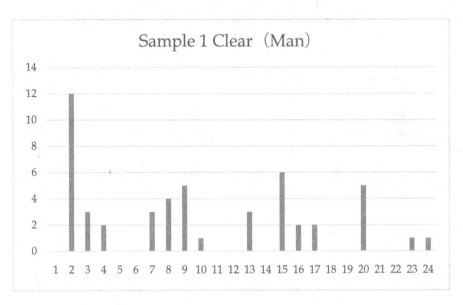

Fig. 4. The distribution of sample 1 clear(M)

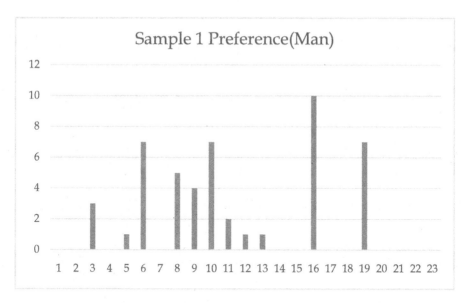

Fig. 5. The distribution of sample 1 preference(M)

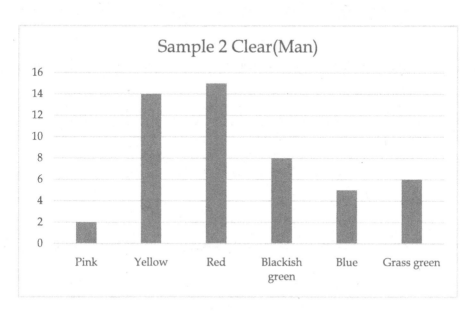

Fig. 6. The distribution of sample 2 clear(M)

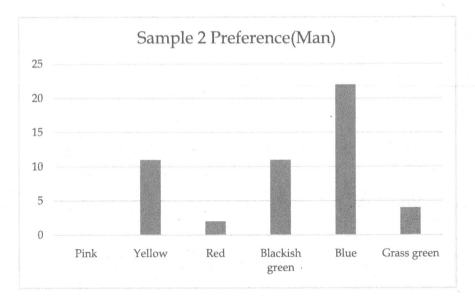

Fig. 7. The distribution of sample 2 preference(M)

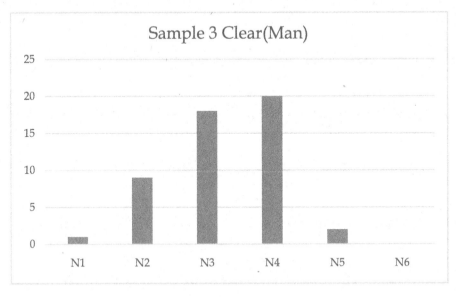

Fig. 8. The distribution of sample 3 clear(M)

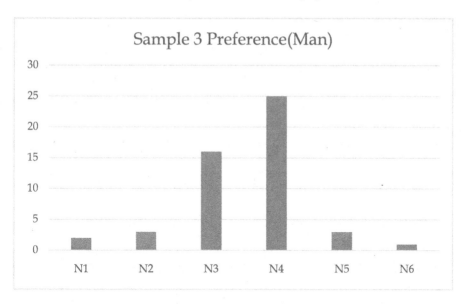

Fig. 9. The distribution of sample 3 preference(M)

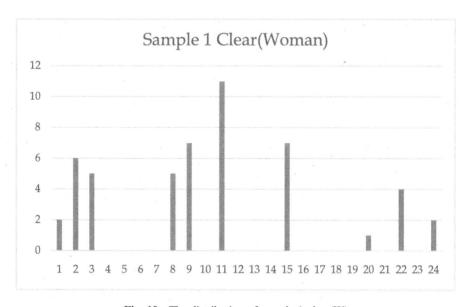

Fig. 10. The distribution of sample 1 clear(W)

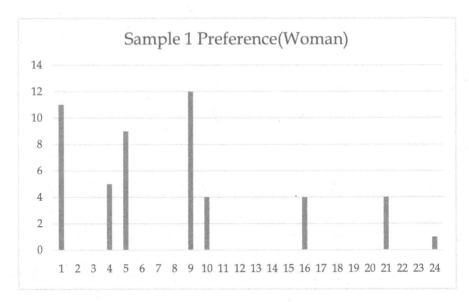

Fig. 11. The distribution of sample 1 preference(W)

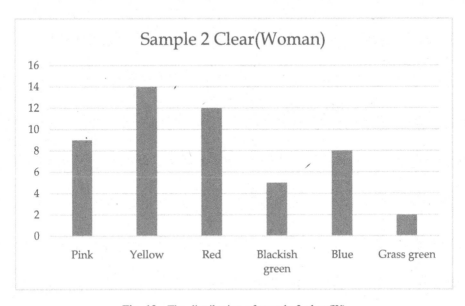

Fig. 12. The distribution of sample 2 clear(W)

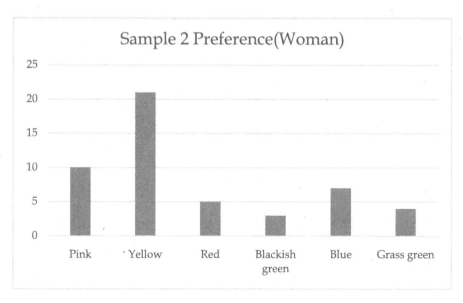

Fig. 13. The distribution of sample 2 preference(W)

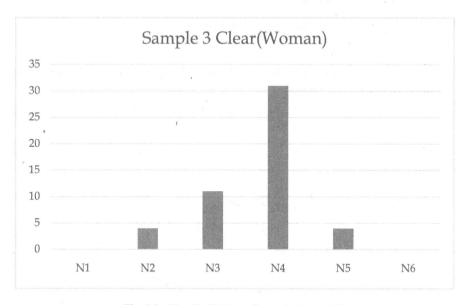

Fig. 14. The distribution of sample 3 clear(W)

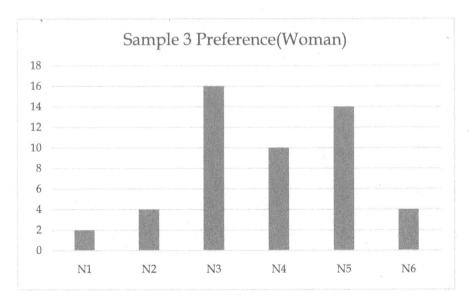

Fig. 15. The distribution of sample 3 preference(W)

4.4   The Analysis of Data Difference

SPSS software 20.0 is used for analysis and the results are as follows:

4.4.1   Descriptive Analysis

Below is the analysis of frequency, that is, the sample frequency, percentage, effective percentage, cumulative percentage.

4.4.1.1 The Clearest

See Tables 1, 2 and 3.

Table 1. PCCS (The Clearest)

Num.	Name	Frequency	Percent	Valid percent	Cumulative percent
1	pR	2	2	2	2
2	R	18	18	18	20
3	rR	8	8	8	28
4	rO	2	2	2	30
5	O	0	0	0	30
6	yO	0	0	0	30
7	rY	3	3	3	33
8	Y	9	9	9	42

(*continued*)

Table 1. (*continued*)

Num.	Name	Frequency	Percent	Valid percent	Cumulative percent
9	gY	12	12	12	54
10	YG	1	1	1	55
11	YG	11	11	11	66
12	G	0	0	0	66
13	bG	3	3	3	69
14	BG	0	0	0	69
15	BG	13	13	13	82
16	Gb	2	2	2	84
17	B	2	2	2	86
18	P	0	0	0	86
19	pB	0	0	0	86
20	V	6	6	6	92
21	bP	0	0	0	92
22	P	4	4	4	96
23	rP	1	1	1	97
24	RP	3	3	3	100

Table 2. Sample of Food Packaging (The Clearest)

Num.	Name	Frequency	Percent	Valid percent	Cumulative percent
1	Pink	11	11	11	11
2	Yellow	28	28	28	39
3	Red	27	27	27	66
4	Blackish green	13	13	13	79
5	Blue	13	13	13	92
6	Grass green	8	8	8	100

Table 3. Color Group of Different Brightness (The Clearest)

Num.	Name	Frequency	Percent	Valid percent	Cumulative percent
1	N1	1	1	1	1
2	N2	13	13	13	14
3	N3	29	29	29	43
4	N4	51	51	51	94
5	N5	6	6	6	100
6	N6	0	0	0	100

4.4.1.2 The Most Favorite

See Tables 4, 5 and 6.

Table 4. PCCS (The Most Favorite)

Num.	Name	Frequency	Percent	Valid percent	Cumulative percent
1	pR	13	13	13	13
2	R	0	0	0	13
3	rR	0	0	0	13
4	rO	8	8	8	21
5	O	9	9	9	30
6	yO	1	1	1	31
7	rY	7	7	7	38
8	Y	0	0	0	38
9	gY	17	17	17	55
10	YG	8	8	8	63
11	YG	7	7	7	70
12	G	2	2	2	72
13	bG	1	1	1	73
14	BG	1	1	1	74
15	BG	0	0	0	74
16	Gb	4	4	4	78
17	B	10	10	10	88
18	P	0	0	0	88
19	pB	0	0	0	88
20	V	7	7	7	95
21	bP	4	4	4	99
22	P	0	0	0	99
23	rP	0	0	0	99
24	RP	1	1	1	100

Table 5. Sample of Food Packaging (The Most Favorite)

Num.	Name	Frequency	Percent	Valid percent	Cumulative percent
1	Pink	10	10	10	10
2	Yellow	32	32	32	42
3	Red	7	7	7	49
4	Blackish green	14	14	14	63
5	Blue	29	29	29	92
6	Grass green	8	8	8	100

Table 6. Color Group of Different Brightness (The Most Favorite)

Num.	Name	Frequency	Percent	Valid percent	Cumulative percent
1	N1	4	4	4	4
2	N2	7	7	7	11
3	N3	32	32	32	43
4	N4	35	35	35	78
5	N5	17	17	17	95
6	N6	5	5	5	100

4.4.2   Chi-Square Testing

$P < 0.05$ is taken as a criteria of statistical difference, the results are as follows:

4.4.2.1 The Clearest

As seen from Table 7, P tested by the chi-square or Fisher for the most favorite colors of packaging bags between different genders is less than 0.05. Therefore, there is the discrepancy of the favorite colors of packaging bags between different genders.

Table 7. PCCS (Chi-Square Testing of The Clearest)

		Gender		X^2(Fisher)	P
		Male	Female		
PCCS	pR	0	2	35.680	<0.001
	R	12	6		
	rR	3	5		
	rO	2	0		
	rY	3	0		
	Y	4	5		
	gY	5	7		
	YG	1	0		
	YG	0	11		
	bG	3	0		
	BG	6	7		
	Gb	2	0		
	B	2	0		
	V	5	1		
	P	0	4		
	rP	1	0		
	RP	1	2		

As seen from Table 8, P tested by the chi-square or Fisher for the most favorite packaging bags of food product between different genders is = 0.150 > 0.05. Therefore, there are no discrepancies of the clearest hue circles between different genders.

Table 8. Sample of Food Packaging (Chi-Square of The Clearest)

		Gender		X^2(Fisher)	P
		Male	Female		
Packaging bags of food product	Pink	2	9	8.004	0.150
	Yellow	14	14		
	Red	15	12		
	Blackish green	8	5		
	Blue	5	8		
	Grass green	6	2		

As seen from the Table 9, P tested by the chi-square or Fisher for the clearest colors between different genders is = 0.090 > 0.05. Therefore, there are no discrepancies of the clearest colors between different genders.

Table 9. Color Group of Different Brightness (Chi-Square of The Clearest)

		Gender		X^2(Fisher)	P
		Male	Female		
Group of brightness	N1	1	0	7.468	0.090
	N2	9	4		
	N3	18	11		
	N4	20	31		
	N5	2	4		
	N6	1	0		

4.4.2.2 The Most Favorite

As seen from Table 10, P tested by the chi-square or Fisher for the most favorite colors between different genders is less than 0.05. Therefore, there is the discrepancy of the favorite colors between different genders.

Table 10. PCCS (Chi-Square of The Most Favorite)

		Gender		X^2(Fisher)	P
		Male	Female		
Color cycle	pR	0	2	35.680	<0.001
	R	12	6		
	rR	3	5		
	rO	2	0		
	rY	3	0		
	Y	4	5		
	gY	5	7		
	YG	1	0		
	YG	0	11		
	bG	3	0		
	BG	6	7		
	Gb	2	0		
	B	2	0		
	V	5	1		
	P	0	4		
	rP	1	0		
	RP	1	2		

As seen from Table 11, P tested by the chi-square or Fisher for the most favorite colors of packaging bags between different genders is less than 0.05. Therefore, there is the discrepancy of the favorite colors of packaging bags between different genders.

Table 11. Sample of Food Packaging (Chi-Square of The Most Favorite)

		Gender		X^2(Fisher)	P
		Male	Female		
Packaging bag of food product	Pink	0	10	27.862	<0.001
	Yellow	11	21		
	Red	2	5		
	Blackish green	11	3		
	Blue	22	7		
	Grass green	4	4		

As seen from Table 12, P tested by the chi-square or Fisher for the most favorite colors between different genders is less than 0.05. Therefore, there is the discrepancy of the favorite colors between different genders.

Table 12. Color Group of Different Brightness (Chi-Square of The Most Favorite)

		Gender		X^2(Fisher)	P
		Male	Female		
Group of brightness	N1	2	2	15.677	0.004
	N2	3	4		
	N3	16	16		
	N4	25	10		
	N5	3	14		
	N6	1	4		

Brief analysis are listed as follows:

(1) There are significant differences of color tendency for the elderly between male and female.
(2) There are significant differences on the length of the wavelength of visual color formed in the eyeballs of the elderly between male and female.
(3) There are significant differences on the hue saturation of the elderly between male and female.
(4) There are no significant differences on the color brightness between male and female.
(5) Women's color recognition is stronger than men, and men have the advantage of unity and decisiveness in choosing color.
(6) In terms of recognition, the majority of men and women choose warm colors.
(7) In terms of preferences, there are obvious differences of preference for the elderly between male and female, which is likely to follow the current color understanding between men and women. Generally speaking, men prefer blue and green and other cool colors, while women have a preference of red, yellow and other warm colors.
(8) In terms of color brightness, the male and female elderly people generally choose the color group of medium brightness, that is, the N4 group, but there are some slight differences in preference, men prefer N3 and N4, while women have a preference for N3 and N5. Therefore, compared with men, women prefer the soft tone with lower brightness.

5   Conclusion

Some research in the journal Gender Biology claim that in the majority of the visible spectrum men and women need longer wavelengths to form the same chrominance in the eye [7]. Based on a survey on Chinese men and female elderly people, it is found that the elderly's preference for color mainly depends on two factors: First, visual factors, for the single color, the elderly prefer the medium brightness color because visual ability of the elderly weakens and the medium brightness color looks more vivid. While more elderly women choose the color red than elderly men. However, there are no significant differences in the aspect of age. In terms of color configuration, the elderly generally has preference in the color or color matching that is bright and easy for visual perception with strong visual impact. For the colors such as red, orange and other warm colors, the same color of red looks more red for men, compared with women. However, for the color of green looks more green for women, compared with men. Second, psychological condition makes most of the elderly need the bright and lively colors due to their psychological need. Therefore, the elderly has a preference of warm color and subconsciously think those sunshine-likely colors symbolize the vibrant life, youth and energy.

Therefore, those factors should be fully taken into account for packaging design for the elderly. In according with people-oriented basic, the correct emotional color with medium saturation and brightness is used to design the packaging of product. However, the relatively distinguished colors neither produce stimulus for the vision of the elderly, nor have color confusion for the elderly with poor visional function. Besides, the large scale color matching that is difficult to distinguish should be avoided including the color white and yellow, blue and gray, blue and green and other colors.

References

1. China Industry Information Network. http://www.chyxx.com/industry/201603/395552.html
2. Narazaki, Y.: Consider the Architectural Design of the Elderly (Illustration). The Disabled, p. 2. Inoue College (2014)
3. Japan Architecture Society: Architectural Design Information Integration (Human, Space Articles), p. 82. Tianjin University Publisher (2003)
4. Xi'an University of Architecture and Technology: Architectural Physics, 3rd edn., p. 130. China Construction Industry Publisher (2014)
5. Wu, S., Yan, H., Shi, X.: The relationship between visual and illumination in the elderly. J. Optom. 6(1), 56–58 (2014)
6. Tang, F.X., Yang, Q.: The Application of Color Emotion in the Packaging of Health Care for the Elderly (02). Drama House (2016)
7. Gender Biology. http://blog.sina.com.cn/s/blog_6812eedd01019jg0.html

Research on the Design of Smart Pension Product Modeling Based on Brand Image

Xinxin Zhang[✉], Minggang Yang, and Yan Zhou

School of Art, Design and Media,
East China University of Science and Technology, M. Box 286 NO. 130,
Meilong Road, Xuhui District, Shanghai 200237, China
y10160052@mail.ecust.edu.cn, yangminggang@163.com,
371047193@qq.com

Abstract. With the deepening of trend and degree on China's aging, the demand of pension services is expanded further. Thus contents about pension services which come from the needs of more families and society are being introduced in the pension industry, and a multi-support system of the old is being formed. Meanwhile, the existing high-technology promotes the conversion of traditional elderly products and convenient smart products under the design idea of "human-oriented". In the development process of smart pension product, apart from the basic functional requirements of the product, the emotional needs of the elderly are needed to parse through the image cognitive process which containing the psychological, experiential, emotional and other aspects, so as to meet the needs of the elderly for the use of functional and kansei image truly. The brand image of product modeling is the brand impression in the minds of users which exists in the concept of consumers', and all the features and beliefs that are imposed upon a product style, being formed in the process of users' cognitive experience after interacting with the product. So it is necessary to grasp the brand image of product form accurately by reading and extracting through the cognitive process for effectively assisting the designers to upgrade the brand value of product modeling quickly. As the information of product modeling is diverse, complex and fuzzy, the image information will appear a dissipation phenomenon during the delivery process. For the sake of the validity to pick up the image information, the theory and method of Kansei Engineering and Information Entropy are used to analyze the brand image of smart pension product modeling in this paper, and also taking the smart bracelet styling as an example to obtain the design factors who can affect the brand image identification of it. Firstly, two methods named KJ method and interview method are used to ensure the research samples and the adjective vocabularies which can describe the image of smart pension product modeling. Secondly, the SD method is needed to grab the consumer's kansei image needs, and an image cognitive space is constructed to count the weight of each target image for analyzing the brand image of smart product modeling. Then, the research samples are deconstructed by using the morphological analysis. Finally, the coupling and the attribute of game between product and design elements as well as design elements and design elements are parsed by the information entropy for gaining the design factors that can affect the brand image identification. Those design factors are also called product design elements which can provide guideline and development ideas for the design of smart pension product.

© Springer International Publishing AG 2017
J. Zhou and G. Salvendy (Eds.): ITAP 2017, Part I, LNCS 10297, pp. 304–315, 2017.
DOI: 10.1007/978-3-319-58530-7_23

Keywords: Brand imagery · Smart pension product modeling · Kansei engineering · Information entropy · Design factor

1 Introduction

With deepening of the aging trend and the rapid development of high technology in China, traditional products of the elderly are converted to the facilitation of smart products. While in the research process of the smart pension products, besides considering the basic functional requirements of the product, it also needs to start from the emotional needs of the elderly to analyze the perceptual information of the elderly cognitive process effectively. Cognitive ability is the most important psychological condition for people to successfully complete their activities, which refers to the ability of the human brain to process, store and extract information. In other words, it is the ability to grasp the relationship between them, the driving force of development, the direction of development and the basic law. However the cognitive ability of people will decline when they are in the old age, and mostly may also decay the ability to extract information, which means can not know the performance of objects [1]. Therefore, this study aims to pick up the image information of the elderly for guiding the design of smart pension product development, the theory and method of Kansei Engineering and Information Entropy are used to analyze the brand image of smart pension product modeling in this paper, and also taking the smart bracelet styling as an example to obtain the design factors who can affect the brand image identification of it.

2 Background

2.1 Aging Society

In the 21st century, the aging of the population has become a common problem facing by the world. The United Nations defines an aging society as a country over the age of 65 with a population of more than 7%. Then, in 2016, the China's elderly population is about 1.1883 billion, accounting for 11.9% of the total population [2]. According to the standards of the United Nations, China has been listed as an aging society, and it makes the silver wave to promote the development of silver-haired market which becoming the hotspot in the future consumer market. Meanwhile, an interpretation of the concept of "People Oriented" is the attention and love from the society for elderly needs, which means not only to provide their physical level of satisfaction, but also should take into account their inner real needs. This study realizes to meet the needs of elderly people to use function and perceptual image by analyzing the image cognition process of the elderly, which includes psychological, experience and emotion.

2.2 Brand Image Needs

People's consumption concept has also changed greatly with the improvement of material and cultural life level. The emotional demand has become diversified and individualized, which reflects people's pursuit of emotional quality and satisfaction of self-realization. The brand image of product modeling is the brand impression in the minds of users which exists in the concept of consumers', and all the features and beliefs that are imposed upon a product style, being formed in the process of users' cognitive experience after interacting with the product. Kansei engineering is a kind of theory and method of using engineering technology to explore the relationship between kansei needs of cognition subject and design elements [3]. In the field of product design, the technical method of Kansei engineering is used to excavate and reveal the potential emotional needs of "human" perception "objects", so as to find the correlation mechanism between the product's emotional images and design elements [4]. Hsin-Hsi Lai used the semantic difference method and the multidimensional evaluation method to explore the relationship between the style and the styling elements of the car side profile [5]. And Ke Shanjun put forward the research method of brand image based on logistic regression, which is aimed at the demand of automobile brand [6]. This study can accurately grasp the brand image of product modeling, through the effective extraction and interpretation of kansei information in "human" cognition process. That is, assisting designers to quickly enhance the brand value of product modeling effectively, and meeting the "people" brand image needs of personalized product development.

2.3   Entropy and Application

Entropy is defined as the degree of system chaos, which also means a measure of the probability that the system is in a certain macro state. Greater the entropy of the system is, more probability that the system is in this state [7]. Claude Elwood Shannon who is an American engineer proposed the concept of information entropy, which is a measure of the amount of information used for the negative entropy, indicating the order of a system [8]. Entropy theory will be applied to the objective analysis of complex image problems in this study. Arnheim who was the earliest person introducing the theory of entropy to the art field studied the perceptions of art works, basing on the Gestalt psychology and Entropy theory [9]. France explored the relationship between the entropy and the system which means an art work, and demonstrated that the chaos of this system can be measured by entropy [10].

3   Methods

As the information which transfers form product modeling is diverse, complex and fuzzy, image information will appear dissipative phenomenon in the transmission process [11]. In order to ensure the validity of the extracted image information, this study uses the theory and method of the kansei engineering and the information entropy to analyze the brand image of smart pension product modeling and evaluate the design elements of the product. The study flow is shown in Fig. 1.

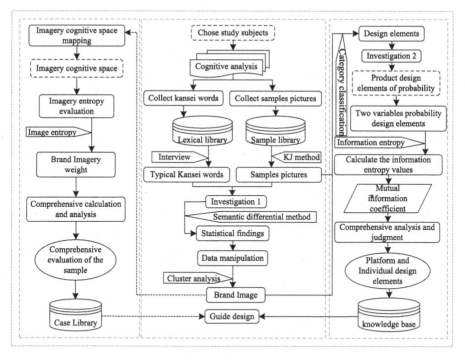

Fig. 1. Study flow

The study flow and steps are described below in five stages:

1. Identify the study samples and the kansei images. The KJ method and Interview are used to screen samples and sensible vocabulary, getting the typical kansei words and the samples pictures.
2. Establish a brand image cognition space basing on the emotional needs of the elderly. The Semantic Differential method is used to evaluate the cognitive performance of the samples, and the images are clustered to draw the brand image collection and image evaluation matrix. Then, constructing a cognitive space of brand image about old people, which takes the elements of brand image as the coordinate axes of spatial model and the image evaluation value as the coordinate value of the sample.
3. Evaluate the brand image entropy of the elderly. According to the image evaluation matrix, the image entropy model [12] is applied to analyze the entropy of brand image in the cognition process of elder image, then getting its weight value. In order to composing an excellent case library which is used to guide product design, weighting is then used to calculate the composite brand image evaluation value of the study samples.

$$I_j = -k \sum_{i=1}^{m} P_{ij} \ln P_{ij} \tag{1}$$

Where I_j is the image entropy value that is calculated from probability P_{ij} which is about the j item target image of the i sample, among these i indicates the study sample which is from 1 to m and j refers to the brand image that is from 1 to n, and the interval of P_{ij} is in [0, 1]. While k is a constant, its value is 1/ln m.

4. Deconstruct the design elements. Category classification is used to analyze the design elements of the study sample, obtaining the design elements set and the modeling feature set of them.

5. Measure the amount of information. By investigating the design elements of the concentration of various design elements of the probability of different shapes, the probability of each modeling feature is the statistics. Then, the information entropy model is applied to calculate the information entropy of a single design element.

$$H = -\sum_{g=1}^{q} p_g \ln p_g \tag{2}$$

Where H is the value of information entropy, and P_g is the probability about the appearance of the q modeling feature which is in the g element. Meanwhile, the relationship between multiple design elements can be explored based on the calculated result, for example, the mutual information entropy between the two design elements named I and II is:

$$H_{I\,II} = \sum_{g=1}^{q} \sum_{g^*=1}^{q^*} p(I_g II_{g^*}) \ln p(I_g II_{g^*}) \tag{3}$$

In the evaluation of product design elements, the mutual information coefficients of the two design elements can be defined by the information entropy of the single design element and the mutual information entropy of the two design elements:

$$\begin{aligned} o_{I\,II} &= \frac{H_I + H_{II} - H_{I\,II}}{H_{II}} \\ o_{II\,I} &= \frac{H_I + H_{II} - H_{I\,II}}{H_I} \end{aligned} \tag{4}$$

The O is the size of the impact between two design elements which named the information coefficient in this paper, containing two aspects. By calculating the mutual information coefficient, we can compare the design elements of the product modeling with each other and obtain the relative importance of each design element, thus can identify the individual design elements and platform design elements of the product modeling, which is conducive to understanding and tapping the individual needs. Finally we may design the product which in line with the people's brand image needs.

4   Case Study

4.1   Identify the Study Samples and the Kansei Images

In this paper, an example of smart bracelet is studied for research. Firstly, collect 86 product pictures from the website, journals and product brochures and other channels. Secondly, obtain the study sample set as shown in Fig. 2 containing the 16 samples that are discussed about 86 cards of the smart bracelet from the experts by using the KJ method. Because this study is to analyze the relationship between product modeling and image cognition, the images are grayscale processed in order to avoid the impact of color on the process of image recognition. Finally, the methods of interview and cluster analysis are used to determine the target image set consisting of five kansei adjectives named comfortable, succinct, slap-up, facile and distinctive.

Fig. 2. Study sample set

4.2   Establish a Brand Image Cognition Space

In order to further determine the brand image of the elderly on the bracelet shape, the semantic differential method is used to analyze the image cognition process of the elderly bracelet modeling, and the SD questionnaire is generated from 16 study samples and 5 target images which have been known in the previous step. Then each participant who is the elderly population scores the study samples for each image, it is means that as the kansei image "Comfortable" for example, "5" is very comfortable, "4" is comfortable, "3" that comfortable, "2" that the general comfort, and "1" that is not comfortable. Finally, we get the evaluation value of the target image of the elderly in each study sample. The results are given in Table 1.

A total of 30 questionnaires have been distributed, of which 26 questionnaires were valid. Then, the cluster analysis is used to analyze the results for reducing the evaluation error. While the representative vocabularies are clustered into three categories which Combined with the image of cognitive space attributes, and the brand images of the bracelet are selected by choosing the nearest image from the cluster center for each

Table 1. Target image evaluation results

Sample	Comfortable	Succinct	Slap-up	Facile	Distinctive
1	3.8	3.5	4.3	3.8	3
2	3.1	3.1	2.4	2.9	2.5
3	3.3	3.1	2.9	2.7	3.6
...	...	...	...	...	...
14	2.9	2.1	2.4	2	2.4
15	2.5	1.6	2.4	2.5	3.7
16	3.5	3.4	2.9	4.1	3.8

Table 2. Lexical classification of target images

Classification	Result	Brand images
1	Comfortable Succinct Slap-up	Comfortable
2	Facile	Facile
3	Distinctive	Distinctive

Table 3. Brand image evaluation matrix

Sample	Comfortable	Facile	Distinctive
1	3.0	3.8	3.9
2	2.5	2.9	2.9
3	3.6	2.7	3.1
4	2.4	4	3.6
5	3.6	2.4	3
6	3.3	2.9	3.9
7	2.9	3.9	2.8
8	3.3	3.8	3.5
9	4.4	3.4	2.4
10	3.4	3.1	3.5
11	3.2	2.5	2.9
12	2.7	2.4	3
13	3.4	3.7	3.3
14	2.4	2.0	2.5
15	3.7	2.5	2.2
16	3.8	4.1	3.3

type of representative. At last, we can get the brand image set and its evaluation matrix, the results are shown in Tables 2 and 3.

Form Tables 2 and 3, the brand image cognition space is set up by Matlab, which is based on the emotional needs of the elderly, as is shown in Fig. 3.

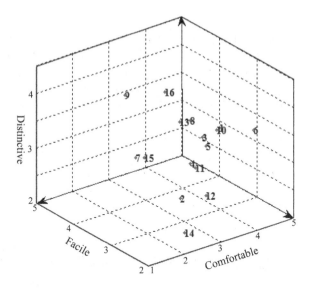

Fig. 3. The brand image cognition space of the elderly

4.3 Evaluate the Brand Image Entropy of the Elderly

Basing on the normalized data from Table 3, the brand image entropy of the elderly is evaluated by Eq. (1). The results are shown as follows:

$$I = [0.9027, \ 0.9271, \ 0.9367]$$

It should be noted here that, when $p_{ij} = 0$, it is shifted to the right by 0.0001 to ensure the validity of the results to minimize the effect of the extreme value 0 on the evaluation results.

4.4 Deconstruct the Design Elements

On the basis of the Table 2 and the Fig. 2, the expert group uses the category classification to deduce the design elements influencing the bracelet image modeling, and determines six design elements which are the material, shape, complex, overall volume, concavity and surface treatment. After that, the modeling features of each design element are analyzed, as shown in Table 4.

4.5 Measure the Amount of Information

In order to know the probability of different modeling characteristics of statistics, designing a questionnaire from Table 3 and Fig. 2, and then having the research. The occurrence probability of the single-design element and two-by-two design elements is obtained by collating the findings, as shown in Tables 5 and 6.

Table 4. Design elements and features

Brand image	Design elements	Design features
Comfortable facile distinctive	*(I)* Material	*I(1)* Hard *I(2)* Soft
	(II) Shape	*II(1)* Square *II(2)* Organic shape *II(3)* Arc-shaped
	(III) Complex	*III(1)* Simple *III(2)* Medium *III(3)* Complex
	(IV) Overall volume	*IV(1)* Small *IV(2)* *IV(3)* Big
	(V) Concavity	*V(1)* Small *V(2)* Medium *V(3)* Big
	(VI) Surface treatment	*VI(1)* No *VI(2)* Yes

Table 5. The single design element

Design elements	Occurrence probability
(I) Material	$P_{I(1)} = 7/16$ $P_{I(2)} = 9/16$
(II) Shape	$P_{II(1)} = 6/16$ $P_{II(2)} = 6/16$ $P_{II(3)} = 4/16$
(III) Complex	$P_{III(1)} = 7/16$ $P_{III(2)} = 6/16$ $P_{III(3)} = 3/16$
(IV) Overall volume	$P_{IV(1)} = 10/16$ $P_{IV(2)} = 6/16$
(V) Concavity	$P_{V(1)} = 6/16$ $P_{V(2)} = 5/16$ $P_{V(3)} = 5/16$
(VI) Surface treatment	$P_{VI(1)} = 8/16$ $P_{VI(2)} = 8/16$

Table 6. The two design elements about *I and II*

Design elements	I(1)	I(2)
II(1)	$P_{I(1)\ II(1)} = 5/16$	$P_{I(2)\ II(1)} = 1/16$
II(2)	$P_{I(1)\ II(2)} = 1/16$	$P_{I(2)\ II(2)} = 5/16$
II(3)	$P_{I(1)\ II(3)} = 1/16$	$P_{I(2)\ II(3)} = 3/16$

Table 7. The information entropy

Design elements	I	II	III	IV	V	VI
H		0.6853	1.0822	1.0434	0.6616	1.0948	0.6931

According to the probability, the information entropy and the mutual information entropy of design elements are computed by Eqs. (2) and (3), and results are shown in Tables 7 and 8. Then, the mutual information coefficient between the design elements are obtained by Eq. (4) and the results are in Table 9.

Table 8. The mutual information entropy

Design elements	I	II	III	...
I				
II	$H_{I\ II} = 1.5607$			
III	$H_{I\ III} = 1.5438$	$H_{II\ III} = 2.0140$		
...	...	...	...	

Table 9. The mutual information coefficient

Design elements	I	II	III	IV	V	VI
I		0.3018	0.2698	0.0947	0.0380	0.1070
II	0.1911		0.1031	0.1048	0.1808	0.0498
III	0.1772	0.1070		0.0715	0.3206	0.0348
IV	0.0981	0.1714	0.1128		0.0355	0.0001
V	0.0133	0.1788	0.3055	0.0215		0.0607
VI	0.1058	0.0778	0.0524	0.0002	0.0959	

Finally, the mutual information coefficient map of the bracelet's design elements is drawn by reading the information in Table 9. As shown in Fig. 5.

5 Results and Discussion

We can conclude from the previous research results about the Fig. 4 that "Comfortable" which is the brand image of the elderly has the highest weight, following by facile and distinctive. The weight values are 0.4167, 0.3122 and 0.2711, that determining the more inclined to care the elderly a sense of comfort in the design process of a bracelet shape. Then, according to the higher composite evaluation value, a case library is also composed from the calculation results are shown in Fig. 4. As shown in Fig. 6.

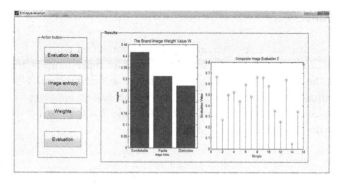

Fig. 4. The calculation results

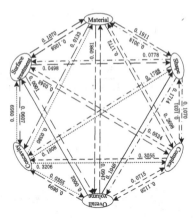

Fig. 5. Map

| 1 | 8 | 9 | 11 | 16 |

Fig. 6. The case library

At the same time, from Fig. 5, the weight values of the design elements are calculated for ranking in the design process that the design factor with larger information coefficient should be given priority in decision-making. And the ranking results named the knowledge base are the concavity, complex, shape, surface treatment, material, and overall volume. Thus the formation of a knowledge base and the case library are used to provide the design idea and direction for the follow-up bracelet design.

6   Conclusion

In this study, we use the kansei engineering and information entropy to analyze the brand image of smart pension product modeling, and we make more consideration for the elderly on the comfort of the heart needs in the design process. While, we also obtain the platform design elements and individual design elements of the smart pension product modeling which affect the brand image that can instruct the follow-up product image design effectively.

References

1. Puyu, Z.: Research on the perceptual design of the elderly. J. Ar. Pan. **5**, 146–147 (1981)
2. A development report of the China's aging cause (2016). http://www.docin.com/p-1392744913.html
3. Mitsuo, N.: Kansei engineering: a new ergonomic consumer-oriented technology for product development. Int. J. Ind. Ergo. **15**, 3–11 (1995)
4. Jianning, S., Pingyu, J., Heqi, L.: Research on kansei image-driven method of product styling design. Int. J. Pro. Dev. **7**, 113–126 (2009)
5. Hsinhis, L., Yuming, C., Huacheng, C.: A robust design approach for enhancing the feeling quality of a product: a car profile case study. Int. J. Ind. Ergo. **35**, 445–460 (2005)
6. Shanjun, K., Ying, W., Zhenbo, C.: The research on brand image for automobile styling based on logistic regression. J. Grap. **37**, 524–529 (2016)
7. Qi, M.F., Fu, Z.G., Jing, Y., Ma, Y.: A comprehensive evaluation method of power plant units based on information entropy and principal component analysis. J. CSEE **33**, 58–64 (2013)
8. Robert, M.G.: Entropy and Information Theory. Springer, New York (2011)
9. Rudolf, A.: Entropy and Art-An Essay on Disorder and Order. University of California Press, London (1971)
10. France, M.M., Henaut, A.A.: Therefore Entropy. J. Leo. **27**, 219–221 (1994)
11. Zhang, Y., Rau, P.-L.P., Zhong, R.: Measuring disengagement and chaos in multitasking interaction with smart devices. In: Rau, P.-L.P. (ed.) CCD 2016. LNCS, vol. 9741, pp. 139–150. Springer, Cham (2016). doi:10.1007/978-3-319-40093-8_15
12. Jianning, S., Xinxin, Z., Nan, J., Xiao, C.: Research on the entropy evaluation of product styling image under the cognitive difference. J. Mach. Des. **33**, 105–108 (2016)

Aging and User Experience

Acoustical Evaluation of Soundscape in Urban Spaces Along Traffic Corridor

Wei Lin[1(✉)], Wei-Hwa Chiang[2], Hsuan Lin[3], and Yi-Run Chen[2]

[1] Department of Interior Design, Hwa Hsia University of Technology,
Taipei, Taiwan
weilin@cc.hwh.edu.tw
[2] Department of Architecture, National Taiwan University
of Science and Technology, Taipei, Taiwan
whch@mail.ntust.edu.tw, pl62@ms3.hinet.net
[3] Department of Product Design, Tainan University of Technology,
Tainan, Taiwan
te0038@mail.tut.edu.tw

Abstract. In recent years, Taiwan's public transport infrastructures at all levels have improved and enhanced public convenience which is including the airport, high-speed railway, metropolitan rapid train (MRT), and so on. The aircraft channel location and highway plane elevated, the formation of the connected trail system and open recreation spaces can provide people holiday gathering and recreation of the important field. The NIMBY effect of the noise in the public open space along the traffic facilities is not reduced, it is the best choice for another area of residents' gathering and recreation on the contrary. For the urban traffic corridor along the adjacent channel system and open space, to the urban soundscape theory as the basis, through the time, energy and space and other factors for the exploring the sound energy distribution of the sound field. In this study, objective physical measurements were taken as an evaluation method, and the equivalent sound level L_{Aeq} (dB) was used to monitor the field, and the sound energy distribution map was drawn from the point, line and region. This paper discusses the relationship between subjective physical measurement and objective evaluations and tries to construct an important exposition of urban soundscape as the research theme of the next stage. The results of this study provide an alternative assessment of the development and sightseeing of urban corridors in terms of urban comfort, which are based on the sound field comfort.

Keywords: Urban soundscape · Sound field comfort · Objective measurements

1   Introduction

Urban development is a collection of industrial development and economic development, with the progress of human civilization and the city development, close to the crowded roads have become the habitat of urban living environments, and thus cause a sense of hearing a certain degree of impact. Acoustic ecology or Eco-acoustics is the study of soundscape research which explores the sound in the biological of live beings and environmental society of interaction relationship. When the face of surrounding sound,

© Springer International Publishing AG 2017
J. Zhou and G. Salvendy (Eds.): ITAP 2017, Part I, LNCS 10297, pp. 319–329, 2017.
DOI: 10.1007/978-3-319-58530-7_24

hearing and living in the natural environment produce a linkage, which interactive relationship is the focus of attention on soundscape. In the early 1970s, Schafer, a Canadian scholar, participated in the creation of the World Soundscape Project (WSP). Its first major project was a field study of the acoustical environment of natural landscape in Vancouver [1–3], it was also the most comprehensive text in the description of soundscape and sound recordings and a series of sound features. Similarly, the British scientist Truax [4] in the West Coast of British Columbia recorded natural soundscapes which were associated relative size of the different sound source volume. Dunn and Van Peer (1999) [5] found that soundscape can transmit the good impression in the environment. In 1969, soundscape researcher M. Southworth also began to explore the sound overall impression of the urban and built environment [6]. Schafer [7] began to attempt to classify the sound data between the country and the city and evaluated them from a historical perspective, and found that specific or repetitive patterns of sound were able to determine the design factors of the soundscape. The function of the sound is important to be able to convey the emotions, when listening to the sound or the virtual signal, the listener has reset the time and space in the memory of the brain [8]. The sound that exists in a particular context is not a natural phenomenon, and every sound is filled with its own vocabulary. "Soundscape" is defined by the International Organization for Standardization (ISO) as "one or more people in the perception, experience, and understanding of the acoustic environment morphology" [9], "soundscape" is also different from the "sound environment", because the former refers to Is the perception of morphology, latter refers to physical phenomena, and both are affected by the environment. "Soundscape", the combination of auditory and landscape terms, in the environment as a whole, the two coexist consistency, the lack of one of them will make the environment seem unnatural [10]. Cai (1998) [11, 12] and Wang (1996) [13] once again define the sound plus the scenery of the composite word, translated into Chinese can be called "Sound landscape" or "Soundscape". Owing to the denseness of the population and the concentration of the metropolitan areas, the annoying voices generated in different urban development stages are considered "noise". After entering the 21st century, most of the international environmental policies focus on noise control in the related studies of economic activity or social science in recent years. However, reducing the noise level does not necessarily improve the quality of life in cities [14–17]. This is why the study of urban sound environment tends to complex, in addition to monitoring the physical basis of information, may have to pay attention to people's actual experience and listening experience. The diversity of the customs and cultures of different countries has become a kind of available "resource" of urban environmental sound, not a kind of "pollution". Brown [18] summarizes the differences between perceived "pleasant soundscapes " and "disturbing noise" and their corresponding differences in characteristics. The impact of sound generated by various infrastructure constructions in people's living environment, such as roads, rapid transit and airports, and the public transport system; whether to re-examine the urban context and development plan from a sound perspective. In particular, Jian Kang, a professor of architecture at the University of Sheffield in the UK, has initiated research in Europe and has devoted considerable attention to soundscape research in North America, East Asia and South Asia, including Australia, Canada, the United States, Japan, China, Hong Kong and Korea [19]. The degree for sound preferences was proposed by Professor Toshimitsu Musha in 1980 [20]. His research mainly focused on the natural factor of wind, chaostic fluctuation (1/fluctuation) has the pleasant characteristics of this fluctuation frequency to which it gives the feeling tends to be positive. The conclusion is that if people like the natural sound which are affected by spectral characteristics of 1/f, but with a sound 1/f spectral characteristics with preference are not accepted necessarily by people in the world, which was related with one's emotions. Consistent with the theory of chaostic fluctuation stimulation can achieve a certain degree of sense of stability. 1/f is defined by as the following formula (1):

$$Log\ Pw = Log\ 1/f\ a = -a\ Log\ f \tag{1}$$

Pw: Sound magnitude (W), F: Frequency (Hz), a: Constance

One of the concepts of the soundscape, as the sound of the existence of the environment, should be accepted by the majority of people, so the first environmental noise to the initial objective to identify the characteristics of environmental sound. How the sound of the city is recognized as the soundscape is generally pleasant to listen to, not necessarily the city noise, including traffic generated by the sound is disturbing voice, Professor Jian Kang notes the current activities and listeners expectation that the visual perception of the sound source plays an important role in hearing the expected perception of the sound. Therefore, the sound energy level is measured by A-decibel dB(A), which is very similar to the frequency response of the human ear. It is the basic unit of sound energy level measurement, and L_{Aeq} and L_{Amax} are the main measurement physical quantities of this study. Most of the measurements of the environmental acoustic energy use sound pressure level (SPL), using the unit for the decibel (dB) that represents loudness, and human hearing and the environment for the decibel standard phase corresponding to the subjective feelings of knowledge has also been discussed. For example, there are many good examples to improve the perception of sound environment characteristics of sound in European cities, with water features and noise barriers embedded in the city's open recreation space, the use of noise barriers block the noise source and the water sound cover the nuisance of background noise. Different water features provide spectral types and different frequency ranges, which can effectively shield traffic noise. Such facilities create culturally significant connotations, such in Sheffield city, fountain water and metal noise barrier facilities, where fountains represent rivers and metals on behalf of the steel industry, symbolizing two important aspects of Sheffield's industrial development and urban planning historical context, in addition to improving the residents and tourists to enjoy the rest of these areas, and rich cultural and educational significance [21]. Through preliminary research on soundscape related three field measurements have been initially completed which are including 1. Sound field is underneath the aircraft channel, 2. Sound field is in the perimeter of high speed rail station and 3. Green belts and recreation areas are along MRT facility. The characteristics of sound field environment are established. The purpose of this study is shown in the following three points:

(1) Distributions of actual sound energy may discuss and sound characteristics of the urban traffic environment are also proposed.
(2) Processes may explore the impact of sound on environmental behavior and provide the proposed model of soundscape analysis.

(3) Research results may present urban planning direction, possibilities with a view to the development of tourism and open space as a national decision-making.

2   Research Methods

Based on the theory of soundscape, this paper defines the sound source types of urban soundscapes and discusses the sound environment of urban public transport corridors around the open space of the airport channel, the space between the high-speed railway stations green belt and the recreational area along rapid transit. The urban soundscape is mainly concerned with the activities of open space, including the fashionable and characteristic business circle in the metropolis. The traffic along the line is close to the high-density residential area and a large number of crowds. The characteristics of the linear greenbelt bring together different groups such as commuting and leisure. Such as the urban corridor along the MRT facility, from the point, line and area distribution, drawing with the characteristics of the sound energy distribution map, with a view to re-interpret the potential of the business district and the traffic node of the green belt of urban identity. The contents and methods of the study are mainly based on the related literature and research. After the establishment of the research process, the objective physical quantities of the auditory aspects are collected and analyzed to sum up their frequency analysis of sound environment. The sound field focused on monitoring traffic noise through the instantaneous acoustic energy to a single event, the acoustic energy over time, can be as an equivalent level Leq described volatility sound energy. Record results following two evaluation indicators, including the volume of noise can process the event (equivalent) L_{Aeq} (dB) and the maximum volume (Maximum) L_{AFmax} (dB). L_{Aeq} is defined by as the following formula (2):

$$L_{Aeq} = 10 \log \left(\sum_{n=20Hz}^{20kHz} 10^{1/10Leq} \right) \tag{2}$$

3   Approaches of Sound Field

The Soundscape triangle, developed by M. Schafer (1978) [1], includes sound marks, foreground sounds and Keynote. The term "Sound mark" derived from the landmark, used to be connected or even think of the unique sound of its source, such as church bells, the signal is noticeable and has been consciously heard the foreground sound, because different from the background sound, it is often organized into a sound code and passes the message. Keynote highlights the tone or tone of a string of sounds, although the main tone is not necessarily consciously aware, it summarizes or condensed a string of sound characteristics. From this, the classification of soundscape are classified by acoustical measurements, and all the collected sounds are decomposed into many elements to be analyzed, which is the basis of the research. In this study, the nodes of traffic facilities may choose which have features as measurement objects. The results of the previous studies are mainly the follow-up work of this study, whether the measured sound energy features are masked in term of the noises or the definition of frequency characteristics.

3.1   Sound Filed is Underneath the Aircraft Channel

Sound field is investigated underneath the aircraft channel which is located at MRT station (Yuanshan Station). Yuanshan Station is located in Taipei Basin in the mountains north of administrative Jiantan slopes with flat terrain area at an altitude of about 153 m, the north side of the river through Keelung. Yuanshan station is currently planning a hub node of "Taipei Flora Expo Park". Building and other facilities in the park of the series as "City museum settlement" recently completed restoration of the music garden, open for the publics, and this is the south side of the base as the opening food court. Since this sound filed is located in the aircraft-landing path, the sound source was generated by aircraft landing frequently which may have an impact on performance and activities in the park. Measuring point a total of three points, take off the next two points (Point A, Point B), another point is set in the Minzu West Road and Yumen Street, the base of the corner (Point C). The sound energy instantly through the sound generated by the aircraft, and synchronized three sets of sound energy instantaneously. The relative positions of three measuring points are shown in Fig. 1.

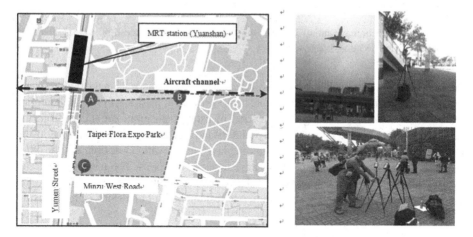

Fig. 1. Three measurement points are illustrated for the real time sound measurement when aircraft instantaneous pass through (left), and figures (right) show the measurements at Taipei Flora Expo Park.

3.2   Sound Field is in the Perimeter of High Speed Rail Station

The second study field is in the vicinity of Hsinchu High Speed Rail Station, which is located in North Taiwan. For the purpose of prohibiting the construction land from the land within 25 m from the centre line of the outer track of the high-speed railway,

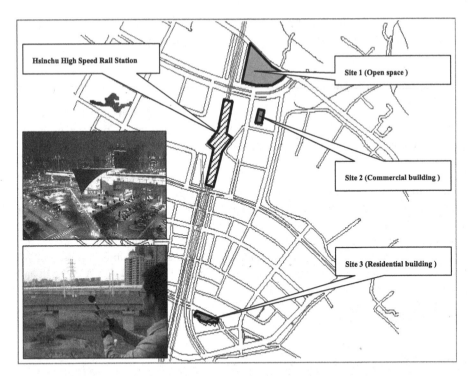

Fig. 2. Three measurement points in the perimeter of Hsinchu high speed rail station and field pictures are abstracted (left side)

the external noise of the building shall be assessed and the distance from the building wall line shall be 1.5 m. Indoor measurements shall be made at least 1.5 m from the interior walls or other major reflecting surfaces. All measuring positions are 1.2 m from the ground or floor. In order to effectively understand the height of the building in the temporary high-speed railway station building level and elevation location, and the other two near the peripheral area of similar base location to assess. The measurement and measurement are three locations, one is the open space (Site 1), the other two are the commercial (Site 2) building and the high rise residential building (Site 3), respectively (Fig. 2).

3.3   Sound Field is Along MRT Facility

Based on previous stage of aircraft measurement, monitoring measurement of greenbelt station and the surrounding sound field space were under progress continually, measurement method are followed by L_{Aeq} equation which are divided into morning, afternoon and evening hours phase, traffic flows information as a reference for the measurement are plotted in Fig. 1(Left). Gray shadows demonstrate the level of transportation level. 12 Measurement locations which are from Yuanshan station to Shuanglian station as also shown in Fig. 3(Right). Preliminary observation is divided into two

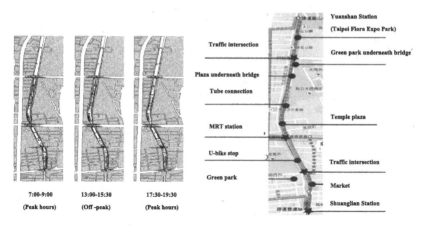

Fig. 3. Traffic flows information with 3 period hours phase as a reference for the measurement are plotted in the left side figure, 12 measurement locations which are illustrated from Yuanshan station to Shuanglian station in the right side figure.

sections, the first part is on the "Human activity", realize the visiting purpose, standing time, frequency of uses and activity behaviors. Second part is on the "Environment", visually observed moving peripheral line configuration of mobile mainly in the green belt, distribution of planting, infrastructure of MRT device, as a reference for future subsequent discussion. As shown in Fig. 1, the 12 locations of measurement are illustrated, the measurement period are divided into peak and off-peak hours, peak distinction from the intersection of the main measuring points, the criteria L_{Aeq} (dB) and the maximum volume L_{AFmax} (dB) are as the evaluation index. After having measurement data in the road and off-peak sections of different time, sound energy distribution are pointed out.

4   Preliminary Results

In addition to the substantial impact of the environment, in the history of culture, human psychology, environmental behavior and ecology of the discussion are also pondering. In the study of sound field survey, due to the highly developed city, adjacent to the transport facilities and the convenience of the road, are important choices for living elements of modern urban residents.

4.1   Measurement Result Underneath the Aircraft Channel

The results of the preliminary assessment of a single aircraft through the event to record the aircraft energy, mainly to the equivalent level of sound level L_{Aeq} sound energy over a period of time to describe the volatility of noise (such as traffic noise) or impulsive noise. The results of the record are the following two evaluation indicators, including the average volume L_{Aeq} (dB) and the maximum volume L_{AFmax} (dB) of the noise event during the process. Mainly to daily flights landing in the Taipei Airport are conducted

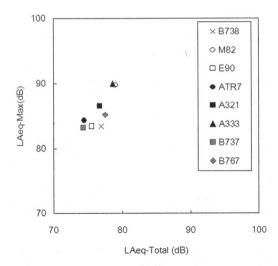

Fig. 4. Point B is illustrated L_{Aeq} (dB) derived from mainly aircraft landed at the Taipei international airport as a function of frequency band comparing the L_{AFmax} (dB).

which are including A321, A333, B738, B767 and other large aircraft. The main aircraft takeoff and landing of the Taipei Airport is based on the No. 10 runway (West→East) as the priority runway, but if there is a more obvious westerly wind will be on the 28th runway (East→West) landing. The maximum noise volume measured for the day is A and B, and the maximum volume is 92.9 dB(A) of M82 and A333, with an average maximum volume of 86.9 dB(A), and all aircraft events are volume is 80.0 dB(A) with an average of 75.4 dB(A). The measurement position (point B) underneath takeoff and descending channel for the instance, the L_{Aeq} (dB) as a function of frequency band comparing the L_{AFmax} (dB) of the aircraft landing sound, as shown in Fig. 4.

4.2   Measurement Result in the Perimeter of High Speed Rail Station

When the high-speed train through, the noise was generated by the value of the content of this stage of assessment. Although the noise value may be reduced by the distance of sound source which is from station body, traffic noise L_{Aeq} (dB) is between 54.1 to 64.8 dB(A). However, up to speed of 250 km/hr through the car close to the high-speed rail station body and pass through the station caused by the impact of the

Table 1. LAeq (dB) at 1/3 octave frequency band for high speed trains pass through

Freq. (Hz)	250	315	400	500	630	800	1 k	1.25 k	1.6 k	2 k	2.5 k	3.15 k	4 k
dB(A)	57.8	54	52.4	58.6	53.5	59.7	60.7	66.7	68	69.7	70	75.8	70

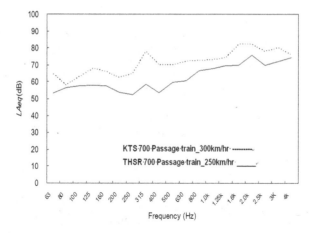

Fig. 5. Measurement results of L_{Aeq} (dB) of THSR (—) in the perimeter of Hsinchu Station at 1/3 octave frequency band compared with the measurements of Korea high-speed railway (KTS) (—) between the station Chunan to Chungwon.

impact of the surrounding area, will make sound noise enlarged. The distance from the centre line of the outer track 50 m, 1.5 m above the ground height of the noise measured by one of third octave band frequency of L_{Aeq} (dB) values is shown in Table 1. The measurement resulted (THSR) similar to the research of distribution at 1/3 octave band of L_{Aeq} (dB) of Korea high-speed railway (KTS) between the station Chunan to Chungwon [22], as measured in the case of the relative position and elevation measurements, measuring 107 classes of trains to speed of 150 to 300 km/hr. Comparison the measurement results of L_{Aeq} (dB) between THSR700 and KTS700 are illustrated in Fig. 5.

4.3   Measurement Result Along MRT Facility

Acoustic energy distribution were illustrated with selected four different measurement locations along the sound field of MRT Yuanshan station to Shuanglian station which are included mainly Yuanshan MRT station, Tatung University Square next to the green belt, temples and Shuanglian station. Energy distribution was interval centre spacing of 5 m outwards, based on the number of 9 measured points and were plotted as a soundscape map, the measurement period is divided into two peak hours (7:00–9:00 and 17:30–19:30) and off-peak hour (13:00–15:30), peak distinction was from the traffic intersection of the main measuring points. Around the MRT Shuanglian station, L_{Aeq} (dB) sound distribution with three periods of hours were illustrated in Fig. 6.

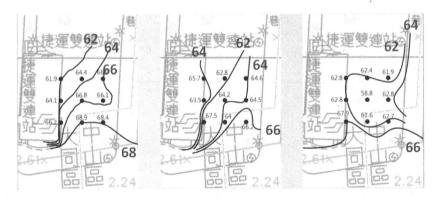

Fig. 6. L_{Aeq} (dB) sound distribution with three period of hours 7:00–9:00 (left side), 13:00–15:30 (middle) and 17:30–19:30 (right side) were illustrated in the around of MRT Shuanglian station.

5 Discussion

It is the primary task of monitoring sound energy along the traffic facilities, and discover whether this frequent impacts of noise may interrupt events in sound field, and then interference problems convert this important hearing characteristics to relative atmosphere of visiting experience. The results of the study have collected all the current sound parameters with sound characteristics, and then confirm the frequency, it should be noted that in the case of urban public space, the overall sound level is higher than the maximum, such as 65–70 dBA, no matter what type of sound source, people will feel annoyed. In this study, reducing noise will become the primary task in the future. However, this study selected the characteristics of the sound field of the characteristics of traffic facilities nodes, a variety of sounds and factors for the re-interpretation of the sound become more important. Some preliminary results are abstracted as followed:

(1) For the urban transport facilities along the open space sound environment, specifically present the status of the characteristics of sound scenes.
(2) Through the survey of interview and field survey, summarize the environment and sound field index and image on the urban transportation node.
(3) Assess the difference between the actual sound energy status and the subjective preference degree in the traffic facilities, and then integrate the interface basis of the future field characteristics and environmental impact.
(4) The data accumulated in this study will help to evaluate the correlation between the physical quantity of the sound field and the subjective preference degree in the public open space along the urban transport facilities.
(5) In addition to the physical characteristics of the field through the physical characteristics of the technology, reproduce the voice of the sound characteristics of environment, complete the subjective preferences adjectives with consultation philosopher experts.

Acknowledgements. The authors wish to thank Professor Wei-Hwa Chiang, Department of Architecture, National Taiwan University of Science and Technology the kindly assistances during the measurement phase.

References

1. Schafer, R.M.: The Vancouver Soundscape. ARC Publications, Vancouver (1978)
2. Schafer, R.M.: A 1996 comparative study: the vancouver soundscape, Records CSR-2CD 9701, Cambridge (1996)
3. Schafer, R.M.: The New Soundscape. Universal Edition, London (1968)
4. Truax, B.: Acoustic Communication. Ablex Publishing, New Jersey (1984)
5. Dunn, D., Peer, R.V.: Music, language and environment. MIT Press J. **09**, 63–67 (1999)
6. Southworth, M.: The sonic environment of cities. Environ. Behav. **1**(1), 49–70 (1969)
7. Schafer, R.M.: The Soundscape: Our Sonic Environment and the Tuning of the World, Rochester. Destiny Books, Vermont (1977)
8. Bricker, K.S., Kerstetter, D.L.: Level of specialization and place attachment: an exploratory study of white water recreationists. Leisure Sci. **22**(4), 233–257 (2000)
9. International Organization for Standardization: ISO 12913-1:2014 Acoustics dSoundscape dPart 1: Definition and Conceptual Framework. ISO, Geneva (2014)
10. Xie, M.Y.: Research on the psychological impact of the visual perception of environmental sounds. Master of architecture thesis, National Chen Kung University (1999)
11. Cai, G.T.: Study on composed exploration of urban residential soundscape. Master of architecture thesis, National Chen Kung University (1998)
12. Cai, G.T., Study on green sound environment of Tainan city. Ph.D. of architecture thesis, National Chen Kung University (2002)
13. Wang, J.J.: Landscape voice: Japanese soundscape exploration. Jpn. Dig. **11**(11), 44–48 (1996)
14. Alves, S., Est_evez-Mauriz, L., Aletta, F., Echevarria-Sanchez, G.M., Romero, V.P.: Towards the integration of urban sound planning in urban development processes: the study of four test sites within the SONORUS project. Noise Mapp. **2**(1), 57–85 (2015)
15. Andringa, T.C., Weber, M., Payne, S.R., Krijnders, J.D., Dixon, M.N., Linden, R.V.D., et al.: Positioning soundscape research and management. J. Acoust. Soc. Am. **134**(4), 2739–2747 (2013)
16. Asdrubali, F.: New frontiers in environmental noise research. Noise Mapp. **1**, 1–2 (2014)
17. van Kempen, E., Devilee, J., Swart, W., van Kamp, I.: Characterizing urban areas with good sound quality: development of a research protocol. Noise Health **16**(73), 380–387 (2014)
18. Brown, L.A.: A review of progress in soundscapes and an approach to soundscape planning. Int. J. Acoust. Vib. **17**(2), 73–81 (2012)
19. Kang, J., et al.: Ten questions on the soundscapes of the built environment. Build. Environ. **108**, 284–294 (2016)
20. Musha, T., Katsurai, K., Teramachi, Y.: Fluctuations of human tapping intervals. IEEE Trans. Biomed. Eng. **BME-32**, 578–582 (1985)
21. Kang, J.: On the diversity of urban waterscape. In: Proceedings of the Acoustics 2012 Conference, Nantes (2012)
22. Kang, D., Lee, S.J., Lee, J.W.: Characteristics of high speed railway noise. In: Proceedings of Inter-noise, pp. 2426–2435. Jeju Korea, 25–28 August (2003)

Elderly Using Innovative Gesture Design of Satisfaction Performance

Shuo Fang Liu[✉] and Ming Hong Wang

Department of Industrial Design, National Cheng Kung University, Tainan, Taiwan
liusf@mail.ncku.edu.tw, wming0403@gmail.com

Abstract. Due to the improvement in medical facilities and care, the elderly have had an increasingly longer life span. At present, many scientific researchers and experts want to probe into the adaptability of the elderly and other relevant issues. With the advancement of medical technology, many countries have paid more attention to the issues about the health of the elderly and expressed the demand for long-term care, so as to establish a complete long-term care service system. This study aims to find out elderly people's demand for long-term care in the future society featuring rapid development and get acquainted with the governance and development trend of the long-term care system. There are a wide range of high-tech products in our daily life, such as cell phones, tablets and personal computers, and they have been very familiar to the public. The multiple use of the cloud service has accelerated the development of smart mobile devices and enabled mobile service suppliers to create new services to meet the needs of the users. The previous studies have shown us the factors which influence the touch gesture of the elderly, and these factors have been taken as the basis of the design of an operating gesture model which satisfies the use need of the elderly. It is believed that the model will greatly benefit the group of people. Moreover, it will give a new direction for the development of various touch mobile devices in the future. According to the findings of this study, the middle-aged and the elderly should use a new design model where the one-finger operating gesture is taken as the basic prototype of the operating system of smart phones. These findings will facilitate the further research on the development of the touch screen user interface.

Keywords: Elderly · Innovative gesture design · Interactive design · Satisfaction performance

1 Introduction

Amid the fast-growing technological landscape, the visual and touch displayer remains a main form of information presentation in the interface of many mobile devices. The current interface of mobile devices like smart phones has significantly facilitated our life. Against such a backdrop, many apps of smart phones have been developed to offer diverse services, including the online payment, the modification of photos, FB, Instagram, LINE and WeChat. Many countries across the world have encountered the problem of an aging population. Early in 1993, Bouma and Graafmans (1992) gave the

© Springer International Publishing AG 2017
J. Zhou and G. Salvendy (Eds.): ITAP 2017, Part I, LNCS 10297, pp. 330–338, 2017.
DOI: 10.1007/978-3-319-58530-7_25

first definition of the technology for the well-being of the elderly: "the technology for the well-being of the elderly is based on the knowledge of aging and focuses on the development of relevant technological and scientific products; it aims to provide the elderly with a sound environment for life and work as well as the supporting medical care".

As smart mobile devices have been adopted by the public and become an indispensable part of people's daily life, whether the operating gesture of these high-tech products is appropriate has become a topic of the academic research on the use of cell phones among the middle-aged and the elderly and on technological innovation.

Multi-functional mobile devices have gradually become ubiquitous devices for information transmission in the daily life and served as an indispensable tool for modern people. An essential service of the present-day technological products is to bring accurate information immediately and send message at any time. E-book reader, tablets and smart touch phones are highly prevalent today. Like a laptop, they are equipped with such functions as the Internet access and document editing and with a screen as big as that of a laptop; moreover, they are lighter and thinner. Therefore, they have evolved into a product of smart mobile device interface which can substitute laptop in recent years.

Additionally, the ever-changing cloud service has contributed to the rapid development of smart mobile devices and satisfied the needs of the users with various mobile services. This has greatly fueled the vigorous development of the mobile device market. For instance, Microsoft has always strived to make their products more efficient, exquisite and humanized (Microsoft surface, 2017). Pitt et al. (2010) argued that smart mobile devices should have the following features: (1) the interface can be controlled through multi-point touch; (2) the hardware is equipped with an acceleration sensor to capture more subtle control based on hand movement, so that the users would have a better access to the Internet and games or finish their tasks in a more efficient way. It is obvious that considering the factors which influence the touch gesture of the elderly to create an operating gesture model which meets the needs of the elderly will greatly benefit the aged. There will be new designs of various touch mobile devices in the future.

These devices will not only possess the advantages of the existing ones but also offer a better touch operating gesture, which will solve the problems in the learning memory among the middle-aged and the elderly and help them acquire the information on the interface of mobile devices in a more efficient way. In the book The Design of Everyday Things published in 2013, Norman proposed the function of natural mapping which could help the users memorize complex information and make the use more efficient. For the elderly, it is rather confusing to think if a product can meet their needs.

As industrial designers, we should be clear about the needs of the elderly and offer the operating gesture suitable for the users according to the principle of general design. According to the research reports on the interface of smart touch devices, the elderly spend more time in getting used to the operation of relevant products. For the old people with clumsy upper limbs, the operation is even more challenging. To date, few studies on the design of the operation gesture of smart phones for the elderly have been done. In terms of gesture control, there have been a wide range of approaches which can be roughly divided into two groups – the two-dimensional gesture and the three-dimensional one.

In a broad sense, they refer to the operation based on the finger or hand touch on the screen in the space of free movement. This study attempts to develop an innovative gesture design model for the operating gesture of smart mobile devices, with the hope of developing the most intuitive and natural gesture operation for the best interaction between products and the elderly. In the innovative gesture design model, only one finger is used for the operation, which is more beneficial for the elderly than the existing operating gestures.

2   Literature Review

According to the authors' relevant studies, the demand for and the understanding of the operation of smart interface devices would change with aging. The young have a better command of technological products because of their excellent physiological state. They perform better than the middle-aged and the elderly in the familiarity with the use and the reaction to the interface operation. In the social structure with increasing aging, the elderly should be able to operate smart interface devices in a more intuitive and efficient way. This will be an issue worthy of special attention in the future.

Today, high-tech products are developing with each passing day, and different brands have launched a multitude of smart mobile interface products. In respect of product value, they emphasize environmental protection, safety, device efficacy and innovative entertainment. Nevertheless, the color of the words on the interface, the product feedback mechanism, the presentation and lightness of the screen, the size of the floating window, and the use gesture often attract less attention. Consequently, a user has to get accustomed to a different operation if he/she buys the products of a new brand; worse still, a different operating gesture requires many attempts, which would result in learning fatigue and even giving up. As for the smart mobile devices where object is selected with only one finger, Saffer (2009) suggested that they should include "tap to select", "slide to scroll", "spin to scroll, and "flick to nudge".

These gestures on the screen interface, which lead to more visual information, are taken as the common gestures, as is shown in Fig. 1. In this study, the authors summarized the types of operating gestures of the common smart phones in the market and found three most frequently-seen operating gestures, namely, "move", "spin" and "zoom". The introduction to the summarized operating gestures is shown in Table 1. The findings of the study by Wang et al. (2015) and Liu (2016) show that it is difficult for the elderly to operate smart mobile devices with two fingers.

Finally, the study proposed the new gesture control model featuring one-finger operating gesture, and the comparison based on the data obtained from the evaluation of feasibility show that the new operating gesture was better than the traditional operating model. Besides, the concepts of human factors engineering are applied to the establishment of the decision-making and evaluation system, the design of modeling development and the presentation development, so as to improve the operating gestures of the elderly on the interface of mobile devices.

Fig. 1. Common gestures

Table 1. Types of existing smart phones and their operating gestures

Type	Move	Spin	Zoom
Samsung NOTE 4		Need to enter the menu of picture editing and tap the function button of spin	
iPhone 4s			
HTC ONE M8		Need to enter the menu of picture editing and tap the function button of spin	
SONY XPERIA Z3		Need to enter the menu of picture editing and tap the function button of spin	
ASUS Zenfone	Its operating gesture of "move" is the same with that of the above phones	Its operating gesture of "spin" is the same with that of the above phones	Its operating gesture of "zoom" is the same with that of the above phones

This study transforms the preliminary results into products that can be further realized in the future. The present invention relates to a method of using single finger for operating touch screen interface. The method for performing a scaling up/scaling down operation comprises: touching a left side region or a right side region of a screen of a mobile device for a predetermined time; displaying a scaling up/scaling down operation interface on the screen of the mobile device; and moving upward or downward to perform a scaling up/scaling down operation. The present invention provides a more intuitive and convenience operation interface, especially for the elderly or disability operator (as is shown in Fig. 6).

A more detailed description of the above operating gestures (move, spin and zoom) is as follows:

1. Move: Place one finger on the displayer of the smart mobile device and press the pictures and message to be moved for 5 ms. Then, the visual effect of mobility will be presented. The finger movement is shown in Figs. 2 and 3.
2. Spin: Currently, spin is an implicit function in most mobile devices in the market; hence, few people know how to initiate the function nor how to operate (as is shown in Fig. 4) when they want to view pictures or have them edited.
3. Zoom: At present, most smart mobile devices adopt the same operating gesture for zooming, where two fingers are placed on any point of the screen. If the two fingers move apart, there will be "zoom in"; if they move towards each other, there will be "zoom out", as is shown in Fig. 5.

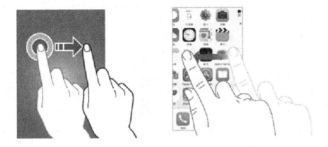

Fig. 2. The finger movement gestures

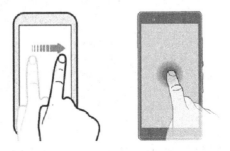

Fig. 3. The finger movement gestures

Fig. 4. Spin gestures

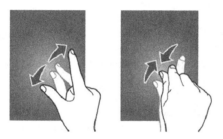

Fig. 5. Zoom in and zoom out gestures

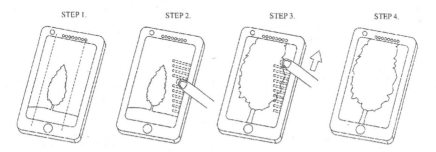

Fig. 6. The non-provisional application claims prioriy from Taiwan patent application no. I-543068, filed on July 21, 2016, the content thereof is incorporated by reference herin.

3 Method

This study adopted the focus group interview to define the operating gestures of smart mobile devices which were the most difficult for the elderly. Then, the three difficult operating gestures (zooming, image capture and spinning) were emphasized. First, 10 subjects used the smart mobile devices familiar to them to perform the three operating gestures. Second, this study turned four experimental samples into an animation and played it for the subjects, so that they learned how to operate the new gesture design model. Finally, the preference of the subjects was measured ("Interested in it", "Want to use it", "Not interested in it", and "Don't want to use it").

3.1 Focus Grouping

- Sample products
  The operating gestures of the majority of present-day smart mobile devices were taken as the experiment samples, and the gestures were divided into "Spin", "Zoom", "Capture image" and "Combined gesture", as is shown in Table 2. With focus on the operating gestures of smart mobile devices among the people aged over 55, this study adopted literature review, questionnaire survey and experiment simulation operation to propose the operating gestures suitable for the elderly; meanwhile, the use evaluation items by Nielsen (1992), including "Learning", "Efficiency", "Memory", "Error", "Convenience" and "Overall satisfaction" were taken into account.

According to Vercruyssen (1996), it was impossible for the elderly to maintain long-term attention and the elderly would feel very tired when asked to do fast or successive scanning. Moreover, they could not make correct judgment if they were asked to finish two or more complicated tasks at the same time (Hartley 1992; McDowd and Craik 1988).

- Subjects
  The average age of the 10 middle-aged and elderly subjects of this study is 60.7, and all of them have used smart mobile devices for over 1 year.
- Process
  First, the subjects were shown the samples of the four operating gestures and how to perform them (for about 5 min). Then, each subject watched the animation (for 10 min) to define which operating gesture is the most suitable for the elderly. Finally, an interview was held with each of the subjects.

3.2 The Subjects' Preference for the Four Operating Gestures

Table 2. Descriptive Statistics

	Age	Have you ever used smart mobile devices?	Sample 1	Sample 2	Sample 3	Sample 4
People 1	67	Yes	Non	Not interested in it/Don't want to use it	Interested in it/ Want to use it	Non
People 2	57	Yes	Want to use it	Not interested in it/Don't want to use it	Interested in it	Non
People 3	73	Yes	Not interested in it/Don't want to use it	Non	Want to use it	Interested in it
People 4	59	Yes	Not interested in it/Don't want to use it	Want to use it	Non	Interested in it
People 5	52	Yes	Non	Non	Non	Interested in it/ Want to use it
People 6	60	Yes	Not interested in it/Don't want to use it	Non	Interested in it/ Want to use it	Non
People 7	54	Yes	Not interested in it/Don't want to use it	Non	Want to use it	Interested in it
People 8	53	Yes	Not interested in it/Don't want to use it	Non	Interested in it	Want to use it
People 9	70	Yes	Don't want to use it	Non	Interested in it	Want to use it
People 10	62	Yes	Want to use it	Non	Interested in it	Non

4   Result

In this study, a human factors investigation into the elderly who have used common touch mobile devices was conducted to detect the problems in the operating gestures of the elderly and summarize the recognitive factors, concentration and preference of the elderly in the use of touch gesture message. Then, the main factors were adopted for the human factors engineering recognition experiment, and we observed the preference of the elderly for the operating gestures in the operation of the touch mobile devices.

Moreover, a subjective scale was employed to measure the significant difference in operating gesture among the elderly. According to the preliminary classification of the common smart phones, the frequently-used operating gestures are "Move", "Spin" and "Zoom". Besides, previous studies and the literatures show that "Spin", "Zoom" and "Capture image" are the three most difficult operating gestures for the elderly.

According to the results of the questionnaire survey on the four innovative operating gestures developed in this study, Sample 1 is the least popular. Some subjects didn't show much interest in Sample 2. Most subjects regarded it as ordinary and found it easy to understand the operation, so there wasn't any strong response to it. What surprised us most were Sample 3 and Sample 4. Most of the subjects were interested in the two operating gestures and want to perform them in reality. The interview indicated that they were curious about the combined gesture (zoom and spin) and the side-zooming.

5   Conclusion

In this study, an innovative interface operating gesture system was designed to reduce the fear and helplessness of the elderly in the operation of smart mobile devices and improve the design of the existing interface operating gestures of smart mobile devices. After probing into the type, method, principle and relevant literatures of the interface operation of smart mobile devices, this study proposed the intuitive operating gestures which are more suitable for the middle-aged and the elderly and analyzed the key factors which influenced their operating gestures and intuition.

By summarizing the design principles and parameters suitable for the development of the interface system of smart mobile devices and delving into the operating gestures and intuition of the middle-aged and the elderly as well as the subjective measurement, this study aims to develop a better gesture-operating system for smart mobile devices to meet the trend of the aging society and create more humanized products to satisfy their needs and improve their life.

Acknowledgements. The authors would like to appreciate that this research is financially supported by MOST (Ministry of Science and Technology) at Taiwan, R.O.C, under the project number: MOST 105-2221-E-006-124. All invited subjects and designers are also appreciated very much.

References

Bouma, H., Graafmans, J.A.M.: Gerontechnology. IOS Press, Amsterdam (1992)

Microsoft Surface. http://www.microsoft.com/surface/

Pitt, L.F., Parent, M., Junglas, I., Chan, A., Spyropoulou, S.: Integrating the smartphone into a sound environmental information systems strategy: principles, practices and a research agenda. J. Strateg. Inf. Syst. **20**(1), 27–37 (2010)

Saffer, D.: Designing Gestural Interfaces. O'Reilly Media, Sebastopol (2009)

Wang, M.-H., Chang, Y.-C., Liu, S.-F., Lai, H.-H.: Developing new gesture design mode in smartphone use for elders. In: Zhou, J., Salvendy, G. (eds.) ITAP 2015. LNCS, vol. 9193, pp. 519–527. Springer, Cham (2015). doi:10.1007/978-3-319-20892-3_50

Liu, S.F., Wang, M.H., Lin, M.C., Huang, T.S.: An ergonomics research for developing senior citizens' mobile devices gesture display. In: Goonetilleke, R., Karwowski, W. (eds.) Advances in Physical Ergonomics and Human Factors, Advances in Intelligent Systems and Computing, vol. 489. Springer, Cham (2016)

Nielsen, J.: The usability engineering life cycle. Computer **25**(3), 12–22 (1992)

Vercruyssen, M.: Movement control and the speed of behavior. In: Fisk, A.D., Rogers, W.A. (eds.) Handbook of Human Factors and the Older Adult. Academic Press, San Diego (1996)

Hartley, A.A.: Attention. In: Craik, F.I.M., Salthouse, T.A. (eds.) The Handbook of Aging and Cognition (1992)

McDowd, J.M., Craik, F.I.M.: Effects of aging and task difficulty on divided attention performance. J. Exp. Psychol. Hum. Percept. Perform. **14**, 267–280 (1988)

A Study of Usability on Internet Map Website

Kuang-Chih Lo[1,2(✉)] and Wang-Chin Tsai[1]

[1] Department of Product and Media Design, Fo Guang University, Jiaoxi, Yilan, Taiwan
kclo@mail.fgu.edu.tw, forwangwang@gmail.com
[2] Graduate School of Design, National Yunlin University of Science and Technology,
Douliu, Yunlin, Taiwan

Abstract. This study assesses a Taiwan Internet Map website by adopting the three commonly used means in usability assessment, namely Coaching method, Interview, and Observation. For determining the problems involving Interface Design and usage, thirty individuals with no prior experience with the website were recruited and underwent a usability assessment for each of the two typical tasks set by the focus groups. The results showed that: (1) Excessive information has been displayed on the homepage, and the ways of categorizing and naming are distinct from public cognition. Base on the principle of minimizing user memory loading, simplifying user interface to the full extent is suggested. (2) The names of options on the user interface should be more in conformity with common language used, and avoid bias that users may associate with. Thus each name of the options shall be amended accordingly. (3) Considering users' reading convenience, the visual design of the web page shall be revised to exhibit simple and consistent text for enhancing reading comprehension. (4) Results of this research provide guidance to website designers to better meet users' needs and preferences.

Keywords: Internet Map website · Usability · Interface design · Map design

1 Introduction

Since the 1980s, the rapid development of computer networking has unfolded a new Internet era that is dominated by transmission and application of graphic messages, notably in the form of maps. Under the Internet environment, the easy and fast upload and download of messages has led to a new species of maps- Internet Map, and created novel scenarios of map cartography and applications. Based on the above background, this research takes the "Taiwan Map", a mobile e-map, as an example to discuss the query design of Internet maps, and uses usability engineering's Focus Groups and Coaching Method to look into the problems users may face with the query interface. Hopefully, the results can be useful reference in the interface design of Internet maps. This research Objectives are following:

(1) With usability engineering, examine the user interface design of a representative Internet map and evaluate its usability.

© Springer International Publishing AG 2017
J. Zhou and G. Salvendy (Eds.): ITAP 2017, Part I, LNCS 10297, pp. 339–347, 2017.
DOI: 10.1007/978-3-319-58530-7_26

(2) Discuss the problems with the use of Internet maps, and analyze the complexity of typical work steps and related user satisfaction; the results hopefully will provide useful reference for future interface design of Internet maps.

2 Literatures

2.1 Internet Map Characteristics

Shi Qingde and Wen Zhuda (2002) suggested the following Internet map characteristics: (1) more convenient map application: the exponential growth of Internet map data sources will make the application pervasive, reaching the so-called evolution of cartographic democratization; (2) ever faster cartography and message delivery: Internet is advantaged in high speed and unrestricted space, allowing conduction of cartography and relevant applications whenever needed; (3) rapid growth of map users: due largely to the constant growth of Internet users; (4) map diversification: map resources are versatile and comprehensive; although current queries are mainly based on the names of streets and venues, more query criteria are expected in the near future; (5) quick updates of map data: constant data updates assure of up-to-date map information; (6) easy processing: the map data are easy to copy and process, greatly reducing the data processing time; (7) personalization and practicality for daily use: the cartography process can be decided by users, fulfilling the so-called user-defined, on-demand maps that satisfy professional and daily needs of individuals and small groups, such as coffee shop maps; (8) dynamic analysis and mobile applications: implementation of geographic visualizations (GVIS).

2.2 Related Studies on Map Information Design

Text labels in map are used for explanation purposes. The place and direction of the texts will also determine whether the user will understand it or not. Phillips (1978) found 5 matters of concern while seeking and studying name of places: 1. Texts with the first letter in capital were easier to be read as compared with texts in all capital letters. 2. Bold fonts did not produce better readability. On the contrary, they made the map looked messy and produced a bad visual effect. 3. There was no close correlation between the choice of font and readability. 4. Texts should be placed in spacious and clear locations. 5. Grades and levels can be differentiated with colors and font size to minimize search time. However, unrelated differentiation will increase search time. Chang Chun-Lan (1993) showed that "lettering" is a general name for texts and numbers on a map, and is one of the cartographic languages. Lettering on a map is made out of 5 elements; the font, font size, text spacing and direction of text, location, and colors. Objects are differentiated by various fonts and colors. The size of the lettering reveals the grade or level of the object and its importance on the map. The location of the lettering and the difference in text spacing and direction of text showed the location, extended direction, and range of distribution of the object. Not long after, Robinson (1995) proposed in the principles of text labeling in map designs that: font size may be used to reflect the grades of a system but must be limited to 3 grades of size only.

2.3 Usability Engineering

In his book "Usability Engineering", Nielsen defines usability as related to all kinds of problems users may have in using products or systems. For the term "usability" comprehensively used in the concept of human-machine domains, Nielsen (1993) argued that evaluation of systems or user interface was not unidimensional; instead, it was composed of 5 criteria: (1) learnability; (2) efficiency; (3) memorability; (4) error rate; and (5) satisfaction. In addition, he also proposed quite a few methods to evaluate usability engineering. Herewith, only the methods used in this research are discussed. They are: (1) Focus Groups: it is a group of people - the users, who discuss a specific problem or interface, from the user perspective, in a more liberal and unstructured approach; (2) Coaching Method: this is an empirical approach with experts providing instant instructions when the testees encounter obstacles in the process of an experiment, so that the experiment can keep going; (3) Interview: recorded data only show what users have done, without elaboration of the causes; therefore, recorded data coupled with subsequent interviews can better display what was happening when the users were using the systems, and elaborately explain interesting phenomena.

3 Research Methods

This research comes with 5 phases: (1) selection of websites for tests: Internet maps that are representative are picked; (2) setup of typical tasks: the Focus Group discusses the queries steps of Internet maps and establishes typical query tasks; (3) implementation of experiments: the testees are asked to execute the typical query tasks and the process flow is recorded; after the queries are finished, a seven-layer subjective satisfaction evaluation and brief interviews are given; (4) decoding the browsing steps: analyze the recorded data of the testees' execution of the typical query tasks, including the steps and time used for the queries and the usability obstacles encountered; (5) comprehensive analysis: after the experiment and interviews, the query modes and evaluation data are integrated and compiled, in search for usability problems.

3.1 Research Scope

Limited to the resources and time, this research only takes the more representative Taiwan Map website (www.map.com.tw) for the experiment. It was a two-week online experiment, from June 22 to July 7 of 2013. This research aims to discuss the usability of the query interface only, not involving the framework and technical aspect of the Internet map itself.

3.2 Experiment Planning

The experiment was conducted in an research office of the Department of Visual Communication Design, National Yunlin University of Science and Technology. The lighting conditions were unified. The tools used include PCs, Hypercam5.0 capture recording software, memorandum, and Microsoft IE V5.0 browser. The 20 testees both males and females, were college students, who are frequent Internet goers (averaged 8 h a week) but had never used this test website before - novice users in terms of this website.

3.3 Typical Tasks

The typical tasks are designed based on the literature information. Five Internet goers with both usability and website design backgrounds were invited to make up a focus group for discussion and setup of the tasks. The group discussion focuses on two aspects: (1) general user motives of querying e-maps and problems they may encounter; (2) most commonly used functions and operations of the target website, and its Internet connectivity allowing users to link through different paths to reach the same destination. Therefore, the principle of setting up typical tasks is to describe the jobs executed, imposing no specific process flow, and the purpose is to observe users' actual query behavior, so that their web browsing patterns can be examined for analysis of the website's usability. This research uses the following two typical tasks:

(1) Search for the location of Yilan County's Dongshan River Water Park and relevant road conditions, and then print out the result and send it out via an email.
(2) Search for the closest path from Taipei City Museum of Art to Printemps Department Store.

3.4 Research Process

See (Table 1).

Table 1. Research steps and relevant contents

Work steps	Description of contents
(1) Experiment preparation	Explains to the testees of the test workflow and things to note
(2) Execution of typical tasks	Prepares a list of typical tasks for the testees to execute, and allows them to, during and after the experiment, raise questions and express comments, which are recorded by the Hypercam software
(3) Likert Scale assessment	After the two typical tasks are finished, uses a Likert Scale (7 layers) to assess the testees' feel about the interface design and their satisfaction
(4) Post-experiment interviews	The interviews are aimed at the browsing behavior, by asking the testees about their hesitation in the workflow as well as questions and suggestions
(5) Data transcoding and analysis	1. The recorded data are transcoded into pure text format for analysis, and then the data of work steps and time spent by each testee in execution of the typical tasks are extracted 2. The ticks made on the Likert Scale by the 20 testees are summed, averaged and converted into percentage to spotlight things to improve
(6) Proposal on interface design	All the test data are compiled and analyzed to determine the website's usability problems, and then interface design suggestions are proposed accordingly
(7) Summarized analysis and conclusions	

4 Results

The research results are discussed in two aspects: one is aimed at the work steps conducted by the users on the typical tasks and the problems they encountered; the other is to explore users' feel about the interface usability and their satisfaction on the design. In the end, all the data are integrated and compiled to conclude the tested website's usability problems and set forth proposals on the design.

4.1 User Query Problems

The analysis of user behavioral patterns on e-map queries is based on the two given typical tasks, from which the users' actual clicking patterns are recorded and analyzed. The most commonly clicked items and webpage links as well as the time spent on each of the objects are observed, and then interviews with the testees are given to find out the causes behind the query patterns, and based on which design suggestions are proposed.

4.1.1 Typical Task I: A Single-Location Query

The testees are asked to execute the query of "where is Yilan County's Dongshan River Water Park located?", and print out the query result and then send it out via an email. The results show most of the testees can easily finish the task, except for a few who encountered some problems at certain points. The subsequent interviews reveal that most of the testees had no idea about what the categorized items on the navigating pages were talking about, and for a novice user, the information volume was too large to decide where to start with, thus they felt negatively about the interface. There are 16 out of the 20 testees who possess this kind of negative perception, in that the webpage contents became identifiable and associated with the users' recognition only after they had spent some time to get familiar with the entire webpage and then gone through trial and error for individual objects, one by one. This experience is like trying a lucky lottery.

Fig. 1. Interface for location search

As for the query patterns, most of the testees clicked the "location" icon to enter the query. The pop-up interface then displays a pull-down menu for the testees to select "Yilan". The webpage also provides an interface for direct type-in of search text, but the too many textboxes can easily confuse the users on which box to fill. About 11 out of the 20 testees mistakenly typed the searched location in the bottom textbox (Fig. 1: box label 4), resulting in wrong search, although they finally completed the search through several times of trial and error. This scenario is further consolidated in subsequent interviews; i.e. people generally do not care about text descriptions (Fig. 1: description label 1), either due to the small font or simply ignorance, and prefer to directly enter the search text via trial and error. Therefore, the user tips should be concise and easy to read, and placed at a noticeable spot on the webpage.

4.1.2   Typical Tasks II: An End-to-End Query

The testees are asked to search for the closest route from the Taipei City Museum of Art to Printemps Department Store. This typical task consists of two queries: first using the "location" function to search and position the museum, and then using the "path" function by entering the road name where the destination (the department store) is located to search for the closest route. The test result shows that most of the testees took some time to learn before being able to finish the tasks, except for two who finished the task in predefined steps, due largely to the occurrence that they could not find the "path" function and not even know how it works. There were 3 testees who had already clicked the "path" function but only to exit for not knowing how to use it, and they finally finished the task after assistance was provided. This scenario was consolidated in subsequent interviews, where most of the testees expressed their problems of finding an one-step "end-to-end" search which is supposed to have by default, thus causing a lot of unnecessary time for trial and error or even give-ups. In the course of executing the task, most testees were using the trial and error approach to first search for the location of the Taipei City Museum of Art, but only to encounter odd problems, such as the descriptive text and markings on the map unable to clearly convey the correct messages they are intended to, let alone indicate which road name is the correct one. The marking of targeted objects is another major issue here. There were 6 testees who executed the location search and got the resulted map display, but couldn't spot the marking of the target. The subsequent interviews reveal that this scenario could happen when the marking is not obviously colored or prompted with text. Therefore, markings should be distinctly colored and prompted with text, in line with the rule of thumb for webpage usability. In the process of typical task II, problems hiked quite a bit. The complex query and poor visual design are to blame. For example, the text arrangement and color design shown on Fig. 3 are not indicative enough - either unclearly marked of the spots or poorly readable of the text. In particular, the unidentifiable colors do not distinguish sections of roads to the destination and, what's worse, the colors are not defined and categorized. Apparently, the coloring and text description on this map need to be redesigned or reinforced.

4.2   Satisfaction Assessment and Post-experiment Interviews

By way of subjective assessment, the Likert Scale was given to the testees to tick on the indicators of operability, sense of design, friendliness, consistency and overall satisfaction, and the result is analyzed to examine the testees' feel about the website usability. The questionnaire analysis of the 20 testees are arranged in Table 2 below.

Table 2. Satisfaction by indicators

	Operability	Sense of design	Friendliness	Consistency	Overall satisfaction
Total score	91	84	90	96	89
Total average	4.19	4.52	5.12	4.61	4.87
Percentage (%)	59.85	64.57	73.14	65.86	69.57

Table 3. Post-experiment interviews and compilation of raised problems

Problem category	Problems raised
Functional design	The system does not have online help or instructions for novice user (2 times) In search for the closest route, user not knowing how to begin with and how to proceed (1 time) The system does not provide detailed addresses for location search (1 time) The zoom in and out buttons are confusing (1 time) The textboxes for starting point and ending point are confusing (1 time) A sense of unfamiliarity for first-time users, short of friendliness (1 time) Using trial and error gives a sense of taking chances by luck in search (1 time)
Query design	The end-to-end function is not found (10 times) Query text can be easily entered in wrong textboxes, resulting failed search (1 time) The query system itself has bugs from time to time (1 time) Too many options to locate the desired ones (1 time)
Hierarchical classification	Classification is not clear (2 times); upper layer is unclearly classified (1 time) To many functions to locate the needed ones (1 times) Users feel like unable to see the whole picture clearly (1 time) The pull-down menu may not contain the location to be searched for (1 time) Do not understand the "path" function and its use (2 times); navigation classification is difficult to understand (1 time) The navigation terminology and classification are difficult to grasp (1 time) Location markings could have been directly indicated on the map (1 time) Wrong clicks because of users' different recognition of classification (1 time)
Visual design	Destination not clearly marked - red dot markings not visible (3 times); locations could have been clearly indicated by direct markings (1 time) Poor coloring (1 time); poor color readability (1 time); road sections not well distinguished by colors (1 time) Colors not defined and categorized (1 time); color markings not explained and poorly designed (1 time) Text on map not visible, unclearly marked, and text size too small (3 times) Easy to enter query text in wrong textbox, resulting in failed search (1 time) Destination should be marked with text; the moving button is weird (2 times) Zoom in and out are confusing (1 time); not knowing the meaning of the 1–7 scale (1 time) The webpage layout is not consistent (1 time); flipping direction is unclear and inconsistent (1 time)

Table 2 shows that operability has the lowest 59.85% scoring, while friendliness has the highest 73.14% scoring. The overall satisfaction has a 69.57% scoring, meaning this website's usability is a bit above medium level. Listed in Table 3 are the testees encountered problems, which are induced into four categories: functional design, query design, hierarchical classification, and visual design, described as follows:

In terms of the functional design, the variety of functions but with a lack of decent arrangement make it difficult for users to decide where to begin with when doing the search. And the lack of online help and instructions for beginners make things worse. Other deficiencies include inadequate address data for location search, confusing zoom in and out buttons, unidentifiable textboxes for correct entry of query criteria; these shortcomings bring in a sense of unfamiliarity and unfriendliness for first-time users, who may do trial and error by taking chances in search for a location.

On the query design, the lack of direct end-to-end (location-to-location) query makes route search very inconvenient. Generally, users perceive a spatial construct through location recognition, therefore most users would prefer to have end-to-end search functions. Other deficiencies of the query design include the easy mistakes of entering search criteria in wrong lower textboxes causing failed queries, as well as system bugs and excessive options. On the hierarchical classification, it presents a substantial gap from what general users would perceive. Detailed questions compiled in the post-experiment interviews are listed in Table 3.

The research results show that the testees regard the classification as unclear and do not know its substances; the excessive functions are not helpful in pinpointing the needed ones and confuse the users; the addresses in the pull-down menu not necessarily contain all the addresses desired for search; and some naming is not consistent with the navigation terminologies and classification, and is difficult to understand. Visual design is decisive on usability. The relevant shortcomings, however, include unclear location markings, unseen red dot markings, and inadequate landmark information. Direct marking with descriptive text is therefore suggested. Color indication can be even more critical.

Most testees regard the map is not appropriately colored, making it difficult to read. For example, the sections of roads in the searched route are poorly colored, the color definition and classification are unknown, and the color markings are neither explained nor well arranged. Also, characters on the map are too small to be clearly seen and pinpointed, location markings are vague, search criteria can be easily, mistakenly entered in the lower wrong textboxes resulting in failed search, the zoom-in and -out buttons and the moving directions are confusing, and the meaning of 1–7 ratio is not well understood. These are the shortcomings to be improved in the visual design.

5 Discussion

This research has executed an experiment in which testees are asked to do two predefined typical tasks of search queries on an e-map, and the problems encountered by the testees during the search are recorded and analyzed, and then post-experiment interviews with these testees are conducted for cross-examination. This research has compiled all the experimental findings and concluded as follows:

(1) In the course of implementing the typical tasks, it is found that the homepage information is way too excessive and the classification and naming convention deviates from the public cognition. Based on the principle of minimal user memory burden, a brevity of user interface is strongly recommended and, specifically, the hierarchy of the data structure on the webpage should be simplified to 3 layers only.

(2) The naming of functional options should be based on the users' language, and associated thinking of the option names is crucial. In other words, the current naming needs a complete overhaul.

(3) For better readability, the brevity and consistency in the webpage visual design is strongly recommended.

(4) Results of this research provide guidance to website designers to better meet users' needs and preferences.

References

Angeli, A.D., Lynch, P., Johnson, G.I.: Pleasure versus efficiency in user interfaces: towards an involvement framework. In: Green, W.S., Jordan, P.W. (Eds.) Pleasure with Products: Beyond Usability, pp. 98–111. Taylor & Francis, London (2002)

Cartwright, W., Crampton, J., Gartner, G., Miller, S., Mitchell, K., Siekierska, E., Wood, J.: Geospatial information visualization user interface issues. Cartography Geogr. Inf. Sci. **28**(1), 45–60 (2001)

Cuff, D.J., Mattson, M.T.: Thematic Maps: Their Design and Production. Methuen and Co Ltd., New York (1982)

de Mendonca, A.L.A., Delazari, L.S.: Remote evaluation of the execution of spatial analysis tasks with interactive web maps: a functional and quantitative approach. Cartographic J. **49**(1), 7–20 (2012)

Fuhrmann, S., Ahonen-Rainio, P., Edsall, R.M., Fabrikant, I., Koua, E.L., Tobon, C., Ware, C., Wilson, S.: (2005)

Genuis, S.K.: Web site usability testing: a critical tool for libraries. Feliciter **50**(4), 161–164 (2004)

Haklay, M., Tobon, C.: Usability evaluation and PPGIS: toward a user-centered design approach. Int. J. Geogr. Inf. Sci. **17**(6), 577–592 (2003)

Keller, P., Keller, M.: Visual Clues: Practical Data Visualization. IEEE Computer Society Press, Los Alamitos (1992)

Kerski, J.J.: The implementation and effectiveness of geographic information systems technology and methods in secondary education. J. Geogr. **102**(3), 128–137 (2003)

Shinshen, G.: Usability engineering based e-commerce webpage evaluation - illustrated with tra web ticketing system. Technol. Sci. **2**(10), 137 (2001)

Shinshen, G.: A retrospective testing on microwave oven usability. Technol. Sci. **3**(9), 223–230 (2000)

Shinshen, G., Jingchun, H., Chengxun, H.: Tourist website interface design and usability study - illustrated with Eztravel, pp. 86–87 (2001)

Liang, C., Wu, J.: WWW homepage design norms. In: Design: Education, Culture, and Technology Proceedings (1999)

Nielsen, J.: Usability Engineering. Academic Press Ltd., London (1993)

How to Enhance Intergenerational Communication? The Influence of Family Orientation and Generation When Using Social Robots as an Intermediary

Fan Mo[✉], Jia Zhou, and Shuping Yi

Department of Industrial Engineering, Chongqing University, Chongqing 400044, China
mofan1992@gmail.com, zhoujia07@gmail.com, ysp@cqu.edu.cn

Abstract. Adopting social robots as intermediaries to help adult children to communicate with elderly parents is a good approach to enhance intergenerational communication. This research aims to analyze the influence of family orientation and the generation of a social robot on learning outcome of conflict issues in dialogue, perceived sociability, and trust with social robots, and the social presence of adult children. The results show that social robots of in-family have better performance than those of out-family in terms of perceived sociability and trust. Elderly parents prefer to communicate family problems with in-family robots that can be considered as family members. Moreover, social robots of older-generation have better performance than those of younger-generation in terms of perceived sociability and trust, and they also improve the learning outcome of conflict issues. However, designing younger-generation robots can improve the social presence of adult children.

Keywords: Intergeneration communication · Social robots · Family orientation · Generation

1 Introduction

Intergenerational communication between elderly parents and adult children can be a severe problem. Most adult children do not live with their elderly parents because they are married and have their own family life, so elderly parents usually communicate with their children by phone, video calls, social network sites, or using a home-based communication system [1–3]. This creates two problems. First, these approaches to communication can cause severe usability problems for elderly parents because they tend to lack the experience of using technology products. Second, elderly parents have different topics, attitudes, and viewpoints from their adult children; hence, they sometimes experience difficulty in comprehending their children in conversation [4].

To deal with these problems, social robots can be used to communicate with elderly parents [5, 6]. However, in existing studies, social robots can only accompany and interact with elderly people [7]. To help parents to understand the attitudes and viewpoints of their children, social robots can act as intermediaries between elderly parents and their adult children. Introducing this sort of information when conversing with elderly parents can be helpful for everyone involved.

© Springer International Publishing AG 2017
J. Zhou and G. Salvendy (Eds.): ITAP 2017, Part I, LNCS 10297, pp. 348–359, 2017.
DOI: 10.1007/978-3-319-58530-7_27

In this research, the social robot is set as an intermediary that can enhance the intergenerational communication. First, we will study the communication between robots and elderly parents. The robot can analyze the content of intergenerational communication such as phone records and present the details that the elderly parents may not understand or the conflict issues that may arise in the phone call. The social robots' characteristics probably have an influence on this process, so this research focuses on the family orientation and generation of the social robot.

2   Literature Review

The aesthetics of social robots can often have a considerable influence on the perceptions of elderly people [8]. The appearance of social robots has been studied and it has been found that the appearance of a robot needs to have the appropriate degree of familiarity and human likeness, based on its application [9]. The results show that people tend to prefer social robots with a more human-like appearance and attributes. However, designing a cartoon image for the robot is a good choice to help it become a companion at home [10].

The role of social robots is an important factor that can influence people's feelings [8]. When it comes to intergenerational communication within a family, family orientation and the generation of the robot probably are major factors that help to determine its role.

First, the generation of social robots probably has a great influence on communication. The young generation and old generation have different thoughts and ideas due to their different experiences; thus, the gap between intergenerational relationships is larger than that between contemporaries [11, 12]. Moreover, elderly people have a reduced cognitive ability, so they can find that comprehending and learning new ideas and things can be difficult [13, 14]. Therefore, elderly people are probably more inclined to talk with contemporaries.

Second, the family orientation of the robot determines whether it is seen to be a member of the family. It has been found that the group orientation of social robots has an influence on people's decision making because they are able to converse with people in group conditions [15, 16]. In a family, it can be speculated that the family orientation of social robots probably has an influence on people's perception while conversing about family issues.

3   Methodology

3.1   Variables

The independent variables are family orientation and generation, which are both characteristics of social robot and within-subject design. Family orientation has two levels: in-family and out-family. Family orientation refers to whether the robot is a family member of the elderly parents. Social robots that are in-family wear an introduction card which is marked with the name of the town where the participants live (i.e. Yuzui town) and the family name of the participants. Social robots that are out-family wear an introduction card which is marked with the name of a city where they do not live (i.e. Chendu city) and only the given name of the robot is used (as shown in Fig. 1). The social robots begin the conversation by introducing themselves and describing their family orientation.

Fig. 1. The introduction cards of in-family social robots (left) and out-family social robots (right)

Generation has two levels: younger-generation and older-generation. Generation determines whether the social robot is a contemporary of the elderly parents or a contemporary of the adult children. For example, social robots of the older-generation have the same age, viewpoints, and attitudes with elderly parents. Therefore, older-generation social robots are set using idioms, life experience, and cases from elderly parents, and they call themselves an elderly parent when conversing with elderly people. Younger-generation social robots are set using catchwords, they use the life experience and case from young people, and they call themselves an adult child.

Both of the variables embody the role delineation of the intermediary robot, which has a considerable influence on the effect of the conversation and on mediation. To control the irrelevant variable, the gender of the social robot and the speed and intonation of its voice are fixed.

There are four dependent variables: learning outcome of conflict issues in the conversation, perceived sociability with robots, trust with robots, and social presence of children. Learning outcome is measured by the judgment accuracy. Participants are asked to decide whether or not twelve additional short dialogues between elderly parents and adult children are related to the content that they have learned. These dialogues are time-consuming in the experiment and according to the pilot tests can be a little difficult for elderly people. Therefore, learning outcome is only tested for the two levels of generation since generation reflects nearly all of the changes of the language features (e.g., person, verb, and cases) in this experiment. Six dialogues are tested for each level of generation. Moreover, perceived sociability with the robot is measured using an aspect from the widely used Almere model [17–19]. Trust with the robot is measured using the questionnaire from the research of Guo, Tan, and Cheung [20]. Social presence of children is measured using existing questionnaires [21–23]. These questionnaires are presented in the Appendix. A five-point Likert scale is used.

3.2 Participants

A total of 14 elderly parents participated in the experiment (9 females and 5 males). They were recruited from the senior center of Yuzui town in Chongqing, China. Their average age is 75.71 (SD = 6.603). A total of 28.57% of older adults have a Junior High School diploma. All of them have adult children who live far away from the hometown. The average number of their children is 2.64 (SD = 1.692). A total of 72.97% of adult children have a Junior High School diploma but only one of them has a high diploma up to bachelor degree level. The average number of face-to-face communications between elderly parents and adult children is three times per month, and the average number of phone calls between them is four times per month. The motivation to join the study is high because the participants have a strong interest in taking an active part in improving the communication between elderly parents and adult children. Moreover, they are highly interested in the social robot and they all enjoyed this experiment.

3.3 Equipment

Two pilot tests were conducted in the participants' home. The formal experiment was conducted in an office of the Citizen School of Yuzui, Jiangbei, Chongqing. In the experiment, the social robot is simulated using a Baymax speaker (A9), which has a cartoon image (as shown in Fig. 2). It connects with a MacBook Air (macOS Sierra version 10.12.1) via Bluetooth. The Wizard of Oz method is used. Two pieces of a soap opera that relates to the phone call between the elderly parent and the adult child were made using Video Studio X5 on an Acer 4750T (Windows 8.1). The material for the short soap opera is filmed using a camera (Sony FDR-AX40). One elderly person and one young person were invited to perform in the film. The voice of the social robot is simulated using iFlytek Voice based on Text to Speech (TTS) speech synthesis. To make the voice easily understood by the elderly participants, a TTS with a Sichuan accent (which is their dialect) was used.

Fig. 2. The simulated social robot

3.4 Conversation Material

Two videos and 41 audio pieces are used in the experiment. The process of using the video and audio material is shown in Fig. 3. When the participants take part in the experiment, certain pieces of the audio (such as all of the audio which is used for transition) are reused. In general, each participant listened to about 64 audio pieces.

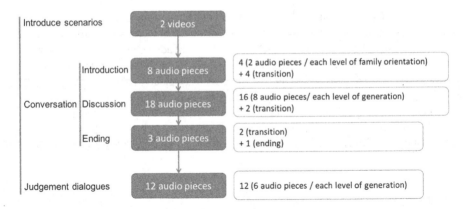

Fig. 3. The process of using the video and audio material

According to the pilot tests, there are two difficulties in designing the conversation. First, designing a long conversation between the social robot and people is difficult because human's dialogue tends to be uncontrolled. To deal with this problem, when the participants digress (such as asking distracting questions or talking about irrelevant content) the transition audio is used to control the dialogue flow. Second, the elderly participants can sometimes be absent-minded during the conversation. To avoid this situation, the duration of each audio is limited to within 20 s. In addition, lots of modal particles are adopted in the social robot's dialogue to improve the emotion and narrative rhythm. Moreover, the social robot is designed to call the name of the participant at the beginning of the conversation, which surprises the participants and makes them focus attention.

In the process of the discussion, there are eight pieces of audio for each level of generation. The eight pieces of audio are used to discuss two issues of conflict; that is, each of the four pieces of audio relate to one issue of conflict. These pieces of audio repeat the conflict dialogue, explain the conflict issue, analyze the cause, and provide advice.

3.5 Procedures

The experiment takes each participant about 60 min. The experimental process is listed as follows. First, the participants are required to complete questionnaires about demographic information. Second, they need to watch a video that tells a simple story about a telephone conversation between an adult child and his elderly parents. Then, the participants communicate with the social robot. After that, the participants are asked to complete questionnaires about perceived sociability and trust with robots and the social presence of children. They are then asked to judge if the short dialogues are related or not. The order of the four conditions was counter-balanced to decrease the learning effect. Each participant was encouraged to individually complete the experiment. At the end, the participants were briefly interviewed about their preferences and other subjective feedback. One experiment field scene is shown in Fig. 4.

Fig. 4. Conversation between an elderly parent and the social robot

4 Results and Discussion

4.1 Perceived Sociability with the Social Robot

The influence of family orientation and generation of the social robot on sociability was analyzed through ANOVA (as shown in Fig. 5). It is found that family orientation has a significant influence on the sociability of the social robot ($F_{(1,13)} = 7.313$, $p = 0.018$). The in-family social robot has a higher level of sociability than the out-family social robot. One possible reason for this is that elderly parents prefer to communicate family problems with family members, and they can open their mind to family members. Therefore, they perceive more sociability when conversing with the in-family social robot. This was confirmed in the interview. Only one female participant expressed that she is likely to communicate family problems with old friends. However, the difference between social robots of younger-generation and those of older-generation is not obvious ($F_{(1,13)} = 3.330$, $p = 0.091$).

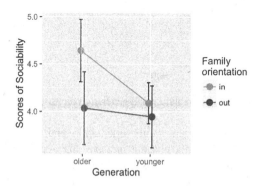

Fig. 5. Influence of family orientation and generation on sociability (error bars = 95% c.i.)

The interaction effects between family orientation and generation are significant ($F_{(3,52)}$ = 4.540, p = 0.006). Post-hoc analysis (Tukey's HSD test) is used to explore the interaction effects. The results show that social robots of in-family and older-generation have a higher level of sociability than those of the other three conditions (in-family and younger-generation: p = 0.051; out-family and older-generation: p = 0.027; and, out-family and younger-generation: p = 0.008). It seems that elderly people perceive a high level sociability with robots when communicating with in-family and older-generation social robots. Furthermore, it is interesting that the generation of the robots does not impact sociability on the whole but it does have an obvious influence on sociability in terms of the robot that is in-family orientation. One explanation for this is that when talking to strangers, elderly people are probably more tolerant and lenient with their age, attitude, and point of view. Thus, there is no difference between older-generation and younger-generation in terms of out-family robots. The combination of in-family orientation and older-generation leads to a significant improvement in the role delineation of the social robot.

4.2   Trust with the Social Robot

The influence of family orientation and generation on elderly people's trust with the social robot is analyzed through ANOVA (as shown in Fig. 6). It is found that family orientation has a significant influence on trust ($F_{(1,13)}$ = 15.14, p = 0.002). The in-family social robot is more trusted by elderly people than the out-family social robot. One possible reason for this is that elderly parents prefer to communicate family problems with family members, and they place more trust in the in-family social robots. The difference between social robots of different generations is not significant in terms of trust ($F_{(1,13)}$ = 2.282, p = 0.155).

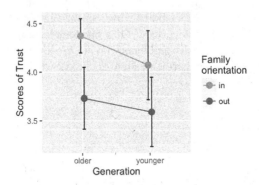

Fig. 6. Influence of family orientation and generation on trust (error bars = 95% c.i.)

The interaction effects between family orientation and generation are significant ($F_{(3,52)}$ = 6.017, p = 0.001). Post-hoc analysis indicates that social robots of in-family and older-generation have a higher level of trust than those of out-family and younger-generation/older-generation (p = 0.002; p = 0.013). This combination performs better in terms of perceived sociability. This advantage is confirmed in terms of trust with social robot. Elderly parents prefer to converse with the social robot of in-family and older-generation since it has high perceived sociability and trust.

4.3 Social Presence of Adult Children

The influence of family orientation and generation on the social presence of adult children is analyzed through ANOVA (as shown in Fig. 7). It is shown that generation has a significant influence on the social presence of adult children ($F_{(1,13)} = 5.494$, p = 0.036). The younger-generation social robot has a higher level of social presence with the adult children when compared to the older-generation social robot. The influence of family orientation on the social presence is not significant ($F_{(1,13)} = 3.247$, p = 0.095). Furthermore, interaction effects between family orientation and generation are significant ($F_{(3,52)} = 3.261$, p = 0.029). Post-hoc analysis shows that social robots of in-family and older-generation lead to a lower level of social presence of adult children than the in-family and younger-generation social robots (p = 0.037).

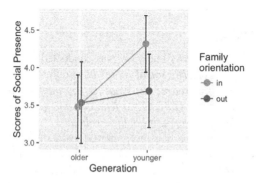

Fig. 7. Influence of family orientation and generation on social presence (error bars = 95% c.i.)

The influence of family orientation is not significant while the influence of generation is significant. This result is different to the results of sociability and trust with the social robot. It seems that when it comes to the adult children's perception of social presence, adopting younger-generation social robots is a good choice. In-family orientation increases the elderly parents' feeling of the social presence of their children when the social robot is younger-generation.

4.4 Influence on Judgment Accuracy

The influence of generation on judgment accuracy is analyzed using ANOVA (as shown in Fig. 8). The results show that the difference between social robots of older-generation and those of younger-generation is significant ($F_{(1,13)} = 4.851$, p = 0.037). In general, the judgment accuracy is relatively low. Participants have an average judgment accuracy of 71.42% (SD = 0.288) after conversing with older-generation social robots, and they have an average judgment accuracy of 47.62% (SD = 0.284) after conversing with younger-generation social robots. One main reason for these results is that the research uses idioms and life experience and cases from elderly parents in older-generation conditions, which are easily understood by elderly people. The interview shows that elderly people cannot understand certain catchwords and they can even miss or do not hear some catchwords.

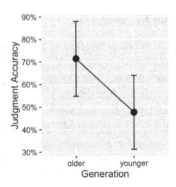

Fig. 8. Influence of generation on judgment accuracy (error bars = 95% c.i.)

4.5   Results of the Interviews

At the end of the experiment, a brief interview was conducted with each participant. The three standard questions are: *(1) The social robots have different family orientations and generations, which is your preference? (2) What do you think about giving the cartoon robot a human characteristic, such as family orientation and generation? (3) What is your advice if you are going to have a social robot in your home?*

As to the first question, seven participants preferred social robots of in-family and older-generation because they thought that communicating with people who were similar to themselves was easier. Among the other participants, two said that they preferred to communicate with social robots of younger-generation and the family orientation of the robot was not important. They considered that the younger-generation can give them the thoughts and ideas of their adult children. One female said that she preferred the social robots of out-family and older-generation because communicating family problems with family members might lead to more trouble and, therefore, communicating with old friends was better. The other three participants did not express any preferences about the family orientation or generation of the robot. In general, the results of this question agree with the results of perceived sociability and trust.

The second question is asked to investigate the participants' feelings about the human-type communication robot with a cartoon image. The results show that the participants did not feel strange when having a conversation with the social robot with a cartoon image. One typical participant said, "I know this is a robot, and its role is fictional, so it is does matter." These results are comparable with the research of Tanaka et al. [24], who used a human-type communication robot with a cartoon image to improve the cognitive ability of elderly women who live alone. As a still robot, it obtains the local optimum of familiarity when it has a cartoon image [10]. It seems that even though they have human characteristics, the application of a cartoon image in social robots is acceptable. In addition, the participants were very surprised when the robot called their names at the beginning of the conversation.

As to the third question, many of the participants mentioned that they want to communicate with the social robot about more topics. The successful introduction of a robot to the home of someone who is elderly probably requires an understanding of their daily life [25] and not only the content of their phone calls.

5   Conclusions

Adopting social robots to communicate with elderly parents has been shown to be a good approach to deal with intergenerational communication issues. In this research, a social robot is used as an intermediary between elderly parents and adult children. The influence of family orientation and generation of the social robot on learning outcome, perceived sociability, trust, and social presence are also investigated.

As to the family orientation, in-family social robots have better performance than the out-family social robots in terms of perceived sociability and trust with the robot. Elderly parents prefer to communicate family problems with in-family robots that can be considered as family members.

As to the generation, older-generation social robots have better performance than the younger-generation social robots in terms of perceived sociability and trust with the robot. Generation also improves the learning outcome of conflict in intergenerational communication. However, designing younger-generation social robots can improve the social presence of adult children.

Three limitations of this study are noted. First, this study recruited homogeneous participants, which may bias the results. Future studies may extend this study to other populations. Second, although this study considered two characteristics of social robots, other critical characteristics should be taken into consideration, such as the robots' gestures and appearance. Third, this study only considered the communication between robots and elderly parents. Future studies should take the communication between the robots and adult children into consideration.

Acknowledgment. This work was supported by funding from the National Natural Science Foundation of China (Grants nos. 71401018 and 71661167006) and Chongqing Municipal Natural Science Foundation (cstc2016jcyjA0406).

Appendix

Perceived sociability with social robots

1. I consider *This* a pleasant conversational partner.
2. I find *This* pleasant to interact with.
3. I feel *This* understands me.
4. I think *This* is nice.

Trust with social robots

5. I believe advice from *This* when I don't know for certain that it is correct.
6. When I am uncertain about a decision I believe *This* rather than myself.
7. If I am not sure about a decision, I have faith that *This* will provide the best solution.
8. When *This* gives unusual advice I am confident that the advice is correct.

Social presence of children

9. Personalness of interaction: Communication through *This* provides a more personal (or impersonal) touch with children.
10. Synchronicity: *This* allows you to have a real-time communication.
11. Feedback: *This* provides quick feedback with children.
12. Familiarity of communicators: *This* allows you to know you are talking with children.

References

1. Muñoz, D., Cornejo, R., Gutierrez, F.J., Favela, J., Ochoa, S.F., Tentori, M.: A social cloud-based tool to deal with time and media mismatch of intergenerational family communication. Future Gener. Comput. Syst. **53**, 140–151 (2015)
2. Muñoz, D., Cornejo, R., Ochoa, S.F., Favela, J., Gutierrez, F., Tentori, M.: Aligning intergenerational communication patterns and rhythms in the age of social media. In: Proceedings of the 2013 Chilean Conference on Human-Computer Interaction, pp. 66–71, ACM, New York (2013)
3. Rodríguez, M.D., Gonzalez, V.M., Favela, J., Santana, P.C.: Home-based communication system for older adults and their remote family. Comput. Hum. Behav. **25**, 609–618 (2009)
4. Williams, A., Giles, H.: Intergenerational conversations young adults' retrospective accounts. Hum. Commun. Res. **23**, 220–250 (1996)
5. Sabelli, A.M., Kanda, T., Hagita, N.: A conversational robot in an elderly care center: an ethnographic study. In: 2011 6th ACM/IEEE International Conference on Human-Robot Interaction (HRI), pp. 37–44. IEEE, New York (2011)
6. Heerink, M.: Exploring the influence of age, gender, education and computer experience on robot acceptance by older adults. In: Proceedings of the 6th International Conference on Human-Robot Interaction, pp. 147–148. ACM, New York (2011)
7. Kachouie, R., Sedighadeli, S., Khosla, R., Chu, M.-T.: Socially assistive robots in elderly care: a mixed-method systematic literature review. Int. J. Hum. Comput. Interact. **30**, 369–393 (2014)
8. Frennert, S., Östlund, B.: Review: seven matters of concern of social robots and older people. Int. J. Social Robot. **6**, 299–310 (2014)
9. Li, D., Rau, P.P., Li, Y.: A cross-cultural study: Effect of robot appearance and task. Int. J. Soc. Robot. **2**, 175–186 (2010)
10. Walters, M.L., Syrdal, D.S., Dautenhahn, K., Boekhorst, R.T., Koay, K.L.: Avoiding the uncanny valley: robot appearance, personality and consistency of behavior in an attention-seeking home scenario for a robot companion. Auton. Robots **24**, 159–178 (2008)
11. Ryan, E.: Aging, identity, attitudes, and intergenerational communication. In: Understanding Communication and Aging: Developing Knowledge and Awareness, pp. 73–91 (2007)
12. Giles, H., Khajavy, G.H., Choi, C.W.: Intergenerational communication satisfaction and age boundaries: comparative Middle Eastern data. J. Cross Cult. Gerontol. **27**, 357–371 (2012)
13. Moller, J., Cluitmans, P., Rasmussen, L., Houx, P., Rasmussen, H., Canet, J., Rabbitt, P., Jolles, J., Larsen, K., Hanning, C.D.: Long-term postoperative cognitive dysfunction in the elderly: ISPOCD1 study. Lancet **351**, 857–861 (1998)
14. Jorm, A.F.: The informant questionnaire on cognitive decline in the elderly (IQCODE): a review. Int. Psychogeriatr. **16**, 275–293 (2004)
15. Rau, P.-L.P., Li, Y., Liu, J.: Effects of a social robot's autonomy and group orientation on human decision-making. Adv. Hum. Comput. Interact. **2013**, 11 (2013)

16. Wang, L., Rau, P.-L.P., Evers, V., Robinson, B., Hinds, P.: Responsiveness to robots: effects of ingroup orientation & communication style on HRI in China. In: Proceedings of the 4th ACM/IEEE international conference on Human robot interaction, pp. 247–248. IEEE, New York (2009)

17. Heerink, M., Kröse, B., Evers, V., Wielinga, B.: Measuring acceptance of an assistive social robot: a suggested toolkit. In: The 18th IEEE International Symposium on Robot and Human Interactive Communication, RO-MAN 2009, pp. 528–533. IEEE, New York (2009)

18. Heerink, M., Kröse, B., Evers, V., Wielinga, B.: Assessing acceptance of assistive social agent technology by older adults: the almere model. Int. J. Soc. Robot. 2, 361–375 (2010)

19. Heerink, M., Kröse, B., Evers, V., Wielinga, B.: The influence of social presence on acceptance of a companion robot by older people. J. Phys. Agents 2, 33–40 (2008)

20. Madsen, M., Gregor, S.: Measuring human-computer trust. In: 11th Australasian Conference on Information Systems, vol. 53, pp. 6–8 (2000)

21. Guo, Z., Tan, F.B., Cheung, K.: Students' uses and gratifications for using computer-mediated communication media in learning contexts. Assoc. Inf. Syst. (AIS) 27, 339–378 (2010)

22. Heerink, M., Kröse, B., Evers, V., Wielinga, B.: Relating conversational expressiveness to social presence and acceptance of an assistive social robot. Virtual Reality 14, 77–84 (2010)

23. Tu, C.-H., McIsaac, M.: The relationship of social presence and interaction in online classes. Am. J. Distance Educ. 16, 131–150 (2002)

24. Tanaka, M., Ishii, A., Yamano, E., Ogikubo, H., Okazaki, M., Kamimura, K., Konishi, Y., Emoto, S., Watanabe, Y.: Effect of a human-type communication robot on cognitive function in elderly women living alone. Med. Sci. Monit. 18, CR550–CR557 (2012)

25. Sabelli, A.M., Kanda, T., Hagita, N.: A conversational robot in an elderly care center: an ethnographic study. In Proceedings of the 6th International Conference on Human-Robot Interaction, pp. 37–44. IEEE, New York (2011)

Factors in Fraudulent Emails that Deceive Elderly People

Jean-Robert Nino[✉], Gustav Enström, and Alan R. Davidson

Department of Computer and Systems Sciences, Stockholm University, Stockholm, Sweden
nino.jeanrobert@gmail.com, guen5897@student.su.se,
alan@dsv.su.se

Abstract. Fraud over the Internet is an increasingly common phenomenon and very common in the form of emails. Though new forms of fraud appear, it is important to look at common denominators that have so far come to light, and try to determine how they should be addressed in order to create a safer stay for everyone on the Internet. With this as motivation, and with a special eye to groups that may be considered especially vulnerable, this study aims to investigate what factors in fraudulent emails that people aged 65 and older have difficulty identifying when they meet them.

The increasing use of the Internet, the target group's vulnerability, and the increasing use of technology in everyday life imply that this kind of fraud is likely to be borne by society to an ever increasing extent. These factors paint a disturbing picture of how the situation is today and the direction in which the phenomenon is headed. It is therefore of interest to clarify which factors come into play in successful attacks against the target group in order to target countermeasures against this form of fraud. To accomplish this, a survey was conducted among residents of a nursing home and members of a Swedish national senior citizen organisation. The results from 122 respondents to our digital questionnaire show that the importance of technical factors in fraudulent email needs to be clarified for the studied group in order for them to make better, accurate assessments of the emails that they meet. The most common factor that the respondents failed to identify were links in the email that looked untrustworthy.

Keywords: Fraud · Phishing · Elderly people · Email · Social engineering · IT-Security in society · Cybercrime · Trust

1 Background

Media has reported on people who have been victims of money, identity or account information theft by trusting fraudsters over the phone, email, social media or other platforms [9]. Such fraud attempts often occur through the Internet with so-called phishing attacks. The method requires little technological skill but relies instead on manipulation and social skills. In order to perform such social engineering, technical equipment, such as telephone and computers is used as a means to reach out to potential victims [16].

Phishing is therefore a form of social engineering, often performed over the Internet. Phishing can be conducted via email but can be carried out via advertisements on

© Springer International Publishing AG 2017
J. Zhou and G. Salvendy (Eds.): ITAP 2017, Part I, LNCS 10297, pp. 360–368, 2017.
DOI: 10.1007/978-3-319-58530-7_28

websites, via chat rooms, social media, etc. The purpose of phishing is to obtain personal information from a user, usually by tricking the user to a website where this information is collected. Phishing often hides behind the guise of a credible organisation or company that pretends to have one or more reasons to ask the user for sensitive information [20].

Email belongs to one of the common forms for fraudsters to initiate contact with potential victims. The email content can contain links or files that install malicious software which can then initiate further contact between the parties [18].

Although web browsers exist that implement some form of protection against phishing attacks [1], none of these are yet capable of guarding against all fraud attempts. The liability ultimately falls on the user when it comes to protecting themselves against this type of attack. To accomplish this, the user needs not only to be aware of the risks, but also be able to apply his or her knowledge in a way that promotes their safety on the Internet.

The age distribution of fraud is relatively even, though is somewhat more common between the ages of 45 to 54 years [15]. The fact that all demographic groups have become more accessible to each other over the Internet, has made them more accessible to the fraudsters who want to exploit and deceive them. According to the Swedish National Council for Crime Prevention (Swedish: Brottsförebyggande rådet) [15], the number of reported fraud attempts more than tripled in the past ten years as seen in Table 1. Computer fraud and scams through the Internet are among the most commonly reported fraud crimes [15].

Table 1. Number of reported fraud attempts between 2010–2015 [15]

Year	2010	2011	2012	2013	2014	2015
Computer fraud reports	25,668	19,960	22,359	32,284	42,883	67,075

According to several sources [3, 5, 21], the elderly demographic is a particularly interesting target for fraudsters. They are often considered to have good credit that can be easily exploited if the offender has access to credit card numbers and personal information. Elderly people are also less eager to report the crime for fear of being further harassed. It often takes a long time for a senior citizen to realise that a fraud has been committed, and with declining memory and cognitive abilities, elderly people find it more difficult to give an accurate testimony of the events of the fraud [3].

2   Known Fraud Factors

Social engineering is deceiving people by applying one or more psychological techniques that are designed to stimulate a response from the victim. The social engineer evokes emotions such as fear, excitement or guilt [14]. Phishing, as well other fraud via email, uses the same techniques. Fraudulent emails usually use captivating language that plays on greed, fear, authority, urgency, curiosity or sympathy [18]. A vivid example from 2015 as seen in Fig. 1, of when these methods are used, is in the case of a fraudulent email claiming to be from Postnord, a Nordic postal operator. Embedded in the email message there is a link that leads the user to a site that downloads a file containing malicious software and that encrypts files on the compromised computer [12].

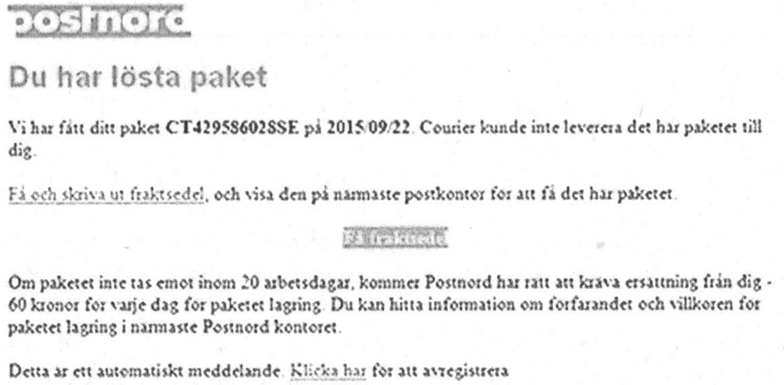

postnord

Du har lösta paket

Vi har fått ditt paket **CT429586028SE** på **2015/09/22**. Courier kunde inte leverera det har paketet till dig.

Få och skriva ut fraktsedel, och visa den på narmaste postkontor for att få det har paketet.

Om paketet inte tas emot inom 20 arbetsdagar, kommer Postnord har ratt att krava ersattning från dig - 60 kronor for varje dag for paketet lagring. Du kan hitta information om forfarandet och villkoren for paketet lagring i narmaste Postnord kontoret.

Detta ar ett automatiskt meddelande. Klicka har for att avregistrera

Fig. 1. An example of fraudulent email that has been circulating since September 2015, claiming to be from Postnord [4].

The email translates to: "You have packages. We received your package CT429586028SE on 2015/09/22. The courier [sic: the correct Swedish term should be "kurir", courier is not a Swedish word] could not deliver this package to you. Get and printing [sic] the shipping label, and show it at the nearest post office to retrieve this package. If the package is not fetched within 20 working days, Postnord will be entitled to claim compensation from you – 60 (Swedish) crowns for each day that the package stored [sic]. You can find information about the procedure and conditions for package stored [sic] in nearest Postnord office. This is an automated message. Click here to unsubscribe [sic]".

The perpetrator tries to stimulate a response from the user by playing on factors such as urgency, fear and greed. The email recipient is given a time frame to carry out the sender's instructions. The use of a deadline in this way is a common strategy used in this type of phishing attack and is used in order to stress the victim into taking an action without due thought [19]. The email preys on the victim's curiosity; a user can be curious about what this package contains, especially if he or she is not expecting a package from Postnord. The use of the company logo, a valid date and a serial number that looks plausible, increases the credibility of the email. However, an attentive reader can react to the fact that the email contains grammatical and spelling errors, which can reduce its credibility. Deliberately using design factors that enhance the emails' perceived authenticity is a factor that affects its efficacy [1].

One of the significant aspects of this type of attack is how well the perpetrator manages to elicit the victim's trust. This is achieved by the offender painting a credible picture of who the purported sender is, i.e. who the email claims to represent. In the field of social engineering this is known as pretexting, a technique frequently used maliciously [8]. After the offender has presented him or herself, instructions or requests often follow. The reasoning behind such requests must seem plausible to the recipient in order for the attack to succeed [14]. In addition to the textual content of fraudulent emails there are technical factors that perpetrators use to deceive the reader. Modern email clients allow for HTML code to be used to format emails and thereby allow for links to be included in the text [11]. This allows linking to a fraudulent website with a text that looks like a genuine URL. An image can also be used as a link to the fraudulent web site. There are web based email clients browsers where the actual URL text/picture reference is automatically displayed in the lower part of the browser [13].

3   Data Collection Method

In order to investigate these issues, the authors conducted a survey with the aid of a digital questionnaire in order to simplify the coding of responses and in order to econ-omise on time and cost compared with physical surveys [10]. The digital questionnaire was conducted in Swedish.

The questionnaire asked several questions about the subject of fraudulent emails and was dependent on the respondent being given the opportunity to respond in free text. The research strategy allowed the collection of data from multiple sources [2], such as social networks as well as in nursing homes for elderly people.

In the questionnaire, the respondent was asked to fill in information about him or herself as a user, including the year in which the respondent was born, how experienced the respondent felt him or herself to be in using computers in general and how often the respondent used email as a communication channel.

The respondent was then presented with a set of emails that were either taken from genuine or fraudulent sources. Participants first answered on whether the email was perceived as genuine or fraudulent. If the email was perceived as fraudulent, the respondent was asked to choose from one or more predetermined factors on which they based their decision. If the respondent did not feel that the predetermined factors could satisfy his or her explanation, an "Other" option was available with the possibility to write in any answer.

Breaking down the essential factors in the success of email fraud in this survey allowed us to see trends among participants' responses. There are several factors associated with this type of attack that affected the outcome. Some of these factors are related and can be divided into themes. An abstraction of these results is shown in the below breakdown.

x Design factors, such as:
o Grammar.
o Professional design (logotypes, formatting, icons and clickable images).
o Overall spelling.

x Technological factors, such as:
o Content of sender's email address.
o Content of possible links.
o Links within email and their actual URL.

x Pretexting factors, such as:
o Presentation of the email subject.
o Emotional factors (greed, fear, urgency, curiosity, etc.).

The respondents were reached through visiting a nursing home in northern Stockholm, Sweden as well as through SPF Seniorerna (an association for pensioners in Sweden). At the nursing home, only elderly subjects who considered themselves to have previous experience of using the Internet were asked. People with diagnosed dementia were not asked to participate in the study.

Permission was also obtained to publish the digital questionnaire within the SPF group on Facebook where they had followers who belong to the target group. The questionnaire was created using Google Forms [6].

4   Results and Conclusions

Respondents were first prompted to give information regarding their birth year, how they felt their user experience with computers and the Internet were, and how often they read their emails. The bar charts in Fig. 2 represent the responses.

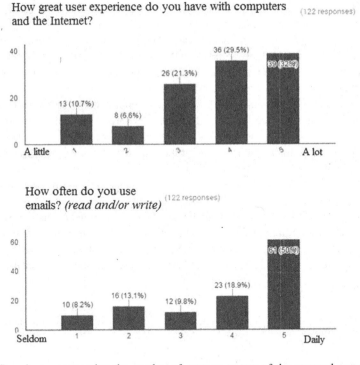

Fig. 2. Bar charts representing the number of answers to two of the personal questions. The X-axis represents the five-scale response option. The Y-axis represents the number of respondents.

In total, 122 respondents answered the questionnaire. The respondents were born between 1928 and 1951. The average respondent's year of birth was 1943.

In the questionnaire, respondents were shown a number of emails they read through and then assessed whether the email was real or fraudulent. If the email was perceived as deceptive, the participant was asked to fill in a number of statements which they based their decision on. These claims were based on the factors identified that are common factors in the fraudulent email.

Participants were given the opportunity to fill in their own reactions in a text field if there was anything else that they felt was suspicious.

When an email message was interpreted as genuine, the respondent was presented with the next email message in order. Tables 2, 3 and 4 show the proportions of correctly identified fraudulent factors in emails.

Table 2. Actual number of correct identifications by each indicative factor: Design factors.

Design factors	Total possible correct identifications	Actual no. of correct identifications	Quota
Grammatical errors	244	98	40%
Spelling errors	366	90	25%
The email lacks professional design	122	43	35%

Table 3. Actual number of correct identifications by each indicative factor: Pretexting factors.

Pretexting factors	Total possible correct identifications	Actual no. of correct identifications	Quota
The sender wants a fast reply	366	68	19%
The email can be perceived as threatening	122	42	34%
What the sender wants to make me do seem unnecessary	244	56	23%
The content seems too good to be true	122	83	68%

Table 4. Actual number of correct identifications by each indicative factor: Technical factors.

Technical factors	Total possible correct identifications	Actual no. of correct identifications	Quota
The sender's address looks unreliable	366	99	27%
Links in the email looks unreliable	366	64	17%

The results showed that respondents were less able to identify technical factors by a ratio of 22%. Respondents were better able to identify fraudulent email when respondents see the email content, formulation and design. The respondents were able to identify pretext factors to 29% and design factors to 32%. The factor in the fraudulent email that was most difficult for respondents to identify was "links in the email looking unreliable".

It appeared that the respondents had primarily been poor at identifying technical factors in the fraudulent email. This suggests that the demographic group is more vulnerable to factors in which the email, for example, includes URLs to malicious sites with apparently trustworthy text links, or where the sender's address looks untrustworthy.

At the time of the study, email clients exist that show the sender's full address rather than just the name of the sender. Google's email client Gmail [7] is an example that provides this feature. It appears that the respondents do not always notice the full email address.

One area for improvement is that the demographic from this study could become better at identifying the technological elements that can reveal the fraud. With this in mind, it would be of interest to see an implementation of a function in email clients or web browsers that could prompt the user to carefully inspect such elements. The sender's address and any URL in the message could easily be identified by a web client and marked as something the user should examine more carefully. Research and development of such a feature could conceivably improve the elderly demographics' chances of protecting themselves from such threats.

5   Related Work

The result of this study is in line with the findings of the study *"Who Falls for phish? A demographic analysis of phishing and susceptibility the effectiveness of the intervention"* by Sheng et al. [17]. The result of this study showed that people with a low user experience of Internet-based services, amongst other parameters, had a greater risk of being deceived on the Internet. The study argues that participants' prior exposure to phishing and total number of years using the Internet, together with a few other parameters, affected the risk of a person being deceived on-line. As a result, people in the 18–25 age group were found to be more likely to fall for phishing attempts than other age groups due to lower level of education and less aversion to financial risk.

Similar to the design of this study, participants of Sheng et al's study were shown both real and fraudulent email in a survey format, in which they had to respond if it appeared fraudulent or not without prior training. There was no detailed information on the elderly populations susceptibility to fraudulent emails in that study.

6   Limitations of the Study

The multiple questions that followed each email gave clues about possible fraudulent factors that may appear in the rest of the email examples. After a participant had seen the different answer options, it could have been possible that the participant looked for things that they otherwise would not have thought of when they were then presented with the next letter.

The questionnaire was answered largely by people with accounts on Facebook. Due to the limitations of tracking the respondents, there was no guarantee that it was an actual person over 65 years who responded to the survey. Since the questionnaire did not require the respondent being logged into any personal account or enter personal information that could link the responses to the individual, there was the possibility that the respondent could answer the survey more than once. Furthermore, the population selection can have been biased given that the survey was digital. The possibility exists that the respondents can have shared the link to the questionnaire with acquaintances who they knew to be very interested or familiar with the subject matter.

As the purpose of the survey was declared when the respondents were asked to identify fraudulent email, this factor could have made the individual more suspicious than if the letter had appeared in a more true-to-life setting. For ethical reasons this was deemed to be the best way to conduct this type of study, i.e. respondents were made aware of the purpose of the study and therefore could be spared possible anguish over the choices they made.

References

1. Blythe, M., Clark, J., Petrie, H.: F for fake: four studies on how we fall for phish. In: ACM CHI Conference on Human Factors in Computing Systems, May 2011. http://citeseerx.ist.psu.edu/viewdoc/download;jsessionid=570414C69898DD2FA38D113C50EA27D3?doi=10.1.1.300.1855&rep=rep1&type=pdf. Accessed 03 Mar 2016
2. Kothari, C.R.: Research Methodology: Methods and Techniques. Google: New Age International (P) Limited, London (2004)
3. Carlson, E.: Phishing for elderly victims: as the elderly migrate to the internet fraudulent schemes targeting them follow (2007). http://publish.illinois.edu/elderlawjournal/files/2015/02/Carlson1.pdf. Accessed 17 May 2016
4. Dagens Industri: Varning för virusmejl från "Postnord" (2015). http://www.di.se/artiklar/2015/9/25/varning-for-virusmejl-fran-postnord/. Accessed 05 Mar 2016
5. Federal Bureau of Investigation. (n.d). common fraud schemes. FBI. https://www.fbi.gov/scams-safety/fraud/seniors. Accessed 24 Jan 2016
6. Google. (n.d.)a. Get started with forms. Google. https://apps.google.com/learning-center/products/forms/get-started/. Accessed 18 May 2016
7. Google. (n.d.)b. Welcome to Gmail. Google. https://www.google.com/intl/en/mail/help/about.html. Accessed 18 May 2016
8. Hadnagy, C.: Social Engineering: The Art of Human Hacking. Wiley, Indianapolis (2010)
9. Lind, J.: Polisen chanslös när bedrägerier ökar lavinartat. Dagens nyheter (2014). http://www.dn.se/nyheter/sverige/polisen-chanslos-nar-bedragerier-okar-lavinartat/. Accessed 02 June 2016
10. Lumsden, J.: Guidelines for the Design of Online Questionnaires. Researchgate (2005). https://www.researchgate.net/publication/44079032_Guidelines_for_the_Design_of_Online-Questionnaires. Accessed 09 June 2016
11. Microsoft: add a hyperlink to an email message (2016). https://support.office.com/en-us/article/Add-a-hyperlink-to-an-email-message-48780838-1b3d-4def-8612-03100491024c. Accessed 17 May 2016
12. Microsoft. (n.d.). Ransomware. Microsoft. https://www.microsoft.com/security/portal/mmpc/shared/ransomware.aspx. Accessed 18 May 2016
13. Milletary, J.: Technical trends in phishing attacks. Carnegie Mellon University, USA (2005). https://resources.sei.cmu.edu/asset_files/WhitePaper/2005_019_001_50315.pdf. Accessed 18 May 2016

14. Mitnick, K.: The Art of Deception. Wiley Publishing, Indianapolis (2002)
15. National Crime Prevention Council: Bedrägerier och ekobrott. National Crime Prevention Council (2016). https://www.bra.se/bra/brott-och-statistik/bedragerier-och-ekobrott.html. Accessed 30 Mar 2016
16. Palmqvist, D.: Social-engineering ett hot mot informationssäkerheten? Sweden: Växjö University (2008). http://lnu.diva-portal.org/smash/get/diva2:205870/FULLTEXT01.pdf. Accessed 05 Feb 2016
17. Sheng, S., Holbrook, M., Kumaraguru, P., Cranor, L., Downs, J.: Who falls for phish? A demographic analysis of phishing susceptibility and the effectiveness of interventions. Carnegie Mellon University, USA. Indraprastha Institute of Information Technology, India (2010). http://lorrie.cranor.org/pubs/papl162-sheng.pdf. Accessed 25 Apr 2016
18. The Swedish Police: Vanliga nätbedrägerier. Polisen.se (2016). https://polisen.se/Utsatt-for-brott/Skydda-dig-mot-brott/Bedrageri/Vanliga-natbedragerier/. Accessed 15 May 2016
19. Tsow, A., Jakobsson, M.: Deceit and deception: a large user study of phishing. Indiana University Bloomington, USA (2007). http://www.cs.indiana.edu/pub/techreports/TR649.pdf. Accessed 02 May 2016
20. United States Computer Emergency Readiness Team: recognizing and avoiding email scams. USCERT. https://www.us-cert.gov/sites/default/files/publications/emailscams_0905.pdf. Accessed 03 May 2016
21. Youngblood, J.: A Comprehensive Look at Fraud Identification and Preventions. CRC Press, New York (2015)

Silent Speech Interaction for Ambient Assisted Living Scenarios

António Teixeira[1,2(✉)], Nuno Vitor[1], João Freitas[3,4], and Samuel Silva[2]

[1] Department of Electronics Telecommunication and Informatics,
University of Aveiro, Aveiro, Portugal
ajst@ua.pt
[2] Institute of Electronics and Informatics Engineering of Aveiro (IEETA),
Aveiro, Portugal
[3] Microsoft Language Development Center (MLDC), Lisbon, Portugal
[4] DefinedCrowd, R. da Prata 80, Lisbon, Portugal
http://wiki.ieeta.pt/wiki/index.php/User:Teixeira

Abstract. In many Ambient Assisted Living (AAL) contexts, the speech signal cannot be used or speech recognition performance is highly affected due to ambient noise from televisions or music players. Trying to address these difficulties resulted in the exploration of Silent Speech interfaces (SSI), making use of other means to obtain information regarding what the user is uttering, even when no acoustic speech signal is produced.

The automatic recognition of what has been said, based only on images of the face, is the purpose of Visual Speech Recognition (VSR) systems, a type of SSI. However, despite the potential of VSR for enabling the interaction of older adults with new AAL applications, and current advances in SSI technologies, no real VSR application can be found in the literature.

Based on recent work in SSI, for European Portuguese, a first working application of VSR targeting older adults is presented along with and results from an initial evaluation. The system performed well, enabling real-time control of a media player with an accuracy of 81.3% and performing classification in around 1.3 s. At this stage, the results vary from speaker to speaker and the system performs better if the words are correctly articulated. The effect of distance of the speaker to the video apparatus (a Kinect One) proved not to be an issue in terms of the system accuracy.

Keywords: Silent Speech Interfaces (SSI) · Visual Speech Recognition (VSR) · Ambient Assisted Living (AAL) · Elderly

1 Introduction

With the increasing percentage of elderly in the world population, Information and communications technology (ICT) providers are more and more challenged

© Springer International Publishing AG 2017
J. Zhou and G. Salvendy (Eds.): ITAP 2017, Part I, LNCS 10297, pp. 369–387, 2017.
DOI: 10.1007/978-3-319-58530-7_29

to help them stay active at their homes. However, the adoption of Ambient Assisted Living (AAL) applications by elderly users strongly depends on its usability and quality of the interaction.

Speech, as we are all aware, is the easiest way for humans to communicate, can be used at a distance while keeping hands free. But in many AAL situations (e.g. noisy environments due to sound of televisions or music), the speech signal cannot be used or speech recognition performance is highly affected. Elderly speech also affects the performance of speech recognizers.

Silent Speech interfaces (SSI) [8], can be used to address these challenges, since it looks beyond the acoustic signal during spoken communication.

Informally, one can say that an SSI system extends the human speech production process by exploring biometric signals other than the voice. In fact, audible speech is just the end result of the complex process of speech production involving, for example, cerebral and motor activities, and a wide range of technologies support the acquisition of data pertaining these different parts of the process. For instance, surface electromyography can capture muscle activity and video can provide data regarding lip movement.

Nowadays, there are several studies in SSI considering every stage of the speech production process (see Sect. 3). Depending on the speech production signal or signals that the SSI system targets, SSI approaches can be either invasive or not. An advantage of vision-based approaches, which target the visible effects of speech (mainly: lips position, jaw position, tongue tip when lips are open), is that they typically require no attachment or insertion of devices. These systems, referred as Visual Speech Recognition (VSR) systems can use different types of cameras (e.g. RGB, depth cameras, etc.).

Despite the potential of VSR for older adults' interaction with new AAL applications and the advances in SSI technologies, to best of our knowledge, no real VSR application can be found in the literature.

Main objective is to develop and evaluate a VSR application, directed to older adults in a real AAL scenario (described in Sect. 2) by leveraging previous work of the authors in SSI [8], multimodal interaction [30] and AAL [7].

Paper is structured as follows: next section presents, briefly, the scenario chosen for the proof-of-concept; Sects. 3 and 4 present some background regarding the process of speech production and a survey of related work in SSI, focusing in VSR; Sect. 5 presents the developed prototype; evaluation results are the subject of Sect. 6; paper ends with conclusions and future work, in Sect. 7.

2   Scenario

For a first proof-of-concept of the potential of SSI for A we chose to develop an application to control a multimedia player in European Portuguese, a relevant scenario for AAL.

The most important areas in AAL are related to allowing the user with some kind of limitations to control entertainment systems, access to social networks, or similar. Controlling such systems allows the user to access to access memories and information from friends and family.

Considering our goal, we chose to take advantage of one of the world's most used open multimedia player, VLC Media Player (VLC) [17]. VLC is seen by users as simple to use and supports a wide range of multimedia formats. Thus, given that it is open source we can adapt it to the targeted AAL scenario.

In VLC it is possible to load a set of videos and then select the video that the user wants to watch. Also, it also supports common media controls such the sound volume, the speed of the video and the stop and play functions. In our scenario these controls are used by detecting the silent speech command, i.e. the movements of the lips and the chin of the user. This allows the user to control the system in a noisy ambient, in case the user wants some privacy or in situations where the user has speech production limitations.

The considered vocabulary is in European Portuguese and the selected words were considered to be the most natural for the targeted scenario. Several iterations were done to reach this set of words. The Table 1 has, in the first column, the set of words chosen in Portuguese and in the second column their translation in English. To help with the recognition accuracy, we avoided phonetically similar words, particularly in commands with two words.

Table 1. Set of words chosen regarding the AAL context of using the VLC

Portuguese	English
Ver filme	Watch a movie
Parar	Stop
Continuar	Continue
Aumentar volume	Increase volume
Baixar volume	Decrease volume
Mais rápido	Faster
Mais lento	Slower
Próximo filme	Next movie

3 Background

Due to the complexity of the speech production and perception process, in this section are presented some topics needed to understand the SSI basics.

3.1 Speech Production

Speech production requires a complex series of events and is considered the most complex motor task performed by humans [29]. In a fluent conversation, we are able to produce two or three words per second.

The speech production process can be divided into several stages [8,9,18]. In order, these stages are, according to [8, p. 4]: (1) Conceptualization and Formulation, (2) Articulatory Control and (3) Articulation.

In the first stage, the brain converts communication intentions into messages, creates linguistic representation required for the expansion of this preverbal messages and produces a phonetic plan [5]. Articulatory control, the second stage, using information from first stage, generates the electrical impulses need to control the articulators. These commands must simultaneously control all the aspects of the articulation, including the lips, jaw, tongue and velum [24]. The changes in articulators, in the last stage, continuously change vocal tract characteristics (mainly shape and stiffness), producing the acoustic speech signal and other effects (e.g., alterations in the face).

In speech production, the articulatory muscles, like the tongue, have a vital role because they can shape the air stream to produce a recognizable speech. Mandibular movement also has an important role in this process. Despite the relevance of cavities, surfaces and organs such as the lungs in speech production, the articulators have a key role in the pronunciation of the different sounds of a language. Their position defines the articulatory and resonant characteristics of the vocal tract.

Articulators can be active or passive. The active articulators include the lips, tongue, lower jaw and velum, being the tongue the most important, as it participates in the production of (almost) all sounds. The passive include the teeth, alveolar ridge and hard palate. Figure 1a sagittal view of several articulators. The most visible effects of the speech production chain are the movement of the lips, tongue, lower jaw and the chin.

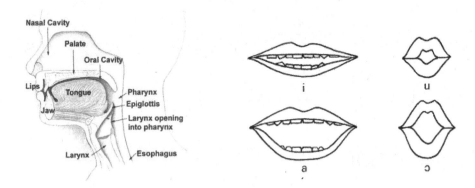

Fig. 1. Sagittal view of the vocal tract depicting its main regions and several articulators [8], at left, and example of visible effects of speech production, at right.

3.2   SSI Basics

A Silent Speech interface (SSI) is a system that interprets human signals other than the audible acoustic signal enabling speech communication [6]. A SSI system is commonly characterized by the acquisition of information from the human speech production process such as articulations, facial muscle movement or brain activity. It is possible to say that the SSI systems extends the human speech production process by exploring biometric signals other that voice, using sensors, cameras, etc. [8].

There are multiple works in SSI done in every stage of the speech production stage. For example, in the first stage (Conceptualization) works were done on the interpolation of the signals from implants in the speech-motor cortex [3] and from Electroencephalography (EEG) sensors [23]. Using information from Articulation stage, works were made regarding the movement of the lips [1,32] or the movements of speaker's face estimated through Ultrasonic Doppler sensing [10], for example.

The usual architecture of a SSI system comprises modules for: signals acquisition and processing, extraction of Features, and classification.

The acquisition of signals from any stage of the human speech production process can invasive or non-invasive and obtrusive or not. An invasive modality needs a medical attention to be used or requires the use of sensors. An obtrusive modality requires wearing some type of equipment, such as, for example sensors.

Choosing the best SSI is not an easy task because they have different advantages and disadvantages regarding price, usability, accuracy, and speaker's dependence.

3.3   Methods to Collect Visual Information for SSI Systems

The most used way to collect visual information from the speech production process is through cameras, non-invasive and non-obtrusive method. There are some different cameras on the market like: RGB cameras that collect information on the color space; and depth cameras, that collect depth information through the stereo vision approach, infrared or time of flight technology.

The introduction Microsoft Kinect for Windows made simple to have both simultaneously, as it provides both types of technologies at an affordable price.

RGB cameras are used to collect information pixel per pixel in a RGB color space (Red, Green and Blue). Today these type of cameras use CMOS or charge-coupled device (CCD) image sensor and operate in general in a Bayer filter arrangement, where green gives twice as many detectors as red and blue (red-green-blue-green (RGBG) color filter array (CFA)) in order to give better luminance resolution than chrominance resolution.

To get the information of depth of the various pixels in a image, depth cameras use one of two different methods [16]: stereo vision or Time of Flight (TOF). Stereo vision uses two (or more) images taken at the same time from separate cameras and the differences are analyzed to yield depth information [2].

Time of Flight cameras (Fig. 2) use modulated infrared light, not visible to humans. Then, a sensor captures the reflected light to extract distance information [15].

Time-of-Flight (ToF) Technology Using Light

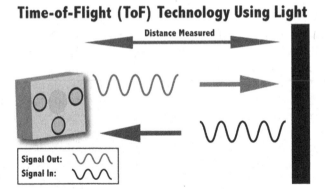

Fig. 2. Simplified illustration of the principle used in Time of Flight depth cameras. [31].

In Visual Recognition Systems, the camera is one of the key issues. The resolution of the camera is extremely important since it will define the detail of each image representing the data collected. Frame rate (fps) is another important specification regarding the amount of information that the camera could record in a second. This becomes a key factor in terms of speech recognition systems considering the movement of the lips.

Microsoft and Prime Sense released the Kinect (for Xbox 360) in 2010. With its 2 cameras and the capability to track 48 points from the human skeleton, this device brought a complete new approach in fields Human Computer Interaction, face tracking, and Audio-Visual Speech Recognition. Despite the many systems created using this versions of Kinect [14,22,35], this camera was far from being perfect due to its low resolution (640 × 480) and limitations of depth information extraction technique (structured light).

Kinect One (see Fig. 3) was release by Microsoft in 2013. This new version brought several improvements such as a better resolution (Full HD, 1920 × 1080 in RGB images); better depth images, thanks to the Time of Flight (TOF) technology; greater accuracy over its predecessor; capability to process 2 gigabits of data per second; capability to track up to 6 skeletons at once; and a wider

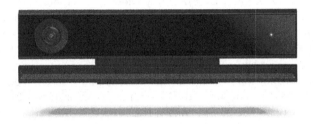

Fig. 3. Kinect one for windows

field of view. This new version soon became an important piece in visual speech recognition systems because of its relation in performance over price.

4 Related Work and State-of-the-Art

In this section is presented some relevant related work in SSI: starting from recent work in SSI in general; continuing with recent work in VSR, the SSI method adopted for the work described in this paper; and ending with information regarding SSI for Portuguese, the language adopted for the worked reported.

4.1 Representative Recent Developments in SSI

EEG is commonly used in SSI, being a representative example the work for Japanese, with EEG signals from 63 channels, by Matsumoto [19], showing that classification accuracies can be improved if an adaptive collection is made. An increase from 56–72% to 73–92% was reported, using SVM with Gaussian Kernel as classifiers.

In 2014 Freitas and coworkers created a multimodal SSI system, for European Portuguese language, combining sensing technologies such as Video and Depth input, Ultrasonic Doppler sensing and Surface Electromyography. These streams of information are synchronously acquired with the aim of supporting research and development of a multimodal SSI [12]. Due to the number and variety of streams, this system continues to be a good example of the state-of-the-art in multimodal SSI. The approach is non-invasive, however it is obtrusive, as EMG sensors were needed for the Surface Electromyography signals (see Fig. 4).

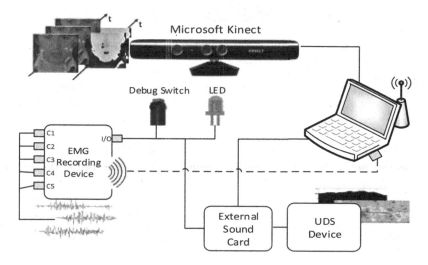

Fig. 4. Diagram of the alignment scheme of João Freitas and co-workers [12].

A vocabulary of 32 words in European Portuguese was used regarding an AAL context, divided in sets of digits, pairs of common words and AAL words.

For classification, Dynamic Time Warping and k-Nearest Neighbor classifiers were used. His results points towards performance advantages using a multi-modal solution to implement an SSI, especially for Ultrasonic Doppler sensing and Surface Electromyography. However, a final conclusion can not be taken regarding which approach represents a higher gain.

The best results had nearly 94% accuracy (for AAL words with features from Video+Depth+UDS+EMG with DTW classification) and the worst were nearly 65% (for a Vocabulary Mix using features from Video+Depth with DTW+kNN classification).

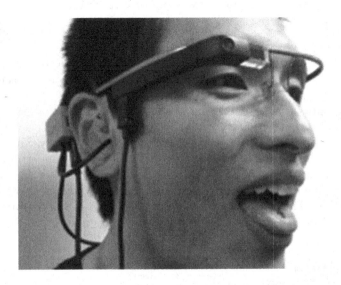

Fig. 5. Tongue magnetometer and Outer Ear Interface [28].

Also in 2014, from Georgia Institute of Technology, USA, a wearable system (obtrusive and intrusive) was created [28] to capture tongue and jaw movements during silent speech in English (Fig. 5).

To achieve that, a two system part was created: one part with a Tongue Magnet Interface, which utilizes the 3-axis magnetometer aboard Google Glass to measure the movement of a small magnet glued to the user's tongue, and the second part a Outer Ear Interface which measures the deformation in the ear canal caused by jaw movements using proximity sensors embedded in a set of earmolds. The classification was done using hidden Markov model-based techniques to select one of the 11 phrases.

During pronunciation of 11 distinct phrases, the average user dependent recognition accuracy was 90.5% using both parts of the system. Using just the part of the Outer Ear Interface (non-intrusive but still obtrusive) the system performs with an accuracy of 85.5%.

4.2   Silent Speech Based on Visual Information

One of the first studies in Visual Speech Recognition (VSR) was in 1994. This study was based on a word recognition system with a lip modeling approach for the recognition task [25]. This system had a 85% accuracy using the height and width of the lips, but only 2 words were tested.

In 2007, Werda created an Automatic Lip Feature Extraction prototype, named as ALiFE, that could automatically localize lip feature points in a speaker's face and carry out a spatial-temporal tracking of these points [33]. The points of interest in Werda work were the top center of the upper lip, bottom center of the lower lip and corners (Fig. 6). By using these points it was possible to extract features like the width (distance between the corners points), the height (distance between the top and bottom points) and also the area consisting of the inside of the mouth. They used multiple speakers in their tests (females and males). French was the used language in the tests and the accuracy obtained was 72.7%.

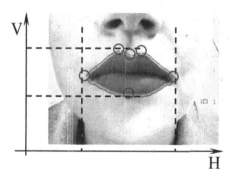

Fig. 6. Points of interest detection by the projection of final contour on horizontal and vertical axis (H and V) [33]

More recently, using the Kinect RGB camera and depth information, without the information of sound (VSR), to obtain 18 points of the lips (Fig. 7) and extracting the angles between all these points, Yargic and Dogan [35] created a system for a Turkish vocabulary of 15 words (color names), obtaining an accuracy rate of 78.2%. They used KNN classifiers.

Another recent VSR system was proposed by Frisky and colleagues [13] applying a video content analysis technique. Using spatiotemporal features descriptors, features were extracted from video containing visual lip information. A preprocessing step is employed to remove noise and enhance the contrast of images of every frame. This system achieved an accuracy between 25.9% and 89.02%.

One of the main features that is extracted in SSI based in visual information are the lips and their position/movement over time. Studies are being developed to find them as accurate and quick as possible [4].

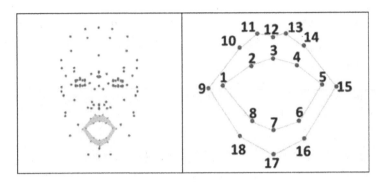

Fig. 7. Features used by Yargi and Dogan: 18 lip feature points and their assigned ID values [35].

4.3   Silent Speech for Portuguese

Regarding the Silent Speech Interfaces (SSI) for European Portuguese (EP), in 2010, Freitas started working, during his PhD, on a solution that addressed the issues raised in adapting existing work on SSI to a new language. Initial work focused on Visual Speech Recognition (VSR) and Acoustic Doppler Sensors (ADS) for speech recognition, evaluating this methodologies in order to cope with EP language characteristics. Dynamic Time Warping (DTW) was used, achieving an Word Error Rate (WER) of 8.6% [9].

In 2013, in a new work on SSI for EP, Freitas et al. [11] selected 4 non-invasive modalities (Visual data from Video and Depth, Surface Electromyography and Ultrasonic Doppler) and created a system that explores the synchronous combination of all 4, or of a subset of them, into a multimodal SSI. For classification, Dynamic Time Warping (DTW), followed by a weighted k-Nearest Neighbor (kNN) classifier, was used. Results showed that a significant difference in recognition rates can be found between unimodal and multimodal approaches, in favor or the latter, and that benefits can be obtained by aligning several modalities, especially when registering Video, Depth and Ultrasonic Doppler, or Video and Depth. Results also indicate a slight better performance when using a decision fusion approach with DTW followed by a kNN classifier [11].

One of the most recent works in a Silent Speech for Portuguese (and also Visual Silent Recognition) is [1]. In his dissertation Abreu used Kinect One to extract geometric and articulatory features from the lips. For the lips' segmentation, Abreu considered two color spaces: RGB and YCbCr. From the RGB frames he used the green channel in order to extract the external points of the lips and from the YCbCr color space the Cr channel was used to obtain the internal points of the lips. After the features extracted, Abreu made some normalizations such as length normalizations to the feature vectors to be sent to the classifiers and some distance normalization.

The selected vocabulary consisted of 25 European Portuguese words, which were divided into 2 sets: one with a widely used set of words used in speech recognition literature, digits from zero to nine and the other taken from a Ambient Assisted Living context.

The classification was done using SVM classifiers and the best accuracy of his system (ViKi - Visual Speech Recognition for Kinect) was 68% based on geometric features and 34% of recognition accuracy based on articulatory features. An hybrid solution using both geometric and articulatory was also tested achieving an accuracy of 49%.

5 Proof-of-Concept Prototype

Our proof-of-concept was developed with the Kinect One camera from Microsoft using VSR of a small set of commands (e.g. "See Movie"), uttered by the user, positioned at some distance of the front of the camera. The recognized commands are passed to VLC player in order to control it.

5.1 Requirements

One of the most important requirement is that the system has to permit some real daily life experiences, for example controlling a television at a certain distance (e.g. from the couch). However, given a typical living room scenario with a television turned on, it is probable to exist some audio noise. In this case, a SSI based on visual speech recognition allows to recognize speech without using acoustic information.

Another requirement is that the proof-of-concept prototype must detect the user's face and start and stop recording data automatically (we excluded push-to-talk solutions). This way a more natural solution is achieved with clear advantages for people with motor limitations.

5.2 Architecture

The system follows the architecture of traditional VSR systems [1,14,27] and takes the advantages of the Kinect One Camera to extract the features from the lips and chin of the user. A diagram with the main actions and modules is presented in Fig. 8.

System architecture follows the classic approach in pattern recognition, integrating feature extraction and classifiers, and is divided into 4 main blocks (Activity Detection, Feature Extraction, Classification and Data Base Creator). There are 2 modes: training and testing/real use. In training mode features extracted are stored in a database, and used to train the classifiers. The test path is the one where the system is used to control the VLC. It cannot be used without a previously creating the database and training the classifiers.

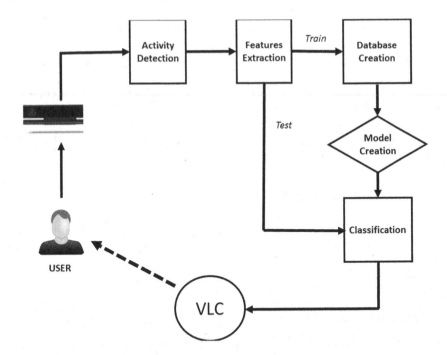

Fig. 8. A diagram illustrating the main modules of the prototype and how they are used. There are 2 modes: training and testing/real use. In training mode features extracted are stored in a database, used to train the classifiers.

5.3 Activity Detection

The first step is the Activity Detection. In this step the system searches for the face of the speaker, when found (with Microsoft Kinect SDK), a rectangular box is drawn surrounding the face of the user from every frame that arrives from the Kinect Camera. The SDK provides additional information like if the speaker is happy, wearing glasses, if the right or left eye is closed etc., as shown in Fig. 9.

For the acquisition to start right from the start of the word, the following process was adopted: first the user has to have the face and lips stable for around one second. Then, the system informs the speaker that it is ready to record a word by displaying a text message and making the window background green in order to be easier for the speaker to see this state change. In the state of Ready to Record, the system starts recording as soon as the speaker opens his mouth (information obtained with Kinect SDK [20]). This is used as an indication that the speaker may utter a command. With the same approach, the system stops recording when the speaker has the face and lips stable for at least one second.

5.4 Features

To build our system we selected the position of the lips and chin as the features for our classifier.

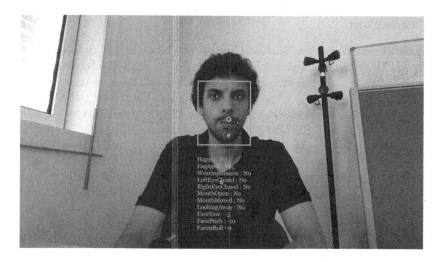

Fig. 9. Face detection by Kinect and other speaker information shown.

In more detail, we extract the position of the lips given by the distance between the upper and lower lip (height) and the distance between the left and right corners (width), the protrusion of the lips (upper lip and bottom lip) and the chin position (x and y coordinates). The position of the lips was chosen because it has proven to give good results in previous works [1]. The chin position was added because of the role of the lower jaw in the human speech production process. To obtain these 6 features we used Kinect SDK, namely the `HighDetailFacePoints` in `Kinect20.face.lib` [21] (Fig. 10).

In order to deal with the different distances between the speaker and the recording device a z-score normalization is applied. To facilitate the Classification stage, we assume a fixed length of 2 s for feature vectors (resulting in feature vectors of 60 dimensions at a 30 fps recording rate).

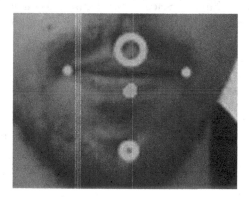

Fig. 10. Points tracked in mouth and chin for feature extraction.

5.5 Classifiers

In terms of classifiers, the Support Vector Machine (SVM), Random Forest, Sequential Minimal Optimization (SMO), AdaBoost and Naive Bayes algorithms available in Weka [34] were evaluated, offline, with databases recorded using the train path of the developed system. We used a linear Kernel for the SVM classifier. This initial list of classifiers resulted from the authors' previous experience in classification tasks in SSI and speech segmentation, such as [26].

As the speed of the algorithm is mandatory for real usage, three classifiers were chosen based in performance and speed in those evaluations: Random Forest, SMO and Naive Bayes Algorithms.

A Winner Take All approach was adopted to combine the decision of these 3 classifiers.

6 Evaluation

Besides evaluating the influence of each classifier and how the distance of the user to the Kinect affected the results, evaluation not included in this paper, the prototype was also tested live with three users. This first evaluation consisted in classifying a word in real time for VLC controlling purposes and was aimed at getting some more insight regarding the system performance to inform future improvements. Speaker dependency of the system was also tested, training the system with a database recorded for one speaker and testing with another. Information regarding participants, databases recorded for training and obtained results are presented in the next subsections.

6.1 Participants

Three persons participated in the evaluation of the system: (a) one of the authors, an Engineering post-graduate student, 23 years old, male; (b) a 22 year old male, also a student of the same course; and (c) a 29 years old female with an MSc in Gerontology and a PhD in Science and Health Technologies, natural from Madeira island, Portugal, and speaking with the regional accent.

6.2 Databases for Training

To train the classifiers to be used in the live evaluation, five different databases were created: 3 databases for Speaker 1 (each recorded at a different distance – 0.6 m, 1 m and 2 m away from the Kinect Camera); 1 database for Speaker 2; and 1 database for Speaker 3. Speakers 2 and 3 recorded at 1 m from the Kinect camera. The databases were recorded at a research lab in low noise conditions. Speaker 1 recorded all the databases without producing audible speech (silent speech) and Speakers 2 and 3 recorded the databases pronouncing the words.

6.3   Results for the Live Evaluation

Live evaluation consisted in classifying a word in real time for VLC controlling purposes. The first tests were performed in matching conditions of test and train regarding speaker and distance (i.e., same speaker and distance in test and database used for training). After, the effect of distance was assessed followed by some speaker dependency tests, assessing if the developed system could perform well when trained with data from other speakers.

Matching Conditions

The results obtained, in terms of hits and misses of the commands are presented in Table 2. Different distances were tested for Speaker 1 since 3 databases were recorded for him.

Table 2. Performance of the system in live evaluation with 3 speakers in matched conditions (test and train using data recorded for the same speaker and distance).

Test speaker	Distance (m)	Hit	Miss	Hit (%)
Speaker 1	0.6	52	28	65.0
	1	44	36	55.0
	2	56	24	70.0
Speaker 2	1	46	34	57.5
Speaker 3	1	25	55	31.3

The best result was achieved for Speaker 1 at a distance of 2 m away from the Kinect, with 70% of correctly detected commands (hits). Speaker 3 had the worst results, possibly influenced by her accent.

Effect of User's Distance to the Kinect

To test the distance dependency, Speaker 1 tested at 2 different distances with classifiers trained with databases recorded at other distances. The following combinations were used: the speaker at 0.6 m from the Kinect and the classifiers trained with the data at 1 m and 2 m; the speaker at 1 m from the Kinect and train data recorded at 0.6 m and 2 m. The results can be seen in Table 3.

The results show evidence that the distance is not an issue (the hits are similar to the ones obtained in Table 2) and show that distance normalization is capable of handling the different user-Kinect distances of a typical AAL scenario.

In Table 3 the best live performance of this work was obtained (81.3%) with the Speaker at 1 m from the Kinect and the training database recorded at 2 m.

Table 3. Effect of mismatch in distance between live test conditions and the databases used to train the system classifiers, for Speaker 1.

Speaker distance (m)	Classifiers trained with (m)	Hit	Miss	Hit (%)
0.6	1	42	38	52.5
	2	44	36	55.0
1	0.6	49	31	61.3
	2	65	15	**81.3**

Speaker Dependency

To finish the evaluation, the speaker dependency of the system was tested. The objective was to understand if the system can be used by an user that has no training data. In other words, if the system can perform with Speaker X, in the Test part, against Speaker Y's data uses for training.

Three tests were made: Speaker 1, at 1 m from the Kinect, with classifiers trained with the databases of Speaker 2 and Speaker 3; Speaker 2, at 1 m from the Kinect, but using classifiers trained with Speaker 1's database, also at 1 m. The results are presented in Table 4.

Table 4. Results regarding speaker dependency tests. Tests by Speaker 1 and 2 with classifiers trained with databases of other speakers.

Tested by	Train database	Hit	Miss	Hit (%)
Speaker1	Speaker 2	14	66	17.5
	Speaker 3	12	68	15.0
Speaker 2	Speaker 1	17	63	21.3

The results shown that the system's accuracy decreases dramatically in comparison to the results obtained for test and train with the same speaker. Analyzing the results presented in Table 4, we can conclude that the system is clearly speaker dependent.

7   Conclusion

In AAL scenarios, means are often needed to control media applications in noisy environments, such as a living room. Thus, this paper describes a first working SSI prototype for Portuguese, potentially relevant for older adults, which allows the control of a media player application at multiple distances using (silent) speech, with promising results.

The developed prototype is divided into the following parts: activity detection (automatic recording based on the movement of the lips), feature extraction, train of classifiers, classification and integration with VLC player. The Microsoft Kinect for Windows was used to capture visual information of the face.

Three different adults, with different ages, genres and accents, tested the system. Using different databases with recordings from each of them, we evaluated different distances between the Kinect and the user, as well as speaker dependency of our solution. The system revealed good performance in real time control of VLC, with an accuracy of 81.3% and 1.3 s taken to perform a classification.

The results show some variation among the users that participated in the study. Some pronounce the words slowly with hyper articulation, others pronounce them fast with small movements of the lips. The system performs better if the words are correctly articulated during all the repetitions and if the words are correctly recorded during the 2 s available to extract the features from the lips and chin. The effect of distance of the speaker was also tested, proving not to be an issue in terms of the system's accuracy.

7.1 Future Work

In terms of future work there are several open possibilities, starting by the control of other relevant applications for AAL scenarios, such as Skype, Youtube, Facebook or Spotify.

Despite the good performance, improvements can be made to the process of command detection, to start recording, and use of a fixed recording time, contributing to an even more natural usage.

The developed system is speaker dependent. Even though it is already useful in many scenarios, and the recording of data for a new speaker is quite simple, evolution to a speaker independent system should be considered.

The evaluation reported, even though it serves the purpose of informing further development of the system, is quite limited. Extended evaluation is needed, and should be implemented to enable a more thorough evaluation of the next prototypes, first with non-elderly and, as soon as system is robust enough, with elderly.

The system created is a Visual Speech Recognition system, non-invasive and non-obtrusive. However, it would be interesting to create and evaluate a multimodal system combining the features used in the created prototype with features from other phases of the humans speech production.

Acknowledgements. Research partially funded by IEETA Research Unit funding (UID/CEC/00127/2013) and Marie Curie Actions IRIS (ref. 610986, FP7-PEOPLE-2013-IAPP). Samuel Silva acknowledges funding from FCT grant SFRH/BPD/108151/2015. The authors also thank the participants in the evaluation.

References

1. Abreu, H.: Visual speech recognition for European Portuguese. Master thesis, Universidade do Minho (2014)
2. Bradski, G., Kaehler, A.: Learning OpenCV: computer vision with the OpenCV library. O'Reilly Media, Inc. (2008)
3. Brumberg, J.S., Nieto-Castanon, A., Kennedy, P.R., Guenther, F.H.: Brain-computer interfaces for speech communication. Speech Commun. 52(4), 367–379 (2010). http://dx.doi.org/10.1016/j.specom.2010.01.001
4. Dalka, P., Bratoszewski, P., Czyzewski, A.: Visual lip contour detection for the purpose of speech recognition. In: Proceedings of the International Signals and Electronic Systems (ICSES) Conference, pp. 1–4, September 2014
5. De Smedt, K.: 11 computational models of incremental grammatical encoding. In: Computational Psycholinguistics: AI and Connectionist Models of Human Language Processing, pp. 279–307 (1996)
6. Denby, B., Schultz, T., Honda, K., Hueber, T., Gilbert, J.M., Brumberg, J.S.: Silent speech interfaces. Speech Commun. 52(4), 270–287 (2010)
7. Freitas, J., Candeias, S., Dias, M.S., Lleida, E., Ortega, A., Teixeira, A., Orvalho, V.: The IRIS project: a liaison between industry and academia towards natural multimodal communication. In: Proceedings of the IberSPeech. Las Palmas, Spain (2014)
8. Freitas, J., Teixeira, A., Sales Dias, M., Silva, S.: An Introduction to Silent Speech Interfaces. Springer, Heidelberg (2016)
9. Freitas, J., Teixeira, A., Bastos, C., Dias, M.: Towards a multimodal silent speech interface for European Portuguese. In: Speech Technologies, pp. 125–149. InTech (2011)
10. Freitas, J., Teixeira, A., Dias, M.S.: Towards a silent speech interface for portuguese. In: Proceedings o the Biosignals, pp. 91–100 (2012)
11. Freitas, J., Teixeira, A., Dias, M.S.: Multimodal silent speech interface based on video, depth, surface electromyography and ultrasonic doppler: data collection and first recognition results. In: International Workshop on Speech Production in Automatic Speech Recognition (2013)
12. Freitas, J., Teixeira, A.J., Dias, M.S.: Multimodal corpora for silent speech interaction. In: LREC, pp. 4507–4511 (2014)
13. Frisky, A.Z.K., Wang, C.Y., Santoso, A., Wang, J.C.: Lip-based visual speech recognition system. In: Proceedings of the International Security Technology (ICCST) Carnahan Conference, pp. 315–319, September 2015
14. Galatas, G., Potamianos, G., Makedon, F.: Audio-visual speech recognition incorporating facial depth information captured by the kinect. In: 2012 Proceedings of the 20th European Signal Processing Conference (EUSIPCO), pp. 2714–2717. IEEE (2012)
15. Gokturk, S.B., Yalcin, H., Bamji, C.: A time-of-flight depth sensor-system description, issues and solutions. In: Conference on Computer Vision and Pattern Recognition Workshopp, CVPRW 2004, pp. 35–35. IEEE (2004)
16. Henry, P., Krainin, M., Herbst, E., Ren, X., Fox, D.: Rgb-d mapping: using kinect-style depth cameras for dense 3D modeling of indoor environments. Int. J. Robot. Res. 31(5), 647–663 (2012)
17. Lanaria, V.: VLC, the world's most popular media player, turns 15 years old: here's why you should download it now (2016)
18. Levelt, W.J.: Models of word production. Trends Cogn. Sci. 3(6), 223–232 (1999)

19. Matsumoto, M.: Silent speech decoder using adaptive collection. In: Proceedings of the Companion Publication of the 19th International Conference on Intelligent User Interfaces, IUI Companion 2014, ACM, New York, pp. 73–76 (2014). http://doi.acm.org/10.1145/2559184.2559190

20. Microsoft: Face tracking (2016). https://msdn.microsoft.com/pt-pt/library/dn782034.aspx

21. Microsoft: high detail face points (2016). https://msdn.microsoft.com/en-us/library/microsoft.kinect.face.highdetailfacepoints

22. Oikonomidis, I., Kyriazis, N., Argyros, A.A.: Efficient model-based 3D tracking of hand articulations using kinect. In: BmVC, vol. 1, p. 3 (2011)

23. Porbadnigk, A., Wester, M., p Calliess, J., Schultz, T.: Eeg-based speech recognition impact of temporal effects. In: 2nd International Conference on Bio-inspired Systems and Signal Processing (Biosignals 2009) (2009)

24. Rabiner, L., Juang, B.H.: Fundamentals of speech recognition. Prentice hall, Englewood Cliffs (1993)

25. Rao, R.A., Mersereau, R.M.: Lip modeling for visual speech recognition. In: Proceedings of the Conference on Signals, Systems and Computers Record of the Twenty-Eighth Asilomar Conference vol. 1, pp. 587–590, 1 October 1994

26. Rodriguez, Y.L., Teixeira, A.: On the detection and classification of frames from European Portuguese oral and nasal vowels. In: Proceedings of the FALA 2010 (2010)

27. Saenko, K., Darrell, T., Glass, J.R.: Articulatory features for robust visual speech recognition. In: Proceedings of the 6th International Conference on Multimodal Interfaces, ICMI 2004, ACM, New York, pp. 152–158 (2004). http://doi.acm.org/10.1145/1027933.1027960

28. Sahni, H., Bedri, A., Reyes, G., Thukral, P., Guo, Z., Starner, T., Ghovanloo, M.: The tongue and ear interface: a wearable system for silent speech recognition. In: Proceedings of the 2014 ACM International Symposium on Wearable Computers, ISWC 2014, ACM, New York, pp. 47–54 (2014). http://doi.acm.org/10.1145/2634317.2634322

29. Seikel, J.A., King, D.W., Drumright, D.G.: Anatomy and physiology for speech, language, and hearing. Delmar Learning, 4th edn. (2009)

30. Teixeira, A., Almeida, N., Pereira, C., Silva, M., Vieira, D., Silva, S.: Applications of the multimodal interaction architecture in ambient assisted living. In: Dahl, D. (ed.) Multimodal Interaction with W3C Standards: Towards Natural User Interfaces to Everything, pp. 271–291. Springer, New York (2016)

31. TeraRanger: Time-of-flight principle (2016). http://www.teraranger.com/technology/time-of-flight-principle/

32. Wand, M., Koutn, J., et al.: Lipreading with long short-term memory. In: 2016 IEEE International Conference on Acoustics, Speech and Signal Processing (ICASSP), pp. 6115–6119. IEEE (2016)

33. Werda, S., Mahdi, W., Hamadou, A.B.: Lip localization and viseme classification for visual speech recognition. arXiv preprint arXiv:1301.4558 (2007)

34. Witten, I.H., Frank, E., Hall, M.A.: Data Mining - Practical Machine Learning Tools and Techniques, 3rd edn. Morgan Kaufmann, San Francisco (2011)

35. Yargic, A., Dogan, M.: A lip reading application on MS Kinect camera. In: 2013 IEEE International Symposium on Innovations in Intelligent Systems and Applications (INISTA), pp. 1–5. IEEE (2013)

A Pilot Interface Evaluation Combined with Three-Dimensional Holography Concept for the Older Adults

Wang-Chin Tsai[1(✉)], Cheng-Min Tsai[2], Hui-Jiun Hu[3], and Kuang-Chih Lo[1]

[1] Department of Product and Media Design, Fo Guang University, Jiaoxi, Yilan, Taiwan
{wachtsai,kclo}@fgu.edu.tw
[2] Department of Creative Product Design and Management, Far East University, Tainan, Taiwan
ansel.tsai@gmail.com
[3] Department of Visual Arts, National Chiayi University, Chiayi, Taiwan
momo@mail.ncyu.edu.tw

Abstract. Due to the rapid growth in the number of elderly people, more and more attention should be paid to interactive products for the elderly. Furthermore, the number of interactive products is increasing because of the development of different display and touch technology. The physiological and psychological degeneration of the elderly could influence the floating display and touch operational ability. The main purposes of this study is to investigate the aging characteristics of the elderly and to develop new guidelines for three-dimensional holography and floating interface design from the concept of welfare and entertainment design. We recruited 30 older adults users (age over 65 years) for this study. Fifteen were randomly assigned to an active Intervention group and were given 3D hologram device rotation operation, and 15 were assigned to a group that used the 2D HoloAD device model rotation operation. 2 series of rotational objects (sphere and cuboid) also constructed and simulated to confirm the performance and feedback during the usage stage. Finally, the results provide insights for related float display and control interface design and develop forming a welfare design perspective.

Keywords: 3D holography · Older adults · Evaluation

1 Introduction

Digital technologies are becoming ubiquitous in everyday life. There is also a trend towards the use of the technology through mobile devices such as smart phones and handheld tablet devices rather than via laptops and personal computers [2]. Access to information and services can be acquired at almost any time and everywhere. However, a large group of people do not engage with these developments. Older adults are now widely understood to be an extremely diverse group and do not uniformly conform to technology averse stereotypes [5]. However, there is reported to be greater fear and anxiety associated with using related technology, and in addition, their assessment of their own skills and abilities, with both using and learning to use them, is generally lower

© Springer International Publishing AG 2017
J. Zhou and G. Salvendy (Eds.): ITAP 2017, Part I, LNCS 10297, pp. 388–396, 2017.
DOI: 10.1007/978-3-319-58530-7_30

than for other age groups. Therefore, use of technology for older people can often be more dependent on the availability of training, and also there seems to be a pragmatic assessment of whether the technology will provide specific desired utility and of the relationship between the perception of this and the perceived difficulty of learning [6].

Moreover, older people have been considered high entertainment users after retirement. Older adults spend far more time watching television than reading newspapers, and they watch more television than any other age group. Of all mass entertainment, television series or shows appears to have the highest credibility. Older viewers are major consumers of television shows, preferring entertainment shows to other programming. At the same time, the elderly are increasingly among the most enthusiastic consumers of new media information. The Cole study also suggested that higher percentages of elderly people than teens use the particular technology. Barnard (2013) suggest that the mobile technology is becoming a functional alternative to future society for many [3]. Many interaction techniques exist in virtual reality (VR) to support 3D manipulations (i.e. 3D elements translations and rotations), such as World-in-Miniature, Virtual Hand or Go-Go techniques are popular in current daily lives for multimedia [1]. More advanced forms of interaction include tangible interfaces such as the Hinckley's puppet and the Cubic Mouse. The above technologies needed not only to find better ways to introduce digital technologies to currently excluded potential users(older adults), but also to improve the design of digital interface in such a way that they are easy to use [4], As information and services are increasingly becoming exclusively accessible via the technology, it is important to understand the reasons why older people have the perception that digital technologies are difficult to use [7, 8], and that some perceive that they are not capable of learning how to use them. In this research, we specifically focus on one of current brand new interaction concept via 3D holography techniques in which involved to manipulate 3D objects for the deeper understanding of entertainment field.

2   Related Works

2.1   3D Holographic Projection

The potential applications of three-dimensional (3D) digital holograms are enormous. In addition to arts and entertainment, various fields including biomedical imaging, scientific visualization, engineering design, and displays could benefit from this technology. For example, creating full-sized organs for 3D analysis by doctors could be helpful, but it remained a challenge owing to the limitation of hologram-generation techniques. 3D holograms, which often appear in science fiction films, are a familiar technology to the public, but holograms in movies are created with computer graphic effects. Methods for creating true 3D holograms are still being studied in the laboratory. For example, due to the difficulty of generating real 3D images, recent virtual reality (VR) and augmented reality (AR) devices project two different two-dimensional (2D) images onto a viewer to induce optical illusions.

2.2 Types of Holography

A hologram is a recording in a two- or three-dimensional medium of the interference pattern formed when a point source of light (the reference beam) of fixed wavelength encounters light of the same fixed wavelength arriving from an object (the object beam). When the hologram is illuminated by the reference beam alone, the diffraction pattern recreates the wave fronts of light from the original object. Thus, the viewer sees an image indistinguishable from the original object. There are many types of holograms, and there are varying ways of classifying them. For our purpose, we can divide them into two types: reflection holograms and transmission holograms.

A. The reflection hologram
   The reflection hologram, in which a truly three-dimensional image is seen near its surface, is the most common type shown in galleries. The hologram is illuminated by a "spot" of white incandescent light, held at a specific angle and distance and located on the viewer's side of the hologram. Thus, the image consists of light reflected by the hologram. Recently, these holograms have been made and displayed in color—their images optically indistinguishable from the original objects. If a mirror is the object, the holographic image of the mirror reflects white light; if a diamond is the object, the holographic image of the diamond is seen to "sparkle."

B. Transmission holograms
   The typical transmission hologram is viewed with laser light, usually of the same type used to make the recording. This light is directed from behind the hologram and the image is transmitted to the observer's side. The virtual image can be very sharp and deep. For example, through a small hologram, a full-size room with people in it can be seen as if the hologram were a window. If this hologram is broken into small pieces (to be less wasteful, the hologram can be covered by a piece of paper with a hole in it), one can still see the entire scene through each piece. Depending on the location of the piece (hole), a different perspective is observed. Furthermore, if an undiverged laser beam is directed backward (relative to the direction of the reference beam) through the hologram, a real image can be projected onto a screen located at the original position of the object.

C. Integral holograms
   A transmission or reflection hologram can be made from a series of photographs (usually transparencies) of an object—which can be a live person, an outdoor scene, a computer graphic, or an X-ray picture. Usually, the object is "scanned" by a camera, thus recording many discrete views. Each view is shown on an LCD screen illuminated with laser light and is used as the object beam to record a hologram on a narrow vertical strip of holographic plate (holoplate). The next view is similarly recorded on an adjacent strip, until all the views are recorded. When viewing the finished composite hologram, the left and right eyes see images from different narrow holograms; thus, a stereoscopic image is observed. Recently, video cameras have been used for the original recording, which allows images to be manipulated through the use of computer software.

2.3 Future of Holography

For now, holograms are static. Recent presentations, such as CNN's special effect of a reporter appearing live from another location, and the late Tupac Shakur "appearing live" at a music festival, are not "true" holograms. However, new holographic technology is being developed that projects 3D images from another location in real time [1]. The images are also static, but they are refreshed every two seconds, creating a strobe-like effect of movement. The researchers hope to improve the technology over the next few years to bring higher resolution and faster and realistic image streaming.

3 Research Method

3.1 Participants

Forty-one older adults (65 years old) people were recruited from Yilan senior learning community centers, and the final 30 (mean age: 66.8 years; 15 female and 15 males participants) met our inclusion criteria. They were all fluent fluency in Mandarin Chinese or Taiwanese; and attend senior learning community centers for exercise or entertained class at least three times a week. Our therapists evaluated whether their physical health would allow them to participate in our study. We recruited only healthy participants because the goal of this research was to evaluate some of the negative effects of aging. Using participants who were already seriously aging or who had already developed Alzheimer's disease would have biased our experiments and their results, especially our usability test to manipulate virtual reality objects of the 2 Holographic projection devices and to continue to pay visual attention to transformed and control virtual 3D models.

All participants were fully informed and had signed a consent form. They were paid a nominal fee of NTD 300 as compensation for their time. Some researchers found that repeated exposure to the prior technology experience with would significantly affect participant performance. Therefore, the participants had not been exposed to the related visual displays in the previous test 2 weeks.

3.2 3D Holographic Projection Device and Apparatus

Our goal for this research was to find empirical evidence for age-related effects of different 3d holography devices characteristics on usability, with the overall aim of understanding how to design interface more inclusively. We sought to identify which 3d holography and content characteristics help or hinder usability, and to determine experimentally whether the effects of those characteristics differ across age groups. Little has been reported in the research literature about holography usability issues that seniors experience, and the 3d material and the interaction situation and our work seeks to take steps to fill that gap. With a view on technology adoption, we focused on the initial usability of created 3d holography device, specifically on two types of 3d material manipulated on the platform.

3.2.1   2D HoloAD Device

The main components used for the **2D HoloAD** were a monitor and a pyramid-shaped form made of reflective acrylic boards. Images in the monitor were presented, using reflection, in the interior of the pyramid form, which was composed of two right triangles as side boards and one isosceles triangle as a front board. They had a separation angle of 45° with the monitor and the ground so that the augmented images would not be distorted. We feed through software with 2D images, it will be converted to a FLV formatted file waiting to be transferred to the device (Fig. 1).

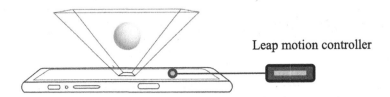

Fig. 1. 2D HoloAD device

3.2.2   3D Hologram Device

3D hologram were a monitor and a boxed-shaped form made of reflective acrylic boards. Images in the monitor were presented, using reflection, in the interior of the pyramid form, which was composed of two side boards and one isosceles rectangle as a front board. They had a separation vertical angle with the Ipad monitor and the ground so that the virtual images would not be distorted. The 3D hologram was set on a wooden box (Fig. 2).

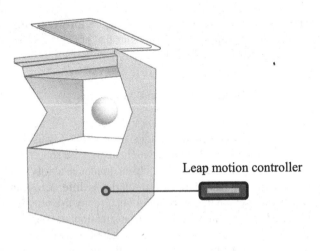

Fig. 2. 3D hologram device

3.2.3   The Leap Motion Device - Operational Characteristics

The leap motion is a kind of operational device. It should first be noted that this device, when capturing hand movement, implements a new way of detecting the human hand and a new means of gesture recognition. Distinguishing it from the Kinect sensor, the producers of Leap Motion claim that this sensor possesses sub-millimeter accuracy. In contrast to devices currently existing in the market, the Leap Motion sensor is under discussion for potential use in interaction applications in virtual interactive environments. We here further outline these features, with greater emphasis than that presented in regarding the usefulness of the Leap Motion device in capturing the configurations of human fingers. Moreover, the Leap Motion device provides a new method that is cost efficient, fast and precise in its capture and digitization of human finger movements.

3.2.4   The 2 Types of Materials

2 sets of 3d objects were used in the study; one set was needed for each of the three dimension-label conditions presented in a floating situation. Objects were selected from the most manipulated of existing basic 3d formation. Figure 3 shows a sample of these 3d objects.

Fig. 3. 3D objects as the 2 experiment materials (sphere and cuboid)

3.2.5   Eye Fatigue

CFF is an effective measure of visual fatigue. It measures the minimal number of flashes of light per second at which an intermittent light stimulus no longer stimulates a continuous sensation. As a highly sensitive and easy-to-use measure, CFF is applied here to evaluate retina functionality. A drop in CFF value reflects a drop in the sensory perception function, attributable to a decrease in alertness.

3.3   Experimental Design and Procedures

A standard experimental desk and chair were provided for experimentation. The experiment environment was standardized. Prior to the experiment each subject was instructed about the purpose and procedure of the study. The sequence of 3d object was randomized for each subject. At the beginning of each manipulated session, the performance was measured as a baseline for comparison. The subject was then asked to control the objects and rotate the star mark to the front side. When the individual found the target, she/he should move the cursor to the object and click the left button of the controller twice to respond 'hit.' The sound feedback also shown to indicate the task is complete. Both control speed performance were measured. In addition, a visual fatigue measure was also taken.

4   Results and Discussion

The summarized ANOVA results are shown in Table 1. The Holography type effect was significant on eye fatigue. The 3d object effect was significant both on control speed performance and eye fatigue. Subject effect was significant on both speed performance and eye fatigue.

Table 1. The average performance of both devices for Sphere and Cuboid objects

Type	Operation time		
	3D hologram device	2D HoloAD device	Sig.
Sphere	18.2(3.2)	23.7(4.5)	**
Cuboid	14.3(2.1)	32.6(5.2)	*
Average	17.4(4.6)	28.6(6.1)	*

4.1 Usability Performance

Control performance was measured by turning and rotating speed. Table 1 shows the average performance of control both Holography types. For the 3D hologram device the average performance time was 17.4(4.6) s. For the 2D HoloAD device the average performance time was 28.6(6.1) s and the control accuracy was 88.2%. On average, controlling the 3D hologram device took 11.2 s less than control the 2D HoloAD device. This may be attributed to the contrast and resolution of the display in a 2D HoloAD device. Also, the subjects were more used to control 3D hologram devices than 2D HoloAD devices. The results also suggest that hand gesture interactions need to be further investigated in terms of their possible advantages over 3D hologram interactions. The study suggests advantages in terms of performance for rotating over traditional tap interactions, in particular for the over 65 age group [7]. However, these differences occurred in tasks where participants had to select one item that did not share the screen with other visual interference items. Given the abundant time of some the participants' strokes when completing rotating tasks, it is unclear whether the advantages would translate to more realistic situations with multiple possible options to select on the 3d Holography device.

Our participants showed great interest in using our holography interface for testing. Many of them said that 3D holography control methods increased their motivation because they were too unlike formal experience, and that they were little care about their hand movement on the test. However, they did not worry about the real performance because the interaction process seemed more like a game, which increased their interest. They also appreciated that the sound feedback interacted with them and guided them during the experiment.

4.2   Eye Fatigue

Eye fatigue was measured by CFF. 3Dholography type had a significant influence on eye fatigue. After control the 3D hologram device, subjects' CFF had an average reduction. This reveals that controlling the 3D hologram device caused less eye fatigue than control the 2D HoloAD device. This is due to the viewing range factors, a larger display facilitated control best, bolstering the subjective assumption that larger holography displays led to better operational performance. In fact, the larger holography displays merely resulted in an improved performance for easy tasks. As rotating tasks became more difficult, smaller holography displays could be resulted in better operational performance.

4.3   Discussion and Future Work

We also found that concrete formation helped older adults, more than the sphere types, to identify objects in the outline with direction indicator for intuitive understanding. Furthermore, we found that the prior experience improved initial usability but did not help older adults. We discuss implications of these findings for designing 3d holography device that are better suited to older adults. Our findings constitute a much needed empirical foundation on age-related differences in 3d object usability and for holography design guidelines targeting older users.

Furthermore, tasks containing clue objects (cuboid) with characteristics were easier to complete than those containing obscure objects (Sphere) without characteristics. The turning-in and –rotating out gestures might solve part of the problem. The other geometry objects without obvious characteristics to facilitate guidance may be one plausible solution [8], but this would require further research.

This research presented the fundamental concept to evaluate and design of an integrated interface that displays "holographic" 3D objects for older adults, allows direct hand-based interaction with the visualized objects, while the older user feels virtual feedback from the objects. This concept will furthermore enable other ways of interaction with more different formation type and feedback factors, such as feedbacks sounds or animation effects affecting the real environment, as well as the real workspace being shadowed by the virtual objects. The next phase of the project will involve the implementation of the designed interface including dynamic, interactive and augmented reality operation, software development, as well as its extensive testing by older users and improvement of the entertainment field based on the holographic feedback received.

Acknowledgements. The authors hereby extend sincere thanks to Ministry of Science and Technology (MOST) of the Republic of China (ROC) for their financial support of this research, whose project code is MOST 105-2410-H-431-013. It is thanks to the generous patronage of MOST that this study has been smoothly performed.

References

1. Argelaguet, F., Anduja, C.: A survey of 3D object selection techniques for virtual environments. Comput. Graph. **3**(37), 121–136 (2013)
2. Baker, P.M.A., Bricout, J.C., Moon, N.W., Coughlan, B., Pater, J.: Communities of participation: a comparison of disability and aging identified groups on Facebook and LinkedIn. Telematics Inform. **30**, 22–34 (2013)
3. Barnard, Y., Bradley, M.D., Hodgson, F., Lloyd, A.D.: Learning to use new technologies by older adults: perceived difficulties, experimentation behaviour and usability. Comput. Hum. Behav. **4**(29), 1715–1724 (2013)
4. Bergé, L., Dubois, E., Raynal, M.: Design and evaluation of an "around the smart phone" technique for 3D manipulations on distant display. In: Paper presented at the Proceedings of the 3rd ACM Symposium on Spatial User Interaction (2015)
5. Czaja, S.J., Lee, C.C.: Information technology and older adults. In: The Human-Computer Interaction Handbook: Fundamentals, Evolving Technologies and Emerging Applications, 2nd edn., pp. 777–792. Lawrence Erlbaum Associates, New York (2007)
6. Hayes, M., van Stolk-Cooke, K., Muench, F.: Understanding Facebook use and the psychological affects of use across generations. Comput. Hum. Behav. **49**, 507–511 (2015)
7. Hu, C., Lin, H., Chen, L.: The effects of screen size on rotating 3D contents using compound gestures on a mobile device. Displays **41**, 25–32 (2016)
8. Knoedel, S., Hachet, M.: Multi-touch RST in 2D and 3D spaces: studying the impact of directness on user performance. In: Proceedings of the 2011 IEEE Symposium on 3D User Interfaces (3DUI), pp. 75–78 (2011)

Personalized Computer Access for People with Severe Motor Disabilities

AsTeRICS, FlipMouse and the Two-Level Personalization Software Engineering Method

Chris Veigl[1,2(✉)], Martin Deinhofer[2], Benjamin Aigner[2], and Klaus Miesenberger[1]

[1] Institute Integriert Studieren, Johannes Kepler University, Linz, Austria
[2] University of Applied Sciences (UAS) Technikum Wien, Vienna, Austria
{veigl,deinhofe,aignerb}@technikum-wien.at

Abstract. As capabilities, preferences and needs of people with disabilities are unique, personalization of ICT-based Assistive Technology (AT) tools is a key factor for their applicability. We developed a set of open source tools for **Component-Based Engineering** which allows an efficient prototyping, parameterization and application of user-driven AT. These tools include the AsTeRICS framework for creation of AT-applications from functional components via visual programming and the FlipMouse universal input system for finger- or mouth control of computers, tablets and smart phones. We present a conceptual framework for a user-centered **Two-Level Personalization** of AT which consists of a development phase, where a solution is modeled and refined in cooperation with a client, and a generalization phase to make this solution configurable via specific parameters which can be tuned when supporting other users in comparable contexts. Experience from customization is then used to improve more generic AT-solution-templates. This fosters a fast and cost-effective development of tailored support for people with disabilities. In this paper we describe in detail the tools and workflows employed. We present a single-subject study based on **Participatory Action Research**, involving a client with multiple sclerosis, and we demonstrate the *Two-Level Personalization* for the creation and evaluation of tailored applications for this client.

Keywords: Assistive technology · Software engineering for accessibility · User centered design · Personalization · Motor disabilities · Multiple sclerosis · Human computer interface · Participative action research

1   Introduction

Disability and demographic change are challenging societies around the world and EU member states in particular [1, 2]. ICT-based Assistive Technologies (AT), eHealth services and modern smart home infrastructures can significantly increase independent living of people with disabilities, allowing them to stay longer in their own living environment. Non-standard Human-Computer Interfaces (HCIs) are required to support people with severely reduced motor capabilities like those with late-stage Multiple Sclerosis (MS),

© Springer International Publishing AG 2017
J. Zhou and G. Salvendy (Eds.): ITAP 2017, Part I, LNCS 10297, pp. 397–415, 2017.
DOI: 10.1007/978-3-319-58530-7_31

Amyotrophic Lateral Sclerosis (ALS) and Hemi- or Tetraplegia. Multiple disabilities – for example a combination of motor restriction and low vision – lead to specific challenges for the selection of adequate assistive tools. Specific needs of users in the range of movement, auditory or visual capability but also preferences and know-how in using a computing platform have to be respected. Use cases may include environmental control, Augmentative and Alternative Communication (AAC), control of specific devices, non-standard user interfaces for computer- or smartphone control and special methods for using the world-wide web or social media platforms. The current market for smart home appliances and AT offers many different products which are not standardized and lack interoperability. This significantly increases the workload for the implementation of tailored assistive solutions, which is one of the reasons why people with highly specific needs still lack in getting access to tailored AT products.

In this work, we present system components and design strategies facilitating user-driven, tailored assistive technology solutions. First we outline the research methodology and the frameworks/tools used - in particular the AsTeRICS construction set and the FlipMouse special input device. Second we introduce the *Two-Level Personalization* method for implementing personalized solutions, where an iterative user-centered design process supports reusability of implemented solutions for persons with comparable capabilities. Third, we apply and evaluate the method in a single-subject study where we develop a set of tailored assistive solutions for computer access together with a client suffering from multiple disabilities. In the final section we discuss our results and compare them with similar research. The involved software modules and hardware designs are available under open source license, inviting for reuse or modification at low cost.

2 Methods and Tools for Personalization

2.1 User Centered Design: Participatory Action- and Single-Subject Research

For the creation and evaluation of the assistive tools developed in this study, we applied user-centered design (UCD) methodologies, in particular the Singe-Subject Research and Participatory Action Research (PAR) paradigms. UCD is often used when ICT solutions are modeled according to individual needs, see for example [19, 20]. The principles of PAR imply that all participants of a study or project are considered as stakeholders or experts and are directly involved in the formative evaluation and indirectly involved in the system/software development process. Researchers and clients are engaged in an equitable relationship where the aim is to solve a problem and generate new knowledge [17, 18]. Single-Subject Research is a method for the development of evidence-based practice in fields with highly individual challenges and research questions, where quantitative measures involving a high number of participants are not possible or feasible [16].

2.2 Component-Based Development for Assistive Technology: AsTeRICS

The Assistive Technology Rapid Integration and Construction Set (AsTeRICS, [3]) was co-developed by the authors together with 9 partnering institutions in course of a collaborative research project funded by the EU-commission under the 7th Framework Program (FP-7). The AsTeRICS framework consists of a Java/OSGI middleware (the AsTeRICS Runtime Environment, ARE), a graphical editor (the AsTeRICS Configuration Suite, ACS) and a set of more than 160 bundles ("plugin"-components) for a flexible creation of assistive solutions [13]. These components are classified into 3 categories: sensors, processors and actuators. Sensors monitor the environment and transmit input information to other components of a model. Processors are responsible for receiving, processing and forwarding this information. Finally, actuators receive data and carry out desired actions [5]. The components expose input- and output ports for data and events and can be connected via the ACS. In the AsTeRICS framework, a model is considered as the container that holds connected components and produces a specific functionality. The runtime environment features dedicated services and communication interfaces (the so-called ASAPI protocol and a RESTful API) which expose functionalities for model management, for example transferring models from ACS to ARE and vice versa, starting and stopping models, modification of parameters of running models, storage and many more. The main components of the AsTeRICS architecture are shown in Fig. 1. For a full description of the capabilities of the API and the xml schema for the model files please refer to [3].

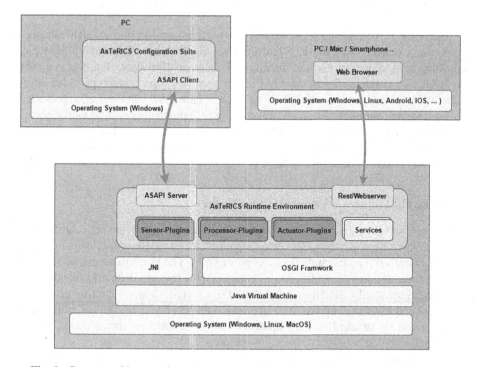

Fig. 1. System architecture, key components and interfaces of the AsTeRICS framework

Examples for sensor components include computer vision (head- and eye-tracking), interfaces to bioelectric amplifiers or simple momentary switches. Actuators include mouse/keyboard/joystick emulation and home automation equipment – for example KNX, enOcean or FS20. An example for the graphical creation of models using the AsTeRICS Configuration Suite (ACS) is depicted in Fig. 2.

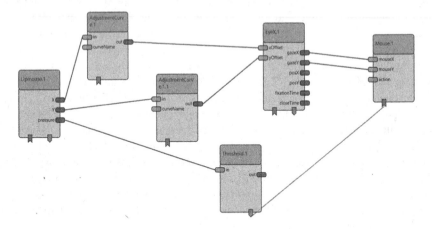

Fig. 2. Construction of an AsTeRICS model using the ACS editor

In course of the ongoing Prosperity4All (P4All) project [4], the AsTeRICS framework was extended with the RESTful interface [6] for controlling model lifecycle, adjusting plugin properties and receiving events or live data. Furthermore, the AsTeRICS Packaging Environment (APE) has been developed, which provides infrastructure to extract a particular set of AsTeRICS-based AT solutions as a dedicated source code repository. Additionally, down-stripped deployment packages can be generated for a given a set of solutions, including native installers. This allows a much better management of different customized versions of the framework which have been tailored to individual users as described in Sect. 3.

2.3   The FlipMouse – A Universal Input Device

For people who cannot move their upper limbs and are thus restricted in using standard input devices for computers, tablets or smartphones, the FLipMouse special input device has been developed by the authors of this paper [7, 8]. The FLipMouse can be actuated via low-force and low-range finger- or lip-movements (using a dedicated mouthpiece) and creates standard USB Human Interface Device (HID) reports - acting as mouse, keyboard and joystick (composite device). As shown in Fig. 3, additional momentary switches can be attached to the FlipMouse and a standard mounting option allows combination with off-the-shelf mounting solutions.

The FlipMouse offers configurable sensitivity for cursor-movement and sip- and puff activities. Up to seven configurations can be stored in the internal EEPROM of the device, which allows the user to switch e.g. from mouse to keyboard mode via a desired action. This offers increased flexibility compared to similar devices available on the market (for example the *LifeTool IntegraMouse* [14] or the *QuadJoy* mouth control device [15]). The configuration editor for the FlipMouse settings is depicted in Fig. 4. Furthermore, the device can learn and replay infrared remote commands. Via a bluetooth low energy (BLE) add-on-module, phones or tablets (including the iPad) can be controlled wirelessly. The FlipMouse can be combined with low-cost eye tracking systems (*Tobii EyeX* [9, 10], *EyeTribe* [11]) allowing significant reduction of jitter and inaccuracies of the eye tracking [5]. For a detailed description of the FlipMouse system and the configurations options please refer to [7].

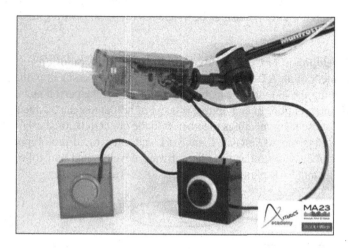

Fig. 3. The FlipMouse alternative input device with attached external switches and mounting option

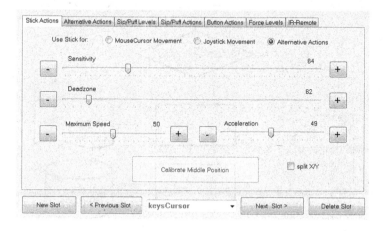

Fig. 4. The FlipMouse configuration editor (detail)

2.4   The *Two-Level Personalization* Method for SW/HW Engineering

Using the AsTeRICS framework, the FlipMouse module and - where reasonable - additional AT tools or software, tailored assistive solutions can be created rapidly. For efficient re-use and sharing of these solutions, we suggest a *Two-Level Personalization* engineering method, which fosters a stepwise refinement and customization of an assistive setup in course of participative single-subject studies, and a final generalization step where successful setups are adapted for generic parameterization. These generic versions of tailored solutions can then be re-applied for persons with similar capabilities and needs.

Level 1: Development of Configurable and Shareable AT Solutions
The development of an AT-solution starts with an initial assessment with the end user (client), querying the individual capabilities and needs of the person and deducing the goals for the intervention. In an iterative process of refinement and evaluation which is performed in subsequent meetings together with the client, a tailored assistive solution is developed using the AsTeRICS framework and other rapid prototyping tools (see Fig. 5). This process is similar to agile software development and follows the user-centered design and PAR paradigms.

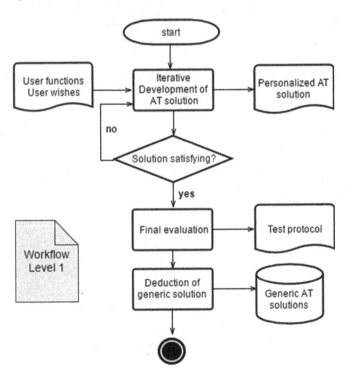

Fig. 5. *Level 1*: Iterative development of personalized AT solutions, deduction of generic solutions

The *Level-1* process yields a set of personalized AT solutions, which are evaluated against the defined goals. When a satisfying result is achieved, this solution is equipped with additional features which make it more flexible and potentially useful for other clients. For example, a small GUI or web-based user interface for changing particular settings of an existing model via the RESTful interface could be added, which allows changing essential parameters also for caretakers and non-experts. This yields the second outcome of the Level-1 process: a *generic version of the tailored solution*, which can be stored in a database for reference solutions and can be reused by the community.

Level 2: On-Demand Personalization of Generic AT Solutions
Existing AsTeRICS-based solutions which resulted from the *Level-1* development process can be picked up on-demand when a tailored solution is required for a new client with similar needs and capabilities, making personalization steps easier and more efficient. Figure 6 illustrates an ideal case where a desired personalization can be achieved solely by changing the provided system properties of a generic solution (via GUI or web interface). If this is not sufficient, model- and system modifications will be applied to the generic solution, re-entering the *Level-1* process.

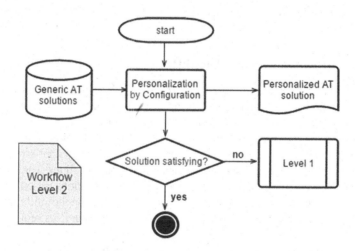

Fig. 6. *Level 2*: Personalization of existing generic solutions

2.5 The AsTeRICS Packaging Environment (APE)

The AsTeRICS Packaging Environment (APE) enables the deployment of stand-alone AsTeRICS-based AT solutions by extracting necessary resources for particular use cases from the complete framework. The resulting "stripped-down"-version of the framework contains only necessary system components (e.g. plugin jar -files, Java Runtime Environment, model- and configuration files) and specific other resources (e.g. images, icons, documentation and license files). This collection can then be hosted as a separate source code repository. Finally, deployment packages for the solution can be created. Several deployment types are supported including a compressed archive (.zip) or native installers for specific target platforms (Windows, Linux, Mac-OS). The installer also contains a native launcher which is integrated into the menu and desktop of the target platform. The installer properties (e.g. application name, version) can be defined and further customization can be done by adding a post-install script. (Please note that some plugins/ components depend on platform-specific code and thus not every AsTeRICS-based solution can be deployed to any operating system or target platform.)

Several APE-based example projects for different use-cases including bioelectric signal processing, camera-based input modalities, Smart Home integration or speech recognition have been provided in the *P4AllBuildingBlocks github-repository*[1]. They can be forked and further customized by other developers or directly be used by care-takers or end-users with IT-background. Additionally, the examples are listed on the developer space platform[2], which was created in course of the Prosperity4All project [4], allowing developers to find AT-related technologies easily.

The *AsTeRICS Ergo repository*[3] is an APE-based solution targeted for occupational therapists with low technical background. The provided simplified web-based user interfaces enable occupational therapists the creation of environmental control setups (e.g. for controlling TV, lights, etc.) for people with disabilities. Using a step-by-step wizard, the user can add remote control commands for infrared- or radio-controlled devices.

2.6 Auto-Personalization Using the GPII

The Global Public Inclusive Infrastructure (GPII) is a cloud-based infrastructure for enabling accessibility of devices and ICT by auto-personalization depending on user preferences and device characteristics [12]. Figure 7 describes the *auto-personalization flow* in GPII: First, a user approaches a device. The user listener notifies the flow manager, which retrieves the user preferences stored in the preferences server and asks the device reporter for device characteristics and installed applications. The matchmaker matches preferences, device characteristics and available solutions (installed or available in the solutions registry). Finally, the life cycle manager applies the solutions and settings using an appropriate settings handler (e.g. for the Windows registry or via a JSON configuration file).

AT solutions created with the *Two-Level Personalization* method and deployed via APE can be registered in the solutions registry so that they can be installed and config-ured by the lifecycle manager, thereby setting model parameters according to the user's preferences. For more information please refer to the GPII Wiki pages [12].

---

[1] Prosperity4All Building Blocks Repository: https://github.com/asterics/P4AllBuildingBlocks.
[2] The GPII developer space platform: http://developerspace.gpii.net/.
[3] AsTeRICS repository for occupational therapists: https://github.com/asterics/AsTeRICS-Ergo.

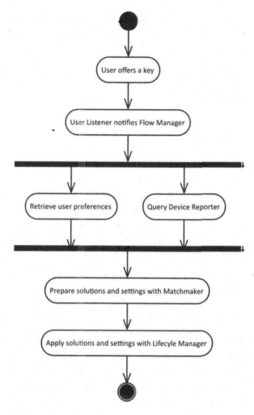

Fig.   7. The   GPII   for   Auto-personalization   flow   (https://wiki.gpii.net/w/
GPII_Architecture_Overview#The_Auto-Personalization_Flow)

3   Single-Subject Research - Evaluation and Results

In this section, the application and evaluation of the *Two-Level Personalization* concept of tailored AT-solutions involving AsTeRICS and the FlipMouse will be described. The applied methodology follows Single-Subject Research and Participatory Action Research criteria, with involvement of one client with multiple disabilities and two Assistive Technology system designers (the authors) who were responsible for the implementation of the AT solutions.

3.1   Initial Assessment

In a first meeting with the client, a holistic understanding of the person and a plan of the interventions were established. For this purpose, an interview was performed where biographic information and details about the kind of disability, personal background, motivation and goals for the ICT-based intervention and other data have been collected. Furthermore, the client read and signed the "informed consent" document which contains information about the nature of the study, his rights - including the right to withdraw from the study at any time - and a data protection agreement. (The photos used in this publication were explicitly authorized by the client.) Based on this information, a plan for the implementation of a first set of assistive solutions and a time schedule for next meetings have been created, initiating the *Level-1 Personalization* phase. The key information from this first meeting will be summarized in the following section.

3.2 Introduction of Client, Setting and Use Cases

P.K. was born 1964 and was diagnosed with multiple sclerosis in 1985. He has lived in a care center in Vienna since 2008. He can move his head and actuate his facial muscles, but no other conscious motor activity is possible. The motor control for his head is limited but precise (lateral movement about 10 cm, dorsal/caudal movement about 5 cm). There are no tremors or involuntary movements involved. P.K. speaks very silently but understandably. He has a very low vision (left eye: 7%, right eye: 12% - diagnosed in 2014 – and his vision has probably gotten worse since then).

P.K. uses a new version of the *Sicare Pilot*[4] environmental control system. The voice recognition works quite well despite P.K.'s whispering voice (commands for changing the TV channel must be repeated several times but are eventually recognized). The primary device controlled by the *Sicare Pilot* is a wide screen LCD TV. P.K. also uses an Android tablet for music playback. The tablet is paired with a stereo music player via Bluetooth. P.K. has an extensive music collection on Google Music and occasionally buys additional albums. The music playback via tablet and *Sicare Pilot* can only be used to start/stop playlists (no selection of individual albums or tracks).

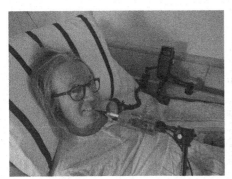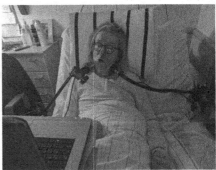

Fig. 8. P.K. using the FlipMouse input device for computer control

Goals of the Intervention
P.K. wants to use a computer for newspaper reading and for listening to music/browsing his music collection (these are the primary use cases). This would considerably increase

---

[4] *Sicare Pilot* environmental control: http://www.nanopac.com/SiCare%20Pilot%20Pro.htm.

his autonomy. If these goals can be accomplished, P.K. would also like to perform internet searches via google and browse arbitrary web pages.

3.3 Iterative Development of *Level-1* Solution

Several interaction strategies were prototyped and tested together with P.K. in course of the first three personal meetings at the care center. Each meeting took about 2–3 h and consisted of an initial interview, followed by an explanation of the planned intervention, the application of the solution and a discussion/evaluation of the advantages and disadvantages. To explore reasonable methods for interaction, the focus was first put on the less complex music player use case.

To facilitate the desired selection of music from P.K.'s music archive, a new AsTeRICS model with a basic selection interface for albums (subfolders in a music directory) was created. In the music player model, a simple graphical user interface with big buttons provides the primary functions including *next/previous folder, enter/exit subfolder, play/stop album*. The folder names and album titles were spoken by a synthetic voice. Furthermore, the 3rd-party screen reader *ZoomText*[5] (commercial software, trial version) was installed on the client's computer. Figure 9 shows the resulting GUI:

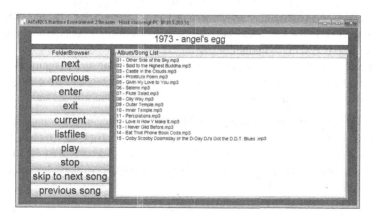

Fig. 9. First version of a GUI-based music player

The initial strategies for enabling P.K an interaction with the user interface were all based on cursor control and deduced from existing generic AsTeRICS models. These strategies were evaluated in the first 3 meetings and involved the following sensor modules:

- Face Tracking for cursor control, using the generic camera mouse model
- Blob Tracking using infrared reflection and head marker (IR-sticker)
- The FlipMouse universal input device, using standard settings for mouth control of the mouse cursor. For this purpose, the FlipMouse was mounted on a *Manfrotto*

---

[5] *Zoomtext* magnification tool and screen reader utility: http://www.zoomtext.at/.

Gelenkarm[6] with *Superclamp*[7] so that it could be precisely positioned. The client could reach the mouthpiece with his lips, the distance of the lips to the mouthpiece was about 5 mm when the client remained in his resting position. The client's bed was adjusted to allow a convenient sitting position (see Fig. 8).

The *ZoomText* screen magnification and screen reader software was configured to apply a very high screen magnification factor (5) and high contrast settings. The "mouse hover" function was activated so that the *ZoomText* screen reader speaks content/captions of UI elements which are located under the mouse cursor. Additionally a big crosshair tool enhanced the visibility of the actual cursor position and a 22" computer monitor was used as primary display. The results were evaluated using qualitative and quantitative methods (observation, recording of results and informal interview) – see Sect. 3.7. The results of the first meetings can be summarized as follows:

- The Face Tracking and Blob Tracking based input methods for cursor control could not be used efficiently: Although a conscious control of the cursor could be obtained, the range of movement was too low and the occurring problems (drifting cursor, lost positioning, etc.) were significant. The Blob Tracking method was also experienced as inconvenient because of the marker which needs to be placed on the forehead.
- Controlling the cursor with the FlipMouse worked well, by touching the mouthpiece with the lips to obtain cursor movement and using sip/puff for clicking. The cursor moved too fast in the first trials, but after reducing sensitivity/acceleration, directional movement was possible without limitation.
- The greatest problem was the low vision of P.K.: despite the high magnification factor, contrast settings and crosshair, P.K.'s visual limitations are too severe for using the GUI as a primary navigation method. The cursor-based navigation was not feasible at all.

These results of the first design iterations led to the conclusion to omit the mouse cursor control completely and create another input interface for P.K. which relies solely on keyboard input. For this purpose, the FlipMouse was reconfigured for cursor key control, so that lip- and sip/puff interactions with the mouthpiece create desired keyboard activity via the FlipMouse device.

3.4   Refinement and Finalization of *Level-1* Solution

In the subsequent meeting and customization steps, a suitable *Level-1 Personalization* was created: The AsTeRICS model for the music player functionality was modified so that it uses the KeyCapture plugin to detect key presses. Six numeric keys (*1/2/3/4/5/6*) were mapped to the music player functions and a dedicated FlipMouse configuration slot was created to send these keys directly from the FLipMouse when an interaction with the mouthpiece takes place (see Table 1).

---

[6] *Manfrotto Gelenkarm* mount: https://www.manfrotto.de/gelenkarm-2-tlg-m-2x16mm-pin.
[7] *Manfrotto Superclamp:* https://www.manfrotto.de/super-clamp-einzeln-verpackt.

Table 1. FlipMouse configuration slot for music player operation via ARE/keyboard emulation

User action (FlipMouse)	Key emulation
Up	key '*1*' - up in the folder list
Down	key '*2*' - down in folder list
Left	key '*3*' - enter subfolder
Right	key '*4*' - exit subfolder
Sip	key '*6*' - stop music playback
strongSip	Not used
Puff	key '*5*' - start music playback
strongPuff	switch to browser/newsreader control (slot 2)

Integrating the Newsreader Use Case

To address the second use case (browser control for reading newspapers on the internet), a second FlipMouse configuration slot was created. This configuration maps the mouthpiece interaction of the user to cursor keys and other special keys which are useful for navigating web pages via a standard web browser with screen reader support (for example skipping to next link/sentence or displaying the bookmark menu – which also places the keyboard focus into the bookmark menu) – see Table 2. The FlipMouse configurations can be switched (from music player to news reader function and vice versa) via a strong puff activity into the mouthpiece. The music player function remains active in the background during newspaper reading. Furthermore, the AsTeRICS model was modified to automatically start the Firefox web browser after system boot. As screen reader solution, the free *NVDA*[8] application replaced the commercial *ZoomText* software which was not necessary anymore because the visual feedback and magnification settings did not yield useful results in the prior trials.

Table 2. FlipMouse configuration slot for newspaper reader/browser control

User action (FlipMouse)	Key emulation
Up	*cursor up* key - go to previous paragraph (*NVDA*)
Down	*cursor down* key - go to next paragraph (*NVDA*)
Left	*shift+tab* key - go to previous link
Right	*tab* key - go to next link
Sip	*alt+left* to go back to previous page
strongSip	*ctrl+b* - to display or hide the bookmark menu of *Firefox*
Puff	*enter* - to follow current link
strongPuff	switch to music player control (slot 1)

Summary of the Finalized Tailored Setup:

- The FlipMouse is utilized as primary interaction aid (two configuration slots for keyboard key creation which can be changed via a strong puff action).

---

[8] *NVDA* screen reader application: https://www.nvaccess.org/.

- *NVDA* screen reader used for auditory feedback.
- The ARE and *NVDA* are started automatically after login. There is no login password so that the menu appears immediately after system startup.
- The primary task of the AsTeRICS model is to capture the keys which are necessary for the music player
- Only one AsTeRICS model is used. The application launcher plugin automatically starts the Firefox browser when AsTeRICS is loaded at system startup.

Utilized Hardware for this Personalized Solution:

- Windows10 laptop (Medion low-cost laptop with Intel Celeron CPU)
- FlipMouse v2.4 with acrylic case[9]
- Mounting solution: *Manfrotto Gelenkarm+Superclamp*
- Adjustable table with wheels for laptop and FlipMouse
- Total hardware cost for this solution: about € 650

3.5 Deduction of Generalization Parameters for *Level-2* Solution

To make the music player applicable in other contexts and for other users, specific parameters were exposed so that they can be adjustable via a dedicated web-based GUI. This GUI can be accessed by any ICT-device with an internet browser. The GUI allows changing the desired keys for using the media player and the root folder for the music archive (see Fig. 10). Thus, different alternative input devices (e.g. momentary switch interface boxes or commercial mouth-control devices) can be supported.

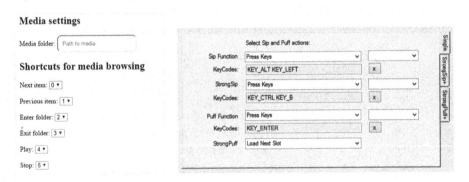

Fig. 10. Settings dialog for generic parameters of the media player use case (left), FlipMouse editor: sip/puff settings for key emulation (right)

For the newsreader use case, a flexible mapping of user activity to system action is already possible via the FlipMouse GUI configuration editor. Several different mappings can be stored in form of FlipMouse configuration files and these files can be provided via the public source code repository together with the *Level-2* AsTeRICS models and other resources. Thus, the utilized keyboard actions for the newsreader use case (e.g.

---

[9] FlipMouse construction kit homepage: http://www.asterics-academy.net/tools/flip.

---

ctrl+b to display or hide the bookmark menu of the Firefox browser) can be provided also for other web browsers or operating system technologies.

3.6 Utilized Quality Indicators for Single-Subject Research

Horner, Carr and colleagues defined a number of quality indicators for Single-Subject Research in special education (see [16]). These quality indicators consider the description of participants and settings, characterization of variables, baseline measures, validity of experimental control and other factors. Although not all quality criteria are applicable for the given study, we present a number of criteria which have been addressed in the evaluation of the tailored assistive solution in Table 3.

Table 3. Quality indicators for the applied Single-Subject Research/evaluation of solutions

Quality indicator	Implementation
Description of participant and physical setting	See Sects. 3.2 and 3.3
Description of the dependent variables	Following dependent variables have been measured repeatedly during user meetings: Task-attainment: success/error ratio Time-to-complete task in seconds Usability-for-client (UFC): low–high
Description of the independent variables	Following independent variables were taken into account and were documented: AT-solution input variant (see Sect. 3.3) Zoom factors for screen magnification Voice selection for screen reader FlipMouse settings: thresholds for sensitivity/key selection/sip- and puff user actions Seating position/tool mounting and orientation
Baseline measures	The baseline conditions were measured in terms of existing capabilities of the user to interact with his environment and ICT-based devices in particular
Experimental control	Results and experimental effects of seven user meetings have been documented and validated
External validity	Until the time of this writing, external validity was only checked with subjects without similar disabilities. This remains to be done
Social validity	Social importance is given by raising self-efficiency, autonomy and communication capabilities of the client. The implementation is cost efficient by using affordable open source tools

3.7 Task Evaluation and Usability Rating

In course of 7 meetings with P.K. at the care center, the assistive solutions have been evaluated along different criteria. The Task-attainment was derived as *successful to unsuccessful trials*. (The trial was successful if a desired task could be performed without help at the first time). The tasks were randomly selected from a list of interactions necessary for the music player- and newspaper reader AT solutions (in course of one session, every task was performed):

- select artist folder, change into artist folder
- select album folder, change into album folder
- play/stop music playback
- exit folder
- switch to newspaper reader functions/switch back to music player
- set input focus to bookmark menu (web browser)
- select desired link in bookmark menu
- skip to next heading/link in news article
- follow link (open new page)/go to previous page

After a trial session, the user was interviewed and he rated usability criteria of the assistive solution. The rated criteria included "ease of use", "efficiency" and "would like to keep solution". In the first 3 sessions, different input variants were evaluated; as expected, the usability was rated low in the first trials where the client could not utilize the provided interaction solutions in a reasonable way. During the 3rd session, the Flip-Mouse-based key input variant in combination with NVDA screen reader (as described in Sect. 3.3) was introduced and this method proved to be useable. In sessions 4 to 7, significant improvements in the client's efficiency using this solution were gained, and the client reported improved usability ratings. In the last evaluation session, about 75% of the tasks could be performed correctly at the first try, and the task completion time decreased to several seconds, indicating that the client learned to use the interaction method more and more efficiently (see Table 4).

Table 4. Evaluation of different solutions in course of 7 user meetings, usability rating

#	Input-method/tools	Evaluated use case	Time to complete	Ease of use	Like to keep?
1	Mouth-based cursor control	Music player	n.a.	Low	No
2	Facetracking based cursor control	Music player	n.a.	Medium	No
3	Blob-Tracking based cursor control	Music player	n.a.	Low	No
4	Flipmouse for key input +NVDA	Music player	~30 s	High	Yes
5	Flipmouse for key input +NVDA	Music player +newsreader	~15 s	High	Yes
6	Flipmouse for key input +NVDA	Music player +newsreader	~10 s	High	Yes
7	Flipmouse for key input +NVDA	Music player +newsreader	~7 s	High	Yes

4   Discussion

In this article, we demonstrate the *Two-Level Personalization* concept for participatory design of assistive solutions in cooperation with end users, which utilizes open source tools and rapid prototyping strategies. In course of a single-subject study, the AsTeRICS graphical construction set was combined with the FlipMouse special input device and 3rd party software to support a client with severely reduced visual and motoric capabilities. Several alternative HCI variants for controlling music player- and newspaper reader applications were prototyped and evaluated, including computer-vision-based cursor control and cursor control via lip movements. An efficient solution which allows the client controlling music player and news reader by key inputs created via the Flip-Mouse was found after 3 meetings and was further evaluated.

In related literature, several systems for computer vision-based mouse cursor control involving head- or eye-tracking are described [5, 10, 21, 22]. Such approaches are hardly applicable for people with low vision. For the client who participated in this study, even high screen magnification and contrast settings did not enable reasonable cursor control via visual feedback, which also prohibited the use of commercial mouth- or lip-controlled input devices [14, 15]. On the other hand, screen readers and supportive tools for people with low vision or blind people often rely on complex interaction via the keyboard and different keyboard shortcuts for navigation. This makes it difficult for people with limited motor control to use such interfaces.

We demonstrated the iterative customization of a suitable unique interaction strategy for our client, which could be achieved with minimal effort and without the need for writing additional programming code, by combining AsTeRICS and the FlipMouse with the *NVDA* screen reader and a standard internet browser. In a final generalization step, useful parameters of the music player solution were exposed to a web-based configuration GUI which allows the application of this use case also for other users and in combination with other special input devices.

In the future, further improvements of the tailored solution are planned, for example adding the possibility to perform a restart or shutdown of the computer via dedicated interaction with the mouthpiece. Quantitative measures of the task completion time will be recorded and evaluated. Furthermore, we would like to test the solutions with other clients and evaluate the parametrization and usability in more detail together with persons who have a non-technical background (e.g. caretakers). Finally, we plan to share the generic solutions in a public repository.

In general this research demonstrates a path how personalization of AT could be implemented at a larger scale by (a) taking care for user involvement and user centered design (Participatory Action Research), (b) reducing technical complexity and efforts through employing Component Based Development, (c) fostering reusability through a *Two-Level Personalization* approach allowing generalization of components and AT solutions through parametrization and (d) sharing components, know-how and solutions. The use cases we worked on proved the viability of the approach but also made clear that more research is needed to improve usability for practitioners without having a strong IT background. More training for therapists and care personnel is needed so that personalization can become an integral part of everyday service provision. This demands for an organizational shift of focus towards using the potential of personalized AT at a larger scale. AT must not be seen as an external resource to be ordered but more as a solution to be built with the users in the service process, based on shared components and know-how. This shift in return would also lead to more and better components featuring increased adaptability through parametrization.

Acknowledgement. This work has been supported by the European Commission as part of the Prosperity4All EU project (Seventh Framework Programme, grant agreement no 610510), and by the Municipal Department 23 of the City of Vienna (Economic Affairs, Labour and Statistics - MA 23) in course of the ToRaDes project (18th Call "Competence Teams for Research and Teaching").

References

1. European Commission: The 2015 ageing report - economic and budgetary projections for the 28 EU Member States (2013–2060), Brussels (2015)
2. Eurostat: Population and social conditions: percentual distribution of types of disability by sex and age group. http://epp.eurostat.cec.eu.int. Accessed 02 Feb 2017
3. AsTeRICS project homepage. http://www.asterics.eu. Accessed 01 Dec 2016
4. Prosperity4All project homepage. http://www.prosperity4all.eu. Accessed 01 Dec 2016
5. Veigl, C., David, V., Deinhofer, M., Aigner, B.: Online offset correction of remote eye tracking data: a novel approach for accurate gaze-based mouse cursor control. In: 7th ICT Innovation Conference, Ohrid, Mazedonia (2015)
6. Komodromos, M., Mettouris, C., Achilleos, A., Papadopoulos, G., Veigl, C., Deinhofer, M., Doppler, A., Schuerz, S.: A runtime middleware for enabling application integration and rapid re-engineering. In: 15th International Conference on Intelligent Software Methodologies, Tools and Techniques, Lamaca, Cyprus (2016)
7. Aigner, B., David, V., Deinhofer, M., Veigl, C.: FlipMouse - a flexible alternative input solution for people with severe motor restrictions. In: 7th International Conference on Software Development and Technologies for Enhancing Accessibility and Fighting Info-Exclusion, 1–3 December 2016. UTAD, Vila Real (2016)
8. FlipMouse project homepage. http://www.asterics-academy.net/tools/flip. Accessed 06 Dec 2016
9. Tobii Gaming homepage. https://tobiigaming.com. Accessed 06 Dec 2016
10. Vazquez-Li, J., Pierson Stachecki, L., Magee, J.: Eye-gaze with predictive link following improves accessibility as a mouse pointing interface. In: Proceedings of the 18th International ACM SIGACCESS Conference on Computers and Accessibility, ASSETS 2016. ACM, New York (2016). doi:10.1145/2982142.2982208
11. Dalmaijer, E.: Is the low-cost EyeTribe eye tracker any good for research? PeerJ PrePrints **2**, e585v1 (2014). https://doi.org/10.7287/peerj.preprints.585v1
12. Raising the floor: the Global Publi Inclusive Infrastructure – GPII. http://gpii.net. Accessed 06 Dec 2016
13. García-Soler, A., Diaz-Orueta, U., Ossmann, R., Nussbaum, G., Veigl, C., Weiss, C., Pecyna, K.: Addressing accessibility challenges of people with motor disabilities by means of AsTeRICS: a step by step definition of technical requirements. In: Miesenberger, K., Karshmer, A., Penaz, P., Zagler, W. (eds.) ICCHP 2012. LNCS, vol. 7383, pp. 164–171. Springer, Heidelberg (2012). doi:10.1007/978-3-642-31534-3_25

14. LifeTool IntegraMouse Plus. http://www.lifetool.at/assistive-technology/lifetool-developments/integramouse-plus.html. Accessed 20 Jan 2017

15. Quadjoy Hands-Free Mouth Mouse. https://quadjoy.com. Accessed 23 Jan 2017

16. Horner, R., Carr, E., Halle, J., McGee, G., Odom, S., Wolery, M.: The use of single-subject design research to identify evidence-based practice in special education. Except. Child. **71**(2), 165–179 (2004)

17. Lindgren, H., Baskar, J., Guerrero, E., Nieves, J.C., Nilsson, I., Yan, C.: Computer-supported assessment for tailoring assistive technology. In: Proceedings of the 6th International Conference on Digital Health (2016). doi:10.1145/2896338.2896352

18. Jansson, M., Mörtberg, C., Mirijamdotter, A.: Participation in e-home healthcare @ North Calotte. In: Proceedings of the 5th Nordic Conference on Human-Computer Interaction: Building Bridges, Lund, Sweden (2008). doi:10.1145/1463160.1463181

19. Dorrington, P., Wilkinson, C., Tasker, L., Walters, A.: User-centered design method for the design of assistive switch devices to improve user experience, accessibility, and independence. J. Usability Stud. **11**, 2 (2016)

20. Torsi, S., Nasr, N., Wright, P.C., Mawson, S.J., Mountain, G.A.: User-centered design for supporting the self-management of chronic illnesses: an interdisciplinary approach. In: Proceedings of the 2nd International Conference on PErvasive Technologies Related to Assistive Environments, PETRA 2009. ACM, New York (2009). doi:10.1145/1579114.1579157

21. Manresa-Yee, C., Varona, J., Perales, F.J., Negre, F., Muntaner, J.J.: Experiences using a hands-free interface. In: Proceedings of the 10th International ACM SIGACCESS Conference on Computers and Accessibility, Assets 2008. ACM, New York (2008). doi:10.1145/1414471.1414528

22. Epstein, S., Missimer, E., Betke, M.: Using kernels for a video-based mouse-replacement interface. Pers. Ubiquitous Comput. (2014). doi:10.1007/s00779-012-0617-z

Digital Literacy and Training

The Positive and Negative Impact of an Intergenerational Digital Technology Education Programme on Younger People's Perceptions of Older Adults

Lisbeth Drury, Ania Bobrowicz[(✉)], Lindsey Cameron, and Dominic Abrams

University of Kent, Canterbury, UK
{l.drury,a.bobrowicz,l.cameron,d.abrams}@kent.ac.uk

Abstract. In order to meet the technological needs of older adults, and ensure digital inclusion, it is important for digital technology designers to accurately assess and understand older adults' needs and requirements, free from the influence of societal assumptions of their capabilities. This study evaluated the impact of an intergenerational digital technology education programme on younger adults' stereotypes of older people. Using an experimental design, results show that compared to a control group, students taking part in the programme subsequently rated older adults as more friendly but less competent. Practical implications for developing intergenerational education programmes are discussed.

Keywords: Older adults · Attitudes · Stereotypes · Digital technology · Intergenerational education programmes

1 Introduction

Although digital technologies have become all pervasive in our increasingly connected digital society, many older adults, aged 65 and above, remain digitally excluded or digitally dismissive; this is despite the general acknowledgement that the internet is important and will become a 'way of life' for more and more people [1]. According to the 2015 report by Foresight, UK Government Office for Science, the rise of digital technologies has been 'a double-edged sword for older people' [2]. On the one hand, digital technologies provide access to local resources and services which national authorities, local authorities and businesses increasingly make available online only. On the other hand, several key barriers to successful engagement with technologies still exist: a lack of understanding and confidence in how digital technologies work, a lack of skills to make the best use of available resources, and the affordability of technologies. Some studies also highlight the fact that digital technologies are not being adopted more widely by the older generation because of a lack of perceived usefulness [3, 4]. This has significant implications for the design community, in particular young digital technology designers, both in terms of technologies they will be designing in the future and the design methods at their disposal which could be used to design digital solutions for those who are not particularly interested in the outcome [4].

© Springer International Publishing AG 2017
J. Zhou and G. Salvendy (Eds.): ITAP 2017, Part I, LNCS 10297, pp. 419–428, 2017.
DOI: 10.1007/978-3-319-58530-7_32

There are social, economic and moral reasons for ensuring technology is appropriately designed for use by older adults [5]. Firstly, it is important that technology is usable by, and accessible to, older adults. Technology is an important tool to support older adults' independence, allowing them to live in their own homes for longer, therefore postponing or avoiding a need for residential social care. Secondly, increasing numbers of active older adults have more free time, therefore offering the technology industry lucrative new product development opportunities. Lastly, moral obligation and legislation (UK Disability Discrimination Act, 1995, and more recently the Equality Act 2010) require that systems are accessible to people with disabilities, who are in many cases older adults. Although technology design often adopts a 'user-centered' approach, it is argued that young designers may find it easier to design technology for a user more similar to themselves and experience difficulties understanding the potential impact of technology on the day-to-day lives of older adults [6]. This gap in understanding can lead to the design of technology based on designers', sometimes patronising, interpretation of older adults needs [5].

The young generation of millennials, which relies on instant communication, social networking, sharing of digital information and informal and rapid connectivity, differs from the older generation in their attitudes towards, purpose for and use of digital technologies. Therefore, there is a need for young digital technology designers to be able to examine and engage with viewpoints of the users of digital technology that they will be designing in future, including older users. Educators are presented with a particular challenge: how to design intergenerational education programmes which help to convey the diverse life experiences and expectations of older users to the technologically literate young generation who are very comfortable with everyday use of digital technologies, but who may lack the understanding of digitally disengaged or digitally dismissive users [7].

1.1 Stereotypes of Older People

Across many western cultures old age is perceived as a time of illness, frailty and dependency [16, 17]. Such prevalent negative age stereotypes can have a detrimental effect on the treatment older adults receive. For example, older workers often experience discrimination in the workplace [18, 19], which can be linked to negative stereotypes such as a lower aptitude to learn, less flexibility and a resistance to change [20]. However, older adults can also be stereotyped positively and can be seen as more moral and wiser than younger adults [21, 22].

These mixed positive and negative representations of older adults can be captured by the stereotype content model [23] which proposes that people from all social groups are evaluated along two independent dimensions: warmth (or friendliness) and competence. Older adults are viewed as warm (positively stereotyped) but incompetent (negatively stereotyped), resulting in a generalised view that they are 'doddering but dear' [24]. This mixed stereotype can result in patronizing, benevolent attitudes and behaviours towards older adults [23] and, in some cases, lead older adults to confirm and internalize negative age stereotypes [25, 26]. One method of reducing stereotyped views of older adults is via increased social contact between generations [27].

Older adults are negatively stereotyped about their ability to interact with new technology [28]. A study invited participants (aged 18 to 72 years old) to rate the skills and abilities perceived as typical of either adults in their 20s or their 60s. Stereotypes rated as typical of younger, but not older adults included learning new skills, using new computer technology (e.g. smartphones), and using social media (e.g. Facebook). Age stereotypes of this nature are likely to hinder the development of technology required by older adults, and may also be strengthened during intergenerational programmes that focus on technology design.

1.2   Intergenerational Education Programmes

For students whose future career may involve addressing the needs of older adults, many educational courses employ intergenerational teaching strategies to provide education and positive intergenerational contact experiences, which also have a positive effect on attitudes towards older adults [8]. Interest in intergenerational programmes which bring together the older population and younger generation with an aim to share experiences, educate, support and engage with each other in the context of digital technologies has been growing steadily in recent years. In 2015 Kaplan et al. conducted a survey of intergenerational technology-focused programmes, which considered the conceptual and practical applications of connecting younger and older generations in the technological domain [9]. Tentative conclusions from this preliminary study indicate that technology can be seen as a powerful tool for intergenerational collaboration and that an increase in digital inclusion may lead to a decrease in social isolation and exclusion.

Intergenerational programmes can bring younger and older people together resulting in positive outcomes. A review of intergenerational case studies across the United Kingdom led by the Beth Johnson Foundation documented a network of over 850 organisations and practitioners who are actively involved in delivering intergenerational programmes [10]. Specifically, studies of intergenerational programmes in education (including technology) generally point to a positive impact such programmes have had on the participants, such as fostering more positive attitudes toward older adults [11]; improving older people's sense of self-worth, health and well-being [12]; improving classroom atmosphere [13], and a higher overall level of social integration [14].

However, a study of intergenerational programmes in Ireland found that while such programmes attract a wide variety of organisations, including public, private and non-for-profit bodies and involve participants from different generations, there is a need to better understand intergenerational practice and involve research institutions in their evaluation [15]. Importantly, one potential drawback of such programmes, particularly those that focus on tasks or areas where older adults are less skilled, is that they run a risk of reinforcing negative age stereotypes by focusing on areas where adults need help, thus they could unintentionally reinforce the impression of older people as incompetent - digital technology is one such context.

1.3 Digital Technology as a Negatively Stereotyped Context

Research shows that intergenerational contact reduces negative attitudes and stereotypes about older adults [29, 30, 31, 32]; including the stereotype that older adults are incompetent [33]. However, it is possible that when the task or context of intergenerational contact highlights or confirms negative old age stereotypes, especially those around dependency or incompetence, this may increase rather than decease stereotypes in this area. Little is known about the effects of intergenerational contact in negatively stereotyped contexts, such as digital technology. Identification of effective training programmes for technology design for older users is essential, and robust evaluation of the impact of such programmes is critical, including their impact on stereotypes of older people.

2 Study Aims

The aim of this study is to evaluate an intergenerational education programme for digital technology students by assessing the degree to which it impacts students' stereotypes of older adults. Whilst contact with older people should improve the participants' perceptions of older adults as friendly, this type of intervention, in a domain where older adults are stereotyped as less competent, risks an increase in the young adults' perceptions of older adults as incompetent.

2.1 Hypothesis

It is hypothesised that compared to a control group who did not take part in the intergenerational education programme, experimental participants who interact with older adults in the negatively stereotyped context will report higher warmth stereotype ratings of older adults but lower competency stereotype ratings.

2.2 Methods

Participants. Participants were eighty-four digital technology students at a University in South East England. The average age of the students was M_{age} 20.42 ($SD = 2.87$). Thirty-nine were males, thirty females and fifteen did not indicate their gender. All participants voluntarily completed paper questionnaires in class. Fifty-one participants had taken part in the intergenerational programme (intervention condition). This consisted of two intergenerational informal but loosely structured conversations, focusing on technology, and was completed as part of their coursework. Thirty-three participants that had not taken the coursework module formed the control group. The data were collected from two waves of the module that was repeated over two consecutive academic years. The final sample consisted of twenty-nine participants from the 1st wave (2014/2015) and fifty-five participants from the 2nd wave (2015/2016). The average age of older adults that took part as conversation partners was 71.52 years old, 41% were male, 45% were female and the gender of 14% of older participants was not identified.

2.3   Design and Procedure

An experimental design was used in which the independent variable was intergenerational contact. Participants were either in the experimental group that experienced contact with older adults as part of the programme or a control group that did not take part in the programme. The dependent variables were stereotypes; warmth and competence.

Participants in the experimental group were instructed to conduct two independent informal guided conversations with an older adult, either face-to-face or via SKYPE. The aim of the conversation was to build rapport with the older adults, share each other's experience of using technology, and identify potential barriers and frustrations. The students recorded and transcribed the conversations, then conducted analysis as instructed by the coursework brief. Both the guidelines for the conversation and the analysis featured focus on variables that had previously been identified as important moderators or facilitators of the successful effects of intergenerational contact on reduced ageism [27]. These conversations therefore focused on the following aspects: common goals, cooperation, institutional support, equal status, good quality contact, self-disclosure, story-telling, shared humour, avoiding incompetency stereotypes, challenging stereotypes, empathy, perspective taking and common in-group identities. Having conducted the conversations, the experimental group submitted their coursework via a Virtual Learning Environment (VLE), after which all participants responded to the stereotype measures.

The participants were informed that participation was voluntary, anonymous and did not form part of their coursework. Full ethical approval for the study was sought and granted.

2.4   Measures

Normative age stereotypes.   In order to measure respondents' awareness of commonly held perceptions of older people participants were asked "What does society in general think of older adults? As viewed by society…" followed by seven items "How competent/confident/ independent/competitive/warm/good natured/sincere are older adults?" on a 7-point scale ($1 = not\ at\ all$, $7 = very\ much$).

Maximum likelihood confirmatory factor analysis was conducted in SPSS to explore the warmth and competence components of the age stereotype measure. This resulted in two factors with an eigenvalue above 1. Together the factors accounted for 60.6% of the variance and a varimax orthogonal rotation showed all items loaded onto one of the two factors, accounting to 31.2% (warmth) and 29.5% (competency) respectively. A chi-square goodness of fit test was non-significant X^2 (8) 5.82, p = .668, indicating the factors are independent of each other. A rotated matrix showing the factor loadings of the items are displayed in Table 1. Items were averaged to create two indices of warmth stereotypes and competence stereotypes.

Table 1. Varimax rotated factor matrix for stereotype warmth and competence factors.

Items	Factor	
	Warmth	Competence
Competent		.89
Confident		.58
Independent		.50
Competitive		.41
Good natured	.82	
Warm	.74	
Sincere	.74	
Cronbach's alpha	.81	.67

2.5   Results

Descriptive statistics To examine whether participants rated older adults as warm or competent one-sample t tests were conducted comparing the mean values to the midpoint (3.5) of the scale responses. The results showed that participants rated older adults as both warm ($M = 4.97$, $SD = 0.96$) t (83) 13.96, $p < .001$, and ($M = 3.88$, $SD = 0.99$) competent t (83) 3.47, $p = .001$. A paired sampled t test was computed to examine the difference in ratings of warmth and competence, revealing that the participants rated older adults as higher in warmth ($M = 4.97$, $SD = 0.96$) than competence ($M = 3.88$, $SD = 0.99$), t (83), –7.31, $p < .001$. Warmth and competence ratings were uncorrelated $r = .02$, $p = .870$).

Inferential statistics To examine attitudinal differences between the experimental and control conditions independent sample t tests were conducted. The experimental group reported higher ratings of warmth stereotypes ($M = 5.18$, $SD = 1.01$) than the control group ($M = 4.64$, $SD = 0.80$), t (82) –2.61, $p = .011$, $d = .59$ and lower ratings of competence stereotypes ($M = 3.69$, $SD = 0.94$) than the control group ($M = 4.16$, $SD = 1.01$), t (82) 2.20, $p = .031$, $d = .48$. Therefore, in line with the study hypotheses, participants who had taken part in the course reported more warmth stereotypes, and less competence stereotypes towards older adults compared to the control group.

3   Discussion

Our study found that compared with the students who did not participate, those students who took part in the intergenerational education programme, in which they conducted conversations with older adults about technology use, subsequently rated older adults higher on warmth (friendliness) stereotypes but lower on competence stereotypes[1]. This

---

[1] Participants' age, gender and prior contact with older adults was also measured and analysed. The results showed that these variables had no relation to participants' stereotypes of older adults and therefore could not be responsible for effects on the outcome of the programme.

suggests that as a result of the programme, students perceived older adults as more friendly but less competent.

The findings are consistent with research showing that intergenerational contact [29] and intergenerational programmes [10, 27] can have a positive impact on impressions of older people. In the case of the current research, an intergenerational education programme boosted perceptions of older people as being 'warm', thus confirming a commonly held positive age stereotype [24]. However, finding that the intergenerational programme increased perceptions of older adults as incompetent, is divergent from other intergenerational contact literature. Tasipoulou and Abrams' analysis of national survey data showed that the more friendships young adults had with older adults the less they agreed that competence declines with age [34]. Findings from the current study however, suggest that in contexts where negative age stereotypes of older adults [31] are salient, or when older adults confirm negative stereotypes about competence, this has a detrimental effect on perceptions of older adults' competence. Therefore, intergenerational contact in these situations exacerbates the already negative societal stereotype of older adults' capabilities [24]. It is noteworthy that students' perceptions of warmth and competence in the current study are not correlated. This demonstrates that the same intergenerational contact experience has independent effects of two outcomes that vary in favourability. This finding is divergent from other intergenerational contact research, which shows an overall positive effect on positive and negative stereotypes [30, 31, 32].

In summary, the findings point to a potential pitfall of some intergenerational education programmes: when the focus is on an area of weakness for older people, such as digital technology, programmes run the risk of strengthening negative stereotypes of older people as being incompetent [24]. Future intergenerational contact research should compare programmes that vary only in the degree to which they highlight negative stereotypes in order to isolate and confirm these effects.

A psychological process that may have contributed to negative effects of the current intergenerational education programme, and others that highlight negative age stereotypes, is that the older adults themselves may have responded to the stereotype. It is possible that discussing technology with a younger adult could have induced a stereotype threat in the older adults. Stereotype threat occurs when an individual is anxious they may confirm a negative stereotype about their social group in a situation linked to that stereotype, and subsequently underperform on the stereotype relevant task [35]. Research shows that both explicit and subtle cues about negative age stereotypes are sufficient to have a detrimental effect on older adults' cognitive and physical performance [25]. In this case, discussing technology with younger adults may have implicitly highlighted the stereotype that older adults are viewed as poor technology users compared to younger adults, resulting in anxiety and less confidence in engaging with the subject.

4   Limitations

The research has some limitations that may impact on the conclusions that can be derived from the current findings. In particular, the number of competence-related items and warmth-related items was unbalanced, which could have led to biasing effects. However, because an average score was used in all analyses, such a biasing effect is unlikely. Additionally, a higher number of participants would improve the robustness of this study. However, because the hypothesis was based on a well-supported theory [37] and reliable measures were employed we are confident in our findings and outcomes.

5   Practical Implications for Educators

In order to include older adults in a society with rapidly changing technology and increase their use of technology it is important that technology is designed with their needs in mind. However, the present research highlights that focusing on these needs presents a problem. On the one hand, the findings demonstrate how intergenerational contact in technology-learning programmes can have a positive effect on perceptions of older adults' friendliness, yet have a negative impact on perceptions of their competence.

Future intergenerational education programmes should aim to counterbalance the detrimental effects of intergenerational contact within negatively stereotyped contexts. For example, experimental research in which young adults collaborated with older adults on tasks at which older adults are stereotypically more proficient, resulted in those young adults being more pro-social in their attitudes and behaviours compared with young adults working on other tasks, or with younger partners [38]. Further studies should examine if highlighting older adults' abilities mitigate the detrimental effects of inter-generational contact in negatively stereotyped contexts.

The results highlight that it is important to be aware that user-centered design strategies involving intergenerational contact (e.g. conversations or interviews) have the potential to increase incompetence perceptions of older adults. In turn, this may hamper young designers' abilities to create technology that fully meets the needs of older adults, by encouraging patronising assumptions of older adults' interaction with, and needs for, technology [5].

These findings underscore the importance of evaluating intergenerational education programmes, as suggested by Finn & Scharf [15]. Comparing outcomes of programme groups to control groups is an important design aspect that helps identify effects attributable directly to the programme. For a review of best practice for intergenerational programmes see [28].

Acknowledgements. This research was supported in part by an Economic and Social Research Council/Age UK CASE award (ES/J500148/1) to the first author. Thanks go to Elizabeth Hunt and Georgina Parker for their assistance with data collection and input.

References

1. Age UK: Introducing another world: older people and digital inclusion (2009). http://www.ageuk.org.uk/professional-resources-home/research/reports/work-and-learning/archive/

2. Foresight: How are attitudes and behaviours to the ageing process changing in light of new media and new technology? How might these continue to evolve by 2025 and 2040? (2015). https://www.gov.uk/government/uploads/system/uploads/attachment_data/file/455176/gs-15-17-future-ageing-attitudes-new-technology-er08.pdf

3. Melenhorst, A.S., Rogers, W.A., Bouwhuis, D.G.: Older adults' motivated choice for technological innovation: evidence for benefit-driven selectivity. Psychol. Aging **21**(1), 190–195 (2006). doi:10.1037/0882-7974.21.1.190

4. Coleman, G.W., Hanson, V.L., Gibson, L., Bobrowicz, A., McKay, A.: Engaging the disengaged: how do we design technology for digitally excluded older adults? Des. Interact. Syst. **2010**, 175–178 (2010). doi:10.1145/1858171.1858202

5. Eisma, R., Dickinson, A., Goodman, J., Syme, A., Tiwari, L., Newell, A.F.: Early user involvement in the development of information technology-related products for older people. Univ. Access Inf. Soc. **3**(2), 131–140 (2004). doi:10.1007/s10209-004-0092-z

6. Keates, S., Clarkson, P.J.: Defining design exclusion. In: Keates, S., Langdon, P., Clarkson, J., Robinson, P. (eds.) Universal Access and Assistive Technology, pp. 13–22. Springer, London (2002)

7. Batchelor, R., Bobrowicz, A.: Empathic and ethical design of technology. In: Stephanidis, C., Antona, M. (eds.) UAHCI 2014. LNCS, vol. 8513, pp. 3–10. Springer, Cham (2014). doi: 10.1007/978-3-319-07437-5_1

8. Levy, S.R.: Toward reducing ageism: PEACE (Positive Education about Aging and Contact Experiences) model. Gerontologist, pii: gnw116. [Epub ahead of print], 1–7 (2016). http://doi.org/10.1093/geront/gnw116

9. Kaplan, M., Sanchez, M., Bradley, L.: Conceptual frameworks and practical applications to connect generations in the technoscope. Anthropol. Aging **36**(2), 182–205 (2015)

10. Hatton-Yeo, A. (ed.): Intergenerational Practice: An Introduction and Examples of Practice (2006). www.ucllouvain.be/cps/ucl/doc/aisbl.../DocPart_Terrain_UnitedKingdomPractice.pdf

11. Knapp, J.L., Stubblefield, P.: Changing students' perceptions of aging: the impact of an intergenerational service learning course. Educ. Gerontol. **26**(7), 611–621 (2000). doi: 10.1080/03601270050200617

12. Park, A-La: The effects of intergenerational programmes on children and young people. Int. J. Sch. Cogn. Psychol. **2**(1), 1–5 (2015)

13. Castro, J.L., González, D.A., Aguayo, I.H., Fernández, E.A.: Perceptions concerning intergenerational education from the perspective of participants. Educ. Gerontol. **40**(2), 138–151 (2014). doi:10.1080/03601277.2013.802182

14. Montoro-Rodriguez, J., Pinazo, S.: Evaluating social integration and psychological outcomes for older adults enrolled at a university intergenerational programme. J. Intergenerational Relat. **3**(3), 65–81 (2005). doi:10.1300/J194v03n03_05

15. Finn, C., Sharf, T.: Intergenerational programmes in Ireland: an initial overview (2012). https://www.ageaction.ie/sites/default/files/attachments/mapping_report_november_2012_web.pdf

16. Levy, B.R., Slade, M.D., May, J., Caracciolo, E.A.: Physical recovery after acute myocardial infarction: positive age self-stereotypes as a resource. Int. J. Aging Hum. Dev. **62**(4), 285–301 (2006). doi:10.2190/EJK1-1Q0DLHGE-7A35

17. Marques, S., Lima, M.L., Abrams, D., Swift, H.J.: Will to live in older people's medical decisions: immediate and delayed effects of aging stereotypes. J. Appl. Soc. Psychol. **44**, 399–408 (2014). doi:10.1111/jasp.12231

18. Gringart, E., Helmes, E., Speelman, C.P.: Exploring attitudes toward older workers among Australian employers: an empirical study. J. Aging Soc. Policy **17**, 85–103 (2005). doi: 10.1300/J031v17n03_05

19. McCann, R., Giles, H.: Ageism in the workplace: A communication perspective. In: Nelson, T.D. (ed.) Ageism, Stereotyping and Prejudice Against Older Persons, pp. 163–199. MIT Press, Cambridge (2002)

20. Posthuma, R.A., Campion, M.A.: Age stereotypes in the workplace: common stereotypes, moderators, and future research directions. J. Manage. **35**(1), 158–188 (2009). doi: 10.1177/0149206308318617

21. Abrams, D., Russell, P.S., Vauclair, M., Swift, H.: Ageism in Europe: Findings from the European Social Survey. Age UK, London (2011)

22. Levy, B.: Improving memory in old age through implicit self-stereotyping. J. Pers. Soc. Psychol. **71**(6), 1092–1107 (1996). doi:10.1037/0022-3514.71.6.1092

23. Fiske, S.T., Cuddy, A.J.C., Glick, P., Xu, J.: A model of (often mixed) stereotype content: Competence and warmth respectively follow from perceived status and competition. J. Pers. Soc. Psychol. **82**(6), 878–902 (2002). doi:10.1037/0022-3514.82.6.878

24. Cuddy, A.J.C., Norton, M.I., Fiske, S.T.: This old stereotype: the pervasiveness and persistence of the elderly stereotype. J. Soc. Issues **61**(2), 267–285 (2005). doi:10.1111/j.1540-4560.2005.00405.x

25. Lamont, R.A., Swift, H.J., Abrams, D.: A review and meta-analysis of age-based stereotype threat: negative stereotypes, not facts, do the damage. Psychol. Aging **30**(1), 180–193 (2015). doi:10.1037/a0038586

26. Levy, B.: Stereotype Embodiment: A Psychosocial Approach to Aging. Curr. Dir. Psychol. Sci. **18**(6), 2–337 (2009)

27. Drury, L., Abrams, D., Swift, H.J.: Intergenerational Connections. Age UK, London (in press)

28. Abrams, D., Swift, H.J., Drury, L.: Old and unemployable? How age-based stereotypes affect willingness to hire job candidates. J. Soc. Issues **72**(1), 105–121 (2016). doi:10.1111/josi.12158

29. Drury, L., Hutchison, P., Abrams, D.: Direct and extended intergenerational contact and young people's attitudes towards older adults. Br. J. Soc. Psychol. **55**(3), 522–543 (2016). doi: 10.1111/bjso.12146

30. Schwartz, L.K., Simmons, J.P.: Contact quality and attitudes toward the elderly. Educ. Gerontol. **27**(2), 127–137 (2001). doi:10.1080/03601270151075525

31. Hale, N.M.: Effects of age and interpersonal contact on stereotyping of the elderly. Curr. Psychol. **17**(1), 28–38 (1998). doi:10.1007/s12144-998-1019-2

32. Hawkins, M.: College students' attitudes towards elderly persons. Educ. Gerontol. **22**(3), 271–279 (1996)

33. Abrams, D., Eller, A., Bryant, J.: An age apart: The effects of intergenerational contact and stereotype threat on performance and intergroup bias. Psychol. Aging **21**(4), 691–702 (2006)

34. Tasiopoulou, K., Abrams, D.: Ageism in Britain. Age Concern England, London (2006)

35. Steele, C.M., Aronson, J.: Stereotype threat and the intellectual test performance of African Americans. J. Pers. Soc. Psychol. **69**(5), 797–811 (1995)

36. Swift, H.J., Lamont, R.A., Abrams, D.: Are they half as strong as they used to be? An experiment testing whether age-related social comparisons impair older people's hand grip strength and persistence. BMJ Open **2**(3), e001064 (2012)

37. Pettigrew, T.F., Tropp, L.R.: A meta-analytic test of intergroup contact theory. J. Pers. Soc. Psychol. **90**(5), 751–783 (2006). doi:10.1037/0022-3514.90.5.751

38. Kessler, E.M., Staudinger, U.M.: Intergenerational potential: Effects of social interaction between older adults and adolescents. Psychol. Aging **22**(4), 690–704 (2007). doi: 10.1037/0882-7974.22.4.690

Playful Method for Seniors to Embrace Information Technology

Jeanette Eriksson[✉]

Malmö University, Nordensköldsgatan 1, 205 06 Malmö, Sweden
jeanette.eriksson@mah.se

Abstract. Digital technology is everywhere today. People who cannot handle digital technology risk to be excluded from the information society. This article reports on how older seniors living in a residential home or participate in day care activities can be introduced to digital technology by playing games. The research was done in close cooperation with seniors and staff from one residential home and two day care centers. The research applied Design Science Research methodology to create a method of how to introduce digital technology to seniors, and to make a game together with the seniors and the staff. In parallel with the research, an implementation process was realized to make digital technology a natural part of the seniors life.

Keywords: Digitalization · Seniors · Residential home · Games · Design science research · Method

1 Introduction

In 2060 the population of senior people in the European Union is expected to be next to one third of the total population [1]. In addition, information technology penetrates the whole society. As it is today 4 of 5 senior Swedes older than 76 years feel not or only partly involved in the information society [2]. The use of Internet among seniors grows, but the proportion of Internet users in the age group of 55 or older is still half the size of the younger age group [3]. This adds up to a risk that a big group of citizens is left out of the society due to their lack of familiarity and knowledge of IT. The issue is more prominent for older seniors at residential homes or day care facilities as they are rarely exposed to new technology. A study of digital exclusion [4] done by the Swedish Local Fibre Alliance, a non-profit association, have identified five obstacles to feel digitally included. These obstacles are (1) lack of access to hardware, (2) lack of access to the Internet, (3) lack of motivation, one perceives no need for, or interest in digital technology, (4) lack of ability, one does not have physical or intellectual capacity to manage hardware and software and (5) knowledge, one needs to understand both hardware and software. All five obstacles are important, but to have access to hardware and the Internet are hygiene factors to be able to participate in the information society. The most important factor to feel involved in the information society is to own a computer of some kind [2] and a first step to make older seniors want to own a computer or tablet is for them to get access to, be familiar with and motivated to use new technology. This paper

© Springer International Publishing AG 2017
J. Zhou and G. Salvendy (Eds.): ITAP 2017, Part I, LNCS 10297, pp. 429–446, 2017.
DOI: 10.1007/978-3-319-58530-7_33

address these issues by introducing digital technology in a sustainable way at residential homes and day care centers[1] for seniors.

To explore how to introduce digital technology at residential homes and day care centers we combined field studies with the Design Science Research (DSR) methodology [5, 6]. The purpose of the field study was to understand the organization and what worked for the seniors, while DSR made it possible to put a design perspective on how to introduce digital technology to the seniors.

Wagner et al. [7] point out seniors' possible lack of motivation to use new technology. There has to be some benefit of the technology to make the use meaningful. There is a belief that new technology may be the key to increased well-being for older adults, but Dickinson and Gregor [8] argues that we should be careful not to be overconfident about the possibilities of technology and believe it always have positive effects. Therefore, the participants should be introduced to new technology with caution and on their own terms. This emphasizes the importance to introduce technology as a gentle slope and in collaboration with the seniors. The intention to learn to use new technology starts with exploring and experimenting with the technology to understand how much effort it is to learn [9]. In such a situation the social environment and the availability of support is of utterly importance [9].

To ensure engagement and motivation to use new technology we have used digital games as a fun and easy way to start exploring the possibilities with digital technology. Gerling et al. [10] have found that players' engagement in games transcend into their everyday life and increased the social interaction which motivates using games as a door to technology as social interaction is a key aspect of well-being and to feel involved.

This article describes how new technology has been introduced to seniors in one residential home and two day care centers. The contribution of the research is a method to make seniors embrace new technology. A method that involves collaboration, engagement, involvement and continuity.

The next section will introduce some related work regarding older adults' use of technology and games for seniors. Thereafter follows a description of the research approach. Section 3 presents the outcome of the research, and how use of digital technology was implemented in one residential home and two day care centers. The paper will end with a discussion and a short summary.

2 Related Work

This section presents related work in relation to three of the obstacles for digital inclusion identified by the Swedish Local Fibre Alliance [4]. That is in relation to motivation and ability to use new technology and the knowledge about the technology. The section ends with a subsection of related work in the area of digital games for seniors.

---

[1] The aim of day care centers is to prevent isolation and contribute to a meaningful life for the participants.

2.1 Motivation to Use New Technology

Seniors are often treated as a homogeneous group, but the reality is different and some seniors are more likely to be left outside the information society [11]. Even if many seniors are interested in new technology, others are not. There are seniors that question why they should use digital technology and accordingly they cannot see the use of it [12]. Younger people may see technology as something that makes things easier such as reading the newspaper on the mobile phone or sending an e-mail instead of posting a letter. The seniors, on the other hand, do not see the technology as a replacement of already established routines, such as sending letters or make a call [13].

It can be challenging to learn how to manage digital technology. Often there is a need for some kind of adaptation of applications and games used by seniors. However, it is rarely done, even if many seniors are interested in digital technology [13]. Nevertheless, senior that have past the learning curve are motivated by, for example, using digital technology to search for information, keep updated with hobbies and keep connected to family and relatives [14]. It is shown that seniors' use of tablets increase the feeling of connectedness and inclusion [15].

A study by Allaire et al. [16] indicate that playing games is positive for successful aging, which could act as a motivating factor. Research also shows that playing games with family members produces positive emotions [17].

2.2 Ability to Use New Technology

Aging results in several changes in, for example vision and motor skills. This influences the seniors' ability to use digital technology. Designers do seldom regard seniors as technology users, which leads to that the graphical interfaces are not customized for this group. In addition most designers have little or no experience of the aging process [18].

There are many practical aspects to consider [19] when developing applications and games for seniors. It is for example important to choose

- sufficiently large text and buttons,
- somewhat larger space between buttons,
- somewhat less pressure sensitive buttons with distinct feedback,
- clear color contrasts in the interface,
- as shallow navigation trees as possible, and
- simple, self-explained user interfaces.

Older adults often also need support for different languages, as they might not speak a second language. In addition, compatibility with different hearing aids might be needed [19]. Vision, hearing and motor skills are often reduced when you get older, but researcher has shown [20] that reaction time is as good as younger people when using pen or voice command as input. On the other hand mouse and keyboard are harder to handle [21]. This is something to consider when developing applications and games.

2.3   Knowledge to Use New Technology

Older adults all have experience of learning and a perception of their self-efficiency [9]. They also have a more or less positive attitude to learning new things. Experiences in school, at work and the social environment establishes a person's attitude to learning [9]. If a person has a negative attitude to learning new things, it is likely that the person reject new technology as something that is too hard to learn. The social environment play an important role for the individuals' motivation to learn about new technology [7]. However, if the senior has an intention to learn the first step is to start experimenting with the technology [9]. This makes the person understand how much effort it will take to learn to use the technology. If it is perceived as too difficult to learn or not useful enough the person may reject the technology, but the threshold can be reduced if there is enough social support and possibilities to get help with technical issues [9]. Research [14] shows that after passing the first difficulties most of the older adults feel enthusiastic to use digital technology.

However, technology evolves constantly and the knowledge has to be updated. Therefore, it is important that the technology use is seen as a continuous activity to, by training in a safe social environment, increase seniors' self-efficacy in the use of computers and mobile devices [7]. Astell et al. [22] state that also older adults with dementia can learn to play games independently preferably in a social context. To allow for exploration of the technology in a socially pleasant environment together with continuity has been very important aspects in the research presented in this paper.

2.4   Games for Seniors

Games may have a positive effect on well-being [23]. However, game developers often make games for people like themselves [14], which leaves seniors behind. The research around digital games for seniors has increased during the last years. One example is Foukarakis et al. [24] who describe a card game for tablets. The game is adjustable according to seniors' ability. The seniors can play the game with friends and family over the Internet. The game can be adjusted to different person by setting the game to adjust to reduced vision or reduced stability in the arms. Seniors tend to prefer games that can be tailored according to ability [25]. Another study [26] shows that seniors think it is more fun to play together on the same screen instead of over the Internet. The seniors prefer playing against the computer to playing over the Internet.

Word puzzles of different kinds and games to find differences in pictures are appreciated by seniors as they are rather simple and the seniors have previous experiences of them [27]. In the contrary, games consisting of small objects or games that require fast reaction is less appreciated [27]. However, reaction speed can be improved by playing games [28].

Wii bowling is a game for the Wii game console. Similar games exist for Microsoft Kinect. Seniors appreciate it [29, 30] as it reminds them of things they have done before. Playing bowling can also be a motivation to be. To play games where you copy a movement, as for example bowling or tennis, may also be a way to perform something you cannot do the same way as before [29, 30].

3   Research Approach

The research was a cooperation between seniors and staff at one residential home and two day centers in southern Sweden. At the residential home lives people with and without dementia, but at the day center all seniors have some form of dementia. The overarching research question has been how to introduce digital technologies to seniors in residential homes and day centers in a sustainable way. For the process to be sustainable, it must operate without researchers or external facilitators in place.

The research was based on user participation and implemented with a combination of fieldwork and the Design Science Research (DSR) methodology [5]. DSR uses iterative development of artifacts to explore the possibilities and shortcomings in the use and design of artifacts. The field study lasted for one and a half year where the researcher visited the residential home or one of the day care centers once a week. There were in total 10 staff members and 21 seniors, age 70 to 89 years old, involved in the research. The aim of the fieldwork was to understand the organization and to learn what works for the seniors. DSR was used to (1) develop a method for introducing new technologies for seniors and to (2) explore how to make games for seniors. The guiding principles of the work has been cooperation, engagement, involvement and continuity for both staff and seniors.

As the access to hardware should not pose obstacles to the project, the researcher bought four 10″ Android tablets with WiFi. Tablets has been shown to be easier to handle than traditional computers as the tablet has a touch screen instead of mouse and keyboard [21].

The research consisted of three overlapping cycles (Fig. 1). In the first cycle, the fieldwork, the researcher chose games for the seniors to try. In cycle two a game, and in cycle three a back-end for tailoring the game, was developed.

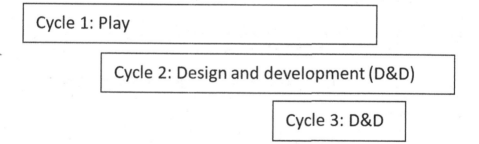

Fig. 1.   Research cycles

3.1   Cycle 1

The manager for the elderly care organization wanted to introduce new technology to the seniors living in the residential home or participated in the activities at the day care center. Thereby Cycle 1 started. In terms of DSR in means that the process was client initiated [5] (Fig. 2).

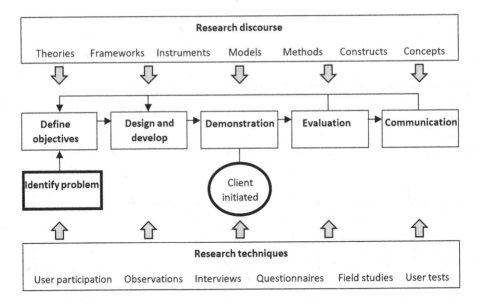

Fig. 2. Design Science Research cycle 1

DSR can start in one of six phases described below. The goal of the first cycle was to define how to implement the use of digital technology in the organization. DSR is an iterative process even if described as linear. The six phases are:

- Problem Identification and Motivation.
  - To identify the difficulties staff perceive as thresholds when introducing tablets in the organization.
    - How to make use of tablets as a natural part of the seniors' life?
    - Which games or apps to use?
- Objective of the Solution.
  - The objectives of a potential solution are identified.
- Design and development.
  - In this cycle, this phase means to design how digital technologies are introduced and used.
- Demonstration.
  - To test different ways to introduce the tablets and games for the seniors.
- Evaluation.
  - Evaluation of what games work and what in the game that works.
  - Evaluation of the practices tested.
- Communication
  - Dissemination of the knowledge obtained from the evaluation to staff members and organizations such as pensioners' associations.

The different research activities in the six phases were common research techniques (Fig. 2) with a focus on user participation. Knowledge within the research discourse informed the different activities.

Through discussions with the staff, it was clear that there was a need for some form of routines or habits to introduce new technology. In both the day care centers and the residential home, there were schedules for other activities. There was a need to set aside time for using digital technology and to explore how to do it. With a different wording, it is about how to make it possible for the seniors to get the knowledge required to be able to handle digital technology. In addition, the question of what games to play aroused. How can you know what games are fun and motivating?

The researcher's aim was to; together with the staff create a process that could work in the organization. The field study made it possible for the researcher to study the result of different methods used to address the perceived difficulties. Cycle 1 resulted in a set of possible ways to design the introduction process, knowledge of what difficulties there are in the tested games, and an understanding of the seniors' interests and their motivation to play digital games.

To try out how to design the introduction of digital technology we tried different settings as the physical environments differed between the residential home and the daycare centers. The settings tried were:

- A small group seniors (4 to 5 people), with one tablet each, played games socializing.
- One staff member, the researcher and a senior played together on one tablet.
- A larger group of seniors sat together when a few seniors played together.
- The tablet was connected to the TV. A group of seniors played together with assistance of one staff member that controlled the game on the tablet.
- The tablet was connected to the TV. A group of seniors played together. The seniors sent the tablet between them.
- The researcher or a staff member played with one senior.

The researcher introduced different games at the visits at the residential home and the day care center. At a initial meeting with two staff members, it was decided to start playing Solitaire, Memory and Candy Crush [31]. We chose Solitaire and Memory because the seniors already knew them, while Candy Crush was chosen because it is a popular game played by both children and adults. The idea was for the seniors to be able to play with their families. The researcher continuously introduced new games based on the seniors' interests. In total 30 games were played. The researcher took notes of observations and conversations during all play sessions.

The researcher evaluated how the introduction process worked by observations, discussions with the staff and the seniors, and by interviews with the staff. How and what was motivating was studied by observations at the play sessions. By discussing the games and by general conversations, the researcher gained information to search for new games. These games where introduced at the next play session.

3.2 Cycle 2

Cycle 1 resulted in knowledge of what works and not. That knowledge acted as input to Cycle 2. Cycle 2 involved development of a game together with staff and seniors. The goal of Cycle 2 was to give the staff a deeper understanding of software and an insight of what is possible to do. Cycle 2 started with a workshop with the staff at the residential home. During the workshop the participants brainstormed, and all the ideas and themes was collected in a mind map. Thereafter all the ideas were discussed based on how interesting they were and what was possible to do within the project. The outcome of the workshop was a decision to make a game that encourage the seniors to do something together and make them talk to each other. It was a problem, especially at the residential home, that the seniors seldom spontaneously talked to each other. It was decided to make a game about the city the seniors live in, and how the city has changed over time. During the workshop, the following requirements were stated:

- The game must be about the city the seniors live in because it is motivates the seniors to engage in the game as it is connected to the seniors reality [27].
- The content must contain pictures of the city to trigger to share memories, which many seniors like [13].
- The game must be social and encourage the players to talk to each other. This is something many seniors appreciate in games [32].
- The game may contain some kind of quiz or treasure hunt to make several players get involved at the same time, which is appreciated by many [33].
- The staff also wanted it to be possible to play the game on the TV [25].
- The game must be kept simple [34].
- The game must be easy to understand [35] if the seniors should be able to play by their own.
- The staff wanted it to be possible for the player to travel along a path and look at pictures and read or listen to stories. This is handle in Cycle 3.
- The staff also wanted to have the possibility to add pictures and stories. This is handle in Cycle 3.

The development consisted of three iterations. The first iteration resulted in a paper prototype, showing how the game could look like and how to navigate the game. The second and third iteration resulted in digital prototypes. One prototype was made in Windows forms as the organization had decided to buy Windows tablets. The decision was eventually cancelled and to be independent of what type of tablets used, a third web based prototype was developed (Fig. 3). The game's name is "Malmö – past and present".

To decide what kind of themes to implement in the game we arranged a workshop with the seniors at one of the day care centers. We used a tourist map of the city and one of the staff members led the discussion. The staff member pointed at different locations on the map and initiated a conversation about what the seniors remembered from the location. The discussion progressed from the memories and themes evolved. The most popular themes were:

- Restaurants and what have become of them.
- Food, now and then.
- Workplaces in the city now and then.
- Streets and squares in the city.
- Celebrities of the city.
- Sports.

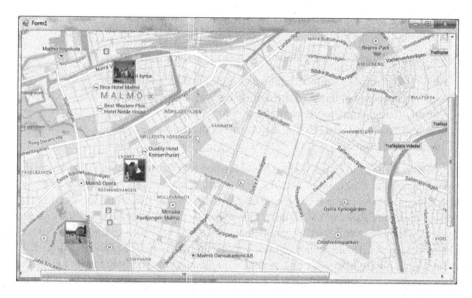

Fig. 3. Third prototype of the game, Malmö – past and present

Five staff members evaluated the first prototype. Both staff members and seniors evaluated the second and the third porotype. The second prototype was play tested by two seniors at one of the day care centers and mainly resulted in some issues concerning usability. The third web-based prototype was tested in three different ways. A group of five deaf seniors at the residential home tested the game by projecting it on the TV and the seniors collaborated to answer the questions. In the same way, seniors at day care center outside the project tested the game. In addition, the game was tested on a senior event and the players maneuvered the game them self. The researchers observed the players during the play sessions and interviewed them after the sessions.

3.3   Cycle 3

Already in the first workshop, the staff members expressed the need to be able to adjust and extend the game to fit the players. They wanted to be able to add their own pictures, stories and travel paths in the game developed, "Malmö - past and present". We created a prototype to show how this could look like. Only one iteration was carried out. The prototype was web based and it was possible to draw travel paths and add stops with pictures and stories. The aim of Cycle 3 was to explore what kind of tailoring the staff members were prepared to do.

The researcher demonstrated the prototype at a meeting with staff members and managers. The evaluation showed that the staff members needed the functionality, but it has to be extremely easy to tailor the game as the managers expressed their concern that the procedure possibly would use too much of the staff's time.

4 Results

This section will describe the outcome of the three cycles with respect to

- what might motivate seniors to play and use digital technologies,
- what has emerged in terms of the ability to play game on tablets,
- learning (knowledge) to use digital technology, and
- how it can be made possible for seniors on residential homes and day care centers to use digital technology.

The Swedish Local Fibre Alience has identified five factors [4] crucial to if a person experience digital exclusion or not. The research described in this article ignores two of these factors, access to the Internet and access to hardware. It is worth mentioning that these to obstacles also were an issue in this research. When the researcher first came to the residential home and the day care centers there was no Wi-Fi available. There was no tablets available for the seniors either. The researcher solved the problem temporarily by providing a wireless router and tablets. The manager solved both issues during the project as the manager thought it is important for the elderly care to keep up with digitalization.

4.1 Motivation to Play

Engagement and motivation is tightly connected. If a game is engaging the player also want to play more and in the case of this project, it means that the seniors get more familiar with digital technology.

During the first cycle, we played about 30 different games with the seniors. Some games was better than others in terms of gameplay, others in accessibility. The visual representation of the game as well as sound effects is important for the motivation. For example, the seniors played Hangman both alone and together. We tried two different versions of the game and in one of the games, the hanged man was rather small. The seniors hardly noticed the man and they felt the game was hard to understand. In the second version, the hanged man was very visible and it was clear when you answered incorrectly, and thereby the game was much more fun to play.

Generally, the seniors appreciated games that they recognized. Puzzles, Memory, Solitaire and other well-known board games were popular. You can question why it is worth playing digital versions of board or card game. There are two reasons. The first reason is what this article want to address, it is important for seniors to be familiar with digital technology and games could be a gateway to other use of the tablet. The second one is that for some seniors it is hard to hold the cards or pick up a piece of a jigsaw puzzle from the table.

Bowling is something many seniors have played previously in life. Bowling on the tablet turned out to be the most popular game for seniors with dementia. The joy the seniors experienced when hit a strike was enjoyable to see. The game used has good sound effect when the skittles goes down and when you hit a strike and it enhanced the experience substantially. The seniors sitting beside the players could not miss the event and they contributed to the game play by cheering. Often the player did not want to hand over the tablet to the co-player as he or she wanted to have another go.

A game similar to bowling is boule. This game was not popular at all. The visual feedback was not as obvious and the game is more complicated in its nature. In addition, boule does not involve fancy sound effects.

Memory also worked well to play together. There is many different memory games and the pictures vary. It was much more motivating for the seniors if the pictures were in line with their interest. One senior was very interested in flowers and chose to play memory with matching flowers. It led to discussions about the names of the flowers and who did grow the flowers in their garden.

One of the games we introduced in the beginning of the project was Candy Crash [31]. It turned out to work badly for the seniors. It was hard for them to understand how you were supposed to change places of the candy to get three or more in a row. Many of the seniors tried to exchange the candy on the diagonal, which is not allowed. When you get some candy in a row, they disappear and others take their place. The game change and the candy moves. In some cases, there is a chain reaction and it was perceived as confusing. It requires a more clear visual cause and effect to make the seniors feel they have control over the game.

Games like Farmvile [36] or Hay Day [37] were you are supposed to manage a farm by seeding and harvesting crops works well if the senior is playing with a staff member. The difficulty with this kind of games is that they often are very detailed with small characters and objects. In addition, it often involves interacting with different characters to get instructions on how to manage the farm. The text in the balloons is often very small and hard to read and sometimes the text is in English. This type of games could be used to have logical reasoning with seniors with dementia: "-Now we have harvested the wheat. What should we do next?" This game concept could be transferred to daily life to discuss daily routines.

In addition, by designing the game, "Malmö – past and present", we experienced how memory could start engaging conversations. For the game to feel engaging over time the game has to be tailorable to fit different seniors, but it also have to be possible to add content to make it more extensive. In the context of "Malmö – past and present" the location triggers memories and the memories have to be collected to act as starting point for new memories and pleasant chats.

4.2 Ability to Play

The research involved playing games with seniors with physical and cognitive impairments and it revealed difficulties of various kinds. A simple thing as holding the tablet may be an issue. Many seniors wants to grab the tablet firmly due to reduced motor skills and then the touch screen does not work as they have their thumb on the screen. We had two types of tablets, black and white. It turned out that the white tablets worked better independent of the color of the game itself as it was easier to see where the frame ended.

Research shows that touch screens are easier to handle than mouse and keyboards [21], but most of the seniors in the project also had difficulties managing the touch screen with the fingers. The men had large hands and it was hard to know where they had touched the screen and if the buttons are close something unpredicted often happened. It ended up in confusion. The way the seniors touch the screen often resulted in nothing happened. When the researcher tried, nothing was wrong. We solved the issue by using stylus. The stylus made it possible to see exactly what was touched. The use of stylus also solved the problem with nothing happening.

The tablets had 10′ screens but, still, the screens are rather small and the space the developers can use is limited, which often led to small text and icons. Naturally, this will cause problem for those with reduced vision. A shiny surface can also be a problem if you play two together.

In some games, you can adjust the difficulty level to challenge the player. In Memory and jigsaw puzzles, for example, a more difficult level will result in more and smaller pieces or the player has to pan the screen to see all the pieces. This functionality was often problematic for the seniors.

One group of seniors was deaf. Game relying on sounds to enhance the game play does not work for this group. Bowling was for example not as popular in this group as in others. Instead, to play this kind of games the game has to be projected on a larger screen for everyone to see.

Many of the seniors participating in the project had some form of dementia. There are even more difficulties for this group of seniors. Human support is important here also when playing digital games. Dementia takes so many forms and the need for support are very different. One difficulty is to remember how to navigate to the desired game. Some remembered some did not. Some of the seniors even forgot how to play in the middle of the game. It would be desirable to have some kind of intelligent support to help remembering what to do next. It is important that this type of support must feel natural and logical, not to be experienced as magical. Astell et al. [22] show how this can be done. It is worth mentioning that managing the tablet itself was no different from the group whiteout dementia.

4.3 Knowledge

The project introduced digital technology by playing games, but after a while, the seniors saw the possibilities with the tablets. They started to use the tablet to search for information. It was common that someone in a middle of a discussion said: "-Use that thing to look it up!" Another way to use the tablets was to look for pictures to illustrate a conversation. For example, one woman was very interested in cars and she wanted to tell the other women what kind of car she had as a young girl. It was very helpful to use the tablet to find a picture of a similar car. Music is also very appreciated and Spotify [38] was used in different ways. At one time, we had coffee while the seniors wished for different songs, just like in an old, Swedish radio program from their youth. We search for the songs on Spotify. The songs spanned from new ones to old, from soft to hard, Swedish and foreign. In addition, "Malmö –past and present" initiated the use of Google Street View. The seniors appreciated it as you can look at where you used to live and where the staff members live.

4.4 Introduction Process

As the physical environment put restrictions on how to introduce digital technology we tried different types of grouping (see Sect. 3.1 Cycle 1). Two types of groups worked less good. One was when the researcher, one staff member and one senior played together. The seniors perceived it as the researcher wanted to check if he or she did the right thing with the tablet. It worked much better if there was just one extra person. It did not matter if it was a staff member or the researcher. It is important with this type of grouping to choose a game designed for two players.

The play sessions where the tablet was connected to the TV and the tablet was passed between seniors in a larger group did not feel comfortable either. You had to be careful when passing the tablet to the next player as the cable was connected to the TV. To use the tablets in this way there has to be a wireless connection between the tablet and the TV. In a large group it is hard for the seniors sitting far away from the TV to engage, especially if a round takes long time. This way of playing works better in a small group of 4–5 seniors sitting close to the TV. To let one person manage the tablet connected to the TV worked well. Our own game worked well this way. The drawback is that only one person have access to the tablet. In a large group, it worked best to let the seniors play together two and two. Both of them could use the tablet and they could help each other. Never the less, small groups work best, both for playing connected to the TV and single player. Even when all the seniors played by themselves, the games initiated conversations.

Parallel with the research cycles there was a discussion of how to implement the process in the organization (Fig. 4). As the head manager of the elderly care was very positive to the initiative to introduce new technology to the seniors and the aim of the project was to create a sustainable process even after the project ended, the manager took actions to ensure such a process, based on the result from the research. It resulted in what was called 'Computer fun' agents. Every sub organization chose a person responsible for the use of new technology. It ensued that seniors could play and use the tablets between the play sessions. The manager also initiated a steering committee. To communicate what was going on in the project there was meetings every second month with the managers, the 'Computer fun' agents and the researcher. The researcher reported the project's status at the meetings. In this way, the knowledge was spread in the organization. The 'Computer fun' agents also met on regular basis to discuss how they worked with the tablets, what applications and games they used, and to share tips of what worked for seniors with special needs. The researcher also participated in the 'Computer fun' agents' meetings. In addition, the researcher started a blog with links to the different games tried and some comments of what was good and bad with the different games. To disseminate the result outside the organization, the researcher communicated the results to senior citizens' associations and in open lectures.

Based on the practice in the project a model (Fig. 5) for how to work, select and choose new apps or games evolved. The 'Computer fun' agents had subsequently a good competence in what apps and games worked in different context, and together they continuously made new experiences. In addition, the 'Computer fun' agents and the rest of the staff had a broad knowledge about the organization and the seniors interests,

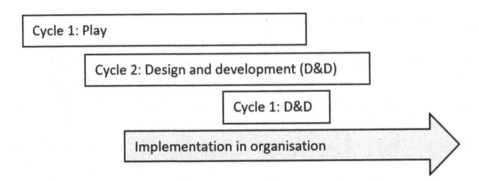

Fig. 4. The implementation process in relation to the research cycles

personality and situation. These competencies are prerequisites to introduce digital technology to the seniors.

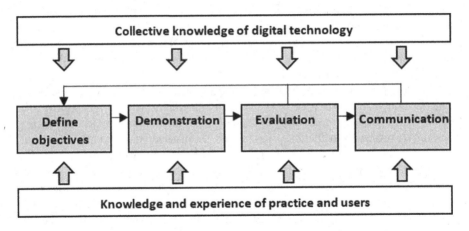

Fig. 5. Resulting implementation model for continuous use of digital technology

The staff knows the seniors and can, based on their needs, decide what goals the game or the app should have. Based on the goals the 'Computer fun' agent choose a game or an app suitable for the senior. One of the staff members evaluates the game or the app by observation and by discussing it with the senior. Then the rest of the 'Computer fun' agents are informed about the result at the next meeting. The knowledge is, in this way, shared by the staff and the collective knowledge increases. The same procedure goes for group use.

5   Discussion

We have seen that games work well as a starting point to learn new technology. It is easy to motivate the seniors to try to play. It feels safe to try a game, as it does not matter much if something goes wrong. This research confirms that many seniors are curious about digital technology [11]. There are also those seniors that cannot see what digital technology can do for them [12], but we have seen that those seniors after a while have felt motivated to play. All the games we have tested have had flaws regarding adjustment to seniors' use. The research presented in this paper confirms all the issues reported by Czaja et al. [18] and van Dyk et al. [19].

Bernard et al. [9] shows how seniors approach new technology and point out the importance of social and technical support to guide the seniors when start using technology. This is confirmed in our studies. Also previous experiences influence how eager the seniors are to embrace the technology [7]. We have seen that too. Some seniors has to be convinced to try and when they did, they were hooked. At some occasions one or two seniors refused to try, but sat for a while and studied the others, after a while they wanted to have a try. This shows that the seniors in some way or another have to be exposed to new technology in a safe way. Wagner et al. [7] confirm this.

The process to implement a working method for using tablets in the residential home has not been easy. Seniors, staff and management were positive, but it is hard to get new routines to work with old ones. The staff members' schedules varies over weeks and the same persons do not work the same time every day. It was hard for the 'Computer fun' agents to put the responsibility on someone else. With a lot of staff participating in the care there was an anxiety that someone would steal the tablets. In the beginning, the tablets were locked in, which made it hard to make spontaneous use of the tablets. Another problem was that the tablets were not charged when someone wanted to use them. It is small practical issues, but they have large impact. At the day care centers, it was easier, as it is the same staff every day taking care of the activities. The tablets were always in full sight and there was routines when to charge the tablets.

The implementation model presented in Fig. 5 revealed itself spontaneously from the work in the project. The project consisted of several cycles: play, design, and development of a game and a backend. The first cycle, to choose and play games, has a self-explaining connection to the implementation model. The other cycles have indirectly influenced the implementation model. By user participation, the participants have gained a better understanding of what technology can mean for the seniors and increased engagement was developed through the work with 'Malmö – past and present'. The staff members gained insight in what is possible, which inspired them to new ideas of how to use the tablets.

Digital technology for older adults with dementia is important as we all live here and now in an information society. Everybody should have the opportunity to feel included even if they cannot use the technology fully with all its potentials. To play games is one way to understand what the technology can do, and the seniors can experience that they know what the grandchildren talk about when they discuss what they do with their computers and tablets.

6   Summary

The method used consists of three overlapping cycles (Fig. 6). In the first cycle, the seniors play digital games. The second cycle is a design phase were seniors and staff, based on the experience of playing existing games come up with ideas for new games.

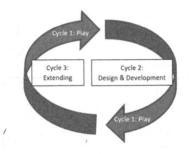

Fig. 6. Overview of the three cycles

The second cycle also involves the development of a game, where the seniors and the staff play test and give input to the development. The third cycle means that the seniors and the staff together add content to the game.

In parallel with the research project, the use of tablets was implemented in the organization. One person per organization was selected to become a "Computer fun" agent, responsible for the use of the tablets. The "Computer fun" agents met regularly to share experiences and offer tips on new applications that are worth trying.

The different cycles all involve collaboration, engagement, involvement and continuity. We have seen how the games and the design activities have created joy and interest. The understanding of the technology has increased amongst the seniors as they recognize what the technology can do for them and the use of digital technology continued after the end of the project.

In conclusion, there was a clear demand from the staff to be able to tailor and extend apps and games to make them useful over time. The research reported in this article just touches the topic. How to achieve tailorability and extendability as a part of game play is something for future research.

References

1. Eurostat, European commission: Population structure and ageing (2013). http://epp.eurostat.ec.europa.eu/statistics_explained/index.php/Population_structure_and_ageing. Accessed 16 Oct 2014
2. Findahl, O.: Svenskarna och internet (2013). https://www.iis.se/docs/SOI2013.pdf. Accessed 8 Feb 2017
3. Eurostat, European Commission: Internet access and use statistics - households and individuals. http://ec.europa.eu/eurostat/statistics-explained/index.php/Internet_access_and_use_statistics_-_households_and_individuals#Internet_activity_by_age_group. Accessed 8 Feb 2017
4. Umecon/Svenska stadsnätsföreningen: En studie i digitalt utanförskap (2016)
5. Peffers, K., Tuunanen, T., Rothenberger, M.A., Chatterjee, S.: A design science research methodology for information systems research. J. Manag. Inf. Syst. **24**, 45–77 (2007)
6. Hevner, A.R., March, S.T., Park, J.: Design research in information systems research. MIS Q. **28**, 75–105 (2004)
7. Wagner, N., Hassanein, K., Head, M.: Computer use by older adults: a multi-disciplinary review. Comput. Hum. Behav. **26**, 870–882 (2010)

8. Dickinson, A., Gregor, P.: Computer use has no demonstrated impact on the well-being of older adults. Int. J. Hum. Comput. Stud. **64**, 744–753 (2006)
9. Barnard, Y., Bradley, M.D., Hodgson, F., Lloyd, A.D.: Learning to use new technologies by older adults: perceived difficulties, experimentation behaviour and usability. Comput. Hum. Behav. **29**(4), 1715–1724 (2013)
10. Gerling, K.M., Schulte, F.P., Masuch, M.: Designing and evaluating digital games for frail elderly persons. In: Proceedings of the 8th International Conference on Advances in Computer Entertainment Technology - ACE 2011 (2011)
11. van Deursen, A.J., Helsper, E.J.: A nuanced understanding of Internet use and non-use among the elderly. Eur. J. Commun. **30**, 171–187 (2015)
12. Pedell, S., Beh, J., Mozuna, K., Duong, S.: Engaging older adults in activity group settings playing games on touch tablets. In: Proceedings of the 25th Australian Computer-Human Interaction Conference: Augmentation, Application, Innovation, Collaboration, pp. 477–480. ACM, New York (2013)
13. Kankainen, A., Lehtinen, V.: Creative personal projects of the elderly as active engagements with interactive media technology. In: Proceedings of the 8th ACM Conference on Creativity and Cognition, pp. 175–184. ACM, New York (2011)
14. Holttum, S.: Do computers increase older people's inclusion and wellbeing? Ment. Heal. Soc. Incl. **20**, 6–11 (2016)
15. Tsai, H.S., Shillair, R., Cotten, S.R., Winstead, V., Yost, E.: Getting grandma online: are tablets the answer for increasing digital inclusion for older adults in the U.S.? Educ. Gerontol. **41**, 695–709 (2015)
16. Allaire, J.C., McLaughlin, A.C., Trujillo, A., Whitlock, L.A., LaPorte, L., Gandy, M.: Successful aging through digital games: Socioemotional differences between older adult gamers and non-gamers. Comput. Hum. Behav. **29**(4), 1302–1306 (2013)
17. Osmanovic, S., Pecchioni, L.: Beyond entertainment - motivations and outcomes of video game playing by older adults and their younger family members. Games Cult. **11**, 130–149 (2016)
18. Czaja, S.J., Lee, C.C.: The impact of aging on access to technology. Univers. Access Inf. Soc. **5**, 341 (2006)
19. van Dyk, T., Renaud, K., van Biljon, J.: Moses – method for selecting senior mobile phones: supporting design & choice for the elderly. In: Proceedings of the South African Institute for Computer Scientists and Information Technologists Conference, pp. 277–285. ACM, New York (2012)
20. Xiao, B., Lunsford, R., Coulston, R., Wesson, M., Oviatt, S.: Modeling multimodal integration patterns and performance in seniors: toward adaptive processing of individual differences. In: Proceedings of the 5th International Conference on Multimodal Interfaces, pp. 265–272. ACM, New York (2003)
21. Motti, L.G., Vigouroux, N., Gorce, P.: Interaction techniques for older adults using touchscreen devices: a literature review. In: Proceedings of the 25th Conference on L'Interaction Homme-Machine, pp. 125:125–125:134. ACM, New York (2013)
22. Astell, A., Alm, N., Dye, R., Gowans, G., Vaughan, P., Ellis, M.: Digital video games for older adults with cognitive impairment (2011)
23. Nguyen, H., Ishmatova, D., Tapanainen, T., Liukkonen, T.N., Katajapuu, N., Makila, T.: Impact of serious games on health and well-being of elderly: a systematic review, pp. 3695–3704 (2017)
24. Foukarakis, M., Leonidis, A., Adami, I., Antona, M., Stephanidis, C.: An adaptable card game for older users. In: Proceedings of the 4th International Conference on PErvasive Technologies Related to Assistive Environments, pp. 27:1–27:7. ACM, New York (2011)

25. Mubin, O., Shahid, S., Al Mahmud, A.: Walk 2 Win: towards designing a mobile game for elderly's social engagement. In: Proceedings of the 22nd British HCI Group Annual Conference on People and Computers: Culture, Creativity, Interaction, vol. 2, pp. 11–14. BCS Learning & Development Ltd., Swindon (2008)

26. Gajadhar, B.J., Nap, H.H., de Kort, Y.A.W., IJsselsteijn, W.A.: Out of sight, out of mind: co-player effects on seniors' player experience. In: Proceedings of the 3rd International Conference on Fun and Games, pp. 74–83. ACM, New York (2010)

27. Vasconcelos, A., Silva, P.A., Caseiro, J., Nunes, F., Teixeira, L.F.: Designing tablet-based games for seniors: the example of CogniPlay, a cognitive gaming platform. In: Proceedings of the 4th International Conference on Fun and Games, pp. 1–10. ACM, New York (2012)

28. Whitcomb, G.R.: Computer games for the elderly. SIGCAS Comput. Soc. **20**, 112–115 (1990)

29. Lai, C.-H., Peng, C.-W., Chen, Y.-L., Huang, C.-P., Hsiao, Y.-L., Chen, S.-C.: Effects of interactive video-game based system exercise on the balance of the elderly. Gait Posture **37**, 511–515 (2013)

30. Kahlbaugh, P.E., Sperandio, A.J., Carlson, A.L., Hauselt, J.: Effects of playing Wii on well-being in the elderly: physical activity, loneliness, and mood. Act. Adapt. Aging. **35**, 331–344 (2011)

31. King: Candy Crush Saga Online – spela spelet på King.com. https://king.com/sv/game/candycrush. Accessed 8 Feb 2017

32. Ijsselsteijn, W., Nap, H.H., de Kort, Y., Poels, K.: Digital game design for elderly users. In: Proceedings of the 2007 Conference on Future Play, pp. 17–22. ACM, New York (2007)

33. Al Mahmud, A., Mubin, O., Shahid, S., Martens, J.-B.: Designing and evaluating the tabletop game experience for senior citizens. In: Proceedings of the 5th Nordic Conference on Human-Computer Interaction: Building Bridges, pp. 403–406. ACM, New York (2008)

34. Thiry, E.: Scenario-based design of a digital reminiscing system for the elderly. In: Proceedings of the 17th ACM International Conference on Supporting Group Work, pp. 299–300. ACM, New York (2012)

35. Spreicer, W.: Tangible interfaces as a chance for higher technology acceptance by the elderly. In: Proceedings of the 12th International Conference on Computer Systems and Technologies, pp. 311–316. ACM, New York (2011)

36. FarmVille | Play the Most Famous Free Online Game | Zynga. https://www.zynga.com/games/farmville. Accessed 8 Feb 2017

37. Hay Day × Supercell. http://supercell.com/en/games/hayday/. Accessed 8 Feb 2017

38. Music for everyone – Spotify. https://www.spotify.com/us/. Accessed 8 Feb 2017

Eliciting Best Practices in Digital Literacy Tutoring: A Cognitive Task Analysis Approach

Kelly S. Steelman, Kay L. Tislar, Leo C. Ureel II, and Charles Wallace[✉]

Michigan Technological University, Houghton, MI 49931, USA
{steelman,cltislar,ureel,wallace}@mtu.edu

Abstract. Responding to the increasing need for all citizens to be digitally literate, our research group has led a program for six years that addresses older adults' questions about digital devices and applications. Our patrons confront a range of socio-technical barriers as they adopt new technology and explore the digital world, and our tutors have developed particular practices to identify and overcome these barriers. Using a cognitive task analysis methodology, we conducted semi-structured interviews with experienced tutors. From these, we derived a set of effective and replicable practices that can form the basis for similar programs elsewhere.

Keywords: Older adults · Senior citizens · Aging · Digital literacy · Computer training · Cyberlearning · Social cognitive theory · Critical decision making

1 Introduction

Older adults are the fastest growing group of Internet users in the US [8], but 41% of older adults still do not use the Internet at all [12]. Several studies have indicated that many older adults are ready and willing to learn about technology, even though it might involve a great deal of time and effort on their part [2]. The benefits clearly outweigh the time and effort required: technology can greatly enhance the lives of older adults by providing social interaction, tools for banking and shopping from home, entertainment, and ways of getting information about healthcare or even contacting healthcare providers. The issue is that older people must be able to acquire the knowledge and skills they need to use technology effectively [11]. Training is critical, especially as success at initial training is one of the primary predictors of whether or not adults continue to use computers [10].

Training can help older adults understand their devices and the software that runs on them, but many psychologists believe that the training needs to be targeted to take advantage of the strengths and compensate for the weaknesses of the adult learner [7]. Several older adult learning training models have been developed. For example, the Industrial Gerontology Model specifies five factors that should be considered when developing training programs for older adults: motivation, structure, familiarity, organization, and time [15]. A meta-analysis

© Springer International Publishing AG 2017
J. Zhou and G. Salvendy (Eds.): ITAP 2017, Part I, LNCS 10297, pp. 447–460, 2017.
DOI: 10.1007/978-3-319-58530-7_34

found that the factor contributing to the largest amount of variance in adult learner performance is self-pacing [5]. Self-paced, goal-oriented training is also recommended because this type of training minimizes working memory demands, which can be an issue for older adults [9].

Our *BASIC (Building Adult Skills in Computing)* program [1,13] is one of many nationwide initiatives aimed at improving the digital literacy of older adults. In contrast to more standard prescriptive, task-focused programming, our self-paced tutoring program focuses on developing digital flexibility, problem solving abilities, and self-efficacy—higher-order skills that are essential for keeping up with the rapid pace of technological change and transferring knowledge from task to task or system to system. Our approach, grounded in Social Cognitive Theory [3,4], emphasizes the roles of observational learning and behavior modeling, learner-led goal setting, and the development of self-efficacy.

Nearly all of the training programs cited in the literature are formal or workplace-based classes rather than the one-on-one tutoring sessions that our program offers. However, our program was designed to incorporate many of the characteristics noted above, such as self-pacing and goal-orientation. As we work to formalize our program, we wanted to discover which other techniques and strategies have emerged from tutoring sessions led by our most experienced tutors. For example, many of our tutors have developed analogies that they frequently use to help learners relate new technology to older systems. Others have honed their skills identifying and addressing errors in learners' mental models of computing. To elicit this expert knowledge, requires a systematic approach. The Critical Decision Method (CDM) [6] is a three-step, semi-structured cognitive task analysis technique that has been successfully used to drive the development of expert systems and training programs.

In the current project, we have adapted the CDM protocol to elicit knowledge from experienced digital literacy tutors in our program. This paper describes our protocol, outlines the steps involved in our tutoring process and the goals of each step, and presents the data we gathered from a set of 12 interviews we conducted with tutors of varying backgrounds. The interviews yielded a wealth of information, and our goal was to classify and organize the data to reveal common themes, tutoring strategies, and obstacles to successful tutoring.

This study was guided by the following research questions:

- What commonalities exist in tutors' stories about their tutoring sessions?
- Which types of strategies are most often used to guide adult learners?
- What types of barriers arise that could derail the patron's learning?
- What are the key attributes of successful tutoring sessions?

The purpose of this narrative study is to analyze the activities, strategies, and tools used to help solve technological issues for older adults in BASIC tutoring sessions.

2   Methods

Participants. Participants included six tutors from our BASIC program, each with two to six years of tutoring experience with older adults. All were current or former Michigan Tech undergraduate (1) and graduate students (5) and faculty (1). Each tutor was interviewed twice, resulting in a total of 12 interviews.

Procedure. The Critical Decision Method (CDM) is an incident-based cognitive task analysis technique. The purpose of the technique is to elicit expert knowledge using a semi-structured interview to help experts tell stories from their field. The interviews were conducted in three sweeps.

- *Sweep 1: Selecting an Incident.* During Sweep 1, we asked the tutors to identify several memorable tutoring sessions. From those sessions, we selected one successful session and one unsuccessful session for further discussion. Success was defined as follows:
  - A successful tutoring session was one in which the tutor (1) understood the patron's request, (2) identified the source of the problem (technical, educational, etc.), (3) determined a solution to the problem or an answer to the question, (4) explained the information clearly to the patron, and (5) felt confident that the patron left the session better equipped to deal with a similar situation in the future.
  - An unsuccessful tutoring session, in contrast, was one in which the tutor either (1) did not understand the patron's request, (2) was unable to clearly explain information to the patron, or (3) did not feel confident that the patron left the session better equipped to deal with a similar situation in the future. Note that we were not necessarily interested in whether the tutor successfully solved the patron's problem. In some cases, doing so may have required advanced technical support or even a new computer. These situations would not be classified as unsuccessful unless the tutor was unable to communicate with the patron as to why he could not solve the problem at that time.
- *Sweep 2: Constructing a Timeline.* After the events were selected, we worked with the tutor to collaboratively draw a timeline depicting the major events that occurred during one of the tutoring sessions. For example, we asked the tutor to consider what happened when the patron arrived, the order in which questions were asked and addressed, any interruptions that occurred during the session, etc. As we moved into Sweep 3, we used the timeline to guide our interview and to elicit additional details about each of the primary events.
- *Sweep 3: Deepening.* In Sweep 3, we went beyond the surface details to focus on what the tutor was thinking during the session. For example, we were particularly interested in the information that our expert tutors use to guide their decision making throughout the help session. How does the tutor identify the patron's knowledge gaps? How does the tutor determine the best way to explain a difficult concept? If there are multiple solutions to a problem, how does the tutor determine which solution best meets the patron's needs? Sweep 3 also aimed to identify common knowledge gaps and socio-technical barriers that patrons frequently encounter.

CDM recommends several categories of deepening probe questions that have proven effective in eliciting expert knowledge [6]. We adapted those questions to our specific domain. A table of these probe questions is included in the Appendix A.

After Sweeps 2 and 3 were completed for one tutoring session, participants were given the opportunity to take a break, and then the process was repeated for the second session. The pair of interviews took approximately two hours to complete, with each interview ranging from 21 to 70 min.

Coding and Analysis. Interviews were digitally recorded, transcribed, and then independently coded by a pair of researchers (the first and second authors). The initial coding focused on a combination of preset and emergent codes. Preset codes included several broad categories, including cues, information use, analogies, standard operating procedures, goals and priorities, and mental models. After the researchers discussed and combined codes, the coded text was reclassified along three dimensions: step in the tutoring process, agent (patron, tutor, task, device, communication, and session), and attribute (agent characteristic, barrier, strategy).

3   Results and Discussion

Analysis of the refined classification codes revealed a sequence of five essential steps to the tutoring process. Not all of our tutors follow these steps exactly, but the majority incorporated the described practices at some point in their tutoring process. These steps are illustrated in Fig. 1. Below we describe the process in detail, and discuss common barriers and strategies at each step.

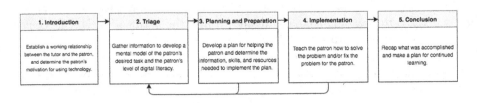

Fig. 1. Model of tutoring process

Step 1: Introduction
Tutoring sessions should begin with an introduction between tutor and patron.

Goal. The goal is to establish a working relationship between the tutor and the patron and to determine the patron's motivation for using technology.

Description. The introduction should begin with the tutor introducing herself to the patron and asking some non-intrusive questions (where are you from, is this the first time you've used our program, what brings you in today, *etc.*). Much of this step might take the form of small talk, with the patron also asking questions of the tutor. The tutor should use this exchange to determine the patron's motivation for using technology. For example, some patrons want to use email or social media to stay in touch with family or friends, while others want to apply for jobs via the Internet. Some patrons may have purchased the device on their own and want to put it to use. Others may have received a device as a gift or feel forced to adopt the technology because there is no alternative means to their desired outcome. Armed with this information, the tutor can begin to assess the urgency or importance of the patron's issue and identify some of the non-technical barriers they may encounter during the session.

Barriers. Patron-tutor rapport and trust is the foundation to a successful tutoring session. Accordingly, tutors tend to struggle when patrons are passive, difficult to talk to, or seem to dislike small talk. Interestingly, the patron's motivation for seeking help and the nature of the desired task can be barriers to building rapport. Patrons who seek assistance to achieve a singular high-consequence outcome, like applying for a job or making money on Craigslist or eBay, may not really be interested in learning and may become easily frustrated by small talk that they perceive as unrelated to their personal agenda. This can be compounded when patrons arrive at the library already overwhelmed and stressed out by their circumstances.

Strategies. To build rapport, tutors must be patient. Tutors should engage in small talk, but spend time carefully listening to identify the patron's specific interests. These will be critical later in the session as the tutor tries to connect aspects of the digital tasks to topics and activities that the patron will find personally relevant. Reading the patron's non-verbal cues can often be key to establishing a strong relationship and choosing appropriate tutoring strategies. Some tutors may be more adept at this than others, but tutor training programs should emphasize how to identify subtle body language, like cautious or tentative movements and tensing, that may indicate the patron a novice or particularly stressed.

Step 2: Triage
Once the patron-tutor relationship has been established, the next step is to assess the situation.

Goal. The tutor's primary goal at this step is to gather information to develop a mental model of the patron's desired task and level of digital literacy.

Description. To begin, the tutor asks the patron to explain verbally, or demonstrate on the device, what he would like to do. The patron's explanation and interactions with the device provides the tutor with many useful insights about the patron, task, and device—each of which may drive the tutor's approach in later steps. As the patron discusses or demonstrates the task, the tutor should consider the following:

– *Patron.*
  • What is the patron's general level of digital literacy?
  • How much is already known about the specific task, relative to how much needs to be taught?
  • What is the patron's style of communication?
  • Is the patron forthcoming or does the tutor need to actively elicit information?
– *Task.*
  • How complex is the desired task?
  • What underlying knowledge or skills are required to complete the task?
  • Can the desired task be accomplished within the time allowed by the tutoring session or should the task be divided into smaller subtasks? If so, which subtasks should be prioritized?
  • Does the task require a one-time change or fix that the patron will never need to do independently?
– *Device.*
  • If the patron is using her own device rather than one provided at the tutoring site, the tutor should inspect it or ask questions to determine its age and condition.
  • Does the tutor have experience with that device or have a similar device on hand?

Barriers. The special terminology of digital technology can be a significant barrier. Terms differ between platforms and software services, and they are in a constant state of flux. Misinterpretation of terms can lead to divergences in understanding that are difficult to identify and roll back.

The fast pace of change in the technology is another barrier. Patrons may experience a constant barrage of small updates or a sequence of intermittent and disruptive major upgrades; they often ignore notifications of such changes, and express frustration and lack of motivation after upgrades cause noticeable changes to established workflows [14]. Hardware and software may be old and outdated—and given many patrons' low level of disposable income, they often are. The incompatibilities faced when trying to use new services on an outdated platform can be confusing and demoralizing.

Patrons' digital literacy levels vary significantly; when they register lack of understanding, it can be unclear what tutors should ask to move the process forward. Cognitive and motor issues can also exacerbate other barriers, as can emotions of fear, embarrassment, and anxiety.

Strategies. Tutors must start out slowly with patrons. A best practice is to listen actively, with neither tutor nor patron using a computing device. Tutors should ask probing "why" questions and encourage patrons to articulate the problem, using their own vocabulary. Through these articulations, tutors try to gauge patrons' level of digital literacy. Cues that may indicate low levels of digital literacy include: use of non-technical or imprecise language; difficulty explaining a problem, even if capable of demonstrating it; little or no experience with email; only knowing one way to access a website (using a shortcut on the desktop to access email); lack of knowledge of common email or word processing functions, like the distinction between "reply" and "reply all" or text formatting options; and slow or tentative mouse, touchpad, or finger (on a touch screen device) movements.

During this time, it is important to manage expectations, set time limits, and prioritize goals.

Step 3: Planning and Preparation
Once the tutor believes he has a clear understanding of the problem space, it is time to begin addressing the problem.

Goal. The goal of this step is to develop a plan for helping the patron and determine the information, skills, and resources needed to implement the plan.

Description. Due to the breadth of issues and questions that patrons bring to the tutoring sessions, the tutor will frequently encounter a task or device with which he is unfamiliar. In these cases, the tutor may need to look up information on the Internet, explore possible options on the device, or consult with another tutor. In situations in which the patron is eager to learn and the process required to find the answer is not overwhelming, the tutor may choose to model how to find the solution, using a talk-aloud strategy to explain his thoughts and actions. If the patron seems overwhelmed or if the process of looking for a solution is unnecessarily complicated, the tutor may simply choose to look for resources independently. The tutor then uses the gathered information to decide how to proceed in helping the patron. If multiple options are available, the tutor may select one based on several factors, including the option's complexity, the time required to teach the option, and the patron's preferences. A final requirement of this step is to create a safe learning environment. This may involve preparing test documents or dummy accounts for patrons to use as they learn the task and practice their skills.

Barriers. Numerous barriers may present at this step, especially if the tutor has had difficulty understanding the patron's description of the problem. Sometimes the task or goal that the patron describes is quite different from the one actually wanted. This may not be readily apparent until after the tutor has developed a plan of action. In other cases, the patron may have provided inaccurate or incomplete information, or the problem may be so complex that the tutor has difficulty prioritizing the steps or determining where to start. Finally, when exploring a patron's device in search of solutions, the tutor may encounter unexpected issues. One common problem is a lack of organization of digital content. Files may also be poorly named. Across a wide range of tasks, tutors reported that they needed to introduce file management skills and work with patrons to set up new folder structures and file naming conventions.

Strategies. Although some patrons may be surprised to learn that the tutor does not automatically know the answer to their questions, many seem delighted to have "stumped an expert." Tutors should be encouraged to tell patrons when they do not know the answer, precisely so they have the opportunity to model their process of finding the solution. As the tutor explores the device or software, he or she should talk aloud and take the opportunity to introduce new terminology. If a patron has been using non-technical language (for example, a patron may refer to documents as "letters" or refer to Microsoft's Internet Explorer or Edge browser as "e" due to the form of the common icon for that application), tutors can mirror this language, but also take the opportunity to connect these terms to their technical component. Another benefit of modeling this search for solutions is that the tutor can reinforce that anyone can find answers through the use of "regular" language for searching.

This step also presents an opportunity for tutors to commiserate with the patrons. When tutors encounter poor design or clunky solutions, they can express their own frustration. In doing so, tutors can help reduce the patron's stress and anxiety and reassure them that this sort of frustration is common and normal.

Finally, tutors should be encouraged to embrace a sandbox philosophy of play and practice. Creating test documents and dummy accounts allows patrons to practice skills without fear of destroying their real files and digital content. It sets up an opportunity for safe, consequence-free play and exploration before transitioning the patron back to the real files to complete the intended task.

Step 4: Implementation

Goal. The penultimate step in the process is to actually accomplish the patron's goal by teaching the patron how to solve the problem and/or fixing the problem for the patron.

Description. This step involves the tutor working with the patron to execute the plan produced in step 3. At this point, the tutor will decide whether the patron will "drive" with the tutor providing ongoing guidance, as needed, or if the tutor will demonstrate first and then ask the patron to repeat the process. As the tutor and patron work through the problem, the tutor may rely on analogies that relate aspects of the digital tasks to other technology or entities for which the patron may already have a mental model.

In select cases, the tutor may determine that the best solution is to complete the task for the patron. Typically this only occurs when the tutor is confident that it is a one-time fix that the patron will not need to repeat on her own, for example, when changing an arcane system setting.

During this implementation process, it is possible that the tutor will encounter a challenge executing the plan or identify an unexpected gap in the patron's knowledge. In these situations the tutor may return to Step 2 (Triage).

Barriers. Implementation may be a period of information overload, where patrons can get lost or sidetracked. Patrons may even react with anger. As the solution plays out, motor skills issues may manifest themselves, and patrons who shun the tutor's exhortations to explore and play may fail to make progress. There is a risk of patrons losing the logical thread of the workflow but failing to admit it; in such cases, the actions do accomplish the goal, but in a way that remains "magical" from their perspective.

Conflicts may emerge at this step if there is a misperception, either on the part of the tutor or of the patron, regarding the patron's level of understanding. A patron may become stubbornly insistent that he understands, not willing to admit that he lacks information. Notes from previous sessions can be a hindrance in this regard: written notes from earlier sessions may be out of date but still convey a false sense of authority. Extensive, repetitious, or disorganized notes can also be a distraction from attention to the tutor and the device and problem at hand.

Strategies. Tutors should encourage patrons to "drive" (manipulate the digital device) as much as possible, with emphasis placed on play, practice, and exploration. In rare occasions, tutors may intervene and perform manipulations—for instance, in the case of a one-time setting change that requires delving into potentially confusing details. In such instances, the tutor must explicitly state why she is intervening. In all cases, either driving or not, the tutor "thinks aloud," modeling her thought process to encourage independence.

Many patrons have knowledge of older technologies or non-technological systems that tutors can leverage to help patrons better understand digital technology. Many tutors have developed sets of analogies that they frequently use:

- An arts and crafts analogy is helpful for digital cut-and-paste operations.
- Experience with Internet Explorer can inform use of File Explorer.
- To explain security-related topics, pop-ups can be likened to someone calling on the phone; if the communication is initiated on the other side, the recipient should demand verification. Likewise, spam can be compared to junk mail.
- To discuss the cues that should be used when assessing the trustworthiness of websites, compare well-established websites to frequently visited Main Street businesses.
- Compare URLs to physical stores or mailing addresses.
- Motivate regular computer updates by invoking recommended regular servicing for cars.
- Compare folders to kitchen drawers and the files to the items you place in them.
- Explain context sensitivity through candles: "If the candle is in the kitchen the power's probably out. If the candle's in the bedroom, it's probably romance."

The patron must be protected from embarrassment and fear. Belittling the patron, and making him feel ignorant or stupid, even inadvertently, is strictly to be avoided. To build up patrons' self confidence, tutors can get them to articulate what they already know, and emphasize that the fault lies with the technology, not the patron. Modeling assertiveness is important: tutors should encourage patrons to take action boldly once they have thought it through sufficiently. Tutors must be aware of anxiety cues and confusion cues, such as hesitation, withdrawal, slower responses, and lack of questions. For patrons experiencing stress, tutors must talk quietly and slowly, and work deliberately.

The sandbox approach, practicing on low-stakes or no-stakes data, is an effective strategy for reducing anxiety. When in the sandbox or manipulating real data, tutors may use back-off statements (e.g., "We don't have to do it this way...") and point out escape routes to earlier safe states. Best practices for staying safe online, such as choosing safe websites and avoiding and detecting viruses, can be woven into the discourse.

Step 5: Conclusion

Goal. The final step requires the tutor to recap what was accomplished and tie up loose ends.

The tutor concludes the session by reviewing with the patron what was done and answering any outstanding questions. If there is time left in the session, the tutor may allot time for the patron to continue practicing the task, providing feedback and assistance when necessary. If there is work remaining to be done, the tutor will explain that and indicate how the patron might proceed (for example, by coming back next week, watching videos online, or having hardware repaired). If the patron took notes during the session, the tutor can review them to ensure there aren't errors and even provide a list of suggested websites or resources that the patron may find helpful. Even if the issue could not be addressed, the tutor tries to end the session on a positive note by reminding the patron what was accomplished and what he learned.

Barriers. The ultimate goal of our tutoring program is to prepare patrons to become independent technology users. Realistically, this is not something that can typically be accomplished in a single tutoring session. Limited time is a barrier. One purpose of this final step, therefore, is to provide sufficient information and resources that the patron can continue to practice and learn at home. Unfortunately, we find that solutions don't always stick. Some patrons forget information between tutoring sessions (or return to seek reassurance that they are doing the task correctly). Others don't practice outside of tutoring sessions.

Many of our patrons rely heavily on taking notes. During the interviews, tutors commented that while note-taking is a useful memory aid, over-reliance on the notes is a barrier to developing true digital literacy skills. Patrons learn to follow steps, but not to explore. Eventually, those who fall into this habit will return to the tutoring program when their step-by-step instructions no longer work for them, perhaps after an update to a website or an application.

Some patrons who are quite capable of completing tasks under the guidance of a tutor continue coming to the program. To some extent, this may be driven by a lack of self-efficacy and a desire to seek assurance from an expert. Others come back to the program when they have something else they want to learn or have additional issues, such as a new device to set up. For other patrons, their return may simply be driven by a desire for the social component of the program.

Strategies. To help overcome these barriers, the session should end with a plan of action. Should the patron plan to attend the program in the future? What can the patron do to practice and maintain the new skills at home? For those patrons who took notes, the tutor may consider reviewing them to check for errors. It is important to avoid embarrassing the patron by calling out errors, but this gives the tutor an opportunity to reinforce the correct steps. The tutor should encourage the patron to practice without the use of the notes, just referring back to them when the patron gets stuck. Finally, the patron should be armed with appropriate resources. Some tutors have a list of trustworthy websites that they share with patrons during the session. Others focus on modeling how to search for answers on Google, YouTube, or other websites.

4 Future Work

Results of the cognitive task analysis have revealed numerous best practices that we believe should be incorporated into tutor training curricula. Our tutoring process is emergent, and effective techniques continue to arise as our tutors gain experience and new tutors appear with new approaches. The results of the cognitive task analysis described here, however, provide us with an initial framework of replicable practices within which we can continue to refine our process.

It is important to note, however, that learning does not begin and end at our tutoring sessions; patrons must reinforce what they have learned through independent practice. Despite our tutors' best attempts to encourage exploration, practice, and play within our tutoring sessions, encouraging patrons to engage in these behaviors independently is a remaining challenge. Patrons may not feel confident about setting up their own sandboxes at home or exploring without the watchful eye of their trusted tutor. Clearly, new techniques are required to reinforce these behaviors as patrons engage in digital tasks. To that end, we plan to focus on web navigation behavior and develop learning support through web components and browser add-ons that mimic tutor best practices—not as a substitute for face-to-face tutoring, but as a complement.

A   Appendix

See Figs. 2 and 3.

Category	Questions
Cues	— What terminology did the patron use when he or she described the problem? Was it technical or non-technical?
	— What did the patron's language use tell you about how much he or she understood about the technology?
	— Was there anything unusual about the manner in which the patron interacted with the technology?
	— Was there anything about the patron's questions or behavior that gave you insight into the patron's cyberliteracy level?
	— Did you rely on any cues to determine whether or not the patron understood what you were saying during the session?
Information	— Did the patron bring a list of questions to the session?
	— Did the patron identify new questions during the session?
	— Did you know the answer to the questions immediately or did you need to investigate the source of the problem or a possible solution?
	— Did you identify any gaps or errors in the patron's knowledge?
	— What information did you need to answer the patron's question?
	— Which pieces of information did you know that the patron did not?
Assessment	— If you had to leave in the middle of a session and needed to explain the patron's problems to another tutor, what would you say?
Decision Making	— At this point in the timeline, what decisions did you have to make?

Fig. 2. Probe questions, adapted from Crandall *et al.* [6].

Category	Questions
Experience	– Do you have any training or past experiences that you felt were particularly relevant to this scenario? – Is there any training you wish you had to better help this patron?
Goals/ Priorities	– What were your specific goals at this point in the timeline? – If the patron had multiple questions, how did you prioritize which one you addressed first or spent the most time on? – What was the most important/critical question that the patron asked during the session?
Analogs	– Did anything about this help session remind you of previous help sessions with other patrons or with this same patron? – Did you have any lessons learned from previous tutoring sessions that you thought might be relevant in this case? – Did you use analogies to help the patron understand the system?
Standard Operating Procedures	– Was the patron's problem typical? – Have you encountered this problem in other help sessions? – Did you feel prepared enough to answer the patron's questions?
Options	– There are often multiple solutions to a problem. Why did you choose the option that you did? – Was there something about this patron that made you select the option that you did? – Do you have any specific rules or guidelines that you follow when you assist a patron? – Do you have a list of resources or tools that you consistently recommend to your patrons? – Do you recommend different solutions depending on the patron? If so, what factors drive your selection?
Mental Models	– At any point in the session, did the patron describe how they thought something (e.g., the cloud, RAM, etc) worked? – At any point in the session, did you describe any concepts by drawing pictures or diagrams?
Guidance	– Did you seek any guidance from another tutor or any online resources during the help session? – How did you know where to look for guidance? Of your options, which source was most trustworthy? – Which source of guidance was the most relevant for this case?

Fig. 3. Probe questions, adapted from Crandall *et al.* [6].

References

1. Atkinson, K., Barnes, J., Albee, J., Anttila, P., Haataja, J., Nanavati, K., Steelman, K., Wallace, C.: Breaking barriers to digital literacy: an intergenerational social-cognitive approach. In: Proceedings of 18th International SIGACCESS Conference on Computers and Accessibility, pp. 239–244 (2016)
2. Aula, A.: User study on older adults' use of the web and search engines. Univ. Access Inf. Soc. 4(1), 67–81 (2005)
3. Bandura, A.: Social Learning Theory. Prentice-Hall, Englewood Cliffs (1977)
4. Bandura, A.: Organisational applications of social cognitive theory. Aust. J. Manag. 13(2), 275–302 (1988)
5. Callahan, J., Kiker, D., Cross, T.: Does method matter? A meta-analysis of the effects of training method on older learner training performance. J. Manag. 29(5), 663–680 (2003)
6. Crandall, B., Klein, G., Hoffman, R.: Incident-based CTA: helping practitioners "tell stories" In: Working Minds: a Practitioners Guide to Cognitive Task Analysis, pp. 69–90. MIT Press (2006)
7. Glass, J.: Factors affecting learning in older adults. Educ. Gerontol. Int. Q. 22(4), 359–372 (1996)
8. Hart, T., Chaparro, B., Halcomb, C.: Evaluating websites for older adults: adherence to 'senior-friendly' guidelines and end-user performance. Behav. Inf. Technol. 27(3), 191–199 (2008)
9. Hickman, J., Rogers, W., Fisk, A.: Training older adults to use new technology. J. Gerontol. Ser. B Psychol. Sci. Soc. Sci. 62(Special Issue 1), 77–84 (2007)
10. Kelley, L., Morrell, R.W., Park, D.C., Mayhorn, C.B.: Predictors of electronic bulletin board system use in older adults. Educ. Gerontol. 25(1), 19–35 (1999)
11. Rogers, W., Meyer, B., Walker, N., Fisk, A.: Functional limitations to daily living tasks in the aged: a focus group analysis. Hum. Factors 40(1), 111–125 (1998)
12. Smith, A.: Older adults and technology use (2014)
13. Steelman, K.S., Tislar, K.L., Ureel, L.C., Wallace, C.: Breaking digital barriers: a social-cognitive approach to improving digital literacy in older adults. In: Stephanidis, C. (ed.) HCI 2016. CCIS, vol. 617, pp. 445–450. Springer, Cham (2016). doi:10.1007/978-3-319-40548-3_74
14. Steelman, K., Wallace, C.: Addressing technology-related anxiety in mobile interfaces. In: Workshop on Designing Mobile Interactions for the Ageing Populations, ACM CHI Conference (2017)
15. Sterns, H., Doverspike, D.: Training and developing the older worker: implications for human resource management. In: Dennis, H. (ed.) Fourteen Steps in Managing an Aging Workforce, pp. 96–110. Lexington Books (1987)

Gamification on Senior Citizen's Information Technology Learning: The Mediator Role of Intrinsic Motivation

Kai Sun[1], Lingyun Qiu[2], and Meiyun Zuo[3(✉)]

[1] School of Business, Renmin University of China, Beijing 100872, China
sun_kai@ruc.edu.cn
[2] Guanghua School of Management, Peking University, Beijing 100871, China
qiu@gsm.pku.edu.cn
[3] School of Information, Renmin University of China, Beijing 100872, China
zuomy@ruc.edu.cn

Abstract. Gamification refers to the use of game elements in a non-game context so as to increase users' engagement and improve their experience. In recent years, gamification has been promoted by both practitioners and scholars as a superior alternative to traditional training methods in terms of improving students' learning process and performance. In this paper, we attempted to verify the effectiveness of gamified training in a unique context, i.e., to help senior users learn new information technology. We proposed a theoretical model to explain why gamification can positively affect senior users' learning experiences and outcomes. Through a laboratory experiment and a pilot study of 9 senior participants, we investigated whether or not gamification can really help improve senior people's learning process and performance. This paper not only extends gamification studies to the context of senior citizen education, its empirical results can also help practitioners design better gamified applications for senior users.

Keywords: Gamification · Senior citizens · Information technology learning

1 Introduction

Gamification refers to the use of game elements in a non-game context to increase users' engagement and improve their experience [1]. Gamification has emerged as a popular trend over the last years [2]. The idea of gamification has been used in industries, community, education, enterprise, environment, government, health, marketing, and social website[1].

Given the potential to increase engagement and enjoyment, practitioners and scholars have been touting gamification as a way to transform education and learning [2–4]. Gamified applications have been used to increase students' participant rate [5, 6] and improve students' learning quality in online learning platform [3, 4, 7]. Some scholars find that students perceive the gamified application as fun, enjoyable and useful [6, 8, 20], and have more positive attitude toward gamified learning methods than

---

[1] http://badgeville.com/wiki/gamification_examples.

© Springer International Publishing AG 2017
J. Zhou and G. Salvendy (Eds.): ITAP 2017, Part I, LNCS 10297, pp. 461–476, 2017.
DOI: 10.1007/978-3-319-58530-7_35

traditional ones [4, 7, 9]. However, some studies also find that gamified education is not as effective as non-gamified learning methods [2].

Based on the literature review, we find there are some limitations in the previous research as follows: First, few of previous researches discuss the mechanism of how gamification affecting learners' intrinsic motivation or performance. In their experiments, whether the application (or learning methods) is gamified or not is the independent variable. Intrinsic motivation and performance are the dependent variables. With comparison between gamified applications and traditional ones, they get the conclusion whether gamification is useful to increase intrinsic motivation and improve performance [2]. However, none of previous research argue why and how gamification can exert this kind of effect. We believe that this question is related to how to choose appropriate elements and design useful gamification application. But, there have been a lack of standards for design and implementation [10]. According to Gartner, by 2014, 80% of current gamified applications failed to meet business objectives primarily due to poor design [11]. Therefore, understanding the mechanism of how gamification elements working is very important for designing successful gamified application.

Second, most of previous research mainly focus on young people (e.g., undergraduate students), but do not prove that gamification is useful for other people with different age (e.g., senior citizens). Since the population is becoming ageing, scholars have paid increasingly more attention to the problems of senior citizen. One of the most important problems is the education and training for senior citizen to catch up with the high-speed development of society, especially the development of information technology [12]. But the traditional training methods are not effective for senior citizen to master the information technology. According to Activity Theory, participating in social activities can improve senior citizens' life satisfaction and enhance their life quality [13]. Therefore, we should discuss whether gamification can improve the quality of new technology-related education for senior citizen.

To sum up, in this paper, we plan to solve the following two questions. First, is gamification useful for senior citizen to learn new IT? Second, what is the mechanism of gamification affecting people's IT learning? This paper is organized as follow: in the second part, we discuss the related theories; in the third part, we propose the hypothesis and build the research model based on related theories; in the fourth part, we conduct a pilot test to answer the two research questions and prepare for the formal experiment; in the fifth part, we demonstrate the results of pilot test; in the sixth part, we discuss the theoretical contribution and practical implication; in the seventh part, we talk about the limitation and future works.

2 Theory

2.1 Gamification

Gamification refers to applying game elements into non-game context to improve users' experience and engagement [1]. The main goal of gamification is not to build a full-fledged game, but rather to apply some game elements to make the system more motivating and fun [9, 10]. According to Hamari, there are some difference between gamification and game: (1) gamification commonly attempts to afford experiences reminiscent of games, rather than providing direct hedonic experiences; (2) gamification attempts to affect motivations (e.g., intrinsic motivation) rather than attitude and/or behavior directly; (3) gamification refers to adding "gamefulness" to existing systems rather than building a full-fledged new game [14, 15].

There are many game elements that have been applied into non-game contexts, such as badge, story, leaderboard, points and so on [1, 9, 14]. In this paper, only the elements of badge and story were used because: First, they are the two most important and frequently used elements in gamification [3, 16]; Second, gamification encompasses so many different game mechanisms in their applications that it is difficult to examine every possible gamification element in one study [2]; Third, we just study gamification in a short term application context. We want to test whether gamification is useful for training senior citizen to learn self-service machine in a short term class. However, points need a relative long term to accumulate. So, we do not use points in our study; Forth, leaderboard is a complicated element in gamification. Many researches about leaderboard have controversial results. For example, in Hanus's research, they find that the leaderboard results in more social comparison and then decreases intrinsic motivation, satisfaction, effort and feeling of empowerment. But in Dominguez and de-Marcos' researches [4, 7], they find the leaderboard can increase students' intrinsic motivation. Therefore, in this paper, we do not include leaderboard.

Badge. A typical gamification method is to use achievement badges. A badge is a graphical icon that appears to users after reaching an achievement or completing certain activities [5, 9, 16].

Actually, badges have no practical value for users. The motivation to pursue badges comes from the emotional reward of achieving challenging goals [9]. The fulfillment of goals gives people the feeling of competence. In psychology, need of competence is a human's basic psychological need [17]. People have the innate desire to fulfill the need of competence and make sure "I am doing very well".

Therefore, a good badge should be designed to offer players timely and informative feedback that they are doing very well and have enough ability to finish the activity [18]. Useful badges should have goal setting to offer challenge and instant feedback about people's ability and "how I am doing". For example, De-Marcos and Dominguez [4, 7] in their papers take badge as an achievement system that reward student immediately on successful task completion. When students obtain badges, they feel that they are performing very well in some way. Consequently, these authors find the achievement system can improve students' learning outcome of operational activities.

Story. A compelling story is important to engage players to participate in activities and achieve the goals [19]. Story elements have been applied in many gamified applications [14]. For example, Li, Grossman and Fitzmaurice in their gamified application design Apollo program as the backstory and they find that the GamiCAD (one example of gamified learning applications) is more enjoyable, fun and engaging [20]. Guin, Baker, Mechling and Ruylea apply a story into online surveys to test if gamification can improve participants' engagement [21]. Flatla and his colleague apply a story into calibration games and find it useful to make user feel more enjoyable than regular calibration procedure, without compromising the quality of the data [22].

In game, stories are used to attract and engage players in two ways: curiosity and situation. Stories in games act as plot hooks. Plot hooks are unanswered questions that keep readers guessing. The uncertainties derived from stories attract players to the question and make they feel compelled to answer [23]. The purposes of plot hooks are to arouse curiosity, create intrigue, and frame puzzles, which all lead the players to ask "what is going to happen next?" [23]. Actually, curiosity give the players the meaning of playing the game [24]. This kind of story is often used in story-driven game, such as Role Play Games (RPG).

In addition to curiosity, stories can provide situations where and when leaners can generalize, comprehend knowledge easily [25]; and use, apply knowledge to real-world problems and requirements [26]. In this way, educational and training games have much in common with problem-based learning or case-based learning [25]. Through stories, metaphor or analogies are given to aid learner in understanding knowledge and skill better [21]. In addition, according to Malone's theory, it is more instructional, when story is designed to indicate how skills might be used in the real-world setting [21]. In this way, story enhance and highlight the meaning of learning [27].

As for gamification in education and training, useful stories are often designed to arouse curiosity and offer realistic situation where knowledge and skills can be applied into. For example, Li uses Apollo Program as backstory where users are responsible for helping NASA build components of a spacecraft [20]. Through the story, users are curious about the learning process and can understand how the skill of Computer Aid Design (CAD) can be used in the real-world setting [6].

2.2 Intrinsic Motivation

Intrinsic Motivation refers to the doing of an activity for its inherent satisfaction and pleasure derived from participation rather than for some separable consequences [28]. Intrinsic motivation is the inherent tendency to seek out novelty and challenge, to extend and to exercise one's capacities, to explore, and to learn. According to Cognitive Evaluation Theory, people's intrinsic motivation can be enhanced by the satisfaction of competence need and autonomy need [17].

Competence. Competence refers to people's capacity for effective interactions with environment in producing desired outcomes and preventing undesired events [17, 29]. According to Deci and Ryan's point of view [17], intrinsically motivated activities involve seeking and conquering optimal challenges. Optimal challenges include elements that are slightly discrepant from, and can be assimilated into, one's existing and organized knowledge or skill structures [17]. And these perceived challenge can stretch out but do not overmatch existing skills [30]. Some psychologists argue the feeling of competence is derived from the match between people's ability and activities' challenge [30, 31]. When people have high competence, they will more concentrate on the activity itself [30], then have more intrinsic motivation [28]. Otherwise they will have less intrinsic motivation with more tension and pressure [17].

Autonomy. Psychologists are most apt to take intrinsic motivation as self-determined [17, 28]. Deci and Ryan [17] use autonomy to refer to the feeling of engaging in activities out of one's own choosing, without external or internal controlling [17, 28].

People engage in an activity just for the satisfactions and pleasure that they can experience, not for external reward or internal pressure [17]. External controlling events, such as reward, punishment, deadline, surveillance, competition and others-administered evaluation, make people finish activity not for activity itself but rather to obtain separate outcomes [17]. Internal controlling is derived from internalized norms, rewards and punishments and is represented as "I should to do" or "I have to do". People like to explore the curious and valuable activities [17]. So, making the activity more curious and valuable can increase people's autonomy. Consequence of Intrinsic Motivation.

Intrinsic motivation can influence people' affect, cognition and behavior [28]. Affective consequences include interest, positive emotions, satisfaction and reduction of anxiety [28]. Intrinsically motivated people will feel more positive emotions, such as interest and pleasure, and less negative emotions, such as anxiety [17]. Cognitive consequence include concentration, attention, good memory, conceptual learning, cognitive flexibility and creative thinking [17, 28]. In some experiments, researchers have proved that intrinsically motivated students learn best, most effectively and most lastingly [27]. Behavioral consequences include persistence at the task, good behavioral intentions and performance [28]. In this paper, we focus on the practical operation of information technology for senior citizens. So, we just examine the effect of gamification on their affective consequence (e.g., technology anxiety) and behavioral consequence (e.g., learning performance).

3   Research Model and Hypotheses Development

The research model is summarized in Fig. 1.

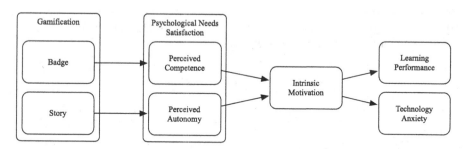

Fig. 1.   Research model

3.1   Badge and Perceived Competence

In this paper, perceived competence refers to senior citizens' perception of their competence to produce desired outcome in the learning context [17, 29]. A badge is a graphical icon that appears to the user after reaching an achievement or completing certain activities [5, 9, 16]. Badges can provide information about learners' behavior and performance, which can reflect their competence and then enhance their intrinsic motivation [17]. In gamification field, useful badges should act as goal setting and instant feedback related to people's ability and "how I am doing". Essentially, goal setting offers people challenge and instant feedback provides information whether their ability and challenge are matched to complete the challenge. If they are matched, obtaining badges is like an encouragement that senior citizens can master the ability of modern IT. Even though they are not matched, people need immediate feedback to judge whether their skills can match with perceived challenges (i.e., proximal goals). Even though they are not doing very well (do not get badge), senior citizens can learn from the timely feedback where the problem is, and then make plan about next stage [17]. Therefore, in gamified context with badges, people are more like to perceive competence. Hence, we propose:

Hypothesis 1 (H1): Participants in the with-badge group have higher perceived competence than those in the no-badge group.

3.2   Story and Perceived Autonomy

In this paper, perceived autonomy refers to senior citizens' feeling of engaging in learning out of their own choosing [17, 28].

Stories, in gamification, usually engage learners by providing a curious situation. As for gamified educational application, story can make senior citizens more curious about what will happen in the next [23, 25]. Then they will behave more actively and spontaneously [17, 23, 25], because curiosity is the basic propensity in human function [17].

Story can also provide a practical situation where and when a senior citizen is able to generalize, comprehend knowledge easily [25]. Furthermore, they can learn how to use and apply the IT to real-world problems and requirements [26] by themselves. So, it is more likely for them to understand the value and importance of learning IT, and learn more actively. Then motivation is internalized and autonomy is increased [17]. Hence, we propose:

Hypothesis 2 (H2): Participants in the with-story group have higher perceived autonomy than those in the no-story group.

3.3   Perceived Competence and Intrinsic Motivation

In this paper, intrinsic motivation refers to the extent of which senior citizens want to study and do exercise, because of the pleasure, enjoyment and satisfaction derived from the study and exercising themselves [17].

Learning new technology-related skill and knowledge itself is able to be intrinsically motivated for senior citizens, because the desire to explore, discover, understand, and know new knowledge is intrinsic to people's nature and is a potentially central motivator of the educational process [17]. Moreover, learning new technology itself is a challenging activity for senior citizens, because of the physical degeneration and social pressure.

According to Cognitive Evaluation Theory, only when people have high competence, they can have enough confidence and focus on the learning activity itself motivation [17]. Then they can have more intrinsic motivation [17]. The need for competence is one of the basic need of human. When it is unsatisfied, it will get human's attention to the gap, so people can not focus on the learning activity itself [17]. Moreover, low competence always accompanies with stress and anxiety, which will result in lower intrinsic motivation [17]. Hence, we propose:

Hypothesis 3 (H3): Perceived competence is positively associated with intrinsic motivation;

3.4 Perceived Autonomy and Intrinsic Motivation

When senior citizens are self-determined or high autonomous to learn modern IT, they have choice and opportunity to be fully involved within learning itself and treat learning activity as something they want to do for the learning's sake [17]. Therefore, a greater opportunity for self-determination frees people to be more intrinsically motivated [17].

When senior citizens perceive their autonomy to be threatened with external controlling events (e.g., peer pressure, "my friends are learning this, maybe I should do this, too) or internal controlling events (e.g., pursuing reputation and under the control of internalized norms), they experience the escaping of controlled and unfree [17]. At such time, they consider that doing the activity is for extrinsic factors rather than the activity itself. They regard their behavior or activity as an instrument to obtain what they want (e.g., reward, reputation, avoidance of punishment) or avoid what they dislike, and their attention are redirected away from the activity itself [17].

In gamification design, more and more designers are aware of the importance of autonomy. One of Cheong's recommendations for gamified design is that participation should be voluntary: "if the participants are forced to undertake the activity, it takes away from its gameful nature" [3]. Hence, we propose:

Hypothesis 4 (H4): Perceived autonomy is positively associated with intrinsic motivation;

3.5 Intrinsic Motivation and Learning Performance

In this paper, completion time of exercise is used to measure senior citizens' learning performance. Completion time of exercise can provide an indicator of how well people learned self-service machine during the training [20].

Intrinsically motivated senior citizens will have more concentration on learning [17, 30]. Under this condition, they are better to think creatively, grasp the meaning of learning materials, and have more flexible cognition [17]. Intrinsic motivation is the natural wellspring of education and achievement. And it can result in high-quality learning and creativity.

When students are intrinsically motivated to learn, they learn better, more effectively and more lastingly [27]. Parker and Lepper, in their experiment, find intrinsically motivated students have greater outcomes of learning programming language [27]. Vansteenkiste et al. find, under the autonomy-supportive context, students who are driven by intrinsic goal have better learning outcome [32]. Hence, we propose:

Hypothesis 5 (H5): Intrinsic motivation is positively associated with learning performance;

3.6   Intrinsic Motivation and Technology Anxiety

Technology anxiety refers to the fear and/or apprehension people feel when considering use or actually using general technology tools [33]. It is characterized as an affection response [34]. Technology anxiety is one of the most important factors in preventing senior citizens from learning modern IT [35].

According to Self-Determination Theory, intrinsically motivated people do something because it is inherently interesting or enjoyable. Then positive emotions will be the consequence of intrinsic motivation [28]. The feeling of positive emotions is the reward for intrinsic motivation [17, 28]. With more intrinsic motivation, the senior citizens will have more positive mood. Therefore, intrinsically motivated learners are less likely to have specific technology anxiety after learning process. Hence, we propose: *Hypothesis 6 (6): Intrinsic motivation is negatively associated with technology anxiety.*

4   Research Method

In the above sections, we discuss the mechanism of gamification theoretically. Next, we did a pilot test to analyze the model, which lay a foundation for future empirical experiment. In our pilot test, we recruit 9 senior citizens (>60-year-old) to join an activity to learn how to use Ticket Vending Machine (TVM). In China, the adoption of TVM is very low for senior citizens. And none of the 9 selected senior citizens knew how to use this machine and had never tried it by themselves before.

In Beijing, China, subway is one of the most widely accepted public transportation ways. In 2008, Ticket Vending Machine (TVM) was first fully used in Beijing subway system. The goal of TVM is to reduce the waiting time wasted to buy ticket in artificial ticket office. However, senior citizens still prefer to buy ticket in the artificial ticket office. They are used to interacting with people, but not with machine. And with the negative news about the malfunction of TVM, it is hard for senior citizens to learn how to use this kind of machine. Therefore, we chose TVM as our experiment scenario. We designed a learning activity to teach senior citizens how to use the TVM and used gamification methods to gamify the process.

4.1   Participants

We recruited 9 senior citizens (>60-year-old), who lived in the community close to our university in Beijing, China. Firstly, we randomly invited 25 senior citizens to join a learning activity, which hosted by the university. Secondly, we deleted 10 people who knew how to use TVM, and 5 people who were not available in our experiment time. Thirdly, we deleted 1 people whose health condition was not good enough to join the learning activity. Finally, we recruited 9 senior citizens who were above 60-year-old.

We classified them into four groups: Badge group, Story group, Badge+Story group and control Group (i.e. not gamified group). The specific information of classification can be seen in Table 1.

Table 1. Demographic information.

	Badge	Story	Badge+Story	Control group
Gender				
Male	0	0	1	0
Female	2	2	2	2
Age				
60–64	0	0	1	0
65–69	1	1	1	0
70–74	1	0	0	0
75–79	0	1	1	1
80+	0	0	0	1
Education				
Elementary school	0	1	0	0
Middle school	1	0	1	0
High school	1	1	0	0
Undergraduate	0	0	2	2
Living condition				
Only with spouse	1	1	1	1
With spouse and children	1	0	2	1
Only with children	0	1	0	0
Income (one year)				
30000–50000	2	2	2	0
50000–100000	0	0	1	2

4.2 Procedure

We developed a Learning System to teach senior citizen how to use Ticket Vending Machine (TVM). In the system there were three parts: (1) video-watching part, watching video to learn what is TVM and how to use it; (2) practice part, practicing on our Learning System. There were three practice sessions. In the first practice session, they bought 1 ticket, but did not change the line; in the second practices session, they bought 2 tickets, but did not change the line; in the third practices session, they bought 2 tickets, but changed the line; (3) test part, doing a test at last. In the practice part, we gamify the system by badge and story.

In the badge group, after every session of practices part, if subjects successfully finished the practices, they could get a Little Red Flower (Badge). The Little Red Flower meant that senior citizens successfully finished the practice. If they performed better than in the last session, they could obtain two Red Little Flowers. Before the practice part, all subjects in Badge group and Badge+Story group were informed the Little Red Flower and how they could them.

In the story group, we provided a story background. In this story, one subject's old friend would come to visit them. And she/he wanted to visit Beijing. So, the subject decided to show the friend around Beijing by subway, because the subway was more convenient and the traffic in Beijing was not good. First, subject would take the subway to train station to pick her/his friend up. Second, they took the subway to The Imperial Palace from train station. Third, they took the subway from the Imperial Palace to The Lama Temple.

In the test part, all subjects took the same examination. After learning process, subject filled up the questionnaire and got the interview. Through the questionnaire, their perception and other psychological state were measured. And through the interview, their opinions about the gamified training method were recorded.

4.3 Measurement

We adapted scales of Intrinsic Motivation, Perceived Autonomy, and Perceived Competence from Ryan and Deci's Intrinsic Motivation Inventory[2]. Six items were used to measure Intrinsic Motivation. Four items were used to measure Perceived Autonomy. Five items were used to measure Perceived Competence. Items of measuring Technology Anxiety were adapted from Meuter and McInerney [33, 36]. Five items were used to measure Technology Anxiety. The time that subjects use in final test refers to subjects' learning performance (See Appendix A).

5 Results

5.1 Descriptive Statistics and Correlation Analysis

Table 2 shows the mean values of constructs. It can be seen from Table 2 that subjects in Badge+Story group have best learning performance (they spent least time in final test). Subjects in Story group have better learning performance than those in Control group and Badge group. Subjects in Badge group have the worse learning performance.

Table 2. Analysis results.

	Badge	Story	Badge+Story	Control	Total
Perceived competence	6.2	5.5	6.7	7	6.4
Perceived autonomy	6.3	5	5.5	5.5	5.6
Intrinsic motivation	7	6.6	7	7	6.9
Technology anxiety	1.8	2.2	1.2	2	1.7
Learning performance	44218	33631.5	22272.3	34352.5	32357.9

Note: Learning performance was measured by the time subjects took to finish their final test.

---

[2] http://www.selfdeterminationtheory.org/intrinsic-motivation-inventory/.

As for perceived competence, subjects in Control group feel the most competent; those in Story group are the least competent. As for perceived autonomy, subjects in Badge group have the highest autonomy; those in Story group have the lowest. As for intrinsic motivation, subjects in Badge group, Badge+Story group and Control are equally intrinsic motivated; those in Story group have the least intrinsic motivation. As for technology anxiety, subjects in Badge+Story group have the least anxiety; those in Story group feel the most anxious.

Although the sample is too small, we can see the trend that subjects in gamification group have better learning performance and lower technology anxiety.

We also did the correlation analysis. In Table 3, it can be seen that perceived competence and perceived autonomy are positively related with intrinsic motivation. Intrinsic motivation are negatively related technology anxiety and learning performance, which means the higher subjects' intrinsic motivation, the better their learning performance is and the lower their technology anxiety is. The results of correlation analysis are consistent with our theoretical model. They demonstrate the relationships of perceived competence-intrinsic motivation, perceived autonomy-intrinsic motivation, intrinsic motivation-technology anxiety and intrinsic motivation-learning performance in some way.

Table 3. Correlation analysis.

		COM	AU	IM	TA	LP
COM	Pearson correlation	1	.000	.630	−.491	−.165
	Sig. (2-tailed)		1.00	.069	.180	.671
AU	Pearson correlation	.000	1	.624	−.205	.136
	Sig. (2-tailed)	1.000		.073	.596	.728
IM	Pearson correlation	.630	.624	1	−.674*	−.086
	Sig. (2-tailed)	.069	.073		.047	.825
TA	Pearson correlation	−.491	−.205	−.674*	1	.081
	Sig. (2-tailed)	.180	.596	.047		.835
LP	Pearson correlation	−.165	.136	−.086	.081	1
	Sig. (2-tailed)	.671	.728	.825	.835	

Note: COM: perceived competence; AU: perceived autonomy; IM: intrinsic motivation; TA: technology anxiety; LP: learning performance. *Correlation is significant at the 0.05 level (2-tailed); The number of sample is 9.

Although the correlation analysis demonstrates the relationships among perceived competence, perceived autonomy, intrinsic motivation, technology anxiety and learning performance, questionnaire data cannot support our expectation. It is because that the small samples result in the insignificant difference among different groups. So, we did another interviews with all subjects to find out what were their opinions about the gamified learning method.

5.2 Interview Results

In the interviews, we used the open questions and asked all subjects to talk about their opinions about the Badge and/or Story. We wanted to find out whether the subjects in

Badge group believed the badge could make them more competent; the subjects in Story group believed that story could make them more autonomous.

Badge and Perceived Competence. Badge, in the gamified learning context, "has not practical meaning" (S10). But, it provides challenge and reflects learners' ability, which helps people feel competent about the activity. In badge group, subjects said that "the badge encourages me and I feel I am capable to finish the exercise" (S1). "I have been off school for a long time. Without this kind of encouragement (of my ability), I do not think I can come back" (S6). And "obtaining a badge after better performance is a good encouragement" (S4), and "it makes me feel confident" (S10).

Story and Perceived Autonomy. In our theory, story has two functions to impact learners' behavior. First, story makes the learning process more curious. Just as one subject (S8) said "the story makes the learning activity more attractive. I want to know what is the next". Second, story can also provide a situation where and when a leaner is able to generalize, comprehend knowledge easily [25] and learn how to use, apply knowledge to real-world problems and requirements [26]. Just like one subject (S6) said "the story makes the learning process more real and can help me understand when and in what situation I can use the TVM". And this design makes them believe "the knowledge is useful in the future" (S10).

In the interviews, most of subject believed that the badge and story can make them more competent and autonomous. And the gamified design can make the learning process more interesting.

6   Discussion

Gamification has become and will become more important in company management, education, marketing and other social application [19]. In this paper, authors discuss the application of gamification in education field, especially for senior citizen's education. As the technology becomes increasingly ubiquitous and common in our daily, how to educate senior citizens to use them is becoming more import social and academic problem [12]. Therefore, authors try to analyze the effect of gamification on senior citizens' learning of information technology (e.g., Ticket Vending Machine).

6.1   Theoretical Contributions

In this paper, we focus on the senior citizens and try to examine the effect of gamified learning method on their learning. Although there are not enough sample in the pilot test, we find in the gamification group, senior citizens have less anxiety and better performance after the gamified learning. They believe that the badge and story make the learning more enjoyable and interesting. In some way, the gamified learning process can help senior citizen master the modern IT better.

In this paper, we try to discuss the mechanism of gamification, through the lens of Motivation Theory [17]. Previous studies pay more attention to the effectiveness test of gamification for younger people, but do not provide the mechanism. Therefore, we attempted to fill this the gap.

Based on the Motivation Theory [17], we believe that the intrinsic motivation is an important factor in influencing people's learning performance and technology anxiety. One of the most important functions of gamification is to offer senior citizens the similar feeling of playing game, without converting learning into a full-edge game [1]. In game, players' intrinsic motivation - doing an activity for its inherent satisfaction and pleasure rather than for some separable consequence [28] - play import role in explaining players' engagement. And in education field, scholars find that high intrinsic motivation of students is related with their high performance [17]. Therefore, we treat intrinsic motivation as the mediator between gamified design and learning results (e.g., performance, anxiety).

Many previous studies also use intrinsic motivation as the bridge between gamified design and learning results [2, 9, 37]. However, not every paper finds the significantly positive relationship between gamified design and intrinsic motivation. So, there may be some factors unfounded between design and intrinsic motivation.

In order to answer the question, we introduce the antecedent factors of intrinsic motivation- perceived competence and perceived autonomy [17]. Perceived competence refers to the people's capacity for effective interactions with the environment in producing desired outcomes and preventing undesired event [17, 29]. Perceived autonomy refers to the feeling of engaging in activities out of one's own choosing, without external or internal controlling [17, 28].

By correlation analysis, we find the significant correlation among perceived competence-intrinsic motivation, perceived autonomy-intrinsic motivation, intrinsic motivation-technology anxiety, and intrinsic motivation-learning performance. Through the interviews, we also find that badge can increase senior citizens' perceived competence, and story can increase their perceived autonomy.

6.2 Practical Implication

In this paper, we find that successful badge design should increase learners' intrinsic motivation through their perceived competence. However, in extant research, many badges are so improperly designed that many researchers find that badge in gamified activities has negative influence on learners' intrinsic motivation and quality of learning [2]. For example, Hanus and Fox [2] argue that the badge system shift students' motivations of learning from intrinsic (i.e., because they want to learn) to extrinsic (i.e., because they want to earn a reward). In their experiment, their badges are designed to ask students to do something that is irrelevant to students' learning performance, such as badge "Go Forth and Multiply". This badge requires student "Go, physically, to the library and find a resource that you cannot find otherwise that could help with a class paper or project, make a copy of it, and bring it into class". Even though students get this badge, they will not feel competent about learning.

In this paper, we also find that successful story design should increase learners' intrinsic motivation through their perceived autonomy. If the story is intriguing and can provide the virtual or real situation where learners can apply the knowledge, it is a proper design to make learners feel that they participate in the learning activity for their own sake. So, just providing an unrelated story as the back-group of the learning process is hard to increase senior citizens' learning performance.

7 Limitations and Future Works

There are some limitations in this paper. First, due to the limitation of sample in the pilot test, the results cannot be concrete enough. In this paper, we just recruit 9 senior citizens to do a pilot test. And the pilot test just shows some superficial results or evidence of the model. We should conduct a concrete empirical experiment to test the model in the future. Second, in order to analyze the different effect of gamification on senior citizen and young people, we should recruit both valid samples of senior citizens and young people to test the model. In out pilot test, we just tried to test the effectiveness of the model for senior citizens. In the future, we should do the test for the young people and explore the difference between them.

Acknowledgement. This work was supported in part by the Fundamental Research Funds for the Central Universities under Grant 10XNJ065, part by National Natural Science Foundation of China under Grant 71273265 and Grant 71472009, part by National Social Science Foundation of China Major Program under Grant 13&ZD184.

Appendix A

Construct	Items	Source
Perceived competence	I think I am pretty good at learning ticket vending machine	Intrinsic Motivation Inventory (IMI)
	After learning ticket vending machine for a while, I felt pretty competent	
	I am satisfied with my performance at this learning	
	I am pretty skilled at using ticket vending machine	
	This was an activity that I couldn't do very well	
Perceived autonomy	While I was learning ticket vending machine, I felt like it was not my own choice to learn (R)	Intrinsic Motivation Inventory (IMI)
	While I was learning ticket vending machine, I felt like I really wanted to	
	While I was learning ticket vending machine, I felt like I had to (R)	
	While I was learning ticket vending machine, I felt like I was active	
Intrinsic motivation	I enjoyed learning ticket vending machine very much	Intrinsic Motivation Inventory (IMI)
	Learning ticket vending machine was fun to do	
	I thought learning ticket vending machine was boring (R)	
	Learning ticket vending machine did not hold my attention at all (R)	
	I would describe learning ticket vending machine as very interesting	
	I thought learning ticket vending machine was quite enjoyable	
Technology anxiety	I am confident I can learn technology-related skills (R)	[33, 36]
	I have difficulty understanding most technological matters	
	Reading a technology manual makes me anxious.	
	I am not comfortable to Learn technology terminology	
	Taking a class about the use of technology make me anxious	

References

1. Deterding, S., Khaled, R., Nacke, L., Dixon, D.: Gamification: toward a definition. In: CHI 2011 Gamification Workshop Proceedings, pp. 12–15 (2011)
2. Hanus, M.D., Fox, J.: Assessing the effects of gamification in the classroom: a longitudinal study on intrinsic motivation, social comparison, satisfaction, effort, and academic performance. Comput. Educ. **80**, 152–161 (2015)
3. Cheong, C., Cheong, F., Filippou, J.: Quick quiz: a gamified approach for enhancing learning. In: PACIS 2014 Proceeding, p. 206 (2013)
4. Domínguez, A., Saenz-de-Navarrete, J., De-Marcos, L., Fernández-Sanz, L., Pagés, C., Martínez-Herráiz, J.: Gamifying learning experiences: practical implications and outcomes. Comput. Educ. **63**, 380–392 (2013)
5. Denny, P.: The effect of virtual achievements on student engagement. In: Proceedings of the SIGCHI Conference on Human Factors in Computing Systems, pp. 763–772. ACM (2013)
6. Dong, T., Dontcheva, M., Joseph, D., Karahalios, K., Newman, M., Ackerman, M.: Discovery-based games for learning software. In: Proceedings of the SIGCHI Conference on Human Factors in Computing Systems, pp. 2083–2086. ACM (2012)
7. De-Marcos, L., Domínguez, A., Saenz-de-Navarrete, J., Pagés, C.: An empirical study comparing gamification and social networking on e-learning. Comput. Educ. **75**, 82–91 (2014)
8. Fitz-Walter, Z., Tjondronegoro, D., Wyeth, P.: Orientation passport: using gamification to engage university students. In: Proceedings of the 23rd Australian Computer-Human Interaction Conference, pp. 122–125. ACM (2011)
9. Hakulinen, L., Auvinen, T., Korhonen, A.: Empirical study on the effect of achievement badges in TRAKLA2 online learning environment. In: Learning and Teaching in Computing and Engineering (LaTiCE), pp. 47–54. IEEE (2013)
10. Seaborn, K., Fels, D.I.: Gamification in theory and action: a survey. Int. J. Hum Comput Stud. **74**, 14–31 (2015)
11. Gartner: Gartner says by 2014, 80% of current gamified applications will fail to meet business objectives primarily due to poor design (2014). http://www.gartner.com/newsroom/id/2251015
12. Ferreira, S., Torres, A., Mealha, Ó., Veloso, A.: Training effects on older adults in information and communication technologies considering psychosocial variables. Educ. Gerontol. **41**(7), 482–493 (2015)
13. Lemon, B.W., Bengtson, V.L., Peterson, J.A.: An exploration of the activity theory of aging: activity types and life satisfaction among in-movers to a retirement community. J. Gerontol. **27**(4), 511–523 (1972)
14. Hamari, J., Koivisto, J.: Social motivations to use gamification: an empirical study of gamifying exercise. In: ECIS 2013 Completed Research, p. 105 (2013)
15. Simões, J., Redondo, R.D., Vilas, A.F.: A social gamification framework for a K-6 learning platform. Comput. Hum. Behav. **29**(2), 345–353 (2013)
16. Antin, J., Churchill, E.F.: Badges in social media: a social psychological perspective. In: CHI 2011 Gamification Workshop Proceedings (2011)
17. Deci, E.L., Ryan, R.M.: Intrinsic Motivation and Self-Determination in Human Behavior. Plenum Press, New York (1985)
18. Charles, D., Charles, T., McNeill, M., Bustard, D., Black, M.: Game-based feedback for educational multi-user virtual environments. Br. J. Educ. Technol. **42**(4), 638–654 (2011)
19. Gartner: Gartner says by 2015, more than 50% of organizations that manage innovation processes will gamify those processes (2011). http://www.gartner.com/newsroom/id/1629214

20. Li, W., Grossman, T., Fitzmaurice, G.: Gamicad: a gamified tutorial system for first time autocad users. In: Proceedings of the 25th Annual ACM Symposium on User Interface Software and Technology, pp. 103–112. ACM (2012)

21. Downes-Le Guin, T., Baker, R., Mechling, J., Ruylea, E.: Myths and realities of respondent engagement in online surveys. Int. J. Mark. Res. **54**(5), 1–21 (2012)

22. Flatla, D.R., Gutwin, C., Nacke, L.E., Bateman, S., Mandryk, R.L.: Calibration games: making calibration tasks enjoyable by adding motivating game elements. In: Proceedings of the 24th Annual ACM Symposium on User Interface Software and Technology, pp. 403–412. ACM (2011)

23. Dickey, M.D.: Game design narrative for learning: appropriating adventure game design narrative devices and techniques for the design of interactive learning environments. Educ. Technol. Res. Develop. **54**(3), 245–263 (2006)

24. McGonigal, J.: Reality is Broken: Why Games Make Us Better and How They Can Change the World, 1st edn. Penguin Press, New York (2012)

25. Smith, A., Baker, L.: Getting a clue: creating student detectives and dragon slayers in your library. Ref. Serv. Rev. **39**(4), 628–642 (2011)

26. Gustafsson, A., Katzeff, C., Bang, M.: Evaluation of a pervasive game for domestic energy engagement among teenagers. Comput. Entertainment **7**(4), 54–66 (2009)

27. Parker, L.E., Lepper, M.R.: Effects of fantasy contexts on children's learning and motivation: making learning more fun. J. Pers. Soc. Psychol. **62**(4), 625 (1992)

28. Vallerand, R.J.: Toward a hierarchical model of intrinsic and extrinsic motivation. In: Zanna, M.P. (ed.) Advances in Experimental Social Psychology, pp. 271–360. Academic Press, San Diego (1997)

29. Venkatesh, V.: Creation of favorable user perceptions: exploring the role of intrinsic motivation. MIS Q. **23**(2), 239–260 (1999)

30. Nakamura, J., Csikszentmihalyi, M.: Flow theory and research. In: Oxford Handbook of Positive Psychology, p. 195 (2009)

31. Csikszentmihalyi, M., Csikszentmihaly, M.: Flow: The Psychology of Optimal Experience. Harper Perennial, New York (1991)

32. Vansteenkiste, M., Simons, J., Lens, W., Sheldon, K.M., Deci, E.L.: Motivating learning, performance, and persistence: the synergistic effects of intrinsic goal contents and autonomy-supportive contexts. J. Pers. Soc. Psychol. **87**(2), 246 (2004)

33. Meuter, M.L., Ostrom, A.L., Bitner, M.J., Roundtree, R.: The influence of technology anxiety on consumer use and experiences with self-service technologies. J. Bus. Res. **56**(11), 899–906 (2003)

34. Barbeite, F.G., Weiss, E.M.: Computer self-efficacy and anxiety scales for an Internet sample: testing measurement equivalence of existing measures and development of new scales. Comput. Hum. Behav. **20**(1), 1–15 (2004)

35. Wagner, N., Hassanein, K., Head, M.: Computer use by older adults: a multi-disciplinary review. Comput. Hum. Behav. **26**(5), 870–882 (2010)

36. McInerney, V., McInerney, D.M., Sinclair, K.E.: Student teachers, computer anxiety and computer experience. J. Educ. Comput. Res. **11**(1), 27–50 (1994)

37. Christy, K.R., Fox, J.: Leaderboards in a virtual classroom: a test of stereotype threat and social comparison explanations for women's math performance. Comput. Educ. **78**, 66–77 (2014)

The Study of Teaching the Smartphone Using in Taiwan's Elderly Population—A Case Study in Learners of the Senior Citizens Academy in a City of Taiwan

Ming-Wei Wang[✉]

Senior Citizens Academy, Chiayi, Taiwan, ROC
louis258306@gmail.com

Abstract. The rapid development of the smartphones, the operation systems and the Cellular network makes the rapid increasing of the population in using the smartphones. The mass production of the smartphones makes the price cheaper, and the using of smartphones is popular. Not only the young people, but also the elderly have begun to use the smart phones and the Cellular network. The office workers use the smartphones and the internet to finish their work, and the elderly use the phones and the internet for convenient life and the connection of their friends and family. More and more elderly want to learn how to use their smartphones and internet. The course in smartphones using becomes more popular in the senior citizens academy.

In this study, we found that the elderly use the smartphones more easily than use the computer. On one hand, the computer using is in home, when the elderly find some problems, they cannot get help immediately. When they have some questions in using smartphones, they will get help easily because they carry the phones with them and they can get help from somebody around them. On the other, the operation of phones is easy than the computer. The using of the smartphones is by fingers, the operating of the computer is by the mouse. To be familiar with the use of the mouse is difficult for the elderly.

We also found that the key point of teaching elderly to use the smartphones is how to use, not how to set their phones. For example, it is important to teach them to use the Facebook by their phones, and it is not very important to teach them how to download the Facebook APP from the Google Play.

It is different between teaching the computer using and the smartphone using. When the elderly come to the academy, the teacher tells them how to read the web, to listen the music, to watch the video by the computer step by step. There are some standard operation processes in using the computer. Now we have to tell them how to use their phone, there are twenty to thirty elderly in one class and they use different brands of the smartphones. The teacher needs to be more patient and teach them one by one.

There are two analysis conclusions in this case study. First, the key point of teaching the smartphones using is the using of the phone or APP, not the phone setting. The phone using is easier than the computer using, but it is still difficult for the elderly to set the user mode or the APP setting on their phones. We suggest that the family or the teacher set up the phone for them to avoid the low learning motivation cause by the difficult setting learning.

© Springer International Publishing AG 2017
J. Zhou and G. Salvendy (Eds.): ITAP 2017, Part I, LNCS 10297, pp. 477–485, 2017.
DOI: 10.1007/978-3-319-58530-7_36

Second, we use more individual instruction to replace the group teaching. Our teach content is the using of the Android cellphone. But each participant owns the different brand of the phone. There are slightly differences of the operation between their phones. The group teaching is not the most suitable teaching method. For example, we would teach them how to use the Facebook on their phones by the group teaching, when we teach them how to set their cellphone to take pictures, the individual instruction is more suitable.

We also found an interesting phenomenon in the teaching. When the elderly people are familiar with the phones using and they often use the instant messaging software on the phone. They used to share a lot of messages on the instant messaging software just as health, philosophy of life, etc. But they don't used to check that the information is true or false. They often share the wrong message on their Facebook or LINE (an instant message software, it is like What's APP) because they don't know the message is wrong. The teacher has to tell them how to distinguish between true and false messages.

Keywords: Smartphone · Cellphone · Elderly · Elderly learning

1   Introduction

The smartphone is a mobile phone that has an independent operating system that can be extended by installing the applications, the games, and the other programs. Its computing power and functionality are superior to the traditional mobile phones. The cellular network, also known as the mobile network is a mobile communication hardware architecture, divided into analog cellular network and digital cellular network. Since the signal coverage of the communication base stations constituting the network coverage is hexagonal, the whole network is named after a cell. When the smartphone and mobile network are combined, our modern digital society is established. When we don't know where we can eat delicious dinner, watch the movies, we used to take our cellphone, and connect the internet to find the information.

The senior citizens academy organize the information application courses in 2008. The candidates must be over 65 years old. The elderly registration is very enthusiastic, because the computer, the Internet is the new technology for them. They know that the new technology would help them to live better. In recent years, under the development of the smart phones, with the mobile network technology, elderly people are eager to access the Internet any time, as the young people around them. So the senior citizens academy organize the course about the cellphones. In the course, we found that a lot of elderly use their cellphone to watch videos on YouTube, to share their pictures on Facebook, to transfer their live on the instant message software like WeChat, Line.

According to our observation, about 10% to 20% of the elderly can use the smart phone independently when the course is completed and they own the ability to search for the information they need on the Internet. 60% to 70% of the elderly can use the instant messaging software to send and receive the messages by the cellphones. About 10% of the elderly are still not familiar with the use of the network when the course is completed.

According to the statistics of the National Development Council of the Republic of China in 2016, the ratio of people over 60 years old using the smartphone to the Internet is 34.8% in 2016, 4.3% growth over 2015. We found that the elderly population also has the demand for mobile Internet, and the demand is increasing year by year.

It is the motivation of this study to create a high-quality learning environment, to reduce the learning burden of the elderly and to improve the learning intention.

2 Literature Review

According to the statistics of the population of Taiwan in December 2016, the total population of Taiwan is 23539816 people, and older than 65 years old population is 3106,105 people, the proportion of the elderly population is 13.20%. In other words, Taiwan will become the aged society in recent years (Ministry of the Interior, Taiwan, ROC 2017). The problems faced by the elderly population will be the focus of our attention.

Elderly education is the teachings of the elderly, and is also a part of adult education (Wang 2004). The 21st century is a lifelong learning century, human beings in order to adapt to the needs of social change must learn four basic learning (Delors et al. 1996): learning to live together, learning to know, learning to do, learning to be. In 2011, when the birth of the first baby boomers in the United States entered the age of 65, it immediately highlighted the importance of Pre-Retirement Education (PRE), which helped individuals to transition from a job role to a retirement role to reduce their likelihood resulting in poorly adapted problems (Anna 2009). The United Nations Educational, Scientific and Cultural Organization (UNESCO) specifically defined that for elderly people, elderly education plays a very important role, emphasizing that elderly educators can no longer look at the problem of the elderly in the context of welfare services, but that learning should be seen as a part of their life.

Through the above literature, we can find that life-long learning is important for elderly people. It would help elderly people to face the transformation of the social roles.

In recent years, Internet continues to develop, not only young people but also elderly people want to learn how to get information in the Internet. In fact, elderly people do not like the imagination of the exclusion of the computers, they are very sure that science and technology affect the multi-level life and the network plays a message communication, contact feelings. For the elderly, the computer is a useful personal tools (White and Weatherall 2000). There is no friendly interface in the use of the network environment and the network equipment. In the development of the Internet and more new media, older Internet learners are vulnerable to social marginalization (Cai and Zang 2003). American scholar Hodse and Lindberg (2002) have also considered the future of the United States in the era of aging, and therefore proposed for the elderly who envisioned web design guidelines: Make your website senior friendly, stressed that any design should consider the actual physiological condition of the elderly.

Through the above literature, we, realize that the elderly is sure about the convenience from the technology, but the design of the operation interface is not friendly for them. An unfriendly interface will lead to the difficulty of learning for the elderly and reduce the willingness to learn. In the process of information education for the elderly, we must think about how to lead the elderly in the unfriendly operating environment to learn and bring their life convenience.

3 Research Methods

Action Research is a process of self-reflection inquiry in the social or educational context. Participants included teachers, students, principals and others. The research aims at rationality and justice of social or educational practices. It helps researchers to understand the practical work, and makes works more efficiently (Carr and Kemmis 1986).

On the teaching part, Action Research is a research method for educational environment. Its purpose is to understand the quality of teaching and looking for a better way to teach (Hensen 1996). It includes the observation of the teaching process, finding and solving the problems, and is a systematic and sequential method for research (Dinkelman 1997).

According to Johnson's book (A Short Guild to Action Research); he pointed out ten characteristics about Action Research:

- Action research is a systematic researching method.
- The researchers have no any presumptions.
- It is not necessary to get the way of research complex.
- It needs detailed plans to collect data.
- The research is no time limit.
- Regular observation is necessary, but it is not necessary to spend a lot of time on observation.
- The research process can be simple and informal, and it can be rigorous and formal, too.
- Action Research requires theoretical foundation.
- Action Research is not a quantitative research.
- When the research result is quantitated, the application of the result will be limited.

The object of the study is 89 elderly students attending the computer courses in the Senior Citizens Academy. The author is the course instructor, his jobs are teaching the elderly students to use the internet, to read the messages on the screen, to input the words (Traditional Chinese characters), etc.

Why did we use the method of Action Research to run the study? We would find something different between the basic research and Action Research (Wang 1997).

	The basic research	Action Research
The training that the researcher need	Researchers need to learn measure, statistics and other methods	Action Research do not need the strict training. The practicing workers would run the study with the help of other academics
Purpose	Research conclusions can be widely used, the purpose of the study is to develop theory and verification theory	The findings can be applied to the specific work environments where participants can conduct on the job training at the same time
How to find the question	Researchers use a variety of ways to define the problem, but usually they are not directly involved in the research issues	The problem defined by the researcher is a problem in the real environment that causes the researcher to plague or affect the efficiency of the work
Hypothesis	Develop specific assumptions and operational definitions that can be tested	The solution to the problem is often regarded as the research hypothesis. Theoretically, the research hypothesis must be quite rigorous
Literature review.	The researchers must have a broad understanding of the current state of knowledge in the field of research, and understand the results of others' research	It is not strictly required the researchers study the data completed
Sampling	The researchers obtained the random or biased samples from the study maternal	The practitioners usually find the teachers and the students in the working environment or themselves as research subjects
The design of the experiment	It is needed to plan before the study running. It is necessary to reduce the errors and the irrelevant variables	The researchers change the way they do during the study to find out that if such changes can improve the working environment. The experimental condition control and error prevention are less important. But the researchers are in the research situation, there may be biased position
Measuring	The researchers choose the most efficient and accurate assessment tool. These assessment tools will be tested before the study takes place	The choice of the measurement tools is less rigorous, the participants lack the use of the measurement tools using training, but they can be assisted by the professional scholars to run the study and find out the results
The analysis of the data	The analysis of the results in the study is one of the purposes of the study, so the research data must be	The research data are analyzed briefly, emphasizing the practicality and feasibility of the

(continued)

(continued)

	The basic research	Action Research
	complex analysis. The use of statistics is very important	research results, rather than presenting the results with a large number of statistics. The researchers attach importance to the information and advice provided by the participants
The application of the research results	In general, the results can be widely used. But in fact, many of the findings can't be applied to the educational environment. The difference between the experience of the researcher and the practitioner creates a serious communication problem	The results of the study can be applied immediately to the practical working environment. But the application of the results is limited, cannot go beyond the scope of the researchers control

Synthesis of the above literatures, there are some reasons that the study was conducted by Action Research.

First, in Action Research, the teacher is also the researcher. In the process fo research, the teacher can take this opportunity to reflect on the content and methods of teaching.

Second, for the research purposes. The purpose of the Action Research can be applied to the specific work environments and improve the method of the teaching and the learning outcomes.

Third, Action Research do not need the strict training. Everyone find some problems, and find some methods to solve. When it is necessary, we can seek the expert assistance.

So, this study run in Action Research.

4 Results

In this study, we find two results.

First, it is important to teach the elderly how to use their cellphones to make their life easily. It is important to teach them how to find and download some interesting APP to make their photos beautiful. It is not important to teach them how to set their cellphones.

To the physical condition of the elderly, their memory capacity is reducing, so it is easier to forget the content of the class. For example, we teach the elderly how to set the Wi-Fi connecting this week, and next week we need to remind them how to do the same thing, or we need to teach them again. They would forget to find the setting on the cellphone to connect the Wi-Fi. So we need to make some notes for them one by one because they don't own the cellphones of the same brand. It is important to teach them how to wake to cellphones up (When we don't do anything on the cellphones in 15 or 30 s, the phones will shut down the screen, and the elderly don't know how to use their fingers to slide the screen to wake the phones up in the beginning of the class.), but it is not necessary to teach them how to set the time change about the screen sleeping because some of them will forget how to make the setting and they will feel troubled. In the first few weeks of the course, we will take them to make some setting that they will use often in the course, for example, to set camera saving the phones in the SD Card. And we will teach them how to connect the network with their cellphones. When they forget the setting, we have to be patient to make the setting for them just like their sitter but not their teacher. Some of the elderly live home alone and their sons and daughters live in another city, so the teacher has to teach them, and has to play the role of the son or the daughter to help the elderly keep on learning sometimes.

Although the elderly's memory capacity is reducing, but some APPs are helpful for their life or for us to take care of their lives. For example, they often transfer the messages by Line APP (an instant message software, it is similar to What's APP). They would show some photos on the Line. When we read their messages, we would know that they are fine and they would feel happy and the sense of accomplishment. They would find some help on the Line also just like that where they can buy something or where they can eat delicious lunch at noon. So we understand that the key point of the teaching is that the using is more important than the setting. It is important to teach them how to transfer the messages by Line but not how to install the Line APP.

Second, we use more individual instruction to replace the group teaching. As we know that every elderly in this course owns his cellphone, so there are many different brands of the cellphones in the class. Although the teaching content is based on the Android system, but there are little differences between the cellphones. The course is going on three hours in a week, and we spend almost half an hour to solve the individual problems. For the reason, we take the individual guidance time every month to solve their problems. We try to do so and find two advantages at least. First, they would not give up learning so easily because of the problems, and they would feel happy because that the teacher cares about their problems and he would spend more time to solve it for them. At the same time the teacher would encourage them to keep learning and make them feel better. Second, the course is going well because we would not stop the course to solve the individual problems. We would solve the problems for them immediately and explain the problems in the individual guidance time. There is an additional advantage in the way: the relationship between the teacher and the elderly would be closer because that the teacher have more time to explain the problems for the elderly and to care for his students.

The individual guidance time makes some elderly and the teacher feel good. The elderly feel ashamed of their questions and don't want to ask questions in front of the classmate because they think their questions are so easy to others. In the individual guidance time, they would feel relax and discuss their questions freely because there are no other classmates watching them and make them nervous. The teacher would run the course smoothly and would not stop the course again and again for just one or two elderly. He would solve the problems intently for the elderly in the individual guidance time.

In this study, we also find that the operation system on the cellphones (Android and iOS) use some professional vocabularies, and it is not the friendly interface for some elderly. The elderly is used to operate the cellphone in the standard thinking. If they would change the picture on the cellphone desktop, their thinking is: first, press the setting icon on the right corner, second, find the display option… etc. But if the position of setting icon changes, they would not know how to operate. In another words, some of they are not used to read the words or don't understand the meanings of the words on the screen. They used to operate the cellphones by memory. If they forget something, they have to get some help. So we suggest that the text used by the system can be more friendly, and we also take the elderly to read the words on the screen, to understand the meanings of the words. It is difficult for the teacher and the elderly. It takes some time to solve the problems, and it is not necessarily to solve the problems. However, we have to try.

There is another interesting finding in the study. When the elderly are familiar with the phones using and they often use the instant messaging software on the phone. They used to share a lot of messages about the health, philosophy of life… on the instant messaging software. But they don't used to check that the information is true or false. So we found that the famous online rumors is shared on the Line. The content of the rumors is about the free gift (just like the key ring). The gift is loaded the tracker, if we take the gift, we also take the tracker with us and make us dangerous. It is a famous rumors in 1970 years, but now it is shared on the Line and make the elderly be afraid. Another rumors is that it is helpful for the cancer patients to drink spirits drinks because the Alcohol will eliminate the cancer cells! To share the messages is very good for their life and inter-personal relationship, but if the messages is wrong, it maybe cause the unnecessary panic. So we have to tell the elderly that how to recheck the correctness of the message.

5 Future Research Directions

1. For the cost considerations, there are more than 25 elderly in a class to learn together. If the students are less than 20 persons in a class, whether the effectiveness of teaching can be improved?
2. We are planning to reduce the weekly class time from three hours to two and an half hour, and there are 30 min to run the individual guidance time. Whether the increase in the individual guidance time would improve learning outcomes?
3. The vocabulary on the cellphones is the same. The factory don't replace the word for the different people. In our country, it is a trouble for some elderly because they don't understand the meanings of the words. Whether the same situation happen in other countries? How do they solve the problem?
4. We are running the new course for the elderly in the day care center. We don't teach them how to connect the internet or how to read on the tablet PC, but we take them to play simple games on the tablet PC. It is not necessary to read words, all the elderly need to do is to distinguish the graphics and the colors, and use their fingers to remove the objects on the screen to finish the games. The elderly in the day care center are over 80 years old, and someone lost the ability of live independently, and someone is illiterate, and most of them have lower active ability. Whether the course help them to live better? Is it possible to combine the courses with medical care as a rehabilitation tool?

References

Wikipedia: Smartphone (2017a). https://zh.wikipedia.org/wiki/%E6%99%BA%E8%83%BD%
E6%89%8B%E6%9C%BA. Accessed 3 Jan 2017

Ministry of the Interior, Taiwan, ROC: Statistical Yearbook of Interior (2017). http://www.ris.
gov.tw/346;jsessionid=3CB07067659DE7A8833A17BB6E3B2593. Accessed 28 Jan 2017

National Development Council, Taiwan, ROC (2017). http://www.ndc.gov.tw/cp.aspx?n=
55C8164714DFD9E9. Accessed 3 Jan 2017

Wang, Z.-Y.: Ethical problems and countermeasures of elderly education in aged society. In: The
Aged Society and the Elderly Education, pp. 31–55. Shi-Da Bookstore, Taipei (2004)

Delors, J., Mufti, I.A., Amagi, I., Carneiro, R., Chung. F., Geremek, B.: Learning: The Treasure
Within. United Nations Educational, Scientific and Cultural Organization, Paris (1996)

Anna, R.: Pre-retirement planning in the workforce symposium to offer tips for creating effective
programs (2009). http://www.mgtncsuedu/index-exp.php/news/article/colleges-pre-retirement-
planning-in-the-work-symposium-to-help-employers-de/. Accessed 16 Apr 2012

Lamdin, L., Fugate, M.: EJder Jeamer: New Frontier in an Aging Society. Oryx Press, Phoenix
(1997)

White, J., Weatherall, A.: A grounded theory analysis of older adults and information
technology. Educ. Gerontol. 26(4), 371–386 (2000)

Cai, Y., Zang, G.-R.: Senior audience and TV drama: the enlightenment from the definition of the
old to the personality psychology on the audience. Chin. J. Commun. 3(6), 197–236 (2003)

Hodes, R.J., Lindberg, D.A.B.: Making your website senior friendly (2002). http://www.nlm.nih.
gov/pubs/staffpubs/od/ocpl/agingchecklist.html. Accessed 14 Nov 2009

Carr, W., Kemmis, S.: Becoming Critical: Education, Knowledge and Action Research. Falmer,
London (1986)

Hensen, K.T.: Teachers as researches. In: Sikula, J. (ed.) Handbook of Research on Teacher
Education, 2nd edn. Macmillan, New York (1996)

Dinkelman, T.: The promise of action research for critically reflective teacher education. Teach.
Educ. 32(4), 250–274 (1997)

Wang, W.-K.: The Method of Education Research. Wu-Nan, Taipei (1997)

Wikipedia: Line (2017b). https://zh.wikipedia.org/wiki/LINE_(%E6%87%89%E7%94%A8%
E7%A8%8B%E5%BC%8F). Accessed 3 Jan 2017

Wikipedia: Android (2017c). https://zh.wikipedia.org/wiki/Android. Accessed 3 Jan 2017

How to Guide the Use of Technology for Ageing-in-Place? An Evidence-Based Educational Module

Eveline J.M. Wouters[1(✉)], Marianne E. Nieboer[1],
Kirsten A. Nieboer[1], Marijke J.G.A. Moonen[1], Sebastiaan T.M. Peek[1,2],
Anne-Mie A.G. Sponselee[1], Joost van Hoof[1], Claire S. van der Voort[1],
and Katrien G. Luijkx[2]

[1] Fontys University of Applied Sciences, Eindhoven, The Netherlands
{e.wouters,m.nieboer,a.sponselee,joost.vanhoof,
claire.vandervoort}@fontys.nl, k.nieboer@upcmail.nl,
marijkemoonen@gmail.com
[2] Tilburg University, Tilburg, The Netherlands
{S.T.M.Peek,K.G.Luijkx}@uvt.nl

Abstract. Aim: Technology is suggested to support ageing-in-place. For care- and technology professionals working with older persons it is important to know how to facilitate the use of technology by older persons. This paper presents the translation of the results of a field study into multilevel and multidisciplinary educational material. Method: During home visits, community-dwelling seniors were interviewed regarding reasons for their level of technology use. All types of technology that could support activities of daily living, were included. Resulting themes formed the basis of the development of personas and scripts for education. Next, lecturers from vocational and higher technical and care education developed an evidence-based educational module from the perspective of professional service provision. Results: 53 older adults were interviewed. The level of technology use is influenced by six themes: challenges in the domain of independent living; behavioural options; personal thoughts on technology use; influence of the social network; influence of organisations; and the role of the physical environment. Four personas were developed, one of which was featured into a film, with twelve separate scenes. For each scene, lessons were developed that consisted of specific questions (first level), in-depth questions (second level) and suggestions for classes (for lecturers). Three personas were translated into case histories. Conclusion: Older adults' perceptions and use of technology are embedded in their personal, social, and physical context. To improve successful technology use to support ageing-in-place, professionals from the domain of care and technology can be trained to be aware of these factors.

Keywords: Technology acceptance · Older adults · Education · Professional service

© Springer International Publishing AG 2017
J. Zhou and G. Salvendy (Eds.): ITAP 2017, Part I, LNCS 10297, pp. 486–497, 2017.
DOI: 10.1007/978-3-319-58530-7_37

1   Introduction

1.1   The Need for Technology

Projected survival the age of 80 has shown marked improvements, and, therefore, it is a challenge how to accommodate and care for an ageing population [1]. As a response, policy makers and professionals, who provide services to older adults with chronic conditions, have placed greater emphasis on stimulating and supporting older persons to stay in their own homes as long as possible [2, 3]. Technology is one of the possibilities suggested to support ageing-in-place for older persons [4]. Examples of technologies are alarm systems, and several tools in the context of eHealth for self-management of chronic conditions, such as diabetes and chronic heart failure [5]. At the same time, the implementation of technology for the purpose of ageing-in-place is often unsuccessful [6, 7].

1.2   Acceptance of Technology

One of the reasons for the limited implementation of technology for ageing-in-place, is that older persons do not accept all technology that is available or offered to them [5]. Themes found in literature associated with acceptance in older persons are concerns regarding technology such as costs, privacy issues and usability; expected benefits of technology, especially increased safety and usefulness; their perceived need for technology, for instance, as related to their health status; available alternatives to technology such as help given by family, social influence (family, friends and professional caregivers); and personal characteristics of older adults themselves, such as the wish to stay in their own homes [5]. Most of the literature on technology acceptance focuses on the pre-implementation phase and mainly considers technology for safety purposes, and, in to a lesser extent, technology for social interaction and support of activities of daily living (ADL) [5]. Other types of technology, such as mobility supporting or household technology, are rarely addressed. More importantly, research to guide factors that influence the post-implementation phase of acceptance and the actual use of technology, is scarce or even non-existent.

1.3   Implications for Professionals and Professionals' Education

For professionals working with older persons, both care professionals and technology providers/installers, it is important to know how to facilitate and stimulate the use of technology by older persons, in order technology to contribute to ageing-in-place. The use of technology in care situations is, for most care professionals, not a topic they are thoroughly acquainted with. Most care professionals have not been educated to explore and use the possibilities of care technology, and do not tend to stimulate the use of technology in their work [8]. Not only care professionals, but also family (informal carers) and technology providers/installers [9] need to get accustomed with a different way of working: together, they form the system in which technology will or will not work for older persons. This also implies that technology implementation converges with social innovation, as work processes will change and new forms of cooperation will evolve [10]. This means that, in the context of making ageing-in-place with technology successful, many professionals from different domains will work together with older adults and their relatives. At this moment, to our knowledge there are no specific evidence-based tools for educational purposes helping (future) professionals to improve technology use by older adults.

The study presented here explored reasons for the use of technology by older persons and transformed the model that evolved into material for the education of care and technology professionals in vocational and higher education.

2 Method

2.1 Introduction

For the purpose of this study, i.e., to design evidence-based educational material to educate professionals to introduce and support technology use for ageing-in-place, three steps were followed. First, interviews were held with older persons living in their own homes, in order to determine factors and the interplay between factors that influence the use of technology. Second, this knowledge and the 'typical cases' were used as a basis to describe personas. Third, an expert group of lecturers in health- and social care, engineering and education, developed the outline for scripts together with the researchers. One script was elaborated into a film and supported by educational materials.

2.2 Interviews

Semi-structured interviews were held at home with 53 older adults. Inclusion criteria were: about 70 years of age or older, living independently, not cognitively impaired. Purposive sampling was used to include different living- and health situations, as well as use of and experience with technology. For more information on sampling, see Peek et al. [11]. Interviews lasted between 90 and 150 min and included visiting the rooms of the house to see which technology was in the house and which was used (or not used) and why. Information on demographic, social and health issues was gathered, as well as on technology use. All technology that was used in or around the house, that used electricity and was in one way or the other, supportive of ADL, was included in this study. Frequency of technology use (for instance, on a daily base), and reasons for using the technology, stopping the use, or contemplating future purchases, were discussed. As a member check, each participant received a summary of the interview [11]. Interviews were always conducted and analysed with two researchers each time (peer-review), using open, selective and thematic coding techniques [11, 12].

2.3 Developing Personas

The researchers who visited the participants and carried out the interviews, also developed the personas. In user-centred design and marketing, personas are fictional characters created to represent the different user types that might use a tool, for

Table 1. Distinctive characteristics for the development of personas.

Technology-related characteristics	Attitude toward technology (including need, interest, willingness to invest)
	Beliefs about technology (including competence, consequences of use)
	Physical characteristics of house and garden relevant for technology use (including Wi-Fi, infrastructure, town/village)
Personal and contextual characteristics	Living situation and marital status
	Physical appearance
	Education
	Financial situation
	Health status
	Social network
	Basic needs (including safety, security, autonomy)
	Frequent activities

instance, a website. Although personas are fictitious, they are based on knowledge of real users and, therefore, require thorough knowledge of users. For the creation of personas, it is advised to interview users in their context [13]. Also in health care, this method has been introduced with the purpose to design intervention programmes [14].

Starting point for the development of the personas was that they had to cover the majority of the factors found in the 53 older persons interviewed and were distinct from each other in aspects such as living and financial situation, educational level, sex, health, basic needs, hobbies, and attitude toward technology. In Table 1, these aspects are summarised.

2.4   Design of the Outline of Scripts

In an expert group of lecturers (n = 12) from two different levels (vocational and higher education), and three different domains (social care, health care and engineering), an outline for the didactic concept was formed. The conditions for this outline were formulated as follows: first, the factors that had emerged from the interviews had to be covered by the educational material; this was a prerequisite, because the educational material was to be evidence-based. Second, as inter-professional education is important in order to prepare students for real-life situations in health care [15], the lessons had to be based on material that was recognisable for all levels and all professions. And third, the material should be a source of inspiration for lecturers, not a checklist, and lecturers should feel invited to use the material as they consider appropriate.

2.5   Development of the Final Scripts and Film

After designing the outline, small expert (sub)groups (n = 2–3) developed specific educational material for different levels and different domains, based on the same fundament, namely the outline of the scripts that were based on the four personas. Thus specific and customised education was developed both for social and health care workers and engineers, on different levels (vocational and higher education). What was developed in these subgroups, was discussed and synthesised into one multi-dimensional module. Apart from that, the scripts were discussed with a professional film director. From one of the scripts a complete film was produced.

3   Results

3.1   Results from the Interviews: Factors Influencing Technology Use

Participants had a mean age of 78 years, 68% female and 71% living alone, while 64% received home care (for details, see Peek et al. [11]). Technologies found and discussed with participants were: technology for personal care (e.g., washing machine, microwave), entertainment appliances, home automation, assistive devices, fitness technology, ICT,

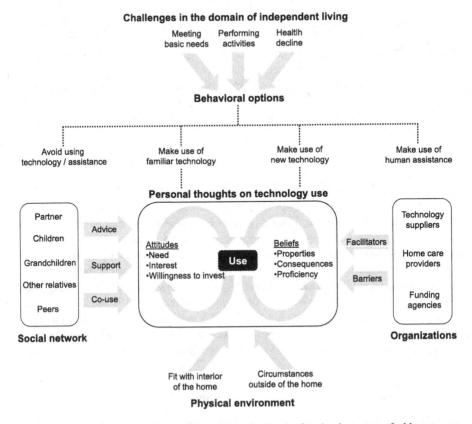

Fig. 1. Conceptual model of factors influencing the level of technology use of older persons who are ageing-in-place (source: Peek et al., Older Adults' Reasons for Using Technology while Aging in Place. Gerontology, 2015, p. 231).

telephones, and transportation devices. Of these, assistive devices were the most often used (used on a daily base), and of technology for personal care, the number of devices per person was highest [11].

Emergent themes related to technology use of this wide range of devices were: challenges in the domain of individual living, behavioural options, personal thoughts on technology use, influence of the social network, influence of organisations and influence of the physical environment [11]. These themes are summarised in Fig. 1 (Conceptual model of factors influencing the level of technology use of older persons who are ageing-in-place). Details on themes and citations of participants can be found in Peek et al. [11].

3.2 Personas

The technology related characteristics and the personal and contextual characteristics of the participants from the interviews were modelled by the researchers in four personas. Together, these personas cover the factors of the conceptual model that was developed. The resulting personas are summarised in Table 2, 'Summary of four personas'.

Table 2. Summary of four personas

Fictional name	Peter	Charles	Maria	Corry
Age & sex	75, male	85, male	78, female	69, female
Living situation & marital status	Married, living together	Widower, living alone	Married, living together (husband 10 years older)	Widow, living alone
Education	Higher technical education	Lower education	Lower vocational education	Secondary school, secretary during working life
Financial situation and attitude	Can support themselves, not always room for extra expenditures	Good pension as a result of sale of company, but doesn't want to spend if not necessary	Frugal. Depends on social security for health care	No financial complaints. Likes luxury and occasionally, to buy on impulse
Health (and health issues)	General health okay. Some arthrosis and hypertension. Some deterioration, especially in the evenings	Has fallen last year, some pain in left hip as a result, perhaps in need of hip replacement. Wants to postpone this	Cares for husband with chronic health problems. Much stress. Has diabetes	Experienced cardiac attack four months ago. She feels good without any consequential complaints

(continued)

Table 2. (*continued*)

Health perception	Doesn't feel impaired in ADL as a result of health issues. Doesn't like talking about his own health	Doesn't like going to the GP. Wants to make his own plans	Always worrying and caring for others. No time to worry about herself	'Use it or lose it' and 'cheer up' are her slogans. She has always been physically active
Social network (including size; important others)	Social contacts are okay (leave out: has to have certain level). His wife also leads an active life. No children	Has one daughter who worries about the safety her father. He fell over recently which feeds the worries	Husband needs much care, can stay on his own for about an hour. One daughter living at an hour driving distance	Has a daughter and two grandchildren that she takes care of twice a week. Lost contact with her son. Grandchildren help her with 'ICT troubles'
Characteristic basic needs (e.g. independence, safety, social contacts, leisure)	Leisure and things to kill time are important since he was pensioned off	Doesn't seek social contact (considers this as being mostly gossip)	Needs her rest, occasionally an outing. Would like her daughter to visit her more frequently, but is afraid to ask	Limited social contacts, apart from her daughter and grandchildren
Activities frequently performed (e.g. as hobby's)	Often goes out with his wife, but also to the bridge club. Lately long distance rides occur less frequently	Likes to watch TV, especially documentaries about nature and history. Often doing small jobs in the home. Has a special shed in the garden for this	Goes for swimming once a week. Would like to go out more often	Uses her laptop for games and pleasure. Goes out occasionally for a weekend 'shopping'. Loves taking care of the grandchildren, but is often very tired afterwards
Attitude toward technology (need, interest, level of	Was always interested in technology. Had worked at 'Philips' (electronics	No special idea or feelings about technology. Technology has to be	Her husband used to buy and install technology. Disturbed by young people	Is interested in technology, especially for 'fun'. Admits not to be able to do without.

(*continued*)

Table 2. (*continued*)

preparedness to invest)	company). Wants to know how technology works and is willing to pay for it and invest energy. For him, technology and health care are not related though	useful. Only spends money on technology if useful	who 'only care for their mobile phone'. She can use all household devices, no need for more	Doesn't think about care technology
Convictions about technology; consequences of the use of technology; skills, characteristics of technology	Considers himself competent in using new technology. Likes to help other persons in using technology. Considers technology important to stay socially connected, such as banking, genealogy research, news)	Technology should be useful or is considered nonsense. Used, in his former business, many (mechanical) tools, but didn't grow up using digital technology	She has little self-confidence in using (modern) technology. Considers household devices as 'totally normal' though as everybody has them	Loves to sit behind her computer. Not afraid to use technology, but sometimes she gets 'stuck' and needs support

3.3 Scripts

The result of the inter-disciplinary expert group meetings was that, in order to create a real-life situation usable by all disciplines, the professional service provision in meaningful and recognisable situations are to be the core of the scripts.

First, this resulted in defining the workflow of activities, in which all professions played a minor or major role. Before being able to define roles, professionals from different domains had to understand each other's roles and language unity was developed. In Fig. 2 ('Workflow of subsequent activities in technology use for support of ageing-in-place by health- and social as well as engineering perspective'), the result is demonstrated. In the first part of the activities 'workflow (Fig. 2, upper part), the care professionals play a major role, whereas in the second part (Fig. 2, lower part), engineers are in the lead. During 'realisation' all professionals are involved. In practice,

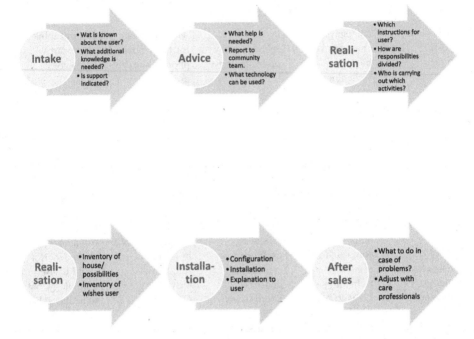

Fig. 2. Workflow of subsequent activities in technology use for support of ageing-in-place by health- and social as well as engineering perspective

and, therefore, also in education, it is important that professionals from both domains are aware of each other's roles.

At each step in the workflow, experts indicated how roles would be divided. For the intake, both vocational and higher educated care professionals are involved. Advice is given by higher educated care professionals, whereas during realisation, both levels are again involved. For the realisation and after-sales steps, both levels of engineering are involved, whereas, the installation is performed by vocational educated engineers.

3.4 Educational Material

Scripts were discussed with a professional film director and discussed with the expert group. This resulted into one detailed script (persona: Charles). This script was divided into 12 separate scenes. For each of these scenes, the expert group developed an educational handout. On one side of this (A4 size) sheet, questions for students are presented, in three different levels of difficulty. The other side contains the model presented in Fig. 1 ('Conceptual model of factors influencing the level of technology use of older persons who are ageing-in-place (source: Peek et al., Older Adults' Reasons for Using Technology while Aging in Place. Gerontology, 2015, p. 231)). Lecturers can use these sheets as such, or use them to inspire the discussion with their students after viewing the scene.

The other three personas are described in one outline each as a case history, with suggestions for questions for students. Of these cases, short film impressions were made.

Finally, a lecturers' instruction guide was made that can also be used by informal caregivers. And, a separate conversation guide for professionals for discussing technology with older persons. All material was presented open access [16].

4 Discussion

4.1 Summary of Results

Six themes dominate the use of technology in older, community-dwelling persons. These themes are: (1) challenges in the domain of individual living, (2) behavioural options, (3) personal thoughts on technology use, (4) influence of the social network, (5) influence of organisations, and (6) the physical environment. In this project, we developed educational material as part of a research project on technology use for ageing-in-place. This resulted in a multi-disciplinary, multi-level module comprising four personas (three presented as cases with questions) and a film, divided into 12 scenes, each enriched with work sheets to inspire the lessons. Additional, a lecturers' guide and a conversation guide for professionals were developed.

4.2 Implications

For technology to support ageing-in-place, factors influencing ageing in place have to be considered in order to promote and support actual use of technology by older persons. This means that in health- and social care, as well as in the domain of installers and technology providers, professionals should address these factors during the entire workflow of service provision. The conversation guide offers opportunities to facilitate this conversation. The educational material offers opportunities to address aspects of barriers for technology use in older adults with students of different backgrounds. In this way students can be more prepared and educated in a realistic manner to their future profession.

4.3 Strengths

The educational module that was developed, is a result of close cooperation between lecturers and researchers. The project, which lasted for four years all together, is an example of how research can have direct implications for practice and education. In most projects, research and education are separate processes. By combining and relating research results to educational possibilities from the start until the end of the process, relevant material could be developed. The module has been used already in vocational and higher education, and in post-initial education. Another strong point of this research project, was the close cooperation between lecturers and researchers of different domains, both from the health- and social care sector, as well as the technology sector.

4.4 Weaknesses

One weakness of the study is that, because of costs only one script has been developed into a film with 12 separate scenes. The other personas and scripts were used as cases and were not translated into film material. On the other hand, this offers future lecturers a range of freedom to use them within their own didactic models. Also, although already used, the educational module has not been formally evaluated. Finally, challenges regarding technology use and acceptance are also relevant for other contexts and professions, that not yet have been addressed. Professionals addressed in this project were mainly nurses and professionals in social care, and engineers. For allied health professions such as physiotherapists and speech therapists, specific educational material should be developed, addressing the specific contexts in which they work.

4.5 Recommendations

It is recommended to evaluate the educational module, both in the vocational school- and higher education environment, and in practice. Specific educational material, addressing relevant contexts of other professionals working in care, especially allied health professions, should also be developed.

Acknowledgments. The authors would like to thank all other participating lecturers of the experts group: Roos Kuster (Summa welzijn), Susan Metz (Summa Zorg), Ilse Vossen (ROC ter Aa Zorg en Welzijn), Hans van der Heijden (Summa techniek), Klaas van den Bos (Summa techniek). Also, all other researchers (Sil Aarts and Maurice Rijnaard) as well as the participants of the interviews, are cordially thanked for their valuable contribution. The RAAK (Regional Attention and Action for Knowledge circulation) scheme, which is managed by the Foundation Innovation Alliance (SIA – Stichting Innovatie Alliantie) with funding from the Dutch Ministry of Education, Culture and Science (OCW), is thanked for their financial support (SIA project number PRO-3-37).

References

1. United Nations: World population ageing (2015). http://www.un.org/en/development/desa/population/publications/pdf/ageing/WPA2015_Report.pdf. Accessed 22 Jan 2017
2. Arai, H., Ouchi, Y., Yokode, M., Ito, H., Uematsu, H., Eto, F., Oshima, S., Ota, K., Saito, Y., Sasaki, H., Tsubota, K., Fukuyama, H., Honda, Y., Iguchi, A., Toba, K., Hosoi, T., Kita, T.: Toward the realization of a better aged society: messages from gerontology and geriatrics. Geriatr. Gerontol. Int. **12**, 13 (2015). doi:10.1111/j.1447-0594.2011.00776.x
3. Vasunilashorn, S., Steinman, B.A., Liebig, P.S., Pynoos, J.: Aging in place: evolution of a research topic whose time has come. J. Aging Res. **12**, 16–22 (2012)
4. Reeder, B., Meyer, E., Lazar, A., Chaudhuri, S., Thompson, H., Demiris, G.: Framing the evidence for health smart homes and home-based consumer health technologies as a public health intervention for independent aging: a systematic review. Int. J. Med. Inform. **82**, 565–579 (2013). doi:10.1016/j.ijmedinf.2013.03.007

5. Peek, S.T.M., Wouters, E.J.M., van Hoof, J., Luijkx, K.G., Boeije, H.R., Vrijhoef, H.J.M.: Factors influencing acceptance of technology for aging in place: a systematic review. Int. J. Med. Inform. **83**, 35–48 (2014). doi:10.1016/j.ijmedinf.2014.01.004

6. Michel, J.P., Franco, A.: Geriatricians and technology. J. Am. Med. Dir. Assoc. **15**, 860–862 (2014). doi:10.1016/j.jamda.2014.09.016

7. Wilson, C., Hargreaves, T., Hauxwell-Baldwin, R.: Smart homes and their users: a systematic analysis and key challenges. Pers. Ubiquitous Comput. **19**, 463–476 (2015). doi:10.1007/s00779-014-0813-0

8. Nieboer, M.E., van Hoof, J., van Hout, A., Wouters, E.J.M.: Professional values, technology and future health care: the view of health care professionals in The Netherlands. Technol. Soc. **39**, 10–17 (2014). doi:10.1016/j.techsoc.2014.05.003

9. van Hoof, J., Kort, H.S.M., Rutten, P.G.S., Duijnstee, M.S.H.: Ageing-in-place with the use of ambient intelligence technology: perspectives of older users. Int. J. Med. Inform. **80**, 310–331 (2011). doi:10.1016/j.ijmedinf.2011.02.010

10. Joyce, K., Loe, M.: A sociological approach to ageing, technology and health. Sociol. Health Illn. **32**, 171–180 (2010). doi:10.1111/j.1467-9566.2009.01219.x

11. Peek, S.T.M., Luijkx, K.G., Rijnaard, M.D., Nieboer, M.E., van der Voort, C.S., Aarts, S., van Hoof, J., Vrijhoef, H.J.M., Wouters, E.J.M.: Older adults' reasons for using technology while aging in place. Gerontology (2016). doi:10.1159/000430949

12. Boeije, H.R.: Analysis in Qualitative Research. Sage, London (2010)

13. Calabria, T.: An introduction to personas and how to create them (2004). http://www.steptwo.com.au/papers/kmc_personas/. Accessed 20 Jan 2016

14. Barbera-Guillem, R., Poveda-Puente, R., Neumann, S., Becker, H., Ramírez, M., Wienholtz, A., Schaedler, I.: Example of the application of the PERSONA methodology in the definition of needs and requirements for the WeTakeCare system. Stud. Health Technol. Inform. **217**, 917–922 (2015). doi:10.3233/978-1-61499-566-1-917

15. Reeves, S., Zwarenstein, M., Goldman, J., Barr, H., Freeth, D., Hammick, M., Koppel, I: Interprofessional education: effects on professional practice and health care outcomes. Cochrane Database Syst. Rev. **23**, CD002213 (2008). doi:10.1002/14651858.CD002213.pub2.16

16. Langer thuis, wat haal je in huis (2016) https://fontys.nl/Over-Fontys/Fontys-Paramedische-Hogeschool/Onderzoek-1/Projecten/Langer-thuis-wat-haal-je-in-huis.htm. Accessed 6 Jan 2016

Exploring the Elders' Information Needs on Home-Based Care: A Community Service Perspective

Zhizheng Zhang[(✉)] and Yajun Li

School of Design Arts and Media, Nanjing University of Science
and Technology, 200, Xiaolingwei Street, Nanjing 210094, Jiangsu, China
450724699@qq.com, lyj5088@163.com

Abstract. It is predicted that by 2030 China will become a country with the highest degree of population aging in the world. Information-based eldercare pattern is the direction for future development of eldercare. Through construction of a hierarchical model of the elders' information needs, in-depth analysis of their contents, and questionnaire survey with the elders, it has been found that many items of information needs are highly recognized by the elders. Cross statistical analysis indicated that information needs in both safety and emotional categories showed significant differences between the gender groups, while those in both physiological and self-actualization categories showed significant differences between the age groups. According to the research results, recommendation is put forward in the end of the paper on design and construction of information-based eldercare platform to help the elder users promote their user experience and information skills.

Keywords: Elderly · Community service · Information-based eldercare · Information needs

1 Introduction

It is estimated that China will enter medium-degree aging society in 2021–2030, and will gradually become a highly aging society, with an average 5.22 million additional elders per year between 2031 and 2050. The above data shows that the degree of China's population aging is constantly accelerating, and that the eldercare pattern is beginning to transit from home-based to community-based eldercare. With information-based community eldercare service as China's mainstream eldercare pattern in the future, the trend of information-based eldercare service will have far-reaching impact on various trades of the society.

Now that the information-based eldercare service has come, in the field of design, close attention should be paid to the needs the elder users have, and the hierarchy and features of their needs. This paper is divided into six parts. Part 2 is literature review of relevant research. In Part 3, the elders' needs are deduced hierarchically, and the model of the elders' information needs is constructed, both according to Marslow's hierarchy of needs. Part 4–5 discusses the questionnaire survey study on the elders' information

J. Zhou and G. Salvendy (Eds.): ITAP 2017, Part I, LNCS 10297, pp. 498–509, 2017.
DOI: 10.1007/978-3-319-58530-7_38

needs. Part 6 looks deeper at the information needs of the elders through statistical analysis. Part 7 gives recommendation on design of information-based eldercare.

2 Literature Review

Current research on the elders carry out studies mainly from the perspectives of the following three disciplines: medicine, psychology, and sociology. Medical and psychological researches focus on the elders' physiological and psychological problems, while sociology studies mainly their social behavior. As this paper discusses the elders' informational needs in community service, the research results currently available are reviewed from the aspects of studies on the elders' needs and informatization of community service.

As a result of the global trend of population aging, research on needs of the elders has caught wide attention among the scholars. Some investigated on the elders' needs of different categories and their degree of life satisfaction through empirical study [1]. Some studied the elders' behavior features, and pointed out the types of services to be provided to them based on these features [2]. Some think that daycare service or housework assistance not only solve the problem of the elders' physiological needs but also help alleviate the psychological burden of their families in looking after them [3].

Some investigated particularly on community care and medical security for the elders based on the characteristics of their needs in medical treatment and care. It was pointed out that community care would certainly become the trend for eldercare, while the elders still had a great deal of difficulties in getting community service and centralized medical service [4]. Some of the scholars think that the users' unfulfilled information needs have been the major obstacle to the development of informatization in community service [5]. Some researches concerned with informatization of home-based eldercare are limited to health and safety aspects. In this study the features of information needs of the elders were understood by carrying out survey with the elders from chosen communities, and making statistical analysis on the survey data.

3 Maslow's Hierarchy of Needs Theory

A hierarchical model of the elders' information needs was constructed in this paper according to Marslow's hierarchy of needs, to classify the information functions into categories. Through methods of questionnaire and mathematical statistics, investigation and data analysis on information needs in home-based eldercare were carried out using questionnaires that had passed reliability and validity tests.

Marslow's hierarchy of needs is one of the important theories of the behavioral science. This theory, which classifies human needs into five levels, i.e. physiological, safety, belonging and love, esteem, and self-actualization, has won wide recognition, and is one of the basic theories of various behavioral science studies. Obviously, we can deduce the elders' needs with the help of Marslow's theory on hierarchy of general needs.

3.1   Hierarchical Model of the Elders' Information Needs

On the basis of Marslow's hierarchical model of needs, the hierarchical needs of the elders were analyzed from the perspective of community service information, and so were obtained the hierarchical model of the elders' information needs (Fig. 1). The model divided the elders' needs into the following five categories: 1. physiological information needs including clothing, food, aboding, travelling, and daily care; 2. safety information needs, covering medical care and old-age support policies; 3. emotional information needs, including information on relatives and friends and group activities; 4. esteem information needs, including both self and social evaluation; 5. self-actualization information needs, including knowledge, skills, and post of duty.

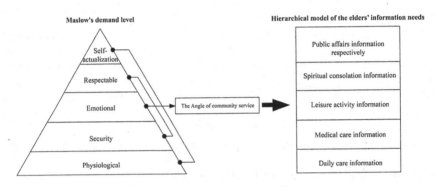

Fig. 1. Hierarchical model of the elders' information needs

The five categories were subdivided to get the information needed at high frequency by the elders (Fig. 2). According to the hierarchical model of the elders' information needs, this research's investigation contents were classified into the following five categories of information: life care, medical treatment & health care, leisure activity, spiritual consolation, and public affairs.

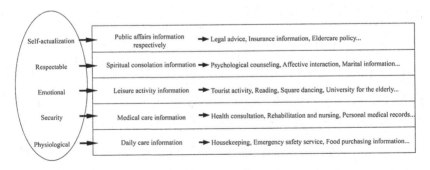

Fig. 2. High frequency elderly demand information

4   Research Design

According to the hierarchical model of the elders' information needs, the questions in the questionnaire, 19 in total, were divided into 5 types. In designing of the questionnaire, we defined first the object and contents of the survey, and then the respondents to the investigation. As the population under the investigation was the elders living at home, before carrying out the big sample investigation, trial visit was done on part of the elders, and the then questionnaires were revised, supplemented, and improved according to the questions emerged in the trial visit, forming the final, complete questionnaire.

The main body of the questionnaire focuses on the information needs in five categories: life care, medical treatment & health care, leisure activity, spiritual consolation, and public affairs. Apart from that the elders were asked how well they would accept the information-based community eldercare service platform.

The respondents of this investigation were urban elders living at home, who were males 65 years or older, and females 60 years or older. Three representative communities were chosen from Nanjing. The three communities' economic status all ranked close to the top among all communities of the whole city. In those communities, 90 questionnaires were distributed, 78 of them were back in total, among which 65 were valid ones after sorting out. The respondents included 30 males and 35 females, or 34 under 70 years old, and 31 of 70 years or older.

4.1   Reliability and Validity Tests of the Questionnaire

As questionnaire survey was the major means for this research, with a view to ensure objectivity and accuracy of the data obtained, we put the questionnaire reliability and validity study in the first place. In the field of social and scientific research, it is generally considered that for a scale or questionnaire with a good reliability coefficient, the reliability coefficient of the total scale is preferably above 0.80, while 0.70–0.80 is considered acceptable. For the scales for various dimensions, their reliability coefficient is preferably above 0.70, while 0.60–0.70 is considered to be acceptable; at the same time, during the reliability test, the corrected item total correlation coefficient (CITC coefficient) value was also considered. Any items whose CITC value was lower than 0.50 were deleted, until the CITC values of all items were greater than 0.50. Meanwhile, should any deletion of a variable be found out to have made the Cronbach α coefficient of the whole dimension higher, then the question item concerned would be deleted to improve the internal coherence of the dimension [6].

The reliability and validity of the questionnaire on information needs of the home-based elders were analyzed with SPSS software. The analysis results showed that the Cronbach α value of information under life care, medical treatment & health care, leisure activity, spiritual consolation, and public affairs categories were 0.705, 0.720, 0.786, and 0.768 respectively, all greater than 0.70, and the CITC coefficient values of the question items corresponding to various information needs were greater than the required value 0.50 without exception, indicating that the questionnaire compiled had good reliability (Table 1).

Table 1. Factor loading of questionnaire questions about information needs

Questions	Daily care	Medical care	Leisure activity	Spiritual consolation	Public affairs
Housekeeping	**0.437**	0.010	0.010	0.008	0.096
Maintenance service	**0.821**	0.168	0.041	−0.320	−0.221
Catering service	**0.765**	0.093	0.167	0.093	−0.161
Emergency safety service	**0.517**	0.130	0.086	0.133	0.125
Daycare center service	**0.679**	0.133	0.006	0.233	0.017
Food purchasing information	**0.702**	0.180	0.112	−0.108	0.149
Health consultation	0.105	**0.671**	0.130	0.047	0.026
Rehabilitation and nursing	0.232	**0.708**	0.132	0.082	0.267
Personal medical records	−0.131	**0.502**	0.122	−0.181	0.076
Tourist activity	−0.062	−0.021	**0.569**	0.011	0.142
Reading	0.276	0.276	**0.632**	0.037	0.078
Square dancing	0.326	0.143	**0.760**	−0.028	0.233
University for the elderly	−0.232	0.123	**0.725**	0.014	0.015
Psychological counseling	0.032	0.155	0.042	**0.573**	0.123
Affective interaction	−0.070	0.087	0.315	**0.623**	0.084
Marital information	0.015	−0.011	0.015	**0.503**	0.095
Legal advice	−0.020	0.066	0.066	0.174	**0.685**
Insurance information	0.157	0.156	0.024	0.205	**0.798**
Eldercare policy	0.032	0.096	0.101	0.084	**0.541**
Eigenvalue	3.482	2.246	1.634	1.342	1.132
Explained variance/%	21.652	19.540	18.043	14.630	11.534
Accumulative explained variance/%	**21.652**	**41.192**	**59.235**	**74.865**	**86.399**

Exploratory factor analysis was performed on the questionnaire items to test its construct validity. The analysis data showed that the KMO value was 0.778, which was greater than the required value of 0.70. At the same time, the result of the Bartlett test of sphericity was 0, indicating that the sphericity test was "significant". The null hypothesis that the correlation coefficient was the unit matrix was rejected, indicating that the correlation coefficient could be used as the classified factor in the factor analysis.

According to the principle of the eigen value being greater than 1, factor extraction was done by varimax rotation. Five groups of combinations were obtained, as shown in Table 1. The five groups of combinations represented respectively the following categories of information function: 'life care', 'medical & health', 'leisure activity', 'spiritual consolation', and 'public affairs'. Their cumulative variance explained was

86.399%. At the same time, the factor loading of various question items were all greater than 0.50, and no question items spanned two groups of dimensions, showing good discriminant validity.

5 Data Analysis

5.1 Basic Analysis of the Investigation Results

Descriptive statistical analysis was performed on the data according to the investigation results. The results are shown in Table 2.

In the six question items in life care information function, to four of them more than 40% gave the answer 'recognized', which were household management service information, emergency safety service information, and maintenance service information, in the order of proportion. The preliminary investigation showed that household management service was one of the most highly demanded services by the home-based elders.

Table 2. Descriptive statistical table of questionnaire data

Type of group	Questions	Recognized (%)	Ordinary (%)	Not recognized (%)
Daily care	**Housekeeping**	77.6	**11.5**	**10.9**
	Maintenance service	69.2	17.5	13.3
	Catering service	50.7	38.6	10.7
	Emergency safety service	**70.5**	**20.4**	**9.1**
	Daycare center service	35.2	29.7	35.1
	Food purchasing information	25.3	43.2	31.5
Medical care	Health consultation	34.7	53.5	11.8
	Rehabilitation and nursing	42.6	30.6	26.8
	Personal medical records	27.5	34.6	37.9
Leisure activity	Tourist activity	59.7	30.5	9.8
	Reading	30.5	35.7	33.8
	Square dancing	**70.1**	**11.6**	**18.3**
	University for the elderly	60.8	12.6	26.6
Spiritual consolation	Psychological counseling	36.4	43.7	19.9
	Affective interaction	57.3	31.9	10.8
	Marital information	23.7	38.3	38
Public affairs	Legal advice	64.2	25.7	10.1
	Insurance information	65.6	27.8	6.6
	Eldercare policy	58.4	30.5	11.1

As they grow older their physiological functions constantly decline, therefore they need assistance from household management services to handle many of their daily affairs. Emergencies, though of occasional occurrence, for instance a fall of an elder at home, could cause immeasurable consequences if the dangerous situation is not handled in time. Therefore, emergency safety service was also recognized by the elders. To other four question items, including catering service information, daycare center service information and food procurement information, most elders ranked them as 'ordinary' in terms of degree of recognition. The demand for these services seemed low, however they might be influenced by other factors. More relevant discussions will be made later in line with the crossover statistical analysis.

In the three items in medical treatment & health care information functions, to most of them such as health consultation and personal medical archive, most elders gave the answer of 'ordinary' in terms of degree of recognition. This showed that, in general, the elders' understanding and receptivity of health care still remained with the tradition of mainly relying on medical treatment, with weak sense of preventative health care. This reflected that the elders were highly dependent of the professional medical institutions, and would be likely to have difficulties in getting medical service in the eldercare service links.

In the four questions of leisure activity information function, to tourist activity, plaza dancing, and elderly university, great majority of the respondents give the answer 'recognized', the sequence being plaza dancing, elderly university, tourist activity, and book reading according to the proportions. It is thus obvious that most elders were in agreement in their needs of and attention to cultural and leisure activities, indicating their high demand of leisure activities. The communities should enhance community cultural and leisure service items, and utilize information application to boost the quality of eldercare by the community.

In spiritual consolation information function, emotional exchange and psychological counselling were highly recognized by the elders. It indicated that the elders' receptivity to spiritual consolation services were still in the initial stage, and great majority of them could not accept this type of service. The home-based elders are relatively lonely, and the current company & chat service can alleviate their feeling of loneliness. Home-based elders whose families are not with them for long need suitable spiritual consolation services to relieve their feeling of loneliness.

In the public affairs information function, all three question items were highly recognized by the elders, in the sequence of insurance information, legal consulting, old-age support policies according to the proportion. It indicated that the home-based elders had an urgent need of public affairs service. Although they chose home-based eldercare, they paid close attention to the welfare provided by the government and insurance benefit provided by the society, which was in line with China's social aging problem of growing old before becoming rich and the social reality of the great burden of eldercare that relied solely on the families.

About how well they would accept the information-based community eldercare platform, most elders expressed their hope that such a platform would provide them with better service. However, many of them also expressed their concerns over how to use the platform, how complicated the operation of the platform would be, and the cost of the service. It is thus clear that multiple aspects have to be taken into consideration in implementing the information-based community eldercare platform.

5.2 Crossover Statistical Analysis on Home-Based Eldercare Service Information Need and Gender and Age

Due to the heterogeneity of the elder population, which was considered in the research, the information needs of the elders might vary among gender and age groups. The functional information and gender and age groups were cross analyzed respectively using data analysis software, to screen more significant differences, which are shown in Tables 3 and 4.

Table 3. Statistical table of gender difference in information needs

Type of group	Gender	Recognized (%)	Ordinary (%)	Not recognized (%)
Psychological counseling	Male	8.1	47.8	44.1
	Female	50.6	39.6	9.8
Legal advice	Male	45.7	38.6	15.7
	Female	74.3	13.9	11.8
Square dancing	Male	3.2	10.2	86.6
	Female	72.8	7.4	19.8
Insurance information	Male	82.4	12.4	5.2
	Female	55.6	39.4	5

Table 4. Statistical table of age difference in information needs

Type of group	Age	Recognized (%)	Ordinary (%)	Not recognized (%)
Tourist activity	≤70	58.1	33.1	8.8
	>70	2.8	29.3	67.9
Catering service	≤70	20.3	31.5	48.2
	>70	60.9	20.2	18.9
Rehabilitation and nursing	≤70	18.9	30.5	50.6
	>70	70.1	10.5	19.4
Health consultation	≤70	13.2	26.5	60.3
	>70	52.8	10.2	37
Daycare center service	≤70	17.9	40.4	41.7
	>70	63.6	10.2	26.2

6   Result and Discussion

6.1   Information Needs Categories with Significant Differences Between Different Genders

1. Gender and differences in needs of psychological counseling information

Analysis based on gender groups suggested that the gender factor played a significant role in needs of psychological counseling information. The male elders' answers to this item were 'recognized' (8.1%), 'ordinary' (47.8%), and 'not recognized' (44.1%), while the female elders' answers to the same were 'recognized' (50.6%), 'ordinary' (39.6%), and 'not recognized' (9.8%). In the chi-square testing, the Pearson square value was 31.25, $P = 0.00 < 0.05$. The null hypothesis of the chi-square testing was equal proportions. The significance level being lower than 0.05 meant that the null hypothesis was false, therefore the elders of different genders had significant difference in their needs of psychological counseling information. It is thus clear that female elders recognized and received psychological counseling significantly better than males did. During the questionnaire survey, female respondents' conversation contents were richer than the males, and the females were more willing to exchange with others than the males were.

2. Gender and differences in needs of legal consulting information

Analysis was performed based on gender groups. The male elders' answers to this item were 'recognized' (45.7%), 'ordinary' (38.6%), and 'not recognized' (15.7%), while the female elders' answers to the same were 'recognized' (74.3%), 'ordinary' (13.9%), and 'not recognized' (11.8%). In the chi-square testing, the Pearson square value was 7.35, $P = 0.025 < 0.05$. Therefore, the elders of different genders had significant difference in their needs of legal consulting information. The results showed that female elders recognized better the policy and legal information needs than the males did, which was probably related to the female's situation as the disadvantaged population compared with the male.

3. Gender and differences in needs of plaza dancing information

Analysis based on gender groups suggested that the gender factor played a significant role in needs of plaza dancing information. The male elders' answers to this item were 'recognized' (3.2%), 'ordinary' (10.2%), and 'not recognized' (86.6%), while the female elders' answers to the same were 'recognized' (72.8%), 'ordinary' (7.4%), and 'not recognized' (19.8%). In the chi-square testing, the Pearson square value was 7.34, $P = 0.026 < 0.05$. The null hypothesis of the chi-square testing was equal proportions. The significance level being lower than 0.05 meant that the null hypothesis was false, therefore the elders of different genders had significant difference in their needs of plaza dancing information. It showed that female elders tended to have higher recognition than the males did in participating plaza dancing activity.

The Chinese male elders tended to choose leisure activities of their personal preference, while the females tended to take part in group leisure activities.

4. Gender and differences in needs of endowment insurance information

Analysis based on gender groups suggested significant gender difference in needs of endowment insurance information. The male elders' answers to this item were 'recognized' (82.4%), 'ordinary' (12.4%), and 'not recognized' (5.2%), while the female elders' answers to the same were 'recognized' (55.6%), 'ordinary' (39.4%), and 'not recognized' (5%). In the chi-square testing, the Pearson square value was 6.59, $P = 0.037 < 0.05$. Therefore, the elders of different genders had significant difference in their needs of endowment insurance information. The investigation results showed that among the samples investigated, the male elders attached more importance to the needs of endowment insurance information than the females did.

Through the above data analysis, it was understood that the female elders showed significantly higher recognition and acceptance level in psychological counseling than the males did; the females recognized better the policy and legal information needs than the males did; while the males attached more importance to needs of endowment insurance information than the females did; and the two gender groups had great difference in recognition level of leisure activity. Needs of safety and emotional information categories showed significant differences in gender.

6.2   Information Needs Categories with Significant Differences in Age

The survey sample was divided into two sub-sample groups according to the age variable, with below 70 years as the young elders, and 70 years or older as the old elders. Cross statistical analysis was performed on each question item and the age group variable. The information needs with significant differences were analyzed as follows:

1. Age and difference in needs of tourist activity information

Cross analysis was performed on age and tourist activity information. Significant differences were found between the two age groups. The answers to this item from the young elders below 70 years were: 'recognized' (58.1%), 'ordinary' (33.1%), and 'not recognized' (8.8%), while the answers to this item from the old elders 70 years or older were 'recognized' (2.8%), 'ordinary' (29.3%), and 'not recognized' (67.9%). In the chi-square testing, the Pearson square value was 37.02, $P = 0.00 < 0.05$. The null hypothesis of the chi-square testing was equal proportions. The significance level being lower than 0.05 meant that the null hypothesis was false, therefore the elders of different age groups had significant difference in their needs of tourist activity information. The result showed that the young elders needed more tourist activity information. The major reason behind it, we think, was that the decline of physical functions with the age increase affected the elders' choice in travelling and touring.

2. Age and difference in needs of catering service information

Cross analysis was performed on age and catering service information. Significant differences were found between the two age groups. The answers to this item from the young elders below 75 years were: 'recognized' (20.3%), 'ordinary' (31.5%), and 'not recognized' (48.2%), while answers to this item from the old elders 75 years or older were 'recognized' (60.9%), 'ordinary' (20.2%), and 'not recognized' (18.9%). In the chi-square testing, the Pearson square value was 15.064, $P = 0.00 < 0.05$. Therefore, the elders of different age groups had significant difference in their needs of catering service information. With the increase of age, higher and higher proportion of the elders attached importance to their choice in catering service.

3. Age and difference in needs of recovery care service information

Cross analysis was performed on age and recovery care service information. Significant differences were found between the two age groups. The answers to this item from the young elders below 75 years were: 'recognized' (18.9%), 'ordinary' (30.5%), and 'not recognized' (50.6%), while answers to this item from the old elderly 75 years or older were 'recognized' (70.1%), 'ordinary' (10.5%), and 'not recognized' (19.4%). In the chi-square testing, the Pearson square value was 7.137, $P = 0.028 < 0.05$. Therefore, the elders of different age had significant difference in their needs of recovery care service information. With the increase of age, there was the trend of growing proportion of the elders who attached importance to their choice in recovery care service.

4. Age and difference in needs of health consultation information

Cross analysis was performed on age and health consultation information. Significant differences were found between the two age groups. The answers to this item from the young elderly below 70 years were: 'recognized' (13.2%), 'ordinary' (26.5%), and 'not recognized' (60.3%), while answers to this item from 70 years old or older were 'recognized' (52.8%), 'ordinary' (10.2%), and 'not recognized' (37%). In the chi-square testing, the Pearson square value was 15.32, $P = 0.00 < 0.05$. Therefore, the elders of different ages had significant difference in their needs of health consultation information. With the increase of age, higher and higher proportion of the elders attached importance to their choice in health consultation information.

5. Age and difference in needs of daycare center service information

Cross analysis was performed on age and daycare center service information. Significant differences were found between the age groups. The answers to this item from the young elders below 70 years were: 'recognized' (17.9%), 'ordinary' (40.4%), and 'not recognized' (41.7%), while answers to this item from the old elders 70 years or older were 'recognized' (63.6%), 'ordinary' (10.2%), and 'not recognized' (26.2%). In the chi-square testing, the Pearson square value was 15.74, $P = 0.00 < 0.05$. Therefore, the elders of different age groups had significant difference in their needs of day care center service information. With the increase of age, higher and higher proportion of the elders attached importance to their choice in daycare center service information.

Through the above data analysis, we got to understand that: the old elders 70 years or older had more needs in catering service, recovery care, health consultation, and daycare center service information; with the increase of age, they attached growing importance to choices in daycare center service, health consultation, recovery care information; and that age made a significant difference in physiological and self-actualization information needs.

7   Conclusions

It was found in the investigation that the following twelve community service information functions for eldercare were highly recognized by the elders: household management service information, maintenance service information, catering service information, emergency safety service information, recovery care information, tourist activity information, plaza dancing information, elderly university information, emotional exchange information, legal consulting information, insurance information, and old-age support policy information.

According to the results of the investigation, the following recommendation was put forward on construction of the information-based community service for home-based elders: The community eldercare service organizations or businesses should provide the home-based elders with the service information that are highly recognized and urgently needed by the elders, for example: household management service information, emergency safety service information, maintenance service information, endowment insurance information, etc. For the service contents whose recognition levels by the elders were 'ordinary' or 'not recognized', for example emotional exchange, psychological counselling, recovery care service information etc., relevant publicity and guidance will be necessary. For information-based service needs related to age and gender, there should be special column dedicated to gender service and a special service space dedicated to the old elders.

Acknowledgement. This study was supported by the National Social Science Foundation of China (Grant No. 16BSH127).

References

1. Barrett, J., Kirk, S.: Running focus groups with elderly and disabled elderly participants. Appl. Ergon. **31**(6), 621–629 (2000)
2. Dunér, A., Nordström, M.: Intentions and strategies among elderly people: coping in everyday life. J. Aging Stud. **19**(4), 437–451 (2005)
3. Chappell, N.L., Funk, L.M.: Social support, caregiving, and aging. Can. J. Aging/La Revue canadienne du vieillissement **30**(03), 355–370 (2011)
4. Abdulraheem, I.S.: An opinion survey of caregivers concerning caring for the elderly in Ilorin metropolis, Nigeria. Public Health **119**(12), 1138–1144 (2005)
5. Boling, P.A., Yudin, J.: Home-based primary care program for home-limited patients. In: Malone, M.L., Capezuti, E.A., Palmer, R.M. (eds.) Geriatrics Models of Care: Bringing 'Best Practice' to an Aging America, pp. 173–181. Springer, Cham (2015). doi:10.1007/978-3-319-16068-9_15
6. Lederer, A.L., Sethi, V.: Critical dimensions of strategic information systems planning. Decis. Sci. **22**(1), 104–119 (1991)

Author Index

Printed in the United States
By Bookmasters